FIRSTHAND AMERICA

FIRSTHAND AMERICA

Brandywine Press · St. James, New York

A History of the United States

FIRST EDITION ★ VOLUME 1

VIRGINIA BERNHARD

DAVID BURNER

ELIZABETH FOX-GENOVESE

EUGENE D. GENOVESE

JOHN McCLYMER

FORREST McDONALD

Library of Congress Cataloguing in Publication Data

Main entry under title:

Firsthand America

Includes bibliographical references and index.
1. United States—History.   I. Burner, David,
1937–   .   II. Burner, David, 1937–   . American
people.
Vol. 1, ISBN 09603726-1-X
Vol. 2, ISBN 09603726-4-4
Combined edition, ISBN 09603726-5-2

PRINTED IN THE UNITED STATES OF AMERICA

Second Printing

About the Authors . . .

VIRGINIA BERNHARD has published a historical novel, *A Durable Fire*, set in seventeenth-century Virginia and Bermuda, as well as a biography of a Texas governor's daughter. Her scholarly articles have appeared in *New England Quarterly*, *Virginia Magazine of History and Biography*, and *Journal of Southern History*. She has coedited the forthcoming *Southern Women: Histories and Identities* (University of Tennessee Press, 1991) and teaches at the University of St. Thomas in Houston.

DAVID BURNER has published several books on twentieth-century American politics, most recently *John F. Kennedy and a New Generation* (1988). His *Making Peace with the '60s* is scheduled for publication by Harvard University Press in 1992. He teaches at the State University of New York at Stony Brook.

ELIZABETH FOX-GENOVESE'S highly-praised recent book, *Within the Plantation Household: Black and White Women of the Old South*, was published by the University of North Carolina Press. Her forthcoming *Feminism Without Illusions* will be published in 1991. She is Eleanore Raoul Professor of Humanistic Studies and Director of the Institute for Women's Studies Department at Emory University.

EUGENE D. GENOVESE has written a number of books, principally on the Old South, including *Roll, Jordan, Roll* (1974). He and Elizabeth Fox-Genovese coauthored *The Fruits of Merchant Capital* (1983). Genovese's *The Slaveholder's Dilemma: Freedom and Progress in Southern Conservative Thought, 1820–1860* will be published in 1991.

JOHN McCLYMER has written *War and Welfare: Social Engineering in America* and has coedited *Images of Women in American Popular Culture* (1985). Professor McClymer, who teaches at Assumption College, has written extensively about pedagogy in *The History Teacher, Teaching History*, and the American Historical Association's newsletter *Perspectives*.

FORREST McDONALD is Distinguished Senior Fellow at the University of Alabama Center for the Study of Southern History and Culture. He has published several pre-eminent studies of the founding of the United States, most recently *Novus Ordo Seclorum: The Intellectual Origins of the Constitution* (1985) and, with Ellen S. McDonald, *Requiem: Variations on Eighteenth-Century Themes* (1988).

About the Firsthand Materials . . .

All comprehensive United States survey textbooks, including this one, give full
coverage to standard political, economic, diplomatic, and legal events. But
these elements of history are largely the story of elites. This textbook also
provides social history captured in the recognizable lives of ordinary people.
Presidents, congressmen, and corporate executives are quoted throughout the
book. So are soldiers, slaves, indentured servants, cowboys, working girls and
women, and civil rights activists. *Firsthand America,* using more than 2000
quotations, therefore gives due place both to the traditional leaders and to the
myriad Americans never named in formal histories.

About the Debates . . .

Textbooks have led generations of students into the comfortable illusion that a single history book can summarize the nation's past. As historians know, it is impossible to resurrect the past exactly. In the reconstruction of events they rely on written records, along with some art objects and physical remains. Yet few occurrences are even recorded in writing. Many documents, moreover, are lost, and the historian can never be certain of having seen every manuscript; or the sources may be too voluminous to read exhaustively. A document carries the point of view, or bias, of the person who wrote it and the time in which it was written. To these documents the historian brings his or her own bias.

Since history, then, is an art of interpretation, two eminent historians, the radical Eugene D. Genovese and the conservative Forrest McDonald, here debate in question and answer form great issues of the American past. Their differences go beyond ideology, and in setting forth distinctive viewpoints these two men may help to crystallize your own thinking. This series of debates will provide material for class discussion or written reports and will demonstrate that there is no fixed truth about the past, which makes it all the more rewarding as an intellectual study. Students in any classroom deserve a challenge; and instructors can employ these verbal interchanges in any way they deem suitable.

The debates will provide theoretical content. But narrative itself is an analytical act. The introductory courses in the other social sciences, so popular and often so simple, fall into easy manipulation of abstract definitions, axioms, dicta, isolated from the facts that might clarify or test them. As fine historians have repeatedly demonstrated, a complex readable story is far more sophisticated for its embracing concrete and sometimes contradictory detail. This textbook, in this sense, offers three different interpretations of the American past: Genovese's, McDonald's and that of its other authors. There are important areas of agreement as well as of argument in the accounts. There is but one past; there are many ways to illuminate that past. We hope this volume will introduce you to the genuine excitement historians have found in casting their own light on the history of the United States.

Acknowledgements

We are eager to receive comments on this textbook from both teachers and students. We welcome corrections, suggestions for fresh firsthand sources, news of omissions, and general criticisms. Please send them to Professor David Burner, History Department, SUNY, Stony Brook, NY 11794.

For various kinds of help and encouragement thanks are gratefully extended to Robert Marcus, Alan January, Jim Moore, Jim Bernhard, Sandy Burner, Robert Burner, David Ellis, Winfrey Purington, Hugh Cleland, Pete Seeger, Robert London, Terry Cooney, Rose Dunne, Terry Bose, Gus Seligmann, Deok-Ho Kim, Mark Buckley, Mark Sullivan, Eric Burner, Mark Hessler, Wilbur Miller, Michael Barnhart, Bonnie Schrack, Jerry Sternstein, Ingrid Scobie, Janet Schmelzer, James Mooney, Steven Boyd, Nick Ucci, and Ron Lee. Special thanks in the preparation of the manuscript are extended to Charlie Peach, who is one, of Baldwin Printing in Waterbury, Connecticut, and his assistants Rosemary Henault and Renzo Melaragno. Enormous help in the preparation of the book came from Thomas R. West of The Catholic University of America; his undergraduate students there are the recipients of courses that are an intellectual awakening.

John McClymer wrote the first appendix, "Succeeding in History Courses," as well as most of the Points To Think About that follow each chapter.

The Authors

Dedication

For Sandy, Diane, Eric and Bob

Contents

Chronology

Hill; Congress adopts its "Declaration of the Causes and Necessities of Taking Up Arms."

1776   Thomas Paine's *Common Sense*; Declaration of Independence; British troops evacuate Boston; Battle of Long Island, New York; British take New York City; Battle of Trenton.

1777   Battle of Princeton; Battle of Monmouth; Battle of Brandywine, Pennsylvania; British occupy Philadelphia; Battle of Germantown; Burgoyne surrenders at Saratoga; Articles of Confederation adopted by Continental Congress, but not ratified by all states until 1781; Washington retires to Valley Forge for winter.

1778   United States concludes military alliance and commercial treaty with France; British evacuate Philadelphia; Seize Savannah, Georgia.

1779   Spain enters the war against Britain; George Rogers Clark captures Vincennes and ends British rule in Northwest.

1780   Americans surrender 5500 men and the city of Charleston, South Carolina; Battle of Camden, South Carolina; Battle of King's Mountain, South Carolina.

1781   Battle of Cowpens, South Carolina; British under Tarleton defeated by Morgan; Battle of Guilford Courthouse, North Carolina; Cornwallis withdraws to coast; Cornwallis surrenders to Washington at Yorktown, Virginia.

1782   Fall of Lord North's ministry.

1783   Treaty of Paris with Britain signed.

1785   Land Ordinance for Northwest Territory adopted by Congress.

1786   Jay-Gardoqui Treaty rejected by Congress; Virginia Statute for Religious Freedom; Shays's Rebellion in western Massachusetts; Annapolis Convention adopts plan to meet in Philadelphia to revise Articles of Confederation.

1787   Federal Constitutional Convention meets in Philadelphia; Northwest Ordinance enacted by Congress. *The Federalist Papers* by Madison, Hamilton, and Jay.

1788   Ratification of United States Constitution by all states except Rhode Island and North Carolina.

1789   First session of Congress meets; Washington inaugurated as first President; Outbreak of French Revolution.

1790   Hamilton's Report on Public Credit; Father John Carroll made first Roman Catholic bishop of United States.

1791   Bank of the United States established; First ten amendments to Constitution (Bill of Rights) adopted.

1792   Washington reelected.

1793   Citizen Genêt Affair; Samuel Slater erects first cotton mill at Pawtucket, Rhode Island; Eli Whitney applies for patent on cotton gin.

1794   Whiskey Rebellion in western Pennsylvania; Battle of Fallen Timbers, Ohio; General Anthony Wayne defeats Indians.

1795   Jay's Treaty with Britain; Pinckney's Treaty with Spain.

1796   Washington's Farewell Address, warning against foreign entanglements and domestic factions; John Adams elected President.

1798   XYZ Affair reported by Adams to Congress; Quasi-war with France on high seas; Alien and Sedition Acts enacted by Federalists in Congress; Virginia and Kentucky resolutions.

1800   Washington, D.C., becomes capital; Thomas Jefferson elected President.

1801   War with Barbary states; John Marshall becomes chief justice.

1803   *Marbury* v. *Madison*, Supreme Court upholds right of judicial review; Louisiana Purchase; Lewis and Clark expedition begun.

1804   Hamilton killed by Vice-President Aaron Burr in duel; Jefferson reelected.

1807   Embargo Act; Robert Fulton's steamboat travels on Hudson River from Albany to New York in 30 hours.

1808   Congress prohibits Americans from participating in African slave trade; James Madison elected President.

1809   Embargo repealed; Nonintercourse Act passed, prohibiting trade with Britain and France.

1810   Macon's Bill No. 2 passed, restoring trade with Britain and France, but providing for trade restrictions to be reimposed on one of the powers if other should abandon its seizure of American ships.

1811   Madison, believing Napoleon has removed restrictions on American commerce, prohibits trade with Britain;

Battle of Tippecanoe, Indiana, in which William Henry Harrison defeats Tecumseh and prevents formation of Indian confederacy.

1812   Congress declares war against Britain; Americans surrender Detroit to British; Madison reelected.

1813   Battle of Lake Erie, Captain Oliver Perry defeats British naval forces; Battle of the Thames; General Harrison defeats British and their Indian allies.

1814   Battle of Horseshoe Bend, Alabama; General Andrew Jackson defeats Creek Indians fighting for British; British burn Washington, D.C.; Commander Thomas Macdonough defeats British fleet on Lake Champlain; invading British turned back at Plattsburgh, New York; Hartford Convention of Federalist delegates from New England; Treaty of Ghent signed between United States and Great Britain.

1815   Battle of New Orleans, Jackson defeats British; *North American Review* founded in Boston.

1816   Second Bank of the United States chartered by Congress; Protective tariff passed; James Monroe elected President.

1818   General Jackson invades Florida to end Seminole War; Rush-Bagot Convention between Britain and United States establishes fishing rights and Canadian boundary.

1819   Depression begins; Adams-Onis Treaty; Spain cedes Florida; *Dartmouth College* Case; *McCulloch* v. *Maryland*.

1820   Missouri Compromise; Reelection of James Monroe without opposition, "Era of Good Feelings."

1822   Denmark Vesey's Conspiracy.

1823   President issues Monroe Doctrine.

1824   John Quincy Adams elected President by House of Representatives after failure of any candidate to win electoral majority.

1828   John C. Calhoun's anonymous *South Carolina Exposition and Protest;* Congress passes "Tariff of Abominations"; Election of Andrew Jackson as President brings victory to new Democratic Party.

1829   Mexico abolishes slavery.

1830   Jackson vetoes Maysville Road Bill; Anti-Masonic Party holds first national party convention.

1831   Nat Turner's slave insurrection in Virginia.

1832   Beginning of Jackson's "war" against Second Bank of the United States (BUS); Special convention in South Carolina nullifies new protective tariff; Jackson relected President.

1833   Congress provides for a gradual lowering of tariffs, but passes Force Bill authorizing Jackson to enforce federal law in South Carolina.

1836   Jackson's "specie circular"; Martin Van Buren elected President.

1838   Aroostook War.

1840   Congress passes Van Buren's Independent Treasury Act; William H. Harrison elected President; Whigs in power; World anti-slavery convention.

1840   American Female Moral Reform Society organized as first national female reform association.

1841   John Tyler becomes President upon Harrison's death.

1842   Webster-Ashburton Treaty settles disputed U.S.-Canada boundary.

1843   First overland caravans to Oregon.

1844   Senate rejects Calhoun's Texas annexation treaty; James K. Polk elected President; Lowell Female Reform Association organized.

1845   Texas enters Union as slave state; John Slidell's unsuccessful mission to Mexico to negotiate purchase of New Mexico and California; Margaret Fuller publishes *Woman in the Nineteenth Century.*

1846   Beginning of Mexican War; General Zachary Taylor invades Mexico from the North; Treaty with Britain divides Oregon Territory along 49th parallel.

1847   General Winfield Scott captures Vera Cruz and Mexico City.

1848   Gold discovered in California; Van Buren, running for President on Free-Soil ticket, receives 10 percent of popular vote; Zachary Taylor elected President; Treaty of Guadalupe Hidalgo ends Mexican War, establishes Rio Grande as border; First Women's Rights Convention at Seneca Falls, New York; Elizabeth Cady

Stanton drafts "Declaration of Sentiments."

1849 California gold rush.

1850 In Congress, sectional debate culminates in Compromise of 1850; Fugitive Slave Law requires federal agents to recover escaped slaves from sanctuaries in the North; Taylor's death makes Millard Fillmore President.

1851 Herman Melville's *Moby Dick.*

1852 Franklin Pierce elected President.

1853 Upsurge of political nativism, the Know-Nothing Party.

1854 Spectacular Know-Nothing election victories; Collapse of Whigs; New Republican Party; Commodore Perry opens Japan to American trade; Kansas-Nebraska Act rekindles sectional controversy over slavery; "Bleeding Kansas."

1856 John Brown's raid at Pottawatomie Creek; James Buchanan elected President.

1857 *Dred Scott* v. *Sanford;* In Kansas, proslavery Lecompton Constitution ratified as free-state men refuse to vote.

1858 Lincoln-Douglas debates.

1859 John Brown's raid on Harpers Ferry.

1860 Democratic Party, deadlocked at Charleston convention, divides along sectional lines at Baltimore; Abraham Lincoln elected President; South Carolina secedes from the Union.

1861 Secession of remaining states of deep South (Texas, Louisiana, Mississippi, Alabama, Georgia, and Florida); Jefferson Davis begins serving as President of the Confederate States of America; Firing on Fort Sumter precipitates war; Secession of Virginia, North Carolina, Tennessee, and Arkansas; Union army routed at first Battle of Bull Run (Manassas); McClellan heads Union Forces; *Trent* affair; Vassar College founded.

1862 Both Union and Confederacy adopt paper money; Union general, U.S. Grant, captures Fort Henry and Fort Donelson; Battle of the ironclads: *Virginia (Merrimack)* vs. *Monitor;* McClellan's Peninsula campaign brings Union army to outskirts of Richmond, the Confederate capital; Robert E. Lee becomes commander of Army of northern Virginia; Confed-

erate victory at second battle of Bull Run; Stalemate between Lee and McClellan at Antietam; Confederate invasion of Kentucky; Lincoln issues preliminary Emancipation Proclamation; Confederate victory at Fredericksburg.

1863 Lincoln issues final Emancipation Proclamation; Confederates defeat Union army under Hooker at Chancellorsville; Lee's invasion of North checked by Union army under Meade at Gettysburg; Grant captures Vicksburg; Draft riots in the North; Confederate army under Bragg defeats Union forces at Chickamauga; Union victory at Chattanooga (Lookout Mountain and Missionary Ridge); Lincoln offers lenient reconstruction program.

1864 Grant named Union general in chief; Grant's direct advance on Richmond checked at the Wilderness, Spotsylvania, and Cold Harbor; Lincoln reelected President; Sherman marches from Atlanta to the sea.

1865 Sherman pushes northward through South Carolina and North Carolina; Lee gives up Petersburg and Richmond; Lee surrenders at Appomattox; Lincoln assassinated; Andrew Johnson becomes President; Johnson moves for speedy, lenient restoration of southern states to Union; Thirteenth Amendment ratified.

1866 Johnson breaks with Republican majority in Congress by vetoing Freedman's Bureau bill and Civil Rights bill (passed over his veto); Congress approves Fourteenth Amendment; Ku Klux Klan formed.

1867 Congress passes Military Reconstruction Act over Johnson's veto; Congress passes Tenure of Office Act and Command of Army Act to reduce Johnson's power.

1868 Former Confederate states hold constitutional conventions, for which former slaves are allowed to vote, and adopt new constitutions guaranteeing universal suffrage; President Johnson impeached; escapes conviction by one vote; Republican Ulysses S. Grant elected President.

1869 Congress passes Fifteenth Amendment; National Women Suffrage Association founded by Elizabeth Cady Stanton and Susan B. Anthony; American Woman Suffrage Association founded by Lucy Stone and Henry Blackwell.

1870   First Ku Klux Klan (or Enforcement) Act gives Grant power to move against white terrorists in South.

1874   Women's Christian Temperance Union organized by Annie Wittenmeyer.

1876   Republicans nominate Rutherford B. Hayes for President; Democrats nominate Samuel J. Tilden. Tilden secures majority of popular vote but electoral vote is in doubt because of disputed returns from three southern states; General Custer's defeat at Little Bighorn; Alexander Graham Bell transmits first telephone message; End of Reconstruction; Declaration of Women's Rights read at Centennial Exposition, Philadelphia.

1877   After political and economic bargaining, Congress creates an electoral commission, which rules that all disputed ballots belong to Hayes, who is inaugurated; *Munn* v. *Illinois.*

1878   Bland-Allison Act; Greenback Labor Movement; "Anthony Amendment" first introduced in Congress.

1879   Frances Willard gains presidency of Women's Christian Temperance Union.

1880   Garfield elected President.

1881   Helen Hunt Jackson, *A Century of Dishonor;* Garfield assassinated; Arthur becomes President.

1882   Pendleton Civil Service Act.

1884   Cleveland elected President.

1885   Josiah Strong, *Our Country.*

1886   AFL Organized; Haymarket Massacre.

1887   Interstate Commerce Act; Dawes Severalty Act; Edward Bellamy, *Looking Backward, 2000-1887.*

1888   Harrison elected President.

1890   Sherman Antitrust Act; Sherman Silver Purchase Act; "Battle" of Wounded Knee; McKinley Tariff; Alfred Thayer Mahan, *The Influence of Sea Power Upon History;* National Woman Suffrage Association and American Woman Suffrage Association merge to form National American Woman Suffrage Association.

1892   Cleveland elected to Presidency again; Homestead Strike; General Federation of Women's Clubs established.

1893-97   Depression.

1894   "Coxey's Army"; Pullman Strike; *Coin's Financial School.*

1895   Venezuelan Boundary Dispute; *United States* v. *E. C. Knight Company.*

1896   McKinley elected President; *Plessy* v. *Ferguson;* National Association of Colored Women founded.

1898   Spanish-American War; Hawaiian Islands annexed.

1899   Thorstein Veblen, *The Theory of the Leisure Class;* National Consumer's League founded.

1899-1900   Open Door Notes.

1900   Gold Standard Act; McKinley reelected.

1901   United States Steel Corporation formed; Platt Amendment; Assassination of McKinley; Theodore Roosevelt becomes President; Hay-Pauncefote Treaty.

1902   Newlands Act.

1903   Departments of Commerce and Labor established; Elkins Anti-rebate Act; Hay-Bunau-Varilla Treaty; Women's Trade Union League founded.

1904   Roosevelt Corollary to Monroe Doctrine; Roosevelt elected President; *Northern Securities Company* v. *United States.*

1905   Portsmouth Peace Conference; *Lochner* v. *New York.*

1906   Hepburn Act; Pure Food and Drug Act; Meat Inspection Act; Algeciras Conference.

1907   Gentlemen's Agreement with Japan.

1908   White House Conservation Conference; *Muller* v. *Oregon;* Taft elected President.

1909   Payne-Aldrich Tariff.

1910   Mann-Elkins Act; Ballinger-Pinchot Controversy.

1911   Triangle Shirtwaist Company Fire.

1912   Socialists nominate Eugene Debs for President; Progressives nominate Theodore Roosevelt on Bull-Moose Ticket; Wilson elected President.

1913   Sixteenth Amendment, the Income Tax; Seventeenth Amendment, Popular Election of United States Senators; Underwood Tariff; Federal

Reserve Act; Charles Beard, *An Economic Interpretation of the Constitution of the United States;* Congressional Union founded by Alice Paul and Lucy Burns.

1914   Federal Trade Commission Act; Clayton Antitrust Act; Margaret Sanger writes *Family Limitation.*

1915   Sinking of the *Lusitania;* National Birth Control League founded by Mary Ware Dennett to include wide middle-class membership.

1916   Adamson Act; Federal Farm Loan Act; Jones Act; Wilson reelected President; Sinking of *Sussex;* National Woman's Party founded as outgrowth of Congressional union and split-off from NAWSA.

1917   United States enters World War I on April 6; Espionage Act; Lever Food and Fuel Control Act; Russian Revolution.

1918   Wilson's Fourteen Points; Sedition Act; War Finance Corporation; Republicans gain control of Congress; Armistice Day, November 11.

1919   League of Women Voters founded.

1919-20   Red Scare.

1920   Palmer Raids, January 2; Harding elected President; Nineteenth Amendment: Women acquire the right to vote; Women's Bureau of the Department of Labor founded; Transportation Act; Sinclair Lewis, *Main Street.*

1921-22   Washington Armament Conference.

1923   President Harding dies, August 2; Calvin Coolidge becomes President; Equal Rights Amendment first introduced by National Women's Party.

1924   Immigration Restriction Act; Dawes Plan; Coolidge elected President.

1925   F. Scott Fitzgerald, *The Great Gatsby;* Scopes Trial.

1927   Charles Lindbergh flies solo across the Atlantic; Sacco and Vanzetti executed.

1928   Hoover elected President.

1929   Black Thursday, October 24 (stock market crash); Young Plan; Ernest Hemingway, *A Farewell to Arms;* Agricultural Marketing Act.

1930   London Naval Conference; Hawley-Smoot Tariff.

1931   Hoover Debt Moratorium; Japanese invasion of Manchuria.

1932   Stimson Doctrine, Reconstruction Finance Corporation; Glass-Steagall Act; Bonus Army; Roosevelt elected President.

1933   "Hundred Days" session of Congress; Agricultural Adjustment Act; Emergency Banking Act; Tennessee Valley Authority; Civilian Conservation Corps; National Industrial Recovery Act; United States Recognizes Soviet Union; Twenty-first Amendment ratified, repealing prohibition.

1934   Gold Reserve Act; Securities and Exchange Act; Platt Amendment abrogated.

1935   National Labor Relations Act; Social Security Act; Works Progress Administration.

1936   Roosevelt reelected; *Butler* v. *United States.*

1937   Administrative Reorganization Act; Congress of Industrial Organizations (CIO).

1938   Munich Agreement.

1939   War breaks out in Europe, September 1.

1940   United States preparedness and defense measures; Battle of Britain; Roosevelt reelected.

1941   Battle of the Atlantic; Lend-Lease Act; Atlantic Charter; Japanese attack Pearl Harbor, December 7.

1942   Battle of Coral Sea; Allied campaign in North Africa.

1943   Casablanca Conference; Allies invade Italy; Teheran Conference.

1944   Invasion of Europe; landing at Normandy, June 6; Roosevelt reelected; Battle of the Bulge.

1945   Yalta Conference; Germany surrenders; Atomic bomb dropped on Hiroshima, August 6; Japan surrenders; United Nations formed; Roosevelt dies; Truman becomes President; Potsdam Conference.

1947   Marshall Plan proposed; Taft-Hartley Act; Truman Doctrine.

1948   Truman elected President; Berlin Blockade; Creation of State of Israel.

1949   North Atlantic Treaty Organization.

1950   Korean War; McCarran Act; Rise of Senator Joseph McCarthy as popular anti-Communist.

1951   General Douglas MacArthur fired by Truman.

1952   Eisenhower elected President.

1953   Stalin dies; Korean ceasefire.

1954   Southeast Asia Treaty Organization; Geneva Conference on Indochina; Senate censure of Joseph F. McCarthy; *Brown* v. *Board of Education of Topeka;* Communist Control Act; Atomic Energy Act.

1955   Geneva Summit Meeting.

1956   Suez Crisis; Eisenhower reelected; Hungarian Revolt.

1957   Eisenhower Doctrine; Sputnik; Eisenhower sends paratroopers to Little Rock.

1958   National Defense Education Act.

1959   Eisenhower and Khrushchev meet at Camp David.

1960   Kennedy elected President.

1961   Bay of Pigs; Berlin Wall; Peace Corps.

1962   Cuban Missile Crisis; President Kennedy appoints Commission on the Status of Women.

1963   Test Ban Treaty; Kennedy is assassinated, November 22; Lyndon B. Johnson becomes President; Betty Friedan publishes *The Feminine Mystique.*

1964   Gulf of Tonkin Resolution passes Senate with two votes against it; Johnson elected President; Civil Rights Act.

1965   Voting Rights Act; Medicare; Elementary and Secondary Education Act.

1966   National Organization for Women (NOW) formed.

1968   Tet Offensive in Vietnam, January-February; Martin Luther King is assassinated, April 4; Nixon elected President.

1969   Moon landing, Apollo II.

1970   American invasion of Cambodia.

1971   Kissinger's secret trip to Peking.

1972   Nixon reelected; Congress passes the Equal Rights Amendment.

1974   Nixon resigns Presidency; Ford becomes President.

1976   Carter elected President.

1977   Panama Canal Treaties.

1978   Camp David Agreements.

1979   Three Mile Island Nuclear Accident.

1980   Reagan elected President.

1980-81   Iranian hostage crisis.

1982   Equal Rights Amendment fails to gain ratification.

1983   Soviets shoot down Korean Airlines jet over Russian airspace; 241 United States Marines killed in airport compound, Beirut, Lebanon; United States invades Grenada.

1984   Ronald Reagan reelected President.

1986   Tax Reform Act

1988   George Bush elected President.

1990   Air Quality Act.

1991-   Crisis in the Gulf.

American Letter for Gerald Murphy

It is a strange thing—to be an American
Neither an old house it is with the air
Tasting of hung herbs and the sun returning
Year after year to the same door and the churn
Making the same sound in the cool of the kitchen
Mother to son's wife, and the place to sit
Marked in the dusk by the worn stone at the wellhead—
That—nor the eyes like each other's eyes and the skull
Shaped to the same fault and the hands' sameness.
Neither a place it is nor a blood name.
America is West and the wind blowing.
America is a great word and the snow,
A way, a white bird, the rain falling,
A shining thing in the mind and the gulls' call.
America is neither a land nor a people,
A word's shape it is, a wind's sweep—
America is alone: many together,
Many of one mouth, of one breath,
Dressed as one—and none brothers among them:
Only the taught speech and the aped tongue.
America is alone and the gulls calling.

It is a strange thing to be an American.
It is strange to live on the high world in the stare
Of the naked sun and the stars as our bones live.
Men in the old lands housed by their rivers.
They built their towns in the vales in the earth's shelter.
We first inhabit the world. We dwell
On the half earth, on the open curve of a continent.
Sea is divided from sea by the day-fall. The dawn
Rides the low east with us many hours;
First are the capes, then are the shorelands, now
The blue Appalachians faint at the day rise;
The willows shudder with light on the long Ohio:
The lakes scatter the low sun: the prairies
Slide out of dark: in the eddy of clean air
The smoke goes up from the high plains of Wyoming:
The steep Sierras arise: the struck foam
Flames at the wind's heel on the far Pacific.
Already the noon leans to the eastern cliff:
The elms darken the door and the dust-heavy lilacs. . . .

This, this is our land, this is our people,
This that is neither a land nor a race. We must reap
The wind here in the grass for our soul's harvest:
Here we must eat our salt or our bones starve.
Here we must live or live only as shadows.
This is our race, we that have none, that have had
Neither the old walls nor the voices around us,
This is our land, this is our ancient ground—
The raw earth, the mixed bloods and the strangers,
The different eyes, the wind, and the heart's change,
These we will not leave though the old call us.
This is our country-earth, our blood, our kind.
Here we will live our years till the earth blind us—

—ARCHIBALD MACLEISH

Mr. Dooley's Advice (1906)

"I know histhry isn't thrue, Hinnessy, because it ain't like what I see ivry day in Halsted Sthreet. If any wan comes along with a histhry iv Greece or Rome that'll show me th' people fightin', gettin' dhrunk, makin' love, gettin' married, owin' th' grocery man an' bein' without hard-coal, I'll believe they was a Greece or Rome, but not befure. Historyans is like doctors. They . . . tells ye what a counthry died iv. But I'd like to know what it lived iv."

FIRSTHAND AMERICA

Columbus—the messenger of the "new heaven and new earth" of the Biblical Apocalypse—planting the cross and giving trinkets to the natives of the New World. *(Courtesy, The Hispanic Society of America, New York)*

CHAPTER 1

Europe and America

CHRISTOPHER COLUMBUS

Son of a Genoese weaver, Columbus was an extraordinary weaver of dreams. In the culture of his Mediterranean, the belief in riches and perfection beyond the sunset was strong, for the only sea route leading outward—going everywhere and nowhere—was west through the Straits of Gibraltar and beyond the Canary Islands. America, where that sea route finally led, was an idea in the mind of Europe, and the writings of Columbus reveal the vividness and extravagance of the idea. It represented wealth, freedom, and happiness, the noble savage and the beckoning mystery of the wild frontier—elements that would later go into the American dream. The new Western hemisphere was also primitive and frightening—full of cannibals by Columbus's testimony. On this fresh, uncharted land Europe could stamp its own shifting character and conflicting desires.

Columbus was a great mariner but an atrocious geographer. Both the strength and the defect helped him to sell his enterprise to the monarchs of Spain. He sharply underestimated the circumference of the globe, placing Asia about 2400 miles from the Canaries of the eastern Atlantic: the actual distance is more than 10,000 miles, most of it vast oceans. Possessed of the intellectual certainty of the self-taught (he had first learned to read as a young man), convinced of the mystical significance of his name (after St. Christopher, who had carried the Infant Jesus across the waters), persuaded that the Bible supported his geographical notions and made likely his discovery of lost Christians, Columbus was an effective salesman for his grandiose project. Besieging King Ferdinand of Aragon and Queen Isabel of Castile for more years than they besieged the Alhambra, he finally got his ships, his crews, his promises of riches, and his striking title "Admiral of the Ocean Sea." And so he set out on what would be an earth-changing voyage, a story endlessly told, rich with symbols of a world's transformation.

He weighed anchor on August 2, 1492, the very day upon which the last Jews who refused to convert to Catholicism had to leave Spain—most of them bound for the more tolerant countries of Islam. "After having turned out all the Jews from all your kingdoms," Columbus records in his first diary entry, "your

highness gave orders to me that with a sufficient fleet I should go." The idea of
a new world as a haven for persecuted people would have astonished
Columbus; the great explorer even gave assurances that he would exclude Jews
from any land he discovered. He envisioned himself the messenger of the
"new heaven and new earth" of the Biblical Apocalypse—in which Jerusalem
is recaptured and the Jews converted—but never realized he had discovered a
new world. He made landfall at the island of San Salvador on October 12, 1492.
After three more voyages Columbus died convinced that he had found the
Eastern Indies, the Orient of India, China, and Japan.

On one voyage, it is written, a tremendous waterspout threatened
Columbus's ship. And he calmed the waters by reading aloud the account in
the Gospel According to St. John of the storm on the Sea of Galilee, tracing a
cross in the sky and a circle around the fleet with his sword. On the same
journey, marooned and starving in Jamaica, he terrified the local Indians into
supplying his crew with food by threatening the divine gesture of removing the
light from the moon—his up-to-date almanac correctly predicted a total eclipse

Tabula Terre Nove, **Map of the New World, 1507–1513.** (*N. Phelps Stokes Collection. Prints Division.*
The New York Public Library, Astor, Lenox and Tilden Foundations)

of the moon. Such were the methods of this man who was at once a modern scientist, a medieval sailor, and a mystic.

The new world that Columbus never knew he had discovered contained wealth beyond his dreams of the riches of the Indies, and offered an opportunity for the expansion of Christianity far greater than his mystical vision. America's nearly twenty million square miles of land and the wealth that lay beneath it would fuel the economy of Europe and offer a haven for millions whose lives his discovery disrupted. Columbus brought back Indian captives, initiating the Atlantic slave trade that would shift to Africa and forcibly disrupt the lives of further millions. It has been suggested that these first transAtlantic slaves brought with them their own revenge, carrying in their bloodstreams the bacillus of syphilis—previously unknown to Europe. It was Columbus, too, who began the colonization of the New World, introducing on the island of Hispaniola an imperialist regime and its murderous course. Among American Indians Columbus Day is not considered a holiday.

The World Stage

At the time of Columbus's discovery of America, Europe was in a state of unending warfare. Europeans fought Europeans as well as Africans and Asians, contending for control of one square mile and another of their subcontinent. Emperors, kings, princes, and dukes laid claims to empires, kingdoms, principalities, and fiefs. Wars in defense of rival claims never ceased. Whatever unity held within European Christendom rested upon the hostility and contempt with which Europeans viewed all other racial, religious, and cultural groups.

The hostility was justified but the contempt was not, for Europe, being one of the least unified, was also one of the most primitive and least potent of the world's great cultures. For some centuries its home territory had been shrinking.

In the twelfth century, the great cultures had arrived at a temporary stalemate. Islam, the most dynamic and aggressive culture on the planet for four centuries, had temporarily spent its force after subduing the Iberian peninsula in Europe, all of North Africa, and Asia Minor as far as northern India. The Moslems retained a commanding superiority over the Europeans in science, technology, warfare, and general learning. It was the Moslems, in fact, who preserved the works of the Roman astronomer Ptolemy, whose estimates of the earth's size guided Columbus. To the east, the Hindu culture continued to dominate the Indian subcontinent, as it had for a thousand years; but the culture had long since passed its zenith and it was torn by revolution and by warfare among scores of provinces, great and small. In the Orient, where printing, paper money, and gunpowder had already been invented, the Sung dynasty dominated a vast area and Chinese culture basked in its golden age; but in the 1120s the Sungs lost half their territory through war and rebellion, and before the end of the twelfth century central Asia had spawned a new Mongol Empire that would rule for a hundred years.

The thirteenth century belonged to the Mongol hordes. In the space of forty years, under the leadership of their ruler, Genghis Khan, these fierce warriors swept over three continents, totally subjugating China and pressing the other three major civilizations into portions of their home regions. They overran all of Russia, subdued and ravaged Slavic eastern Europe, and thrust into the Germanic lands. There the onslaught against Europe stopped, for the interior mountains were not suitable to the Mongol style of mounted warfare. Then the hordes swung south to devastate Islamic territory. Western India fell, and then the Near East, and westward the Mongols swept until 1260, when Islamic forces stopped them just short of Egypt. Thenceforth, the Mongols expanded no more; they held on for a century and then, as abruptly as they had risen, they retreated and declined into impotence.

The Mongol occupation quickened Europe's economy and in ways that would have vast consequences. When the Mongols seized land to the east, the wealthiest and

While Europeans were developing an interest in science and commerce, primitive peoples half a world away were expressing cultures of their own. Mask. Nootka people. West Vancouver, Canada. *(Courtesy, The Menil Collection, Houston)*

nearly twenty years in the Far East, mostly in service at the court of Genghis Khan's grandson, the emperor Kublai Khan. Marco Polo's journal gave Europeans their first direct information about the geography and civilization of the Orient, quickened their curiosity, and introduced them to a host of Chinese technological and scientific advances—including gunpowder. Through such borrowings, and by their own ingenious improvements on them, the Italians started Europe along the way to the technological superiority that would, in time, make Europeans masters of the world.

The Ottoman Turks But Europe's time was yet to come: for at the beginning of the fourteenth century, just as the menace of the Mongols was abating, the Moslems rose again, this time under the most terrible group of all, the Ottoman Turks. Before this wave of Islamic fury had spent itself, the Ottoman Empire would

Figure of kneeling woman with child. Western Sudan: Djenne culture. *(Courtesy, The Menil Collection, Houston)*

most advanced centers in Europe were the great city-states of northern Italy. Venice and Genoa in particular had gained large profits by supplying and transporting the armies of the Crusades, a series of wars against Islamic territory along the eastern Mediterranean and particularly in the ancient Christian Holy Land. Venice and Genoa then established themselves as the principal entrepôts for the importation of spices, silks, and other commodities from the Far East. During the Mongol years, trade from the East came overland across Asia to the Byzantine Empire, the easternmost portion of the Christian world, and then by sea to Venice and Genoa. To exploit this trade the Italians, using Portuguese and Italian Jews as intermediaries, borrowed extensively from the technological and scientific storehouse of the Moslems. They learned to use the lateen rigging, which enabled vessels to sail toward the wind, and acquired a knowledge of mathematics, astronomy, and navigation that was far superior to any then current in Europe. Late in the thirteenth century a Venetian, Marco Polo, spent dominate a land mass extending ten thousand miles, from the Danube River to the Red Sea, and including North Africa, Egypt, Syria, Persia, and the Arab peninsula. Through their advanced seamanship, the Moslems would dominate the entire Indian Ocean as well.

This expansion had drastic effects on economic conditions in Europe. Eastern commodities could no longer be carried overland to Constantinople; they now went by water to the Red Sea or the Persian Gulf, and thence overland, through a series of what were in effect toll stations, to Mediterranean ports in Africa and Asia Minor. The price of spices rose greatly, with severe consequences to Europe. Spices—cinnamon, cloves, pepper—were a necessity, not a luxury: Europe suffered from a chronic shortage of winter feed for cattle, and the spices were needed as preservatives for the huge amount of livestock slaughtered every autumn. The population of Europe, moreover, began to increase rapidly at this time, which meant that Oriental spices were becoming scarcer and dearer as the demand was becoming greater. By 1453, when Constantinople fell to the Moslems, old trade patterns with the East had been thoroughly disrupted, and Europe's strength was at its lowest in centuries.

Portugal's Crusade by Sea

Europe desperately needed a way of coping with the Moslems and trading with the East. Portugal found it. The people of that tiny kingdom, free for three centuries from Moslem domination but struggling for survival in a rocky and barren land, had turned to the sea, first as fishermen, then as traders. As seagoing traders whose home base was in the southwestern corner of Europe, and on the Atlantic, not the Mediterranean, they understandably thought of an indirect route to the spices that Europe needed. Western Africa below the Sahara had gold and ivory in abundance, and with these Europe could buy spices. Overland, through the Moslem territories of northern Africa, the black kingdoms that ruled western Africa and controlled the ivory and the gold could be reached only through Moslem intermediaries. But if Europeans could find a sea route around Africa to the East, they could bypass the Moslems, establish trade relations with the blacks, and simultaneously edge toward the Orient.

African Art (1200–1700). Figures like this one were sometimes given to tribal girls when they came of age. It is decorated with cowrie shells from the Indian Ocean, which were used as currency in many parts of Africa. (*National Museum of Denmark, Department of Ethnography*)

The black peoples Europe was seeking to trade with were impressive. In the area drained by the Senegal and Niger rivers, the rulers of Ghana, Mali, and Songhay had successfully established imperial domains; and in a vast territory extending from the Gulf of Guinea to the plains on the edge of the Sahara, and from the Atlantic Ocean deep into the interior, subsidiary kingdoms ruled. Those black kingdoms that had converted to Islam or come under its influence had developed written languages; and all of them possessed most of the other attributes that Europeans regarded as the marks of civilization, including agriculture, metal tools, political organization, professional armies, social stratification, cities, creative arts, and regular international and intercultural trade.

Prince Henry the Navigator The man who directed Portugal's efforts to take advantage of all this was Prince Henry the Navigator. Henry began his explorations in 1415. At the age of twenty-one this extraordinary young man retired from the court and from politics, became governor of the southernmost province of Portugal, and began building a strange settlement there, on Cape St. Vincent—"where endeth land and where beginneth sea." For the next forty years he gathered sailors, astronomers, map makers, instrument makers, and ship builders from all over Europe, and subsidized expeditions to explore the west coast of Africa, seeking "to reach India by an ocean route." Overcoming the fears of superstitious sailors that ships would run into boiling hot waters at the equator, Henry's grand and audacious Portuguese undertaking was only temporarily set back by his death in 1460. In 1487 Bartholomeu Diaz, his ship blown off course by a gale, rounded the southern tip of Africa. Then in 1497, Vasco da Gama made his celebrated voyage around the Cape of Good Hope to India with a four-vessel fleet, returning two years later with a cargo of pepper and cinnamon. Within twenty more years Henry's dream was fulfilled, for Portugal had established a maritime empire that extended the full breadth of the Indian Ocean.

Other Europeans, inspired by the Portuguese, sought to share in the glory and profit of war and trade in the East. None reckoned that they could overtake Portugal in the race around Africa, but several thought they might find an alternate course. It was reasonably well known that the earth was round. And since America was not known to exist and even knowledgeable Europeans underestimated the earth's circumference, they thought that a daring sailor might easily reach the Orient by sailing west from Europe. The most persistent of seamen who so reasoned was Christopher Columbus. "It is useless to complain," he told his crew in 1492, "I made this voyage to go to the Indies, and shall continue until I find them, with God's help." His voyages profited from Prince Henry's development of a small sailing ship, the caravel. Its hull design and sail plan enabled the caravel to sail closer to the wind and therefore faster than earlier ships. Now mariners could go as far as they wished with assurance that they could return. And so Columbus made his spectacular voyages, thinking that he was finding the Orient but in fact opening a new continent to Europeans.

The Spanish Empire

The consequence of Columbus's voyages was a flurry of efforts by other Europeans to capitalize on his findings. The Portuguese did little, for they were convinced that Columbus had not reached Oriental islands. Other European monarchs, including the Kings of England and France, backed voyages upon Columbus's mistaken belief that he had found the Indies, or a passage to them. Henry VII of England sponsored voyages by the Italian John Cabot in 1497 and 1498. Cabot explored the American coast from Labrador to Chesapeake Bay and discovered vast areas teeming with fish; but found neither spices nor a passage to India. Instead, as a contemporary noted, Cabot "found his new lands only in the ocean's bottom, to which he and his ship are thought to have sunk, since, after that voyage, he never heard of more." Henry's England profited little from these and two additional expeditions. French and Venetian efforts were likewise unprofitable, and both kingdoms had pressing preoccupations, and so they, like England, soon abandoned the search. Hence, for nearly a hundred years

The Great Temple of Tenochtitlán reconstructed by Ignacio Marquina from descriptions by Spanish conquerors and existing Aztec monuments. (*Courtesy, American Museum of Natural History*)

Spain had a virtual monopoly on exploration and discovery in the New World.

Explorers for Spain

The greatest of explorers sailing under the Spanish flag was, of course, Columbus himself. Columbus made four voyages in all (1492–93, 1493–96, 1498–1500, and 1502–04). He visited most of the major islands of the Caribbean, Trinidad, the northern coast of South America, and the Central American mainland from Honduras to Panama, and planted colonies in several of these places. In Cuba one of Columbus's sailors reported "many people, with a firebrand in the hand, and herbs to drink the smoke thereof." By the 1600s tobacco-smoking would become the rage all over Europe. In nonmaritime activities, Columbus proved inept. He so neglected and mismanaged the colonies that he had to be removed as governor; and when he died in 1506 he was still convinced that what he had explored was part of Asia. Columbus's reports of the new land's abundance and its natives' childlike innocence planted in the European mind the image of an earthly paradise, a lost Eden inhabited by noble savages, that would shape ideas about the New World for centuries to come.

One of Columbus's contemporaries, an Italian navigator named Amerigo Vespucci, first convinced Europe that Columbus had discovered a new continent. After sailing along the coast of what is now South America in 1501, Vespucci described the land and its people, marvelling, like Columbus, at their unspoiled nature:

> The inhabitants of the New World do not have goods of their own, but all things are held in common. They live together without King, without government, and each is his own master. . . . There is a great abundance of gold, and by them it is in no respect esteemed or valued. . . . and surely if the terrestrial paradise be in any part of this earth, I esteem that it is not far distant from these parts.

In 1507 a German cartographer, impressed by Vespucci's writings, named the new land "America" in his honor. It was Columbus, however, who would eventually have a day named for him, and the feminine "Columbia" would become the poetic synonym for the young United States. Vespucci's detailed descriptions of terrain, plants, and people added greatly to European knowledge and understanding of the shape and size of the New World. Henceforth all Europe knew America for what it was, a new continent and a barrier between Europe and Asia.

Voyages of exploration

Nothing of any recognized value had yet been found in America, and so the problem now was to find a strait through a land mass of unknown size. In 1513 a Spanish explorer, Juan Ponce de Leon, visited what is now the southeastern United States. He named the area Florida, meaning in Spanish "full of flowers." A chance discovery in 1513 stimulated the search for a passage to the Orient. Vasco Nuñez de Balboa, a Spanish adventurer, led a band of followers in search of gold in Central America, crossed the Isthmus of Darien, and sighted the Pacific. Spain promptly planted a colony in the vicinity, and explorers, encouraged to learn that the two oceans were separated only by an extremely narrow strip of land, renewed their hopes. After the coast of Central America and Mexico had been fairly thoroughly cruised, the most promise of finding a route lay to the south. And in 1519 Ferdinand Magellan, a Portuguese sailing under Spanish auspices, set out on his monumental voyage.

On September 20 he set out with five small ships and 275 men; three years later, on September 8, 1522, one worm-eaten ship and eighteen survivors sailed into the harbor at Seville. Magellan had been killed by natives in the Philippines, but his place in history was assured. His expedition, sailing around South America, across the Pacific, through the Indian Ocean, around Africa, and back to Spain, was the first to circumnavigate the globe. It added enormously to Europe's knowledge of the world and demonstrated for all time that it was not feasible for Spain to try to compete with Portugal in the East by sailing west. The route was simply too difficult; and besides, by the time Magellan's vessels reached the Indian Ocean the Portuguese had already established the bases that made them dominant in the entire area. In 1519, while Magellan's ships were nearing Tierra del Fuego, another voyage of discovery brought the first Europeans to what is now the Texas Gulf Coast. Searching like Magellan for a route to the Orient, Alonso Alvarez de Piñeda and his 270 men visited the mouth of the Rio Grande River before returning to Spain. Other nationals, much later, would resume the search for a northwest passage to the Pacific, but from the time of Magellan's voyages Spain had to be content with exploiting what it could in America.

| **The Aztecs, Incas, and Mayans** | The early Spanish settlements in the West Indies proved reasonably prosperous, establishing some |

economies based on cattle raising with Spanish labor and others founded on sugar planting with Indian slave labor. But raising cattle and growing sugar were not the kinds of activities that quickened the imagination or filled the treasuries of the Spanish monarchs. Far more exciting were rumors of highly civilized kingdoms in the interiors of Mexico, Central America, and northwestern South America, and of their stores of gold and silver. An expedition set out in 1519 to find, conquer, plunder, and Christianize these kingdoms. In command was Hernando Cortez, a thirty-two-year-old soldier and adventurer.

The Aztecs under the emperor Montezuma II, who believed himself a god, had dominated the valley of Mexico since the early 1300s. From their capital city of Tenochtitlán (now Mexico City), they sent out war parties to exact tribute from other tribes. In the capital the Aztecs had surgeons and hospitals as advanced as the best in Europe, but they also practiced human sacrifice. They worshiped many gods but particularly Quetzalcoatl, the feathered serpent, and the bloodthirsty Hummingbird, who demanded human offerings. In the space of only four days the Aztecs once sacrificed 80,000 human beings at the altar in Tenochtitlán. In 1519 as news of the Spanish encroachments reached him, Montezuma's astrologers forecast a war of the gods and he stepped up the ritual murders, which understandably weakened the loyalty of his subjects. When the emperor finally realized that the Spanish were not gods, he fought ably and might have defeated them. But during the siege of his city, smallpox decimated the Indian population.

The Aztecs, like the later Indian tribes Europeans encountered in America, had developed no immunity against the perennial European epidemics. Between 1500 and 1600 the native population of New Spain declined from some twenty-five million to about one million.

In a matter of months Cortez had penetrated the heart of the Aztec Empire and slain Montezuma, though it took two years to complete the systematic looting and destruction of Tenochtitlán and the total subjugation of the Aztec people. In the next few years Cortez's lieutenants brutally conquered the 400-year-old Mayan empire of Central America. And in 1532 an obscure adventurer, Francisco Pizarro, led a tiny band into Peru, seized and executed the Incan leader, Atahualpa, and on behalf of the King of Spain placed himself at the head of an empire of six or eight million souls. Finally, the Mayans of the southwestern Mexican coasts, literate and skilled, were subjugated. Only Brazil, awarded to Portugal by the Treaty of Tordesillas of 1494, remained outside the empire of the Spanish *conquistadores*.

In each instance the Spaniards consolidated their conquest with ease, partly because of their superior weapons, cunning, and aggressiveness, and partly because most of their victims were accustomed to total obedience, and so mastery over them required little more than the defeat of their existing masters. In each instance, the conquerors reaped fantastic wealth in gold and silver.

For the next hundred years, reports of the

Machu Picchu, the mysterious "Lost City of the Incas," 50 miles from Cuzco, Peru. Used by the last Inca ruler as an impregnable refuge from Pizarro and his conquistadores, it clings to a ridge 2000 feet above the Urubamba Valley. Abandoned after the Spanish conquest, it was unknown for centuries until rediscovery in 1911. *(Braniff International)*

New World's fabled treasures circulated throughout Europe. This description of a Peruvian garden, written by the illegitimate son of an Inca princess and a Spanish laborer, appeared in a work published in England in 1625:

> This Garden was in the Incas time a Garden of Silver and Gold, as they had in the Kings' houses, where they had many sorts of Hearbes, Flowers, Plants, Trees, Beasts great and small, wilde, tame: Snakes, Lizards, Snailes, Butterflies, small and great Birds, each set in their place. They had . . . Fruit-trees with the fruite on them all of Gold and Silver, resembling the naturall. They had also in the house heapes of wood, all counterfeit of Gold and Silver, as they had in the house royal: likewise they had great statues of men and women, and children . . . All the Vessel[s] . . . for the Temple's service, Pots, Pans, Tubs, Hogsheads, was of Gold and Silver, even to the Spades and Pickaxes for the Garden.

In 1528 Panfilio de Narvaez led 400 men to search for gold in Florida. Shipwrecked on the coast, the expedition was destroyed, but four survivors, including Narvaez and a black man named Estebanico, wandered in the

Texas wilderness for seven years before making their way to Mexico City. A few years later Hernando de Soto landed in the Tampa area in 1539 en route to the Mississippi River. No permanent settlements resulted from any of these early Spanish explorations.

In the 1540s de Soto and Francisco Vasquez de Coronado separately explored parts of the present-day United States for gold. De Soto, after landing on the west coast of Florida, led his men into North Carolina, turning westward and ending near Memphis, Tennessee, where he died in 1542. Ultimately, over 300 of his followers made their way back to Mexico via the Mississippi River. Coronado moved northward out of Mexico and probably traveled as far as Kansas. When he returned to Mexico he made clear that the fabled "seven Cities of Cibola," cities said to be made of gold, did not exist and that there was little else in the area to attract settlement.

Spanish exploration of the California coast also occurred in the 1540s. In 1542 Juan Rodriguez Cabrillo, a Portuguese explorer in the employ of Spain, hoped to discover the Northwest Passage between the Pacific and the Atlantic oceans. He first sailed into San Diego Bay and later went northward, perhaps as far as Oregon. Following Sir Francis Drake's claiming of California for the English, the Spaniards, fearing they might lose the region, sent Sebastian Vizcaino in 1602 to report about California to the Spanish monarch. Vizcaino recommended to the King that Spain establish colonies there, but further Spanish activity along the west coast would await the passing of nearly a century.

The French, however, in 1564 established a colony, Fort Caroline, near present-day Jacksonville. French Protestants, called Huguenots, remained in this colony until the Spanish massacred them. In 1565 the Spanish founded St. Augustine, the first perma-

Francisco Vasquez de Coronado, one of the earliest Spanish explorers of Mexico and the American Southwest, in a 1905 painting by Frederic Remington. *(Copyright 1905 by P. F. Collier and Son)*

nent settlement in what would one day become part of the United States. The Indians here introduced tobacco pipes to France and England: "The Floridians," said an English visitor, "have a kind of herb dried who with a cane and an earthen cup on the end, with fire, doe suck through the cane the smoke thereof, which smoke satisfieth their hunger." St. Augustine provided the base from which the Spanish would attempt to teach their way of life to the Florida Indians.

| Spanish Rule   By 1550, with the major centers of settled population in tropical America under Spanish control, Spain had imposed over the entire area a highly centralized imperial system. It differed greatly from the later British Empire. The Roman Catholic Church, through its missionary orders, vigorously pursued the spiritual conquest of the Indians and obtained a considerable measure of power in its own right, more or less independent of the lawyers who ran the imperial administration for the King. The empire had a fairly rigid class and caste system. At the top were the Spaniards who held most of the political and religious offices. Next came the Creoles, or pureblood Spaniards born in America, who held the larger landholdings or *encomiendas*. But the bulk of the population was made up of pure Indians and the *mestizos*, people of mixed Indian and Spanish blood, ultimately the most numerous element in the population. In the Spanish island plantations there was a still lower group, the black slaves. For all its faults, and for all the follies of the Spanish Kings, the Spanish empire thus organized flourished for more than two and a half centuries, and for much of the time made Spain the foremost power in the world. Then by the 1700s a newer British empire to the north, peopled by vigorous farmers, craftsmen, merchants, and seafarers prospering amidst considerable political freedom, would grow in strength while the hierarchical Spanish empire—its far-flung boundaries a source of unending trouble—declined.

Yet the Spanish empire endured for four hundred years. It has left its legacy in the United States in a growing number of Spanish-speaking citizens and a distinctive Hispanic culture in the Southwest.

England: The Sceptered Isle

| Henry VII   When Henry VII, the first Tudor King, ascended the throne in 1485, the royal treasury had been depleted by a long civil war, the War of the Roses. The throne itself was insecure, a number of ruthless and powerful noble families supporting the claims of various pretenders.

Henry might have been expected to secure his position in the traditional way, allying himself with various groups of nobles and playing them off one against the other. Instead, he built up the independent power of the Crown by taking a number of commoners into the government and launched a direct attack on the nobles who would not support him. As the principal instrument for this attack he created, with the consent of Parliament, the Court of the Star Chamber, through which people could be seized, tried without a jury, and punished by fines so heavy as to be confiscatory. In these early days the Star Chamber functioned and was looked upon as a protector of the common people against the tyranny of the nobles. By its means Henry weakened and divided the nobility, strengthened the Commons—the House of Parliament that was more representative of the people—and won the respect of the populace. To replenish the royal treasury, Henry managed his fiscal affairs efficiently and frugally (he paid John Cabot £10 for his 1497 voyage to America). He chose his wars carefully, acting only when he was likely not only to win, but also to reap profit from plunder or from ransoming captives. By the time he died in 1509 his dynasty was firmly secured, and the royal treasury was the richest in all Europe.

| Henry VIII   His son and successor, Henry VIII, began his reign by dissipating the royal treasury in little more than a decade. By the early 1520s, as a result of his own extravagance and overambitious meddling in continental politics and wars, the treasury was bare. The problem increased when the first great influx of American gold and silver into Spain inflated European prices.

Just at this time, a number of circumstances

coalesced to induce Henry to another radical measure. Of the six children borne by Henry's wife Catherine of Aragon, only one daughter survived and Catherine was unable to have more; and so the Tudor dynasty was in danger of having no successor to the throne. In addition, Henry fell passionately in love with Anne Boleyn, who was willing to marry the King but refused to become his mistress. Henry turned to the Pope with a request for an annulment, which might readily have been granted except that the Pope was virtually a prisoner of King Charles of Spain, Catherine of Aragon's nephew. The request was refused, and in 1529 Henry called Parliament into a historic session that lasted seven years. Before it was dissolved, a new Church of England had cut all ties with Rome.

That opened the way for a solution to Henry's financial problems. He confiscated the property of the church monasteries, which brought him nearly a sixth of all the land in England. Over the years Henry sold most of the land, mainly to the landholding classes on all levels, including many city merchants. A number of the new owners quickly resold their lands to smaller holders, and this somewhat broadened the landholding class. The releasing of land from the control of the Church, the consequent growth in the number of landholders, and the commercial activity that the sale of the lands awakened together modernized the English economy.

The break gained for England the zealous enmity of its traditional ally, Spain. That enmity intensified with the accession of Philip II to the Spanish throne in 1556; for Philip was fanatically dedicated to using all the wealth and power of the Spanish Empire to suppress Protestantism.

| Elizabeth I   And so when Queen Elizabeth, Henry VIII's daughter by Anne Boleyn, ascended the throne in 1558—after a turbulent and bloody eleven-year interval in which her half-brother Edward and her Roman Catholic half-sister Mary each occupied the throne for just over five years—England's internal order and external relations had been fundamentally rearranged.

Elizabeth faced spiraling prices and had no more monasteries to confiscate. One solution was for England to obtain a share of Spain's gold and silver through direct trade with Spanish colonies, and for Elizabeth to augment her treasury either by taxing or licensing this trade or by going into secret partnership with the English traders.

For a while such undertakings were entrusted to private enterprise. The first outsider to exploit this market was the Englishman John Hawkins. The two Old World commodities most in demand in Spanish America were cloth and slaves, the first a product of England and the other easily obtainable in Portuguese West Africa. In 1562 Hawkins acquired 300 black slaves and sailed with them to Hispaniola, where he sold them at a handsome profit; he received payment in sugar and hides, which he sold for further profit in Europe. On his second venture the queen and several members of her Privy Council were Hawkins's secret partners, and he again made a whopping profit, this time mainly in silver. Subsequent ventures were handicapped by a Spanish crackdown and by 1569 trade was thoroughly closed to outsiders. Within another four years, more or less open conflict between the Catholic and the Protestant countries had begun, the Dutch having allied themselves with England. For the next thirty years, British and Dutch ships engaged in smuggling to Spanish America and in systematic plunder of Spanish shipping.

The greatest of the English captains in these enterprises was Sir Francis Drake, kinsman of Hawkins. Drake conducted a brilliant and profitable privateering raid in 1573, viewed the Pacific Ocean from the Isthmus of Panama, and resolved "to sail an English ship in these seas." He launched his most spectacular venture five years later. With secret authorization and an investment from the queen he crossed the Atlantic, passed through the Strait of Magellan, plundered Spanish shipping off South America, captured a shipload of Peruvian silver, explored the Pacific coast of North America, crossed to the East Indies, concluded a treaty with a sultan who was at war with the Portuguese, bought several tons of cloves, and sailed home by the Portuguese route around Africa, returning with glory and magnificent treasure of £2,500,000—a return of 4700 percent on the Queen's investment. Meanwhile, Elizabeth encouraged Martin Frobisher and John Davis in their exploration of North America for a northwest water passage to Asia, and granted Humphrey Gilbert and his

Sir Walter Raleigh, encouraged by Queen Elizabeth to colonize North America, explored a new region which the monarch, known to history as the Virgin Queen, named Virginia in honor of herself. *(Courtesy, N.Y. Public Library, Picture Collection)*

half-brother Walter Raleigh a charter to colonize "remote heathen and barbarous lands not actually possessed by any Christian prince or people," and providing for settlers to "enjoy all the privileges of free denizens and persons native of England." When Drake came home from his spectacular circumnavigation of the world in 1581, the queen knighted him on the quarterdeck of his ship, the *Golden Hind*, and rejected all attempts by Spain to recover the stolen booty.

Open war with Spain soon followed. Spain under Philip II had had more than enough of Elizabethan "sea dogs," and the somber Catholic zealot Philip was committed to rewinning England and Calvinist Scotland for the Roman Catholic Church.

Naval warfare began in 1584. Elizabeth sent troops to aid Protestant Holland in its long struggle to retain its independence from the Spanish Crown. Drake set forth with more than twenty men-of-war and a royal commission to attack the Spanish position in America. In the ensuing year Drake wreaked

considerable devastation in the West Indies and sacked Santo Domingo. In 1587 he conducted an audacious raid that sank much of the Spanish fleet in its home harbor at Cadiz.

Philip of Spain then ordered the construction of an "Invincible Armada" of 132 vessels carrying 3165 cannon. The British hurriedly prepared for defense by constructing a more numerous though less heavily armed fleet, and one far better suited to fighting in rough seas. The Spanish were handicapped by being required to move on orders from Madrid. The English were infinitely more flexible. In a great naval battle in July 1588 the British outmaneuvered the Spanish in the English Channel and defeated the great Armada. Most of the Spanish vessels that escaped fled north hoping to return home by circling the British Isles, only to be destroyed by a storm off the Hebrides.

At the time of Elizabeth's death in 1603, the English people, a scant three million, but proud, aggressive, and prosperous, had gathered the energy that would propel them into virtual domination of the world.

English Colonization

While the Spanish were planting their colonies in the New World, Englishmen had given little energy to colonization. The English at the time of Henry VII as well as in Elizabeth's reign had sent voyages of expedition to North America in search of a northwest passage to the Orient, and Elizabethans had made some effort to colonize; but much of the activity of the English in the Western Hemisphere had been in trade with the Spanish colonies, with or without the acquiescence of Spanish authorities, and in plunder of Spanish shipping.

In the late sixteenth and the early seventeenth centuries, however, the idea of colonization found its promoters and publicists. One of the most dedicated of these was a clergyman named Richard Hakluyt. In *A Discourse Concerning Western Planting* in 1584 he argued that colonization would greatly benefit England. It might "stop the Spanish King from flowing over all the face of that waste land of America." Hakluyt noted that America had

plenty of excellent trees for masts, of good timber to build ships and to make great navies, of pitch, tar, hemp, and all things needed for a royal navy, and that for no price, and without money or request. How easy a matter it may be to this realm, swarming at this day with valiant youths, rusting and hurtful by lack of employment . . . to be lords of all those seas.

Hakluyt wrote that the many "wandering beggars of England, that grow up idly, and hurtful and burdensome to this realm, may there be unladen . . . to their own more happy state." Actually, England was far from overpopulated; but the poor who were packed into London gave the impression that the whole island was crowded beyond its resources. Other publicists for colonization insisted that Christians had a duty to do missionary work among the American Indians. Adventurers hoped that colonization would be profitable in its own right; they hoped also that colonies in North America, which James I recognized as belonging to the Spanish Crown, might provide an occasion for renewed war with Spain and renewed plunder.

The English after 1600 began crossing in large numbers to North America and the West Indies. In the first century of colonization, some 400,000 Britons embarked for the New World. Some searched for wealth, and some for a modest prosperity in the new lands. Many came for reasons connected with the religious controversies of the seventeenth century. Both the economic and the religious motives would leave their marks on American history, but first the English had to come to terms with the native Americans.

The First North Americans

Though the English, Spanish, and French languages and cultures ultimately dominated North America, the continent was first the domain of the Indians. The pre-Columbian story belongs largely to prehistory, that state of human development preceding adequate written records. And Spanish explorers and conquerors damaged what little written evidence existed in their attempt to weaken Indian beliefs. Our knowledge of early American Indians therefore can be reconstructed only from bits and scraps: tools, bones, pits, pots, graves, weapons, and garbage.

When Columbus landed in the West Indies, calling the people he met "Indians," the "New World" was new only to the Europeans. Neither Columbus nor the Norsemen who had touched Newfoundland and possibly present-day New England centuries before discovered the New World. The natives the European explorers came upon had discovered the continent in far prehistoric times. They came from Asia, of an Oriental stock, possibly mingled with some traces of European and African blood. The time of their arrival is subject to dispute. Once a thousand-mile land bridge, which geographers call Beringia, stretched between Siberia and Alaska. It existed fifty thousand years ago during the early part of the most recent Ice Age, sank below sea level, resurfaced about fifteen or twenty thousand years ago as the last Ice Age made its final surge, and disappeared again about ten thousand years ago. The migration from Asia occurred during one or more of the Beringian periods. Anthropologists and archaeologists agree that humankind came to North America at least twenty thousand years ago, and reached the southern tip of South America by about 8000 B.C.

Early Indians in North America were seed gatherers and game hunters, living in bands of twenty to fifty people. Some ten thousand years ago, they learned to remove flakes from stone, forming what are called "Folsom points," which made them more efficient hunters, though they continued where possible to drive big game such as mammoths, bison, deer, and antelope off cliffs or into swamps preparatory for the kill. Gradually diets diversified to include raccoons, opossums, shellfish, and sea animals in some areas. As the Ice Age retreated and the continent dried, great forests grew in the east and north of North America; the bow and arrow aided in the kill of small, swift woodland animals. Hooks, nets, and weirs caught fish and snared ducks. Desert Indians relied increasingly on plants, ground seeds, berries, bulbs, and nuts. About seven thousand years ago American natives, like peoples elsewhere around the world, developed agriculture. In comparison with modern technologies, basic agriculture seems simple; but in comparison with hunting and the gathering of wild plants it is a major, sophisticated control of the environment. Efficiency in food growing increased populations and quickened village life. Plant domestication emerged first in the Mexican highlands, and then spread north and south. It probably reached the peoples north of Mexico about three thousand years ago.

The degree to which this agricultural revolution had developed among the North American Indians varied widely at the time of Columbus's arrival. Hundreds of tribes speckled the continent, separated into the numerous linguistic and cultural groups that scholars today define.

The Indians of the Far North, across Canada and Alaska, were few. Divided into two major language groups, Algonquin and Athabascan, they included such tribes as Algonquin, Beaver, Chippewa, Cree, Chowo, and Yellowknife by present designations. Since the growing season was too short for agriculture, they gathered berries, plants, and nuts, and hunted caribou, moose, deer, elk, muskox, and buffalo. Nomadic Indians used portable tepees; others built sturdy log homes. The Far North Indians appear to have fought rarely.

A unique hunter-gatherer culture existed in the northwest corner of the present-day United States. The Northwest Coast Indians, their population stretching from northern California to southern Alaska, probably never developed agriculture. The Bella Coola, Chinook, Klikitat, Nootka, Quinault, and Tlingit Indians harvested the oceans and rivers, taking salmon, steelhead, inland trout, shellfish, sea lions, sea otters, and whales. In the lush forests, they hunted bear, caribou, deer, elk, and moose. Unlike most Indians north of Mexico, these people were not very egalitarian. A few families accumulated wealth in canoes, blankets, or hammered copper sheets. Lavishing wealth brought magical power over others, and these extraordinarily competitive Indians therefore held ceremonial feasts called "potlatches"; the hosts fed their guests and displayed, gave away, or even destroyed valued possessions. Like the hunter-gatherer Far North Indians, the Northwest Coast tribes had no pottery; they used wood for masks, grave markers, and utensils. The abundant redwoods, cedars, firs, and pines served as posts, beams, siding, and gables for their homes, and as raw material for the huge sixty-foot seagoing canoes that could carry up to sixty men. The Northwest coasters kept alive the myths surrounding their pantheon of gods by enacting religious dramas.

To the south of the coast tribes lived an Indian culture between the Cascade-Sierra Nevada ranges and the Rockies, in what is now called the Great Basin. Food was not abundant in this semi-arid land. Animals were scarce, and few edible plants could survive the droughts. Small Indian bands often ate rats, snakes, grasshoppers, grubs, and roots.

A North Pacific Coast Indian village as depicted in a nineteenth-century painting by Arthur A. Jansson. Indians in this region probably never developed agriculture, relying instead on fishing and hunting for food. *(Courtesy, American Museum of Natural History)*

The California Indians had an easier economic life. They lived in villages, hunted small game, fished and gathered wild plants, seeds, and nuts, and hand-crafted some of the finest basketry in the world.

The land between the Mississippi River and the Rocky Mountains belonged to the Plains Indians. Until the mid-1500s the Plains Indians preferred a more settled agricultural life in villages near rivers. When the agricultural product was insufficient, they would venture onto the plains and, when possible, stampede buffalo off cliffs. By the end of the sixteenth century the Plains Indians had domesticated the wild ponies, descendants of horses brought by the Spanish. The only North American Indians to adopt the horse culture, they quickly became superb horsemen. As mounted warriors and hunters they would roam the plains for nearly three hundred years. When they stayed in their permanent villages, they built homes of log framing covered with brush and dirt. When they traveled, they lived in portable tepees.

Another combination of hunter-gatherer and settled agrarian culture occupied much of the Southwest. These southwestern Indians showed remarkable ability to adapt to the arid buttes, mesas, and steep canyons in the northern part of this area and the flatter desert country to the south. The Anasazi, whom the Navaho call "the Ancient Ones," and their descendants, the Pueblos, Hopi, and Zuni, built cliff dwellings, some with as many as 800 units, centering around the point where Colorado, Utah, New Mexico, and Arizona meet. This more advanced agrarian culture developed specialization in work, yet sophistication did not lead to hierarchy: religious and military leaders worked much like anyone else. Pueblos were peaceable, preferring to pull up the ladders to their adobe homes when attacked. When an Anasazi killed someone, even in self-defense, elaborate purification preceded his reentry into the village. This peaceful, advanced culture faded, possibly because of a prolonged thirteenth-century drought and growing population pressures from the north. The chief invaders were the Navaho and Apache, both warlike Plains Indians related to the Athabascan language tribes of northwestern Canada.

The territory of the eastern woodland Indians extended from Canada to the Gulf of Mexico and from the Mississippi River to the East Coast. They belonged to three major language groups: Algonquin, Iroquian, and Siouan.

From about 400 B.C. to 550 A.D., in parts of what are now Ohio, Indiana, Illinois, Missouri, Michigan, and Wisconsin, a culture known as the Mound Builders flourished, leaving behind huge earthen burial mounds, some covering hundreds of acres. Ornaments and tools of bone, shell, and copper found in these mysterious mounds suggest that these Midwestern Mound Builders traded with areas as far away as the Gulf Coast and the Southwest. For unknown reasons, their culture died out long before the Europeans came. Another Indian culture, that of the Temple People of the Mississippi Valley, began around 900 A.D. and lasted until the late 1500s. They left enormous flat-topped earthen pyramids containing exquisitely-made jewelry, pottery, and agricultural implements with obvious Mexican influence. Hundreds of these mounds were scattered from present-day Illinois to the Gulf Coast states, and a number of them still remain. The Cahokia Mounds, near Collinsville, Illinois, are the remains of a city of over 20,000 with more than 100 mounds. The largest one rises in terraces to one hundred feet in height and covers fourteen acres. It is the largest prehistoric earthen structure in the New World.

On the eve of European discovery several Indian cultures dominated the eastern woodland, the third of the continent bordering the Atlantic. The eastern Algonquins occupied the Atlantic coast from Labrador to present-day North Carolina. Deep in the interior, on the Western Great Lakes, a northern and western Algonquin culture shared many of the traits of its eastern relatives. The Iroquois peopled the area between the two Algonquin cultures, from the Great Lakes to the central Appalachians. They included the Hurons, located north of the lakes; the Five Nations (Cayuga, Onondaga, Oneida, Mohawk, and Seneca) of the Mohawk Valley; and a conglomerate of related tribes including the Cherokee, Tuscarora, Moneton, and Monacan in the central and southern Appalachian Mountains. The Muskogean culture occupied the lowlands of southeastern North America.

The Five Nations confederation, founded around 1570, numbered perhaps 10,000 peo-

"They have likewise a notable way to catche fishe in their Rivers, for whear as they lack both yron, and steele, they faste unto their Reedes or longe Rodds, the hollowe tayle of a certain fishe like to a sea crabbe in steede of a poynte, wehr with by nighte or day they stricke fishes, and take them opp into their boates."—Hariot (1590). John White, *The Manner of Their Fishing*, drawing 1585. *(Courtesy, British Museum, London)*

ple by the year 1600. Its purpose was to eliminate blood feuds and cope with the nagging conflicts with nearby Algonquins, which may have resulted from population growth generated by improved agriculture. According to Iroquois legend, the leader credited with solving these problems was a chief named Hiawatha, who apparently lost relatives around 1450 and, rather than taking blood revenge, recommended that a ritual bereavement replace the vendetta, that retaliations be forbidden, and that a council of forty-nine chiefs make decisions for all the villages. Thereafter villages of the Five Nations were bound together for internal peace and external defense. A sixth tribe, the Tuscarora, joined in 1722. Communal sharing extended to land use, the hunt, and the home. Although plowed by a family, the land was not owned, and although one hunter might outdo another, the kill was distributed. Families might live together in one house, but no single family owned it. If one person went hungry, all did.

Women dominated familial lineages and were influential in Iroquois politics, although the Senecas did not give women the right to vote or serve on tribal councils until the 1960s. The families included the oldest female and her daughters, immature male children, and sons-in-law. Married men joined the family of their wives. Women initiated divorce by throwing their husbands' belongings outside. In politics women picked replacements for vacancies in the council of forty-nine, and influenced village decisions behind the scenes. The women farmed, controlling the villages, while the men warred, fished, and hunted; women could sometimes veto military expeditions by refusing to supply footwear or food.

Although the Iroquois did compete among themselves in hunting, fishing, and fighting, child raising encouraged egalitarianism. Youngsters were rarely punished physically, and were expected to err as they imitated adults. This freedom continued as the child grew up. Without specialized legal personnel, laws, or jails, acceptable behavior was maintained by the ostracism and consensus that are typical of many small agricultural communities.

Among themselves, then, the Iroquois were civilized people, in some ways more civilized than the Europeans. Yet they do not deserve to be romanticized as a lost, virtuous civilization destroyed by white invaders. Like Europeans and white Americans, they could be as ruthless toward people outside their polity and culture as they were civil to their own kind. Algonquins and others knew the Iroquois as cruel warriors.

Indians in the Americas had too little technology and were too divided to stop the European newcomers. The very lack of unity among North American natives meant that each group would have to find its own way to accommodate the increasingly numerous and powerful Europeans.

The Columbian Exchange

The contact between Europe and America led to what has come to be called the "Columbian exchange," a redistribution of peoples, animals, and plants around the world. With contact came radical changes in life around the globe. By 1500 Europe had a population of 75 million, and perhaps one hundred million Indians may have lived in the Americas, perhaps ten million of those in what are today the United States and Canada. But European conquest and disease decimated American Indians to about five to ten percent of their earlier numbers. As the years passed the native populations were replaced by Europeans in three major patterns. The Spanish and Portuguese intermarried with highland Indians and lowland black slaves to form the mestizo, mulatto, and zambo populations that dominate Latin America. The English in the West Indies and the southeast coast of the present-day United States, failing to enslave the Indians, established hierarchical societies based on the labor of blacks imported from Africa. And in the northeast, English colonists developed exclusively European communities, largely segregated from Indian villages.

Animal and food plant exchanges accompanied Indian-European contact. Domesticated animals—pigs, goats, horses, cattle, and sheep—accompanied Europeans to America, along with wheat, rye, barley, oats, rice, melons, coffee, dandelions, sugar cane, and olives. The plants that American Indians made available to the rest of the world now constitute one-third of the world's food supply: Indian corn, beans, squash, pumpkins, white potatoes (which first went from South America to Europe and finally, through the Scotch-Irish, to North America in the eighteenth century), tomatoes, peppers, and peanuts. Tobacco, drugs such as cocaine, novocaine, and quinine, and the strains of cotton in modern use also entered the world market from the Americas.

Some of the biological exchange also involved microscopic life in the form of diseases. Indians had developed no immunity to measles, chicken pox, smallpox, and whooping cough, from which they had been isolated by three thousand miles of ocean. These diseases devastated American Indians, killing far more than did conquest. In 1520 an Indian recalled that the smallpox in Peru

spread over the people as great destruction. . . . Very many died of it, they could not stir; they could not change position, nor lie down on one side, nor face down, nor on their backs. And if they stirred, much did they cry out.

In the early 1620s one European observer wrote that the Massachusetts Bay Indians

died on heapes, as they lay in their houses, and the living, that were able to shift for themselves, would runne away and let them dy, and let there Carkases ly above the ground without burial. . . . And the bones and skulls upon the severall places of the habitations made such a spectacle after my coming into those parts, that as I travailed in the Forrest nere the Massachusetts, it seemed to me a new found Golgotha.

And Europeans may have contracted syphilis from Americans. While medical historians cannot definitely attribute the disease to the Indians, circumstantial evidence suggests an American origin. Traces have been found in Indian but not European bones in pre-Columbian times. The first recorded case appeared in Cadiz, Spain, soon after Columbus returned from America. In any event, about ten million Old World people died of syphilis within the next fifteen years.

Central and South American gold and silver enriched European monarchies and stimulated trade and industry. European merchants prospered from the trade in American agricultural raw materials. While European ethnocentricity increased among those who judged superiority on such bases as written languages, military technology, and Christianity, America also provided a storehouse of information in the natural sciences and contributed to the intensification of scientific inquiry. Europeans were captivated by the notion of the "noble savage" and took that mythic creation into their political and moral philosophies. The very idea of a new and open land enlarged the vision of human possibility.

In America, Europeans adopted Indian ways. Beside eating Indian foods, they wore moccasins, snowshoes, ponchos, and parkas, plied rivers and lakes with canoes, and rested in hammocks. They played lacrosse, built homes of adobe, and rode on dogsleds and toboggans. The early European settlers followed Indian trails, smoked native tobacco, and used native medicines. Indian names entered English usage. They would serve for nearly half of the eventual state names—from Connecticut and Alabama to Iowa, Texas, and Wyoming—and were used for many rivers and cities.

Besides declining in numbers, the original Americans underwent enormous cultural changes. Indian lands shrank as the plow, lumbering, cattle, and sheep permanently transformed the eastern woodlands. Other changes in Indian life were largely a matter of choice. European knives and guns improved hunting. The horse gave the Plains Indians mobility to hunt buffalo and raid settlements. Iron pots replaced pottery and baskets. Sheep made possible the beautiful wool blankets of the Pueblos. The iron hoe and plow increased agricultural productivity, and the metal fish hook enhanced catches. Many natives also responded to the lure of profit from the fur trade. European demand for pelts soon outstripped the animal population near the sea coast, and some tribes had to abandon older settlements in favor of new ones farther inland, eventually depleting animals there, too. The pelts purchased not only European weapons and utensils but also alcohol.

American natives borrowed selectively from the Europeans, but Indian cultures persisted. Material and economic incentives and the need for alliances against other tribes may have lured Indians to change their ways, but they never adopted European political, social, or religious values and customs. No evidence shows that Indians sought to live permanently among the newcomers, although there were a substantial number of "white Indians," Europeans who lived permanently among Indians. In North America, Indians were not conquered and enslaved to the extent that occurred in Latin America, and so were able to maintain a largely separate racial and cultural existence. They interacted with the Europeans primarily in trade and war with disastrous results for both sides.

Points To Think About

1.   The New World's gold and silver, pouring into European coffers, transformed the Old World's economy from a medieval system, in which most people bartered for their goods and little money changed hands, to an early modern economy based on hard currency (gold and silver coins) as a medium of exchange. As trade expanded, the need for credit grew apace. Lenders were, as always, being asked to risk their money; but the risks were far higher than today's. Ships were small and fragile. A storm could turn an otherwise successful venture into a total loss. So interest rates—the money charged for credit—were high. Yet any interest at all the medieval church viewed as usury, a sin against the virtue of charity. Medieval Catholicism taught the individual to seek for meaning and for salvation in the community. The Church urged everyone to find a place in the order of creation and faithfully fulfill the duties of that station.

The various faiths of the Reformation, on the other hand, all began with the notion that each person must find his own way to God. And each must seek to glorify God by succeeding on earth.

For ordinary people, mobility, social or spatial, was unusual. Individuals expected to live and die in the same social class and in the same town or village as their ancestors. The burgeoning world of commerce encouraged individual initiative and industry, and at the same time the Protestant Reformation told the individual to seek God for himself. Perhaps it was only a matter of time until the ordinary individual, living in a world of monarchies, would want to govern himself.

2. Christopher Columbus set sail in the very year that Ferdinand and Isabella succeeded in driving the Moors off the Iberian peninsula, thereby unifying Spain under a strong central government. That 1492 marks both events is no coincidence. Imperialism and the modern nation-state go hand in hand. Spain's early lead in the race for control of the non-European world came exactly because Spain was the first large European state to develop a modern, unified government. France and England did not succeed in doing the same until near the end of the sixteenth century. So it is no mystery why England was a comparatively late entrant in the imperialist sweepstakes.

Imperialism awaited the formation of the centralized, bureaucratic state. This has led some historians to say that empire-building is what marks the transition from medieval to modern history. It is tempting to say still more. Can we say that impe-rialism is a by-product of the formation of the modern nation-state? Typically, that formation involved expansion of some kind.

3. The emergence of England as a modern nation-state reflected more than changes in the role of the monarchy or the growth of a centralized bureaucracy. It also involved profound economic and social changes. In the first half of the sixteenth century British exports of woolen goods grew enormously. This new source of prosperity caused English landlords to shift from farming to sheep-growing on a wide scale, a change that altered the society as well as the economy of the English countryside. Small farmers, most of them tenants, were driven from the land. These people wandered from place to place looking for work. Downturns in demand for cloth produced wholesale unemployment. The Crown sought to control prices and wages in an attempt, largely unsuccessful, to mitigate the resulting distress. The government also passed a number of laws designed to punish vagabonds, robbers, poachers, and others whose distress made them careless of property rights.

Colonies seemed the perfect solution to these new problems. Not only would they lead to increased trade, but they would also provide a place for the surplus population to go in the chartered trading colonies. Thus it can be said that the United States began as a business venture.

Suggested Readings

Any study of the voyages of discovery can begin with Samuel Eliot Morison's works: *The European Discovery of America: The Northern Voyages, A.D. 500–1600* (1971) and *The European Discovery of America: The Southern Voyages, A.D. 1492–1616* (1974). Morison examines in impressive detail, and from an extraordinary number of unpublished sources, the personalities and the routes followed by the great navigators who explored the continents. Both works have been abridged into a single volume: *The Great Explorers: The European Discovery of America* (1978). A beautifully illustrated book on the period of discovery is Richard Humble, *The Explorers* (1979). J.A. Williamson's *Sir Francis Drake* (1966) is a stirring biography, and Kenneth Andrews's *Elizabethan Privateering* (1964) is exhaustive. See also Ralph Davis, *The Rise of the Atlantic Economies* (1973), Charles Gibson, *Spain in America* (1966), and R.C. Padden, *The Hummingbird and the Hawk* (1967).

On American Indians, Wilcomb Washburn's *The Indians of North America* (1975) is both well written and well illustrated. An important environmental study is William Cronon's *Changes in the Land: Indians, Colonists, and the Ecology of New England* (1984). *The Columbian Exchange* (1972) by Alfred W. Crosby, Jr., shows how ways of life were altered in both hemispheres. *In The White Man's Indian: Images of the American Indian from Columbus to the Present* (1978), Robert Berkhofer, Jr. skillfully applies the analytical devices of anthropology and the behavioral sciences. Elizabeth A. H. John, in *Storms Brewed in Other Men's Worlds: The Confrontation of Indians, Spanish, and French in the Southwest, 1540–1795* (1975), tells the shockingly neglected story of the settlement of the Southwest. On white-Indian relations, see Gary Nash, *Red, White, and Black* (1974), and Karen O. Kupperman, *Settling with the Indians; The Making of English and Indian Cultures in America* (1980), which finds similarities as well as contrasts. See also Margaret Connell Szasz, *Indian Education in the American Colonies* (1988).

FORREST McDONALD

As with any complex historical process, there was no simple explanation for Europe's discovery of the New World and expansion over it. Surely greed, power, and religion were part of the story, but these motives were old long before Columbus set sail.

Portugal and Spain began their explorations largely for religious reasons. The Age of Discovery was but another chapter in their long warfare for Christianity against Islam. Finding gold and silver in the Americas was a coincidence that spurred further explorations. The Spanish Kings, having expelled the last of the Moors, found a new religious warfare that would use every ounce of gold and silver they could take from the New World during the next two hundred years: the suppression of the Protestant Reformation.

Other nations of western Europe sent expeditions in search of windfall wealth, but none was successful. Then during the seventeenth century the age of colonization began. When we speak of colonization, however, we really refer to the British. In the Spanish and Portuguese empires the vast majority of subjects were of native descent. The Dutch, Swedish, and Danish colonies were minuscule. France claimed a huge area, but few Frenchmen settled the lands. On the North American continent, small numbers of French occupied military and fur-trading posts and lived among the Indians, often intermarrying with them. On the Caribbean islands a few grew extremely rich from the slave labor of large numbers of blacks. The French crown was interested in colonies to increase royal revenues and to control political factions at home through the granting of lucrative monopolies. Even stronger was France's desire to gain strategic advantage over England.

In England King James I (1603–1625) actively promoted resettlement to maintain political and religious order at home. England had suffered a long period of poor harvests and was thought to be overpopulated; sending Englishman abroad was a way of averting the dangers posed by religious and political radicalism. But James also believed in colonization as a means of pacifying, Christianizing, and "civilizing" native populations. He chartered colonies on the Scottish Island of Lewis and in Northern Ireland as well as in America. Charles I (1625–1646), seeking to establish religious uniformity, both persecuted dissenters and encouraged them to emigrate. Charles II (1660–1685) dispensed colonial charters as a means of paying his political and monetary debts. Unrestricted emigration persisted until the early nineteenth century simply because no one thought it worth the trouble to stop it.

The reasons for migrating were varied. A sizable number of people went involuntarily: blacks were forcibly transported to the New World, and many Irish and Scots were deported for rebellion or for nonpolitical crimes. The Puritans left largely for religious reasons, though the push of hard times and the pull of opportunity contributed. Quakers also emigrated to escape religious persecution, as did some Catholics. But after 1689, when the greatest emigration took place, most who left were in flight from grinding poverty; and most of these earned their passage by selling themselves into indentured servitude for four to seven years. Others went because they did not like the changes taking place in their homelands. And many went just from a spirit of adventure.

The nature of the emigration helped stamp the American character indelibly. It took initiative, enterprise, and courage to venture to the New World. And thus, though the settlers came mainly from the lower to middle orders of the population, they were a pre-selected, hardier breed than the kinsmen they left behind. America was blessed from the start.

Why did Europeans Colonize?

EUGENE GENOVESE

Of British North America Professor McDonald says, "It took initiative, enterprise, and courage to venture to the New World. And thus, though the settlers came mainly from the lower to middle orders of the population, they were a pre-selected, hardier breed than the kinsmen they left behind." But why should Professor McDonald limit that description to British North America? It applies nicely, for example, to Brazil; no word need be altered. The Northern colonies of British North America, to be sure, were settled primarily by Europeans of initiative, enterprise, and courage, while Brazil was settled by a much smaller number relative to the African slaves imported to do the work. Those Africans had their share of initiative, enterprise, and courage, but of a different order and necessarily put to different uses, such as slave rebellion. The Southern colonies of British North America and the British West Indies, which for a long time were the most lucrative of colonies, resembled Brazil. But throughout the New World, settlers both African and European, were well endowed with the virtues Professor McDonald lists.

In what, then, was British North America "blessed," as Professor McDonald says? Initiative, courage, and enterprise the British settlers shared with the Spanish, Portuguese, Dutch, and others. But the English had developed and disciplined these qualities in a new kind of society. Long before the industrial revolution the English had come to live among one another in freedom. Their ties to their lords and to the land had been steadily eroded, and with those ties the protection and security supposedly conferred by feudal relations. The great English revolutions of the seventeenth century legally and constitutionally consolidated this historic transformation in social relations. Those who came to North America, however traditional they may appear when compared with later generations, were products of this revolutionary new social system. For better or worse they were independent in a way in which the Spanish and Portuguese, even the haughty aristocrats who defiantly stood on their feudal liberties, were not. The British settlers brought new institutions to match their new sentiments, sensibilities, and ways of thought. Those institutions embodied large concessions to the rights of individuals and would eventually spark a great revolution against Britain, carried out in defense of the British liberties that recent centuries had wrought.

The emerging modern personality and modern institutions rested on private property—on the right of everyone to own land and other property. Those who did not own real property owned property in themselves; they could sell their labor-power to the highest bidder. And, if lucky, they could apply their earnings to the purchase of real property, which itself was increasingly clear of traditional obstacles to sale, and was abundant in the New World.

Private property, as the modern Western world defines it, has been intimately connected with the expansion of freedom, but it can also be the enemy of freedom. My private property intrudes upon your free space, or fences off from you the land or other wealth with which you could have expressed your freedom. The institution of slavery in the new colonies was the clearest instance in which property turned against freedom. But even today, over a century after the end of slavery, the systems of private property that attended the growth of freedom choke off the possibilities for a full development of freedom and justice. When freedom and property landed together on the shores of British North America, they were to begin a long, complex, and tortured relationship.

Diagram of the attack on the Pequot Fort on Mystic River. Led by Captains John Mason and John Underhill, the colonial forces set fire to the fort, burning alive between 400 to 700 men, women, and children. From an illustration, artist unknown, accompanying John Underhill's *Newes from America*, London, 1638. *(Courtesy, Rare Book Room, New York Public Library)*

CHAPTER 2

British North America

PURITANS AND PEQUOTS: THE INVASION OF NEW ENGLAND

In the late sixteenth and early seventeenth centuries, disruption and violence
marked the history of the region we now call New England. Shortly before
1600 a powerful and warlike tribe from the upper Hudson pushed its way into
the Connecticut Valley. Originally called Mohegans, these people earned by
their brutal conquests the name Pequot—"destroyer" in the Algonquin dialects
of New England. Soon they dominated the valley, terrorizing and exacting
tribute from the Narragansetts to the east, the Montauks to the south on Long
Island, the Nipmucs to the north, and the Podunks, Wongunks, Siciaoggs, and
other tribes to the west.

New England was a poor, hard, thinly populated land. The total population
in 1600 was perhaps 25,000, a population density of about one person per four
acres. The various tribes, none larger than 4000 people, lived in relatively
settled territories, moving about among winter, summer, and autumn quarters
to sustain their mixed farming and hunting economy and to escape into more
sheltered valleys for the winters. The white man's later image of them as
nomadic hunters was as false as William Bradford's sense of their numbers
when he spoke of "a hideous and desolate wilderness, full of wild beasts and
wild men." Warfare over boundaries, hunting lands, and the like was common
enough, but most encounters were no more than skirmishes affecting only a
few braves on each side. Diplomacy was as intricate and complex as in Europe:
most tribes had traditional rivals as well as slowly shifting alliances.

During the winter of 1616–17 an epidemic of smallpox suddenly decimated
many of the tribes. No Indian would have connected this mysterious visitation
with the occasional and usually friendly encounters with European fishermen
drying their catches on the beaches in summer or trading a few items for furs
and skins or food; but these were the source of the disease that wiped out as
much as one-third of the area's population. Thousands more would die during
the winter of 1633–34 from a similar outbreak. Since these epidemics did not
stretch beyond the region, the New England Indians found themselves even

less capable than before of withstanding the depredations of the powerful border tribes. But then potential allies—white settlers equipped with modern firearms—suddenly arrived from Europe.

Despite the many obvious cultural differences and the language barrier between English settlers and Indians, the Pilgrims and after that the larger Puritan settlement in Massachusetts Bay received a generally friendly welcome. Puritans also made an effort to convert the Indians to Christianity. Trade, Indians perceived, made tribes rich and powerful and usually ended with their acquiring firearms. At first the needs of the two cultures seemed compatible. The English settlers understood the strongly hierarchical structure of most tribal government. They carefully purchased land titles granting the Indians the right to continue to hunt or fish.

Misunderstandings nonetheless turned into resentments and finally conflict. Neither Puritan governors nor tribal sachems could control all that occurred in each trading venture or settlement. New England attracted not only well-disciplined Puritans, but many a reckless adventurer seeking fortune and excitement. Thomas Morton, famous for his colony's merriment and frolic about the blasphemous maypole, was expelled from the colony in part for the "many wrongs hee hath done them [the Indians] from tyme to tyme." Massachusetts court records are full of attempts to punish and make restitution for the deception, sharp dealings, kidnappings, and little battles that marked many encounters between newcomers and natives. By the early 1630s the number of English colonists was far larger than that of any single tribe; by mid-decade there were probably as many English as Indians in New England. And as the Massachusetts Bay colony grew in size, the disposition to impose order on Indians grew likewise. When settlement expanded into the Connecticut Valley, where the Pequots had already shredded the tissue of intertribal diplomacy, war broke out.

An eighteenth-century poet chronicler of the Pequot war blamed the Pequots for provoking war by killing three Englishmen: *"First, helpless Stone! they bade thy bosom bleed,/A guiltless offering at th' infernal shrine/Then, gallant Norton! the hard fate was thine,/By ruffians butcher'd, and denied a grave/Thee, generous Oldham! next the doom malign/Arrested; nor could all thy courage save/Forsaken, plunder'd, cleft, and burried in the wave."*

That John Stone, the victim, had already been banished from New England under penalty of death for larceny, adultery, and attempted murder of the governor of Plymouth lends some force to the Pequot claim that his killing was under dire provocation. Norton was in cahoots with Stone; and Oldham, apparently, met his fate at the hands of the Narragansetts—who remained allied to the British—rather than the Pequots. Despite these uncertainties, the Puritans, goaded by their Indian allies and perhaps nervous over the religious schisms occurring in the colony, dispatched ninety men under John Endicott on a mission of destruction. Endicott's orders included putting to death all Indian men on Block Island. When the band of Englishmen with guns was frustrated by the Indians' retreat into swamps, they fired all their wigwams, destroyed all their possessions, then wantonly "destroyed some of their dogs."

The Pequots replied in kind. Ambushing five men near Saybrook, they dispatched three immediately and roasted one alive; "the other came down drowned to us . . . with an arrow shot into his eye through his head." Similar fates befell about thirty white settlers in the next year before skirmishes and ambushes turned into a full-scale war of extermination, whose genocidal intent was expressed in the Reverend Thomas Hooker's admonition "not to do this work of the Lord's revenge slackly."

The Pequot war was not an early version of cowboys and Indians. There was not a white and an Indian side. The climactic battle pitted Mohegans (who had broken with the Pequots), Narragansetts, and Englishmen against the Pequot fort on Mystic River within which somewhere between 400 and 700 men, women, and children perished by fire, musket ball, or arrow in less than an hour's time on May 26, 1637. God, so the Puritan commander reported, had "laughed his Enemies and the Enemies of his People to Scorn, making them as a fiery Oven. . . . Thus did the Lord judge among the Heathen, filling the Place with dead Bodies."

The Town of Secotan, by John White, depicts a seventeenth-century Indian village in Virginia. English colonists traded trinkets, glass beads and tin whistles, for Indian corn. *(Courtesy, Virginia State Library)*

Early Southern Settlements

| **Roanoke and**
| **Jamestown**
The history of British settlement of North America begins with a tale of mystery. Late in the sixteenth century a group of adventurers, among them the courtiers Sir Humphrey Gilbert and his half-brother, Sir Walter Raleigh, had developed plans for establishing settlements in the New World. The mercantile and maritime adventurers of the seventeenth century were of the lusty and aggressive character that had marked the Elizabethans. They were eager to exploit the American continent that Europeans only a few decades earlier had considered no more than an annoying obstacle on the route to the Orient. Gilbert left for the New World in 1583, but after reaching Newfoundland he and two of the expedition's five ships went down during a fierce autumn storm. Sir Humphrey's ship, as an observer reported, was "devoured and swallowed up of the sea."

In 1584 under Raleigh's sponsorship another voyage explored the coast of what is now North Carolina. One of the leaders of this expedition wanted to name the new land "Wingandacoa," a word he had heard the Indians use, but Queen Elizabeth I and Raleigh chose "Virginia," in honor of Elizabeth, the Virgin Queen.

In 1585 Raleigh sent over a hundred men to establish a settlement at Roanoke, a small wooded island off the coast of present-day North Carolina. They found the Indians inhospitable and returned home after a year. In 1587 Raleigh, still determined to "plant a colony," sent 115 settlers, this time including seventeen women, under the leadership of John White, whose watercolors of the Indians and wildlife would furnish Europeans with some of their first views of the New World. At Roanoke, White's daughter Elenora, wife of Ananias Dare, gave birth to a daughter, "the first Christian born in Virginia." The infant was appropriately named Virginia.

Sometime between 1587, when John White and the supply ships left Roanoke, and 1590, when he was finally able to return, Virginia Dare and all the rest of the colonists vanished. To this day no one knows what became of them. England's war with Spain and the battle of the Spanish Armada in 1588 had

prevented a resupply mission to the Roanoke colonists until 1590; by then it was too late. White's journal records his fruitless search:

> We espied towards the north end of the island the light of a great fire through the woods, to the which we presently rowed. When we came right over against it, we let fall our grapnel [anchor] near the shore, & sounded with a trumpet call, & afterwards many familiar English tunes of songs, and called to them friendly, but we had no answer. . . .
>
> In all this way we saw on the sand the print of the savages' feet of 2 or 3 sorts trodden that night, and as we entered up the sandy bank upon a tree, in the very brow there were curiously carved these fair Roman letters, C R O: which letters presently we knew to signify the place, where I should find the planters seated, according to a secret token agreed upon between them & me. . . .

Though Raleigh sent another expedition to look for the Roanoke colonists in 1602, no further trace of them was ever found.

In 1612 William Strachey, a Virginia colonist, reported hearing that "the men, women, and children of the first plantation at Roanoke were . . . miserably slaughtered" by the Indian chief Powhatan, though they "had peaceably lived and intermixed with those savages, and were out of his territory."

Other reports from America nevertheless whetted English appetites for more colonizing ventures. One account described the shellfish as "exceeding good and very great," and characterized the Indians as "courteous" and "gentle of disposition." Another found the Atlantic coast's crabs "rather better in taste than ours, one able to suffice four men." The Indians were "kind and loving," and "a very witty and ingenious people, apt both to understand and speak our language." In 1603 a sea captain exploring what would become New Hampshire reported seeing "goodly groves and woods and sundry beasts, but no people."

In 1606, two groups of investors, one in London and one in Plymouth, formed joint-stock companies and petitioned the King for charters of incorporation for the purpose of colonizing North America. Both companies were chartered, the Plymouth Company for operations in the northern part of the continent, the Virginia Company in the southern;

but councils named by the King controlled each of the ventures.

In May 1607 the Virginia Company sent three small ships, the *Susan Constant, Discovery,* and *Godspeed,* with 105 men and boys to plant a settlement called Jamestown.

In the first seven weeks they built a log fort, planted "good store of wheat," "built some houses," and enjoyed fishing in a river "so stored with sturgion and other sweet fish as no man's fortune hath ever possessed the like." But soon disease and hostile Indians took their toll, and of the original 104 English settlers, only 38 were alive in January 1608 when the Virginia Company's supply ships returned.

At first the colony was governed by an unwieldy and bickering council, which meant in practice that it was not governed at all; and many settlers took to wandering into the interior to hunt or to search for gold, leaving no one to do the work of building the settlement and making it self-sufficient. In 1608

one of the settlers, twenty-seven-year-old John Smith, became president of the local council. He took charge, declared that "he that will not work shall not eat," and ensured the permanence of the settlement.

Smith also made a fragile peace with the Indian chief Powhatan, who commanded some 1500 warriors in the area surrounding Jamestown. On one occasion, Powhatan's ten-year-old daughter, Pocahontas, "a well-featured but wanton yong girle," interceded with her father on Smith's behalf, and later became a frequent visitor to the English settlement. As the Virginia Company sent more colonists (including the first "Gentlewoman and woman servant" to arrive at Jamestown) in 1608, food remained in short supply, and the arrival of nearly 300 new settlers in the summer of 1609 plunged the colony into chaos. There was barely enough food for the 200-odd settlers already there, and bitter quarrels arose. The newcomers were part of the largest expedition—9 ships and 500 colo-

Jamestown, founded in 1607, fared better than the Roanoke settlement. Though ravaged by disease and Indian attacks, the settlement survived and Virginia became the preeminent Southern colony. (*Courtesy, American Historical Society*)

nists—yet sent out by the Virginia Company. The flagship *Sea Venture* and two other vessels had disappeared in a hurricane. In September 1609 Smith was severely injured by an exploding bag of gunpowder, and had to return to England.

In the winter of 1609–10 there occurred what came to be called the "Starving Time," in which the Jamestown colonists, according to one report, ate

> dogs, cats, rats, and mice, . . . boots, shoes, or any other leather . . . and those being spent and devoured, some were forced to search the woods and to feed upon serpents and snakes and to dig the earth for wild and unknown roots where many of our men were cut off and slain by the savages.

Of nearly 350 colonists left in Virginia when Smith and five of the ships departed, about 100 survived: 60 men, women, and children at Jamestown, and another 40 or more at a fort downriver. In May 1610 Deputy-governor Gates and 150 survivors of the *Sea Venture* shipwreck arrived, and they and the rest of the colonists decided to abandon Jamestown. In June, sailing downriver, they were met by the new governor and three ships carrying 300 colonists and a year's supply of food. All returned to Jamestown, and England's fragile little colony endured.

Back in England a faction in the company arose, headed by Sir Edwin Sandys, one of the most influential leaders of Parliament. He recruited support from small shareholders in the company and in 1618 succeeded in overthrowing the old management.

Under a new charter the Virginia Company, in order to attract more investors and more settlers, granted a "headright" of fifty acres of land per person to all individuals who came on their own or brought others to Virginia. With aggressive recruiting the Company poured some 3,500 newcomers into the colony between 1618 and 1621, more than twice the number who had emigrated since 1607. But in 1622, before the Indians massacred 347 settlers, Virginia's English population was slightly over 1,300. Diseases—salt poisoning from the saline James River, dysentery, typhoid—and hardship took a fearful toll. One colonist thought that "more doe die here of the disease of their mind, then of their body."

At its own expense the Company undertook to send to Virginia a variety of craftsmen and a number of female settlers, "young maids," who would make the colony's economy more self-sufficient and its life more tolerable. The company relaxed its governing rules, provided that settlers continue to be governed by English law and have the rights of Englishmen, and gave settlers a voice in the management by allowing them to elect representatives to an assembly. The House of Burgesses, the first colonial legislature in North America, began meeting in 1619.

Also in that year, according to a letter written by colonist John Rolfe, a Dutch ship brought "20 and odd Negroes, which the governor and cape merchant bought . . . at the best and easiest rate they could." This is the first mention of blacks in Virginia. Their status is not clear from the existing records, and it is possible that these first blacks were treated much the same as the colony's white servants. The origins of slavery are obscure,

John Smith, one of the original settlers of Jamestown, wrote a history of the colony. Smith's presidency of the local council was a critical factor in the survival of the settlement. *(Scribner's Archives)*

and the institution itself evolved slowly as the number of blacks grew in the seventeenth century. A 1625 census lists a total of twenty-three blacks—eleven men, nine women, and two children—in a population of 1,275. Despite the determined efforts of the Virginia Company, the colony had not flourished. The shocking mortality rate and the Company's virtually empty treasury led to a dissolution of the Virginia Company in 1624, and Virginia became a royal colony governed directly by the crown. Relations with the Indians worsened after the massacre. One colonial official exulted that "now we have just cause to destroy them by all means possible." On one occasion, the colonists lured a band of peaceful Indians into drinking a toast with poisoned wine, killing "some two hundred."

By the 1620s the colony was exporting in considerable quantity a valuable crop, tobacco, which appealed to Europeans. King James I published a pamphlet that denounced smoking as

> a custom loathsome to the eye, hateful to the nose, harmful to the brain, dangerous to the lungs, and in the black stinking fumes thereof, the nearest resembling the horrible smoke of the pit that is bottomless.

But the King's perception failed to dissuade seventeenth-century smokers, some of whom may have read a 1614 pamphlet by an Edinburgh physician. He claimed that tobacco would cure asthma, shortness of breath, coughs, ulcers, colic; "yea almost all diseases," and that smoking "prepareth the stomach for meat, it maketh a clear voice, it maketh a sweet breath, it cleareth the sight, it openeth the ears, it comforteth the nerves. . . ." Whatever the eventual impact on European lungs, tobacco ensured a long and prosperous history for the preeminent southern colony.

The New England Puritans

In 1607, as the first Englishmen reached the Jamestown peninsula, others were thrown into jail for trying to leave England. In Lincolnshire, William Brewster, leader of a group of religious dissenters known as Separatists, and his young friend, seventeen-year-old William Bradford, were among those imprisoned several months for trying to emigrate to Holland. Separatists, so called for their desires to separate from the Church of England, incurred the wrath of King James I, Elizabeth's successor (1603–1625) and the first of the Scottish Stuart monarchs, who declared that a Separatist was like "a rat to be trapped and tossed away."

James wished to be the undisputed head of the Church of England, sharing no significant authority with Parliament. And the Church he wanted would have more of ritual and hierarchy than suited the consciences of the Separatists and other strict English Protestants. Those who did not wish to separate but merely to simplify the Church's structure and practice—making it, so they thought, more Protestant—came to be known as Puritans.

Brewster, Bradford, and a small group of Separatists fled to the Netherlands in 1611, and in 1620 cemented an agreement with the London Company of Virginia to finance their emigration to America. In September 1620 the 180-ton bark *Mayflower* left Plymouth Sound with 102 colonists, and after a voyage of 65 days they reached Cape Cod on November 9. William Bradford recorded their arrival in his journal:

> Being thus arrived in a good harbor, and brought safe to land, they fell upon their knees and blessed the God of Heaven who had brought them over the vast and furious ocean, and delivered them from all the perils and miseries thereof, again to set their feet on the firm and stable earth, their proper element. . . . They now had no friends to welcome them nor inns to entertain or refresh their weather-beaten bodies; no houses or much less town to repair to, to seek for succour. . . . And as for the season it was winter, and they that know the winters of that country know them to be sharp and violent, and subject to cruel and fierce storms, dangerous to travel to known places, much more to search an unknown coast. Besides, what could they see but a hideous and desolate wilderness, full of wild beasts and wild men—and what multitudes there might be of them they knew not.

Estimates place the Indian population of New England in 1620 at 15,000 to 18,000, and at least one of them spoke English. Squanto, or Tisquantum as he called himself, was a Pawtuxet Indian who years before had been taken to England by English explorers, converted to Christianity, and had returned to find that his entire tribe had succumbed to smallpox. Settling among the Wampanoags near the coast, Squanto befriended the Pilgrims, served as their interpreter in negotiations with the Wampanoag chief Massasoit, and showed them how to fish and "set their corn." The grateful Pilgrims, who celebrated their first Thanksgiving in October 1621, viewed Squanto as "a special instrument sent of God."

Since the *Mayflower* had landed outside the boundaries prescribed by the Virginia Company charter, that document would have no authority. To secure their government in this unknown land, the leaders of these Separatist Pilgrims drafted an agreement that has come to be known as the Mayflower Compact, embodying the principle of government by majority rule. Every adult male signed it, and it has held a special place in the American imagination ever since, as a cornerstone of democratic government. With William Brewster as their first governor, the Pilgrims named their colony Plymouth, after the English seaport they had left behind. In 1691 Plymouth colony would become part of the larger Puritan colony of Massachusetts.

During James's reign and that of his son and successor, Charles I, supporters of the Church clashed with Puritans, while an overlapping constitutional controversy took place between champions of royal authority and champions of the rights of Parliament. The arguments between royalists and Puritans would bring on several years of armed warfare, beginning in 1642 and ending in a victory for Parliament and Puritanism, the execution of Charles I in 1649, and the transformation of England into a kingless Puritan state that lasted from 1649 until 1660.

In the late 1620s Charles hoped to get Puritans to leave England and to this end maintained a policy of continuous though mild persecution while offering them generous, even lavish, grants for settlement in America. One such grant went to a group of Puritans for settlements in the Leeward Islands of the West Indies, and another went to the Massachusetts Bay Company. Charles also granted a charter to George Calvert, Lord Baltimore, for the establishment of a colony north and east of Virginia, where Roman Catholics would be permitted to settle.

Boston

The Massachusetts Bay Company, organized in 1628 by a group of well-to-do English Puritans, received from the King a charter granting it land in present-day New England. Members of the Company signed a document, known as the Cambridge Agreement, to settle with their families in the new land, provided that they be allowed to take the charter and government of the Company with them. Nothing in the charter required the Company to maintain headquarters in England, and the transfer was arranged. The Company elected as its governor John Winthrop, a solid country squire. Within the year Winthrop and ten other members of the Company had set sail for America with a fleet of eleven ships carrying 800 adults and children with them. They arrived in Massachusetts in July 1630. In the next decade, as persecutions of Puritans increased, more than 20,000 would come to New England in what has been called the Puritan Migration. From the start, the immigration of families distinguished the settlement of New England. The presence of nearly as many women as men among the Puritans guaranteed that the settlement would grow in population. Women's presence further guaranteed the accomplishment of basic domestic tasks necessary for survival. Perhaps because of that, these New England colonists, with the exception of those at Plymouth the first winter, did not suffer the dreadful mortality of Virginia's early years. By the end of 1630 the Puritans had established six settlements besides Boston.

Housing was primitive at first. Some colonists borrowed from the Indians and erected wigwams. One settler recalled

> We built us our wigwam, or house, in one hour's space. It had no frame, but was without form or fashion, only a few poles set together, and covered with our boat's sails, which kept forth but a little wind, and less rain and snow.

Others dug cellars. The Puritan historian Edward Johnson wrote that they

> burrow themselves in the Earth for their first shelter under some Hillside, . . . make a smoky fire against the Earth at the highest side, and thus . . . provide for themselves, their Wives, and little ones, keeping off the short showers from their Lodgings, but the long ones penetrate through to their great disturbance.

Some years later, Johnson described the finished houses, observing that

> the Lord hath been pleased to turn all the wigwams, huts, and hovels the English dwelt in at their first coming into orderly fair, and well-built houses, well furnished many of them, together with Orchards filled with goodly fruit trees, and gardens with variety of flowers.

Land was not sold, but was allotted by the governing council at fifty acres for each head of a household, plus fifty acres for each family member, and more "according to their charge and quality." The Puritan communities, as John Winthrop said, would have "some rich, some poor." Equality was not a Puritan virtue, but industry was, and the Puritans were not averse to making a profit.

While they saw themselves as a religious people specially chosen by God and believed that "God sifted as a whole nation that he might bring choice grain over into this wilderness," they realized that not everyone had come to New England for religious reasons. One colonist wrote in 1630 that

> Intentions are secret; who can discover them? Necessity may press some, novelty draw on others, hopes of gain in time may come to prevail with a third sort, but that the . . . sincere and godly part have the advancement of the *Gospel* for their main scope I am confident.

The Massachusetts Bay Company, like other English business corporations of the time, was governed by its voting members, or "freemen." At first the only members were the stockholders, but in 1631 the government of the Company and therefore of the colony admitted to membership more than a hundred adult male settlers. Subsequently all male members of Puritan congregations were admitted as freemen. Like the original governing body, this extended body was constituted on the assumption that men only were fitted for governance and would naturally speak for the women of their families when speaking for themselves. The charter provided that Company members gather as a General Court four times a year, and that between times management be in the hands of a governor, deputy governor, and council of eighteen "assistants," all elected annually by the freemen. The organization that the Massachusetts Bay Company possessed for the conduct of its business was now the government of the colony, and Winthrop, the Com-

pany governor, was the governor of the colony. As the colony expanded, legislation by the entire body of freemen became unwieldy, and after 1634 they annually elected representatives from each settlement. This general structure of government—governor, council, and assembly—formed the type for most subsequent governments established in British America.

A PURITAN MEDICAL REMEDY, 1656
For all sorts of agues, I have of late tried the following magnetical experiment with infallible success. Pare the patient's nails when the fit is coming on; and put the parings in a little bag of fine linen and tie that above a live eel's neck, in a tub of water. The eel will die and the patient will recover.

The Puritan government enacted into law the biblical injunctions against drunkenness, adultery, murder, theft, and violations of the Sabbath, and otherwise attempted to regulate the religion and morality of the people. Yet Massachusetts Bay was not a theocracy: its ministers did not run the government. And as the colony developed in the seventeenth century, it was by no means a guilt-ridden, pleasure-denying society. Its members engaged in lively and profitable commerce; they developed a bright if decorous social life and did not prohibit alcohol; and well-educated Puritans read secular as well as religious literature. Government of the church was the domain of the members of the congregation; and the government of the town was also the domain of the members of the local church.

Puritan Theology   Economic ambition had combined with religion in the founding of the colony, and many settlers had land or opportunity as their motive. The prevailing creed, however, was Puritan. This creed was heavily influenced by the Swiss theologian John Calvin, best known for his belief in predestination: that those who were to be saved had been so chosen from the beginning of time. Calvin's premise might be taken to mean that there was no need to make any effort to be moral and good since nothing could alter the individual's predestined fate. Not so: orthodox ministers in Massachusetts observed that religious "conversion," an intense personal experience by which individuals came to know that they were saved, would be attended by diligent pursuit of a "calling," or earthly occupation and a life of fervent prayer and good works. Idleness was a sin. Devout Puritans tried to lead good lives and thereby demonstrate to themselves that they were among the saved or, as they called it, the "elect." And while the Massachusetts Puritans were as convinced as all their contemporaries in English society of the superiority of men to women, and the need for men to govern the "weaker sex" firmly, they did hold women accountable for their own souls, and as responsible as men to meet their obligations to God—in a manner appropriate to their sex.

Not all Puritans reasoned the same way from these premises, and not all agreed even on the principle of cooperation among congregations. One who shared none of the Puritans' values was Thomas Morton, an adventurer whose followers fraternized with the Indians and enjoyed drinking freely and dancing around a maypole at Mt. Wollaston, near Plymouth. The Puritans disapproved of his conduct and shipped him back to England in 1628. Settlers who shared Puritan values but disputed specific points of the colony's religious practices were a good deal more troublesome.

| **Rhode Island**   In 1631 Roger Williams, a clergyman of great personal charm, arrived in Massachusetts. He began immediately to point out the numerous defects he saw in the Massachusetts scheme of things, declared the colony's charter invalid because it did not purchase the land from the Indians, and delivered such seditious doctrines as that no government should have authority over religious matters. Such was Williams's appeal that he became minister of the congregation in Salem despite his views; but when large numbers began to share those views the government found it necessary to banish him, lest the foundation for all authority in Massachusetts be undermined. In 1636 he went down the coast to Narragansett Bay, established a settlement he named Providence, which he said would be a "shelter for persons distressed of conscience," and for almost half a century presided as the spiritual head of what became the colony of Rhode Island and Providence

Plantations—a haven for religious nonconformists. Roger Williams is sometimes mistaken for an early secular liberal. He was not. His opposition to government coercion of conscience was founded in his intense religiosity, not his concern for civil liberties. Williams was a Separatist. This group wished not to control and reform the church established and enforced by government, but to separate themselves from all state religion as a sinful worldly institution.

In 1638 the colony's authorities tried and banished another religious dissident. Anne Hutchinson, the daughter of a minister, wife of a prosperous cloth-merchant, and mother of eleven children, had arrived with her family in 1634. She soon emerged as a charismatic amateur theologian. Holding informal meetings in her home to discuss the Sunday sermons, she began to propound what was to orthodox Puritanism a heresy: grace is God's free gift; it cannot be earned by faith and good works.

Anne Hutchinson, carrying to an extreme an application of Calvinism, also represented

Roger Williams, banished from Salem for arguing that government has no authority over religious matters, founded Providence, Rhode Island. (*Courtesy, The Rhode Island Historical Society*)

The New England Colonies

an implication of Protestantism known as Antinomianism, which by a rough translation from the Greek means "against the law." It amounts to the belief that the Christian, where love of Christ burns in the human spirit, is no longer under the cold law of reason, custom, and government.

Hutchinson's words found a receptive audience among some women who were conscious of regularly risking their lives—and confronting eternity—in childbirth, and among those merchants who favored the development of a more mobile and commercial society in the new world. Even the most learned ministers had difficulty in countering the hair-splitting logic of her reasoning. As increasing numbers of Bostonians embraced Anne Hutchinson's doctrines, she became even more dangerous to the established authorities than Roger Williams had been. John Winthrop described her as "a woman of a haughty and free carriage, of a nimble wit and active spirit . . . more bold than a man." Spurred on by Winthrop, the authorities reacted sharply, accusing her and her followers of heresy. She was condemned by both civil and religious authorities and banished. She and her family, along with a number of loyal followers, moved to Rhode Island.

In the 1630s other Massachusetts colonists settled elsewhere, most simply out of an urge to have more room to move around in, physi-cally and politically. In 1635 a group settled along the Connecticut River. The Reverend Thomas Hooker led his flock west also, to establish Hartford. In 1639 these new towns, choosing to place themselves outside the jurisdiction of Massachusetts, drew up an agreement called the Fundamental Orders. They established their own government, which differed from the one in Massachusetts in a single important feature: suffrage was not confined to church members. In 1638 English immigrants set up the rigid religious community of New Haven.

The Colonies on Their Own

| Maryland   In the 1630s religion was the primary motive for the founding of another colony to the south of the Puritans. In England the elaborate rituals of Roman Catholicism, far more than those of the Anglican religion of the Stuart monarchy, clashed with the plain worship of Puritans and Separatists. Henrietta Maria, the wife of Charles I, who came to the throne in 1625, was a Catholic, and in the later years of Charles's reign, attendance at Mass in the queen's Catholic chapel would become popular among some upper-class Englishmen. Yet Roman Catholicism was officially a forbidden religion, and Catholics were isolated within an England of Protestants—Anglican, Puritan, and Separatist. One of these Catholics was Sir George Calvert, Lord Baltimore, who wanted to expand his holdings in land. The charter of 1632, by which the Crown granted to his son Cecilius the vast estate that would become the colony of Maryland, constituted the fulfillment of the plans George Calvert had begun.

Maryland was the first proprietary colony, a colony founded not by a joint-stock company as were Virginia and Massachusetts Bay but by a close-knit group, family, or an individual. Later the Carolinas, New York, New Jersey, Pennsylvania, and Georgia also would begin as proprietary colonies. Lord Baltimore had the authority to set and collect rents, issue legal writs, appoint administrative officials, confirm laws, and supervise the defense of the colony. The only important limitation required the proprietor to make laws "with the advice, assent, and approba-tion of the freemen of the province," a provision that led Baltimore to establish an elective assembly similar to Virginia's House of Burgesses.

The colony remained small. Founded with 2,000 colonists in 1634, it had less than 6,000 in 1660. Most heads of families were small planters, cultivating tobacco for export. George Alsop, an indentured servant, wrote in 1666:

> They whose abilities cannot extend to purchase their own transportation over into Mary-Land, (and surely he that cannot command so small a sum for so great a matter, his life must needs be mighty low and dejected) I say they may . . . go over into this Province and there live plentiously well. . . . He that lives in the nature of a Servant in this Province, must serve but four years by the Custom of the Country; and when the expiration of his time speaks him a Freeman, there's a Law in the Province, that enjoyns his Master whom he hath served to give him Fifty Acres of Land, Corn to serve him a whole year, three Sutes of Apparel, with things necessary to them, and Tools to work withall; so that they are no sooner free, but they are ready to set up for themselves, and when once entred, they live passingly well.

Roman Catholics never settled in Maryland in large numbers, and Protestants soon sought greater influence. During the 1640s the militant Protestantism of the period of the English Civil War put the Calvert family on the defensive. In 1649 the Maryland assembly adopted an act, framed by Lord Baltimore in response to pressures in England and America and in response to his own conscience, that guaranteed religious toleration to all Christians. And during the 1650s a Protestant faction wrested control away from the proprietor. Lord Baltimore regained authority in 1660. But Maryland never fulfilled his early plans to be a haven for Roman Catholics. And Maryland, like the New England colonies and Virginia, felt the shock waves from Civil War and revolution in England.

| The Beginnings of "Salutary Neglect" | In 1642 the Puritan Parliament in England began open warfare with the Royalists. Parliament triumphed in 1647, and in 1649 executed Charles I. Then for eleven years a nation without a monarch was given over to experimentation in politics and in the shaping of a virtuous Protestant society. Parliament made the country into a Commonwealth that soon gave way to a Protectorate under Oliver Cromwell. In 1660, not long after the death of Cromwell and the succession of his son to the Protectorate, a Parliament tired of the unsettled times invited a Stuart to resume the monarchy, and Charles II became King after years of exile in Europe.

From the Civil War until the restoration of the Stuarts, England was occupied with argument, war, and experiment, and the colonies were orphaned, virtually independent of the mother country. During these times they matured institutionally and socially.

New England vs. Virginia   From the beginning the settlers in New England differed fundamentally from those in Virginia. The New Englanders (Rhode Islanders always excepted) had a tight cooperative community, based upon a shared devotion and a shared theology. A spirit of adventure and a quest of private fortune had prompted Virginians, by and large, to move to America. To the extent that they had any common loyalty, it was to the King and his bishops. Natural conditions strongly reinforced the initial tendencies of both groups of settlers. In New England a rocky soil and a lack of navigable streams discouraged large-scale agriculture, and small subsistence-farming communities, each with its church, were the form of settlement. In Virginia, by contrast, fertile soil intersected by rivers and tidal creeks encouraged the cultivation of tobacco as a cash crop. Settlers established their plantations "stragglingly and scatteringly, as a choice veine of rich ground

invited them, and the further from neighbours the better." In the 1640s the experience of isolation that resulted from the English Civil War drove the two groups of colonies into courses of development at once different and similar.

When the war broke out, the Puritan magistrates in New England formally dissolved their connections with the Crown. Various of the colonies, partly to establish more regular and consistent relations with the Indians in the wake of the Pequot War of 1637–38, acted as Indians had learned earlier to act: they formed the New England Confederation for mutual defense and general cooperation. Rhode Island was excluded, on the ground that it was a sinkhole of depravity and heresy. The sense of a common identity among the members of the Confederation hardened through their isolation from England and their sense of being surrounded by enemies: not only hostile Indians, but belligerent French trading posts to the north, and prosperous and militarily strong Dutch trading settlements to the south in New Netherland, a colony established in 1624. During the turmoil in England the New Englanders took to the sea, ventured into occasional trading activities with the West Indies, and therein laid the foundations for New England's robust maritime future.

In Virginia the colonial government likewise separated itself from England, but for the opposite reason. Virginia proclaimed its loyalty to Charles I, and when the Puritan Parliamentarians won the Civil War Virginia declared its allegiance to the Stuart heir-in-exile, Charles II. The English Puritan Commonwealth government in 1652 appointed four commissioners, and sent two armed vessels to bring the Southern colony into line, and though the royal governor, Sir William Berkeley, wanted to resist, he was overruled by the council and assembly. The commissioners made few requirements except for the election of Puritan governors, and during the remaining years before the restoration of Charles II, Virginia virtually governed itself without interference from the Puritan government in England.

When the Civil War broke out in England the flow of Puritan immigrants to New England stopped, but by the time the war was over in 1647 it had become clear that the population of the colonies was increasing as fast as ever. In New England the increase de-

Pilgrims Going to Church, a nineteenth-century painting by George Boughton. The original Massachusetts settlements were governed by and for the orthodox Puritans, but by the 1660s other settlers and congregations were laying the basis for religious pluralism. (*Courtesy, New York Historical Society, New York City. From the Robert L. Stuart Collection*)

rived from an extremely high birth rate; in Virginia it sprang from a new immigration, first in trickles and then in waves, of fugitives from Puritanical repression that was unfolding in England.

After about 1650, New England's economy began to boom. The Puritan emphasis on industry as a spiritual value had brought material prosperity to John Winthrop's "Citty upon a Hill." One colonist had declared in 1630 that "There is nothing to be expected in New-England but competency to live on at the best, and that must be purchased with hard labor," but some New Englanders amassed substantial fortunes as the seventeenth century progressed. This quickening of economic activity turned heads away from the Puritan founders' original purpose and attracted profit seekers who remained outside the religious community. And by the 1650s Puritans uneasily noticed that many of their children were not undergoing the conversion experience required for church membership. If the trend continued, Puritans feared, the bulk of the population would soon be outside the church.

In 1662 a meeting of Puritan ministers ar-

rived at a solution to the problem of declining church membership. The ministers agreed to admit the grown children of church members into partial fellowship even though the children could not give evidence of grace. To preserve the church's purity, the ministers excluded these "halfway" members from participation in the sacrament of Holy Communion. This Half-Way Covenant did revive lagging church membership, but it also showed that the Puritans' early dreams were yielding to practicality. Churches must be kept filled, even though, as one Concord man complained, "in the extreme seasons of heat and cold we were ready to say of the Sabbath, 'Behold what a weariness.'" The colony of Massachusetts, and even the church itself, were no longer a community of saints.

Boston by the late 1660s was a town

furnished with many fair shops; their materials are brick, stone, lime, handsomely contrived, with three meeting houses or churches, and a townhouse built upon pillars where the merchants may confer; in the chambers above they keep their monthly courts. Their streets are many and large, paved with pebble stone, and the south-side adorned with gardens and orchards. The town is very rich and populous, much frequented by strangers; here is the dwelling of their governor. On the northwest and northeast two constant fairs are kept for daily traffic [trade] thereunto. On the south there is a small but pleasant Common where the gallants a little before sunset walk with their *Marmalet*-madams [prostitutes] . . . till the nine o'clock bell rings them home to their respective habitations, when presently the constables walk their rounds to see good orders kept, and to take up loose people.

| **Mayflower Compact**

New England in its first four decades had established institutions that have profoundly influenced the American perception of democracy. The Mayflower Compact of 1620, the agreement among the Pilgrims aboard the *Mayflower* to bind themselves into a single government, resembles that primitive contract among free individuals that political philosophers in early modern times have imagined as the beginning of all government. And so the Mayflower Compact has existed in the American imagination ever since, as though those early settlers had reenacted the very foundation of government. The granting of the vote in Massachusetts Bay to all male members of Puritan congregations gave that colony a moderately democratic government. That government granted considerable autonomy to the towns; and the New England towns, with their meetings at which the citizens debated local issues, are distinctive of the region today. In their own church activities, the Separatist and the New England Puritan churches rested power not in bishops—they had no bishops—but in the congregations. Americans since then have pointed to those early churches, as much as to colonial governments, as nurturing the American democratic spirit.

It is easy, and in part correct, to trace American democracy to those early New England institutions. But neither the Mayflower Compact nor the government of Massachusetts Bay nor the church polity of the New England congregations sprang from anything close to a conscious modern democratic theory. Each of the three came out of its own special circumstances and needs.

When the Mayflower dropped anchor at Cape Cod she was far outside the boundaries of the London Company's charter. Bradford, Brewster, and others feared that since their charter had no authority, some of the colonists might "use their owne libertie, for none had the power to command them." A need for law and order, not a desire for democratic government, inspired the Mayflower Compact. To agree among themselves to have a government was a simple, necessary act. And the Compact did not project an independent government: it specifically declared allegiance to the King of England.

The suffrage in Massachusetts Bay represented the fusion of the organization of a business company with that of the New England Puritan congregations. That English joint-stock companies gave a vote to each shareholder for the conduct of business was, of course, not theoretical democracy but a practical arrangement among people who had chosen to pool their resources for some enterprise. No one in seventeenth-century New England believed in democracy as a desirable form of government. "If the people be governors," said John Cotton, "who shall be governed?" In making all male members of Puritan congregations voting freemen of the Massachusetts Bay Company and therefore voting freemen of the colony, the government of Massachusetts Bay was acting in a practical manner to hold settlers who might otherwise have refused to live within the reach of the colony.

Within the Puritan and the Separatist congregations, members were spiritual equals, of a sort. While women could be of the elect and therefore could be full members of congregations, they could not be ministers or members of the governing body of the church, and they could not voice their opinions too loudly, as Anne Hutchinson had proved. The Puritans' concept of equality derived from the doctrine, which no modern democrat would accept, that they belonged to the special, chosen assembly, selected for salvation from the beginning of time. Members were spiritual equals, but only because there can be no inequality among saints.

Yet even if the early institutions of New England did not derive from any philosophical notions of equality or democracy, they deserve a place in the history of American democracy. The manner of their formation represents the way in which many of the nation's political and social institutions came into being—neither by theory nor by ancient custom but by matter-of-fact response to conditions and needs.

New Colonies

While the Virginians and the Puritans were establishing settlements other colonies were taking shape—some founded for religious reasons and some for a variety of other motives.

Until the middle of the seventeenth century the division of British North America into colonies had been on a patchwork basis. In 1660, when England abandoned the Puritan government and returned the throne to the Stuart family, some settlements had no official sanction. The new King Charles II had to give these some legal status, and he also wished to reward his loyal supporters. His government and that of his successor James II also proceeded to provide for further colonization.

Earlier in the century lands lying within the present states of New Hampshire and Maine had gone to individual proprietors receiving authority from the Crown, but that authority was shadowy and from time to time Massachusetts Bay had extended its government to settlers there. By 1679 New Hampshire became a royal colony, while Maine stayed with Massachusetts until 1820.

Connecticut and Rhode Island were quickly provided for. In 1662 the towns in the Connecticut valley received a charter from Charles. The charter, to the displeasure of New Havenites, placed the strict Puritan town of New Haven within the same colony as the more liberal settlements of the Connecticut valley. The Puritan government of England at Roger Williams's urging had granted a patent to Rhode Island. In 1663 Charles granted a charter to that democratic collection of towns. The grant confirmed the policy of religious freedom that had made Rhode Island a haven for religious dissenters. Their charters gave to Connecticut and Rhode Island the privilege of governing themselves. Therein appeared a colonial form, the charter colony, taking its place alongside the proprietary colony such as Maryland, owned by a single individual or

The island of Manhattan, looking southwards toward the town of New Amsterdam, ca. 1679, province of the Duke of York. *(Courtesy, New York Public Library, Picture Collection)*

small group, and the colony owned by a joint-stock company, like Massachusetts. Before long the British American mainland would contain more royal colonies, with governors appointed by the Crown.

| **New York**   Since earlier in the century the Dutch West India Company had owned New Netherland, the territory that is now the state of New York. In 1626 a Dutch trader had bargained with the Indians for Manhattan Island, which the Dutch wanted as a trading post. Tradition has it that goods worth about $24.00 purchased the site, which the Dutch named New Amsterdam. By the 1660s the colony had no single character or purpose. New Englanders (including the widowed Anne Hutchinson, who, along with five of her children, was killed by the Indians in 1643) and Dutch had settled on Long Island. A collection of Dutch, English, and other European peoples dwelt in the little village of New Amsterdam, which lived off the fur and land trade and whatever other commerce the colony could offer. Farther up the Hudson were the beginnings of a system that would leave its mark on New York society for two centuries and more, in which patroons—the word suggests the English "patron, patrician," or aristocrat—presided over huge farming estates and their workers. The Dutch West India Company had extended over New Netherland a loose control under directors-general and provided local self-government and freedom of religion. The company was not able to turn a profit from the fees, taxes, and duties it imposed on the colony, and in 1654 it went bankrupt.

Charles II, continuing the commercial conflict with the Netherlands that the Puritan Commonwealth had entered, in 1664 seized New Netherland bloodlessly, the famed and magnificent temper of its governor, Peter Stuyvesant, proving to have some mixture of prudence. (The Dutch would briefly retake the colony in the 1670s.) Charles II gave the province to his brother James, the Duke of York, and it became New York; the town of New Amsterdam also took that name. James's lieutenant in the colony proceeded to work out a set of laws. The scheme gave the freeholders—in essence, the landholders—of the colony the vote for town officials, but insured that the Duke would hold ultimate power. There was to be freedom of religion, though

each town was required to sustain a church. To two Royalists, Lord Berkeley and Sir George Carteret, the Duke transferred the conquered Dutch territory that received the name New Jersey, so named in honor of Carteret's earlier defense of the English Channel island of Jersey against the Puritans. Berkeley and Carteret then offered freedom of religion and granted to the freeholders the right to elect representatives who, along with a governor and council appointed by the proprietors, would legislate for the colony; the proprietors retained the authority to annul the laws.

| **The Carolinas**   In 1663 a group that included Berkeley and Carteret became the proprietors of Carolina. In a charter of 1665, wherein Charles extended the boundaries of Carolina, the King affirmed the right of the inhabitants to liberty of religion. The proprietors provided for a legislature elected by the freeholders, but retained the right to revoke laws. In 1669 Lord Ashley, one of the proprietors, and his secretary, the political philosopher John Locke, designed "The Fundamental Constitutions of Carolina," conceiving an elaborate and fanciful scheme for the colony, with a hereditary nobility and a feudal serfdom which was never realized. Toward the end of the century Carolina was centered in two unconnected locations: in the north, benefiting from migration from Virginia, a society of small farmers; and in the south, around the seaport of Charles Town (Charleston) a cluster of Virginians, migrants from the Northern colonies, English immigrants, Scots, French Protestants called Huguenots, and planters from the British West Indies. The economy of the southern part of Carolina subsisted in part on the fur trade with the Indians. The colonists from the West Indies were familiar with slavery, and the settlers around Charles Town were beginning to grow rice with slave labor. North and South Carolina both possessed self-government under ultimate proprietary control but each would eventually become a royal colony with a Crown-appointed governor by 1729.

| **Pennsylvania**   In 1681 an upper-class Quaker, William Penn, received from Charles II a proprietary grant to "Pennsylvania." Penn had already joined other Quakers in purchasing from Carteret

the proprietary rights to part of New Jersey.

The Quakers, so called because of the trembling that overcame them at their meetings, when individuals were possessed by an "Inner Light," were a sect whose members refused to bear arms or take oaths. They, like the Puritans, were persecuted in England.

Penn's grant derived in part from the earlier friendship between Charles and Penn's father; Charles owed Penn £16,000 for services rendered by the father, an admiral, and the grant was made in payment of that debt. The charter to Pennsylvania required that William Penn enforce British trading acts, permit appeals from Pennsylvania courts to the King, submit all Pennsylvania laws to the King for approval, and upon request from twenty colonists, provide an Anglican minister—a minister of the established Church of England. The King reserved the power to impose taxes "by act of Parliament." In all other respects Penn was free to govern his colony as he pleased.

In an elaborate *Frame of Government*

(1682), Penn provided that the governorship of the colony would go to the proprietor or his deputy, and that legislative power would be vested in a council and an assembly, both elected by the freeholders of the colony. He proposed to earn an income from his colony by collecting rents from the settlers, and to attract the settlers by advertising widely the good land, free government, and religious liberty available in the colony. The campaign was an immediate success. Quakers flocked to Pennsylvania from England, Holland, Germany, Wales, and Ireland. Many non-Quakers went as well, for in the wake of the reestablishment of the Stuart monarchy, a new wave of refugees poured out of England; and a group of German Mennonites, driven from their homes by the continental religious wars, also emigrated to Pennsylvania. By 1720 the capital, Philadelphia, the "City of Brotherly Love," had a population of 10,000, and by the 1770s would be the largest city in North America.

Penn also possessed deeds to what is now

Penn's Treaty with the Indians, by Benjamin West. The Quaker William Penn's historic treaty with the Delaware Indians in 1682 created a peaceful settlement in Pennsylvania. *(Courtesy, Pennsylvania Academy of Fine Arts)*

Delaware, though the grounds of his legal claim to govern "the Territories," as the lower region was called for a while, were unclear. In the first decade of the eighteenth century Delaware, settled in part by Swedes,

in effect would separate from Pennsylvania, though both colonies continued to have the same governor. In 1776 Delaware would become a separate state.

The Colonies and the Crown

The Navigation Acts and Mercantilism In 1651 the government of the Puritan Commonwealth had passed a Navigation Act aimed at building up the shipping of England and the empire. The government was particularly interested in excluding from English and colonial posts the ships of the fellow Protestant nation of the Netherlands, with which the Commonwealth was in close economic competition. The Act provided that no ships except those belonging to the people of England or her colonies could carry Asian, African, or American goods into England or the colonies.

After Charles II reestablished the English monarchy in 1660, his ministers and Parliament, building on principles established by the Navigation Act of 1651, enacted a broad program designed to stimulate England's economic growth and to transform the scattered American settlements and East Indian trading posts into a world empire. The primary aim of the mercantilist program was to make England and its overseas colonies a vast, closed trading area, as self-sufficient as possible, protected by an enlarged navy, and serviced by an expanded merchant fleet. Each part of the empire was supposed to specialize in supplying the products and services for which it was best suited, and thereby contribute to the well-being of all the other parts and to the strength of the whole. The colonies would provide the mother country with raw materials—goods that England could not produce economically—such commodities as lumber, naval stores, fish, tobacco, indigo, and West Indian sugar. The colonial products would be sent only to Britain, but would have a monopoly on the English market. Insofar as was feasible, the colonies would not engage in manufacture, but would buy their finished goods from England. All products would be subject to customs duties and would be carried only in English or colonial ships.

Two major acts laid the legal foundations of the system: the Navigation Act of 1660 and the Staple Act of 1663. The Navigation Act restricted all colonial trade to vessels owned and manned primarily by Englishmen or British colonists, and required that certain enumerated articles produced in the colonies—tobacco, sugar, indigo, and ginger—be shipped only to Britain or to another English colony. The Staple Act required that most goods imported into the colonies, whether they originated in Britain or in foreign parts, must be shipped from a British port. The Staple Act aimed to benefit the Crown by increasing the customs revenues on exports from England; to help English exporters by giving them a monopoly of the colonial market (even as the Navigation Act gave colonial producers a monopoly of the English market); and to protect the colonists by confining their trade to shipping lanes that could be patrolled and protected by the English navy.

For all the laxity of its enforcement, the new commercial system was an immediate success. English commerce boomed and the merchant fleet became the largest and most profitable the nation had yet known. This was not surprising. Simply by virtue of establishing the system England took exclusive possession of a large and growing colonial trade. Besides the mainland colonies, England's island possessions also prospered under this new system. These included Bermuda, founded in 1612, and the West Indies colonies of St. Christopher (1624), Barbados (1627), Nevis (1628), Montserrat and Antigua (1632), and Jamaica (1655). The West Indies, booming with the rapid expansion of sugar production, welcomed the naval protection afforded by the new system, for the Caribbean was teeming with pirates. The tobacco colonies, Virginia and Maryland, paid perhaps a bit more for freight than they had before, and tobacco prices continued to decline until the 1690s, but the establishment of a great central marketing system in England facilitated an enormous increase in production that in the long run more than compensated. By 1680, for example, the two colonies were exporting over seventeen million pounds of tobacco a year. The New England colonies, being free to elect their own governors, were also free to ignore the Acts of Trade when it was to their advantage. Thus they profited from trade with the enclosed imperial market as well as from the protection of the English navy, and otherwise did as they pleased. Consequently, the merchant fleet of New England, built by a burgeoning new local industry, grew even faster than that of Old England.

Another Restoration policy, the resumption of discrimination against those who dissented from the Church of England, also promoted New England's prosperity. A new wave of dissenters went to America in flight from this policy, and in the 1660s the population of New England increased from about 33,000 to some 52,000.

During the Restoration the colonies cultivated that independence that they had already enjoyed in the days of the Commonwealth. The Massachusetts Bay Colony led the way.

Massachusetts: Resistance to the Crown From the outset of the Restoration Massachusetts was troublesome. It secretly harbored three of the men condemned to death for the execution of Charles I (despite the fact that there was a £100 bounty on their heads and anyone caught assisting them would be drawn and quartered alive). Massachusetts ignored the Navigation Acts; and it violated its charter by retaining on its statute books a number of laws, particularly those concerning religion, contrary to the laws of England. Very early, Charles II sent orders commanding Massachusetts to make its laws conform to those of England. The colony did temporarily stop persecuting the Quakers—it had executed several—and did modify its laws concerning suffrage, but neither action was taken in response to the King's orders, which the colonial assembly flatly ignored. And so, when the British mission to seize New Netherland from the Dutch was dispatched in 1664, Charles sent four commissioners along to investigate the New England governments.

The commissioners encountered no difficulty in Plymouth, Connecticut, or Rhode Island, but when they arrived in Boston they

The Thirteen Original Colonies

Name	Founded by	Year	Made Royal	Status at Revolutionary War
1. Virginia	London Company	1607	1624	Royal
2. New Hampshire	John Mason and others	1623	1679	Royal
3. Massachusetts	Separatists and Puritans	1620–30	1691	Royal
4. Maryland	Lord Baltimore	1634	———	Proprietary (controlled by proprietor)
5. Connecticut	Emigrants from Massachusetts	1635	———	Charter
6. Rhode Island	Roger Williams	1636	———	Charter
7. North Carolina	Virginians	1653	1729	Royal (separated informally from S.C., 1691)
8. New York	Dutch	c.1613		
	Duke of York	1664	1685	Royal
9. New Jersey	Berkeley and Carteret	1664	1702	Royal
10. South Carolina	Eight nobles	1670	1719	Royal
11. Pennsylvania	William Penn	1681	———	Proprietary
12. Delaware	Swedes	1638	———	Proprietary
13. Georgia	James Oglethorpe	1733	1752	Royal

met with a reception that was at once icy and bold. The magistrates referred the commissioners to the Massachusetts Bay Charter of 1629, refused to submit to investigation, and publicly forbade the citizens to offer any testimony. The commissioners returned to England, and three of them recommended to the King that the charter be revoked. The open defiance might have provoked not only a revocation of the charter, but armed suppression of the colony as well. But the confrontation came just at the time England was suffering from the London plague, a great fire in that city, and military reverses abroad. For the next six years Massachusetts, together with the other colonies, was largely ignored, and could take advantage of the situation.

Massachusetts did so. The price of tobacco fell in 1667 to about half a penny per pound. Under normal circumstances, about half the tobacco shipped to London was reexported to the Continent through Holland, and though the English market had vanished the European market continued to exist. So the merchants of New England, ignoring the Acts of Trade, carried tobacco directly from Virginia to Holland, and from 1667 to 1672 reaped considerable profits for themselves and improved Virginia's tobacco prices in the bargain.

Virginia, the most royalist of all settlements, and New England, the least, had become equally disenchanted with the government in London. And in the late summer of 1675, both colonies were subjected to difficulties that would have strained any loyalties.

| **Renewed Conflicts with Indians** | The difficulties in both places resulted from the renewal of Indian hostilities, and the ultimate wellspring of the trouble was the ambitions of France. Since the massacre of 1622 in Virginia and the Pequot War of 1637–38 in Massachusetts, the Indians had gradually and peacefully retreated to the interior rather than face the devastating fire of English muskets. But in the late 1660s the French adopted a broad strategy of encircling the English colonies with settlements along the St. Lawrence, the Great Lakes, and the Mississippi, and forged alliances with the Indians between their own settlements and those of the English. The five Iroquois nations of New York had for long been enemies of the

French and their Indian allies. Hence the new French policy forced the Iroquois back. They, in turn, pushed back the Algonquin tribes of New England and the Susquehannocks of what is now Pennsylvania, with the result that in the 1670s they clashed with the English to the east, and the Susquehannocks engaged in hostilities with the colonists to the south.

In New England the fighting was known as King Philip's War. Philip, a Wampanoag chieftain whose people were already hemmed in between rival governments and land speculators in Rhode Island and Massachusetts, was pressed to the point of desperation by the Iroquois drive; and just at that time the Massachusetts government ordered the Indians to disarm. They responded in the only way they could, by attacking the English settlements. The Indians did not fight according to the rules of formal territorial warfare, European-style: a contest in which the only combatants and subjects of attack were uniformed armies, and in which both sides campaigned until one or the other surrendered. The Indians fought only intermittently, and regarded all men, women and children included, as fair prey. There was considerable barbarism on both sides. But the colonists had the advantage of superior arms and superior organization. Not everyone was eager to fight. Two Boston men said they "would be hanged drawne and quartered rather than goe." Another colonist petitioned the authorities:

> The Petition of Nathaniell Bylfield Humbly Sheweth that your Peitionour is a Stranger in the Country: and Lately married and is now Prest to goe out to Warr against the Indians: And where as the Law of God is plaine: in 24 Dewter: 5: That when a man hath taken a new wife he shall not goe out to warr.

The New England Confederation mobilized about a thousand men and conducted a ruthless, systematic, relentless campaign, and by 1676 the Indians had been thoroughly defeated. King Philip's War cost the English settlers about a sixth of their adult males and the destruction of about twenty towns. During the entire campaign, the English government sent no help.

Instead of help, a special agent of Charles II, Edward Randolph, arrived in Boston to convey new royal instructions and to investigate the enforcement of the Navigation Acts.

After a less than cordial reception and a cursory investigation, Randolph submitted two reports to the Crown. He charged Massachusetts with refusing to comply with the Navigation Act, executing English subjects for their religious faith, denying appeals to the King's Privy Council, and refusing to take the oath of allegiance.

Massachusetts continued to be obstinate. The General Court declared that

> Wee humbly conceive that the laws of England are bounded within the four seas, and doe not reach America. The subjects of his majesty here being not represented in Parliament, so we have not looked at ourselves to be impeded in our trade by them.

The General Court refused to recognize Randolph as customs officer, set up its own customs office, and imprisoned the deputies Randolph had appointed. Randolph reported on the conduct of the colony. When Massachusetts did not satisfactorily reform its behavior, court proceedings began against the colony. In 1684 the Massachusetts Bay Company lost its charter and Massachusetts became a royal colony.

Bacon's Rebellion in Virginia

In the summer of 1675, bands of Susquehannock Indians, fleeing the Iroquois, crossed the Potomac River into Virginia. Relations between the back-country Indians and the Virginia planters deteriorated until a planter's herdsman was killed, several Indians (including five Susquehannock chiefs under a flag of truce) were killed in retaliation, and the whole Potomac frontier erupted in raids and counterraids. Thomas Mathew described the colonists' fears:

> In these frightfull times the most Exposed small families withdrew into our houses of better Numbers. . . . Neighbours in Bodies Joined their Labours from each plantation to others alternatively, taking their Arms into the Fields, and Setting sentinels; no Man Stirrd out of Door unarm'd.

The royal governor of Virginia, William Berkeley, sought to stop the outbreak, but he did so from premises and with policies that were certain to alienate the frontiersmen. A staunch, pigheaded royalism guided Berkeley's policy. He had been royal governor from 1642 to 1652, had suffered humiliation and exile under the English Puritan regime, and had been restored with the Stuarts in 1660; thereafter, he would not yield an inch of the royal prerogative. Indeed Charles, in his gratitude for such loyalty, rashly proclaimed Virginia as one of his kingdoms, coequal with England, Scotland, and Wales. As part of the restored royal authority, according to Berkeley, Indians became subjects of the King, on an equal footing with the English colonists, and were therefore entitled to the protection of royal justice. No warfare upon the Indians was to be tolerated, despite the Indian attacks—which Berkeley regarded as minor frontier incidents and impediments to the lucrative fur trade with the Indians. Berkeley met the crisis by raising funds to rebuild the frontier forts and to pay and equip a band of mounted rangers, and by prohibiting fur trade by any but a handful of traders whom he himself licensed. The new tax was ill calculated to please the frontiersmen, and the new trade regulations threatened the ambitions of a number of frontier fur traders, land seekers, and border barons.

The malcontents soon raised a leader who was willing to defy the governor: Nathaniel Bacon, the governor's nephew, recent settler in the interior of Virginia, artful demagogue, unscrupulous royalist adventurer and lawyer who had been trained at the Inns of Court in London. Bacon held that the Indians were not subjects of the Crown but were outside the law and could be attacked by any Englishman so disposed. In May 1676, without a commission from the governor, Bacon marched at the head of an expedition that descended upon the Roanoke River to destroy a Susquehannock village. He was promptly accused of treason, but the governor pardoned him when he acknowledged his offense.

Meanwhile Bacon, along with a goodly number of other radicals, was elected to the House of Burgesses. They proceeded to push through a series of enactments, collectively known as "Bacon's laws," which reversed most of Berkeley's Restoration policies by liberalizing voting, tax, and religious regulations. Bacon himself had little or nothing to do with all this. Instead, he took up his military career again. He raised an army of 500 men, marched on the colonial capital at Jamestown, forced Berkeley to commission him as a militia captain, and set about looking for more Indians to kill.

And now the tobacco planters demonstrated what recent royal and parliamentary policies had accomplished. The planters professed no allegiance at all to Parliament, and their loyalty to the Crown had become only formal, devoid of any personal commitment. When Governor Berkeley again declared Bacon a rebel, many planters and their wives—some of whom became Bacon's active supporters—swore their allegiance. In 1676, they held to their oath, enabling Bacon to drive Berkeley's forces out of Jamestown and burn the village to the ground. On both sides, women and children were involved. Loyalist forces threatened rebel families, and Bacon used loyalists' wives as hostages during his attack on Jamestown. The rebellion revealed class tensions as well as political differences. One female partisan of Berkeley wrote to a friend that the "differences with in our selves

being far greater than those without, and a reason why the other [the Indian problem] was not before remedied." Order was restored in the ensuing months, largely as a result of Bacon's death from the "bloody flux" (dysentery) in October. Berkeley regained control and proceeded to hang twenty-three of the rebels, causing Charles II to remark, "The old fool has hanged more men in that naked country than I have done for the murder of my father." The King sent a royal commission to Virginia to investigate the rebellion, and the seventy-year-old Berkeley was recalled to England, but he died before he could give his side of the story.

The Dominion of New England

With the death of Charles II in 1685, his brother James became King. James II soon suppressed a rebellion led by a pretender to the throne. Thereupon James proceeded to try to strengthen the power of the Crown and to bring back Roman Catholicism. But the King's most ambitious project for the establishment of royal rule, and for bringing some coherence to the government of the colonies, was the Dominion of New England. New Hampshire, Massachusetts, Plymouth (not yet absorbed into Massachusetts), Connecticut, Rhode Island, New York, and the Jerseys were all to be governed by one governor and his council, without the interference of representative assemblies. James appointed as governor of the dominion, Sir Edmund Andros, a former governor of New York and a staunch Church of England man, who arrived in Boston during 1686. "The fox," said the Puritan clergyman Cotton Mather, "has been made master of the hen house."

| **Sir Edmund Andros**   The new system made a great deal of administrative sense. For the first and only time in the history of the English empire in America, England had a colonial system that was, at least on paper, as efficient as those of France and Spain. Andros's administration was in many respects both shrewd and enlightened. He left most of the existing laws in force. He respected the established churches and schools—though in his attempts to provide for the Church of England

he antagonized Puritans. His observance of Christmas, which Puritanism rejected for savoring of ritual and Catholicism, drew the indignant notice of Samuel Sewall. A prominent and devout Puritan, Sewall made a dour comment in his diary on December 25, 1686 (a Sunday): "The Christmas keepers had a very pleasant day." For the most part Andros left the towns in control of their own local affairs—and the town and congregation constituted the primary unit of government in New England. But he could also govern with a strong hand; for example, he offered the merchants of his dominion the protection of the Royal Navy if they cooperated with him and threatened them with its great destructive power if they refused. Andros tempered his unpopular measures skillfully.

While he antagonized the merchants of Boston, Newport, and New York by insisting on enforcement of the Navigation Acts, he also reversed his earlier policy and stopped offering pirates haven in these principal ports. Though he may have reduced the merchants' profits, he reduced their risks as well. Again, Andros provoked considerable grumbling by declaring that the Massachusetts Bay government had proceeded illegally in granting land for town settlements. The grumbling was aggravated when he ordered all landholders, present and prospective, to obtain land titles from the governor and pay quitrents as well. But virtually everyone was confirmed in his title to the land he already possessed, the rents proved to be nominal

Edmund Andros, governor of the Dominion of New England from 1686–1688, being taken prisoner in Boston. Though this was triggered by rumors of a popish plot, opposition to Andros stemmed from the colonists' belief that he was limiting local self-government. *(Scribner's Archives)*

and were not collected, and it turned out to be far easier to obtain land from the new governor than it had been from the Puritan government.

Andros also levied taxes without legislative approval, but they were no larger than they had been when duly elected representatives levied them. Andros further encroached upon the principle of local self-government by ordering that town meetings be held no more than once a year and that control of the militia be vested in the governor; but the towns customarily met officially only once a year anyway (they met once a week at church congregations, and that Andros did not change), and as it happened Andros never had occasion to call out the militia.

In short, Andros's innovations directly challenged the professed principles of the New Englanders, but altered the daily lives of most of them precious little. It is uncertain whether this experiment in enlightened despotism would have won over New Englanders inclined to hostility toward outside rule, and more especially rule by a communicant of the Church of England. The Dominion of New England was never put to the full test, for it failed in England. James II's undoing came in 1688 after he had alienated his strongest supporters by attempting to go too far too fast in his efforts to restore Roman Catholicism. Even the Tories, the party more sympathetic to the privileges of the Crown, were antagonists. Rich country gentry, who made up much of the strength of the Tories, were wedded to the Church of England; and some of them feared that full restoration of the Roman Church might include restoration of its lands, which happened now to belong to them. Even then, James might have prevailed but for a sudden change in the prospects for the royal succession.

The Glorious Revolution James was in his fifties and his only children were two daughters, Mary and Anne, both by his first wife and both devoutly Protestant; his second wife, an Italian princess and a Catholic, had borne him no children. Most Englishmen, however much they despised the King, therefore thought it better to wait out the papist storm as they had the Puritan, on the theory that little permanent harm could be done before James died and the Crown passed to a Protestant. But in June of 1688 the queen had a son, and that opened the possibility of a permanent Catholic succession. It seemed to be now or never for English Protestantism; and so a group of prominent Englishmen conspired to invite William of Orange of Holland, husband of James's daughter Mary, to rescue England from Catholic tyranny. William accepted and on November 5 landed with a force of about 14,000 at Torbay, in southwestern England. General John Churchill and Colonel Percy Kirke led a carefully planned desertion of great numbers of royal troops, and much of the remainder of James's army refused to obey their Catholic commanders. James was left defenseless, and in December he fled to the continent. Eight weeks later William and Mary became joint sovereigns of England.

Governor Andros was in Maine when he got news of William's landing, and he returned to Boston to prevent an anti-royalist reaction. But he had neither army nor police, and rioting broke out in response not to James's removal but to rumors of a popish plot. Andros fled to the local fort, but before the end of the day he and the other royal officials surrendered and were jailed. A Puritan oligarchy governed the colony for two months, until a new General Court could be elected. In July Andros was ordered to return to England.

As soon as the news of Boston's uprising reached New York that colony too was swept with a great fear of a popish plot, and three of its counties, those populated mainly by Puritans, threw out the royal officials and elected their own. In New York, Jacob Leisler, a successful German trader, led a group that ousted Andros's deputy governor and established a provisional government with Dutch support. At first Leisler had little backing outside the city, but soon French-inspired Indian raids in the upper part of the colony lent gruesome reinforcement to the rumors of a papist and Indian campaign to massacre Protestants. Leisler offered discipline, order, and military strength, and became in fact governor of the entire colony for two years, until a new royal governor arrived. Then Leisler and his son-in-law were hanged and drawn and quartered for treason. One spectator at the execution reported that "The shrieks of the people were dreadful." The

New York Assembly declared that "These were days of wrath and utter darkness."

The Jerseys and Pennsylvania adjusted to the new regime in England with little drama. In Maryland a group of colonists calling themselves the Protestant Association forced the resignation of the governor appointed by the Catholic, Lord Baltimore, brought back the assembly, which had been dissolved, and petitioned the Crown to take over the colony. In Virginia the dominant planters announced their support of William and Mary and their confidence that James's governor would be removed, which soon happened. Settlers in Northern Carolina turned on the proprietary governor, who fled to Charles Town and temporarily set up a government there. Soon afterward the proprietors suspended him.

The Ideology of Revolution The philosopher of the English revolution was John Locke. At the behest of various champions of the revolution, Locke published in 1689 and 1690 several essays, notably the *Second Treatise on Civil Government* and *An Essay Concerning Human Understanding*. Locke argued that man is born innocent, capable of good or evil, a creature whom conditions will mold. He reasoned that man had once lived in a state of nature, in accordance with the laws of nature (or of God), which endowed man with rights to life, personal freedom, and the property that he accumulated through honest labor. But in the natural state the strong prey upon the weak, and so men had formed societies and created governments. Governments existed by virtue of voluntary agreements, or contracts, between governed and governors, and their function was to protect the individual's natural rights to life, liberty, and property. The government of James II, founded upon such a contract, had been legitimate until the King broke the contract by depriving people of their natural rights, in effect declaring war upon his subjects. The people therefore had no recourse but to overthrow James's government and to establish a new contract with a new sovereign who seemed more likely to abide by his agreements, William of Orange.

To make legitimate the Glorious Revolution, a Convention Parliament proclaimed early in 1689 a Declaration of Rights that a formal Parliament enacted, under the title of Bill of Rights; William and Mary approved it later the same year. The Bill of Rights established, for all time, limits upon the English monarchy and judiciary. The Crown could no longer make or suspend laws, levy taxes, or maintain standing armies without the consent of Parliament, which was guaranteed frequent meetings, free elections, and free debate. Some ecclesiastical courts were eliminated and others had their powers reduced, and in all courts every person was guaranteed trial by jury and protected from excessive bails and forfeiture of estates before conviction.

Equally important was a series of steps taken to regularize, modernize, and render more flexible the system of public finance, which had previously occasioned such destructive conflict between the Crown and Parliament. Henceforth Parliament did not merely grant monies, but controlled their expenditure as well. To that end, it began to make specific appropriations for specific purposes, and to require estimates and accounts of expenditures.

As a part of the process of putting things in order, Crown and Parliament again attempted to bring order to affairs in America.

| **England Tries Again: The Navigation Act of 1696** | In 1696 William III commissioned a new body, the Board of Trade, to supplant the Lords of Trade (1660). |

It was empowered to supervise trade, recommend appointments of colonial officials, and review colonial laws to see that none interfered with trade or conflicted with the laws of England. Since the 1660s the colonists had taken advantage of England's political preoccupations to profit from illegal trade. It was possible to do so largely because enforcement of the earlier Navigation Acts had depended more upon private morality, supplemented by generous rewards to informers, than upon efficient administrative machinery. The new Navigation Act of 1696 sought to change that. Colonial governors were now held responsible, on penalty of forfeiture of office, for violations of the law. Regular customs officers were now appointed for each colony, whereas previously there had been only a few officers who had moved about from one colony to another. Trials for violations of the law were to be in admiralty courts, where proceedings were not encumbered by juries.

But the new system could not overcome the physical circumstances in English America, which were not conducive to efficient supervision of trade. Effective customs operations require concentration of shipping, and in much of America such concentration was not feasible. Tobacco, for example, which was by far the most valuable product of the mainland colonies, was normally loaded on ships directly at the plantations along the rivers of Virginia and Maryland and on Chesapeake Bay. Short of placing customs officers on every plantation or stationing armed ships at every river and inlet, it was virtually impossible to prevent masters of local, New England, or foreign vessels from carrying tobacco anywhere they pleased.

For the enforcement of anything like the Navigation Acts England had as yet no tradition of civil service, royal or parliamentary, in the colonies or at home. Posts were filled through influence, bribery, or other corrupt means more commonly than through regard for honest and efficient administration. Colonial service attracted the least savory of a generally unsavory lot, not only because life in the colonies was far from desirable to most courtiers, but also because the rewards for legitimate service there were small. In all the colonies except Virginia and Barbados the governor was dependent upon the local assembly for his salary, and the customs officers were paid out of fees and fines, not the royal treasury. Accordingly, many of those who filled imperial positions were quite amenable to bribes, offered in exchange for looking the other way when colonials proposed to trade outside the rules established by the Navigation Acts.

By and large, the imperial commercial system worked when it was to the mutual advantage of the colonies and the mother country to abide by it; which is to say, it worked for about three-quarters of the trade affected by the Navigation Acts. Otherwise it was generally ignored, except when the Royal Navy was not engaged in war and had nothing better to do than police the seas against pirates and smugglers.

In the years following the Glorious Revolution of 1688–89 colonial governments underwent a reorganization that replaced the firmer rule the monarchy under James II had tried to maintain over several of the colonies—but gave the Crown a tighter control

James Goodwyn, *American Sleigh Ride.* (*Courtesy, Museum of Fine Arts, Boston*)

than had been the case for much of the seventeenth century. Connecticut and Rhode Island retained their self-government, and the Penn family, after losing the original charter to Pennsylvania, regained the proprietorship of that colony. In 1691 the Crown took over Maryland, though the Calvert family retained property rights there. But then the Calvert family converted from Roman Catholicism to the Church of England, and in 1715 it was given back its proprietary rights to the government of Maryland. In the colony founded as a refuge for Roman Catholics, people of that faith now lost the right to vote and their right to worship was limited. Virginia, Massachusetts, and New Hampshire were now royal colonies. In 1702 New Jersey too became a Crown colony, and by 1729 North Carolina and South Carolina each became a separate Crown colony.

Within a few years after the Glorious Revolution, then, British North America had the kind of government and the relationships to Great Britain that would determine its course until the American Revolution. At a time when in England power was going increasingly to Parliament, government in the Crown colonies was in effect being unintentionally divided. In the eighteenth century governors and councils appointed by the monarch would often clash with elected assemblies that alone had the authority to tax the colonists, and therefore had the authority to withhold money from a governor in the pursuit of his policies. The Navigation Acts, with further legislation in the eighteenth century, would in time lead to major conflict with the government in Great Britain. The foundations had been laid for a grand but restless empire.

Points To Think About

1. The New World was not new to the Indians. Neither was it a wilderness. Nor did they incline to the view that Providence had reserved it for reformed Christians. The various tribes had their own projects for their own portions of a land that they did not know as a single continent, projects that they attempted to preserve in spite of the continuing incursions of Europeans.

The first and most important effect of European settlement was the spread of European diseases to Indians who had no immunities against them. A second effect was to upset the Indian balance of power, since those tribes which traded with the Europeans acquired firearms in exchange. These new weapons encouraged their possessors to attack other tribes—a development which, in the long run, could only weaken the Indians and strengthen the Europeans.

Rapid population growth caused colonists to encroach upon Indian lands within a generation of first settlement. Indians would resist, often with some initial success, but the superiority of European arms coupled with tribal rivalries would, in the end, lead to Indian defeat. The badge of defeat was a treaty which would guarantee to the Indians permanent rights to their remaining land. The treaty would be observed until population pressures brought new white settlers into Indian lands. This cycle would repeat itself for the next two hundred years.

2. The American colonists of the seventeenth century faced the challenge of developing new political institutions. So, of course, did the nations of Europe. But while Europeans were solving their problems by centralizing power and developing bureaucratic procedures, the colonists found themselves practicing a decentralized politics. While Europeans, furthermore, were strengthening the executive, colonists were coming to rely increasingly on the legislative branch of government. And while European nations—with the partial exception of England—were becoming more autocratic, Americans, perhaps without realizing it, were opening their political system to ever wider levels of participation.

Political participation widened not only because property ownership was widespread. Also widespread was the experience of social mobility. Because it was possible for those who began with little or nothing to rise to a decent competence there seemed little need to restrict political participation unduly. Colonial practice, in other words,

came before theory; and Americans ever since have tended to believe that practice should take precedence over theory.

The early colonists were eager to transplant European institutions and practices, but the very act of creating new communities forced them to perfect the arts of local government and to think about representative government in a new way. Their colonial governors, often royal appointees, had sweeping powers in theory but little knowledge of local needs. So colonists turned to the popularly elected lower house of their legislatures for leadership. Thus, as the years passed, they gained practical experience in governing themselves.

3. Societies, it would seem, sooner or later develop a sense of their special mission or role in history. In the Russia of the Tsars, for example, Moscow was thought to be the "Third Rome," the successor to Rome and Constantinople as the capital of true Christianity. France, during its revolutionary era, proclaimed itself the carrier of political freedom to the rest of the world. China and Japan have also developed distinctive notions of their special historical destiny. So it is not surprising that Americans also developed an ideology of their special place in history.

As early as 1630 John Winthrop was reminding the first Puritans of their mission:

> Wee must consider that wee shall be as a citty upon a Hille. The eyes of all people are upon us. Soe that if wee shall deale falsely with our God in this worke wee have undertaken, and soe cause him to withdraw his present help from us, wee shall be made a story and a by-word through the world.

As Winthrop's words suggest, this idea that America was to be an example to the other nations of the world derived in large part from his Puritan conviction that the Reformation was a continuing process and that God had saved America for settlement by adherents of reformed churches. Americans, Puritans and other Protestants believed, were a chosen people—latter day Jews—and America was to be a new Israel. Reinforcing this religious interpretation was the secular belief that whoever controlled this vast continent would necessarily, in time, take a leading role in world affairs. America was, after all, a new world.

So however small the first beginnings, they were immediately enhanced by this vision (largely borne out) that the American colonies were the start of a vast new chapter in human history. Americans found congenial this notion of themselves as a model of mankind, and not only because it was so flattering. The first colonists were people whose lives contained more than a full measure of upheaval, danger, suffering, and uncertainty. They needed to ask themselves why they were making the sacrifices involved in leaving the familiar scenes of home; they needed a heroic vision of themselves, and the notion of America as a "Citty upon a Hille" provided one.

Suggested Readings

The study of the massive migration of Europeans to America must begin with Bernard Bailyn's *The Peopling of America: An Introduction* (1985). Karen O. Kupperman's 1984 study, *Roanoke: The Abandoned Colony,* is a thoughtful, well-reasoned account of the "lost" settlers. Edmund S. Morgan wrote the brilliant *American Slavery, American Freedom* (1975), which serves as a fine introduction to colonial Virginia. Alden Vaughan illuminates the early history of the colony in *American Genesis: Captain John Smith and the Founding of Virginia* (1975). On the founding of New England, Edmund Morgan's *The Puritan Dilemma: The Story of John Winthrop* (1958) has become a classic, while John Demos, *A Little Commonwealth: Family Life in Plymouth Colony* (1970) uses material culture as well as psychology to reconstruct everyday life. New England towns and Puritan ideas have inspired a number of first-rate studies including Kenneth Lockridge, *A New England Town: The First Hundred Years* (1970), and Philip Greven, *Four Generations: Population, Land, and Family in Colonial Andover, Massachusetts* (1970).

Sumner Chilton Powell, *Puritan Village* (1966), was one of the first of the town studies. Robert Middlekauff, *The Mathers: Three Generations of Puritan Intellectuals* (1971), and Sacvan Bercovitch, *The American Jeremiad* (1978) add to the earlier work of Perry Miller. See Miller's brief *Errand into the Wilderness* (1956) for a distillation of parts of *The New England Mind: From Colony to Province* (1953). See also Charles L. Cohen, *God's Caress: The Psychology of Puritan Religious Experience* (1986). The definitive study of the Anne Hutchinson controversy is still Emery Battis, *Saints and Sectaries: Anne Hutchinson and the Antinomian Controversy in the Massachusetts Bay Colony* (1962). On King Philip's War see Edward Douglas Leach, *Flintlock and Tomahawk: New England in King Philip's War* (1965).

Stephen Webb's study of Bacon's Rebellion, *The End of American Independence* (1984), sees that event as an important turning-point in Britain's relations with the colonies. Thad Tate and David Ammerman, *The Chesapeake* in the *Seventeenth Century* (1979) is an excellent collection of essays.

☆ ☆ DEBATE ☆ ☆ ☆

FORREST McDONALD

It is fashionable to accuse the white man of every manner of crime against the American Indians. They are generally depicted as simple, peaceful, happy, and free people who were perfectly attuned to nature and had wondrous things to teach the whites. The invaders burst into this paradise of the "noble savage," plundering, slaughtering, and stealing land. Of all the burdens of guilt that white Americans must bear, we are frequently told, the injustice committed against the Indians is among the heaviest.

It is a bum rap. The doom of the Indians was sealed the moment outsiders began to set foot in America, and would have been if the invaders had been saints or had come from Africa or Asia. The people of the Old World had developed immunities to a wide variety of diseases, but the native Americans had not. As soon as Europeans and Indians made contact, Indians started to die in epidemic proportions. During the first fifty years after the Spanish arrived, well over nine-tenths of the roughly six million inhabitants of the Aztec and Incan empires died of smallpox. Measles and other infectious diseases took additional droves. Gradually, as contacts spread over the two Americas, nearly ninety-five percent of the remaining Indians died in epidemics. Later, diseases such as malaria and yellow fever, brought over from Africa, resulted in more deaths. No question of morality is involved: nothing the newcomers did, apart from simply being there, had anything to do with the demise of the native American. (There is an object lesson in humility here: it is presumptuous if indeed not blasphemous to blame ourselves for things that are entirely beyond human control.)

The idea of the noble savage is a sentimental dream. Mexico and Peru were highly civilized, but the vast majority of the people there were for practical purposes slaves of their rulers. By far most of the Indians elsewhere were by European standards dirty, treacherous, ignorant, and superstitious. Tribal warfare—which routinely included theft, arson, rape, and torture as well as the indiscriminate slaughter of women, children, and the aged—was almost continuous. For most of the Indians, as for Thomas Hobbes's man in a "state of nature," life was "poor, nasty, brutish, and short."

The question of Indian lands is a complex one. The lands did not belong to the Indians, for they had no concept of private ownership of property in land. It is true that various tribes occupied hunting grounds that they considered the collective possession of the tribe; but there was nothing sacrosanct about such possession, for neighboring tribes were wont to seize control of the lands whenever it struck their fancy and they had the chance to do so. British Americans regularly purchased titles to Indian lands they occupied. This must have struck the Indians as a humorously fair bargain, being paid for something that was not theirs to sell and that other Indians would have taken by force.

One special aspect of relations between the English and the Indians requires brief notice. The English had been hardened by a long history of dealing with the Irish, the Highland Scots, and the Welsh. They had regarded these tribal Celtic peoples as a dangerous nuisance, as contemptible savages whose periodic attacks (often in alliance with France or Spain) led to costly wars, as an almost subhuman species who occupied but did little farming on land that Englishmen could put to profitable use. English settlers in America consciously saw the Indians as being replicas of the "wild Irish" and were disposed to treat them accordingly. This meant, among other things, that English colonists rarely intermingled with Indians and almost never married them. Anglo-Americans did not face the problem of assimilating or Europeanizing the natives and did not change their own ways to accommodate the ways of the Indians. That made the experience of Englishmen in America radically different from that of their Spanish, French, and Portuguese counterparts.

Were the Indians Victims?

EUGENE GENOVESE

I have some sympathy for Professor McDonald's outburst against the silly moralizing that tries to make Americans out to be premature Nazis. Those who find Americans especially wicked, either absolutely or relative to the Third World peoples, might profitably study the Mongol conquests; Muslim slave-trading in Africa; slaughters of Hindus and Muslims in India; the career of the Zulus before the Europeans did unto them what they had been doing unto other black Africans; the periodic and often sadistic butchering of peasants by German, Japanese, Russian, and many other ruling classes across the globe. Cortez could not have conquered the great Aztec empire without the support of the "Indian" peoples whom the Aztecs had conquered, exploited, oppressed, terrorized, and tortured.

I do not, however, find helpful a substitution of conservative cant for liberal cant. The forcible reorganization of the native economy and the destruction of much of traditional social and cultural life are brutal, however much hostility the old culture may have contained. And the story of the European conquest of the American Indians will not be complete without some account of the slaughters and the enslavement of the subject peoples.

If the Indians were "by European standards, dirty, treacherous, ignorant, and superstitious," they were indeed a bad lot. Let us start with "dirty." The Europeans who landed on the African coast, looking for gold and slaves, sickened the natives by their stench and filth. The Africans could not believe that human beings could be as filthy as the Europeans were. Could the Indians really have outdone them? Treacherous. Toward whom? About what? Did the United States government ever make a treaty with the Indians that it did not break? Were the Indians more treacherous than the princes of Renaissance Italy, those much admired benefactors of the early modern world? More treacherous than the Borgia Pope Alexander VI or his famous daughter Lucrezia? More treacherous than the British in Ireland, than Francis II of France toward his fellow Catholics during the religious wars? This charge, like that of "ignorant," is offensive primarily for being meaningless. Of "superstitious" I shall say little. Since Protestants have always denounced Catholics for being superstitious, we should hardly expect them to treat with respect the religious beliefs of American Indians, Africans, or Hindus.

The question of Indian land is more serious. Professor McDonald employs the concept of "private property" as though such property, in its modern form, has always existed. But in fact private property as an absolute possession of an individual or business corporation is a recent legal and social construct. Even under late European feudalism, property was in some sense collective, not individual or "absolute." What Europeans did to the Indians, as to the Africans and others, was to swindle them, either by the simple device of imposing on the transactions their own harshly modern idea of property, or by making deals with corrupt leaders who were alienating common property without legal or moral authority.

Let these matters pass, and with them any attempt to do justice to the culture of the Indian peoples. Yet even from a Eurocentric perspective the conquest of the continent from the Indians—their expulsion as well as their slaughter—had fearful consequences. It contributed mightily to the deepening, broadening, and hardening of a racist arrogance and inhumanity that would extend, in even more virulent form, to the black people who were being brought in as slaves. That racism, to which the war on the Indians contributed so much, has poisoned American life. Even those who are disposed to take lightly the treatment of the Indians—to excuse it, to explain it, to place it in tendentious perspective—ought to be willing to ponder the cost our nation has been paying.

Gallows Hill, Salem, Massachusetts, where the witches were hanged.

CHAPTER 3

The Developing Colonies

THE WITCHES OF SALEM

In 1692 the Devil assaulted the seaport town of Salem, Massachusetts, with an unparalleled fury. This village of a few hundred people was invaded by scores of warlocks and witches, men and women who had covenanted with the Devil to make mischief, to drive little children mad, to sicken and kill livestock and people. One witch, it seemed, had caused the deaths of fourteen members of a single family. The jails bulged with over a hundred prisoners awaiting trial, including a four-year-old child bound for nine months in heavy iron chains. Twenty-seven people eventually came to trial; the court hanged nineteen—fourteen women and five men—as witches. One man refused to enter a plea, and suffered *peine forte et dure:* heavy weights were laid on Giles Cory's body until, still refusing the plea, he was pressed to death.

The trouble had begun innocently enough: "Conjuration with sieves and keys, and peas, and nails, and horseshoes" at first seemed harmless activities with which to pass the New England winter. But these games turned serious when grim-visaged parents tried to discover what was causing their children's "fits" and "distempers." Salem Village's minister, Samuel Parris, was the first father to react. His nine-year-old daughter, Betty, and her eleven-year-old cousin, Abigail Williams, had fallen into "odd postures" and "foolish, ridiculous speeches." The concerned father called in a local doctor who, diagnosing no physical illness, raised suspicions of the "Evil Hand"—witchcraft.

This was a reasonable supposition. Everyone knew about witchcraft. Just as those who were saved covenanted together to form a church, so, too, some of those who were damned made a pact with the Devil. They "wrote in his book," joining his legions for the thrill of conjurations, midnight frolics, obscure or perhaps obscene rituals, and the power to harm their neighbors. Waves of witchcraft had swept across Europe for the past two centuries as the Reformation inspired a direct struggle between Christ and the Devil. Do not "suffer a witch to live," the Bible commanded, and tens of thousands, mostly women but many men as well, had been burned or hanged as the Evil One's followers.

Before 1692, the Devil had paid small attention to New England, except through the incursions of his New World minions, the Indians. Forty-four cases, three hangings, no burnings—such was the entire history of New England witchcraft before Betty and Abigail's malady spread to seven adolescent girls in Salem Village. Under intense questioning, and responding to this attention with yet further manifestations of demoniac possession, the girls named three women as the source of their sufferings. These were likely candidates. Sarah Good, daughter of a well-to-do innkeeper, had steadily tumbled down the social ladder; she was in 1692 a surly, pipe-smoking beggar whose "muttering and scolding" seemed to cause cows to die. Sarah Osborne's name swirled in contention and scandal: her battle with her own sons for control of her first husband's estate, her liaison with the Irish indentured servant who became her second husband. And there was Tituba, the slave woman who had introduced Betty and Abigail to the practices of voodoo she had learned in the West Indies. At the pre-trial examination Tituba readily and noisily told the audience of townspeople and "possessed" girls what they wanted to hear. For three days, she regaled them with stories of her comportings with the Devil and with witches Sarah Good and Sarah Osborne, of midnight sabbaths and rides through the air with Satan, whom she described as "a thing all over hairy, all the face hairy, and a long nose." She had seen the Devil's "book" and although she could not read, she had counted nine names in it. Nine names! There were more witches: soon the girls, shrieking, contorting, sobbing hysterically, dredged up still more names. Not all were outcasts like Sarah Good, Sarah Osborne, and Tituba; not all were from Salem. The jails groaned; the gallows rope snapped. The girls' madness, for the better part of a year, infected a whole society. When they began to accuse prominent citizens—some Boston clergymen, for instance, and the governor's wife—the Reverend Cotton Mather, his father, the Reverend Increase Mather, and some other ministers recommended the cessation of the trials. (Cotton Mather, like everyone else in the seventeenth century, believed in witches, but he also believed in science. He would have his day in 1721, when to combat popular fears of the new medical practice of inoculation for smallpox, he allowed his son to be inoculated. Among Mather's critics was a young journalist, Benjamin Franklin.) In 1692 reason returned to Salem; probing questions were asked; the jailed were sent home and pardoned.

The girls' part in it is easiest to explain. The life of young girls in Massachusetts Bay was dull in the best of times. "I am not fond," wrote Cotton Mather, foremost Puritan minister, "of proposing *Play* to children, as a Reward of any diligent Application to learn what is good; lest they should think *Diversion* to be a better and nobler Thing than *Diligence*." While young men, sent to school and taught to pray and work, could at least look forward to the adventure of choosing careers, girls could do little more than wonder "what trade their sweethearts should be of." It is understandable that when the little girls dabbled in magic with Tituba, their slightly older friends and relatives joined the only excitement midwinter had to offer. (Many teen-aged girls—including most of the "afflicted" ones—did not live at home where parents might spoil them, but were sent to relatives' or neighbors' houses to learn their adult roles and to be evenly disciplined.) Once the adults began to fuss over their fits, how could the young resist pursuing their adventure and showing their power over the adult community, particularly over the married women who laid on endless chores and discipline? Even these antics would have been relatively harmless had not the adults panicked. It is their role, not the children's, that cries out for explanation. Forty years later, when children in Northampton behaved the same way, their minister, Jonathan Edwards, read the cues differently. Under his inspired counseling, the young people's fits and sobbing fueled the start of a great religious revival.

In Salem the witchcraft epidemic had fed upon local conflicts as people from different political and clerical factions hurled accusations back and forth. For Salem was an angry place. Town and countryside were sharply diverging. Conservative back country farmers smarted under the growth of commercial capitalism and its accompanying secular style. Sons coming of age found difficulty establishing themselves as land became increasingly scarce. The values of Puritanism itself seemed more and more in question as ministers bemoaned the "declension" from the piety of the colony's founders three generations before. And since 1684 the colony of Massachusetts had been without a charter. Would the old land claims be valid under a new one? Would voting still be restricted to church members? Nearly every adult must have been startled at a changing world crowding in on what had been for two generations a largely fixed culture. Men and women who were supposed to practice Christian unity engaged year after year in lawsuits over boundaries and legacies. Like the witches, they were at war with their neighbors, disrupting the church and government, bursting the old molds. Were they too possessed? How much easier it must have been to blame everything on the literal bewitchment of enemies rather than on their own bewitchment with the new and perhaps dubious values and goals that were transforming John Winthrop's "Citty upon a Hill" into a secular society.

So historians and sociologists have reasoned. But there is a simpler explanation. For all the learning, the sobriety, the orderliness, the industry that New England Calvinism could muster there was within it from the beginning something close to hysteria. Other outbreaks of hysteria have appeared in various forms throughout America's history. In the 1950s the American playwright Arthur Miller wrote "The Crucible," a play about the Salem witch trials. He wrote it at the height of another hysteria—Senator Joseph McCarthy's "witch hunt" for Communists at the beginning of the Cold War.

The Settlements Become a Society

In many instances what the seventeenth-century promoters of colonization promised had come true: people of ordinary means in the Old World improved their fortunes in the New. As one promotional tract put it, people "which go away from hence very poor, may within a little while become very rich." Another promised that "they that here were needy & of mean estate may there arise to be ... men of substance and good ability." Many colonists proved John Smith's statement that a man who came to America "with nothing but his hands" could "by industry quickly grow rich." For the colonist willing to work, economic opportunity, if not riches, lay everywhere. The forests were thick with fine timber for ships' masts and lumber. The soils of Virginia and the Carolinas hungered to be planted with tobacco and rice. The New England seacoasts invited the forming of a great mercantile and seafaring culture; nearby were the teeming fish banks of Newfoundland. And everywhere there was land: land to plant with American corn and other

Meetinghouse, Plymouth, Massachusetts, built in 1683. In the early years of colonization a New England town's meetinghouse served both as church and town hall. *(Courtesy, Colonial Society of Massachusetts, Boston)*

subsistence foods, land to test for the possibility of new commercial crops, land to flee into, away from civilization and its troubles, land to settle with religious communities that Europe would not tolerate.

Take today's crowd at a Yankee Stadium double-header and scatter it along the East Coast, and you will have the entire European population of this land in 1660. Though the death rate in Virginia in the earliest times had been terrible, the population of the colonies was growing, by births in some regions and elsewhere by immigration. From about 65,000 in 1660 the total population had reached 265,000 by 1700. Throughout the colonies, stable, self-perpetuating growth depended upon the presence of women in their child-bearing years who could marry the male settlers. Where the ratio of men to women remained very high—3 to 1 in the Chesapeake, and as many as 9 to 1 in the fishing settlements in Newfoundland—it took considerable time for the settler population to reproduce itself. Even at the end of the century the European population was a sprinkling of people at the eastern edge of the American continent. The British government, when it thought about this land at all, saw it as part of a commercial and territorial empire, and granted chunks of it to courtier proprietors, or legislated for it with the Navigation Acts, or otherwise tried to control it. Colonists were keenly aware of their place within that empire, and such things as the Navigation Acts and the Dominion of New England reminded them of it. Meanwhile they were forming societies of their own, establishing ways of life that did not subordinate themselves to the needs and programs of the empire. But colonial societies did not simply develop spontaneously within the rich land and opportunities of the continent; they took much of their shape from the societies of the Old World.

The New England Colonies

Everyday Life   The early New England settlers gathered into communities that duplicated something of the physical arrangement of the English villages they had known. An English family did not live in isolation on the land it worked. Homes were close together in the village, and each family worked plots of the surrounding lands. The system was well suited to the needs of the first generation in New England. On a stubborn soil in a harsh winter climate and under threat of Indian attack, that generation sought to establish a stable and comfortable life. For several generations in Massachusetts, attendance at church was required of everyone, including nonmembers; and the centrality of the churches in the life of the colony was further reason for the colonists to cluster into villages. By the eighteenth century, however, young men seeking farm land had to go farther afield, or be content with smaller plots as fathers parcelled out family holdings to sons. Neighbors sometimes coveted each other's land, and social tensions rose. But the village pattern that had developed in the early years left its permanent stamp on New England: and the system of town meetings, in which local citizens directly make decisions that elsewhere in the country are left to elected or appointed officials, persists to this day.

Even in the seventeenth century New England, at least in its most settled portions, was a remarkably well-educated region, possibly one of the most civilized places in the English world. Harvard College, America's

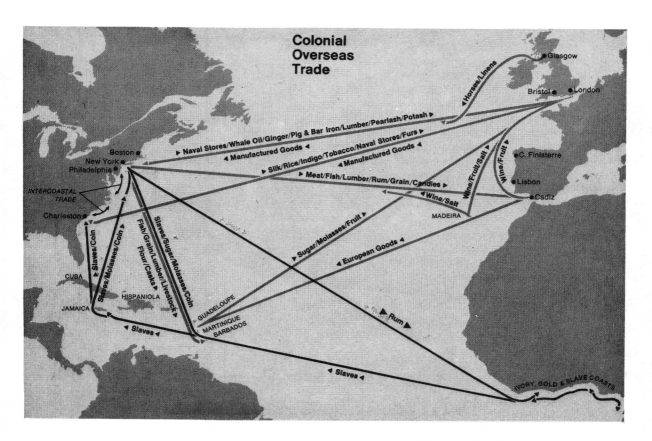

Colonial Overseas Trade

first institution of higher learning, was founded in 1636, primarily to educate young men for the clergy. The government of Massachusetts Bay had the towns provide free elementary schools—although girls were not expected to benefit from them and women's literacy lagged far behind that of men. Boys and girls alike read the *New England Primer*, published in 1691:

> In *Adam's* fall
> We sinned all.
>
> Thy life to mend
> This *Book* attend.
>
> The *Cat* doth play
> And after slay.
>
> A *Dog* will bite
> The thief at night.
>
> An *Eagle's* flight
> Is out of sight.
>
> The idle *Fool*
> Is whipped at school.
>
> As runs the *Glass*,
> Man's life doth pass.

Scholars have rejected the notion that New Englanders were black-clad haters of life, the world, and pleasure. In 1725, for example,

the *Boston News-Letter* complained that people "could hardly hear the minister's first prayer for the rustling of silk gowns and petticoats." That same year there was a horse race on Boston Common with a prize of "a velvet Saddle with Silver Lace." Most New Englanders did not even wear black, although they would have been happy to do it. Black was the color not of grimness but of wealth and prominence.

New England settlers imported English class distinctions, yet here as in other matters the land and conditions of the New World modified the institutions of the old. Class distinction in New England meant not the presence of a powerful aristocracy but a somewhat milder component of the English system of class, a deference on the part of the majority toward the "better sort," people of greater wealth, schooling, and political position. But class distinctions were growing more difficult to maintain. As one New England minister observed, "The Misery and Iniquity of it is, the inferior sort of People will be clad in as Costly Attire as the Rich and Honourable."

The diarist Samuel Sewall and others like

him might grumble at Edmund Andros for celebrating Christmas, but Sewall and other Puritans enjoyed good food and drink. New England sermons could employ an imagery beautiful in its homespun "plain style," and educated New Englanders enjoyed not only religious but secular literature written in the language of everyday life. Sermons and history dominated colonial reading, but there was also an audience for poetry that ran from the religious doggerel of Reverend Michael Wigglesworth's "Day of Doom" to the delicate lyrics of Anne Bradstreet's "To My Dear and Loving Husband:"

> If ever two were one, then surely we.
>   If ever man were lov'd by wife, then thee;
> If ever wife was happy in a man,
>   Compare with me ye women if you can.

Colonists also read newspapers, beginning in 1704 with the *Boston News-Letter* and the *New England Courant* (run by Benjamin Franklin's brother) in 1721.

As New England's economy matured, colonial merchants found it necessary to buy large quantities of manufactured goods from England. New England was almost entirely dependent upon England for clothing, for almost all tools beyond the most primitive, for muskets and other firearms, and for clocks, compasses, and a host of other instruments. The New Englanders drank oceans of tea and used considerable quantities of spices, which could be legally obtained only through the East India Company in London; and despite recurring waves of puritanical hostility toward the consumption of luxuries, they sought and bought the finer things of life when they were able. "Those flags of pride," said Cotton Mather to his Sunday-best-dressed congregation, "are they paid for?" And since New Englanders could not grow staples, such as Virginia's tobacco or the sugar of the West Indies, that would pay the mother county for imports, the region's balance of trade with Great Britain was invariably unfavorable.

Prosperity

Despite the trade imbalance, the years from about 1715 to 1755 were a time of great prosperity. The port of Boston serviced "annually between three and four hundred ships, great and small," trading not only with "the English and other European nations," but with the mainland and Caribbean colonies as well, exchanging "beef, pork, fish, and other provisions . . . for rice, pitch, tar, rum and sugar, and spices and logwood." It is not true that, as myth once had it, New England's commercial success was based upon hauling freight or upon the slave trade. The colonial merchants were never more than marginally engaged in either of these maritime activities. The key to the New Englanders' system was the great sugar plantations of the West Indies. These were not self-sufficient, for it was uneconomical to waste the labor of slaves on growing staple food when it could be bought so cheaply and land was so valuable. The sugar islands were also deficient in timber suitable for providing the bare necessity of wood products, even including staves for making containers in which to ship their sugar. By supplying the West Indies, New England's entrepreneurs made enough profit not only to pay what they owed for imports, but to provide employment for their whole population.

New England farmers produced fruit, beef, pork, butter, and cheese for the West Indian market, and many also raised cattle, horses, and chickens for live export. Fishing expanded enormously and became highly commercialized after 1715. By the 1730s as many as 150 new fishing vessels were being built annually, and the number of people employed in the fisheries was more than 5,000. Whaling developed as an additional specialty in some places, notably Nantucket, where it was even more valuable than fishing.

In the early days, when settlements were concentrated along the seacoast and immediately to the interior from Boston and the other ports, farmers produced marketable timber from the trees they felled to clear their lands for the plow. But timber is a bulky commodity and the only practical way to transport it is by river; and south of Salem the Massachusetts coast was almost entirely devoid of streams that extended as much as five miles into the interior. New settlers in towns beyond that distance developed the practice of burning the trees they felled and making the ashes into potash and pearlash; these could easily be carried to port towns for merchants who found a ready market for them in England. But the change also meant that the supply of lumber from Massachusetts and Connecticut dwindled just at the time the demand for lumber products in the West Indies was expanding rapidly. For this expanding market, a commercial lumber industry was developed after about 1720 in New Hampshire and the province of Maine, where there were magnificent stands of white pine and the river systems afforded convenient transportation.

The merchants of New England secured their provisions for the West Indies from the local farmers by selling them goods imported from England, but the owners of fishing fleets and lumber camps and their employees consumed little of such commodities. The fishermen and lumber workers did, however, consume one thing abundantly, and that was rum. Accordingly, New England merchants made a practice of importing West Indian molasses for part of the goods they sold in the islands; the molasses was then manufactured into rum to trade for more lumber or fish.

Payment of the duty on molasses that the British government imposed in 1733 would have been detrimental to New York and Pennsylvania and ruinous to New England. So the merchants in those places did what American businessmen would do ever after when the law ran counter to their interests: they simply ignored the law. It was easy enough to do, for Britain's machinery for collecting customs and preventing smuggling in America was as yet primitive, and many customs officials were amenable to bribery. The passage of the Sugar Act of 1733, therefore, in no way altered the course of New England's economic growth, except to place the entire economy upon illegal foundations.

The Middle Colonies

New York, Pennsylvania, New Jersey, and Delaware contained by the mid-eighteenth century a varying mix of population. People of Dutch ancestry in New York were retaining their ethnic identity, Scotch-Irish and Germans had settled in Pennsylvania west of the Quakers, and there were Swedes to their south. Philadelphia was a principal landing place for immigrants who in the eighteenth century moved to British America by the hundreds of thousands. Each successive wave of immigrants sought land for settlement in the immediate vicinity, until all the cheaply available land in the Middle colonies was taken up and it became necessary to push toward the interior and toward the back country of the South.

| **German Immigrants** Many if not most German immigrants came as redemptioners, paying for their passage by binding themselves to serve as laborers for five to ten (normally seven) years before becoming freemen and ordinary settlers. Gottlieb Mittelberger, a German immigrant, described the arrival of indentured servants in Philadelphia around 1750:

> When the ships finally arrive in Philadelphia after the long voyage only those are let off who can pay their sea freight or can give good security. The others, who lack the money to pay, have to remain on board until they are purchased and until their purchasers can thus pry them loose from the ship. In this whole process the sick are the worst off, for the healthy are preferred and are more readily paid for. The miserable people who are ill must often still remain at sea and in sight of the city for another two or three weeks.

Then, migrating to the back country, former German redemptioners settled in a broad area extending twenty to a hundred miles west of the Delaware River. They picked the choicest lands, especially those in the limestone valleys, cleared their farms slowly but thoroughly, and built solid buildings upon them. Because of the care with which they proceeded, by the time they were able to produce for market they could bring in regular and bountiful harvests. Their principal crop was wheat, which became the second great staple (or third, if New England fish be counted) to be produced in British North America. Virginia tobacco of course was the first.

The Germans continued to arrive at a steady rate, about 2000 a year, from 1717 until about 1750. By the 1730s they were beginning to overflow the Middle colonies. Thenceforth, they proceeded to the Pennsylvania back country and headed south, settling the Cumberland Valley in Pennsylvania and Maryland and much of the Shenandoah Valley of Virginia.

By and large, wherever they went the Germans kept to themselves, retaining their own ways and making no effort to become involved in the political or social life of the colonies they inhabited. They tended to cluster in groups that had little to do even with one another. They represented a wide variety of religious sects, Reformed, Mennonite, Dunker, Moravian Brethren, Schwenkfelder, and even Roman Catholic. Considerably more numerous and far more disruptive were the descendants of the Scottish Protestants who had settled in Ulster in the North of Ireland. The total number of Scotch-Irish immigrants was around 250,000.

The Scotch-Irish   The first wave headed for New England. The Ulstermen, like the Puritans, were Calvinist, but the congregation-based church polity of New England was incompatible with the Scotch-Irish polity, with its more centralized Presbyterian church structure. Besides, the New Englanders were exclusive almost by instinct, welcoming no foreigners. What was more, Boston and its vicinity had no excess land and no shortage of labor; the inhabitants feared that immigrants would become just so many paupers to feed from the resources of their meager land; and New Englanders generally regarded the Ulstermen as illiterate, slovenly, and filthy. A few thousand immigrants of the first wave landed in Boston and, with difficulty, founded settlements around Worcester and along the Merrimac Valley of New Hampshire, but irate mobs greeted subsequent boatloads at the docks and refused to let them land.

The remainder of the first wave of Ulstermen and the overwhelming majority of future shiploads headed for Philadelphia, along with the Germans. The Scotch-Irish also followed the same routes to the interior, but there the resemblance between them and the Germans ends. For reasons of preference as well as circumstance, the two groups of immigrants did not mix. The pattern of settlement, all the way down through the Virginia valley, was that the German firstcomers farmed staples on the rich bottom lands and the Ulstermen who came later raised cattle and corn on the hillsides and poorer lands. And whereas almost all the Germans could be expected to be industrious, frugal, orderly, and peaceful, many of the Scotch-Irish worked by fits, drank prodigiously, and were quick-tempered, impetuous, and likely to pick up stakes and move for no apparent reason. And yet, having a zeal for education deriving from their Presbyterianism, the Scotch-Irish founded schools and colleges on a scale that no other group of Americans ever

approached. They loved freedom, by which they meant the right to be left alone to be themselves, and were quick to fight for it. In constant friction with the Indians, Scotch-Irish often did not hesitate to slaughter them or involve colonial authorities in wars with them. They became avid politicians, skillful and disputatious, and regularly demanded a voice in the lawmaking process when the law affected their way of life, but they totally disregarded the law when it did not suit them. By the late 1730s Ulstermen were filling the Shenandoah Valley of Virginia; by the late 1740s they were spilling out over the Piedmont Plateau of southern Virginia and central North Carolina; and a decade later they were invading the uplands of South Carolina.

Amidst enormous growth in population—from more than 75,000 in 1715 to 400,000 by the 1750s—the economic and political life of the Middle colonies developed rapidly. The economy grew even faster than the population and, as had been the way in New England and the tobacco colonies, proceeded along two lines: development of small-scale production of tools and other equipment for the expanding population, and development of production for trade in international markets.

In the colonies to the north and the south, by far the biggest portion of the business was selling land, but in the Middle colonies, for different reasons in each, the population at large could not participate in this lucrative enterprise. In New York the governors and assemblies continued the policy, originated by the Dutch, of granting land only in huge tracts—and only to themselves and their friends and relations. The great patroons, as the Dutch called them, who received the grants were more often interested in leasing the lands than in selling them. In Pennsylvania and Delaware the land belonged originally to the Penn family as proprietors, and all proceeds from sales and rentals went to them. In New Jersey, too, the land belonged to small groups of proprietors, and though the system of land disposition was always complex the profits from land sales went to these small groups.

Philadelphia   The supply of craftsmen, the abundance of raw materials, and the insatiable market combined in the Middle colonies to breed a thriving industry in farm implements, other hardware, clocks, locks, guns, flints, glass, stoneware,

The Middle Colonies.

paper, nails, and woodwork. The port of Philadelphia burgeoned: by the mid-1730s several hundred vessels were entering and clearing the port every year. At first most of these vessels belonged to others, but then Philadelphians began to acquire their own ships, and with this development came an-

other, the establishment of a shipbuilding industry and such linked activities as importing and processing naval stores and manufacturing ropes, anchors, and sails.

By the 1730s, Philadelphia (like New York City to a lesser extent) had begun to emerge as a major export and import center. Among the exports were beef and pork, which, along with the livestock, were produced mainly by the Scotch-Irish. These products found ready markets on the sugar plantations of the West Indies. More important were wheat and flour, produced by the industrious Germans and the scores of mills that sprang up along the Delaware and Schuylkill rivers. The Navigation Acts did not confine colonial wheat and flour to the English market. Some went to the West Indies and much to the European continent, where Philadelphia merchants could acquire bills of exchange and goods for trade in England. This made Philadelphia a principal importing center for English manufactures in North America.

By mid-century, Philadelphia was fast becoming America's richest and largest city. A visitor in 1744 observed that

> In this city one may live tolerably cheap, as to the articles of eating and drinking, but European goods are extravagantly dear. Even goods of their own manufacture—such as linen, woolen, and leather—bear a high price. Their government is a kind of anarchy (or no government), there being perpetual jars betwixt the two parts of the legislature. . . . There is polite conversation here among the better sort, among whom there is no scarcity of learning and good sense. The ladies, for the most part, keep at home and seldom appear in the streets, never in public assemblies, except at the churches or meetings; therefore I cannot with any certainty enlarge upon their charms, having had little or no opportunity to see them either congregated or separate, but to be sure the Philadelphia dames are as handsome as their neighbors.

In another decade or two Philadelphia would be the second largest city and second busiest port in the entire English-speaking world. New York's port also thrived, though it developed much more slowly. The colony's restrictive immigration and land policies kept New York from developing anything like Philadelphia's business of transporting and supplying newcomers, and it also had a smaller productive base for its international trade. But the Iroquois Indians in New York's interior did trap some furs themselves and also served as middlemen between the Albany traders and many of the western Indians, who trapped furs in enormous quantities and were eager to sell them. The fur trade was profitable, and so for a time New York's prosperity matched that of Philadelphia, although its population grew more slowly.

Quaker Influences

William Penn's plans late in the seventeenth century for Pennsylvania had been ambitious. The colony would be a place of love and harmony. Penn had established friendly relations with the Indians. The very act of establishing a government that could back up its laws with force meant that whether or not Penn, like other Quakers, would oppose all wars among nations, he was not prepared to practice a Quakerism of total nonresistance at home. But one of his schemes provided that imprisonment would be humane and seek the reformation of criminals. For a short period Pennsylvania actually attempted a system of imprisonment for reform of criminals—an experiment that prefigured the modern penitentiary. The earliest Quakers had been given to fits of emotionalism accompanied by disruptive behavior, but Penn prized more sober virtues and conduct. An account that he wrote of Pennsylvania, translated into German, Dutch, and French and published on the European continent as well as in Britain, invited solid, industrious farmers and craftsmen to settle in the colony. His Quakerism, then, cherished the compound of spirituality and virtuous worldliness that has been characteristic of the Society of Friends ever since.

In Penn's lifetime political disputes broke out in Pennsylvania. And in the years after his death the colony became quite different from the harmonious commonwealth he had envisioned. The presence of the Scotch-Irish on the frontier guaranteed that the Indians would receive something other than the treatment Penn would have wanted for them. The tide of immigration made the Quakers a minority in the colony, though a wealthy and powerful one, and Quakers lost favor with the proprietors when the sons of William Penn left the Society of Friends for the Church of England. To promote and protect their interests in the face of these reversals, the Quakers gathered allies and formed a political faction called variously the Quaker party and the Anti-Proprietary party. Their wealth and influence normally gave them control of the legislature. Arrayed against them in the Proprietary party were the Scotch-Irish (who were perhaps America's least peaceful people), most frontiersmen, and a considerable number of non-pacifist Germans.

In contrast to the popularly based politics

ESTIMATED POPULATION OF AMERICAN COLONIES:
1630 TO 1750

	1630	1650	1670	1690	1730	1750
White						
New England	1,796	22,452	51,521	86,011	211,233	349,029
Middle Colonies	340	3,786	6,664	32,369	135,298	275,723
Southern Colonies	2,450	22,530	49,215	75,263	191,893	309,588
Black						
New England	0	380	375	950	6,118	10,982
Middle Colonies	10	515	790	2,472	11,683	20,736
Southern Colonies	50	705	3,370	13,307	73,220	204,702
Total White	4,586	48,768	107,400	193,643	538,424	934,340
Total Black	60	1,600	4,535	16,729	91,021	236,420

of Pennsylvania, politics in New York was aristocratic. The colony did have numerous and vociferous lower elements, fighting one another as well as the upper classes and clamoring for a voice in government: but the lower classes largely canceled one another out in antipathies among Scotch-Irish and New Englanders and New Yorkers, among Presbyterians and Congregationalists and Dutch Calvinists, among tenant farmers and squatters and the plain folk of the city. Such of these inhabitants as could vote were normally easy for the landed aristocrats to manage, for they voted orally, in public, and were therefore amenable to bribery and pressure when mere deference failed to secure their vote.

The Southern Colonies

| **Southern Plantations** The upper South, unlike New England, had land suitable for the growth of a great commercial staple crop. And since Virginia planters had never been interested in setting up villages with churches as the focus of their life, society in Virginia spread out into tobacco plantations of various sizes—the average was about 200 acres. The majority of Virginia's colonists were small farmers, the independent yeomen whom Thomas Jefferson, years later, would call "the chosen people of God." A visitor to the colony in the 1680s described their life:

They usually plant tobacco, Indian corn, wheat, peas or beans, barley, sweet potatoes, turnips, which grow to a monstrous size and are very good to eat. They make gardens as we do in Europe. . . . So much timber have they that they build fences all around the land they cultivate. A man with fifty acres of ground, and others in proportion, will leave at least twenty-five wooded, and of the remaining twenty-five will cultivate half and keep the other as a pasture and paddock for his cattle. . . . Some people in this country are comfortably housed; the farmers' houses are built entirely of wood.

This observer also commented upon the houses of the wealthier planters:

Those who have some means, cover them inside with a coating of mortar in which they use oyster shells for lime; it is as white as snow, so that although they look ugly from the outside, where only the wood can be seen, they are very pleasant inside, with convenient windows and openings. They have started making bricks in quantities, and I have seen several houses where the walls were entirely made of them. . . . They build also a separate kitchen, a separate house for the Christian slaves, one for the Negro slaves, and several to dry the tobacco so that when you come to the home of a person of some means, you think you are entering a fairly large village.

The Southern Colonies.

In the tobacco colonies as elsewhere, labor was in short supply. Until the end of the seventeenth century the major solution in all the colonies was to import indentured servants. In exchange for passage money to America, servants were obliged to work for a number of years for the employer—usually seven years, sometimes fewer. The paper on which the agreement was written would then be torn in two, the servant receiving one piece and the master the other. Each thereby had evidence that he or she had been a party to that specific agreement, for the jagged indentations along the tear line of one piece would fit exactly into those on the other.

Although the supply of white indentured servants dwindled by the late seventeenth century, the demand for them did not. A Maryland agent in 1774 requested

40 or 50 indented servants, or as many as the ship will conveniently bring. I think they will turn a profit. . . . Tradesmen and farmers answer best, next to them common laborers, the fewer women the better.

Tradesmen—blacksmiths, bricklayers, carpenters and the like—were in great demand. One indentured servant in Maryland observed that "Tradesmen hear lives like gentlemen." He lamented that he had been "born under a bad planet, or else, i mite

[have] had a trade or two and not a suffered the heate of sun from day break tell dark" working in the fields. Such servitude existed throughout the colonies, but it was most pronounced in the South.

Throughout the seventeenth century the colonists had tried unsuccessfully to enslave Indians, especially those captured in the Pequot War and King Philip's War, but the native Americans often proved intractable and could easily run away on the mainland. Enterprising New Englanders sold a number of these captives to colonists in Bermuda and the Caribbean.

Perhaps as many as two-thirds of the people who emigrated to North America during the colonial period came as servants. The lot of a servant varied according to the custom of the region and the temperament of the mas-

As this eighteenth-century advertisement suggests, tobacco-smoking was popular in Europe. Tobacco profits, based on the labor of slaves, were popular in Virginia.

ter. In Virginia in the 1650s a colonist wrote that

> The labour [that] servants are put to, is not so hard nor of such continuance as Husbandmen, nor Handecraftmen are kept at in England, as I said little or nothing is done in winter time, none ever work before sun rising nor after sun set, in the summer they rest, sleep or exercise themselves five houres in the heat of the day. Saturdayes afternoon is always their own, the old Holidayes are observed and the Sabboath spent in good exercises.
>
> The Women are not (as is reported) put into the ground [fields] to worke, but occupie such domestique imployments and houswifery as in England, that is dressing victuals, righting up the house, milking, imployed about dayries, washing, sowing, etc. and both men and women have times of recreations, as much or more than in any part of the world besides. . . .

Such accounts must be weighed against newspaper notices for runaway servants like these:

> *Philadelphia, April 14, 1748.*
> Run away from Samuel Lippincott of Northampton in the county of Burlington, an Irish servant Maid, named Mary Muckleroy, of a middle Stature: Had on when she went away, a blue and white striped gown, of large and small stripes, cuffed with blue, a white muslin handkerchief, an old blue quilt, a new Persian black bonnet, a new pair of calf-skin shoes, a fine Holland cap, with a cambrick border, an old black short cloak lined with Bengal, blue worsted stockings, with white clocks, a very good fine shirt, and a very good white apron. She took with her a sorrel horse, about 14 hands high, shod before, and paces very well. It is supposed there is an Irishman gone with her. Whoever takes up and secures the said woman and horse, so that they may be had again, shall have Three Pounds reward, and reasonable charges paid by
> *Samuel Lippincott*
> —The Pennsylvania Gazette, April 16, 1748. . . .

> *Philadelphia, June 8. 1749.*
> Run away from *Nicholas Bearcraft* of *Hunterdon County,* a Black Wench, named *Hecatissa* alias *Savina,* Country born, about 27 Years of Age, short Stature, gloomy down Look, often troubl'd with the Cholick, it is thought she may be gone towards Maryland. Whoever takes up and secures said Wench, so that she may be had again, shall have *Twenty Shillings* Reward, and reasonable Charges, paid by
> NICHOLAS BEARCRAFT.
> –The Pennsylvania Journal, June 8, 1749. . . .

Slavery

Through most of the seventeenth century slavery had not been of major importance on the American mainland. Not until the eighteenth century would black slavery become entrenched on a large scale in British North America. There was a perpetual shortage of labor in the colonies, but as long as the farm unit remained small and was worked by the owner alongside his family and such indentured servants as he could afford, servants who spoke English were preferred to others.

Only gradually in the seventeenth century did black slavery develop. In Virginia, for example, with a population of 15,000 at mid-century, there were only about 300 blacks, and not all of these were slaves. Some of these lived as free men and women in the colony's early years, and some even acquired land of their own. They could say, as did a black landowner named Anthony Johnson, "I know myne owne ground and I will worke when I please and play when I please." At one time he owned 250 acres on Virginia's Eastern Shore, and employed servants of his own, including at least one black man who was his "slave for life."

At first even large planters shunned slaves as expensive and subject to a high mortality in a new land. The black population in the English colonies grew very slowly. The first blacks in the English colonies had arrived in Virginia in 1619, but as late as 1680 there were still no more than 3,000 in Virginia and fewer than 7,000 in all the mainland colonies combined. English common law had no concept of slavery, and for a time slaves may have been in a legal position somewhat like that of indentured servants. Records in the middle of the seventeenth century referred to slaves as "servants for life."

But then in the 1680s and the following decades a series of developments combined to establish slavery firmly, though still on a modest scale, in the tobacco-growing colonies of Virginia and Maryland, and at the same time to establish a prosperous gentry as the ruling class. A change in the laws of both colonies finally made it legal and even easy to buy land in large tracts. Despite a rapid increase in production, tobacco prices remained fairly high from about 1684 to about 1703. In these circumstances small farm units began to give way to sizable plantations, where workers could be employed efficiently in gangs. At just this time, the Royal Africa

Company and other groups of English merchants were beginning to dominate the African slave trade and were looking for markets. Competition between slave traders of several nations, moreover, temporarily reduced the profits of supplying blacks for West Indian sugar plantations, so the English were willing to sell slaves in Virginia and Maryland at bargain prices.

By the early 1700s Virginia and Maryland were importing thousands of African slaves and laying the foundation for the plantation system of Southern agriculture. Slavery acquired a sharper legal definition. A Virginia law of 1662 declared that "all children born in this country shall be held bond or free only according to the condition of the mother," ensuring that children of slave women would be slaves as well. Other laws restricted blacks from "walking abroad on nights meeting together" without their master's permission. By the early eighteenth century slavery was fully defined as a legal institution in the colonies. By 1710 there were well over 30,000 slaves in Maryland and Virginia in a total population of about 120,000. By 1740 the numbers had grown to 84,000 blacks in a population of 296,000. New England, by contrast, had only 8500 blacks in a population of nearly 290,000. Slavery spread throughout the colonies, but never in the concentration it achieved in the plantation economies of the South. Most of the blacks came from West Africa, a settled area in which agriculture, mining, and handicrafts were well established, and they adapted reasonably well to work on American farms and plantations. Not all blacks were eager to obey their new masters. An English visitor in 1746 observed that

> a *new Negro,* if he must be broke, either from obstinacy, or, which I am more apt to suppose, from greatness of soul, will require more hard discipline than a young spaniel. You would really be surprised at their perseverance; let an hundred men show him how to hoe, or drive a wheelbarrow; he'll still take the one by the bottom, and the other by the wheel, and they often die before they can be conquered.

One colonist thought that slaves were probably treated better than indentured servants:

> Negroes being a property for life, the death of slaves, in the prime of youth or strength is a material loss to the proprietor; they are, therefore, in almost every instance, under more comfortable circumstances than the miserable European.

On a tobacco plantation the atmosphere was generally healthy and the labor to be done, though fussy and tedious, was not back-breaking. It became both possible and profitable for a plantation owner to encourage both breeding and some semblance of family life among his slaves. Around the 1720s the slave population in the Chesapeake colonies began to reproduce itself, kinship networks formed, and a semblance of a slave community developed. Slaves on small plantations might visit friends or relatives on larger ones; husbands and wives (slave marriages were not recognized by law) if owned by different masters might spend Sundays together.

Developments in Virginia In the early 1730s there began a remarkable economic boom in Virginia. Before it had ended the entire area from Pennsylvania to South Carolina had been transformed.

Part of the boom was in tobacco prices. They climbed back from the depressed levels that had prevailed for much of the seventeenth century, and despite a great increase in production, prices remained high enough to make tobacco planting profitable for most of the next three decades. The plantation system spread rapidly, and slavery spread with it. An enormous volume of importations as well as natural increase doubled the number of slaves in Virginia to 60,000 in 1740, pushed it past 100,000 in 1750, and took it to 140,000 in 1760.

Meanwhile, land sales surged in Virginia. When the Penn family in the 1730s raised the prices and rents on Pennsylvania lands, Scotch-Irish and German immigrants flooded to the west and south. As they poured southward down the great valley of Virginia, North Carolina and Virginia both promised freedom of worship for Presbyterians, and Virginia and Maryland liberalized their land policies. These measures stimulated a thriving sale of land, and Virginia in particular moved to capitalize on it. Planters and other influential inhabitants of the old tidewater settlements began to realize that there was as much money to be made from selling land as from selling tobacco, and perhaps a great deal more. The members of the House of Burgesses, in collaboration with the governor and his council, began to grant large blocks of interior lands to themselves: sometimes for nominal sums, sometimes for nothing, sometimes in exchange for their services in attracting new settlers to the colony.

In mid-century the southern colonies, like the Middle colonies, were thriving, and their growth and prosperity were largely a function of the arrival, on a grand scale, of newcomers of non-English stock. For a variety of reasons, however, the immigrants (or rather the white immigrants) did not much affect the social and political life of the South, except in the back country.

The system that evolved in Virginia was designed to insure the primacy of a class that can best be termed gentry. The gentry were not of the same class as the royal officials, and did not possess the wealth of the largest planters and land speculators. But by education and the size of their lands they stood apart from their neighbors and from the Scotch-Irish and Germans of the backwoods. Their position of leadership came in large part of the willingness of their humbler neighbors to grant it to them, a habit of deference on the part of the lowly toward people of education and political training. That deference was easily and happily given, for the gentry were generous to those below them. A Fairfax County candidate for the House of Burgesses named George Washington provided 160 gallons of liquor for the county's 400 voters and, after the election, invited his supporters to a victory ball and supper. "Treating" voters was accepted practice, both in England and the colonies. In Virginia they called it "swilling the planters with bumbo [a punch made with rum]." On one occasion in Hanover County, the sheriff closed the polls "because the candidates had distributed too much strong liquor among the people." No great social or economic gulf, in fact, separated the gentry from other white Virginians. In a generation or two, a family might acquire the land, the schooling, and the sense of social responsibility that would place it in the gentry class and elect some of its men to office.

The social preeminence of the Virginia gentry was reinforced by the rules governing politics. Institutional power was concentrated into three overlapping organizations: the vestrymen of the local parishes of the established Church of England, the justices of the peace who constituted the county courts, and the popular branch or lower house of the House of Burgesses. The electorate, those who chose the rulers on all levels, consisted of free white adult males, members of the Church of England, who owned at least twenty-five acres of improved land and a house or fifty acres of unimproved land, or a town lot in the county in which they voted or stood for office. Almost every white male who was not a tenant or a servant could vote, and for legislators the Virginia voters respectfully selected members of the gentry.

The Carolinas and Georgia The institution of slavery was rapidly spreading in another quarter, on the rice plantations of South Carolina (and, a little later, of Georgia). Slavery was a part of life in South Carolina almost as soon as the colony passed beyond its primitive frontier stage. Many of the early settlers were immigrants from Barbados, where slavery had long been firmly established, and they brought their slaves with them. Of the roughly 3,900 inhabitants of the colony in 1690, about 1,500 were slaves. Then, in the early decades of the eighteenth century the South Carolinians began large-scale rice cultivation in the coastal swamps, and with a phenomenal increase in rice production, slavery increased apace. South Carolina exported 394,000 pounds of rice in 1700, 1,600,000 pounds in 1710, 6,400,000 in 1720, 18,700,000 in 1730, and 43,000,000 in 1740; in the same years the number of slaves in the colony increased from 2,400 to 30,000. From 1720 until the Civil War, slaves outnumbered whites about two to one in South Carolina.

No gentle village-and-manor system developed in South Carolina. Rice was grown in the coastal swamps, where the climate was hot and humid and teemed with malaria and other disease. The work was possible only for strong young adult males, and even many of these died from overwork and disease within five to seven years. For the few slaves, most of them women and children, who lived in or near the master's house and worked as menial servants, life was tolerable and could even be pleasant, but for the field hands it was hell. Many a Carolina slave escaped from his master and found refuge among the Creek and Seminole Indians to the south, despite a law permitting any white to shoot on sight a slave who left his plantation without a written pass from his owner. There were isolated uprisings, and in 1739 slaves on several plantations rose in a rebellion that was not put down until twenty-one whites and forty-four blacks had been killed and scores more of both races had been wounded. Thirty more slaves were killed in the Stono Rebellion that same year.

In the early 1700s North Carolina rapidly became even more separate socially and economically from its sister colony. The Virginia planter William Byrd looked down upon the back-country denizens of North Carolina and Virginia, condemning them for their idleness:

Indian corn is of so great increase, that a little pains will subsist a very large family with bread, and then they may have meat without any pains at all, by the help of the low grounds and the great variety of mast that grows upon the high-land. The men for their parts, just like the Indians, impose all the work upon the poor women. They make their wives rise out of their beds early in the morning, at the same time that they lie and snore, till the sun has run one third of his course, and dispersed all the unwholesome damps. Then, after stretching and yawning for half an hour, they light their pipes, and, under the protection of a cloud of smoke, venture out into the open air; though if it happens to be ever so little cold, they quickly return shivering into the chimney corner. When the weather is mild, they stand leaning with both their arms upon the cornfield fence, and gravely consider whether they had best go and take a small heat at the hoe: but generally find reasons to put it off till another time.

John Brickell, another observer, had a more positive view of the North Carolina settlers:

They marry generally very young, some at thirteen or fourteen, and she that continues unmarried, until twenty, is reckoned a stale maid . . . Both sexes are very dexterous in paddling and managing their canoes, both men, women, boys, and girls, being bred to it from their infancy. The women are the most industrious in these parts, and many of them by their good housewifery make a great deal of cloth of their own cotton, wool, and flax, and some of them weave their own cloth which with which they decently apparel their whole family though large. . . . The men are very ingenious in several handy craft businesses, and in building their canoes and houses; though by the richness of the soil, they live for the most part after an indolent and luxurious manner; yet some are laborious, and equalize with the Negroes in hard labour. . . .

Plantation slavery was slow to take root, for the colony was covered with thick pine forests, was too dry to permit rice cultivation, and lacked the access to the sea that was then necessary to the growth of tobacco plant-ations. Until well into the eighteenth century North Carolina's principal products were the naval stores that could be extracted from the pines: tar, pitch, rosin, turpentine, and masts and spars. After 1705, the British government subsidized the production of all these commodities.

Georgia, founded in 1733, the last British colony to be established in America, developed slowly until the 1760s. In 1732 James Oglethorpe, a Tory member of Parliament, had received a charter to plant the colony. He conceived of it as a refuge for paupers and debtors, and as a laboratory for experiments in social and religious reform, but for the first twenty years of its existence the colony served mainly as a buffer between South Carolina and the hostile Indians to the immediate south along with the Spanish colony in Florida. Thereafter, Georgia began to develop on a more permanent basis, largely through the establishment of slavery and a rice plantation system much like that of South Carolina.

During the colonial period few whites protested the use of slaves. Quaker meetings in and around Philadelphia regularly denounced slavery, but many Quakers themselves acquired slaves. John Woolman, an itinerant Quaker preacher, said that "though we have made slaves of the negroes, and the Turks made slaves of the Christians, I believe that liberty was the natural right of all men equally." A pamphlet denouncing slavery, Samuel Sewall's The Selling of Joseph, was published in Boston in 1701, but Cotton Mather piously informed a group of blacks that slavery was "what God will have to be the thing appointed for you."

In the Northeast, where at about the middle of the eighteenth century a small but substantial portion of the populations of Boston, Philadelphia, New York City, and Newport, Rhode Island were slaves, most worked as craftsmen, laborers, or personal servants rather than as field workers. In New York City in 1712 a slave uprising involving two dozen blacks resulted in the deaths of nine whites. Punishment was swift and cruel: thirteen slaves were hanged, one left to die in chains, three burned at the stake, one burned over a slow fire for ten hours, and one broken on the wheel. In 1741 two New York blacks who burned several barns were executed at once, as fearful whites thought that "had not the merciful hand of providence interposed

. . . in one and the same night the inhabitants would have been butchered in their houses by their own slaves and the city laid in ashes." In Philadelphia, Benjamin Franklin owned slaves as house servants for thirty years, although he favored the abolition of slavery. In 1757 he made provision in his will for the freeing of "my Negro man Peter and his wife Jemima." In Rhode Island, New Jersey, New York, Pennsylvania, and Delaware, however, slaves worked for commercial farmers or in some places for small manufacturers.

In the colonies as a whole, the institutions of the Old World were neither disappearing nor remaining intact, but instead were accommodating themselves to the opportunities the American continent offered. Customs and institutions became more open. Indentured servants could look forward to freedom and perhaps to entry into the propertied classes. A large part of the population could vote or otherwise engage in local government. And yet, while so much of British civilization was becoming freer in North America, the new land had begun to cultivate the institution of slavery, unknown in Britain for centuries. Freedom and slavery were growing up together.

The Great Awakening and the Enlightenment

In the 1730s, a fervent new religious movement—Pietism on the Continent, Wesleyanism in Britain, and the Great Awakening in America—began to infect the ministry and to spread rapidly everywhere. A new enthusiasm for religion and moral reform appeared almost simultaneously in continental Europe, Great Britain, and the colonies. The message of the new religion was essentially the same, whatever its form: that the way to salvation lay not in faithful performance of sacraments and rituals as the Catholics and Anglicans had always maintained, or a life of good works, but simply in opening the heart to God through prayer. A simple and total act of faith in God's goodness and mercy would bring to the faithful an unspeakably profound experience of personal conversion and salvation.

As John Winthrop and those who banished Anne Hutchinson had argued in the 1630s, any such doctrine is potentially dangerous to an established social order, for it implicitly vests in the individual alone the capacity to judge the moral rectitude of his own behavior. The new pietist faith of Anglo-America was disruptive. It advocated the separation of converts from others and their formation into small groups, and aimed at the immediate reform and the final transformation of all of man's ways—to serve the coming of the Kingdom of Heaven on earth.

In the colonies the Great Awakening had its beginnings in 1734, when the Reverend Jonathan Edwards, pastor of the church in the small frontier town of Northampton, Massachusetts, a community of about 200 families, noticed a "religious concern on people's minds." As the winter of 1734 progressed, Edwards noticed that "There was scarcely a single person in the town, either old or young, that was left unconcerned about the great things of the eternal world. Those that were wont to be the vainest, and loosest, and those that had been most disposed to think and speak slightly of vital and experimental religion, were now generally subject to great awakenings." Edward's account of the Northampton revival, *A Faithful Narrative of the Surprising Work of God*, published in 1737, may have prepared the way for the preaching of George Whitefield, the eloquent young English clergyman who arrived in America in 1739.

George Whitefield

Various French, German, and Dutch ministers were associated with revivalism, and John and Charles Wesley were the most important figures involved in England. The most influential of all in British America was George Whitefield. After receiving some training at Oxford, Whitefield had persuaded the bishop to ordain him before he was of canonical age. In his maiden sermon, this restless, charismatic preacher raved and exhorted, sang and shouted, wept and thundered and, it is said, drove fifteen people mad.

Whitefield made his first evangelical tour to America in 1739 at age twenty-five, preaching under the open air and converting hundreds in Georgia, and returned two years later to conduct a great revival in New Eng-

The eloquent British revivalist preacher George Whitefield fueled the Great Awakening on several evangelical tours. *(Courtesy, National Portrait Gallery)*

land. The New England and mid-Atlantic tour was the greatest triumph of Whitefield's career, though he made several successful trips to America during the next thirty years. In 1740 the populace was ready for him, if only out of restlessness, boredom, or economic troubles. The brief revival that Jonathan Edwards had conducted five years earlier in Northampton, Massachusetts, had already primed New England. Edwards had carried the right message, and with Whitefield's personal magnetism and style might have set the region aflame himself. The clergy of New England was at first also energetic in support of the crusade by Whitefield and his followers and imitators, in the understandable if mistaken belief that a new outburst of religious zeal would reinvigorate and thereby preserve a church that had lately lost much of its following. So Whitefield infused New England, along with most of the other British colonies, with enthusiastic piety that matched any that Americans had ever experienced.

In Philadelphia Whitefield managed to affect even that lover of reason, Benjamin Franklin, as the latter recorded in his *Autobiography:*

> I happened . . . to attend one of his sermons, in the course of which I perceived he intended to finish with a collection, and I silently resolved he should get nothing from me. I had in my pocket a handful of copper money, three or four silver dollars, and five pistoles in gold. As he proceeded I began to soften, and concluded to give the coppers. Another stroke of his oratory made me ashamed of that, and determined me to give the silver; and he finished so admirably, that I empty'd my pocket wholly into the collector's dish, gold and all.

"Enthusiastic" Religion The impact of the Great Awakening was not quite what the ministry that welcomed Whitefield had expected. The number of active participants in church affairs doubled, trebled, and quadrupled, and for the first time in years religion attracted the enthusiasm of the young; but the effect was to divide the church everywhere. Much of New England, for example, became divided into fiercely hostile camps of "Old Lights," or defenders of the existing order, and "New Lights," who embraced the new piety.

The Great Awakening had its philosophical connections with more sober forms of Protestantism that had preceded it. Puritans, like other Protestants, had taken the conversion experience very seriously, and even after the Half-Way Covenant of 1662 a conversion experience was a requirement for admission to full church membership among New England Puritans. But the Puritan congregations had not demanded the violent outpourings of emotion that revivalism sometimes identifies with religious experience. The Great Awakening was the earliest large instance of a revivalism that has become a recurrent phenomenon in American Protestantism. Like the Great Awakening, moreover, American religion since has emphasized the experiential component of religion. In breaking open churches that had been stable and undivided, the Awakening is suggestive of the tendency within Protestantism to multiply churches and sects. And the Awakening introduced America to a movement that John and Charles Wesley were spreading within the Church of England: Methodism, a faith

SINNERS IN THE HANDS OF AN ANGRY GOD *by Jonathan Edwards.*
Among the preachers associated with the Great Awakening, Edwards is the most famous.
His sermons embodied the tremendous emotionalism of a powerful religious revival.

The God that holds you over the pit of hell, much as one holds a spider, or some loathsome insect, over the fire, abhors you, and you, and is dreadfully provoked; his wrath towards you burns like fire; he looks upon you as worthy of nothing else, but to be cast into the fire; he is of purer eyes than to bear to have you in his sight; you are ten thousand times so abominable in his eyes, as the most hateful and venomous serpent is in ours. You have offended him infinitely more than ever a stubborn rebel did his prince: and yet it is nothing but his hand that holds you from falling into the fire every moment: it is ascribed to nothing else, that you did not go to hell the last night; that you was suffered to awake again in this world, after you closed your eyes to sleep; and there is no other reason to be given, why you have not dropped into hell since you arose in the morning, but that God's hand has held you up: there is no other reason to be given why you have not gone to hell, since you have sat here in the house of God, provoking his pure eyes by your sinful wicked manner of attending his solemn worship: yea, there is nothing else that is to be given as a reason why you do not this very moment drop down into hell. . . .

How dreadful is the state of those that are daily and hourly in danger of this great wrath and infinite misery! But this is the dismal case of every soul in this congregation that has not been born again, however moral and strict, sober and religious, they may otherwise be. . . . There is reason to think, that there are many in this congregation now hearing this discourse, that will actually be the subjects of this very misery to all eternity. We know not who they are, or in what seats they sit, or what thoughts they now have. . . . It would be no wonder if some persons, that now sit here in some seats of this meeting-house in health, and quiet and secure, should be there in hell before tomorrow morning.

that stressed both religious feeling and a morality of self-discipline and hard work. In the nineteenth century the Methodist and Baptist churches, well adapted in structure, practice, and belief to spread to the frontier and the back country, would become one of the largest denominations both in cities and in the countryside and a notable influence on American ideas of morality.

| **The Enlightenment** The energies of revivalism were directed against reason, or at least the cool, detached reason that opposed bursts of emotion. But there began in Europe around the middle of the eighteenth century a movement called the Enlightenment. Some Europeans thought themselves to be living in the Age of Reason; and the Enlightenment, with its confidence in reason, soon reached American shores.

It began to glimmer in the glass jars of Benjamin Franklin's electrical experiments in Philadelphia. In 1749 Franklin was "chagrined a little that we have hitherto been able to discover nothing in the way of use to mankind," but by 1752, with his now-famous kite experiment, he had proved that lightning and electricity were one and the same. His practical invention of the lightning rod soon followed. On one occasion he nearly electrocuted himself attempting to roast a turkey, but by the late 1750s Franklin had acquired an international reputation for his contributions to science.

In its European form, the Enlightenment practiced an abstract kind of thinking known as deductive logic, a reasoning that begins with general principles and then applies these to particular cases or details. Philosophers of the Enlightenment, for example, abstractly defined large, general "laws of nature," which could be laws governing the material world or natural laws fixed in human beings; and having determined the laws of nature that applied to human beings, Enlightenment thinkers considered what particular kind of government would best serve or express these laws. The European Enlightenment would make for great advances in science; and its political thought, much of which presumed that the laws of nature make

NATHAN CALE, *a farmer and carpenter of Connecticut, breathlessly anticipated George Whitefield's great sermon.*

There came a messenger and said Mr. Whitfield preached at Hartford and Weathersfield yesterday and is to preach at Middeltown this morning at 10 o clock. I was in my field at work [and] I dropt my tool that I had in my hand and run home and run thru my house and bade my wife get ready quick to goo and hear Mr. Whitfield preach at Middeltown. And [I] run to my pasture for my hors with all my might, fearing I should be too late to hear him. I brought my hors home and soon mounted and took my wife up and went forward as fast as I thought my hors could bear, and when my hors began to be out of breath I would get down and put my wife on the Saddel, and bid her ride as fast as she could, and not Stop or Slak for except I bade her. And so I would run until I was almost out of breth, and then mount my hors again, and so I did severel times to favour my hors. . . .

When we came within about half a mile of the road that comes down from Hartford, Weathersfield and Stepney to Middeltown, on high land, I saw before me a Cloud or fog, rising—I first thought—off from the great river. But as I came nearer the road I heard a noise, something like a low rumbling thunder, and I presently found it was the rumbling of horses feet coming down the road and this Cloud was a Cloud of dust made by the running of horses feet. It arose some rods into the air over the tops of the hills and trees. And when I came within about twenty rods of the road, I could see men and horses Slipping along in the Cloud like shadows. And when I came nearer it was like a stedy streem of horses and their riders, scarcely a horse more than his length behind another, all of a lather and fome with swet, ther breth rooling out of their noistrels. . . . Every hors semed to go with all his might to carry his rider to hear the news from heaven for the saving of their Souls. It made me trembel to see the Sight.

We went down in the Streeme. I herd no man speak a word all the way, three mile, but evry one presing forward in great haste. And when we gat down to the old meating house, thare was a great multitude. It was said to be 3 or 4000 of people assembled together.

We gat of from our horses and shook off the dust, and the ministers was then coming to the meating house. I turned and looked toward the great river and saw the fery boats running swift forward and backward, bringing over loads of people. The ores rowed nimble and quick. Everything—men, horses and boats—all seamed to be struglin for life. The land and the banks over the river looked black with people and horses all along the 12 miles. I see no man at work in his field, but all seamed to be gone.

When I see Mr. Whitfield come upon the Scaffold, he looked almost angellical—a young, slim, slender youth before some thousands of people, and with a bold, undaunted countenance. And my hearing how God was with him everywhere as he came along, it solomnized my mind, and put me in a trembling fear before he began to preach, for he looked as if he was Cloathed with authority from the great God.

---

all human beings equal in rights, contributed to the modern political revolutions seeking freedom and legal equality.

Numbers of American writers later in the century were much under the influence of the political as well as the scientific Enlightenment in Europe, talked of the "laws of nature," and argued in the language of the Enlightenment for liberty and equality. But some historians have identified a difference in emphasis between the European Enlightenment and its American counterpart. Americans tended more than European philosophers of the time to follow not deductive reasoning but a kind of thought that is now called empiricism, a reasoning that begins with the observation of particular details rather than with speculation about general principles. American thinkers confined much of their work to looking at plants and animals, to experimenting with practical gadgets, or to solving concrete practical problems of government.

Empiricism produced early and important scientific studies in America. In 1715 eleven-year-old Jonathan Edwards studied a spider's habits and recorded his observations in an essay, "Of Insects." But he forsook science for

George Whitefield and John Wesley promised salvation to those who opened their hearts to God through prayer. To them was offered eternal life in the New Jerusalem depicted in this drawing; to others the door to Hell stood open. (*Courtesy, Scribner's Archives*)

theology. Late in the seventeenth and early in the eighteenth century the New Englanders Thomas Brattle and Thomas Robie made a number of astronomical observations that proved useful to Newton and other Europeans, and the Royal Society in London published papers by John Banister, Cotton Mather, and Paul Dudley on American flora and fauna. Eliza Lucas Pinkney's observations pioneered the cultivation of indigo, which became widespread as a cash crop. Mathematical observations of note came from John Winthrop IV, Ezra Stiles, and David Rittenhouse. Perhaps the crowning American scientific achievements were Benjamin Franklin's experiments in electricity, particularly his demonstration that lightning is elec-

trical. Possibly as important as these scientific discoveries were the mediums through which scientific knowledge was introduced and spread.

The most advanced were the colleges, along with philosophical and scientific societies, the most important being the American Philosophical Society, established in Philadelphia in 1743. Most colleges started during the colonial period were founded by religious groups. Harvard (1636) and Yale (1701) were Congregationalist, the term that came to be used for New England Puritanism, with its placement of church government in the hands of the congregation. William and Mary (1691) and King's College (1754, later renamed Columbia) were founded by Anglicans. Rhode Island College (1764, later Brown) was Baptist, Queen's College (1766, later Rutgers) was Dutch Reformed, and the College of New Jersey (1746, later Princeton) was Presbyterian. The only nonsectarian college founded in the colonial period was Franklin's Academy, established in 1751, which became the University of Pennsylvania in 1791. Dartmouth became a college in 1769 after having been established much earlier as an Indian missionary school. King's College and Franklin's Academy introduced practical courses in agriculture, navigation, and astronomy.

Higher education was available to a much wider spectrum of classes in the colonies than in England. The prestigious institutions of higher learning were reserved for males. During the eighteenth century, a few private academies for women were founded, but systematic attempts to provide even for the education of upper-class girls would not emerge until after the Revolution. The colonies did produce some well-educated and even learned women, but these women had invariably benefited from private instruction from tutors who had been hired for their brothers or cousins. In general, female literacy continued to lag behind male literacy.

| The Press   On the popular level, scientific and other information was spread mainly through newspapers. Laws in Massachusetts and Connecticut required every town to provide a school at which children could learn reading and writing. Elementary schools, established most zealously by Congregationalists and Presbyterians, gave America a much higher literacy rate than Europe possessed: ninety percent

AN EARLY HARVARD RIOT (1639)

College students have long complained about the quality of food in university dining rooms. If this very first American instance of an incipient food riot is typical, they have good reason for their complaint. Mistress Eaton, the cook and author of this letter, was wife of Harvard's first headmaster, Nathaniel Eaton. Both lost their jobs when students protested the severe discipline that Mr. Eaton dispensed and the atrocious food that his wife served.

For their breakfast, that it was not so well ordered, the flour not so fine as it might, nor so well boiled or stirred, at all times that it was so, it was my sin of neglect, and want of that care that ought to have been in one that the Lord had intrusted with such a work. Concerning their beef, that was allowed them, as they affirm, which, I confess, had been my duty to have seen they had it, and continued to have had it, because it was my husband's command; but truly I must confess, to my shame. I cannot remember that ever they had it, nor that ever it was taken from them. And that they had not so good or so much provision in my husband's absence as presence, I conceive it was because he would call sometimes for butter or cheese, when I conceived there was no need of it; yet, forasmuch as the scholars did otherways apprehend, I desire to see the evil that was in the carriage of that as well as in the other, and to take shame to myself for it. And that they sent down for more, when they had not enough, and the maid should answer, if they had not, they should not, I must confess, that I have denied them cheese, when they sent for it, and it have been in the house; for which I shall humbly beg pardon of them, and own the shame, and confess my sin. And for such provoking words, which my servants have given, I cannot own them, but am sorry any such should be given in my house. And for bad fish, that they had it brought to table, I am sorry there was that cause of offence given them. I acknowledge my sin in it. And for their mackerel, brought to them with their guts in them, and goat's dung in their hasty pudding, it's utterly unknown to me; but I am much ashamed it should be in the family, and not prevented by myself or servants, and I humbly acknowledge my negligence in it. And that they made their beds at any time, were my straits never so great, I am sorry they were ever put to it. For the Moor his lying in Sam. Hough's sheet and pillowbier, it hath a truth in it: he did so one time, and it gave Sam. Hough just cause of offence; and that it was not prevented by my care and watchfulness, I desire [to] take the shame and sorrow for it. And that they eat the Moor's crusts, and the swine and they had share and share alike, and the Moor to have beer, and they denied it, and if they had not enough, for my maid to answer, they should not, I am an utter stranger to these things, and know not the least footsteps for them so to charge me; and if my servants were guilty of such miscarriages, had the boarders complained of it unto myself, I should have thought it my sin, if I had not sharply reproved my servants, and endeavored reform. And for bread made of heated, sour meal, although I know of but once that if was so, since I kept house, yet John Wilson affirms it was twice: and I am truly sorry, that any of it was spent amongst them. For beer and bread, that it was denied them by me betwixt meals, truly I do not remember, that ever I did deny it unto them; John Wilson will affirm, that, generally, the bread and beer was free for the boarders to go unto. And that money was demanded of them for washing the linen, it's true it was propounded to them, but never imposed upon them. And for their pudding being given the last day of the week without butter or suet, and that I said, it was miln of Manchester in Old England, it's true that I did say so, and am sorry, they had any cause of offence given them by having it so. And for their wanting beer, betwixt brewings, a week or half a week together, I am sorry that it was so at any time, and should tremble to have it so, were it in my hands to do again.

or more could sign their names in New England, fifty to sixty percent in Virginia, and somewhere between these figures among the Scotch-Irish.

In 1725 the British mainland colonies still had only five newspapers. Then along with the rapid expansion of commerce and land settlement came a proliferation of newspapers: by 1765 there were twenty-five. In 1766 the *Massachusetts Gazette* boasted that it "circulates mostly in the Country, especially on the Great Western Road to Worcester, Springfield, Northampton, Hartford, New Haven, etc." Four-page weeklies were filled with advertisements, notices of arrivals and departures of ships, and reprints of news that had appeared months earlier in European journals. But as time went by the colonial newspapers printed more and more articles, written by their readers, in which the nature of man, society, and government was endlessly explored, and so it was largely through the newspapers that Americans formed their opinions of themselves and their world. The *Virginia Gazette* pointed out in 1766

> the advantages of a well conducted newspaper ... especially at a crisis, which makes a quick circulation of intelligence peculiarly interesting to all the American colonies. ... The interests of religion and liberty we ever think it our duty to support.

Following the English lead, the colonies also began to produce a few journals such as the *Lady's Magazine* and the *Gentleman's and Lady's Town and Country Magazine* that catered to the female members of polite society.

Colonial America provided an important incident in the development of freedom of the press. In 1735 Peter Zenger faced a charge of libel for publishing in his newspaper an attack by the former chief justice of New York on actions of the governor of the colony. The counsel for Zenger argued that since the statements printed in the paper were true they were not libelous. The jury agreed, and returned a verdict of not guilty. The effect of the verdict was to establish the principle that only false statements are libelous, and thereby to free newspapers to widen the range of their commentary and criticism.

The American Character

British Americans were energetic or at least busy; or rather, enough of them were that way to give the impression that busyness was a central attribute of American life. Having vast quantities of good unoccupied land at their disposal and having accepted population explosion as a social norm, they had become eager and avaricious speculators in land: the fever for land, for seizing the main chance and growing wealthy through big land deals, reached epidemic proportions. Americans seemed ambitious, optimistic, presumptuous, and—compared to

Europeans and despite having developed their own forms of social deference—egalitarian. An English visitor in Connecticut in 1750 remarked that "their government, religion, and manners all tend to support an equality. Whoever brings in your victuals sits down and chats with you." Europeans were inclined to view Americans as bumpkins for those reasons and because all but a few lacked the finer social graces. They were in fact quite cosmopolitan, for their daily existence and their very survival depended upon keeping abreast of events all over the Atlantic world. So, at least, they believed. And having a higher literacy rate than perhaps any nation of Europe, they read newspapers and exchanged letters avidly.

But there was also some social timidity, which Americans have never completely lost. Their fear of being isolated from Europe led them to slavish imitation of the London fads and styles in clothing, architecture, and entertainment. Americans drank coffee and tea incessantly, but the most common form of release among men was alcohol; they consumed prodigious quantities of wine and rum, and many of them drank whiskey, gin, and beer as well. Women of Nantucket Island in Massachusetts were addicted to opium, and it is not unlikely that opium and other drugs were in use among women elsewhere to ease the pain of childbearing and "female complaints." It is also possible that the black slaves knew (as their masters apparently did not) the anesthetizing joy of smoking hemp, for Africans had cultivated and used marijuana and hashish for ten centuries and more, and hemp was fairly widely grown in the South for use in rope making.

But the most important generalization applicable to these early Americans is that they defied generalization, for heterogeneity was their very essence. Americans were pluralistic in other than their ethnic and religious backgrounds. Colonial America at mid-century was a kaleidoscope of regions and societies changing over time. From the 150-year-old tidewater Virginia plantations, to the newly-plowed red fields of Georgia, from the urban bustle of Boston and Philadelphia to the remote villages and farms on the frontier, generalizations are difficult. And with each locality, multiple forms of social stratification existed. Each community— the town in New England, the manor in New York, the county or parish elsewhere—

had its own hierarchy, which sometimes did and sometimes did not correspond to the gradations of power and status in the colony as a whole. The most common determinants of social rank were wealth, occupation, and ethnic stock, but the most important determinant involved connections and sponsors, especially with officials or families of high station in England.

The distinction between male and female remained a fundamental determinant of an individual's social opportunities, but in any given instance wealth, inherited social status, and family membership could outweigh gender. The familial, or dynastic, character of colonial politics cast women as pawns in the use of successful marriages as a base for alliances, but family connections could also permit women, either married or single, to play significant political roles in exceptional circumstances. In 1647 Margaret Brent administered Maryland as the executrix of Governor Leonard Calvert's estate, although her subsequent request for two seats in the Maryland legislature—one as executor, the other on the basis of her own holdings—was denied. Most women, however, spent their lives firmly under the governance of their fathers, husbands, and male kin to whom they were considered constitution-ally, intellectually, and often morally inferior.

According to the Puritan leader John Winthrop, a woman's husband "is her lord, and she is subjected to him, yet in a way of liberty, not of bondage: and a true wife accounts her subjection her honor and freedom." A Puritan clergyman likened the family to "a little commonwealth" with the father as its undisputed head. Women were supposed to be subject to their husbands in all matters. Women when they married normally lost whatever property rights they might have had. As the eighteenth-century jurist William Blackstone put it: "Husband and wife are one and that one is the husband." Husbands were expected to govern their wives with gentleness and love whenever possible, but an unruly wife required stronger measures.

The laws of Massachusetts differed from those of England in restricting the husband's right to correction. Wife-beating with a stick that was larger than one inch in diameter was prohibited. But even the gentler laws of the new world did not interfere with "corrections" or "chastisements" administered with switches of the proper size. And the Puritan emphasis on the responsibility of the individual to God did not encourage women's equality in religious institutions; Puritan fathers

Captains from Surinam, by John Greenwood. *(Courtesy, Art Museum of St. Louis)*

were especially fond of St. Paul's dictum: "Women, keep silent in the churches." By the end of the seventeenth century, women usually outnumbered men in church congregations. By the nineteenth century the predominance of women in church attendance would be noticeable in many congregations, but it did not open to women the role of minister or church leader. And women were almost entirely excluded from all forms of politics.

The inferiority of women to men, like women's necessary subordination to men, was the dominant view of gender relations and one of the most widely shared assumptions throughout the colonies. It has nonetheless been argued that women enjoyed a better position in the New World than women in the old, then or earlier. This view rests in part on the assumption that since women remained in short supply throughout the seventeenth century they were especially valued. But there is little evidence to suggest that simply because the authorities tried very hard to encourage women to emigrate to the colonies the reigning idea of women's nature and worth actually changed very much. The incentives offered to women had to do more with improving their social and economic position among other women than with improving the status of women relative to men.

As one Maryland man observed, "The women that go over into this province as servants, have the best luck here as in any place in the world besides; for they are no sooner on shoar, but they are courted into a Copulative Matrimony. . . ." A Virginia colonist advised single women to

> sojourn in a house of good honest repute, for by their good carriage, they may advance themselves in marriage . . . loose persons seldome live long unmarried, if free, yet they match with as desolute as themselves, and never live handsomly or are ever respected.

It is possible that New World conditions did, at least initially, bring women somewhat greater freedom in their daily lives—and perhaps even somewhat greater respect as individuals. But when women strayed out of their assigned roles they were rapidly accused of insubordination, of defying the order of God and man, and even of familiarity with the Devil. Sometimes the courts stepped in, as in Salem in 1678 when Bridget Oliver, accused of calling her husband "old rogue" and "old devil" was "ordered to stand with her husband, back to back, on a lecture day in the public market place, both gagged for about an hour with a paper fastened to each of their foreheads, upon which their offence should be fairly written." In 1715 when Cotton Mather's third wife criticized him he accused her of "Madness" and demoniacal "Possession."

If free white women in colonial America were assigned a subordinate status, female indentured servants were doubly subordinate. In 1756 a young serving-girl in Maryland wrote to her father that she was "toiling almost day and night," had "scarce any thing but Indian corn and salt to eat," and had "no

Puritan women in their Sunday best. Some wore masks to protect themselves from wind and sun.

shoes nor stockings to wear . . . what rest we can get is to rap ourselves up in a blanket and ly upon the ground." Indentured women were seldom allowed to marry, and the "secret marriage of servants" was forbidden by law in some places. Most masters reserved the right to lengthen the period of service if the woman became pregnant. The possibility of marrying better than they might have married in England offered the main incentive to single female immigrants, and delaying marriage for the normal minimum of the seven years of indenture often meant that the female servant might marry only after several of her child-bearing years had passed and after brutal work in a harsh climate had perhaps undermined her health. Those who did get pregnant during their term of indenture were sometimes the victims of the sexual exploitation of the same masters who then punished them for their pregnancy. A Virginia law of 1662 addressed this problem: "Whereas by act of assembly each woman servant got with child by her master shall after her time by indenture or custom is expired . . . be sold for two years . . ." Masters justified extension of service on the grounds that pregnancy reduced the woman's capacity to work, and in most cases extension far exceeded the time missed. A poem speaks in the voice of an indentured servant who, after recalling her happier days and more attractive appearance in England, laments her condition in the New World:

> In weeding Corn or feeding Swine,
> I spend my melancholy Time,
> Kidnap'd and Fool'd, I thither fled,
> And to my cost already find,
> Worse Plagues than those I left behind.

The hardships that weighed on female indentured servants weighed even more heavily on slave women who lacked the minimal rights and promise of eventual freedom that masters accorded to indentured servants. Initially, slave women were as scarce relative to slave men as indentured females were to indentured men. African societies placed a high value on women, or at least on their productive and reproductive abilities, and so African slave-traders often withheld women from the slave trade. Many women who were transported to the New World had been separated from their families. Children taken with their mothers might not survive the Atlantic crossing or might be separated from their mothers after their arrival in America. Black women, like black men, participated in revolts aboard slave ships. In the early years of slavery in the colonies, the ratio of men to women was too high for the newly enslaved population to reproduce itself. Only in the eighteenth century did a community of slaves begin to take shape in the Chesapeake colonies and South Carolina. By then, some slave women were forming stable unions with slave men and bearing their children. But the legality of slave marriages was never recognized in law. And slave women, even more than indentured women, lacked any resources to oppose the sexual exploitation of the master or other white males. Most slave colonies forbade interracial fornication, but enough black women bore mulatto children—either because they had been raped, or because they had established a relationship with a man who was not black—to make the status of mulatto children a pressing legal question. In most Latin American slaveholding countries many masters acknowledged their mulatto offspring and freed them, so a distinct class of free mulattoes emerged. In

Jersey Nanny, by John Greenwood. The opportunities open to women in the colonies were limited. *(Courtesy, Museum of Fine Arts, Boston)*

English America, such acknowledgments and manumissions were less common: there were many mulatto slaves, and free mulattoes simply joined the class of free blacks. No child born of a slave mother, whoever its father, could escape slavery without formal manumission.

| **Women's Legal Rights** | The law severely circumscribed the status of most women. The general presumption that all women should come under the authority of some man governed their lives whether their status be slave, indentured, or free. Only adult single or widowed free women could act in their own name or hold or dispose of property for themselves. These legal barriers to all forms of female independence derived primarily from the English common law, which assigned all minor children to the authority of their fathers and viewed all married women as "femmes coverts"—or, literally, covered women. New World practice apparently modified the severity of this legal doctrine; some widows who remarried signed contracts with their husbands-to-be prior to marriage and thus preserved control of their own property. In Braintree, Massachusetts, John French, upon his marriage to Eleanor Veazie in 1683 had to agree "not to meddle with or take into his hand any part of her estate wherein she is invested by her former husband. . . ." Women were also known to act in a legal capacity on their own or their family's behalf. Wills reveal that at least some women did bequeath property to heirs of their own choosing. In 1667 Martha Emons, a Boston widow, left to her son Benjamin

> that feather bed which be best liketh, with the bolster & pillow, the new coverlet, a pair of blankets, curtains, hangings, the bedstead I now lie on, two pair of my best sheets, a pair of pillow biers, my silver beaker & silver spoon, & of my other goods, as pewter, brasse & old bedding. . . .

Law in some colonies such as Massachusetts and Connecticut also permitted women somewhat easier access to divorce than they had in England, and the records reveal that at least some women took advantage of the opportunity. But formal divorce was never common and some states, notably South Carolina, prohibited it absolutely except by act of the legislature. And, in a predominantly rural society, most women had few opportunities to live comfortably on their own. Men had difficulty managing an agricultural household without a woman; women alone faced even greater obstacles. By the eighteenth century, single and widowed women were occasionally running small businesses, managing shops, or otherwise supporting themselves and perhaps their children.

Whatever the limitations imposed by the law, in practice married free women probably enjoyed considerable feelings of importance to the survival of their households. Their work was as important to the survival and solvency of those households as was that of their men. Most white women who survived their child-bearing years—normally from marriage in their early twenties until their early forties—bore about eight children. Some bore more, and many lost one or more in childbirth or infancy. In addition to this vital contribution, most women shouldered a significant portion of the labor necessary to the household. They were responsible for cooking, for the making of many household necessities such as candles and soap, for washing, for sewing, and frequently for making clothes. This labor could include heavy tasks such as carrying the water for cooking and washing from stream or well to the house. Women also usually assumed responsibility for certain kinds of agricultural labor, such as milking cows, tending gardens and keeping chickens. When circumstances required, especially at harvest time, they worked in the fields beside men. But the indispensability of women's labor to colonial society did not necessarily result in any permanent improvement either in women's status, or in the general view of women's position in society. The women themselves recognized the importance of their contributions. But it is doubtful that many colonial women gave any thought to equality with men, or if many colonial women aspired to male status. Many, however, doubtless aspired to lives of greater ease.

The woman of the day who enjoyed the greatest freedom did not work alongside her husband, but could enjoy the more leisured life of the colonial aristocracy. She might acquire something of the more serious education provided for her brothers. By the eighteenth century, she was likely to have silver instead of pewter, an ample supply of linen for beds and tables, silks and laces to wear, looking glasses, cupboards and chests from Europe, books, periodicals, and more. But the comfort of her life depended upon the labor of other women—slaves or servants—who performed the tasks from which wealth had liberated her.

| Children   In a land where labor was scarce, children also contributed to the livelihood of the family. Colonial Americans had no concept of adolescence. But if familial responsibilities came early, the opportunities of a new land also provoked tensions within the family, frequently pulling children away from home. The apparent disruption of family life in the New World was a frequent source of complaint and worry. The president of King's College, Samuel Johnson, bemoaned that "it is obvious that our youth are apace running headlong into all sorts of debauchery and uncontrolled indulgences, which I doubt not is . . . chiefly owing to the fond indulgence of their parents."

Every colony had laws demanding obedience from children; the potential punishment for disobedience in Massachusetts and Connecticut was nothing less than death. In New Haven in 1656, for example, the law stated that "If any child or children above sixteen year[s] old, and of competent understanding, shall curse, or smite, his, her, or their natural father or mother, each such child shall be put to death. . . ." Furthermore, "stubborn rebellious" sons sixteen or older who refused to obey the "voice and chastisement" of their parents were also subject to the death penalty. Such laws, however, were rarely, if ever, enforced. Existing records do not reveal that any court ever resorted to such extreme punishment. In fact, by allowing such cases to be tried, these laws guarded against parental abuse at the same time that they sought to curb recalcitrant children. Colonial law reflected the belief that the community, acting through the courts, had an interest in maintaining order within individual families.

New England also assumed the burden of providing formal education. A Massachusetts statute of 1641 anticipated the nineteenth-century community provision of schooling for all members of society. And as society became more secular, so did education; the inculcation of civic virtue and good citizenship took priority over religious instruction.

Yet most young people learned pedagogical and vocational skills within their families.

Alice Mason, 1670. Artist unknown. Puritans thought of their children as miniature adults fully responsible for their moral behavior. *(National Park Service, Adams National Historic Site, Quincy, Massachusetts)*

If a son did not want to learn his father's trade, then he might be apprenticed into another family for study under the direction of the master. Whatever young colonials failed to absorb from elders they had to learn on their own. Colonial newspapers and almanacs, such as Ben Franklin's *Poor Richard's Almanac*, served as early home study guides.

| Courtship   Though marriages were often arranged by parents or at least had to have parental approval, courtship had its prescribed rituals. The custom of "bundling," a betrothed couple's spending the night in bed together—but fully clothed—was much practiced, especially during the cold New England winters. An English visitor to the Carolinas in the early 1700s described a similar practice among the Indians there:

> When any young Indian has a mind for such a girl to his wife, he, or someone for him, goes to the young woman's parents, if living; if not, to her nearest relations, where they make offers of the match

BUNDLING

Courting couples had little privacy to hug and kiss. A sensible solution, to these sensible people, was to take the beloved under the covers. The results were unpredictable, as this nineteenth-century poem suggests.

Whether they must be hugg'd or Kiss'd when sitting by the fire
Or whether they in bed may lay, which doth the Lord require?
In Genesis no knowledge is of this thing to be got,
Whether young men did bundle then, or whether they did not.
The sacred book says wives they took, it don't say how they courted.
Whether that they in bed did lay, or by the fire sported.

Young miss, if this your habit be, I'll teach you now yourself to see:
You plead you're honest, modest too, but such a plea will never do;
For how can modesty consist, with shameful practice such as this?
I'll give your answer to the life: You don't undress, like man and wife.
That is your plea, I'll freely own, but who's your bondsman when alone,
That further rules you will not break, and marriage liberties partake?
But you will say that I'm unfair, that some who bundle take more care,
For some we may in truth suppose, bundle in bed with all their clothes.
But bundler's clothes are no defense, unruly horses push the fence.

---

betwixt the couple. . . . The man pays so much for his wife, and the handsomer she is the greater price she bears. Now it often happens that the man has not so much of their money ready as he is to pay for his wife, but if they know him to be a good hunter, and that he can raise the sum agreed for, in some few moons, or any little time they agree, she shall go along with him as betrothed, but he is not to have any knowledge of her till the utmost payment is discharged; all [of] which is punctually observed. Thus they lie together under one covering for several months, and the woman remains the same as she was when she first came to him.

Courtship and marriage across racial boundaries were discouraged, and in some colonies, illegal. A 1691 Virginia law aimed to prevent

that abominable mixture and spurious issue which hereafter may increase in this dominion, as well by negroes, mulattoes, and Indians intermarrying with English, or other white women, as by their unlawful accompanying with one another. . . .

Such couples were to be "banished and removed from this dominion forever." Particularly in the cities, courting customs changed rapidly, disturbing the older generation, shocking rural visitors, and even surprising foreign observers. A young man described a party he went to in Quaker Philadelphia:

"Seven sleighs with two ladies and two men in each, preceded by fiddlers on horseback" rode to a public house where "we danced, sung, and romped and ate and drank, and kicked away care from morning till night, and finished our frolic in two or three sideboxes at the play." A British traveler in Virginia in 1755 reported that "dancing is the chief diversion here," and another was shocked at the widespread dancing of "jigs." Claiming that the dance was borrowed from the slaves, the proper Englishman found it "without method or regularity: a gentleman and lady stand up, and dance about the room, one of them retiring, the other pursuing, then perhaps meeting, in an irregular fantastical manner." Serenading under the window of a favored lady also came into vogue during the late colonial period. Sometimes the gentlemen first lubricated their throats at a local tavern, yet women reportedly considered the midnight visitation and inevitable disharmony a high compliment.

Like folk songs everywhere, those of colonial America revolved around courtship, unrequited love affairs, or doomed lovers. Many American ballads came from Britain; "Greensleeves" was one of the most popular and graceful tunes, and it provided the melody for about eighty different sets of lyrics. Compare the lyricism of the English "Greensleeves" ("Alas, my love/You do me wrong/To cast me off/Discourteously. . . .") with the blunter expression of the native song "Springfield Mountain," the first popular folk song known to be native to the colonies in both words and music:

On Springfield Mountain there did dwell
A lovelie youth I knowed him well....
He had scarce mowed half round the field
When a poison serpent bit at his heel....
They took him home to Mollie dear,
Which made him feel so verie queer....
She also had a rotten tooth
And so the poison killed them both.

America in 1750

| **The Colonies and the Empire** By the middle of the eighteenth century thirteen contiguous British colonies were clustered on the North American mainland. Together they contained well over a million inhabitants. Rhode Island and Connecticut existed by virtue of corporation charters that vested the power of government in the body of freemen. The Penns' Pennsylvania and Delaware and the Calverts' Maryland were proprietary colonies, whose administration had fallen to the heirs of the original proprietors. The proprietors had the title to all the land, and the nominal power of government, though as a result of various charters and agreements they actually appointed or served as the executive branch only, while the legislative power resided in the inhabitants. In 1752, when Oglethorpe's proprietorship was terminated, Georgia became a royal colony. None of the seven other provinces of the Crown had begun as royal colonies. Virginia and Massachusetts had been the possessions of business companies; others had been proprietary colonies; for a time there was no one clearly official government for New Hampshire. In the royal colonies the executive branch, consisting of a governor and a council that in some colonies also functioned as an upper house of the legislature, was appointed by the crown, as were some of the colonial judges.

The Board of Trade, a fifteen-member agency of the Crown, exercised general supervisory power over the entire overseas empire. It selected most royal officials for the colonies and reviewed all legislation passed by the colonial assemblies; of about 8,500 colonial laws passed in the entire period prior to 1776, all were at least nominally reviewed and 469 were rejected. The Board had established vice-admiralty courts in five mainland colonies, with jurisdiction over the acts of Parliament and the various orders concerning trade, other maritime activity, and the conservation of timber for the Royal Navy. Appeals from these courts went to the High Court of Admiralty in London until 1748, after which the Admiralty court shared jurisdiction with the Board of Trade. Appeals from colonial courts on all other matters went to the King's Privy Council, some of whose members also sat on the Board of Trade; all told, something like 1,500 court decisions were appealed prior to 1776. This jerry-built structure, cumbersome enough in theory, was doubly so in practice, for officials were generally slipshod, inefficient, and negligent in executing their duties. That left the royal governors as the principal instruments of the royal will in the colonies, but since the governors normally received their salaries from the local legislatures they were prone to identify themselves less with the Crown than with the richer and more powerful colonials.

| **The Imperial System** The system of imperial regulation that the colonies followed or evaded as expediency demanded was not an effort to build up the prosperity of the mother country at the expense of the colonies. It aimed at protecting the empire as a whole and encouraging each part to do what it could do best.

The Navigation Acts gave a monopoly of the carrying trade within the empire to ships of England and the colonies, with crews made up mostly of colonists or Englishmen. The acts not only protected the American carrying trade but stimulated the shipbuilding industry in British America. Another measure of the imperial system gave the tobacco colonies a monopoly for their product. The Wool Act of 1699, the Hat Act of 1732, and the Iron Act of 1750 did shield producers in the home country against potential competition from American makers of these goods. But at the moment there was not enough colonial production of wool, hats, or iron to make them competitive with British producers. The Molasses Act did injure the colonial manufacture of rum, or would have done so if colonists had obeyed it, but its object was to protect other colonists, those of the British West Indies, against foreign competition.

The imperial system, then, was designed to nourish the whole empire and each of its parts, and the scheme was intelligent within the understanding available to statesmen at that time. By the eighteenth century, not long after the Navigation Acts, an economic concept, centuries long in development, known as mercantilism had gained full expression. It held that a nation or empire should increase its wealth, measured in gold, by policies that insure it will sell more abroad than it imports. By that standard much of the imperial system could claim to be sound economics. Not until a little later would economists be arguing extensively for free trade among nations, unhindered by protective legislation, as the best means of enriching each of the traders. But to colonists aware that the imperial system was the work of a government in which they had no direct voice, every item of the system that seemed to clash with their interests could turn them suspicious of the motives of the mother country. In the meantime, Britain and the colonies alike profited from a vast, enclosed common market.

The informal adhesives of the empire were somewhat stronger than the formal. The colonies and the mother country had common enemies, France and Spain, and that alone was enough to hold the empire together. Beyond such tangible considerations were common language, customs, constitutional and legal institutions, and above all pride in a heritage of freedom, of sharing the celebrated "rights of Englishmen."

| **Political Theory** All British subjects, whether they resided in England or the colonies, shared a pride in the British constitution. This unwritten foundation of Britain's political system was an aggregation of custom, law, and precedent developed over several centuries. By the 1700s it had achieved a fine balance among the classic forms of government: monarchy, or rule by the one; aristocracy, or rule by the few; and democracy, or rule by the many. Englishmen believed that each needed to be checked by the other two, or it would degenerate into an evil: monarchy would fall into tyranny, aristocracy into selfish domination by the wealthy and powerful, democracy into mob rule. The British government, according to this concept, contained an element of each of the three forms. The Crown represented rule by the one; the House of Lords represented the titled aristocracy, the privileged few; the House of Commons represented the democracy. In the British system, the theory went, each of the three was properly restrained by the other two.

Theory was one thing, but practice was another. The House of Commons did represent, directly or indirectly, a considerable range of British public opinion. But it was not democratic. For the most part only the propertied classes, and not all individuals within these, had the privilege of voting for members of the Commons. And the Commons did not balance neatly against the Lords. Interests represented in the House of Commons could be as hostile to one another as to the aristocracy. The monarchy in the later years of the century did wield much power, but it was no longer able to rule by sheer sovereign will and command. Its strength now lay in its ability to influence Parliament through the appointments and other royal favors at its disposal. It was closer to being the leader of a political party then to being an independent branch of government balancing and restraining the rest.

Much of what remained of the presence of the Crown in British political thought was a fiction that theorists thought it convenient to abide by. It was believed that for every country, there must be a sovereignty, a single individual source of all legal authority. The British throne, so tradition claimed, constituted this sovereignty within the empire. Whatever legitimate power the Lords, the Commons, or the courts possessed was by grant of authority from the monarch. Those who held to this idea were perfectly aware that in fact Parliament could pretty much do as it pleased, constrained only by the monarch's power to make appointments and to influence parliamentary votes.

Eighteenth-century observers, in fact, perceived the politics of their time as a corruption of a system that had once been pure. Beginning in the 1720s, when party politics was developing in the mother country, political essays attacking the King's ministers and claiming evil designs againt English liberties were common in London periodicals. Literate and concerned colonists read these, too, and kept a watchful eye on ministerial policies. By the 1760s it would take little to convince Americans that they, too, were endangered by a vast, evil conspiracy of corrupt officials to take away the sacred rights of Englishmen everywhere. The belief that an ideal government should combine the three elements—monarchy, aristocracy, and democracy—and that the British system had once possessed the right combination, persisted into the early days of the independent United States. It provided a model for the Constitution, where the President provided government by the one, the Senate—for which the Constitution did not require popular elections—provided rule by the few, and the House of Representatives supplied rule by the many.

By 1750 the governments of the royal colonies—all the colonies except Rhode Island and Connecticut—also appeared to reflect the structure of the British government. The governor, appointed by the Crown, had the authority to veto legislation passed by the colonial assembly and to call or dissolve the assembly. The governors' powers in the colonies were not identical to those of the monarch in Britain, but the governors, like the crown, could be described as providing government by the one. While some governors were upper-class Americans, the Crown more often appointed someone from Britain. A council, drawn for the most part from among the wealthier or more distinguished colonists and in most royal colonies appointed by the governor, could amend or reject legislation by the more popular branch of the colonial legislature and served as the highest court in the colony. A political theorist might have described the council as supplying government by the few. The other branch of the legislature, called in most colonies the assembly, provided government by the many. Throughout British America be-

tween fifty and seventy-five percent of adult white males possessed enough property to vote.

| **How Much Democracy?** Why were the colonies so much more nearly democratic politically than Great Britain? No passionate commitment to the idea of universal equality had moved proprietors, companies, and colonial leaders to provide for broad distribution of the right to vote, or led Kings and the rest of the British government to accept the arrangement. Voting in England was restricted to persons owning at least a "forty-shilling freehold" (land that produced a yearly income of forty shillings). But land was scarce in England, and comparatively few people could vote. In America land was abundant, and a modest property requirement comparable to that in England was easily met. Thus the franchise in the colonies was wider by accident, not by design. Not only was voting more widespread in America, but the number of voters was constantly growing as new immigrants became settlers, as new communities formed and elected their own representatives to colonial legislatures. And so much of colonial British America enjoyed a democracy that had little ideology to it, representing instead something of British tradition and much of the realities of colonial life.

Still, the colonies were not democratic by modern standards. People voted, but governors not chosen by the people could veto legislation. Wealthy elites ruled, but ordinary folk were untroubled by that rule, since, being democratic by circumstance rather than by ideology, they had no philosophical reason to be troubled; they were prepared to offer to people of wealth and standing a certain deference.

By no means all white American males could vote. There were laborers and seamen with almost no property, and paupers with none. In Philadelphia on election day in 1742 some sailors without the vote rioted in anger at the unwillingness of the Quaker-dominated assembly to provide measures for military defense—a common complaint also among the Scotch-Irish voters on the Pennsylvania frontier. The incident gives witness both that a disfranchised class existed and that it was prepared to make its own political mark. As a general rule, women were similarly disfranchised, but there is no record of their having protested their condition. Since in principle married women could own no property without very special legal arrangements, and since officially no women performed military service, they could not claim the two main justifications for a vote. Colonists of both genders widely shared the basic

assumption of their society that public affairs were the business of men. And finally, throughout British America the institution of slavery mocked whatever democracy white Americans practiced.

And so democracy in British America was incomplete, and, for the most part, unintentional.

Points To Think About

1. The most significant fact about the Salem witchcraft trials is that they were the only outburst of their kind in colonial America. Similar episodes were relatively commonplace in England and Europe during the seventeenth and early eighteenth centuries. As important as it is to ascertain why the trials occurred, it is even more important to determine why there were no other Salems. This is the kind of question historians rarely ask and are not particularly well suited to answer. Their whole training is directed to explaining what did happen.

One way of approaching the question is to isolate the features of Salem village life that set it apart from other colonial communities. Perhaps these peculiarities account both for why the witchcraft scare happened in Salem and for why nothing like it happened elsewhere. But there was little in the community's economic situation, or its ethnic or religious makeup, that set it apart from other New England towns. The strains introduced by the growth of a market economy, for example, were felt in many other places. What Salem village conspicuously lacked were social and governmental mechanisms for resolving conflict. The village had originally been part of the town of Salem and continued to look to the town for leadership. When villagers found themselves at odds over the choice of the minister, they turned to the town for guidance. The minister was expected to provide moral leadership. Disputes between neighbors or family members were routinely referred to him. Normally the minister's moral authority was sufficient to cause the disputants to accept his advice. But this could never work in Salem village, where acceptance of the minister's authority had never been unanimous. As a result, grievances persisted, and old resentments festered. The sorts of normal social pressures that the average community had managed to deal with built up to the flash point in Salem village.

The witchcraft outburst can be seen as testimony of a sort to the effectiveness of colonial so-

cial arrangements elsewhere. Every community had its own problems, of course, but normally colonists could feel confident that they would be solved in an effective and legitimate way. Only in Salem village did they seem *devilishly* recalcitrant.

2. Prior to the Great Awakening most colonists had thought of conversion as an individual experience. It became, under the ministrations of the "New Light" ministers, a communal event that lasted but a few days or even hours. The New Light preachers appealed to the hearts of their listeners. While some, like Jonathan Edwards, maintained a dignified tone, others thundered forth. And all used emotionally charged and dramatic images (see the excerpt from Edwards's "Sinners In The Hands Of An Angry God") designed to bring their hearers to an immediate awareness of their needs for salvation.

In seeking after conversion in their sermons, the "New Lights" took what had been an intensely private experience and made it public. In so doing they created an emotional atmosphere at their meetings unlike anything that had come before. People cried out—presumably under the conviction of sin. They wept, they groaned, they fell to their knees. Some lost consciousness. And, most critically, the excitement was contagious. Whole gatherings experienced the drama of conversion together.

Those used to the old ways, called "Old Lights," were horrified. This was not religion, they thought, it was mass frenzy. And so the first of several battlelines over the Awakening was drawn. Established congregational churches often split. New Lights refused to heed a minister they regarded as cold or lifeless or spiritually dead; the Old Lights roundly condemned the excesses of the Awakening.

Several important questions were at stake. The Awakening led many to challenge or even condemn the authority of the established clergy. New Lights defied the traditional deference paid to learning. They encouraged laymen and, sometimes, lay women to lead prayers and even on occasion to preach. Their lack of training was no handicap, said New Light ministers. Instead it was an advantage. New Lights spoke straight from the heart. Their sentiments were not filtered through so much useless learning.

In these ways, the Awakening proved a disruptive experience in much of colonial America. It led to a proliferation of churches, divided religious authority, and enabled ordinary men and women to challenge their betters.

In another sense the Great Awakening drew the colonies together. George Whitefield's tours and the reports of revival meetings from New England to Georgia, often printed in colonial newspapers, were one of the first shared experiences that helped unify thirteen separate colonies.

3. The rapid growth of the British colonies during the eighteenth century convinced many contemporaries that the Americans would in time be independent or that the seat of empire, as Benjamin Franklin once prophesied, would move to their side of the Atlantic. The sheer size of British North America, the rapid growth of its population, and the wealth of its resources all plainly forecast its ultimate preeminence or independence. Yet these facts do not explain the reasons why the revolution took place when it did. Nor do they explain why the revolution took the form that it did. The patterns of colonial government offer a readier explanation.

The colonies had long benefited from "salutary neglect." Imperial control had been intermittent at best. This meant that the colonists grew used to regulating most of their affairs. Furthermore, they experienced little difficulty in evading those few imperial regulations they did find bothersome. This happy state of affairs encouraged Americans to think of themselves as partners in the British imperial enterprise. They thought of possessing all "the rights of Englishmen," for example. And they engaged in several wars with France as patriotic Englishmen. They saw an identity of interest between themselves and the mother country.

The colonists, often without fully realizing it, had embraced one vision of mercantilism while the British government embraced another. Mercantilism taught that there was a limited amount of wealth and power and that the various nations of the globe were engaged in an unending struggle to get their shares. But while the colonists thought of themselves as equal partners successive governments in England thought of the colonies not as partners but as subordinates, existing to benefit the mother country through whatever policies she designed.

Suggested Readings

For an important and recent overview see John J. McCusker and Russell R. Menard, *The Economy of British America 1607–1789* (1985). On the New England and the southern colonies see Michael Zuckerman, *Peaceable Kingdoms: New England Towns in the Eighteenth Century* (1970) and Allan Kulikoff, *Tobacco and Slaves: The Development of Southern Culture in the Chesapeake, 1680–1800* (1986). Paul Boyer and Stephen Nissenbaum attribute the witchcraft hysteria in Salem to a rift in the social structure ultimately traceable to an emergent mercantile capitalism. See *Salem Possessed: The Social Origins of Witchcraft* (1974) and, in three volumes, *The Salem Witchcraft Papers: Verbatim Transcripts of the Salem Witchcraft Outbreak of 1692* (1977). John Demos's excellent 1983 study, *Entertaining Satan*, offers a broad view of the episode.

People of Paradox (1980) is Michael Kammen's venture onto the perilous ground of national character. He finds the hallmark of American society to be contradictions ("biformities") and tensions within colonial life that contributed to the formation of a peculiar American style reconciling a European sense of order with a New World thirst for freedom. A good brief view of the early American economy is Gary M. Walton and James P. Shepherd, *The Economic Rise of Early America* (1979). The early history of blacks in America is brilliantly analyzed in David Brion Davis, *The Problem of Slavery in Western Culture* (1966) and Winthrop Jordan, *White Over Black* (1968).

On colonial women the classic is Julia Cherry Spruill, *Women's Life and Work in the Southern Colonies* (1938), to compare with a newer work by Laurel Thatcher Ulrich, *Good Wives: Image and Reality in the Lives of Women in Northern New England, 1650–1750* (1982).

Richard Hofstadter's *America at 1750* (1969) is a social history of the thirteen colonies; the late author's lucid, crisp style freezes a moment in history for close scrutiny and ready understanding.

FORREST McDONALD

The Puritans endowed the future republic with much that is good. They bequeathed us what were once known as the middle-class virtues, or what Professor Fox-Genovese may call bourgeois values. They taught us to believe that people justify their existence by the work they do; that every man is responsible for the welfare of himself and his family; and that the community is obliged to care for the needy, but only if misfortune has made them unable to care for themselves. The Puritans taught cleanliness, honesty, and thrift, obedience to law, involvement in the affairs of the community, respect for learning, deference toward elders and those in authority, and above all reverence toward God. To the extent that Americans still treasure such values, the Puritans have enriched us.

But the Puritans also implanted defects in the American character. Puritanism had much in common with two ancient, perverse Christian heresies, Gnosticism and Manichaeism. "Gnostic" stems from the Greek word *gnostikos,* meaning to know; the gnostics regarded themselves as having "knowledge of the divine mysteries reserved to an elite." The Puritan counterpart was the "elect": the chosen few whom God has predestined for eternal salvation and incidentally for blessings in this life. As a theology this doctrine became unfashionable, but its psychological substance has endured. Partly it persists as a craving for knowledge of absolute truth that is a mark of the ideologue. Partly it persists in an attitude of superiority: he who is chosen "knows" absolutely and this knowledge entitles him to invade, regulate, and direct the lives of the non-elect—for their own good, of course.

Manichaeism, a species of gnosticism, was the belief that two gods divide and contend for the cosmos, a God of Light and pure goodness and a God of Darkness and pure evil. The Puritan equivalent of Manichaeism was the inability to distinguish among gradations of good and evil, the belief that things were all one or the other, which in turn led to an inability to compromise, to accommodate, or to accept things as they are. Evil became something external rather than something carried in the heart of every individual.

Puritanism was therefore a contradictory force. During hard times its ethic of work, frugality, and self-reliance was constructive, and during such times Puritans were too busy trying to keep their heads above water to cause any mischief. But they could not stand success: in times of general prosperity nearly everyone enjoyed material abundance, which was inherently sinful and also contrary to the belief that only a few were chosen.

The Puritans responded to sinfully prosperous circumstances in one of two characteristic ways, both destructive. One was to pronounce the whole of society hopelessly corrupt and to drop out, to join with a few like-minded souls and to make a world apart. Countless variants of dropping out have occurred throughout American history and are with us today.

Another response was not to leave the world but to cleanse it of its evil, and this usually meant isolating a single, external source of all evil and seeking to exorcise it. During the seventeenth century the source was identified as supernatural: the devil seduced some people (most often women) and made them witches. Later the demons became secularized: In the eighteenth century the demons were the ministers of George III; in the nineteenth they were variously alcohol, the slaveocracy, and the plutocracy; in the twentieth they have ranged from the immigrant hordes to the Communist conspiracy to the military-industrial complex to simply the "system." In all of its forms the urge to cleanse the world of evil reflects a primitive fear of the God of Darkness.

Do We Need Puritan Virtues?

ELIZABETH FOX-GENOVESE

Yes, I do call Puritan values bourgeois, a term difficult to define but suggestive of a people hardworking, thrifty, smug, complacent, conventional, and greedy for money. I agree with Professor McDonald that at least some of the bourgeois values are a great legacy to modern civilization. I also agree with his eloquent testimony to the contributions of the Puritans and with his sober estimates of the good and bad effects of Puritanism on our national character and personality as Puritanism became secularized, democratized, and absorbed by later generations whose ethnic and social origins were far removed from Puritan Britain.

I would also caution that those values intentionally spoke in the male voice and for men's purposes. Puritanism did insist upon doctrines that seemed to promise equality among individual souls, but in practice mainstream Puritanism never fully divorced souls from the bodies they inhabited. And it largely accepted the assumptions of the day that men should dominate women, should govern households and families, should speak in churches. Within Puritanism lay a temptation, which most Puritans resisted, to turn away from all outward laws and teachings and rely instead on emotions and impulses that the believer could identify with divine grace. This Antinomianism, as it was sometimes called, could imply that all social distinctions are false, impudently discarding grace and instead exalting human virtues or learning or wealth or ancestry. In England the more radical Puritans spoke of the equality between men and women, criticized the institution of marriage, occasionally favored free love, and frequently encouraged women's prophecy.

But even the radicals did not always seriously question the natural relations of dominance and dependence between men and women: female prophets often captured an audience precisely because they were seen to be transcending women's normal roles. The very irregularity of their behavior was accepted as proof of their special relations with God. Yet irregular behavior sometimes got women in trouble; it could be seen as proof that they were witches. And when, in the early Massachusetts, Anne Hutchinson claimed to challenge the authority of John Winthrop and other Puritan fathers, she was publicly tried and censured for behavior unbecoming a woman and for beliefs incompatible with Puritan orthodoxy, and then banished.

Hutchinson's case reveals a deep contradiction in Puritan thought between the egalitarian spiritual ideology and the acceptance of unequal relations in the world, a contradiction that would plague the legacy of Puritanism to our own time. The Puritans do not stand alone in their failure to implement the more radical implications of their beliefs, but in questioning hierarchy in theory while continuing to accept manifestations of it in practice, they allowed Puritan belief and practice to be invoked for contradictory purposes. It could be used to justify rebellion as the legitimate expression of conscience in the English and American revolutions, or it could be used to condemn rebellion as an illegitimate attack on the social order and the individual's place in it, as in the cases of Anne Hutchinson and Roger Williams. The confusion for both the Puritans and their heirs is one of the ironies of American history.

The Death of Wolfe, by Benjamin West. Though Wolfe was killed in action at Quebec, the British victory there marked a turning point in the French and Indian War. *(Courtesy, National Gallery of Canada)*

CHAPTER 4

An Independent Spirit
1763–1776

THE PLAINS OF ABRAHAM

At 2 a.m. on September 13, 1759, Major General James Wolfe ordered two lanterns raised to the maintop shrouds of his British flagship, the *Sutherland,* anchored on the St. Lawrence River. It was the signal to attack the French fortress of Quebec, which lay on the heights 175 feet above the dark river.

The attack had been long delayed. Wolfe and his army of redcoats, Scottish highlanders, and American rangers had arrived before the French stronghold the previous June, fighting a score of skirmishes with the French-Canadian militia, their Indian allies, and the crack French regulars of the Guyenne, Royal Roussillon, Bearn, La Reine, and La Sarre regiments. By now the brief Canadian summer was nearly spent, and the bitter northern winter would soon descend. The British naval commander, faced with the prospect of being trapped by ice, was threatening to sail home with his fleet.

Wolfe and his men were confident. They were fewer than the French, but what they lacked in numbers they made up in morale and experience. In the boat taking him to the French side Wolfe himself, as though with some premonition of what was about to happen to him, recited Gray's "Elegy in a Country Churchyard." It contained the line "The paths of glory lead but to the grave."

As the small boats carrying the British troops edged along the darkened north bank of the St. Lawrence a French sentry shouted: "what regiment?" A highland officer responded in fluent French: "the Queen's." The boats were allowed to pass. Soon after, they touched the bank close to where Wolfe some days before had spied a zig-zag path up the steep cliff that separated the river from the plain stretching before Quebec city. Twenty-four volunteers leaped out and, grabbing trees and bushes, pulled themselves up the plateau. Hundreds more followed.

The invaders spied a small French encampment. They immediately attacked, captured two of the French soldiers, and put the rest to flight. Hearing the triumphant shouts of his men above, Wolfe and his remaining force disembarked and scaled the cliff by way of the path to join the advance party.

As morning broke with clouds and threatening rain, 4000 British troops drew themselves up in battle order on the Plains of Abraham a mile west of Quebec, the center of French power in America where General Louis de Montcalm commanded 14,000 troops.

In the walled city itself, news of Wolfe's surprise move provoked great alarm. For many weeks the *Quebeçois* had endured bombardment from the British fleet and army. Much of the city was in ruins, although it was packed with refugees from the countryside who jammed into every remaining dwelling and spilled over into the town's hospitals, convents, and public buildings. Worse than the physical devastation and discomfort was the political confusion in the city. Montcalm, a forty-four-year-old veteran of France's wars, had been pulled from retirement to command His Majesty's troops in distant Canada. The civilian leader was Pierre de Rigaud, the Marquis de Vaudreuil, a Canadian-born son of a previous governor of Canada. The two men did not get along, and their lack of rapport would hurt France in the hours ahead.

As news spread of the British success in scaling the heights, the French and Canadians poured out of the town to assemble on the plain outside the walls. Montcalm asked the city commander to send him big guns from the palace battery, but was given only three on the plea that the rest were needed to defend the town itself. Montcalm might have waited for troops from Vaudreuil, but the governor too held back, fearing, apparently, to be part of any defeat while at the same time reserving the right to arrive in time to claim credit for any victory. As his men formed ranks, Montcalm rode back and forth along his lines brandishing his sword and urging his troops to show their mettle for France and for the King.

At 10 a.m. the French, with the white-clad regulars in the center and the Canadians at either end, started forward against the double-ranked British, firing and shouting. The redcoats and highlanders advanced a few yards and then stopped. When the two lines were within forty paces the British commander ordered his men to fire. Two precise volleys rang out like single shots, and then a ragged clatter followed as the men reloaded and fired at will. When the smoke lifted, it was clear that the battle was over. As far as the eye could see, the field was covered with French dead and wounded, 1400 in all. The French troops still on their feet had stopped short and were milling around in a confused mob. The British officers now gave the order to charge. The cheering redcoats ran forward with their bayonets poised. The highlanders dashed ahead yelling in Gaelic and brandishing their broadswords. Leading the charge of the Louisburg Grenadiers was Wolfe himself. At that moment of triumph the British general was struck in the chest by a French bullet and taken to the rear. A few minutes later he died.

By now the French were fleeing pell-mell to the safety of Quebec's walls. Borne along with the human tide was Montcalm, still mounted. Close to the walls a British shot hit him in the thigh and passed along it to lodge in his stomach. The French commander was escorted through the city gate by three soldiers and brought to the military surgeon. But nothing could be done, and he died the next day.

Meanwhile the timid Vaudreuil, despite the urging of his senior officer, refused to move his large remaining force against the exhausted British. When reinforcements arrived under the Chevalier de Levis several days later, it was too late: Montcalm's successor at Quebec had already surrendered the city to Brigadier General James Murray.

Nonetheless, fighting continued for some time before French Canada was completely subdued. In early spring 1760 the French tried to retake Quebec from the British, but were beaten. That summer British troops from three directions descended on Montreal, the last remaining French strong point in Canada. On September 8 Vaudreuil surrendered all of French Canada to the British.

The great war between France and Britain went on officially for three and a half more years before the negotiators at Paris signed a peace treaty in 1763. In reality, it had ended on the cloudy battlefield at Quebec, where both brave commanders surrendered their lives.

The French and Indian War

A World War for Empire News of Wolfe's victory deeply affected the North American public. The young hero had given his life to save Protestant America from Catholic France and his sacrifice took on epic proportions. Grateful for the victory and moved by the young general's death, thousands of King George's subjects sang the words to Gray's "Elegy" in taverns all over the colonies.

Since the last years of the seventeenth century Britain and France had been rivals in Europe and wherever their empires clashed. The War of the League of Augsburg, waged from 1689 to 1697, had led to French and Indian raids on New England's frontier, and New England attacks on the French in Canada. As one Massachusetts man put it, "We shall never be at rest until we have Cannida." The British colonists called this conflict King William's War. The War of the Spanish Succession, from 1702 to 1713, again had produced its small counterpart in America, Queen Anne's War. So far the colonial fighting had been border raids between British and French colonists, sometimes employing their Indian allies. The American phase of the War of the Austrian Succession, which took place from 1740 to 1748, was called King George's War. New England troops won an important victory in the capital of Louisburg, which guarded the entrance to the St. Lawrence River. Colonists were disappointed when Britain returned Louisburg in the Treaty of Aix-la-Chapelle. Then in 1756 Britain and France began a seven-year world war for empire. The fighting in North America became known as the French and Indian War. The victory of Britain in 1763 more than doubled the territorial extent of overseas domain it had been building for a century and a

half. And then, as an indirect result of the same war, it lost almost all of that empire in a decade and a half.

Though they had claimed and occupied much of North America for more than a hundred years, the French had by no means settled it. During the seventeenth century explorers such as René La Salle pushed down the St. Lawrence River into the center of North America and down the Mississippi River. The vast area of New France, comprising most of present-day Canada, the Ohio Valley, the Mississippi, and lands to its west, constituted a serious threat to the English colonies. France established a brisk fur trade with Algonquin-speaking Indian tribes and introduced guns to their Indian allies. As French traders moved along the St. Lawrence and into the Great Lakes region, they established Indian alliances that would later aid them in fighting the English. There were only about 55,000 French settlers in North America, the overwhelming majority in the far Northeast and along the St. Lawrence River and the remainder distributed in widely scattered trading posts on the Great Lakes and the Ohio and Mississippi rivers. Quebec and Montreal were the only towns of consequence on the St. Lawrence, and New Orleans the only one of importance on the Mississippi. As buffers between their own settlements and those of the aggressive, coast-bound British Americans, the French had long depended upon the friendly but subject Indians. A sudden establishment of favorable relations between the British Americans and the Indians upset all balances and jeopardized the entire French position in North America, for the greedy, land-hungry British Americans outnumbered the French Americans by almost thirty to one.

A view of Fort Ticonderoga on Lake Champlain, New York. This was a strategic battleground in several wars. *(The Crown Collection in the British Museum)*

Skirmishes in the Ohio Valley
The new governor of Virginia, Robert Dinwiddie, had instructions to promote the concerns of the Ohio Company, a business interested in the Ohio Valley lands, but to do so without antagonizing the French. Accordingly he dispatched a seven-man mission, which included a twenty-one-year-old surveyor named George Washington, to urge the French to respect British rights in the area. The mission was politely received and, with equal politeness, informed that the construction of Fort Duquesne would begin in the spring. The place where the fort was to be located, the site of present-day Pittsburgh, was in territory then claimed by Virginia. Upon being told of the French intention, Governor Dinwiddie rushed a work force to the area

with instructions to build a British fort on the spot. To protect the workers young Washington followed with troops a little later, quite unaware that the French had expelled the work force almost immediately upon its arrival. In May 1754 Washington was encamped at Great Meadows on the Monongahela when he learned of the existence of a small French force a few miles ahead. He ordered a precipitous night march and attacked the French, capturing twenty-one and killing ten. Then he pushed on until he learned that the French were about to attack him in force. He retreated and hastily threw up a stockade, imaginatively called Fort Necessity. In June his force of 150 grew by 200 more men, and on July 3 he was attacked by 500 French and 400 Indians. After a nine-day siege Washington surrendered. The future commander of the American forces had had his first taste of battle, and the French and Indian War had begun. "I heard the bullets whistle," Washington wrote to his half-brother, and there was "something charming in the sound."

It took European statesmen two years to complete the necessary formalities of choosing up sides (France and Austria, later joined by Spain, against Great Britain and Prussia) and reaching a state of official hostility. Meanwhile, French and English Americans were busily engaged in killing, enlisting for that purpose the aid of various Indian tribes.

| **Albany Plan of Union** | Even before Washington's abortive expedition, the Board of Trade had ordered a conference of colonial officials, and even as Washington was blundering in the wilderness a congress was in session in Albany, New York, attended by delegates from the New England colonies, New York, Pennsylvania, and Maryland. Schemes for uniting the colonies were afloat at the congress. The Pennsylvania delegation, led by Benjamin Franklin, proposed what is known as the Albany Plan of Union. The plan called for a president-general for the British colonies, to be chosen and supported by the Crown, and a grand council, representing the several colonies in proportion to their contributions to the colonial treasury. This agency was to have general legislative and taxing powers for the purpose of defense and Indian relations. The delegates approved the plan with modifications, but the colonies rejected it. The first effort to establish an American union was stillborn. The colonial legislatures had been jealous above all of sharing their power to tax. That jealousy would later involve them in a revolution against Great Britain.

Braddock's Defeat   As hostilities continued on the frontier it remained obvious that some sort of plan would have to be devised for coping with the French in America. Though eminent Londoners were preoccupied with the gaming tables, court intrigues, and other pressing pursuits, someone in the capital did come up with a vague plan of action. Official British policy was to engage in what, at a later day, would be called limited warfare. Two British regiments at half-strength, the rest to be made up of colonial militiamen, would march up from Virginia and capture Fort Duquesne. Another and similar force, to be gathered in New England and New York, would seize Crown Point on Lake Ticonderoga and Fort Niagara. General Edward Braddock, a sixty-year-old veteran with forty-five years' military experience, was put in charge of the campaign.

Braddock arrived in Virginia early in 1755, then delegated responsibility for raising troops for the multiple attack, and chose Washington as one of his aides-de-camp. In June he started over the mountains with a force of over 1400 men and 150 wagons, cutting a road through the wilderness as he went. In an open space near Fort Duquesne on July 9 French and Indian forces fighting from behind cover surprised Braddock's troops. Some of the Virginia troops abandoned the close-ranked, conventional eighteenth-century military formation and tried to fight in the frontier manner, which meant using cover. Some of Braddock's British regulars attempted the same thing, but Braddock and his officers ordered them back into line, where they were slashed by enemy fire until they broke. Many ran, as George Washington said, "as sheep pursued by dogs." By the next evening Braddock's forces had been destroyed; General Braddock himself was killed. Of 1,459 men, 977 were dead or wounded. In the North, the planned expedition on Fort Niagara, directed by the new Governor William Shirley of Massachusetts, got as far as Oswego, half the distance, before being defeated. The campaign to take Crown Point, led by colonist William Johnson, brought no further British victories.

Attack on Canada   By the middle of 1756 the French had taken the offensive, and throughout 1757 French forces won victory after victory. Then a new expedition, commanded by General John Forbes and composed of 6,000 men, began in the fall of 1758 to cut its way through the forests of western Pennsylvania toward the forks of the Ohio. The French defenders of Fort Duquesne, deserted by their Indian allies as Forbes's army drew near, blew up their stronghold and fled to Canada in November of 1759. Forbes immediately began to reconstruct the fort, rechristened Fort Pitt. Settlers began to pour into the area despite British orders. Another expedition, commanded by William Johnson, directed a

French troops being reviewed in Quebec, an almost impregnable fortress commanded by Louis Joseph Montcalm. *(Courtesy, William H. Coverdale Collection, and the Canada Steamship Lines Limited, Montreal, Canada.)*

force of 3500 Americans, 2500 British regulars, and 1000 Indians against Fort Niagara, with the aim of cutting off Montreal and Quebec from the Great Lakes region. The expedition marched in the spring of 1759 and achieved total victory. A force commanded by Sir Jeffrey Amherst was directed to move north from New York City, clear the French posts on Lake Champlain, bypass Montreal, and lay siege to Quebec from the southwest. General James Wolfe was ordered to move with a combined army and naval force up the St. Lawrence and attack Quebec from the other side. Amherst's expedition took both

Ticonderoga and Crown Point, but was so slow in the doing that it was forced to stop on Lake Champlain for the winter of 1759–60. That left Wolfe to attack Quebec alone, and Quebec was protected by a high rock cliff that made it the most formidable natural fortress in America. The French commander at Quebec, Montcalm, remained inside the fortress, confident that high cliffs would prevent any attack on Quebec from the southwest by way of the Plains of Abraham. The ensuing battle was a momentous occasion for the future of North America.

Imperial Reform

The French and Indian War as a whole was an invigorating experience for Americans. They had fought well in a score of battles from Canada to the Caribbean. After 1763

they would exhibit a new confidence and a new pride in what they, mere provincials before, could accomplish.

The elimination of France as a major

power in North America enhanced this new spirit. For a century New France and then Louisiana, representing absolutism and clericalism, had hung like a sword over Anglo-America, forcing the colonists to acknowledge dependence on the British army and navy. The Treaty of Paris in 1763 changed all this. To Great Britain, which had already won Canada by the surrender of Montreal in 1760, France now relinquished all claims to America east of the Mississippi. Spain, an ally of France, turned over Florida to the British. In compensation for Spanish losses, the French gave Spain New Orleans and all their possessions west of the Mississippi. Now that the most dangerous foreign power had been removed, the colonists were free to reassess their relationship with the mother country.

The British were aware of the possibility of change in the colonial temperament. During the negotiations at Paris the Duke of Bedford spoke for returning Canada to France to prevent Americans from growing too mighty and asserting their independence. Bedford's views were overruled, but in later years there were those who believed that the conquest of New France had been a mistake. During the fierce debate between the colonies and Britain that preceded independence, the loyalist governor of Massachusetts, Thomas Hutchinson, noted:

> Before the peace of 1763 I thought nothing so much to be desired as the cession of Canada. I am now convinced that if it had remained to the French none of the spirit of opposition to the Mother Country would have yet appeared and I think the effects of it worse than all we had to fear from the French or Indians.

Renewed Conflict with Indians By the war's end, moreover, it had begun to look as if Britain would have to maintain a permanent and expensive military force in America. France was down but not out. Unreconciled to Britain's triumph, the French were reportedly rebuilding their navy in preparation for further war. More immediately, the Indian tribes in the West were becoming a problem. During the war American settlers and Indian traders had flooded into the trans-Appalachian region in the wake of British victories over the French. The newcomers often plied the Indians with rum and then "bought" their lands

for a few cheap goods and rifles and powder. These difficulties would become worse once the Americans poured across the mountains in force after 1763.

Even before the British could formally announce policy the Indian frontier exploded. One of the Indian leaders was the Delaware Prophet, a visionary and seer who assured his followers that if they rejected the European's ways, they would regain their former strength and former lands. The other, the Ottawa chief Pontiac, led his warriors in May 1763 against the British fort at Detroit and came close to taking it. Pontiac's attack commenced a massive Indian uprising all along the northern frontier; by June only three major British military posts remained.

The British quickly struck back. Two columns went to the relief of the surviving posts. One, led by Colonel Henry Bouquet, forced Pontiac to accept a truce. Soon after, Pontiac's chief allies made peace with the English, and before long Pontiac himself "smoked the calumet" (peace pipe) with the British and Americans. On the Pennsylvania frontier in 1764 a band known as the Paxton Boys attacked some peaceful Indians and then marched on Philadelphia, "uttering hideous cries in imitation of the war whoop" and bent on killing the Indian refugees who had fled to the capital for protection. Benjamin Franklin persuaded them to petition the assembly instead of invading the city.

The End of "Salutary Neglect" The French forced the British government to focus attention on American affairs as never before, and the experience was an eye-opener. As British officials saw it, the Americans had behaved badly. Their illegal trade with the enemy had profited them and made the war more costly in men and money. The war, meanwhile, had burdened Great Britain with a huge debt. British officials argued that the easy and benign policy of governing the colonies by "salutary neglect," a policy of leaving the colonies alone, would have to be replaced by a tighter, more rational, and financially sounder system. The Americans were not unaware of these arguments. Colonial spokesmen pointed to heavy local taxation for the repayment of the colonial war debt. Colonists were also prepared to argue that the Navigation Acts worked to pull wealth from the colonies into Britain. Since the dispute was over money, each side was inclined to feel itself the victim.

The chief advocate of the British position was George Grenville, Chancellor of the Exchequer and King George III's chief minister following the retirement of William Pitt, the great wartime leader. Grenville was a man of limited vision who treated the empire as if it were a business concern. As a contemporary noted, Grenville judged "a national saving of two inches of candle . . . a greater triumph than all Pitt's victories." He soon initiated measures to reduce British expenses and to generate income for the mother country.

Grenville first took aim at policy toward the West and the Indians. To generate orderly settlement and to prevent further Indian wars caused by land-hungry settlers, the Proclamation of 1763 set the limit of colonial settlement at the crest of the Appalachians. All colonists west of that line must "forthwith . . . remove themselves." British military authorities would now be in charge of all Indian territory west of the mountains; all traders in Indian territory would have to be licensed, and they could trade only at designated points under British military supervision. The Proclamation was soon followed by a flurry of measures designed to raise revenue in America whenever the colonists might refuse to provide for their own defense.

The intention of the Revenue Act of 1764, a revision of the Sugar Act of 1733, was to increase the scanty receipts of the British customs service in America. The law added a dozen items to the list of "enumerated" American articles that must go first to Britain to be taxed before they could be sent elsewhere. The law also established a new set of taxes for goods imported into the colonies and set up new admiralty courts with power to enforce their collection with the aid of general search warrants called "writs of assistance." The most important change affected the trade between the mainland colonies and the West Indies. Molasses was the chief raw material in the making of rum, a major New England industry. For many years American merchants had relied on the French and Dutch Caribbean islands for this product, which was cheaper there than in the British Caribbean islands. By smuggling, the colonists had evaded the high tax Britain had imposed on foreign-produced molasses.

John Singleton Copley's portrait of Paul Revere represents him as a silversmith and craftsman. Revere also cast cannon for the army and designed the state seal still used by Massachusetts. *(Courtesy, Museum of Fine Arts, Boston)*

Because the duty of sixpence a gallon had been uncollectable, the British now cut the duty in half—but determined to collect the money.

A second measure of 1764, the Currency Act, struck at the practice of issuing legal tender, or paper money. The colonials believed paper to be an indispensable medium of exchange in a chronically coin-poor community. British merchants had long complained, however, that the paper issued under the colonial legal-tender laws was a cheap and flimsy currency. Its use by Americans, especially Southern planters, in payment of their debts to British creditors, amounted to a scaling down of the debt. The right to issue legal tender had already been forbidden the New England colonies. Now, the prohibition would extend to the Middle and Southern colonies as well.

Americans did not take these new measures lightly. The Proclamation of 1763 threatened the ambitions of land speculators, Indian traders, and would-be settlers in the West alike. For the moment, the reaction was comparatively mild. Americans interested in western development simply ignored British policy and went ahead with their own plans. As George Washington wrote a fellow land speculator: "any person who . . . neglects the present opportunity of hunting out good Lands and in some measure marking and distinguishing them for his own . . . will never regain it." Reaction to the Revenue and Currency Acts was more vigorous. A Boston town meeting listened to James Otis's impassioned attack on writs of assistance and condemned

the Revenue Act as taxation without representation. The *New York Gazette* reported that in New Haven:

> The young Gentlemen of Yale have unanimously agreed not to make use of any foreign spiritous liquors. . . . This will not only greatly diminish the Expences of Education, but prove, as may be presumed, very favourable to the Health and Improvement of the Students.

A group of Boston merchants, joined by the city's artisans, resolved to boycott several items imported from Britain. By the end of 1764 a limited boycott of British goods had spread to several other colonies.

The Stamp Act Crisis

Trouble awaited the Grenville program. But few people could have anticipated the full extent of American hostility to British policy. Then came the Stamp Act—the first attempt to impose an internal tax on American colo-

nists, a tax on their activities within their own localities. Previous taxes had been external; they had applied to American commerce with the outside world.

Grenville must have realized the danger in

Reaction to the Stamp Act by the *Pennsylvania Journal*, "The Times are Dreadful, Dismal Doleful Dolorous, and Dollar-less," reflected the widespread anger among the colonists.

the new policy, for when he asked for a tax that would apply directly to transactions in America rather than to overseas trade, he promised to consider other means of raising revenue in the colonies if Americans objected. But he gave the colonial legislatures little time to respond. When their London agents, including Benjamin Franklin, the agent for Pennsylvania, tried to induce Grenville to withdraw the stamp tax proposal, he refused.

In February 1765 the Chancellor of the Exchequer introduced the fatal measure to a poorly attended session of the House of Commons. The debate, though brief, was significant as an expression of the different views of the colonies that were then current among Englishmen.

Speaking for Grenville, Charles Townshend gave voice to a widespread condescension toward Americans that would poison relations between the two peoples. Townshend called Americans "children planted by our care." They had been "nourished up" by British "indulgence" and protected by British arms. Would "they grudge to contribute their mite" to relieve the British people from "the heavy burdens" they suffered?

Townshend's remarks offended Colonel Isaac Barré, an officer who had fought under Wolfe and unlike other upper-class Englishmen argued for relaxing the bonds of empire. Townshend was seriously mistaken, Barré declared. The Americans had been planted not by British care, but rather by British oppression which had driven so many refugees to the New World. Nor were they nurtured by British indulgence. Rather they "grew by your . . . neglect of 'em." Indeed, Barré said, these "sons of liberty" had suffered under greedy British officials for many years. Nor had they been protected by British arms; they had nobly fought for themselves.

Americans would cheer Barré's words, and "patriot" organizations would soon adopt "Sons of Liberty" as their name. But Parliament was unmoved. On March 22, 1765, it passed the Stamp Act, taxing newspapers, almanacs, pamphlets, legal documents, insurance policies, dice, playing cards, and other items. These taxes would be paid in the form of a stamp, purchasable from officials to be chosen from among Americans residing in the colonies, and placed on the specified documents. England had a similar tax, and Gren-

ville expected the law to raise £60,000 of the £300,000 needed to maintain the British military establishment in North America. Tax evaders could be tried in vice-admiralty courts, which had no juries.

News of the Stamp Act's passage reached America in mid-April. Although the act would not take effect until November 1, consternation was immediate and almost universal. By this "single stroke," wrote the conservative jurist William Smith of New York, Britain had "lost . . . the affection of all her colonies." The *New York Gazette* lamented that "every good patriot's heart should be broken by the spectacle of his country, fainting and despairing, hourly expecting to be utterly crushed by the cruel rod of power." One anonymous poet invited the world to

Come, see our Poor, and bring a bit of Bread!
Come, see our Liberties without a Head!
Come, see our Trade declining more and more,
And ragged Want approaching ev'ry Door!

In the Virginia House of Burgesses at Williamsburg the young lawyer Patrick Henry denounced the measure in a speech that has become famous. "Caesar had his Brutus; Charles the First his Cromwell; and George the Third—[here tradition has it that the House Speaker interrupted with a shout of "Treason!" but Henry continued] may profit by their example. If this be treason, make the most of it." Although some doubt exists that the eloquent and ringing version well known to generations of American school children represents Henry's actual words, he apparently came close to suggesting rebellion. After this speech the delegates at Williamsburg adopted a set of resolutions proclaiming that the House of Burgesses possessed the "only and sole power to lay taxes . . . upon the inhabitants of this colony," and that Virginians were "not bound to yield obedience to any law" that Parliament might pass to tax them. Various versions of these Virginia Resolves appeared in colonial newspapers, serving as "an alarum bell to the disaffected." Soon almost all the other colonies had adopted similar resolutions. In June 1765, when the Massachusetts General Court proposed that representatives of all the colonies meet in New York in October to consider joint action against the detested measure, nine of the colonies quickly accepted the invitation.

Violence

Long before the Stamp Act Congress assembled, Americans resorted to more than words to express their indignation.

| **Sons of Liberty** In August Boston's newly formed Sons of Liberty hanged in effigy the man who was to be the new tax commissioner, Andrew Oliver. Oliver was a brother-in-law of Lieutenant Governor Thomas Hutchinson, great-great grandson of the Anne Hutchinson who had clashed with the Puritan ministers of Massachusetts Bay more than a century earlier. Later the mob tore down a house that Oliver had allegedly built to serve as his tax office. The crowd next marched on Oliver's home and broke all the windows. The following day Oliver resigned his tax commission.

The Boston Sons of Liberty next attacked the house of William Story, deputy register of the admiralty court, smashed down the doors, and burned Story's public and private papers. Another contingent sacked the home of the comptroller of customs, carried away his records, and pillaged his wine cellar. On August 26 the mob targeted Hutchinson's three-story brick mansion. The swarm battered down the walls, burned the furniture, destroyed the library, tore windows and doors from their frames, drank all the liquor, and even cut down the trees in the Hutchinson yard. Individuals also stole £900 in cash and walked off with the family silver. Hutchinson, who escaped through his back garden, had actually opposed both the Revenue Act and the Stamp Act.

The mob's fury appalled even some patriots. The Boston town meeting condemned the rioting, and the authorities issued a warrant for the arrest of the Sons of Liberty leader, Ebenezer McIntosh, but the damages were never repaid.

In Newport, Rhode Island, a crowd burned and sacked the homes of "Tories" (so called after the more conservative of Britain's political parties), who defended British authority. In Newport as in Boston, the mobs forced the Stamp Act collector to resign. Connecticut patriots conducted a mock trial of stamp distributors. New York Sons of Liberty vented their fury on the house of the British military commander who had sworn to "cram the Stamp Act down the people's throats." In the words of one observer of the attack, "The Beds they cut open, and threw the Feathers abroad, broke all the Glasses, China, Tables, Chairs, Desks, Trunks, Chests." They then started a fire, threw all the remaining furnishings into it, "drank or destroyed all the Liquor," and left the major's garden in ruins. In Charleston, capital of South Carolina, a mob attacked the house of the prominent merchant Henry Laurens, suspected of being the future stamp distributor. Only Laurens's bold denials kept the irate patriots from doing harm to him and his property. In Philadelphia an angry crowd surrounded Benjamin Franklin's house, but some of his friends dissuaded the rioters. Agent Franklin wrote to a friend, "I took every step in my power to prevent the passing of the Stamp Act; nobody would be more concern'd in interest than myself to oppose it, sincerely and heartily."

So it went from colony to colony. Everywhere Tories were intimidated, and collectors forced to surrender their commissions. When the stamps finally arrived, there was no one to sell them or to see that they were affixed to the designated documents.

Crowds like those that roamed the streets during the Stamp Act crisis would appear in later confrontations between colonists and the British government. They were, in fact, a feature of eighteenth-century politics. Across the Atlantic, the London mob was a menacing presence to the government. And before the end of the eighteenth century, the Paris mobs of the French Revolution would enter history.

| **The Stamp Act Congress** In the early fall of October 1765, twenty-seven delegates from nine colonies— all but New Hampshire, North Carolina, Virginia, and Georgia—convened in New York to consider united action against the detested law. This Stamp Act Congress was relatively conservative, but its Declaration of Rights and Grievances effectively summed up most of the colonists' complaints. Taxation, the Declaration asserted, could be imposed only by the people's consent, "given personally, or by their representatives." Trial by jury, ignored by the new admiralty courts, was an inherent right of Englishmen. The Stamp Act as well as the other recent measures restricting American commerce, the Congress declared, must be repealed.

Far more effective than the words of the

Demonstrations erupted throughout the colonies in response to "taxation without representation." In New England, suspected supporters of the hated Stamp Act were hanged in effigy. (*Scribner's Archives*)

towns, thousands of workingmen lost their jobs as the workshops and mills dependent on the American market slowed and then stopped.

The man who now had to face the uproar was the Marquis of Rockingham, who had succeeded Grenville as prime minister in July 1765. Rockingham's group drew its support largely from the merchants and manufacturers and was particularly sensitive to their plight. Leading the battle for repeal in Parliament was William Pitt, the great wartime prime minister. Pitt eloquently defended the colonists' rights. "The Americans," he declared, "are the sons, not the bastards of England." The Stamp Act must "be REPEALED ABSOLUTELY, TOTALLY, IMMEDIATELY. . . ." In March 1766 Parliament complied. But at the same time, to satisfy its more authoritarian members, it passed the so-called Declaratory Act, asserting its power to make laws binding the American colonies "in all cases whatsoever."

Few Americans took note of the Declaratory Act amid general rejoicing at the end of the detested stamp tax. Merchants immediately abandoned their nonimportation agreements and placed large orders with British

Stamp Act Congress were the actions of businessmen in the major American port cities. Two hundred New York merchants agreed not to take new orders for British goods so long as the Stamp Act remained. They were joined by the traders of Philadelphia, Boston, Salem, and other ports. Meanwhile, November 1, the date when the Act was supposed to take effect, rolled around. For a while business was disrupted, since very little could be done legally without the stamps. Slowly it resumed without them. The law was dead.

The British government could not ignore the American response to the Stamp Act. Some Englishmen were outraged at American defiance. Dr. Samuel Johnson, the critic and lexicographer, called the opponents of the Act "incendiaries" and "fractious demagogues." But others, particularly merchants who found their American business dwindling, sympathized with the Americans and bombarded Parliament with petitions for repeal of the measure. In Manchester, Leeds, Nottingham, and other English industrial

A teapot celebrating Parliament's repeal of the Stamp Act in March 1766. (*Courtesy, Essex Institute, Salem, Massachusetts*)

suppliers. New York City voted to erect statues to Pitt and George III. Other towns and villages put up monuments to Pitt, the "Great Commoner." The ordinary people rang church bells, put lighted candles in their windows, and fired off guns. The Boston Sons of Liberty built on Boston Common "a magnificent pyramid, illuminated with 280 Lamps." Crowning the pile was a box of fireworks that went off at dusk to splendid effect.

In the words of a popular song, written for the great occasion:

In spite of each parasite, each cringing slave,
Each cautious dastard, each oppressive knave,
Each gibing ass, that reptile of an hour,
The supercilious pimp of abject slaves in power,
We are met to celebrate in festive mirth,
The day that gave our freedom second birth,
That tells us, British Grenville never more
Shall dare usurp unjust, illegal power,
Or threaten America's free sons with chains,
While the least spark of ancient fire remains.

Conditioned by the rhetoric of opposition politics between Tory and Whig factions in England, which often hinted at ministerial corruptions and designs to take away English liberties, the colonists vented their wrath on Grenville and remained fiercely loyal to King George III.

| **Not Yet Americans** | The colonial protest over the Stamp Act in 1765 did not deny that Parliament had the right to legislate for the empire or to regulate trade with foreign nations. Noteworthy also is that the protesters proudly identified themselves as British, entitled to the right of Englishmen to be free of any taxation except such as they had consented to. British history provided sources for the distinction that colonists continued at least for a short time to make between taxation, which must be by the consent of those being taxed, and legislation, which did not require popular consent. The colonies had always agreed that Parliament could legislate for them as in the regulation of their trade by the Navigation Acts, the Sugar Act, the Hat Act, and so on. But in their comparatively brief history the colonies had come to believe that only their respective assemblies could tax them. Parliament had never before attempted a direct tax, and the colonists appealed to time-honored precedent in their arguments. In past centuries English monarchs had needed money for essentially private projects, such as wars on foreign soil for the extension of their personal domains. For these and other objectives they would call Parliaments representing the various classes of the kingdom and ask for money to be raised by taxes. And so the idea formed that taxes are a gift from the people to the sovereign, and as a gift must of course be given freely rather than by coercion. Law, on the other hand, is according to this theory an act of sovereignty, an expression of the will of the monarchy, and can apply even to a population that has not agreed to it.

Actually, by the eighteenth century the real power to make law in Britain was almost wholly in the hands of Parliament, and so the distinction was nearly irrelevant there. But the colonies were in another situation. They had assemblies, elected by a considerable portion of the people, that made local laws and raised local taxes. And in their view they had no representatives in the British Parliament. From a transAtlantic perspective, however, as British subjects they were "virtually represented," since Parliament—in theory, at least—represented the people of the entire realm. The word "representation" carried quite different meanings in England and America, and the mother country remained unmoved by colonial cries of "taxation without representation." Parliament could impose regulatory laws on the Americans, since in doing so it was acting as the agent of the Crown, in which all authority to regulate rested.

Even angry colonists, then, still saw themselves as part of the empire, subjects of the King, honoring the authority of Parliament, sharing in the rights that belonged to the British nation and history. But recent events had made them touchy; they were developing a habit of asking large questions about the legitimacy of the actions of the British government; and in the Stamp Act Congress they had gained experience in confronting Great Britain not as Virginians or people of Massachusetts but as united colonists, as Americans. Soon political theorists in the colonies would be abandoning the distinction between internal and external taxation, denying the validity of both and claiming they were victims of a sinister plot against English liberties. Then they would eventually question whether Parliament had the right to legislate for them at all.

Blunder Again

After the repeal of the Stamp Act in 1766 Americans did not rejoice for long. That same year Parliament, in an attempt to reduce expenses associated with the colonies' defense, had passed the Quartering Act. It required the colonies to provide the king's troops with barracks and furnish them with "candles, firing, bedding, cooking utensils, salt and vinegar, and five pints of small beer or cider, or a gill of rum per man, per diem." For a year or two the colonies complied. Then, in 1767, the New York assembly, believing the colony overburdened, refused. New York was the headquarters of General Thomas Gage, commander of British forces in America. In retaliation, Parliament suspended all acts of the New York provincial legislature until it should vote money for the army.

| **Townshend Duties** Many British leaders still wanted colonials to pay a larger share of colonial administrative and military costs. In early 1767, Charles Townshend, then Chancellor of the Exchequer, unveiled his program. The colonies had successfully resisted the Stamp Act, which had taxed their internal business without their consent. But since the colonials themselves had not yet challenged Parliament's right to tax their external commerce, Parliament might still impose an import tax. Capitalizing therefore on the distinction between "internal" and "external" taxation, Townshend proposed taxing a wide range of colonial imports including glass, paper, lead, and tea. These duties, he argued, would raise badly needed funds and also teach the disruptive colonials that Parliament had the authority to tax them. He further proposed creation of a new American customs service as well as a crackdown on New York's continually defiant assembly. After Parliament enacted all these potentially explosive measures, the ministry indicated its determination to enforce the trade laws. In the fall of 1767 when the Acts went into effect, Parliament appointed several unpopular officials to the new customs board and established the body's headquarters in Boston, the center of opposition to stricter commercial regulation.

In some areas, enforcement of commercial regulations broke down almost completely. A Boston ship's captain, Daniel Malcom, drew a pistol on two revenue agents searching for illegal wine in his basement. Returning with the sheriff and a search warrant, the agents discovered the captain's house surrounded by a crowd of his friends, and the harried sheriff avoided a direct confrontation only by stalling for time until the search warrant expired. After the disgusted officials departed, Captain Malcom treated his protectors to buckets of smuggled wine. Such cases were not infrequent.

Investigating past enforcement, Townshend's customs board discovered only six seizures and one smuggling conviction in all of New England during two and one half years. Mobs rescued three of the seized ships, and colonial juries acquitted two other defendants. Initially the new customs officials fared little better, enforcing restrictions only enough to enrage colonial merchants. The same Captain Malcom brought an entire load of illegal wine into Boston on small boats during the night and then boldly sailed his empty ship into port the next day. The vessel's water line clearly revealed his subterfuge, but enraged customs officers could find no Bostonian who would testify against him. In June 1768 a British customs official was locked in the cabin of John Hancock's sloop *Liberty* while the crew unloaded untaxed madeira wine. When customs officials seized the vessel, the patriots forced them to flee to the British garrison at Castle William, where they appealed for British troops to help keep order.

| **Another Boycott** Conditioned by the Stamp Act, Americans were sensitive about any further extension of British power, and an outcry greeted the Townshend Duties. That the duties did not constitute an internal tax made slight difference. This time, though, leading merchants and lawyers kept dissent under control. In each colony, the Sons of Liberty and the merchants adopted strict non-importation agreements. Early in 1768 the Boston patriot leader Samuel Adams drew up a "circular letter" laying out British misdeeds and suggesting united colonial actions. The Massachusetts General Court approved it, and so did several other colonial assemblies. Governor Francis Bernard of Massachusetts did not approve, and dissolved the General Court. In South Carolina, the legislature resolved that

until the colonies were restored to their former freedom by repeal of the Townshend Duties the people of the colony would refuse to import any of the manufactures of Great Britain. South Carolinians would practice the "utmost economy in our persons, houses, and furniture, particularly that we will give no mourning, or gloves, or scarves at funerals."

Colonial leaders fully recognized that they could not expect to enforce non-importation without the fullest possible cooperation of all members of society, notably women. In Virginia "An Address to the Ladies" asked them to forswear imported finery:

> And as one all agree that you'll not married be
> To such as will wear London factory,
> But at first sight refuse, tell them such you do
>   choose
> As encourage our own manufactory.
> No more ribands wear, nor in rich dress appear,
> Love your country much better than fine things,
> Begin without passion, 'twill soon be the fashion
> To grace your smooth locks with a twine string.

Women, as homemakers responsible for clothing and feeding their families, were among the principal consumers of those products, especially luxury items of dress, and beverages like tea, that were not made in the colonies.

One boycott supporter wrote that "the *greatest difficulty* of all we have to encounter . . . is, to persuade our wives to give us their assistance, without which 'tis impossible to succeed." Many women were eager participants in the non-importation movement. One poem claimed that women could do more than men to bring Great Britain to terms. The Sons of Liberty, according to this anonymous poet, were

> Supinely asleep, and depriv'd of their Sight
> Are strip'd of their Freedom, and rob'd of their
>   Right. . . .
>
> Let the Daughters of Liberty, nobly arise,
> And tho' we've no Voice, but a negative here,
> The use of the Taxables, let us forbear.
> Stand firmly resolved and bid Grenville to see
> That rather than Freedom, we'll part with our Tea.

Numerous newspaper writers vehemently urged women to refrain patriotically from purchasing tea, and women of all classes were soon caught up in the political excitement. A New York newspaper reported that even the "peasants and their housewives" had begun "to dispute on politics and positively to determine upon our liberties."

Many women apparently welcomed this appeal to contribute to the defense of colonial interests. One woman declared "Though a female I was born a patriot and can't help it if I would." Certainly non-importation could not have been as successful as it was without women's cooperation. In 1774 for example, John Adams's landlady refused to serve him any tea, even though he requested smuggled tea on which no duties had been paid.

The Townshend Duties and the non-importation movement also encouraged a great deal of pamphleteering advocating a new imperial relationship with more freedom for the colonists—or, rather, with the liberties of Englishmen that they claimed already to possess. The most effective and eloquent of these arguments was John Dickinson's *Letters from a Farmer in Pennsylvania* (1768). Posing as a simple Pennsylvania yeoman, Dickinson cautioned against violence and expressed an affection for "mother Britain" that foreshadowed his later refusal to sign the Declaration of Independence. But on the question of British taxation he was adamant. "Let these words be indelibly impressed on our minds," he concluded

> —that we cannot be free without being secure in
> our property—that we cannot be secure in our
> property if without our consent others may as by
> right take it away—that taxes imposed on us by
> Parliament do thus take it away.

And Dickinson meant all taxation, taxes on imports as well as on internal business.

| Lord North

In the summer of 1768 Governor Bernard called on British authorities for troops to restore order in unruly Boston and prevent a repetition of the *Liberty* incident. In September the new British prime minister, Lord Frederick North, ordered two regiments of redcoats from Ireland to the rebellious Massachusetts capital despite threats of armed resistance by the Sons of Liberty.

Meanwhile, North and his colleagues were having second thoughts about the Townshend Duties. Widely evaded, the taxes brought in virtually no revenue. Particularly galling was the smuggling of untaxed Dutch tea into the colonies. And non-importation agreements had reduced annual exports to America. The British government was in a quandary: repealing the duties would end non-importation, but it would also be the second time the British government had backed down.

In the end, the North ministry yielded to American pressure, but in a grudging and halfhearted way that only highlighted British weakness without calling forth American gratitude. In 1770 Parliament allowed the Quartering Act to expire and rescinded the taxes on glass, paper, and painters' colors; it also reduced the tea tax from twelve to three pence a pound, but did not repeal it.

This partial repeal ended the boycott. It did little to end resentment of Britain—as one American merchant remarked about the repeal: "Doing things by Halves of all others [is] the worst Method." Many fundamental disagreements with Britain persisted. The whole question of the constitutional relationship between mother country and colonies was still unsettled. What body, colonists asked, was the ultimate source of authority in America, the colonial legislatures or Parliament? By now some colonists were advocating an American relationship with Great Britain resembling that of the later British dominions within the British Commonwealth: the King of England would also be King of Massachusetts, New York, Virginia, and so forth, but each American colony would be autonomous in all its domestic affairs. Few, if any, thought of complete independence. Americans remained proud of their British heritage and of the rights of "free-born Britons." Even the most ardent patriots still insisted that they merely wished to preserve these rights from the arrogant usurpers who had gathered around the King.

The Boston Massacre

Quartering British Troops In the months following repeal of the Townshend Duties, resentment toward Britain remained particularly strong in Boston. Aside from the longstanding grievances the Boston townspeople shared with other communities, there was the question of the recently arrived troops. If Massachusetts was not at war, what justified the sending of soldiers to Boston Common?

Before the British regiments arrived in the fall of 1768, the Boston town meeting called upon the people of the city to arm themselves and demanded that the governor call a meeting of the General Court, which he had dissolved in June. When Bernard refused, the patriot leaders called an assembly of the colony's towns as a substitute for the General Court. This "convention" helped to acquaint the citizens of smaller communities with the view of the radical leaders of the capital, and it demonstrated that John Hancock (Harvard '54) Boston's richest merchant, John Adams (Harvard '55) the prominent lawyer, his cousin Samuel Adams (Harvard '40), the failed brewery owner who found his true calling in political activism, and the rest spoke for a large number of the colony's people, not just for the merchants and artisans of the metropolis.

The day the convention adjourned, the British troops dispatched by North arrived in Boston harbor, protected by guns of British men-of-war. While the city's dubious citizens looked on, the soldiers debarked at the Long Wharf and marched up King Street to the music of drums and fifes. It was a moving sight, even for the most dedicated radicals. The men's red tunics, criss-crossed by white straps, and their black three-cornered hats were far more colorful than modern uniforms. Towering over the regular troops were the grenadiers, chosen for their height, a feature emphasized by their tall, mitre-shaped bearskin caps. The grenadier officers wore crimson sashes and carried swords at their sides.

Boston's pleasure at the bright display soon faded, however, and the troops found it no pleasure to be quartered among a hostile populace. While their officers had no difficulty finding good lodgings with wealthy Tories, the city council refused to assign barracks for the troops, and soldiers had to be scattered around the town at whatever empty buildings, generally workshops and warehouses, the British could rent.

"Lobsterbacks" Before long, the patriots' worst fears were realized. The bored troops turned for solace to Boston's cheap rum and loose women. To get money for their dissipations, many engaged in petty theft. Inevitably they got into fights, especially with sailors in the local taverns. When winter came many soldiers deserted, and although the citizens of the Massachusetts countryside had little reason to love the "lobsterbacks," they also re-

Engraving by Paul Revere depicting Friday, September 30th, 1768, when British "Ships of War, armed Schooners, Transports, etc., came up the Harbour and Anchored round the Town; their Cannon loaded." *(Courtesy, The I. N. Phelps Stokes Collection, The New York Public Library)*

fused to help the military authorities return them to duty. The colonists saw the redcoats as an army of occupation and both sides traded insults.

On Friday, March 2, 1770, a civilian rope-maker, William Green, asked a soldier passing by, Patrick Walker of the Twenty-ninth Regiment, whether he wanted work. Such part-time jobs were permitted to off-duty soldiers, and Walker said yes. Green responded: "Then go clean my shithouse." Walker retorted in kind and left, threatening to come back with some friends. Soon afterward he appeared with forty of his mates, led by a tall, black regimental drummer. The soldiers, armed with clubs, sailed into Green and his friends, who defended themselves with sticks. When other civilians joined in, the soldiers retreated.

All that weekend rumors circulated that the soldiers intended revenge. And so they did. On the night of Monday the 5th, bands both of soldiers and of citizens roved the icy streets of Boston looking for trouble. It came

at Private White's sentry post adjacent to the Custom House, when a wigmaker's apprentice baited White until the sentry hit him with the butt of his gun. When the apprentice fled, a British sergeant pursued him, brandishing his musket.

News of the fight spread quickly, and a half-dozen young men descended on the sentry post screaming "Lousy rascal! Lobster son of bitch!" Soon the swelling crowd pelted White with snowballs and jagged chunks of ice, crying "Kill him, kill him, knock him down." Finally Captain Thomas Preston, officer of the day, decided he must save White even at the risk of a serious confrontation. With six grenadiers he marched on the beleaguered sentry post and surrounded White. But with angry civilians pressing on him from every direction, Preston now found that he could not return to the safety of the barracks. He tried to persuade the crowd to disperse, but they responded by daring the soldiers to shoot. At this point someone struck one of the redcoats with a

JOHN TUDOR, *a Boston merchant, described the "Massacre" in his diary:*

On Monday Evening the 5th current, a few Minutes after 9 O'Clock a most horrid murder was committed in King Street before the Customhouse Door by 8 or 9 Soldiers under the Command of Capt Thos Preston drawn of from the Main Guard on the South side of the Townhouse.

This unhappy affair began by Some Boys & young fellows throwing Snow Balls at the sentry placed at the Customhouse Door. On which 8 or 9 Soldiers Came to his assistance. Soon after a Number of people colected, when the Capt commanded the Soldiers to fire, which they did and 3 Men were Kil'd on the Spot & several Mortaly Wounded, one of which died next morning. The Capt soon drew off his Soldiers up to the Main Guard, or the Consequencis mite have been terable, for on the Guns fiering the people were alarm'd & set the Bells a Ringing as if for Fire, which drew Multitudes to the place of action. Lev^t Governor Hutchinson, who was commander in Chefe, was sent for & Came to the Council Chamber, w[h]ere som of the Magistrates attended. The Governor desired the Multitude about 10 O'Clock to sepperat & go home peaceable & he would do all in his power that Justice shold be done &c. The 29 Rigiment being then under Arms on the south side of the Townhouse, but the people insisted that the Soldiers should be ordered to their Barracks 1st before they would sepperat, Which being don the people sepperated about 1 O'Clock.—Capt Preston was taken up by a warrent given to the high Sherif by Justice Dania & Tudor and came under Examination about 2 O'clock & we sent him to Goal [jail] soon after 3, having Evidence sufficient, to committ him, on his ordering the soldiers to fire: So aboute 4 O'clock the Town became quiet. The next forenoon the 8 Soldiers that fired on the inhabitants was allso sent to Goal. Tuesday A.M. the inhabitants mett at Faneuil Hall & after some pertinant speches, chose a Committee of 15 Gentlemⁿ to waite on the Lev^t Governor in Council to request the immediate removeal of the Troops. . . .

(Thursday) Agreeable to a general request of the Inhabitants, were follow'd to the Grave (for they were all Buried in one) in succession the 4 Bodies of Mess^s Saml Gray Saml Maverick James Caldwell & Crispus Attucks, the unhappy Victims who fell in the Bloody Massacre. On this sorrowfull Occasion most of the shops & stores in Town were shut, all the Bells were order'd to toll a solom peal in Boston, Charleston, Cambridge & Roxbery. The several Hearses forming a junction in King Street, the Theatre of that inhuman Tradgedy, proceeded from thence thro' the main street, lengthened by an immence Concourse of people, So numerous as to be obliged to follow in Ranks of 4 & 6 abreast and brought up by a long Train of Carriages. The sorrow Visible in the Countenances, together with the peculiar solemnity, Surpass description, it was suppos'd that the Spectators & those that follow'd the corps amounted to 15000, som supposed 20,000. Note Capt Preston was tried for his Life on the affare of the above Octob^r 24 1770. The Trial lasted 5 Days, but the Jury brought him in not Guilty.

club, knocking him off his feet. The soldier fired, forcing the crowd back. Now another British soldier fired, this time hitting Sam Gray in the head. A third pulled the trigger of his musket and hit Crispus Attucks, a black man, in the chest. By the time the shooting stopped, three Bostonians lay dead and two others were mortally wounded.

The whole city might have erupted in a bloody rebellion, but Lieutenant Governor Hutchinson intervened, and by promising a quick investigation and punishment of the guilty parties prevented a blow-up. Preston and his men were arrested and confined to jail pending trial. Patriot silversmith Paul Revere quickly made an engraving of the "Bloody Massacre." Phillis Wheatley, a seventeen-year-old slave girl who had published her first poem at age thirteen, wrote that "AMERICANS were burden'd sore/When streets were crimson'd with their guiltless gore!" Patriotic propaganda notwithstanding, the trial itself was conducted with propriety and fairness. Captain Preston hired as coun-

Phillis Wheatley. *(Courtesy, Library of Congress)*

avoid any suspicion that the Massachusetts courts would not give the accused a fair trial.

In the end, Preston and his men were acquitted. Adams demolished the charge that Preston had given the order to fire. He and Quincy appealed for fairness. "The eyes of all are upon you," Quincy told the jurors. It is "of high importance to your country, that nothing should appear on this trial to impeach our justice or stain our humanity." The two defense lawyers called witnesses who demonstrated that the soldiers had been taunted and abused beyond bearing. Some soldiers were convicted of manslaughter but punishments were light. Massachusetts justice had been vindicated.

The trial eased angers in Boston and the colonies as a whole. It was followed by a period of relative calm in relations between Britain and the colonies. During these months the non-importation agreements totally collapsed, despite the attempts of more radical patriots to continue them until tea too was exempted from duty. At Samuel Adams's suggestion the Boston town meeting organized a "committee of correspondence" to keep other towns informed of British and loyalist actions. "Let every town assemble" said Adams. "Let associations and combinations be everywhere set up, to consult and recover our just rights." The idea spread quickly to other colonies. Adams exulted, "where there is a spark of patriotic fire, we will enkindle it." Actually, little had happened to settle fundamental differences, but for a time both Americans and Englishmen chose to believe that reason had prevailed.

sel two prominent Boston patriots, John Adams and Josiah Quincy, who took the case out of a combined concern for the colony's and their own good names. Patriots wished to

The *Gaspée* Affair

Then in June 1772 came the *Gaspée* affair. Rhode Island, one of the two colonies whose charter did not require a Crown-appointed governor (Connecticut was the other), had long been notorious for ignoring imperial trade laws. For years, Rhode Island's many coves and inlets had sheltered smugglers who defied the customs authorities with impunity. To stop the traffic, the British authorities finally dispatched the ship *Gaspée* to Narragansett Bay. Tricky tides ran the ship onto a sandbar near Providence. That night a band of Rhode Island Sons of Liberty boarded the stranded *Gaspée,* overwhelmed

its captain and crew, and burned the vessel to the waterline.

The British were outraged. Civilians had attacked one of the King's naval vessels in performance of its lawful duties. British authorities immediately appointed a commission of inquiry, with power to send suspects to England for trial. Despite a £500 reward, the commission—stymied by the refusal of witnesses to testify against the culprits, many of them substantial citizens of the colony— adjourned without fulfilling its mission.

The *Gaspée* affair had important consequences. British officials concluded that the

" 'The Bloody Massacre perpetrated in King Street, Boston on March 5th, 1770, by a party of the 29th Reg [iment].' Engrav'd, Printed and Sold by Paul Revere, Boston."

patriots would stop at nothing, and resolved to take a harder line. The patriots themselves were angered by the authorities' intention to drag men off to England to stand trial for crimes committed in America. It violated one of the elementary "rights of Englishmen,"

and they determined to prevent it from taking place. British officialdom announced, moreover, that the salaries of both the governor and the judges of Massachusetts were now to be paid by the Crown.

The Boston Tea Party

The East India Company Another brief period of calm followed the *Gaspée* affair. Then came swift events that ripped apart the old empire. The shock came from an unexpected source. In 1773 the East India Company was on the verge of financial collapse. Since the seventeenth century the company had exploited India as its private corporate enterprise. Many company officials had become rich through bribery and special privileges, but the company itself had suffered. One of its few remaining assets, 17 million pounds of tea held in its London warehouses, remained unsold because of the American boycott, and also because heavy taxes made it too expen-

sive in Britain itself. Why not, Lord North asked, drastically reduce the English tax? With only three pence per pound to be paid on arrival in America, the tea would become so cheap that it would undersell smuggled Dutch tea. The tea would sell widely and the East India Company would be saved from ruin and the government would at last raise some much-needed revenue from the troublesome mainland colonies. This plan received legislative form in the Tea Act of 1773.

What North did not foresee was that Americans would perceive this scheme as an insulting bribe and a tax—even a three-penny one—they were opposed in principle to pay-

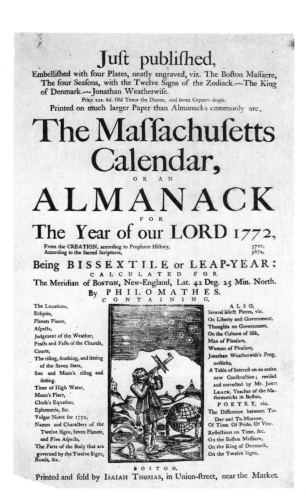

The Massachusetts Calendar or an Almanack of
1772 included "reflections" on worldly affairs—
the Boston Massacre—as well as other-worldly
concerns such as the signs of the Zodiac.
(Courtesy, American Antiquarian Society)

ing. To make matters worse, he consigned
the East India Company tea exclusively to
colonial merchants who favored British policies and obeyed the trade laws.

A wiser statesman would have seen the
consequences of the Tea Act. But North,
though witty and energetic, was a hardliner
on America who had supported the Stamp
Act and opposed its repeal, and had endorsed
the Townshend Duties. Such a man could
not have anticipated what would now take
place.

News of the new British affront enraged
the radicals. In New York City, most of the
merchants resolved that the tea would not be
sold. The patriot citizens of Philadelphia met

and adopted resolutions declaring that since
"the duty imposed by Parliament upon tea
landed in America is a tax on the Americans,
or levying contributions on them without
their consent, it is the duty of every American
to oppose this attempt." Along the Delaware
River, a "Committee of Tarring and Feathering" threatened captains of vessels carrying
tea that their cargo would bring them "into
hot water." In Charleston, patriot pressure
also frightened off tea importers. But, as
usual, Boston responded more violently than
any other town.

Governor Hutchinson warned the British
authorities soon after the Tea Act passed that
"at and near Boston the people seem regardless of all consequences. To enforce the Act
appears beyond all comparison more difficult
than I ever before imagined." If Hutchinson
had allowed this perception to guide him, disaster might have been avoided. But, though
he was American born, as governor of a British colony he felt bound to enforce the law,
and when three tea-carrying cargo ships arrived in Boston harbor he determined that
they must unload, come what may.

▌The Tea Party   On the evening of December 16, 1773, a gathering of
perhaps 8000 men—most of the able-bodied
males in this town of about 17,000—assembled at Old South Church. They were there
to hold a town meeting, to ask that the hated
tea not be landed. Their request was not
granted, and at the end of the meeting Sam
Adams rose from his seat and said "This
meeting can do nothing to save the country."
As if by prearranged signal, as soon as the
meeting adjourned, a band of men disguised
as Mohawk Indians rushed down Milk Street
to Griffin's Wharf. Three companies of these
instant Indians rowed out to the anchored tea
ships, boarded them, split open the tea
chests, and dumped their massive contents
into the waters of the harbor. Their mission
accomplished, the men quickly and quietly
dispersed.

George Hewes, one of the "Indians" involved in the tea party, recalled later that he
took

a small hatchet, which I and my associates denominated the tomahawk, with which, and a club, after
having painted my face and hands with coal dust in
the shop of a blacksmith, I repaired to Griffin's
wharf, where the three ships lay that contained the
tea.

Hewes wrote later that

> There appeared to be an understanding that each individual should volunteer his services, keep his own secret, and risk the consequences for himself. No disorder took place during that transaction, and it was observed at that time that the stillest night ensued that Boston had enjoyed for many months.

The British saw the Boston Tea party as an outrage and they determined not to let it go unpunished. In Parliament William Pitt and the eloquent Irish member Edmund Burke warned that punitive measures would lead to revolt. Burke urged the government to let Americans tax themselves, and not worry about whether they were legally required to obey Parliament. But the Burkes and the Pitts were a minority. Other politically influential Englishmen believed, as one expressed it, "that the town of Boston ought to be knocked about their ears and destroyed."

Determined to prevent the Americans from ending all parliamentary control, North introduced the Boston Port Bill. Until Massachusetts had paid for the tea destroyed, a naval force would close Boston Harbor to shipping. Troops withdrawn from the town to Castle William following the Boston Massacre would reenter the city.

Fury in Boston itself was predictable. The town meeting sent a circular letter to the other colonies, declaring that

> This attack, though made immediately upon us, is doubtless designed for every other colony who will not surrender their sacred rights and liberties into the hands of an infamous ministry. Now therefore is the time when all should be united in opposition to this violation of all the liberties of all.

Indignation swept the colonies.
The Reverend Joseph Fish of Stonington, Connecticut, wrote to his daughter:

> I don't remember any time, since I lived, so alarming as these, on account of the tyrannical measures which the ministry at home have taken & are designing to take against the colonies. They seem (by accounts sent over) determined to distress us to the last degree, if not to destroy us, unless we submit to the yoke of slavery they have prepared for us.

In November 1774 Fish's daughter, Mary Noyes, wrote to her parents that "There has not one drop of Tea been drink'd by any one of our family but only two afternoons when I had very particular company."

Messages of sympathy for Boston's plight poured in from every colony. In Virginia, George Washington urged his fellow patriots to support the Bostonians. We must not "suffer ourselves to be sacrificed by piece meals," he wrote. The Virginia House of Burgesses convened in the Raleigh Tavern in Williamsburg after the Tory governor refused to let it sit at the capitol, and there it called for a continental congress to meet to consider united action. Similar calls came from New York, Providence, and Philadelphia. Everywhere Americans recognized that a final crisis had been reached, and in North Carolina patriot groups began to arm and drill in preparation for combat.

The closing of the port of Boston was the first in a series of parliamentary measures of 1774, known collectively as the Coercive or Intolerable Acts. The Administration of Justice Act declared that if any royal official were sued for carrying out his official duties, he could have his trial transferred out of unfriendly Massachusetts to Britain, where he would face a more favorable jury. The Massachusetts Government Act struck a severe blow at self-government by taking away from the provincial legislature many of its powers of appointment and giving them to the royal governor. Henceforth the governor, not the assembly, could appoint the council, and juries were to be summoned by sheriffs rather than elected by the town meetings, which could be called only by the governor. A new Quartering Act housed British troops in private homes instead of barracks.

Another measure passed in 1774, the Quebec Act, was not intended as punishment, but so offended the colonists that it is often included among the Intolerable Acts. This law established a permanent government for the conquered province of Canada that provided few of the rights the English colonists enjoyed. It also extended toleration to the predominant religion of Quebec's inhabitants, Roman Catholicism. And the law extended the boundaries of Quebec south to the Ohio River into a region claimed by Virginia, Connecticut, and Massachusetts.

The First Continental Congress

In Carpenter's Hall, in Philadelphia, early in September 1774, the first Continental Congress assembled in response to what many colonists perceived as Parliament's oppression.

BOSTONIAN JOHN ANDREWS *described the tea controversy in a series of letters to his brother:*

November 29th [1773]. Hall and Bruce arriv'd Saturday evening with each an hundred and odd chests of the detested Tea. What will be done with it, can't say: but I tremble for ye consequences should ye consignees still persist in their obstinacy and not consent to reship it. They have softened down so far as to offer it to the care of Council or the town, till such times as they hear from their friends in England, but am perswaded, from the present dispositions of ye people, that no other alternative will do, than to have it immediately sent back to London again. . . . Y^e bells are ringing for a general muster, and a third vessel is now arriv'd in Nantasket road. Handbills are stuck up, calling upon Friends! Citizens! and Countrymen!

December 1st. Having just return'd from Fire Club, and am now, in company with the two Miss Masons and Mr. Williams of your place, at Sam. Eliot's, who has been dining with him at Col^o Hancock's, and acquaints me that Mr. Palfrey sets off Express for New York and Philadelphia at five o'clock tomorrow morning, to communicate ye transactions of this town respecting the tea. . . . The consignees have all taken their residence at the Castle, as they still persist in their refusal to take the tea back. Its not only ye town, but the country are unanimous against the landing it, and at the Monday and Tuesday Meetings, they attended to the number of some hundreds from all the neighboring towns within a dozen miles. . . .

December 18th. However precarious our situation may be, yet *such* is the present calm composure of the people that a stranger would hardly think that ten thousand pounds sterling of the East Indian Company's *tea* was destroy'd the night, or rather evening before last, yet its a serious truth; The affair was transacted with the greatest regularity and despatch. . . . A general muster was assembled, from this and all ye neighbouring towns, to the number of five or six thousand, at 10 o'clock Thursday morning in the Old South Meeting house, where they pass'd a *unanimous* vote that the *Tea* should go out of the *harbour* that afternoon, and sent a committee with Mr. Rotch to ye Custom house to *demand* a clearance, which the collector told 'em was not in his power to give, without the duties being first paid. They then sent Mr. Rotch to Milton, to ask a pass from ye Governor, who sent for answer, that "consistent with the rules of government and his duty to the King he could not grant one without they produc'd a previous clearance from the office."—By the time he return'd with this message the candles were light in [the] house, and upon reading it, such prodigious shouts were made, that induc'd me, while drinking tea at home, to go out and know the cause of it. The house was so crouded I could get no farther than ye porch, when I found the moderator was just declaring the meeting to be *dissolv'd,* which caused another general shout, out doors and in, and three cheers. What with that, and the consequent noise of breaking up the meeting, you'd thought that the inhabitants of the infernal regions had broke loose. For my part, I went contentedly home and finish'd my tea, but was soon inform'd what was going forward: but still not crediting it without ocular demonstration, I went and was *satisfied.* They muster'd, I'm told, upon Fort Hill, to the number of about two hundred, and proceeded, two by two, to Griffin's wharf, where Hall, Bruce, and Coffin lay, each with 114 chests of the *ill fated* article on board; the two former with *only* that article, but ye latter arriv'd at ye wharf only ye day before, was freighted with a large quantity of other goods, which they took the *greatest* care not to injure in the least, and before *nine* o'clock in ye evening, every chest from on board the three vessels was knock'd to pieces and flung over ye sides. They say the actors were *Indians* from *Narragansett.* Whether they were or not, to a transient observer they appear'd as *such,* being cloath'd in Blankets with the heads muffled, and copper color'd countenances, being each arm'd with a hatchet or axe, and pair pistols, nor was their *dialect* different from what I conceive these geniusses to *speak,* as their jargon was unintelligible to all but themselves.

Twelve colonies were represented. The popular royal governor had dissuaded Georgia patriots who were trying to pass a resolution to send a delegation. Of the fifty-six delegates, twenty-two were lawyers, and most of the others were planters or merchants. Almost all had been prominent in the affairs of their individual colonies, and many had belonged to the committees of correspondence.

The delegates did not all agree on the best course. Some held it sufficient to petition the King informing him of wrongs done the colonists and asking that he intervene. The Massachusetts delegates, led by John and Sam Adams, along with Christopher Gadsden of South Carolina, Charles Thomson of Pennsylvania, and Patrick Henry and Richard Henry Lee of Virginia, favored retaliatory measures such as a new non-importation agreement and a blunt refusal to pay for the tea dumped at Boston.

The delegates quickly demonstrated an emerging sense of continental unity and shared nationality. Patrick Henry, in a sample of his famous oratory, sounded the new note. "The distinctions between Virginians, Pennsylvanians, New Yorkers, and New Englanders," he declared, "are no more. I am not a Virginian, but an American." All imperial government, he continued, was at an end. "All Distinctions are thrown down. All America is thrown into one mass." Henry was exaggerating, but the Congress would help to create a new feeling that Americans all shared a common destiny.

It was a radicals' convention. In the midst of the deliberations the delegates received a set of resolutions adopted by a convention recently held in Suffolk County, Massachusetts brought posthaste by Paul Revere. These declared that Americans should not obey any of the Coercive Acts, and declared the Quebec Act "dangerous in an extreme degree to the Protestant religion and to the civil rights and liberties of all America." Citizens should "use their utmost diligence to acquaint themselves with the art of war as soon as possible, and do, for that purpose, appear under arms at least once every week." Until redress was obtained, non-importation of all British goods should be the rule. Over the strong objections of conservatives, the Congress endorsed the "Suffolk Resolves."

When it came to resolutions of their own, the delegates disagreed. On one side were the moderate Joseph Galloway of Pennsylvania and his supporters, who proposed a "Plan of Union" that would establish an overall government for the colonies with a president-general appointed by the King. This official would exercise authority over a grand council selected by the various colonial assemblies. Together the president-general and the grand council would constitute an "inferior branch" of the British Parliament. Radicals in the Congress, correctly perceiving this as a scheme to freeze into law the colonies' political subordination to Britain, defeated it. The radicals' own plan—which was adopted—denounced the Coercive Acts as oppressive and unconstitutional and condemned the various revenue measures Parliament had passed since 1763, the enlargement of the vice-admiralty courts' jurisdiction, the maintaining of a British standing army in America, and the dissolution of colonial assemblies by British authorities. The Congress also adopted a plan known as the Continental Association, a stringent set of regulations virtually cutting off all commercial relations with Britain until American grievances had been redressed. A final resolution called for a second Congress to meet on May 10, 1775, if by that time Britain still refused to yield.

Toward Lexington

The work of the Congress pleased many colonists. Following adjournment the Pennsylvania Assembly gave the delegates a dinner at the City Tavern, where their work was toasted and praised. Patriots throughout the American community congratulated Congress for its efforts. Tories were dismayed and depressed by what had transpired in Philadelphia. Governor William Franklin of New Jersey, Benjamin Franklin's Tory son, noted that the Congress had left Britain "no other alternative than either to consent to what must appear humiliating in the eyes of all Europe, or to compel obedience to her laws by a military force." The Franklins, father and son, became bitter political enemies. A Massachusetts Tory insisted that the men at Philadelphia had made the "breach with the parent state a thousand times more irreparable than it was before." A New York loyalist charged that the Congress had *"erected itself into the supreme legislature of North America."*

In England itself, high officials were thunderstruck. British merchants once more became a voice for conciliation. So did Pitt and Burke.

Lexington and Concord In the fall of 1774 in Boston, events moved toward a showdown. For months the army commander there, General Thomas Gage, had been reinforcing the British garrison so that by the end of 1774 there were eleven battalions of redcoats, some four thousand men, in the city and at Castle William. Patriots armed and drilled. Outside the city, bands of militia ready to "meet at one minute's warning equipped with arms and ammunition," and calling themselves Minute Men patrolled the countryside and made it dangerous for British troops to leave the city

even on official business. Before long, Gage began to feel as though he were under siege and fortified Boston Neck against the time when he might actually be attacked. The Massachusetts provincial congress had ordered the stockpiling of arms and ammunition at nearby Concord. A Bostonian reported seeing "twenty load covered with dung go out of town . . . but lately all carts have been searched by the guards, and unluckily last Saturday evening a load of cartridges were seized pack'd in candle boxes." Within a few months, the colonists secreted some twenty thousand pounds of musket balls and cartridges, plus a considerable number of tents, axes, spades, and supplies of beef, flour, rice, butter, and hogsheads of rum—all hidden in private houses and barns in Concord. The town's men and women helped to manufacture still more supplies: cartridge boxes, belts, and holsters. A fifteen-year-old girl supervised the young women of the town in manufacturing cartridges. As one Concord resident observed, "the people are ready and

First published in 1775:- the First engraved Print published in Connecticut.

Drawn by Earl & engraved by A.Doolittle in 1775   Re-Engraved by A.Doolittle and J.W.Barber in 1832

BATTLE OF LEXINGTON.

1. *Major Pitcairn at the head of the Regular Granadiers.-2. The Party who first fired on the Provincials at Lexington.*
3.*Part of the Provincial Company of Lexington.- 4. Regular Companies on the road to Concord.- 5. The Meeting house*
at Lexington.- 6. The Public Inn.

At the Battle of Lexington, April 19, 1775, British troops quickly overwhelmed the small band of minutemen. *(Courtesy, The I. M. Phelps Stokes Collection, The New York Public Library)*

Following their rout at Lexington, farmers and minutemen surprised the British at the North Bridge in Concord and sent them into retreat to Boston. *(Scribner's Archives)*

determine[d] to defend this Country Inch by Inch." Elsewhere in New England armed patriot militia seized British military supplies and arms. To English officials and American Tories, the patriots' insistence that they were still loyal to the King by now seemed rank hypocrisy. A patriot called the redcoats "debauched Weavers' 'prentices, and fops who would not, and indeed could not, fight." From a people who had fought beside the British in the French and Indian War came boasts that "lobsterbacks" would be no match for hardy American yeomen in a fair fight.

Relations between Boston patriots and British authorities reached the flash point early in 1775. There was a brawl between butchers and redcoats at the public market. Then British troops tried to confiscate military supplies at Salem, but were turned back by Sons of Liberty. As Massachusetts continued to brace for war, in Virginia the eloquent Patrick Henry, speaking before the House of Burgesses, made what would become one of the most famous speeches in American history:

Our chains are forged, their clanking may be heard on the plains of Boston! The war is inevitable,—and let it come! . . . Gentlemen may cry peace, peace—but there is no peace. The war is actually begun! The next gale that sweeps from the north will bring to our ears the clash of resounding arms! Our brethren are already in the field! Why stand we here idle? . . . Is life so dear, or peace so sweet, as to be purchased at the price of chains and slavery? Forbid it, almighty God! I know not what course others may take; but as for me, give me liberty, or give me death!

The anniversary of the Boston Massacre in March became a second occasion for friction when some British officers heckled the patriot leader Joseph Warren as he was delivering a commemorative oration.

At about this time spies for the British informed General Gage that the minutemen were collecting arms and ammunition at Concord, a few miles outside of Boston. In addition, the Massachusetts legislature, in defiance of Gage's orders, was holding meetings at Concord. In mid-April Gage laid a plan to capture the arms and perhaps seize some of the rebellious patriot leaders.

On the evening of April 18, 1775, a force of 700 redcoats set out for Concord. Patriots in Boston quickly learned of the move and dispatched William Dawes and Paul Revere to alert the minutemen and the patriot leaders that the British were coming. Revere was captured and Dawes turned back, but another rider conveyed the news to the patriots at Concord in time. When the British reached nearby Lexington after marching most of the night, they discovered seventy armed minutemen lined up on the town commons shivering in the early morning chill. The British commanding officer, Major John Pitcairn, immediately rode toward them shouting: "Ye villains, ye rebels, disperse! Lay down your arms!" At the same time the British light infantry began to run forward to intercept the Americans, who retreated to a stone wall at the edge of the field. Tradition has it that their commanding officer Captain John Parker, said, "Stand your guard. Don't fire unless fired upon. But if they mean to have a war, let it begin here." No one knows which side fired first, but at the wall the minutemen stopped and fired off a ragged volley, wounding one redcoat and Major Pitcairn's horse. The British replied more effectively, killing eight of the Americans and wounding nine others.

As the British reassembled to move on Concord, the Massachusetts countryside rose in fury. By the time the redcoats had arrived at their destination, a large force of armed and angry farmers had collected to intercept them. As one of the soldiers recalled:

> We marched down . . . about a mild [mile] or mild [and a] half, and we see them acomming, we halted and stayd till they got within about 100 Rods then we was orded to the about face and marched before them with our Drums and fifes agoing. . . . We had grand musick.

The British forces entered the town, and the militia took up a position beyond the town's center. In the meantime, Concord's women did their best to conceal the precious stores of military supplies. A servant girl at the tavern kept British soldiers out of such an arsenal by declaring it was her own room and forbidding them to enter. An elderly widow raised the alarm when a fire set by the British spread to the courthouse. When the Americans began to advance on their enemy, the British tried to withdraw. At this point the minutemen fired, killing three and wounding a dozen of the redcoats.

Now began a long, dismal, and bloody British retreat from Concord all the way back to the safety of Boston. As they plodded back, the British soldiers took a withering barrage from behind hedges, trees, houses, and stone walls. A British lieutenant, seeking to explain the debacle, reported that his men had been attacked "from all sides but mostly from the rear, where people had hid themselves in houses till we had passed, and then fired." At Lexington the original British force picked up reinforcements from Boston. After a short wait to rest the exhausted Concord contingent, the combined force resumed the retreat to Boston. Once again, they came under devastating fire. One of them wrote to England that "even the women had firelocks. One was seen to fire a blunderbuss between her father and husband from their windows. There they three, with an infant child between them, soon suffered the fury of the day." Many were hit. Occasionally detachments broke off from the main body to charge a knot of Americans or to loot the houses along the road.

At one place British troops broke into a deacon's house, and his wife recorded that many of them "entered our house by bursting open the doors, and three of the soldiers broke into the room in which I then was laid on my bed, being scarcely able to walk from my bed to the fire and not having been to my chamber door from my being delivered in childbirth to that time. One of said soldiers immediately opened my [bed] curtains with his bayonet fixed and pointing . . . to my breast. I immediately cried out, 'For the Lord's sake, don't kill me!'

He replied, 'Damn you.'

One that stood near said, 'We will not hurt the woman if she will go out of the house, but we will surely burn it.'

I immediately arose, threw a blanket over me, went out, and crawled into a corn-house near the door with my infant in my arms, where I remained until they were gone. They immediately set the house on fire, in which I had left five children and no other person; but the fire was happily extinguished when the house was in the utmost danger of being utterly consumed."

The British arrived back in Charlestown in the evening and counted their losses. Despite their contempt for amateur soldiers they had to admit that the colonists' fire was often deadly. Of the 700 men sent to Concord, 73 had been killed, 174 wounded, and 26 reported missing. Only by the sheerest good luck had the Americans been prevented from cutting off the whole force and capturing it. The Americans had won a victory against the finest troops of Europe.

Amos Farnsworth, a Concord farmer-turned-soldier, wrote that "Surely God has a favor towards us . . . thanks be unto God that so little hurt was done us when the balls sung like bees round our heads." A piece of doggerel commemorating the battle taunted the British troops:

How brave you went out with muskets all bright,
And thought to befrighten the folks with the sight;
But when you got there how they powder'd your pums,
And all the way home they pepper'd your bums,
And is it not, honies, a comical farce,
To be proud in the face, and be shot in the a-se.

A New York paper remarked that the British troops "were roughly handled by the Yankees, a term of reproach for the New Englanders, when applied by the regulars." It was about this time that the song, "Yankee Doodle," with various lyrics, became popular. Tradition has it that the original was a British tune, sung to make fun of the Americans, who then adopted it as their own.

After April 19, 1775, there was no turning back. From that day until July 2, 1776, the Continental Congress, in its desperate efforts to resolve the crisis, was, as John Adams said, caught "between hawk and buzzard." General Gage warned the British government: "These people are now spirited up by a rage and enthusiasm as great as ever People were possessed of, and you must proceed in earnest or give the Business up." A Philadelphia woman wrote to a British officer:

I have retrenched every superfluous expense in my table and family. . . . Tea I have not drunk since last Christmas, nor bought a new cap or gown since your defeat at Lexington, and what I never did before, have learnt to knit, and am now making stockings of American wool for my servants, and this way do I throw in my mite to the public good. I know this, that as free I can die but once, but as a slave I shall not be worthy of life. . . . All ranks of men among us are in arms. Nothing is heard now in our streets but the trumpet and drum, and the universal cry is "Americans, to arms!"

Yet in the ensuing months thousands of native-born Americans would become Tories, partisans of the King. Loyalism would prove especially strong among certain groups of Americans. Natives like Thomas Hutchinson who had close ties to the British government were natural loyalists. Anglican ministers who recognized the King as head of the Church of England also tended to take the British side, as did many Anglican laymen, especially in New England, where they formed an unpopular minority. Loyalists were not invariably rich with a large property stake in society. Besides loyalist merchants, officials, and planters, there were also loyalist mechanics, farmers, and small shopkeepers. In the western Carolinas, where small farmers known as "regulators" had rebelled against low-country domination in the 1760s and early 1770s, there was some loyalist sentiment. Angry at the seaboard Carolina gentry for denying them representation in the colonial assemblies and for crushing their rebellion by force of arms, some of the western farmers chose the King's side after 1775, if only because the low-country Carolina planters and merchants had chosen the opposite side. There were even slave loyalists. When the royal governor of Virginia appealed to the slaves to help the Crown against its enemies among the planters, many would respond.

Like the loyalists, the patriots came in different shapes and sizes. If many Anglican clergymen chose the King, almost all Congregational and many other dissenting ministers chose Congress. In the major port towns—Boston, Newport, New York, Philadelphia, and Charleston—artisans, apprentices, and laborers were rebels. But so were the merchants, especially those who felt threatened by the trade regulations that had been piled on top of the Navigation Acts since 1763. The landed gentry of New York split. Families such as the Delanceys took the King's side; the Schuylers and the Livingstons, equally wealthy and aristocratic, supported Congress. In Virginia and the Carolinas, the patriot leaders were almost all Anglican gentlemen, many of them, men such as George Washington, Henry Laurens and Thomas Jefferson, were owners of large estates and scores of black slaves.

One reason for the diversity in both loyalist and patriot ranks was the diverse nature of colonial society itself. Since the close of the French and Indian War there had been a wave of immigration, much of it non-English stock. From 1760 to 1775 more than 221,000 newcomers had taken up residence in the mainland colonies. Only about 30,000 of these were English. The rest were Irish, Scots, Germans, and 84,000 were blacks from Africa. Except for the blacks, who were brought mostly to the South as slaves, in the decade and a half before the American Revolution these new settlers poured into all the colonies, taking jobs, acquiring land, joining churches, holding office. Some 20,000 of them settled in New England, increasing that region's population by 59 percent from 1760 to 1780. In New York the population increased by 39 percent from 1760 to 1770, and grew another 29 percent in the next decade. Pennsylvania grew by 40 percent from 1760 to 1776. Just at the time of tension with the mother country, colonial communities were adjusting to the pressures of new growth, and assimilating a sizable number of Americans who lacked the long tradition of reverence for the English Crown and its institutions. It is small wonder that there were clashes.

"Bunker Hill" and the Drift Toward Independence

The response of patriot leaders to the events in Massachusetts was prompt and vigorous. In Massachusetts the Provincial Congress, as the illegal colonial legislature was called, authorized the raising of troops and appealed to the other colonies for aid. Before long, several thousand militia from Rhode Island, Connecticut, and New Hampshire, along with contingents of Indians, were pouring into the colony and assembling in a ring around Boston, where Gage's troops were encamped. The American general in charge was Artemus Ward; his subordinates included the talented Nathanael Greene and Israel Putnam.

In some ways the besiegers of Boston were in worse shape than the besieged. The hastily-assembled colonial troops lived without sufficient tents and amidst filth. They were unused to the standards of hygiene necessary where men lived together in masses, and before long, dysentery and other diseases invaded the American camp. The British in Boston, on the other hand, seemed to be living off the fat of the land, well housed and well supplied with food and necessities. At the end of May 1775, Gage was joined by three other high-ranking British officers, Sir William Howe, Sir Henry Clinton, and John ("Gentleman Johnny") Burgoyne. Howe took over command from Gage, who remained as civilian governor of the colony.

| **Bunker Hill**   Sooner or later, Howe would have had to attack the troops surrounding Boston, but they forced his hand by fortifying Breed's Hill, across the Charles River from Boston and within cannon range of the city. On June 17, 1776, the British navy began to bombard the new fortifications. Confident that the untried amateur soldiers under Colonel William Prescott's command could not stand up against redcoats in a regular battle, Howe and his fellow officers decided to make a direct attack on the entrenched Americans. Troops of grenadiers and light infantry, with packs containing three days' rations, were ferried across the Charles to Charlestown peninsula.

As the British troops landed on the beach, the Americans waited silently. When the redcoats prepared to charge, Prescott gave the order to fire. There was a great crash and a cloud of smoke; scores of Welsh Fusiliers fell. In seconds the light infantry regiment was fleeing in panic, leaving behind its wounded, its dead, and most of its equipment. Meanwhile the tall grenadiers were advancing on Breed's Hill in well-dressed lines. When the redcoats were within twenty yards of the American position a volley rang out, knocking down scores. The grenadiers, unlike the Welsh Fusiliers, continued to advance, their bayonets fixed. The Americans, now almost within spitting range, continued to fire away. Finally the grenadiers too broke ranks and fled.

Howe was not finished. Once more he ordered his men against the American position. Once more they were mowed down and retreated. Again Howe ordered his men to attack, this time without their heavy packs. By now the Americans were low in ammunition. Assuming the battle was over, many had disobeyed their officers and had begun to leave for home. Despite heavy casualties, this time the redcoats drove the Americans off the hill and took possession of the Charlestown peninsula.

The British had won, but at what a price! Over a thousand redcoat casualties, with over

The Battle of Bunker Hill (actually Breed's Hill), June 17, 1775. The British won but suffered a great number of casualties. For the Americans it was a moral victory.

two hundred killed. Almost fifty percent of the British troops engaged were either dead or wounded. As Howe commented: "A dear bought victory, another such would have ruined us."

The battle, misnamed "Bunker Hill," was of vast symbolic importance. To Americans it was a great moral triumph. Combined with Lexington and Concord it had demonstrated that American militia could stand up to the best the British could throw against them. In reality, the Americans, with 15,000 men encamped around Boston, could have done much better with sufficient training. Far too many had been insubordinate; some had been cowards. The Americans' staff work and supply services had been poor. Finally, American success had been due as much to British errors in using a frontal assault as to their own planning. Still, the Americans had reason to be proud and to look to the future with some hope.

Washington Takes Command Meanwhile, the Second Continental Congress had assembled in Philadelphia, as scheduled, in early May. Among its first acts was the choice of commander for the whole Continental army who would take charge of the troops around Boston. Following the advice of John Adams to make a bid for unity by choosing a Southerner, Congress appointed George Washington of Virginia on June 15, just days before Bunker Hill. The tall Virginian, who had appeared in Congress in his militia colonel's uniform, won out over Boston merchant John Hancock, who reportedly hoped for that position. Congress also voted to raise six companies of riflemen from the Middle colonies and the South to join the New Englanders at Boston and decided to issue bills of credit to support the accelerating rebellion.

Despite the outbreak of hostilities, Congress resisted a final political break with Britain. There were some like Sam Adams who favored a bold declaration of American independence. His cousin John, however, urged the delegates to accept the advice of Massachusetts and endorse the formation of new constitutions for each colony to break the tie with England. These independent states, he believed, would ally themselves in a continental league that would be equivalent to an independent nation. But even this oblique road to independence did not please most of the delegates, who still hoped for British conciliation.

Meanwhile, George Washington's appointment filled him with "inexpressible concern." Other Americans exulted in having a leader at last. By the fall of 1775, babies were being named after him, and the poet Philip Freneau saw the tall Virginian as a classical hero:

> See WASHINGTON New Albion's freedom owns,
> And moves to war with half Virginia's sons;
> Bold in the fight, whose actions might have aw'd
> A Roman Hero, or a Grecian God;
> He, he, as first, his gallant troops shall lead. . . .

Phillis Wheatley wrote, "A crown, a mansion, and a throne that shine,/With gold unfading, WASHINGTON! be thine." She sent her poem to General Washington, and he wrote to thank her, adding, "If you should ever come to Cambridge, or near head-quarters, I shall be happy to see a person so favored by the Muses."

Washington arrived in the Boston area after Bunker Hill to find the largely New England army a disappointment. The Yankees, the Virginian complained, were "an exceedingly nasty and dirty people," excessively concerned with money. Other observers found the troops enterprising, though highly individualistic, and unwilling to submit to discipline or even call their officers by official titles. The new commander-in-chief had his work cut out for him in seeking to turn this ragged collection of farmers and mechanics into an army and to combine it smoothly with the regiments of Virginians, Marylanders, and Pennsylvanians who began to arrive at Cambridge.

In these months of 1775, and virtually all through the war, one of the general's chief problems was simply to keep his force intact. Few Americans considered military service a full-time occupation. Farmers were willing to enlist for a few months, especially in the winter or after the crops had been planted. But when needed at home, or when confronted with long stretches of idleness, they grew restless. Some simply deserted. Others waited until their term of enlistment had ended and, regardless of the military situation, went home.

Grant Wood, *Daughters of Revolution*. The artist captured a later proud group of upper-class women who could trace their ancestry to the American Revolution. (*Courtesy, The Edwin and Virginia Irwin Memorial*)

The Second Continental Congress appointed George Washington commander of the Continental army. A few years earlier he had hoped to get a commission as an officer in the British army. *(Courtesy, The Pennsylvania Academy of the Fine Arts)*

❚ Early Fighting Even before Washington arrived to construct a Continental army out of fifteen thousand individualists encamped outside Boston, the war was not marking time elsewhere. In May of 1775 a force of Massachusetts men and Vermonters under Ethan Allen and Benedict Arnold had attacked and captured the small British garrison at Fort Ticonderoga on Lake Champlain. The Americans acquired valuable military supplies, including one hundred cannons. In August the captured British post became the jumping-off point for an attack on Canada led by General Philip Schuyler of New York and the British-born Richard Montgomery. On November 13, 1775, Montgomery captured Montreal. Meanwhile, Arnold, with one thousand vol-

unteers from Washington's force, set out across Maine heading toward Quebec City. He reached the British fortress in November and was joined by Montgomery and his men. The combined little army attacked the city in a howling snowstorm. In the battle Montgomery was killed and Arnold wounded. A hundred Americans were killed and four hundred captured. With his pitiful remnant Arnold continued to besiege the town all through the winter. In the spring he gave up the siege and returned home.

In Virginia the royal governor, the Earl of Dunmore, had gathered the colony's loyalists together at Norfolk, formed them into a small army, and set them to destroying patriot-owned plantations. In November, Dunmore issued a proclamation establishing martial law and calling on all citizens to support the King. He also offered freedom to all slaves who would desert their patriot masters and join his forces. This proved to be a mistake. Dunmore's little army did attract some runaway slaves, but white Virginians feared nothing more than a slave uprising, and Dunmore's proclamation may have pushed many of the undecided into the patriot camp. When Dunmore sallied out of Norfolk with his mixed band of loyalists and blacks, he was defeated. Soon after, he loaded his blacks and loyalists aboard ships and abandoned Norfolk to the Americans. In February 1776 he returned and set fire to the city.

While Americans and Englishmen were sporadically killing one another in the fields and forests of North America, efforts were being made to bring the two sides together. In July 1775 Congress adopted the Olive Branch Petition announcing continued American attachment to the King and asking him to desist from further hostile acts until some scheme of reconciliation had been arranged. It also adopted a "Declaration of the Causes and Necessities of Taking Up Arms." This document did not proclaim independence, but pronounced American determination to refuse submission. Several weeks later, Congress rejected Lord North's proposals of February, by which the British government offered to forgo parliamentary taxes on any colony that would agree to tax itself for defense and to pay its own expenses.

Congress adjourned in August 1775, but reconvened in mid-September with a full representation from all thirteen colonies. In early November, members learned that the King had rejected the Olive Branch Petition and declared the colonies in open rebellion. On December 6 Congress responded to the King's declaration by disavowing American allegiance to Parliament, but acknowledging continued allegiance to George III.

As these proposals and counterproposals flew back and forth across the Atlantic, Americans were moving rapidly toward practical self-government. Congress established a Continental army. It appointed commissioners to deal with the Indian tribes and set up a post office department. In October 1775 it organized a navy. Its most momentous act was to appoint in November a five-man Committee of Secret Correspondence to negotiate with potential allies abroad. In December the Committee made contact with a French agent, who informed it that France would aid the colonists against the British. Soon after, the French Foreign Minister, Comte de Ver-

gennes, consulted his Spanish counterpart regarding joint action to aid the Americans. When the Spanish gave their approval, Vergennes ordered a large amount of munitions to be sent to the Americans through a "front" company, Hortalez et Companie. In April 1776 Congress responded to these French moves by opening American ports to the commerce of all nations except Britain.

About that time twelve-year-old Jemmy Noyes of Connecticut, visiting New York City, wrote to his grandmother:

> I see four large ships there; one a seventy gun ship; and I saw the King's statue, and he sat on a great horse, both covered over with leaf gold; and the King had one bullet hole through his cheek, and another through his neck, and they talk of running his Majesty up into bullets for he and his horse are made of lead.

Common Sense and The Declaration of Independence

A final wrench to the remaining ties of empire came with the publication of *Common Sense*, a hundred-page pamphlet composed by a recently arrived Englishman, Thomas Paine. Written with extraordinary passion and eloquence, *Common Sense* denounced the institution of hereditary kingship. "For all men being originally equals, no *one* by *birth* could have a right to set up his own family in perpetual preference to all others forever," Paine declared. George was a "royal brute," not the generous father of his people, and Americans had no reason to continue to obey him or remain his subjects. George III was not a royal brute, but *Common Sense* was an important document in the modern rejection of the whole system of hereditary rule.

The pamphlet had an electrifying effect. Perhaps a million Americans read it as it passed from hand to hand, and were profoundly affected by its message. Washington noted that it was "working a powerful change in the minds of men." After reading it, he himself ceased to toast the King, as he had done till now through thick and thin.

The Declaration of Independence On April 12, 1776, the North Carolina Convention authorized the colony's delegates in Congress to vote for independence. The Virginia legislature followed soon after. On June 7

Richard Henry Lee, responding to the House of Burgesses, offered a motion in Congress that "these United Colonies are, and of a right ought to be, free and independent states, and that all political connection between them and the state of Britain is, and ought to be, totally dissolved." Despite John Adams's earlier remark that "Every post and every Day rolls in upon Us, Independence like a Torrent," the delegates were not unanimous in support of such a bold move.

Congress responded by appointing to frame a statement of independence a five-man committee consisting of Thomas Jefferson, John Adams, Benjamin Franklin, Roger Sherman, and Robert Livingston. The group chose Jefferson to write a first draft. At thirty-three the tall Virginian was one of the youngest members of Congress. But he was also a man of great charm and eloquence, with a reputation as a scholar.

Jefferson's Declaration of Independence is one of the most eloquent and moving endorsements of human freedom and equality ever composed. With simplicity and directness the document captures the essence of the ideas that numbers of European political philosophers had articulated, among them the seventeenth-century English Whigs who had overthrown James II and helped establish England's constitutional monarchy. The document announces that "all men are created equal" and "endowed by their Creator with certain unalienable Rights," more especially "to Life, Liberty and the pursuit of Happiness." Governments exist only to "secure these rights." When a government becomes "destructive of these ends," it is "the Right of the People to alter or abolish it" and establish a new one that will respect them.

Americans today do not have to be reminded that the framers of the Declaration of Independence did not intend the reference to "the People" to imply that all inhabitants of a country should be active participants in the political life of the nation. The Congress was accustomed to institutions that defined a portion of the population as expressing the will of the whole. Masters were seen as speaking for servants; husbands for their wives. A few months prior to the signing of the Declaration, Abigail Adams had written to her husband, John Adams, that she longed "to hear that you have declared an independency." And, she added, for the new code of laws "which I suppose it will be necessary for you to make I desire you would Remember the Ladies, and be more generous and favourable to them than your ancestors."

Abigail Adams was not claiming citizenship or equal political rights for women. She sought only that the lawmakers "not put such unlimited power into the hands of the Husbands." For, she reminded her husband, "all Men would be tyrants if they could." John Adams' wife marvelously adapted the revolutionary vocabulary of her day to women's situation as she understood it. She accepted women's domestic role, but sought to introduce greater freedom for women into the domestic sphere. Should men fail to reduce their own domestic tyranny, she warned, the ladies would surely foment their own "Rebellion." And any notion of the Declaration as a democratic and egalitarian document will have to take account of the existence of slavery, about which the members in their deliberations showed a flicker of conscience, but little more.

The rest of the Declaration was a detailed indictment of King George III, not the real culprit, Parliament. Here Jefferson marshaled virtually every American grievance, both immediate and of long standing, against Britain and defended the actions of the colonists during the years since 1763. All pointed toward one inescapable end: "these United Colonies are, and of Right ought to be, Free and Independent States." "With firm reliance on the Protection of Divine Provi-

Detail from the Declaration of Independence, celebrated by the American artist John Trumbull. *(Courtesy, Yale University Art Gallery)*

dence," the Declaration concluded, "we mutually pledge to each other our Lives, our Fortunes and our sacred Honor."

That the list of accusations largely exaggerates the actions of the British is to be expected of a document intended to justify a revolution. More puzzling at first glance is that the Declaration makes out the King to be the villain. George III, to be sure, had been among the most eager advocates of a policy of forcing the colonists into submission, but it was Parliament that had been the effective agent of repression. The attack on the King, foreshadowed in Paine's *Common Sense*, signifies that by now the leaders of the rebellion were looking beyond the details of the colonial quarrel with Britain and seeking to justify the Revolution as a struggle against monarchy.

Adams, Franklin, and the rest of the committee suggested a number of changes, primarily stylistic. Congress as a body, when it received the draft, struck out several phrases and clauses, including an attack on the slave

COMMON SENSE *by Tom Paine*
Paine's rousing pamphlet circulated by the tens of thousands and galvanized sentiment against England in the spring of 1776.

The sun never shined on a cause of greater worth. 'Tis not the affair of a city, a county, a province, or a kingdom; but of a continent—of at least one-eighth part of the habitable globe. 'Tis not the concern of a day, a year, or an age; posterity are virtually involved in the contest, and will be more or less affected even to the end of time by the proceedings now. Now is the seedtime of continental union, faith, and honor. The least fracture now will be like a name engraved with the point of a pin on the tender rind of a young oak; the wound would enlarge with the tree, and posterity read it in full grown characters. . . .

Small islands not capable of protecting themselves are the proper objects for government to take under their care; but there is something absurd in supposing a continent to be perpetually governed by an island. In no instance hath nature made the satellite larger than its primary planet; and as England and America, with respect to each other, reverse the common order of nature, it is evident that they belong to different systems. England to Europe: America to itself. . . .

O ye that love mankind! Ye that dare oppose not only the tyranny but the tyrant, stand forth! Every spot of the old world is overrun with oppression. Freedom hath been hunted round the globe. Asia and Africa have long expelled her. Europe regards her like a stranger, and England hath given her warning to depart. O receive the fugitive, and prepare in time an asylum for mankind.

---

trade. On July 2 the Congress voted to accept it, and John Adams wrote to Abigail that on that date would be

celebrated by succeeding generations as the great anniversary festival. . . . It ought to be solemnized with pomp and parade, with shows, games, sports, guns, bells, bonfires and illuminations, from one end of the continent to the other, from this time forward forevermore.

In the next few days the Declaration was read to large gatherings of Americans throughout the self-proclaimed independent country. In Philadelphia John Nixon, head of the city guard, read the document to a large audience in the State House yard. When he finished, the crowd cheered. In New York, the officers of the Continental army, after hearing the Declaration read, all "went to a Publick House to testify to . . . their joy at the happy news of independence." The next day the statue of George III in New York City was "pulled down by the populace," and its 4000 pounds of lead were melted down for musket balls. Bostonians celebrated by removing the plaque bearing the King's coat of arms from the State House wall and burning it.

The United States dates its independence as a nation from July 4, 1776. On that day the Congress adopted the Declaration. On Au-

Windsor chair, reputed to be the sort used by Thomas Jefferson while he wrote the Declaration of Independence, probably made in New England, mid-eighteenth century. *(Courtesy, Index of American Design)*

gust 2 the official copy (the original, one observer remembered, was "scored and scratched like a schoolboy's exercise") was ready for signing. Then (and not on July 4) the 55 delegates signed it. Now there could be no turning back. Victory would mean that the efforts at Philadelphia had not been in vain. Defeat might mean the surrender of lives, fortunes, and sacred honor. The die was cast.

Points To Think About

1.   The Stamp Act crisis was in several senses, as Edmund S. Morgan points out, the "prologue to the Revolution." What made it particularly so was that, as in later conflicts, the disgruntled colonists along with their opponents were stating the clash as a matter of absolute principle. It was a foretaste of the peculiarly intellectual flavor of the American Revolution.

The colonists objected not simply to the particular exercise of power (which, however ill-advised, was anything but tyrannical), but to what it boded for the future. Americans of the revolutionary generation had a positive genius for searching out the farthermost implications of every British action. Hence they devoted their most vigorous condemnations not to the Stamp Act but to the principles it embodied. The British were equally sensitive to questions of principle. For them, too, the Stamp Act quickly ceased to be a mere means of raising revenue and became instead a test of parliamentary authority. Each party, believing that the other was aiming at the total overthrow of legitimate law and justice, assumed that it had to defend itself by the assertion of its absolute and inviolate rights.

Why did two peoples—both reputed to be intensely practical and uninterested in theoretical issues—see every disagreement over colonial policy as involving critical questions of principle? The answer, in large measure, rests in each side's reading of the other's intentions. The colonists saw the Stamp Act as only the first step in an elaborate plot to deprive them of their rights and reduce them to a state of slavery. The British government saw American resistance to the act as signifying disregard for its authority.

Both sets of suspicions were initially mistaken. Parliament did not wish to enslave America. It wished merely to oblige the colonists to pay a larger share of the expenses of running the empire. The colonists did not wish to be independent. They wished simply not to be taxed internally without their consent. But the intense suspiciousness both sides displayed meant that their expectations, however wrong initially, quickly became self-fulfilling prophecies. Colonial intransigence provoked ever sterner measures from Parliament. Meanwhile, the colonists advanced ever greater claims to home rule, culminating in the Declaration of Independence.

2.   The American colonists after 1763 were, on the one hand, deeply suspicious of every parliamentary act and, on the other, avowed admirers of the British constitution as the finest form of government ever wrought by the hand of man. Both the suspicion and the admiration were sincere. For Americans believed that the British constitution was being systematically undermined. The term they used was "corruption" and they meant by it more than simple venality.

The genius of the British constitution, all agreed, lay in its exquisite balance. Under it the King ruled, but ruled in Parliament. Both houses had to consent to all decrees. The House of Lords was composed of the hereditary nobility. Its role was to temper the popular enthusiasms of the Commons on the one side, and the tendencies of the Crown on the other to be tyrannical. The Commons represented the "people," an undifferentiated term applied to all who were not of noble birth. It represented the ruled; yet as the Commons grew more important throughout the century, supplying the Crown with ministers to oversee the management of the realm, it began to take on more and more executive functions. Americans, in their own Constitution, would reinstitute the distinction between the legislature and the executive that had marked seventeenth-century British practice, a distinction that they believed had guarded against corruption.

Corruption, so concluded the critics, arose in part out of this gradual merger of executive and legislative functions. The king's ability to appoint to high office members of Parliament or their relatives enabled him to forge a working majority in the House of Commons. This, to American colonists, was a clear perversion of the British constitution. Moreover, this political corruption seemed, in colonial eyes, to mirror the larger social corruption of Georgian England. Colonists thought it a land given to luxury and pleasure, and London appeared to be a capital of vice. Americans contrasted the simplicity of their own society with the imperial pomp they found in England. This distrust of elaborate ceremonials, luxurious dress, and highly polished manners persisted well past the revolutionary era in the cult of republican simplicity.

3. In the eighteenth century the popularly elected lower houses of the legislatures in the royal colonies protested against whatever they found to be heavy-handed in imperial policy or in the conduct of governors. In time the lower houses came to argue that since colonists were entitled to "the rights of Englishmen," they were entitled to representation in any body that governed them. The full implication of this argument, which it took a generation or more to realize, was that, since colonists were not properly represented in Parliament, only the lower colonial houses could legitimately pass laws for British America.

Some British defenders of the existing arrangement argued that the colonists were already "virtually" represented in Parliament and needed no other voice in the imperial government. A member of Parliament, so the concept of virtual representation argued, spoke not only for his own constituency but for other constituencies with similar interests. This reasoning would hold that a member of Parliament from a seaport town in England also represented Boston or New Yorkers. It made a certain sense to the English because the franchise in Britain was severely limited. But virtual representation made no sense on the other side of the Atlantic.

Suggested Readings

Recent works on the revolutionary era include Bernard Bailyn's *Voyagers to the West: A Passage in the Peopling of America on the Eve of the American Revolution* (1986), Peter Shaw, *American Patriots and the Rituals of Revolution* (1981), and Richard Beeman's *Patrick Henry* (1982).

Bernard Bailyn's *The Ideological Origins of the American Revolution* (1967) and Morton White's *The Philosophy of the American Revolution* (1978) are readable intellectual histories of the Revolutionary era. Kenneth Silverman, *The Cultural History of the American Rvolution* (1976) is a detailed analysis of relationships between politics and the arts. Changes in social history during the period are treated in J. H. Huston and S. F. Kurtz, *Essays on the American Revolution* (1973), while Gary Nash studies the importance of cities in *The Urban Crucible: Social Change, Political Consciousness, and the Origins of the American Revolution* (1979).

Pauline Maier traces the rise of popular hostility to England in *From Resistance to Revolution* (1972). See also Edmund and Helen Morgan, *The Stamp Act Crisis* (1953); Benjamin Labaree, *The Boston Tea Party* (1964), Hiller Zobel, *The Boston Massacre* (1970), and David Ammerman's *In Common Cause: The American Response to the Coercive Acts of 1774* (1974). Esmond Wright provides a British view in *Fabric of Freedom, 1763–1800* (1961). Lexington and Concord are beautifully studied in Thomas Fleming's *The First Strike* (1978). See also Robert Gross, *The Minutemen and Their World* (1976), Benjamin Quarles, *The Negro in the American Revolution* (1961). Ira Gruber, *The Howe Brothers and the American Revolution* (1972), and Charles Royster, *A Revolutionary People at War* (1979).

☆ ☆ DEBATE ☆ ☆ ☆

FORREST McDONALD

Revolutions, we customarily think, are born amidst the poor and oppressed. The crowds call for bread and for release of political prisoners whose bodies are broken with torture. In the American Revolution the colonists were indeed reacting in anger. The King, wrote Thomas Jefferson in the Declaration of Independence, had "sent hither swarms of officers to harass our people, and eat out their substance. . . . He has plundered our seas, ravaged our coasts, burnt our towns, and destroyed the lives of our people." But the anger in America was not about torture or the extremes of poverty.

We also expect revolutions to make for violent change—the destruction of a ruling class, the overthrow of political institutions, and even the coming of a revolutionary style of dress and behavior. The French Revolution popularized short hair, mustaches, and modern trousers, and revolutionists addressed one another as "Citizen," as Russian Communists would later call one another "Comrade."

By such measures as these, the American Revolution was no revolution at all. Rather, it was an attempt by all classes of Americans to conserve what they already had. The leaders of the American Revolution did not come from some oppressed lower class and certainly did not speak for any such class. They were people of wealth and more particularly wealth in land. Though it was far easier in the colonies than in any part of Europe to move upward in property and social position, the gates to wealth and power had been steadily closing for a generation by the time of the Revolution. Everywhere in the colonies a relative handful of large landholding or merchant families dominated society as well as government. Intent on preserving their privileges against British attempts to rule the colonies more closely, these families might talk loudly in favor of the rights of the people, but they were not eager to share their power with the lower orders.

Yet the small farmers, the frontiersmen, and the craftsmen who supported the Revolution did not resent the leadership of these powerful families, or at any rate not enough to turn against them. Here a family of the common people could obtain a slice of land; or if that family lived in one of the young American cities, its members could do well in a craft or trade or perhaps rise into the prosperous mercantile class. As conservatives, well satisfied with their basic condition, common people joined with the wealthy in resisting the efforts of the British to impose change on the colonies.

Britain, the colonists believed, had once been a virtuous agricultural nation, with a balanced government, honest labor on the land and craftsmanship in the cities, and direct honest trade among individuals—it had been, in effect, a society much like their own. But Britain, so they decided, had now sunk into corruption, enslaved to money that brought monopolies, standing armies, and vicious government hungry for tax revenues. Britain had actually given birth to a modern, dynamic, expanding economy that would greatly improve the well-being of its inhabitants. This the Americans were perhaps too hidebound to see. They learned to believe only the worst, and to fear that sooner or later the British would attempt to impose their sinister system upon the colonies. As the imperial crisis deepened in the 1760s and 1770s, that fear grew into a widespread conviction that just such a thing was happening, and then into something approaching a delusion. Finally, the Americans saw no way of preserving their own agricultural and mercantile paradise except to declare their independence. In this sense the American Revolution was a conservative crusade against the forces of modernism.

The American Revolution, then, was culturally, politically, socially, and economically a conservative movement. But there were ironies in the colonists' successful defense of their established ways. Their victory brought great change. The new states found themselves unable to deal with their problems, and soon they had to create a central government with far greater powers than any that Parliament had dared to exercise.

What Kind of Revolution?

EUGENE GENOVESE

Was the American Revolution a conservative movement that somehow produced unintended radical results? No, it was truly radical. Where in the world have conservatives reacted with anything short of hostility to slogans like "All men are created equal"—the slogans under which Americans took up arms? Who else except European radicals welcomed the direct participation of the common people in rebellion, or in any major political action? Where else before the French Revolution did a national movement bring about a republic, surely the most radical political experiment since Cromwell's Puritan government in England over a century earlier?

While many leaders of the American Revolution were indeed wealthy and even aristocratic, the Revolution meant the triumph not of an aristocracy but of people who owned only small amounts of property. Professor McDonald speaks of the satisfaction the colonists took in their prosperous circumstances, and he is right. They had reason to be satisfied. The natural richness of the continent had made possible a wide distribution of property. Americans rose in anger against British taxes imposed on their property without their consent and against restraints on the trade that their property provided. And it was precisely in being a victory of independent owners of small property that the Revolution was radical rather than conservative. It represented the furthest point of social transformation that the European world had so far achieved. The old order in Europe was a society of great families, and of peasants who worked but did not own the land. Only in European cities did there exist a class of self-reliant property owners somewhat like Americans. And as the French Revolution would make clear, that class threatened the aristocracy.

The fledgling American republic threw down the gauntlet to monarchical and aristocratic Europe. In breaking with the theory and practice of established hierarchy, it challenged not merely the ruling classes of Europe but all old ideas of rank and privilege. Creating a large republic shorn of King or nobles constituted a radical act of the first order. European political theory at the time assumed that only an Athenian city state or a small territory like that of the Netherlands could exist without a hereditary monarch. It is no wonder that conservatives feared and hated the new American nation.

To invent more democratic institutions is to engage in a radical act. The equality that the Declaration of Independence enshrined was not total nor was it intended to be. The reservations, however, did not amount to limits on the notion of equality. The founders of our nation said what they meant and meant what they said: in fundamental human and political respects all men are created equal. The politics of the new nation excluded women, children, servants, blacks in general, and slaves in particular, but this was understood not to qualify the principle of equality among men but to qualify the definition of "men." Only free adult males, according to the beliefs that then prevailed, were full and equal members of the political process. And while the victors in the Revolution did have hopes that slavery might one day disappear, they did not desire much more in the way of further change. But the language of the Declaration and the ideal of equality had a power to press far beyond all that, and in the course of the nation's history to awaken demands for a real social and political equality that would include all races, women as well as men, the poor along with the prosperous.

The economy of small independent property-owning that triumphed in the Revolution, moreover, contained the conditions for its own eventual destruction. That economy made possible the accumulation of wealth by mercantile and industrial capitalists. And capitalism, for all its beliefs in the rights of property, does not make for a society of individual property holders. To the contrary, it turns the population into wage earners who receive their subsistence from the hands of employers. And in the years to come, economic inequality, like the inequalities of race and sex, would collide politically with the egalitarian morality that the Revolution had fixed in the nation's conscience.

A stereotyped nineteenth-century representation of *The Death of Jane McCrea,* by John Vanderlyn. McCrea's murder in 1777 by Indian allies of the British aroused the entire region against Burgoyne and his troops. *(Courtesy, The Wadsworth Atheneum purchased from a subscription in 1855.)*

CHAPTER 5

Revolution and Independence 1776–1787

VICTORY AT SARATOGA

Of all the generals sent by Great Britain to subdue the American rebels, the one the colonials most enjoyed hating was "Gentleman Johnny" Burgoyne. To a generation bred on tales of English decadence, corruption, and arrogance, he was the ideal enemy to defeat in the critical battle of the Revolutionary War— the Battle of Saratoga, New York in 1777. "Sir Jack Brag" (as one song called him) was rumored to have told the King that "with one regiment he could march triumphantly through all the American colonies."

Burgoyne initiated his campaign in 1777 with an infuriating proclamation denouncing "the present unnatural Rebellion" as "the compleatest System of Tyranny that ever God, in his Displeasure, suffered, for a Time, to be exercised over a froword (sic) and stubborn Generation." He threatened the rebels with "the Indian forces under my direction—and they amount to thousands."

Burgoyne's pomposity offered rich opportunity for parody, but the campaign that he directed was no joke. Colonial leaders had long worried that the British might become "masters of the Hudson River," which would "divide our strength, and enfeeble every effort for our common preservation and security." As originally planned, one army of British, Hessian, and Indian troops would march down from Montreal, while a second came from the West through the Mohawk Valley, and a third up the Hudson from New York City, all to converge on Albany. Along a line from New York to Montreal they would create a chain of forts to cut off New England, the heartland of rebellion.

The campaign began with a signal British victory on July 6, 1777, the capture of Fort Ticonderoga, key to the lake route to Albany. King George III is said to have shouted on receiving the news: "I have beat them! I have beat the Americans." Alexander Hamilton was a better prophet than the king: "I am in hope," he wrote, "that Burgoyne's success will precipitate him into measures that will prove his ruin. The enterprising spirit he has credit for, I suspect may easily be fanned by his vanity into rashness."

Burgoyne immediately blundered. Deciding that he now had ample time to move his army a mere seventy miles to Albany, he set out through the woods rather than following Lake George. Hauling fifty-two cannon, his enormous wardrobe, his ample wine cellar, and a female entourage along a route obstructed by hundreds of trees that the Americans had felled, Burgoyne covered twenty-three miles in twenty-four days. Then, at Oriskany and Fort Stanwix in the Mohawk Valley, in tough hand-to-hand fighting, the Americans soundly defeated the British army advancing from the West. Meanwhile the murder and scalping of a young New York woman, Jane McCrea, by Burgoyne's Indian allies sent the citizens of the upper Hudson Valley into a fury at the British, who had been paying Indians for the scalps of revolutionists.

"Miss McCrea," wrote patriot commander Horatio Gates to Burgoyne, "a young lady lovely to the sight, of virtuous character and amiable disposition, engaged to be married to an officer in your Army, was with other women and children taken out of a house near Fort Edward, carried into the woods, and there scalped and mangled in a most shocking manner. . . . The miserable fate of Miss McCrea was particularly aggravated by her being dressed to receive her promised husband, but met her murderer employed by you."

Burgoyne, fearing mass desertion by his Indian allies, refused to execute her murderer and thereby aroused the entire region: for one of the few times in the war, militiamen and volunteers came and stayed to fight. When Burgoyne sent out a force to gather supplies in Vermont, two thousand minutemen from Vermont, New Hampshire, and Massachusetts threw the British back with heavy losses.

Short of troops, hungry for supplies, and facing a large and capable continental army well supported by local militia, Burgoyne was now in serious trouble. Nonetheless, as Hamilton had predicted, his vanity drove him to fight. Crossing the Hudson he stood at Saratoga facing Gates's army, which held a commanding position behind powerful fortifications built at the direction of a Polish engineer, Thaddeus Kosciusko. On September 19, Burgoyne threw his troops into action against Gates at Freeman's Farm. The battle sapped British strength while Gates easily reinforced his army. With supplies running low, Burgoyne had to decide whether to fight again or retreat. Of course he fought and on October 7, in the second battle of Saratoga, again suffered heavy losses. His position completely untenable—only the women in his company, whom the chivalrous Americans would not shoot, could get water from the nearby river—Burgoyne surrendered. A popular topical verse said it all:

> Burgoyne, alas! unknowing future fates,
> Could force his way through woods,
> but not through GATES.

The Armies

The King's and Patriot Armies

A soldier of the Revolution who overheard talk in the ranks of the King's troops might have caught the sound of various accents from the British Isles, or American accents, for there were several loyalist regiments among the Crown troops. And it is likely that he would have heard German. In the eighteenth century a nation might rent whole military units from such rulers as were willing to go into the business, and in the course of the war the British rented nearly 30,000 troops from German princes, including the Hessians from the principality of Hesse-Cassel. The regular British army also contained many Germans recruited by contractors. The patriot army, like the troops who were to fight for the Union in the Civil War nearly a century later, was itself a little congress of nations and ethnic groups, as were the colonies themselves. New England Yankees, descendants of German and Scotch-Irish immigrants, and Southerners of varied ancestry in the British Isles were prominent. The Continental army, like the loyalist forces in Virginia, contained black recruits.

In the American navy, which preyed on British commerce, the *Bon Homme Richard* can exemplify the diversity of the ethnic and national strains that could collect under a single flag. This ship, the conqueror in 1779 of the British warship *Serapis*, had been supplied by France. It was under the command of John Paul Jones, a Scotsman who had come to America not long before the war. Only a minority on board the *Bon Homme Richard* were clearly definable by residence as American. By their side were seamen from Scotland and Ireland, Scandinavians, Portuguese, and a French unit of marines. In the course of the war there were deserters from the patriot forces to the King's troops, and from the King's to the patriot, which added to the diversity in both armies.

Types of Warfare

The British were not scrupulous in their methods of recruitment. British prisons yielded some recruits for the army, and strict enforcement of the vagrancy laws helped, for enlistment was a way to avoid prison. But harsh British military discipline

A British sentry in full regalia; the colonists wore simpler uniforms or their ordinary clothes.
(Courtesy, The New York Public Library, Astor, Lenox and Tilden Foundations)

turned the recruits into a fighting machine that operated according to set of prescribed rules for battle. The officers of each army would march the troops as close to the enemy as possible. The soldiers, placed in several parallel ranks, one behind the other, would fire in unison taking careful aim, for the troops on the other side were also closely packed. The troops might thereupon have time to reload and fire at will, as the British had done on the Plains of Abraham against the French defending Quebec. But reloading was a lengthy process, and in place of a second volley the soldiers might charge with bayonets, which in the eighteenth century were a major weapon. What a European army needed from the bulk of its troops, then, was not literacy, technical or administrative skills, or initiative in the performance of a job, the properties that twentieth-century armies demand, but the ability to go through the formal operations of eighteenth-century manual of arms: to stand or kneel in rank and not break under fire, to shoot or to charge at the proper time. The disposition of troops in a battle, one rank behind another, had as one of its objects to prevent the front ranks from fleeing. British discipline produced an army that could endure much enemy fire without breaking. But under sufficiently heavy fire, the best of soldiers could break.

| Patriot Troops The patriot forces contained both local militias and Continental army troops. Congress had no power to conscript troops, and so it had to assign quotas to the states for the Continental army and let each state decide how to fill them. Congress, also lacking the authority to tax, even had to requisition money from the states and hope that they would fulfill their obligations. More effective, perhaps, were the bounties that states offered, which later in the war were supplemented with a draft. A state, in turn, might impose quotas on towns, and they could pay men to enlist. States also raised their own militias, in which discipline was likely to be light. After Washington took command outside Boston, he induced about 10,000 militiamen to join the Continental army. The army of the Revolution was a foreshadowing of something more modern than the King's troops: it represented the beginnings of a citizens' army, like those that have fought in the major wars since the French Revolution; and like citizens' armies since then, it had to find ways of dealing with the reluctance of citizens to join.

As the patriot troops differed from the Crown forces in their recruitment, they differed at least somewhat in methods of fighting. At the beginning of the war outside Boston, soldiers had been electing their own officers, and it was some time before the practice was ended. The Continental army had to instill discipline, which was difficult among soldiers who had no thought of becoming long-term military professionals. General Nathanael Greene remarked of the militiamen: "They are naturally brave and spirited, as the peasantry of any country, but you cannot expect veterans of a raw militia from only a few months' service." In 1778 Washington put the Baron von Steuben, a former captain in the Prussian army recommended by Benjamin Franklin, in charge of training the troops. Von Steuben made an army out of the rag-tag Continentals, commanded a division, and became an American citizen after the war. These forces—the "summer soldiers" and the "sunshine patriots" of Thomas Paine's pamphlet—did not remain consistent or predictable in size. Citizen soldiers, committed more to their families than to army life—many of them were farmers who knew that the year's crop depended on the accomplishment of seasonal tasks—might decide to go home to plow, returning to the army if and when they felt like returning, as this Connecticut militia man did:

> I was att my house in bed, between Brake of Day and Sunrise. I hard the Signel of an-larm by the fireing of thre Cannon . . . I turn'd Out and ask'd my wife to git Brakefast as soon as possabel for I must go off. I went Down on the hill . . . Whare the fleet was in fare Site in a line acrost the haber. There was 15 Sale of Ships an other Square rig'd Vessels, besides other Vesels. I came home. My brakefast was redy. After Brakefast . . . My hors Being redy I Slung my Musket & Cartrig Box and mounted with my littel Black Boy to bring the hors Back . . . After I got Under Way my wife Called to me pretty loud. I Stopt my hors and ask'd her What She wanted. Her answer was Not to let me hear that you are Shot in the Back.

It is perhaps to be expected that soldiers so averse to military discipline and the formalities of eighteenth-century battle should become known for fighting as individuals, firing from behind cover rather than in ranks, and taking aim. Some Americans were expert marksmen and used the Pennsylvania rifle, which was accurate at longer distances than the smooth-bore musket. The colonists' method of fighting from cover had come from their fighting the Indians, who also fought as individuals and had never read a military manual. These tactics infuriated the British, who thought the colonists unprofessional or cowardly.

In tactics, as in constituting a citizen army, the patriot troops seem more modern than their British and Hessian opponents. A British survivor of Concord remarked of the Americans:

> Whoever looks upon them as an irregular mob will find himself much mistaken. They have men amongst them . . . who know very well what they are about, having been employed as Rangers against the Indians and Canadians, and this country being much covered with woods, and hilly, is very advantageous for their method of fighting.

Midshipman Augustus Brine, 1782, by John Singleton Copley. *(Courtesy, The Metropolitan Museum of Art)*

A Marylander found the means of fighting almost embarrassing:

> Our northern Generals have introduced a new system for conducting this war, which subverts every principle in the art of war adopted by other States, for instead of instructing their troops in the principles of military discipline, preparing and encouraging to meet their enemies in the fields and woods, they train them to run away and to make them believe they never can be safe unless under cover of an intrenchment, which they would rather extend from the North to the South pole than risque an engagement.

The picture that comes down to us of the American crouched behind a stone fence and picking off soldiers in the bewildered British ranks may owe much to the work of the Mas-

sachusetts farmers at Lexington and Concord. During much of the war, Americans
fought on the open field, managing as much
of conventional warfare as training could
teach them and their inclinations allowed.

And in the course of the fighting, the Continental army developed a pride in itself as a
seasoned and knowledgeable fighting force.
If few of its troops wanted to become permanent professionals, if most of them like citizen soldiers in other wars wanted a quick return to their homes, they were nonetheless
more than farmers or artisans who had picked
up a gun for a scrap or two with the British;
they were now real soldiers of a trained and
national army. That meant that they were a
major embodiment of the new nation itself.

The women who accompanied the army
in diverse capacities also contributed to its
being a people's army, an incorporation of
American society. Only officers were provided with quarters that could accommodate
their wives, but other women frequently
accompanied the army as camp-followers,
laundresses, nurses, cooks, and provisioners.
Wives might also accompany husbands to the
actual field of battle and assist them by such
tasks as fetching the water required to keep
the cannon functioning. It is not certain that
the legendary Molly Pitcher actually existed,
but many women did what has been attributed to her: they brought their husbands
water for the cannon, and then took over firing it themselves after their husbands had

been wounded. Some women actually disguised themselves as men and fought unde-
tected for long periods. Others capitalized on
their femininity to serve successfully as spies
and messengers.

The many American women who did not
participate in battle or accompany the armies
also frequently provided important services
that today would be the responsibility of the
military authorities. They provided lodging
for officers or allowed their homes to be
turned into prisons and hospitals, and a vast
network of women emerged to make shirts
and knit stockings for the American soldiers.
As this letter illustrates, some women even
raised money for Washington's army.

Philadelphia, July 4th, 1780.
Sir,
The subscription set on foot by the ladies of this
City for the use of the soldiery is 200,580 dollars,
and £625 6s.8d. in specie, which makes in the
whole in paper money 300,634 dollars.

The ladies are anxious for the soldiers to receive
the benefit of it, and wait your directions how it can
best be disposed of. We expect some considerable
additions from the country and have also wrote to
the other States in hopes the ladies there will adopt
similar plans, to render it more general and
beneficial. . . .

E. Reed

Nothing better illustrates the impact of the
war on American society than the extensive
participation of women. The war effort fully
mobilized the nation.

The Course of Battle

**The Critical
Battles,
1776–1778**
Against the rebels Britain
massed an overwhelming
force. Only days after Congress proclaimed indepen-
dence in July 1776 a huge British fleet—a
"forest of masts"—sailed into New York harbor: 32,000 soldiers with 11,000 sailors man-
ning thirty major ships of the line and dozens
of transports. The commanders, General William Howe and his brother Admiral Richard
Howe, aimed at establishing a principal base
in New York, isolating New England from
the other states, and providing easy communication between New York and Canada.
One British force would descend from Canada by way of Lake Champlain and the Hudson River; the main force would strike New

York City from the sea. Meanwhile, the British fleet's blockade of the coastline was intended to deprive the Americans of both income and supplies from trade. The Howe
brothers had brought with them instructions
from Lord North to sue for peace. The "revolting colonies," said the Prime Minister,
"cannot last long." But he was mistaken, and
the peace overtures were ignored.

The Howes' upstate campaign was never
effective. The brilliant tactics of Benedict Arnold in his courageous stand against a superior enemy fleet on Lake Champlain delayed
a British thrust southward for a year. The British strike against New York City, on the other
hand, was child's play. Washington unwisely
divided his makeshift army, sending about

half of his troops to Long Island while the rest stayed on Manhattan. English ships slipped around both islands to block retreat, while Howe's soldiers attacked Brooklyn Heights, inflicting heavy losses. Realizing his mistake, Washington skillfully retreated across both islands into New Jersey, although his army was now demoralized and in disarray. It was, Washington lamented, a "disgraceful and dastardly" flight. With the retreating army was volunteer aide-de-camp Thomas Paine, who wrote in a widely-distributed pamphlet, "These are the times that try men's souls. The summer soldier and the sunshine patriot will, in this crisis, shrink from the service of his country; but he that stands by it now, deserves the love and thanks of man and woman."

Wishing to negotiate with the revolutionaries, not destroy them, Howe pursued them only as far as the Delaware River. Washington used this pause to regroup his armies, and on Christmas night of 1776 returned to the attack. After a daring military maneuver across the icy Delaware River, his army pounced on a camp of Hessian mercenaries at an outpost in Trenton, New Jersey. One of Washington's soldiers recalled that the crossing of the river took place on "as severe a night as I ever saw—the frost was sharp, the current difficult to stem, the ice increasing, the wind high and at eleven it began to snow." The Hessians, who had gone to bed drunk and confident that no army would attack on such a hallowed occasion, were quickly overwhelmed. Nearly a thousand were captured. A week later Washington struck again, outmaneuvering a British force at Princeton and driving the enemy back to the Hudson before both armies went into hibernation. Washington took up winter quarters in the hills of western New Jersey; Howe diverted himself in New York "in feasting, banquetting, and in the arms of Mrs. Loving. . . ." He had fumbled a chance to end the war quickly.

In 1777 Britain's army renewed its efforts to occupy major coastal cities and isolate

Washington Crossing the Delaware, by Emanuel Leutze. On Christmas Eve, 1776, General George Washington led his troops across the icy Delaware River, a maneuver that surprised the Hessian troops at Trenton and led to a much-needed American victory. This romantic mid-nineteenth-century painting is, however, filled with historical inaccuracies and unlikely poses. Which ones can you spot? *(Courtesy, The Metropolitan Museum of Art)*

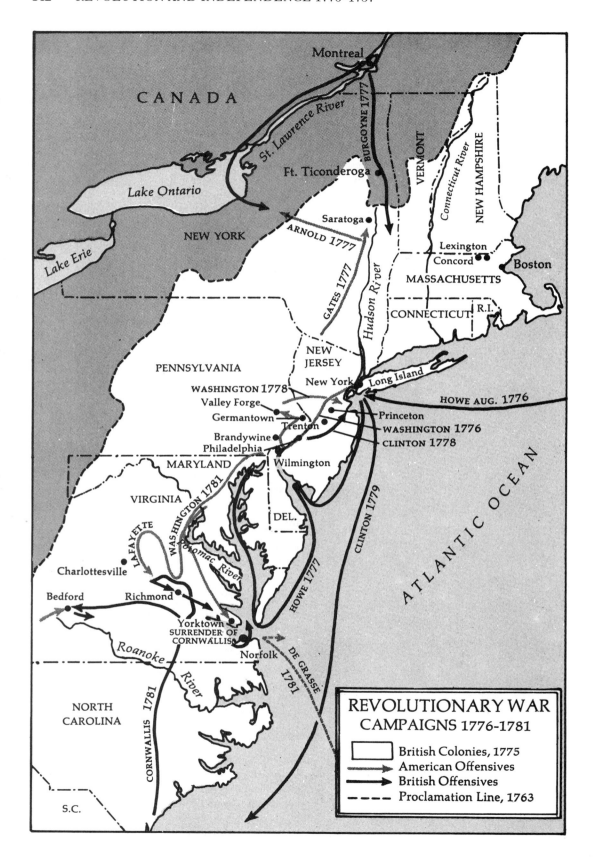

CANADA

St. Lawrence River

Lake Ontario

Lake Erie

NEW YORK

Montreal

BURGOYNE 1777

Ft. Ticonderoga

VERMONT

NEW HAMPSHIRE

Connecticut River

Saratoga

ARNOLD 1777

GATES 1777

Hudson River

Lexington
Concord
Boston

MASSACHUSETTS

CONNECTICUT   R.I.

PENNSYLVANIA

NEW JERSEY

New York   Long Island

HOWE AUG. 1776

WASHINGTON 1778
Valley Forge
Germantown
Brandywine
Philadelphia
Trenton
Princeton
WASHINGTON 1776
CLINTON 1778

MARYLAND

Wilmington

WASHINGTON 1781

VIRGINIA

Potomac River

DEL.

CLINTON 1779

ATLANTIC OCEAN

LAFAYETTE

Charlottesville

Bedford   Richmond

HOWE 1777

Yorktown
SURRENDER OF
CORNWALLIS

Norfolk

DE GRASSE 1781

Roanoke   *River*

NORTH
CAROLINA

CORNWALLIS 1781

S.C.

REVOLUTIONARY WAR
CAMPAIGNS 1776-1781

British Colonies, 1775
American Offensives
British Offensives
Proclamation Line, 1763

New England. In July General Howe embarked from New York with 15,000 men, sailed around to land at the head of Chesapeake Bay, and began fighting his way north toward Philadelphia. Washington and his troops scurried overland to meet the British at Brandywine Creek, but could not turn them back and made an orderly retreat. By September 26 Washington had lost a fifth of his total force and Howe had occupied Philadelphia—forcing Congress to flee to the Pennsylvania interior. On October 4, at the Battle of Germantown, Washington executed a series of intricate maneuvers that placed him in a position to destroy Howe's main encampment, but the American troops became lost in a heavy fog and at one point even fired on one another. Only General Nathanael Greene's skillful retreat prevented disorder. Humiliated, Washington's remnant of an army was forced to spend a half-frozen and half-starved winter near Valley Forge, one of the few iron foundries still in patriot hands. One of Washington's soldiers wrote in his diary:

> I am ashamed to say it, but I am tempted to steal fowles if I could find them, or even a whole hog, for I feel as if I could eat one. . . . At 12 of the clock at night, Providence sent us a little mutton, with which we immediately had some broth made, & a find [fine] stomach for same. Ye who eat pumpkin pie and roast turkies, and yet curse fortune for using you ill, curse her no more, least she reduce your allowance of her favours to a bit of fire cake, & a draught of cold water, & in cold weather too.

One of Washington's officers was more philosophical:

> When it is taken into consideration that our army was not more than one-half the numbers of our enemy, and all things were well appointed and equipped with them, but our army not so . . . we did, I think, as well as could be expected. . . . We had our solacing words always ready for each other,—"Come boys, we shall do better another time,"—sounded throughout our little army. Had any man suggested, merely hinted the idea of giving up . . . he would have been knocked down. . . . Such was the spirit of the times. . . .

Civilians suffered too. In October 1777 when Burgoyne's troops came into the Hudson Valley, one family hid in a swamp, and when they returned home their daughter recalled that "our crops and our cattle, our sheep, hogs, and horses, were all gone . . . yet we . . . thanked God sincerely that our house and barns were not destroyed."

The victory of the United States at Saratoga in October 1777 more than made up for any losses. It revived patriot morale, secured a crucial European ally, France, which transformed the war.

The French Alliance   As early as 1775, the Continental Congress had sent agents to France. Some, like Silas Deane and Arthur Lee, had arranged a trickle of loans and shipments of military supplies. The small Dutch island of St. Eustatius in the Caribbean served as a transit point: French ships unloaded munitions there, and patriots picked them up. Late in 1776, Congress sent Benjamin Franklin to Paris to negotiate an alliance. But King Louis XVI hesitated. His government was nearly bankrupt; his Spanish allies feared that the example of the Revolution might encourage revolution among their own colonies; the armies of the United States seemed weak. It seemed enough to have the secret trade in military hardware supporting the patriot armies, accomplishing French objectives by tying Britain down in a protracted war. However much Franklin's republican wit and easy charm captivated courtiers at Versailles, diplomatic grace could not, by itself, gloss over hard realities. For two years, Franklin moved through France, winning many friends for the new nation and establishing his own formidable reputation. But for the time being the King avoided any overt alliance.

Nonetheless, France and Spain did see opportunities. King Louis yearned for revenge against an old enemy, while Spanish courtiers in Madrid feared the mushrooming British empire in the New World. After the Battle of Saratoga opponents of the war in Britain persuaded Parliament to open peace negotiations, and by early spring 1778 a delegation under the Earl of Carlisle was on its way to the colonies with an offer of limited autonomy within the British empire. Fears that the Americans might accept such terms, along with the encouragement that the victory at Saratoga gave to France, finally prompted Louis XVI and his foreign minister to offer Congress a formal alliance. The patriots ratified the bargain on May 4, 1778, only weeks before the Carlisle commissioners arrived in Philadelphia. With the entry of France into the conflict, the American Revolution became a world war.

In the dark and drifting time from 1778 to 1780, the United States could not find a winning strategy, neither could British generals defeat Washington's army or control the countryside. One major difficulty for the British was the sheer vastness of the country. The redcoats fought at the end of a 3,000-mile line of supply; slow-moving ships could not maintain large land armies. Americans, on the other hand, could attack like guerrillas and then easily escape across rivers into forests. Short of occupying the whole country—a physical impossibility—His Majesty's generals could find no way to strike some final, decisive blow that would crush the rebellion once and for all. Nor did the British have the ruthlessness to destroy the morale of the patriots. Fighting to bring the rebels back into the empire, some of the British soldiers sympathized with the Americans' cause. Besides, the rules of eighteenth-century warfare did not scorch the earth or brutalize the population. Lord Dunmore, the last royal governor of Virginia, had offered freedom to slaves who fled their masters or fought the rebels, but most remained with their owners. As British strategy failed to divide the states or to quell the rebellion, Parliament grew increasingly restless with the war.

A Passive Strategy

American strategy played upon British weakness. Unable to dislodge the redcoats from major seaport cities or confront their superior numbers in pitched battles, Washington adopted a policy of "watchful waiting." Patriot forces often conducted guerrilla warfare against isolated British units or their supply columns. Washington hoped to wear down the resolve of the British to continue the war or to force them into a situation in which he could make a decisive strike.

Washington needed time, and yet the new nation found even this passive strategy difficult to execute. Most men shunned enlistment in the Continental army, especially as patriotic fervor subsided after 1776. Farming required the most work in spring and early fall, precisely those times most favorable for battle. The sense of a common nationhood was as yet half-formed, and state governors maintained tight control over their local militias, sometimes not letting them leave the state. Many Americans, fearful of military authority and centralized power, refused to pay taxes to support Washington's troops, and so the regular army lacked not only soldiers but also arms and equipment. The national government, too, lacked sufficient revenue; unable to levy taxes itself, it was dependent on inadequate state contributions. To finance the war the Continental Congress printed millions of paper dollars popularly called "continentals." This flood of currency drove up prices mercilessly. After the French alliance Congress, unwisely assuming that the French would help pay its bills, printed still more paper money. By 1780 few merchants or farmers would accept "continentals" in payment for supplies. Washington had to resort to impressment—forced sales on credit—to provision his troops. Localism hampered Congress in other ways, too. It could not act without the approval of nine of the thirteen states, a rule that allowed the smaller states to intrigue for large gains as the price of their consent. And the government conducted the war through cumbersome committees. A serious lack of manpower and money, compounded by provincialism and defects in organization, hampered the new nation's effort to survive.

During the war some Americans deplored frivolity as wasteful of money and energy, and at odds with the sobriety needed in a time of national crisis. In the interest of economy, Congress had officially condemned balls and entertainments. A while later it condemned plays put on by officers and men of the Continental army stationed in Philadelphia as "disagreeable to the sober inhabitants" of the Quaker city. Moralists condemned the growing "licentiousness"—gambling, cockfighting, and wenching—that developed whenever large numbers of young men congregated together in barracks and military encampments.

The moralism of the early wartime years did not last. As the conflict dragged on, standards relaxed. To relieve the tedium of sacrifice and offset the general gloom, urban Americans sought out amusement and pleasure. Officers of the British military and naval forces occupying New York opened the "Theater Royal" and sold hundreds of tickets for benefit performances to succor "the Widows and orphans of those who have lost their lives in his majesty's service." Patriots, too, organized theatricals and gave balls and suppers for the officers of the Continental army.

In the winter of 1778–79 the new British

commander-in-chief in America, General Henry Clinton, lacking sufficient troops to pacify the North, shifted British operations to the South, where he anticipated aid from the large loyalist population. Washington, unable to mount a two-front war, remained encamped outside British-occupied New York City.

One boost to American morale was the unexpected naval victory of John Paul Jones's *Bon Homme Richard* over the British warship *Serapis* in September 1779. When asked if he wished to surrender at one point during the battle, the intrepid Jones replied, "I have not yet begun to fight."

By 1779 the war had reached a stalemate. Both sides reduced the scale and intensity of the fighting in North America as skirmishes there simply became part of an international war. Now forced to defend as well their possessions in India and the Caribbean, the British withdrew ships and men from America. France, benefiting from England's distress, was slow to aid the patriot forces. For a year after the unsuccessful battle of Monmouth, New Jersey, in June 1778, Washington's beleaguered army had mounted no major offensive. Civilian morale sagged; unrest mounted in the army.

In 1780 General Benedict Arnold, reprimanded for misuse of his powers while he was commander at Philadelphia, began treasonable negotiations with the British to turn over West Point. When his activities were discovered he fled to the British, who made him a brigadier general.

In the South the British took Savannah and Charleston and encouraged the loyalists to make war on their patriot neighbors. In these circumstances the war in the back country became uncharacteristically savage. At Waxhaw Creek, South Carolina, in May 1780, Colonel Banastre Tarleton's British troops massacred a Virginia regiment that had surrended. According to an eyewitness,

> Not a man was spared . . . and for fifteen minutes after every man was prostrate [the Tories] went over the ground plunging their bayonets into everyone that exhibited any signs of life, and in some instances, where several had fallen one over the other, these monsters were seen forcing their steel through several bodies at once.

The term "Tarleton's Quarter" became a rallying cry among Southern patriots.

In the North, discord plagued Washing-ton's army. Bonuses paid to new recruits outraged some Pennsylvania troops, and on New Year's Day 1781, they mutinied and marched on Philadelphia to seek redress from Congress. Only promises of quick relief persuaded them to return to camp. Three weeks later some New Jersey troops mutinied, and two soldiers were executed.

Then, in the summer of 1781, the war turned in favor of the rebels. Congress centralized the administrative departments and enacted a new financial program under the direction of Robert Morris. Supplies were soon flowing to the army again. Meanwhile French money and manpower finally began to arrive in significant amounts. And on the military front Washington in August 1781 received word that a French fleet and 3,000 troops were enroute to Chesapeake Bay. Joining with other French forces in New York, Washington at last had a chance to strike.

In the Carolinas, harassed by guerrillas and "tired out marching about the country in quest of adventures," General Charles Cornwallis marched his army north toward Virginia for the purpose of cutting rebel communications between North and South. Counting on protection and supplies from the seemingly invincible Royal Navy, he repeatedly violated one of the cardinal rules of warfare: never let your forces be backed up to the sea, where retreat is impossible. In August 1781 Cornwallis made the fatal blunder: he moved his army onto a narrow peninsula between the York and James rivers near Yorktown and encamped there. Soon the French navy was at his back and a combined force of 9000 Americans and 7800 French began to besiege him by land. Hopelessly trapped, he surrendered his whole army on October 19, 1781.

An American at Yorktown wrote in his diary an account of the final days of the war:

> 17th.—In the morning, before relief came, had the pleasure of seeing a drummer mount the enemy's parapet, and beat a parley, and immediately an officer, holding up a white handkerchief, made his appearance outside their works; the drummer accompanied him, beating. Our batteries ceased. An officer from our lines ran and met the other, and tied the handkerchief over his eyes. The drummer sent back, and the British officer conducted to a house in rear of our lines. Firing ceased totally.
> 18th.—Several flags pass and repass now even without the drum. Had we not seen the drummer in

CORNWALLIS COUNTRY DANCE

The General Cornwallis's retreat and advance across Carolina and Virginia in 1781 reminded an American balladeer of the contemporary "contre" dance, where two facing lines move back and forth. The English dance tune to which the ballad is set became popular in early nineteenth-century music halls as "Pop Goes the Weasel."

Cornwallis led a country dance the like was never seen, Sir,
Much retrograde and much advance, and all with General Green, Sir.
They rambled up, they rambled down, joined hands, and off they run, Sir,
　of General Green to Charlestown, the Earl to Wilmington, Sir.

Quoth he, my guards are weary grown with doing country dances.
They never at St. James had shown at capers, kicks, or prances.
No men so gallant there were seen while saunt'ring on parade, Sir,
　or dancing o'er the park so green, or at the masquerades, Sir.

Good Washington, Columbia's sons, whom easy nature taught, Sir,
Now hand in hand they circle round in ev'ry dancing mood, Sir,
The gentle movement soon confounds, the Earl's day draws near, Sir,
　the gentle movement soon confounds, the Earl's day draws near, Sir.

His music soon forgets to play; his feet can't move no more, Sir,
And all his men now curse the day they jigged to our shore, Sir.
Now, Tories all, what can you say . . . Cornwallis is no griper,
But while your hopes are danced away, it's you that pay the piper.

his red coat when he first mounted, he might have beat away till doomsday. The constant firing was too much for the sound of a single drum; but when the firing ceased, I thought I never heard a drum equal to it—the most delightful music to us all.

19*th*.—Our division man the lines again. All is quiet. Articles of capitulation signed; detachments of French and Americans take possession of British forts. Major [Alexander] Hamilton commanded a battalion which took possession of a fort immediately opposite our right and on the bank of York river. I carried the standard of our regiment on this occasion. On entering the fort, Baron Steuben, who accompanied us, took the standard from me and planted it himself. The British army parade and march out with their colors furled; drums beat as if they did not care how. Grounded their arms and returned to town. Much confusion and riot among the British through the day; many of the soldiers were intoxicated; several attempts in course of the night to break open stores . . . our patrols kept busy. Returns of British soldiers, prisoners six thousand, and seamen about one thousand. Lord Cornwallis excused himself from marching out with the troops; they were conducted by General O'Hara. Our loss said to be about three hundred; that of the enemy said not more than five hundred and fifty. Fine supply of stores and merchandise had; articles suitable for clothing were taken for the use of the army. A portion furnished each officer to the amount of sixty dollars.

Diplomacy Wins Independence

The defeat at Yorktown was by no means a military disaster for the British, since they still held America's major seaports. But what Yorktown did accomplish was to dramatize how slender were the possibilities for eventual British victory against the combination of American armies and guerrillas and French power. Another vital consideration was that an end to the fighting in North America would free badly needed fleets and armies to fight in the West Indies and India. Early in 1782, Parliament forced Prime Minister North out of office and demanded negotiations with the United States. Although

George III disagreed, most of his subjects thought that a generous peace might conciliate the former colonists, and even draw them back into the British orbit.

| **The Peacemaking** — The Americans, too, were ready to end the war. In the Continental Congress one overworked member complained that "the little leisure we have is not sufficient for the common functions of life & exercise to keep us in health." "I heartily desire to be at home," wrote another. The Continental Congress was near collapse, and local loyalties and interests were continuing to strain against the national purpose. In Congress, planters worried about "getting home to their plantations at a season in which planters in general have so very much to attend to." One lawyer complained, "I have lost my Clients the benefit of a Circuit and now despair of doing any thing the ensuing Term." Said another, "This trade of patriotism but ill agrees with the profession of a practising Lawyer." (There were some benefits: one delegate enjoyed dining "in the company of a number of very fine ladies, who seemed not averse, to a small Squeze from a Member of Congress.")

The victory at Yorktown, however welcome, was more lucky circumstance than a triumph of superior military power or skill. Chances for a large territorial settlement and the prospect of better relations with Britain, a dangerous adversary for any nation so exposed to attack from the sea, understandably attracted many Americans. In fact, the Congress authorized its negotiating team, headed by Benjamin Franklin, to accept almost any treaty that included independence and a withdrawal of British troops. With their mutual interests so aligned, the two enemies seemed likely to conclude a quick agreement.

Yet negotiations dragged on for nearly two years. The Franco-American alliance of 1778 bound the United States not to make a separate peace. In turn, Louis XVI and his minister Vergennes, in order to gain Spanish support, had promised ministers in Madrid much British territory as booty, especially strategic Gibraltar. The Spanish, moreover, wanted to confine the United States to the area east of the Appalachian Mountains. Although Spain could expect few concessions from Great Britain, it could hold up indefinitely a settlement between Britain and the United States. America now had more to lose from its friends than from its enemies.

At last, Franklin broke the diplomatic logjam by violating the terms of the alliance with France and opening separate negotiations with English agents. The French, themselves weakened by a long and costly conflict, were not much upset, for Franklin's maneuver had in effect rescued them from an embarrassingly democratic ally. Once started, talks progressed steadily. The series of treaties that ended the war, collectively known as the Treaty of Paris, was signed on September 3, 1783. England granted independence and promised to withdraw all of its troops from the colonies. The new nation acquired a huge dowry of land: from the Atlantic seacoast to the Mississippi River. Its boundaries in the north with Canada remained vague, and redcoats still occupied forts south of the Great Lakes. The Gulf coast was ceded to Spain, although both Americans and Englishmen were guaranteed navigation rights on the Mississippi. Britain successfully demanded that "no unlawful impediment" block the collection of prewar debts Americans owed to British merchants. The treaties also pledged the United States to make restitution to loyalists who had suffered financially during the Revolution. British merchants did succeed in closing the Americans out of imperial commerce, a serious loss for the young nation. Despite these concessions and the lack of adequate enforcement procedures, the Americans had benefited handsomely from European rivalries. War and diplomacy created a new nation with boundaries generous enough to insure future growth and prosperity.

The Revolution at Home

| **Prosperity and Inflation** — Eight years of warfare not only profited many individuals but also invigorated the whole economy. An immense amount of money in circulation raised the price of nearly everything. The Continental Congress and the state governments spent nearly $200 million in hard money, followed by many more millions in paper currency. British soldiers and purchasing agents

poured another $50 million into the economy. All this money created an extraordinary demand for commodities and, of course, persistent inflation resulted. Yet few Americans suffered economically. War stimulated production. The need for uniforms and arms, for example, produced rapid growth in the textile and iron industries. Merchants' inventories and farmers' crops grew in value. Bankers lent at high rates of interest to importers and privateers—goods brought through the British blockade commanded enormous profits. State and local governments often imposed price and wage controls, a device used since the Middle Ages to control inflation. Congress regulated monopolies and prevented exports of crucial raw materials. More and more local economies were coming together into a broad national market.

Despite occasionally rigorous local efforts at regulation, the pressures of wartime inflation produced extensive black markets. Shopkeepers and small farmers preferred to deal with Englishmen and private citizens who spent silver and gold coin. An indignant Pennsylvanian angrily refused to sell his grain to one of Washington's agents, saying, "Your money's not worth a damn continental." The phrase caught on. Throughout most of the war, private citizens prospered while the government and army suffered penury and hardship. This paradox so angered Washington that he proposed hanging all profiteers.

| **Land and Slavery, Freedom and Religion** | Major changes occurred in the pattern of land ownership after the war. Prob- |

ably a quarter of the population was loyal to the British Crown, either openly or secretly. By 1778 all thirteen states had confiscated the property of those who "took refuge with the British tyrant." Some 100,000 already had left the country, most for Canada or England, and their estates were sold for money to support the patriot cause. Much of the confiscated land was bought up by rich speculators or other large landowners, not by tenants and small farmers, who rarely had enough money to buy in places already settled. Instead, many of them and their children looked westward to the mountains and beyond. Even before the war ended, thousands had migrated, going into what were to be Tennessee and Kentucky, into northern New England and northern New York.

The Revolution also made for a rhetoric of liberty that stumbled against the reality of human bondage. "How is it," chided the crusty British writer Samuel Johnson, "that we hear the loudest yelps for liberty among the drivers of Negroes?" A group of blacks in Boston announced to the General Court that

Bonds paying 6% per year were sold to finance the Revolution. The inflation rate was much higher.
(Courtesy, Chase Bank Collection of Moneys of the World, New York)

their race looked for "great things from men who have made such a noble stand against the designs of their *fellow-men* to enslave them." During the war over 5000 blacks served in the American army and navy. Several states granted freedom to slaves who served in the military. Soon a voluble antislavery movement emerged. Philadelphia Quakers had formed the first antislavery society in 1775. In most Northern states, slavery was not a large part of the economy, and patriot leaders struck decisively at the institution. In 1781 a Massachusetts judge declared:

> As to the doctrine of slavery and the right of Christians to hold Africans in perpetual servitude, and sell and treat them as we do our horses and cattle, nowhere is it expressly enacted or established. It has been a usage—a usage which took its origins from the practice of some of the European nations, and the regulations of British government respecting the then Colonies, for the benefit of trade and wealth. But whatever sentiments have formerly prevailed in this particular or slid in upon us by the example of others, a different idea has taken place with the people of America, more favorable to the natural rights of mankind, and to that natural, innate desire of Liberty, with which heaven (without regard to color, complexion, or shape of noses . . .) has inspired all the human race. And upon the ground our Constitution of Government, by which the people of this Commonwealth have solemnly bound themselves, sets out with declaring that all men are born free and equal—and that every subject is entitled to liberty and to have it guarded by the laws, as well as life and property—and in short is totally repugnant to the idea of being born slaves.

Some people may have felt the irony of the inscription on the Concord gravestone of John Jack, a slave who bought his freedom in the 1760s and died in 1772:

> God wills us free; man wills us slaves.
> I will as God wills; God's will be done.
> Here lies the body of
> JOHN JACK
> a native of Africa who died
> March 1773 aged about 60 years
> Tho' born in a land of slavery,
> He was born free.
> Tho' he lived in a land of liberty, he lived
> a slave. . . .

Slavery was outlawed in Massachusetts and Vermont, while New York and Pennsylvania adopted plans for gradual emancipation. After the war Congress prohibited slavery in the Old Northwest, the western lands north of the Ohio River. But along that part of the Eastern seaboard that lay south of Penn-sylvania, antislavery proposals foundered. There plantation owners like Washington and Jefferson granted that slavery was immoral and violated the republican spirit, but saw no way to abolish it without alienating large numbers of slaveowners—a group whose support was critical to the new nation's government. Of slavery itself Jefferson wrote, "We have the wolf by the ears; and we can neither hold him, nor safely let him go."

The Revolution also affected religion. Most states "disestablished" churches, ending the special privileges or civil functions of particular sects. Only Massachusetts and Connecticut still collected taxes to fund a state church; the other states viewed competing religions as equal in the eyes of the law. Tolerance did not extend to atheists, however, and most state legislatures established a religious test (aimed against Jews and Catholics) for holding public office. Blasphemy remained a crime punishable by imprisonment.

Documents like Thomas Jefferson's Statute of Religious Freedom in Virginia, finally enacted by the Virginia legislature in 1786, granted tolerance for the free practice of religion, not a guarantee of rights for nonbelievers. If narrow by twentieth-century standards, the statute was for its time a model, proclaiming to the rest of the world an example of the nation's new freedom.

How Revolutionary? Historians have argued fiercely about whether or not American society became more open, more fostering of upward mobility, during the Revolutionary era. Certainly some older marks of privilege did disappear. Since feudal times European law, seeking to keep intact the property of the upper classes, had enforced the principle of entail, that property could be passed on only within the same family, and the rule of primogeniture, that it could not be divided in inheritance but must go to the eldest son. Such rules had survived in some colonial laws, applying at least in cases in which a landowner had not provided otherwise in a will. These laws were now swept aside as relics of an age of artificial privilege and inequality. In addition, the emigration of thousands of loyalists left many local political offices vacant and created new opportunities.

Yet America remained firmly under the

control of an elite that had never had a fixed membership. Revolutionary ardor hardly touched the traditional "politics of deference" south of Pennsylvania. There the local gentry kept control over tidewater society and government. In Philadelphia, New York, and Boston a coalition of lawyers, merchants, and landowners dominated the cities after the war, much as it had before. The rich held disproportionate power in the Continental Congress. Robert Morris, for example, a merchant and speculator who served in the early 1780s as the nation's chief treasury official, possessed a fortune of $8 million.

American political rhetoric, in the heady days that followed the Revolution, exalted liberty and equality. Yet the kind of freedom and the kind of equality that Americans thought of was a stable sort, among farmers, artisans, shopkeepers, and landowners secure in their lives and possessions.

The American Revolution and its aftermath, then, presented no scenes of revolutionary crowds pitted against a besieged upper class. What happened instead was a rational application of the principle, pronounced in the Declaration of Independence, that governments derive "their just Powers from the consent of the governed." Under the new state constitutions drafted during the war, legislatures welcomed representatives from backcountry areas; the middling ranks of society—small farmers, local businessmen, and artisans—came to occupy office in larger numbers; and bills of rights prefaced many constitutions. Everywhere governors lost power: elected assemblies gained control of patronage and tax matters; only in Rhode Island, Georgia, and Vermont did state governors have the power to veto legislation. Legislators stood for election each year. In Pennsylvania, a new constitution abolished altogether the legislature's upper house, traditionally the bastion of the wealthy. Pennsylvania's candidates for election were forbidden to give "meat, drink, money, or otherwise" as gifts to voters.

New York experimented with the secret ballot instead of voice voting, claiming that the ballot "would tend more to preserve the liberty and equal freedom of the people."

Some less democratic practices lingered. Property ownership was still a requirement for voting in many states; high political office still required the ownership of large amounts of land. Upper chambers of most state legislatures could block the demands of the major-ity, and unfairly apportioned assemblies mocked the popular will in South Carolina, Virginia, and Georgia. In Georgia, for example, the piedmont—the inland region toward the mountains—contained three-fourths of the population yet received only one-fourth of the seats in the assembly, which tidewater plantation owners still rigidly dominated. Nonetheless, in all the colonies government officials were elected, lower houses had most of the power, and state officials proved extremely susceptible to public opinion. Many people never before interested in politics had discovered their voice. Individuals of every class now found themselves taking part in a democracy of public discussion and common action—a democratic activity more basic than the formal democracy of the vote.

The Revolution had made much of liberty, but the meaning of the word must not be confused with the twentieth-century concept of freedom. It did not mean the liberty to be private, to withdraw property and energies from uses that might serve the public good. Liberty was perceived as the proud possession of republican citizens simple in habits, industrious, generous, quick to engage in public service. The word "republic" had to eighteenth-century revolutionists a noble ring. It recalled the austere city states of Greece, the stern citizenry of Rome, the stately Roman senators. To be a citizen of a republic, theorists held, was to be an actor in a continuing civic life, a contributor to the common good.

| **Women and the War** | The war also affected the lives, and perhaps the self-image, of women. Many |

had participated in the war effort, either at the front or on the homefront. Many more had become accustomed to discussing politics and military news. Some few, like Mercy Otis Warren, who first wrote anti-British plays and then a history of the Revolution, engaged directly in propaganda. Others, like Abigail Adams, took over the management of farms and businesses about which they had previously known little. In this sense, the war years offered many women an education in independent action. One such woman was Deborah Franklin, Benjamin's wife, who was obliged to do without him for ten years, while he served as colonial agent in England prior to the outbreak of the revolution. In 1765, during the Stamp Act crisis, she wrote to him:

By the laste packit thair was a letter from mr. Jackson to you the poste Came in laite att night I did not know hough to ackte as you had not sed aney thing to me a bought what I shold due with the letters had it a bin direckted to the Speker I shold a sent it to Mr. Fox but in the morning Billey Franklin Came to town and he and Mr. Galloway Came . . .

We have nothing stiring amoungst us but phamlits and Scurrilitey but I have never sed or dun aney thing or aney of our famely you may depend on it nor shall we. . . .

Few, if any, colonial women translated their revolutionary experience into a demand for political rights or equality with men, despite Abigail Adams's warning to her husband that "If particular care and attention is not paid to the ladies we are determined to foment a rebellion, and will not hold ourselves bound by any laws in which we have no voice or representation." But many women must have emerged from those years with greatly increased confidence in their own abilities. Those women who had worked together in the Ladies Association that organized a national fund drive to collect money for the American troops had also experienced the power and satisfaction of women's collective action. That experience would be multiplied in the many women's voluntary associations that emerged in the early nineteenth century. "I expect to see our young women forming a new era in female history," said Judith Sargent Murray in 1798. Her expectations were somewhat premature.

By and large, women did not gain independence from the Revolution in the same sense that most free men gained it. During the final decades of the eighteenth century single, property-holding women were allowed to vote in New Jersey, but that was not typical and New Jersey rescinded this limited suffrage at the beginning of the nineteenth century. Few Americans of either gender seriously contemplated political rights for women, and some women may have actually lost independence during the revolutionary

period. Certainly the Revolution did not noticeably improve married women's standing in law in general, or their right to hold property in particular. Yet in one respect the Revolution brought significant improvement in the status of women—the ideal of virtuous "republican motherhood." A version of it was set forth in the commencement oration at Columbia College in 1795:

> Let us then figure to ourselves the accomplished woman, surrounded by a sprightly band, from the babe that imbibes the nutritive fluid, to the generous youth, just ripening into manhood, and the lovely virgin. . . . Let us contemplate the mother distributing the mental nourishment to the fond smiling circle . . . watching the gradual openings of their minds, and studying their various turns of temper. . . . the Genius of Liberty hovers triumphant over the glorious scene.

This suggested that women —"Republican mothers"—deserved a special kind of independence and dignity within the domestic sphere. There they would contribute their special qualities of nurture to the raising of virtuous young republicans to ensure the future of the new nation. But in this respect as in so many others the slim advantages gained by free white women did not extend to black slave women, whose experience looked more like a grim caricature than like an extension of the sanctity and dignity of motherhood.

Although institutions such as the Young Ladies' Academy, founded in 1786, encouraged young women to exercise their minds, women who knew too much were frowned upon. An anonymous essay in a Philadelphia newspaper in 1805 reflected the prevailing view of the intellectual woman:

> A woman who is conscious of possessing more intellectual power than is requisite in superintending the pantry, and in adjusting the ceremonials of a feast . . . is by the wits of the other sex denominated a learned lady. She is represented as disgustingly slovenly in her person, indecent in her habits, imperious to her husband, and negligent of her children.

The Articles of Confederation

The New Government The Continental Congress that convened in May 1775 following the battles at Concord and Lexington sat in continuous session until 1787. Members came and went, but during this wrenching and momentous

period Congress operated with remarkable effectiveness. While drafting a new form of government (the Articles of Confederation) Congress also raised an army and appointed its commander-in-chief, negotiated with the enemy, authorized a navy, and sent agents and commissioners to France, Spain, Prussia, Austria, and Tuscany. It issued millions of dollars of paper money. And that Congress, meeting within the red brick walls of the Pennsylvania State House, declared that "these United Colonies are, and of Right ought to be, Free and Independent States."

In June 1776, almost simultaneously with the resolution that led to the Declaration of Independence, Richard Henry Lee proposed a permanent new government to represent all the states. In July, John Dickinson of Pennsylvania, chairman of the committee appointed to draw up the plan of government, submitted his proposals. Dickinson's scheme contained several controversial features. The new Congress was to have broad powers, including the right to establish state boundaries and to dispose of unoccupied western lands. Each state would have one vote, regardless of its population and the number of representatives it actually sent to Congress.

The Dickinson proposals came under immediate attack in open Congress. The large and influential state of Virginia, which claimed much of the trans-Appalachian West, opposed granting the new government sweeping powers over lands. Many of Virginia's most prominent leaders had for years anticipated selling western lands to the farmers whom they expected to pour over the mountains when peace returned. On the other hand, delegates from states such as Maryland and Pennsylvania, owning no western lands as far inland as Virginia claimed, wanted the United States as a whole to acquire the lands toward the Mississippi. Only in this way, they insisted, could Americans from all parts of the new nation benefit from these millions of fertile acres. The delegates also fought over the voting provision. Large states wanted voting by population size. The small states supported the Dickinson proposal. By their reasoning, allotting one vote to each state meant that the new government was a league of sovereign states, while apportioning representation to the states on the basis of their population would suggest, they thought, that the power of the new government flowed directly from the American people, bypassing the states. Some members of Congress feared even the Dickinson document for giving too much power to the central government. This issue would arise again in the debates on the Constitution of 1787, and, in fact, the question of states' rights would be a perennial problem in American politics.

The Articles

For almost a year and a half, amidst the smoke and flames of war, Congress debated the powers of the new government. One New Jersey man thought that "Congress have not reserved enough power for themselves." Opponents of the original proposal succeeded in adding to it a provision that Congress could exercise only those powers specifically delegated to it by the states. Another change was a victory for Virginia. Under strong pressure from that land-rich state, the delegates at Philadelphia agreed to drop the provision that Congress would control the new nation's western lands. With these modifications accepted, Congress in November 1777 adopted the Articles of Confederation and sent the new frame of national government to the states for ratification. A New Hampshire man observed that all thirteen must approve it "for this Simple Reason that when any Society Gets Divided in Sentiment it is verry hard to unite them."

Twelve states swiftly ratified the Articles. Maryland, however, held out for the original proposal that Congress control western lands and refused to ratify until it was restored. A number of prominent Virginians, including Thomas Jefferson, had a grander vision of the West than merely as a mammoth, overgrown Virginia. The great interior valley of North America, they believed, should be carved into new, self-governing states, rather than remain colonies of the seaboard. For the good of the whole nation they were willing to surrender their own state's claims. Under their influence, Virginia ceded its western lands to Congress, and in 1781 the Articles of Confederation finally went into effect. It pledged all the states to "a firm league of friendship" with one another, and committed them to mutual support against attack. It gave to Congress sole power over foreign affairs and over the issues of war and peace. Congress would also deal with the Indians, and the states agreed to surrender to one another all escaped criminals and to give "full faith and credit" to court orders, sentences, and other judicial decisions of other states.

On March 1, the day of ratification, artillery on land and aboard vessels in the harbor boomed out a salute to the new government. That evening Philadelphia's citizens enjoyed

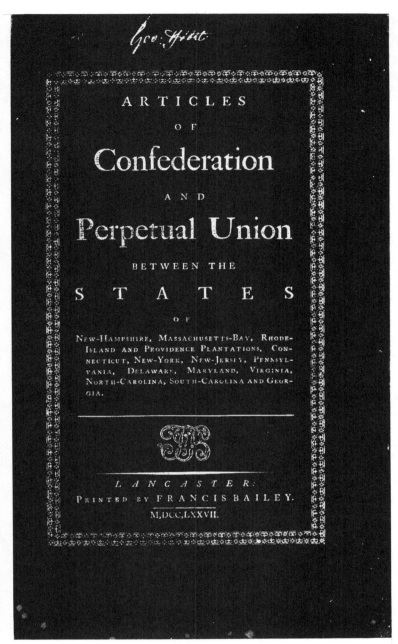

The Articles of Confederation and Perpetual Union Between the States pledged the thirteen states to "a firm league of friendship" with one another but failed to create a strong national government.

an opulent "collation" presided over by Congress's chief executive officer and watched a brilliant display of fireworks. The *Pennsylvania Packet* rhapsodized over the historic event: "Thus has the union, begun by necessity, been indissolubly cemented. Thus America, (like a well constructed arch . . .) is growing up in war into greatness and consequence among the nations."

The *Packet's* editor spoke too soon. From the very first, the Articles proved inadequate as a basis for dealing with the difficulties of a new nation. The Confederation amounted to a league of virtually independent sovereign states, not a modern nation. The new government lacked one vital power—the power to tax or the power to force the states to levy taxes in its behalf. Congress had to depend on contributions from the states. Nor could it regulate trade and commerce among the states. Any attempt to change or modify the Articles required the agreement of all the states. There were no executive and no national judiciary. Under this instrument of government, however weak, Americans did succeed in bringing the war to a successful conclusion. But the Confederation's authority would be too feeble to garner the fruits of victory and manage demobilization successfully.

The "Critical Period"

| **Debt Problems** During the months following Yorktown, the strains of nationhood, no longer obscured by military events, became painfully apparent. By early 1783 discontent plagued the army. Officers protested Congress's failure to establish a promised pension system for discharged veterans. In early March a group of officers at Newburgh, New York, threatened a military coup until Congress found the means to provide the officers with five years of full pay in lieu of the pensions.

The rank-and-file soldiers still had not received their pay. Congress simply could not raise the money. In the end, Congress discharged most of the troops without meeting their demands. Most of them rushed back to civilian life with little fuss, but several hundred marched to Philadelphia protesting their shabby treatment. Unable to meet the soldiers' demands and terrified by the angry troops, the Congress fled first to Princeton, then to Annapolis, and finally came to rest in New York, which remained the national capital for several years.

Some patriots despaired over the pitiful state of the national government. Congress could pay neither its troops nor its creditors. The war had been financed by a combination of loans, paper money, and, in the case of several states, some taxes. The paper money had seriously depreciated; in 1781 Congress announced that it would not give in exchange to holders of paper currency the hard coin (specie) that in those days was considered to be the only reliable money. Other sizable obligations remained. Congress had borrowed directly from its own citizens, issuing IOU's in exchange for supplies, food, services, and cash. It had also borrowed from Dutch bankers. The states had similar problems. Massachusetts and a few others imposed high taxes to pay their debts; most were content to default like the Confederation government.

The story of one Rachel Wells is particularly revealing of the problems faced by the impoverished states:

> To the Honnorabell Congress I rachel do make this Complaint Who am a Widow far advanced in years & Dearly have ocasion of ye Interst for that Cash I Lent the States. I was a Sitisen in ye jersey when I Lent ye State a considerable Sum of Moneys & had I justice dun me it mite be Suficant to suporte me in ye Contrey whear I am now, near burdentown. I Leved hear then . . . but Being . . . so Robd by the Britans & others i went to Phila to try to get a Living . . . & was There in the year 1783 when our assembley was pleasd to pas a Law that No one Should have aney Interest that Livd out of jearsey Stats . . .
>
> Now gentlemen in this Liberty, had it bin advertised that he or She that Moved out of the Stat should Louse his or her Interest you mite have sum plea against me. But I am Innocent Suspected no Trick. I have Don as much to Carrey on the Warr as maney that Sett now at ye healm of government. . . . your asembly Borrowed £300 in gould of me jest as the Warr Comencd & Now I Can Nither git Intrust nor principall Nor Even Security. . . . My dr Sister . . . wrote to me to be thankfull that I had it in my Power to help on the Warr which is well enough but then this is to be Considered that others gits their Intrust & why then a poor old widow to be put of[f]. . . .
>
> god has Spred a plentifull table for us & you gentelmen are ye Carvers for us pray forgit Not the Poor weaklings at the foot of the Tabel ye poor Sogers [soldiers] has got Sum Crumbs That fall from their masters tabel.

These unpaid public debts cast a pall over the nation in the years after the war. How could such a country not be an object of scorn in the eyes of the whole world?

| **Trouble with Spain** Spain controlled both Florida and the lower reaches of the Mississippi, including the important port of New Orleans. By the end of the Revolution 50,000 American farmers lived on the "Western waters" in Kentucky and Tennessee, and many more

Americans were eagerly awaiting the opportunity to cross the mountains to the fertile lands of the Mississippi Valley. If these people were not to remain subsistence farmers, they would need outlets for their wheat, pork, beef, corn, and forest products. The route over the mountains was too difficult for the shipping of bulky products, but the great river that flowed to the Gulf of Mexico was a cheap and safe natural highway. Raft-like flatboats could be constructed of local lumber and loaded with barrels of pickled beef, pork, and grain to float with the current to New Orleans. There the rafts could be broken up and sold for lumber, and the barrels reloaded on ocean-going vessels to be carried to the Atlantic coast ports, the Caribbean islands, or Europe. The farmer could then buy some horses and return to Kentucky with some cash in his pocket and manufactured goods in his saddlebags. Control of New Orleans, then, gave Spain a strong hand in dealing with the United States.

In 1784 the Spanish government announced that it was closing the Mississippi to American commerce. Now only Spanish subjects could use the river and the port of New Orleans. All others would be arrested.

Westerners threatened to raise ten thousand troops to march on New Orleans. Some listened to British agents who promised protection if they would reunite with Great Britain. Washington, seriously worried at the prospect of national dismemberment, reported after a long journey through the frontier that "the western settlers . . . stand as it were upon a pivot. The touch of a feather would turn them any way."

America's diplomatic weakness was soon confirmed. Negotiations began in 1785 between Spain and America over the "right of deposit" at New Orleans—in effect, the right to use the port there for foreign trade. Dour, tight-lipped John Jay, Congress's Secretary for Foreign Affairs, met with the suave and charming Don Diego de Gardoqui, Spain's negotiator. The Spanish emissary knew that the powerless Americans were in no position to threaten Spain, and refused to grant the major American demand, the right of deposit, although he was willing to make minor boundary adjustments along the West Florida border and allow some American trade within the Spanish empire. Congress refused to accept the treaty, and it died. New Orleans

remained a tight cork bottling up the mouth of the Mississippi.

Trouble with Britain The British, who could make more trouble for the new nation than Spain, had no reason to wish the Americans well. In 1783 Lord Sheffield, a prominent member of Parliament, published a pamphlet urging the British government to deny the Americans the trading rights within the empire that they had enjoyed before 1776. The "American states," Sheffield noted, could not "act as a nation," and so were "not to be feared as such by us." In July 1783 the Privy Council issued an order that closed the British West Indies to most American commerce.

This order dismayed farmers of the Northern states, who had long sent their surplus provisions to Jamaica, Barbados, and the other British islands. It also hurt the New England fishing industry, which had supplied the sugar plantations with dried cod and mackerel, and the merchants of New York, Philadelphia, Salem, and Boston who had carried these goods. The shipping industry employed hundreds of seamen, and thousands more in such related occupations as shipbuilding and the making of sail and rope. The British Caribbean planters connived at the smuggling of needed products, but this scarcely made up for the damage to American interests.

The Americans were in no position to retaliate. The British, of course, needed the American market for their manufactured goods. In the immediate postwar period, in fact, British goods flooded the United States, causing severe distress among American artisans and manufacturers who could not compete with the cheaper English commodities. Paying for imports from Britain also drained gold and silver coin from the nation. Several states, urged on by mass meetings of artisans and craftsmen, imposed duties on foreign goods. But the British found ways of sending their product through adjacent states that had no such taxes. Efforts to erect trade barriers among states created bad feeling between neighbors. Merchants of New London, Connecticut, boycotted New York; New Jersey taxed the New York lighthouse at Sandy Hook.

Under the peace treaty ending the war, the British had granted the United States all the territory south of the Great Lakes and north of the Spanish possessions—all the way to the Mississippi River—and had promised to give up their military posts in the Northwest "with all convenient speed." For many months, however, they refused to remove the garrisons. The British did not wish to abandon their Indian allies and were reluctant to surrender the rich fur trade. They justified their delay by citing two provisions of the peace treaty: the promise that the Americans would do nothing to prevent British creditors from collecting millions of pounds in prewar debts, and the assurance that Congress would try to get the states to compensate loyalists for their wartime losses. The states had not yet fulfilled either of these promises, and Congress was powerless to compel compliance. The governments of Virginia and Maryland, dominated by planters, wrote off about £2,000,000 in private debts that their citizens owed to British merchants.

The Confederation tried to achieve a settlement of these issues. John Adams, the American minister to England, threatened, pleaded, and cajoled, in an effort to persuade the British to relent on trade and meet their obligations under the peace treaty. But British officials presumed the weakness of the United States and dug in their heels.

| **Barbary Pirates** One final confrontation came close to being the most humiliating of all. For many years the deys and pashas of the Barbary Coast states of North Africa, Algiers, Tunis, Tripoli, and Morocco had preyed on European commerce. Most European nations either paid blackmail to these corsairs or provided naval protection for their own commerce. So long as the Americans were dependents of Great Britain, the British navy and treasury had covered them as well as Englishmen. After independence this protection ceased. In 1785 the New England ship *Maria* was captured by Algerians, who stole its merchandise, stripped the crew of all their clothes and possessions, and then sold them into North African slavery. American merchants demanded that Congress respond to such ruthless attacks. But without a navy or the means to create one, the Confederation government could do nothing to overawe the Barbary pirates. Congress did manage to raise $80,000 to buy exemption from the

deys, but this was so little that only the Moroccan leader concluded a treaty. In a few years, under the administration of John Adams, the American navy would so punish the pirates as to free the country from further trouble with them. It was to be one of the most assertive acts of the new nation.

| **Paper Money** Creditors of the new government, whether original holders of Congress's securities or speculators in them, had no more reason to respect the new government than did foreign nations. They had little hope of ever being paid. Farmers who had supplied commodities to the British West Indies and southern Europe, merchants who had traded with these regions, and all those in the port towns who had relied on this trade for a living saw their economic horizon shrink. Equally aggrieved were craftsmen and artisans in the towns who found their businesses and jobs wiped out by the deluge of cheap British goods.

Debtors, too, found times hard and sought to offset the difficulties they encountered. One favorite scheme of debtor groups to counteract the postwar deflation was state-issued paper money. When paper money is in circulation a unit of money tends to decline in value more quickly than when the only currency is in hard money of gold or silver. That is because the quantity of gold and silver is limited while paper can be printed in any amount a government chooses. Even when the understanding is that the government will give gold or silver to any holder of paper money who demands the exchange, the government can print more paper than it possesses in gold and silver, hoping that it will never be asked to exchange all the paper for metallic coin. The more paper money a government prints, or even the greater the public expectation that the government will flood the economy with paper, the less will be the value of any single unit of currency. A paper currency would therefore be to the advantage of debtors, for they would be able to pay their debts with units of money cheaper than those they had borrowed. In Maryland indebted planters supported paper-money schemes, and in Pennsylvania and South Carolina merchants endorsed them. Not only were planters and merchants often in debt themselves, but many believed that the lack of paper money made all business hard to conduct and contributed to the depressed state of the economy.

In a number of states, however, paper money became in effect a way of confiscating a part of creditors' property. In North Carolina, Georgia, and New Jersey the paper money issues authorized by the state legislatures quickly depreciated, yet creditors were forced to take it at face value. The most noto-

rious case occurred in 1786 when Rhode Island issued an avalanche of paper money. These notes were legal tender, so if any creditor refused to accept them the bills could be deposited with a judge and the debt legally canceled. Many Rhode Island merchants closed their doors rather than accept the notes. Creditors fled the state to escape debtors anxious to pay them in depreciated paper.

Daily Life

Farmers and Planters Despite the problems of government in the "Critical Period," in the summer of 1787 most ordinary Americans went about their daily affairs without giving too much thought to the concerns of the new nation. The vast majority of the 2.5 million Americans of 1780—say, ninety percent—made their living from the soil. They were by no means all alike. Some 600,000, virtually all living south of Pennsylvania, were black slaves. Another considerable group was made up of white tenants or indentured white servants. A few thousand Americans, mostly in the South—though some were to be found in the Hudson Valley and a few other spots as well—were owners of great estates or plantations. The largest group, perhaps sixty percent, was made up of free farmers who owned their own land.

Yeoman farmers who owned their hundred to two hundred acres of land outright were especially numerous in New England, Pennsylvania, New Jersey, and the back-country and mountain areas of the Southern states. Those who lived close to cities or were connected to them by good roads or navigable rivers produced crops not only for themselves and their families but also perhaps for distant markets in the West Indies, the Mediterranean, or Newfoundland. These farmers were by no means rich; the trade provided the means to buy a few luxuries and goods they could not themselves produce. Families were generally large, and children helped. Their labors created modest comfort and a rough abundance of food, clothing, and shelter even among the subsistence farmers.

A few got rich cultivating the soil: tobacco growers in Maryland and Virginia, the rice

planters in South Carolina and Georgia, the New York landlords who grew grain and raised livestock. The traveler encountered many fine houses along the streams and inlets of the Chesapeake region, in the Caro-

A lady's dressing table of the era, made in Baltimore. Patriotic touches, like the eagle that surmounts the mirror, are characteristic of post-Revolutionary times.

Head of a Negro, by John Singleton Copley. By 1780, some 500,000 slaves worked the lands of the South *(Copyright © 1983, Founders Society, Detroit Institute of Arts)*

lina and Georgia sea islands and coastal lowlands, and in the Hudson Valley. Most of these houses built since the 1740s were of brick with plaster trim, designed in the gracious Georgian style with evenly spaced windows and classical cornices and moldings over windows and doors. With large ballrooms, imported English furniture, and many bedrooms, these structures attested to growing affluence and sophistication.

Merchants and Townspeople   Maritime merchants of the port cities constituted another wealthy class. In Boston the average merchant left $5000 in real estate and personal property to his heirs at a time when few laborers earned more than fifty cents a day. A few merchants were fabulously rich. Sharing in the prosperity in about equal measure were lawyers and doctors, especially those who practiced in the larger communities. Instead of country homes the urban rich had large townhouses surrounded by gardens. These men and women, like their counterparts in the country, ate elaborate meals, dressed in silk and fine broadcloth, wore wigs or powdered their hair, and traveled by coach or on horseback.

The towns were busy with the work of shopkeepers, innkeepers, clerks, seamen, la-

borers, and artisans. A day laborer's wages could keep a young man in modest comfort, but not a married man with a family. Porters, pick-and-shovel workers, and the like could make ends meet only if their wives worked as seamstresses, laundresses, or servants. Skilled craftsmen, on the other hand, had little trouble earning a good living. Many carpenters, blacksmiths, shipwrights, tailors, cordwainers, barrelmakers, masons, printers, and other artisans owned their own shops. Some craftsmen became fairly prosperous. One tailor, for example, had a house and land worth $1130, a silver pocket watch, silver buckles for his shoes, two gold rings, six silver spoons, and furniture and household goods worth $375.

Churches   Sunday was a day of rest not only in Congregational New England, but also in the Middle states and the South, where there were many Baptists, Methodists, and Presbyterians, as well as Episcopalians. Religious observances were more than a quest for solace in an uncertain world, or traditional observances imposed by community pressure. They were also social events. People dressed up not only for the minister but for one another. And church was one of the few meeting places for young men and women. Many a courtship began in church under the watchful eyes of parents and older brothers and sisters.

Members of the evangelical sects, such as the Baptists, Methodists, and "new light" Presbyterians, found deep emotions in church attendance and did not confine their religious participation to Sundays. Beginning in the 1780s, great revivals periodically swept the back country, especially in the South. Many of these were held in churches; others took place at temporary encampments in open places where hundreds of pious people came for several days to listen to eloquent preachers exhort sinners to repent their evil ways, turn to God, and find everlasting salvation. More sedate people despised these camp meetings; they sneered at the "ranting" preachers and expressed horror at the shrieks, jerks, and groans of the listeners caught up in the emotions of the event. Critics also claimed that these camp meetings were opportunities for the nubile young to indulge their awakening sexual appetites. An Episcopalian clergyman observing a Carolina back-country Baptist revival saw

Pat Lyon at the Forge, a nineteenth-century painting by John Neagle. Many skilled craftsmen owned their shops and had little difficulty earning a good living. Lyon, at the time a prosperous man, had once been jailed for debt in the building shown behind him. *(Courtesy, Museum of Fine Arts, Boston)*

"Extravagancies—One on his knees in a Posture of Prayer—Others singing—some howling—These Ranting—Those Crying—Others dancing, Skipping, Laughing and rejoycing. Here two or 3 Women falling on their Backs, kicking up their Heels, exposing their Nakedness to all Bystanders." But however unseemly or disreputable, the camp meeting provided an important emotional release for rural Americans whose lives otherwise were largely bound up in a round of monotonous toil.

Amusements The ten percent of Americans who dwelt in substantial towns or cities enjoyed more varied lives. Cities were centers of culture. Boston, New York, Philadelphia, and Charleston had theaters where traveling companies performed the works of Shakespeare and other English playwrights. There were subscription concerts in several cities, and in Charleston the St. Cecilia Society, founded in 1762, the oldest musical society in America, imported musicians from Philadelphia and New York. In Boston in 1786 a "Concert of Sacred Music" with seventy performers played to an audience of 2,000. There were no art galleries or museums, but a handful of distinguished painters—Charles Willson Peale, John Singleton Copley, Benjamin West, John Trumbull, and Gilbert Stuart—were the equals of Europe's artists. Their battle scenes and portraits captured the Revolution for posterity.

In addition to concerts and plays in the cities, there were dances, horse races, and celebrations of public events. During and after the war the anniversary of the signing of the Declaration of Independence became a general occasion for bonfires, fireworks, and noisy parades. In Philadelphia, news of the treaty of peace set off a surge of revelry so boisterous that prudent citizens feared for the safety of their property.

Then, as today, Americans were susceptible to fads and crazes. A peculiar one of the Confederation period was for balloons, the first of which, inflated with hot air, had recently been launched in France. The idea that the human race could free itself from the force of gravity seized the public's imagination. By midsummer 1784 it was said that nothing attracted attention unless it had the word "balloon" attached to it. Fashionable people wore "balloon" ornaments and a farmer hawking his vegetables in town sold them as "fine balloon string beans."

Progress Under the Confederation

Expanding Commerce With the break from England, American merchants, no longer hindered by the Navigation Acts, began direct trade with parts of Europe from which they had been virtually excluded. Soon American vessels were showing up regularly in the harbors of Sweden, Holland, and Denmark, and even faraway Russia.

Still more interesting was the new trade with the Far East. In 1784 Robert Morris and some partners fitted out the 360-ton *Empress of China* with a cargo containing ginseng root, which the Chinese believed increased sexual potency. The vessel sailed for Canton around the Cape of Good Hope. It returned to New York the following year with tea, silk, chinaware, cotton cloth, and other goods that earned a profit for the promoters of almost $40,000. In a few years American ships were rounding Cape Horn, scudding up the Pacific coast to the region north of California, picking up otter skins in the Pacific Northwest, and sailing on to Canton. On one such voyage in 1792, Captain Robert Gray discovered the mighty Columbia River. These voyages provided a much-needed outlet for American commodities, and at the same time created a taste for Chinese furniture, housewares, and textile patterns, as well as an interest in Chinese civilization.

| **The Public Lands**   The peace treaty of 1783 had left the United States with a princely landed domain. Between the Appalachians and the Mississippi, stretching from Canada in the North to Florida in the South, lay enough unoccupied real estate to provide every free American family of 1775 with a tract of 750 acres, or over one square mile of land. The Indians, especially the Shawnee, Wyandot, Iroquois, and Miami in the North, and the Cherokee, Choctaw, and Chickasaw to the South, claimed millions of acres as their hunting grounds; most stood ready to resist any white settlers who would come to occupy their lands. Isolated settlements of French farmers and merchants were still scattered through the region, at Vincennes in present-day Indiana and at Kaskaskia, now within the state of Illinois.

The legal rights to this magnificent region were ambiguous. Virginia, with the broadest claims, had ceded its lands to the Confederation government. But other states tried to hold substantial portions of the West, a number of them awarding some of this land to their war veterans. Bit by bit, the states gave up their claims in favor of the nation, retaining in most cases only small parcels. For many years, however, state and federal claims overlapped.

Some Americans, especially Easterners who feared the political eclipse of their own part of the country, wanted the new region to remain secondary to the older states, with new settlers denied full representation in Congress. Others hoped to see equal states carved out of the region. Supporters in the older states saw the public domain as a source of federal revenue. One obvious maneuver was to sell the land at high prices—for immediate returns. Large wholesale parcels could be sold to land speculators, who in turn could profit by retail sales to settlers. But farmers argued that cheap land should be available for all Americans.

The Land Ordinance of 1785 was one of two measures in which the Confederation government laid down its basic policy toward the West and the public domain. It provided first for a careful survey of the land and then its division into townships six miles square, these to be divided into thirty-six sections, each one square mile, or 640 acres. Half the township might be sold as a unit; the other half would be offered on the market only in single sections. Actual sales at auction to the highest bidder started with a minimum price of a dollar an acre. Congress reserved four sections of each 36-section township for later use and kept one to sell for revenue to maintain local schools.

The Land Ordinance did not please everyone. Its minimum price and prescribed plot size meant that a pioneer farmer needed at least $640 to acquire a farm—in those days, a hefty sum. At the same time, the ordinance favored the establishment of family farms over speculation. Congress soon violated its own principles, however, by also selling almost two million acres of land to a group of speculators organized under the name of the Ohio Company, granting them an option on an additional five million—all for well under a dollar an acre.

| **The Northwest Ordinance**   Before long, Congress also reached a decision on the political organization of part of the trans-Appalachian area—the region bounded by Pennsylvania on the East, the Great Lakes to the North, the Mississippi on the West, and on the South the Ohio River. The Northwest Ordinance of 1787 was a milestone in the progress of Americans across the continent. This ordinance, along with the Land Ordinance, represented a triumph of statesmanship for the Confederation Congress. Borrowing from an earlier plan proposed by Jefferson, the Ordinance laid out the process by which the Northwest might eventually become a group of self-governing states, equal in all respects to the original thirteen. In time the area would be carved into between three and five territories, governed initially by officials appointed

A tray from the late eighteenth or early nineteenth century, depicting the rare sight of a black minister preaching to the flock. *(Rhode Island School of Design)*

by Congress. When a territory acquired a population of five thousand adult males, it would be allowed to elect an assembly and could send a non-voting delegate to Congress. With a population of sixty thousand free inhabitants, the territory became eligible to apply for admission as a fully equal, self-governing state. The final section of the Ordinance of 1787 reflected the most liberal spirit of the Revolutionary era. All residents of a territory would enjoy complete freedom of worship, full representation in the territorial assembly in proportion to their numbers, trial by jury, and other fundamental protections to both persons and property. In a provision that would later take on great significance, slavery was forbidden in the whole of the vast region.

There remained an important Western problem that the Confederation government could not solve: what to do with the Indians. In 1784 Congress had sent five commissioners to meet with the tribes of the Northwest in an effort to open the eastern portion of the region to white settlement. At Fort Stanwix the commissioners got the Iroquois to surrender their claims for a few trinkets. Next, they coerced the Chippewa, Ottawa, Wyandot, Shawnee, and Delaware into giving up most of their Ohio lands. The resentful tribesmen quickly repudiated these agreements and were soon trading blows with the frontiersmen now pouring into the Ohio country. The government sought to pacify the irate Indians by promising them additional gifts, while at the same time it strengthened the army garrisons in the West.

The Drive Toward the Constitution

The move to convert the Confederation government into a more effective political instrument had begun when the war ended. In 1783 nationalists had devised a scheme to grant Congress the right to collect duties on imported liquors, sugar, tea, coffee, cocoa, molasses, and pepper; each state would collect the duties at its own ports and then remit them to the Confederation treasury. This plan was submitted as an amendment to the Articles, and so required the agreement of all the states. New York, however, refused to accept it.

In 1784 a representative from Delaware wrote a fellow member that the "situation of Congress is truly alarming; the most important business pending and not states enough to take it up. . . ." Another member declared: "The Congress is abused, laughed at and cursed in every company."

As Congress declined to little more than a sleepy debating society, the future of national affairs passed into the hands of men who thought, as Alexander Hamilton of New York put it, "continentally." In early 1785, commissioners from Virginia and Maryland met at Washington's home, Mount Vernon, to discuss common problems concerning navigation of the Potomac River, which separated the two states. So successful was this meeting

The Constitution, mural by Barry Faulkner, showing James Madison presenting the Constitution to Washington and the Convention. *(Courtesy, The National Archives, Washington, D.C.)*

that it led to calls by Virginia for a larger con-ference on commercial cooperation to meet at Annapolis the following year. Only twelve delegates from five states turned up at An-napolis, however, and so consideration of the planned agenda was postponed. Instead the delegates, led by Hamilton, drew up a pro-posal for a new convention, to meet at Phila-delphia in May 1787, to discuss every issue necessary "to render the constitution of the Federal Government adequate to the exigen-cies of the Union." Congress received this proposal and cautiously endorsed it.

By the time of the Philadelphia meeting, all doubts moderate Americans may have en-tertained about the need for a stronger cen-tral government had been shattered by the farmers of western Massachusetts. One state that took its wartime debt seriously, Massa-chusetts had imposed heavy taxation on its citizens to meet this obligation. At the same time, farm prices declined. There were ef-forts to relieve by issues of paper money the distress of farmers who had gotten into debt. But in Massachusetts creditor groups de-feated the attempts to issue paper currency. In the Berkshire hills of western Massachu-setts, where few farmers had ready cash, many lost their land for non-payment of debts or taxes. The troubles that followed made it look as though anarchy threatened at least a portion of the new republic.

The American Star, by Frederick Kemmelmeyer. (*Courtesy, The Metropolitan Museum of Art*)

Points To Think About

1. The excitement of warfare obscured important changes within American society. The long struggle for independence accelerated forces and trends already apparent in the colonies before it began. The Revolution was, as one historian has written, "a struggle not only for home rule, but also over who should rule at home." The colonial elite aimed at preserving much of the old order so beneficial to it. Laborers, artisans, and small farmers often challenged, sometimes successfully, traditional prerogatives. Yet revolution in America involved no wholesale redistribution of property or wealth, no long-term change in the control of government. The War for Independence stopped short of creating an egalitarian society; it is doubtful that most patriot leaders wanted one. Most people simply yearned for the restoration of harmony and for economic advancement. The colonists, now citizens, wanted to build, not destroy.

2. The war had unified the thirteen mainland colonies and helped create a sense of shared nationality. Separate political and social entities in 1775, they learned much about cooperation between 1763 and 1783. But were they truly a nation? Previous republics had always been small, homogeneous city-states. Never had one been so large in extent. Could this unusual creation called the United States survive as an independent republic? Many Europeans—and some Americans thought not.

3. American statesmen and writers knew the history of Greece and Rome. They looked for examples of what they called "republican virtue:" patriotism, honesty, simplicity, the rejection of wealth and luxury. It was natural for Americans to suppose that the ancient republican spirit might have a rebirth on the American continent amid a free and industrious people uncorrupted by the vices of older civilizations. The idea of virtuous republican simplicity survived into the early years of the United States, expressing itself particularly in Jeffersonian politics. It was not until the twentieth century that Americans would fully relinquish the values of a simple agrarian republic for those of a modern, urban, industrial nation.

Suggested Readings

A recent study by a master historian is Edmund Morgan's *Inventing the People: The Rise of Popular Sovereignty in England and America* (1988). Also provocative are Michael Kammen, *A Machine that Would Go of Itself: The Constitution in American Culture* (1986) and John P. Diggins, *The Lost Soul of American Politics: Virtue, Self-Interest, and the Foundations of Liberalism* (1984).

Garry Wills's, *Inventing America: Jefferson's Declaration of Independence* (1978) is a readable and engaging study of the intellectual background of America's first national document. And Will's *Explaining America: The Federalists* (1981) offers a fresh reading of constitutional work. Gordon Wood's *The Creation of the American Republic, 1776–1787* (1969) explores the relationship between ideology and social and political reality. In *We the People: The Economic Origins of the Constitution* (1958) and *E Pluribus Unum: The Formation of the American Republic, 1776–1789* (rev., 1979), Forrest McDonald presents the Founding Fathers not as the self-interested businessmen an earlier twentieth-century generation of scholars had described but as statesmen committed to the founding of a secure republic. On the Anti-Federalists see Stephen Boyd, *The Politics of Opposition: Anti-Federalists and the Adoption of the Constitution* (1979) and Robert Rutland, *The Ordeal of the Antifederalists and the Ratification Struggle of 1787–88* (1966).

Jackson Turner Main stresses class and sectional differences in *The Social Structure of Revolutionary America* (1956) and subsequent studies. Other important works are Mary Beth Norton, *Liberty's Daughters: The Revolutionary Experience of American Women* (1980) and Linda Kerber, *Women of the Republic: Intellect and Ideology in Revolutionary America* (1980). A nationalist account of the confederation era is J. N. Rakove, *The Beginnings of National Politics: An Interpretive History of the Continental Congress* (1979).

☆ ☆ DEBATE ☆ ☆ ☆

ELIZABETH FOX-GENOVESE

Was the American Revolution, whether conservative or radical for men, a revolution at all for women? The previous debate between McDonald and Genovese scarcely touches the question. Presumably the two gentlemen assume that women, confined as they should be to the custody of their husbands and fathers, experienced the Revolution as members of families and social classes. Women gained or lost as their men gained or lost. Their independent political rights were not an issue.

When Abigail Adams wrote to her husband that he should "remember the ladies," she was asking that the domestic powers of husbands be reduced and, above all, that they cease behaving like tyrants within the household, but she was not asking that women be allowed to participate in government. During the second half of the eighteenth century advanced advocates of women's rights were insisting on women's capacity for an essentially female excellence, not asking that women be recognized as functionally interchangeable with men.

In effect, the American Revolution strengthened gender as a form of social classification. If previously women had been able to relate to the polity—or at least the public area—as delegates of families on occasion when family and class membership superseded gender membership, then after the Revolution they related to the polity as women first and members of families or classes second. This intensification of gender as a form of social classification has led historians to argue that women actually lost opportunities as a result of the Revolution.

Others contend that women gained through their heightened identification with other women, through the emergence of a recognizable "woman's sphere" within which they forged tight bonds of sisterhood. But neither of these developments ties the short-term changes of the Revolution very closely to the long-term changes in society. So the question remains: If the Revolution did not result in women's inclusion in the polity, if the new republic did not welcome women as citizens, what did the specific political transformations offer women?

What changed was that the view of women as women—what it meant to be a woman—improved. Previously seen as potentially dangerous and deviant, as possible witches or probable shrews, women were suddenly seen as the mothers of citizens and the republic. Where they had previously been bound to labor under the direction of the male heads of their households, they now were ascribed governance of the home. The ties that bound women to their gender tightened, but their gender gained status. The belief that women had a particular feminine sensibility legitimated their demands for education, though an education different from that for men; the conviction that they were capable of superior moral purity and had special insights into the human condition legitimated their concern with social problems, as long as they did not take those concerns into the political sphere; the respect and self-respect that they had won legitimated their quest for excellence within their own sphere.

The record then leaves us with a paradox. The most important results of the Revolution were political and resolutely excluded women. The indirect results were social and ideological and attempted to circumscribe and control women. But in contributing to a clearer definition of women as women, these results also undercut the time-honored vision of women as inferior or lesser men. By proposing that women should aspire to excellence in their own sphere, they allowed that women *could* be excellent. Once that possibility had been granted, it remained only a matter of time until women would begin to claim that they could be excellent in roles previously ascribed to men.

Women and the Revolution ☆

FORREST McDONALD

The Revolution was even more of an all-male phenomenon than Professor Fox-Genovese imagines. The principles of republican theory were familiar even to the common man in America, and Americans had fashioned their state constitutions upon those principles. What does all this have to do with the role of women in the Revolution? Republicanism totally and expressly excluded them.

The word "republic" derives from the Latin *res publica,* meaning the public thing or that which is of concern to the public. "Public," in turn, comes from the same Latin root as pubic, meaning maturity or manhood. Women were necessarily excluded, as were children, slaves, and the propertyless; for all these descriptions of people were dependent, which was regarded as incompatible with the full status of manhood. (Unlike "public," the "people" and "popular" were terms that included everybody).

It was universally agreed that the activating principle of a republic was and must be public virtue. This did not mean benevolence, kindness, thoughtfulness, or any of the other attributes associated with the idea of Christian charity. Rather, "virtue" stemmed from the Latin *virtus,* meaning manliness; it connoted courage, strength, virility, self-sufficiency. To say that public virtue must activate the republic, then, is almost to be redundant: it means that manly men must attend to those matters which are of concern to men. The opposite of virtue, in eighteenth-century usage, was "effeminacy," which was used interchangeably with "vice" and "luxury."

John Adams had a great deal to say on the subject. When the principles of a republic were pure, he wrote, it was "productive of everything, which is great and excellent among Men." But "there must be a positive Passion for the public good, the public interest, Honor, Power, and Glory." This public passion "must be Superior to all private Passions. Men must be ready, they must pride themselves, and be happy to sacrifice their private Pleasures, Passions, and Interests, nay, their private Friendships and dearest Connections, when they stand in Competition with the Rights of Society." As for women, "their delicacy renders them unfit for practice and experience in the great business of life, and the hardy enterprise of war, as well as the arduous cares of state."

A less rigorous form of republican theory, popular among Americans outside of New England, also had little place for women. Agrarian republicanism, formulated by the seventeenth-century English political theorist James Harrington, held that ownership and cultivation of the land bred independence and manly virtue, and contended that if most of the people did own and cultivate their own land the supply of public virtue would always be adequate for the support of the republic. The great mass of the white adult males in America were in fact owners and cultivators of the soil, but the consequence for women was to deprive them of part of the limited role that Professor Fox-Genovese depicts them as having had in the early republic. They could be mothers of the sons of the republic, it is true, but they could not have the dominant role in child rearing. The menfolk were physically present almost all the time in the vast majority of American households; female children were required to be dutifully submissive to them, males to be respectfully imitative of them. In other words, after the first few years mothers were normally excluded from the shaping of the characters of their sons. Not for another generation, when increasing numbers of men began to go into manufacturing, commerce, and other urban pursuits that kept them away from home all day, did women begin to take over the rearing of their sons.

In the summer of 1786, farmers' discontent over taxes broke into rebellion when Daniel Shays and his band attacked state troops at Springfield, Massachusetts, an action that was soon quelled. *(Drawing by Howard Pyle, Courtesy, The Library of Congress)*

We the People 1787–1800

SHAYS'S REBELLION (1786–1787)

On a snowy January afternoon at Springfield, Massachusetts, a rag-tag army of 1,200 farmers advanced towards the federal arsenal building. They were angry because the state legislature had ignored the petitions of hundreds of debt-ridden farmers whose farms and homes were in danger of foreclosure for failure to pay taxes. At their head was Daniel Shays, a former captain in the Continental army, now a destitute farmer unable to pay his state taxes. Near the arsenal, General William Sheperd and 600 militiamen waited, their cannons trained on Shays and his men. When the farmers came within a hundred yards of the arsenal, the cannons belched fire and smoke, the attackers faltered, and four fell dead. The rest broke ranks and retreated in disarray.

On January 27 General Benjamin Lincoln and a hastily-recruited force of over 4,000 men joined Shepherd at Springfield and pursued the embattled farmers across western Massachusetts to the village of Petersham. On February 4, 1787, this little army surprised the rebels and captured 150 of them. The rest fled, and Shays escaped across the snow-covered hills to Vermont.

Shays's Rebellion, as it was called, alarmed many Americans who feared that the new Confederation government was too weak, and that the country was on the verge of anarchy. "Every man of sense," said Congressman Fisher Ames, "must be convinced that our disturbances have arisen more from the want of power than the abuse of it."

In 1782 the Massachusetts state government, in order to pay off its Revolutionary War debts, had required all taxes to be paid in specie—hard money—instead of depreciating paper money, so that the state could afford to pay off its notes and bonds at their full face value. But for many people, coin was hard to come by. Especially in the four westernmost counties was the tax burdensome. Foreclosures were growing each year with no relief in view and little chance of redress from the legislature, which was controlled by the maritime and mercantile interests of the eastern part of the state.

In the best tradition of revolutionaries the farmers held protest meetings, drafted petitions, and organized committees of correspondence, using the methods they had perfected in the struggle against Great Britain a decade before. Conservatives in Boston, however, condemned this extra-legal action: "Let the majority [of the legislature] be ever so much in the wrong," legislative action was still the only course "compatible with the ideas of society and government." One of the loudest voices raised against the rebels was that of Sam Adams, the former revolutionary.

The farmers were not disposed to listen. Their wrath focused on the county courts, where judges were busily ordering forced sales of land to pay taxes and reimburse creditors. In August 1786, 1,500 farmers of Hampshire County prevented the meeting of its Court of Common Pleas. A few weeks later, at Worcester, a hundred men armed with swords, muskets, and clubs blocked the judge from entering the courthouse. The insurgency quickly spread across the western part of the state, and even far into the east, a mob breaking up the court session at Concord. When the rebels threatened to obstruct the Supreme Court at Springfield, Governor James Bowdoin called out the militia to protect it. In September Shays and a group of about 500 farmers successfully challenged the militia and forced the court to adjourn. Then the governor called for additional forces to protect the arsenal from seizure, and the January clash with rebel forces took place.

A popular ditty about Daniel Shays made the rounds in Massachusetts:

My name is Shays; in former days   Within the State I lived of late
In Pelham I did dwell sir.   By Satan's foul inventions
But now I'm forced to leave the place   In Pluto's cause against the law,
Because I did rebel, Sir.   I raised an insurrection.

In the annual spring elections, John Hancock replaced Bowdoin as governor, and a new slate of legislators who were mostly sympathetic to the farmers' plight took control. With a "total change of men," said Noah Webster, "there will be, therefore, no further insurrection, because the Legislature will represent the sentiments of the people." Hancock pardoned Shays; the legislature passed laws offering tax relief and exempting clothing, household items, and tools from seizure for debt. The rebellion was over, but concerns about the stability and order of the young republic remained.

Not all farmers had supported Shays. Jonathan Smith wrote: "I am a plain man, and I get my living by the plow." He spoke to his fellow "plow-joggers": "I have lived in a part of the country where I have known the worth of good government by the lack of it. The black cloud of Shays rebellion rose last winter in my area. It brought on a state of anarchy and that led to tyranny."

Yet the uprising alarmed many Americans. In a letter to a friend Washington could have been speaking for many who had fought for their independence. "I am mortified beyond expression," he wrote, "that in the moment of our independence we should by our conduct render ourselves ridiculous and contemptible in the eyes of all Europe." Richard Henry Lee of Virginia declared: "We are all in dire apprehension that a beginning of anarchy with all its calamitys has approached, and have no means to stop the dreadful work." The rebellion was an argument for Washington's conviction: "I do not conceive we can exist long as a nation without lodging, somewhere, a power which will pervade the whole Union in as energetic a manner as the authority of the state governments extends over the several states."

The Constitutional Convention

The scene now shifted to Philadelphia and the coming conference. With its 40,000 inhabitants, the city was the largest in the United States. During the postwar period it had suffered like other ports from the decline of foreign trade. Nonetheless, it remained a bustling community whose neat, tree-lined streets reflected the original orderly plan of its founder, William Penn, and the sobriety as well as the prosperity of its Quaker elite. The delegates who gathered in 1787 in Independence Hall were a mixed lot. Several men of great intellectual force and ability were prominent national leaders; still others scarcely contributed at all to the deliberations and disappeared from history after their brief day at the convention. Together this group of delegates from a settlement on the edge of a wilderness were to produce one of the most remarkable political schemes in the history of Western civilization.

The Founding Fathers The presiding officer, George Washington, richly honored as the commander in chief of the Continental forces that had defeated the British and made independence possible, enjoyed enormous prestige throughout the nation. His opening appeal to "raise a standard to which the wise and the honest can repair" set the tone for the solemn deliberations that followed. Nearly as eminent was Benjamin Franklin, fresh from the triumphs he had won as minister to France and chief negotiator of the peace treaty. Though now eighty-one and somewhat infirm, Franklin could still inspire confidence and rally support. Both men favored a stronger central government.

Yet a short and lively Virginian, James Madison, proved more important at the Convention than either of these two commanding figures. A close friend of Jefferson, a man of wide reading and deep reflection, Madison would be the major architect of the Constitution. A few of the more able men present at Philadelphia during the spring and summer of 1787—Robert Yates of New York, Luther Martin of Maryland, and George Mason of Virginia, for example—remained defenders of local power against expanded federal authority. Most of the delegates, however, were strong nationalists who wished and expected to remake the federal government into an effective instrument of the national will. Perhaps the convention's most extreme nationalist was New York's Alexander Hamilton, who had scant use for the states at all and would prefer to see them reduced to little more than administrative units.

All through the Philadelphia summer the fifty-five delegates in Independence Hall argued, negotiated, maneuvered, and deliberated. Nearly all of them lawyers and educated men, they drew on their knowledge of history, especially the experience of the ancient Roman republic. They also culled ideas from the political thinkers of their time, most notably Montesquieu, Harrington, and Blackstone. But ultimately their own common sense, their experience of government, and the interests of their states and their sections guided their decisions. Said John Dickinson, "Experience must be our only guide. Reason may mislead us."

Federalism

All agreed that the new government must be strong without being oppressive, and the delegates kept striving to balance liberty and order. The Constitution they finally produced represents a series of compromises between strong government and government limited in the interests of freedom, between national and local authority, and between the interests of the large states and the interests of the small.

Virginia and New Jersey Plans As debate opened Edmund Randolph of Virginia presented a proposal by his friend Madison. The Virginia Plan, as it would come to be called, recommended a new national legislature representing not the states, as the Confederation Congress did, but the people. The new body was to have two houses. The numbers that each state would have in both houses was to be proportionate either to the state's population or to its wealth. The voters of each state would choose directly their representatives to the lower house, and that state's delegation would select the state's delegates to the upper house. On other matters delegates in both houses were to vote as individuals, not as members of separate state delegations. The new Congress could define the powers of the federal government and overrule the states, appoint a national executive, and choose a new national judiciary.

The Virginia Plan came under immediate attack. Many delegates believed that it veered too far toward nationalism, practically obliterating the states as governing units. It also smacked of favoritism: the largest and richest states such as Virginia, Massachusetts, or Pennsylvania would have many more delegates in the new Congress than the smaller or poorer states such as New Hampshire, Georgia, and Rhode Island.

Opponents of the Virginia Plan countered with a scheme submitted by William Paterson of New Jersey. The New Jersey Plan provided for all the states to have equal representation in a single-chamber legislature. This new Congress would regulate foreign and interstate commerce, levy tariffs on imports, and impose various internal taxes. It would also choose the officers of the executive and judicial branches. All those powers not specified were to remain with the states.

For many weeks, debate swirled around these two proposals. Attacks on the Paterson proposal pointed out the injustice of allowing, say, the voice of a few thousand New Jerseyites to equal the voice of many more Virginians. The small-state people complained that under the Virginia Plan the three largest states could outvote virtually all the others together. The Randolph scheme raised another difficulty: who were to be counted as "population"? Should slaves, who could not vote, be considered the equals of freemen for purposes of representation? If so, the Southern states, with their many slaves, would have many more delegates in proportion to their voting population than the Northern states.

A Balanced Government

The Connecticut Plan, the chief among the compromises that the Convention finally hammered out, established a two-house national legislature. In the lower, the House of Representatives, the people of each state would be directly represented in proportion to population. In the upper, the Senate, each state legislature would elect two members regardless of population. A later arrangement determined that a slave would be treated as three-fifths of a person for the purpose of calculating representation in the House of Representatives. The new Congress was given broad powers over foreign and interstate commerce, permitted to levy taxes directly on citizens, and awarded the sole right to coin money and regulate its value.

Borrowing from the British Constitution's model of "mixed" government (monarchy, aristocracy, democracy embodied in King, Lords, and Commons) and from Enlightenment political thought a system of "checks and balances," the delegates set alongside Congress two other equal branches of government, the executive and the judiciary. The president, or executive, would be chosen by a group of "electors" in each state, the electors being in turn selected by any method each state legislature deemed best. The judicial branch, headed by a Supreme Court, would be selected by the president with the approval of the Senate. To insure the judges' independence from political pressure, the Convention provided that they would serve for life and could not have their salaries reduced. The president, too, would be independent of Congress. His term of office would last four years regardless of what Congress thought of him, and he could be re-elected.

Each branch of government—executive, legislative, and judiciary—was empowered to check the others, so that no one branch could become tyrannical. The president held the power of veto over laws enacted by Congress, although this veto could be overridden by a two-thirds vote in both houses. He would choose all federal judges, ambassadors, and high officials of executive departments, including what would later come to be called his "cabinet." But most of these appointments had to be confirmed by a two-thirds vote of the Senate. The Supreme Court, having jurisdiction over violation of federal laws and over suits between citizens of different states, was also going to exercise its own important brake on the other two branches. Though the Constitution contains no clause giving the Supreme Court and the lower federal courts the power to declare a federal law to be in violation of the Constitution, the Court soon after its establishment was to conclude that by implication it possessed that authority, and it has exercised that implicit power ever since Congress, in its turn, could put on trial and remove from office for bad conduct both the president and members of the judiciary.

Congress itself had a built-in check. The delegates at Philadelphia expected the House of Representatives to be the branch more responsive to the people as were the lower houses of the state legislatures, many of which still had property requirements for holding office. Under the Constitution the only requirements for Congressional office were that the candidate be a United States citizen, a resident of the state that elects him, and at least twenty-five years old. Under the original terms of the Constitution, members of the Senate were to be elected by the state legislatures rather than directly by the people of each state. The upper house would accordingly, the delegates believed, tend to be above public whims. Since any measure would have to pass both chambers to become law, the Senate could check the House and vice-versa. As a means (the Convention hoped) of assuring protection against excessive taxation, it was provided that all money bills would have to originate in the House.

By September 1787 the new Constitution had assumed its essential form. At times the debate had grown heated. Franklin had proposed that a chaplain open each session with a prayer for divine guidance. At least three delegates objected so strenuously to what the majority had wrought that they left Philadelphia in disgust. Many of those who stayed were not much happier. A substantial number of delegates continued to complain that the Constitution conferred too much power on the federal government. At least one delegate, Alexander Hamilton, believed it created too weak a government for America's needs.

Gouverneur Morris of Pennsylvania wrote a preamble to the document, and on September 17, with only three members abstaining (George Mason of Virginia said that he would rather cut off his right hand than sign the new document), the delegates affixed their signatures to the Constitution. Now it awaited the approval of Congress—and the people.

Ratification

On September 20, 1787, the Confederation Congress in New York received the Constitution composed in Philadelphia. A few members protested, calling it the work of a "dark conclave." One of its sharpest critics was the man who first proposed independence in 1776: Richard Henry Lee of Virginia. Opposing him was his cousin "Light Horse Harry" Lee, a young ex-cavalry officer and the future father of Robert E. Lee, who would lead an army against the Union in 1861. The majority agreed to transmit the Constitution to the states for ratification or rejection by special state conventions. For over a year, national political discussion would revolve about whether to accept the new Constitution or continue with the Articles.

By early 1788, five states, either unanimously or by overwhelming majorities, had ratified the Constitution. Elsewhere, especially in Massachusetts, Virginia, and New York there was a strong opposition.

Said the *Massachusetts Gazette:* "It is impossible for one code of laws to suit Georgia and Massachusetts." Amos Singletary, a self-described "poor" person of Massachusetts, put his case:

> We fought Great Britain—some said for a three-penny tax on tea; but it was not that. It was because they claimed a right to tax us and bind us in all cases whatever. And does not this Constitution do the same?
>
> These lawyers and men of learning and moneyed men, that talk so finely and gloss over matters so smoothly, to make us poor illiterate people swallow down the pill, expect to get into Congress themselves. They expect to be the managers of this Constitution, and get all the power and money into their own hands. And then they will swallow up all us little folks, just as the whale swallowed up Jonah!

Several leaders believed that the new frame of government offered insufficient protection from tyranny. One critic thought that

> The idea of an uncompounded republick, on an average, one thousand miles in length, and eight hundred in breadth, and containing six millions of white inhabitants all reduced to the same standard

of morals, of habits, and of laws, is in itself an absurdity, and contrary to the whole experience of mankind.

What these men wanted was a "bill of rights" that would defend personal freedoms against federal power.

The Anti-Federalists, the opponents of the Constitution, have been called "men of little faith." Beneath their specific objections to one or another provision of the new constitution lay a deep-seated distrust of all government no matter what form it might take. Governments are dangerous, said the Anti-Federalists, because they are composed of men, and men are corrupted by the exercise of power. Thus Anti-Federalists sought to limit the power of government.

One farmer complained that under the new Constitution "The purse-strings are given up. . . . The sword is also given up by this system. Is there no danger in giving up both? . . . In case of war, the last man and the last penny would be extorted from us."

In the same spirit Anti-Federalists believed that terms of office should be brief (usually this meant annual elections) so that the people could speedily turn out oppressive officials. And, of course, they opposed appointive offices. The obligation to run for office would itself, they thought, partially restrain tyrannical office-holders. Said one skeptical Anti-Federalist, "Every thing is to be done by our own representatives, who are to be good men. There is no security that they will be so, or continue to be so."

On June 21, New Hampshire became the ninth state to ratify and, by the terms of its own ratification provision, the new Constitution was now technically in effect, for nine states had accepted it. Yet two very important states, New York and Virginia, had not yet acted, and without them the new union would be like the limbs of a tree lacking a trunk. The Federalists desperately needed the two big states.

In Virginia the formidable Patrick Henry, James Monroe, and George Mason led the Anti-Federalists. Favoring the Constitution were James Madison, Edmund Randolph, and, above all, George Washington. The expectation that the state's most revered statesman would be the first President of the Republic made the Federalists difficult to stop. In the end Virginia ratified, but like Massachusetts requested a bill of rights.

The Federalist Papers and The Bill of Rights

Now the struggle shifted to New York. The inclusion of that state, with its great port and strategic mid-continental location, was essential if the union was to work. But for a while it seemed as if New York would refuse to enter the new union. The convention that assembled in Poughkeepsie was under the control of the state's stalwart Anti-Federalist governor, George Clinton. Arrayed against Clinton and his supporters, however, were John Jay, Secretary of Foreign Affairs, and the strong-willed Hamilton. Soon these two New York Federalists, joined by James Madison, were engaged in a war of words with their Anti-Federalist opponents. Day after day the *Independent Journal* carried the closely-argued essays in which the three men, writing under the common name "Publius," explained the virtues and necessity of the new Constitution. Dealing both with immediate concerns and universal political values, these eighty-five pieces—in 1788 published under the collective title *The Federalist*—constitute a classic commentary on the nature and purposes of government. Publius's articles, however, did little to change the minds of the Poughkeepsie delegates, most of whom were Anti-Federalists. More important was pressure from New York City, where merchants and artisans threatened that if New York State did not join the Union, New York City would. On July 25, 1788, after an impassioned personal address to the delegates by Hamilton, the state ratified the new frame of government.

Samuel Nasson, a saddlemaker, nicely caught the harmony between his view and the thinking that had driven the movement for independence:

> The eighth section [of the Constitution] provides that Congress shall have power to lay and collect taxes, duties, imposts, excises, etc. We may, sir, be poor; we may not be able to pay these taxes, etc. We must have a little cornmeal and a little meat, whereon to live, and save a little for a rainy day. But what follows? Let us see "To raise and support armies." Here, sir, comes the key to unlock this cabinet; here is the means by which you will be made to pay taxes! A standing army! Was it not with this that Caesar passed the Rubicon, and laid prostrate the liberties of his country?

Anti-Federalists wished to protect the people against government, but that does not mean that they trusted the individuals who

The Federal Plan Most Solid & Secure
Americans their Freedom Will Endure
All Arts Shall Flourish in Columbia's Land
And All her Sons Join as One Social Band

SOCIETY of PEWTERERS

SOLID AND PURE.

A silk banner carried by the Society of Pewterers of New York City in the Federal Procession, July, 1788, celebrating the impending ratification of the Constitution. (*Courtesy, The New-York Historical Society, New York City*)

collectively make up the people. Individuals who gain power, they believed, are too weak to wield it justly: they will succumb to the temptation to be tyrannical. But, as James Madison pointed out in *The Federalist* the same human weakness that makes government dangerous also makes it necessary.

Federalists were themselves men of little faith. They shared with their political opponents the same dour view of human nature. The difference was that they feared government less and people more. Hence they were eager to shield much of the government from direct popular control. Only the House of Representatives would be directly answerable to the people, and then only once every two years. The Senate would be elected by the state legislatures, the president by the electoral college. The judiciary would be appointed, and would hold office indefinitely. Each branch of the government would balance the others so that no one individual or party could work its will.

In March 1788 the Federalists received a

setback when Rhode Island rejected the Constitution. As the state where conflict during the Critical Period between debtors and creditors had been the most intense, Rhode Island represented the one clear case of a division along economic lines. The merchants and professional men, smelling certain defeat, boycotted the referendum, and their absence gave the Anti-Federalists a margin of ten to one. But Federalist victories by large majorities soon followed in Maryland and South Carolina.

The battle, in effect, was over. Rhode Island and North Carolina were still outside the new Union, but they did not seem essential. One North Carolinian grumbled, "We see plainly that men who come from New England are different from us. They are ignorant of our situation, they do not know the state of our country. They cannot with safety legislate for us." In November 1789 North Carolina officially ratified the Constitution and entered the Union. Reluctant Rhode Island joined at last in 1790. After setting up electoral procedures, the old Congress then quietly passed out of existence.

When the body of electors—called the "electoral college" voted on February 4, 1789, every presidential vote cast went for Washington, with John Adams of Massachusetts receiving the vice presidency. Newly-elected representatives and senators set out for the nation's temporary capital, and on March 4, 1789, the first Congress under the new Constitution assembled in New York City. Federal Hall, the former city hall, was still being remodeled and the new Senators and Representatives took their seats amidst the carpenters' noise and flying sawdust. The confusion and disorder caused little harm. Only eight Senators and thirteen Representatives had slogged their way through the muddy roads of spring to take their oaths of office that opening day.

Senator William Maclay of Pennsylvania wrote to his friend Benjamin Rush on March 9: "I never felt greater mortification in my life to be so long here with the eyes of all the world on us and to do nothing is terrible."

April 14, 1789, Washington received formal notice of his election. Two days later he wrote in his diary, "About ten o'clock I bade farewell to Mount Vernon . . . and with a mind oppressed with more anxious and painful sensations than I have words to express, set out for New York." There, in the nation's temporary capital, on April 30, he was sworn into office and delivered his first inaugural address. The celebration in New York when Washington came to the city for his presidential inauguration exceeded anything previously seen in the young nation. The barge that brought the President-elect across New York harbor from New Jersey was surrounded by large and small vessels of every sort, full of cheering passengers. Washington made his way through streets lined with exu-

berant citizens. At night the city was illuminated with bonfires, and happy celebrants crowded the city's thoroughfares and coffee-houses.

The next few months were busy ones. In the fall, Congress drafted a Bill of Rights, the first ten amendments to the Constitution, which the prescribed three-fourths of the states quickly ratified. The first eight amendments placed certain fundamental restraints on the power of the federal government over ordinary citizens. Congress could not limit free speech, interfere with religion, deny to the people the right to keep and bear arms, require the quartering of troops in private homes, or allow homes to be searched by federal authorities without search warrants. Persons accused of crimes could not be made to testify against themselves, nor could the federal government deny the citizens trial by jury or deprive them of life, liberty, or property "without due process of law." The central government could not impose excessive bail or "cruel and unusual punishments." Amendment IX ordained that the rights included in the earlier list did not exclude others; Amendment X provided that those powers not given to the federal government or denied the states should belong solely to the states or the people.

Never before had any single document enumerated so clearly and emphatically the rights of private citizens. The Bill of Rights became, accordingly, a landmark in the history of human liberty. But the Bill applied to the federal government only. It was recognized that most of the states had similar provisions in their own constitutions. But what if a state chose to violate fundamental human rights; would a citizen have any official or agency to turn to? That question would not be answered until the twentieth century.

The Hamiltonian Program

| **The New Government** | Friends of the Constitution composed most of Congress. Many members had been present at Philadelphia during the momentous summer of 1787 to write the new frame of government, and the majority hoped to carry out the purposes of the nationalists:

to make the United States a going concern and create respect for the republic among the older nations of the world.

Yet the first deliberations were nearly farcical. For three weeks the members debated the proper title of address for the president. Vice President John Adams insisted that

The votes of nine states were needed to ratify the Constitution of the United States. *(Courtesy, American Antiquarian Society)*

without some such title as "His Elective Highness" or "His Excellency," the president might be mistaken for the head of a volunteer fire company or leader of a cricket club. Adams's opponents believed any such title would be "aristocratical," unrepublican. They mocked the pudgy vice president's serious concern, and took to calling him "His Rotundity." Senator Maclay wrote about Adams in his diary:

> May 2, 1789—He is not well furnished with small talk more than myself and has a very silly kind of laugh. I have often looked with the utmost attention at him to see if his aspect, air, etc. could inspire me with an opinion of his being a man of genius; but . . . no; the thing seems impossible . . .
> June 22—His pride, obstinacy, and folly are equal to his vanity.

Secretary of State Jefferson, on the other hand, impressed Maclay with his nonchalance:

> Jefferson is a slender man; has rather the air of stiffness in his manner; his clothes seem too small for him; he sits in a lounging manner, on one hip commonly, and with one of his shoulders elevated much above the other; his face has a sunny aspect; his whole figure has a loose, shackling air. He had a rambling, vacant look, and nothing of that firm, collected deportment which I expected would dignify the presence of a secretary or minister. I looked for gravity, but a laxity of manner seemed shed about him. He spoke almost without ceasing. But even his discourse partook of his personal demeanor. It was loose and rambling, and yet he

scattered information wherever he went, and some even brilliant sentiments sparkled from him. The information which he gave us respecting foreign ministers, etc., was all high-spiced.

Washington himself settled the momentous issue of his title. Though protective of his dignity on all occasions, he preferred to avoid "monarchical" trappings. He did travel through the streets in a gilded coach and held "levees," formal receptions for visitors and guests, but he would not accept a title of any sort. He wished to be addressed as "Mr. President"—the same as when he had presided over the Convention of 1787. From the beginning, Washington's commanding presence lent the new government some badly needed respect and dignity. Besides his title, the first chief executive set other precedents for the conduct of the presidency. Early in his administration Washington, taking literally his power to "make treaties" with "the advice and consent of the Senate," appeared before the Senators to explain an Indian treaty. After an awkward debate a Senator proposed referring the treaty to committee. The President, offended by this snub, stormed out, saying that he would "be damned" if he would ever come back. He did return once, but no other President has attempted to discuss treaties personally with the entire Senate.

Meanwhile, Congress had set up three major executive departments, State, War, and Treasury, and appointed a Postmaster General. It also passed the Federal Judiciary Act, which specified that the Supreme Court was to consist of a chief justice with five associates. John Jay, the first Chief Justice, resigned to run for governor of New York in 1795, saying that under "a system so defective, the court would not obtain the energy, weight and dignity which are essential . . . nor acquire the public confidence and respect which, as the last resort of justice of the nation, it should possess." At Jefferson's urging the justices discarded the wearing of wigs, which he said made "the English Judges look like rats peeping through bunches of oakum." It also established a system of federal courts and created the office of Attorney General as the government's chief law officer.

In response to one of the new government's most pressing concerns, that of providing itself with revenues, Congress passed the nation's first tariff, setting low duties on a host of imported goods. Congress now had the means to pay the army and official salaries, and to begin to meet its debts. But those debts were still troublesome. By 1789 they amounted to about $52 million—$40 million owed to Americans, and $12 million due foreigners. In addition to these obligations of the federal government, there were also the still-unpaid state debts, amounting to about $25 million.

Few people doubted that the foreign debt must be paid in full. Otherwise, the United States would not earn the respect of foreign powers or be able to borrow abroad again. But what about the domestic debt? Speculators had bought Continental IOU's for a song from those who had actually given the wartime Congress money or supplies to fight the British. Should these speculators alone benefit by the improved credit of the national government, or should the original holders also get something? And what about the state debts? Many Southern states had already paid off these obligations while many Northern states had not. If the government were to "assume" or take over these obligations, the residents of the Middle states and New England would benefit at the expense of those south of Pennsylvania. Congress turned over to Alexander Hamilton, Washington's Secretary of the Treasury, the problem of how to handle the debt as well as other pending financial questions.

| **Alexander Hamilton**   A young man of thirty-five, Hamilton was a former aide-de-camp to Washington who had married into the prominent Schuyler family of New York. Able, handsome, and well-connected, he had risen high in New York political life after his army service despite his West Indies origin and his illegitimate birth.

Hamilton was a nationalist, lacking the emotional attachment that men like Jefferson and Madison felt for the local community. Like many other veterans of the Continental Army, he recalled bitterly the petty jealousies and selfishness of the states during the Revolutionary War. He had so little respect for the states that at the Constitutional Convention he had proposed their virtual elimination. He prized banking, trade, and manufacturing, and believed that the United States could not afford to remain an agricultural nation, producing raw materials for Eu-

rope. Britain, rapidly becoming the industrial workshop of the world, must be America's example, he claimed. This required a vigorous central government commanding its citizens' loyalty. Hamilton was skeptical of human nature. Men of the Enlightenment, such as Jefferson, tended to believe that human beings were inherently more good than evil, social and political evil being the result largely of evil institutions. Freed of these, mankind would flourish. Hamilton believed that the people tended to be "ambitious, vindictive, and rapacious." He wrote, ". . . they seldom judge or determine right."

Congress's problem was Hamilton's opportunity. The new Secretary of the Treasury seized the occasion to advance some of his fondest political and economic hopes. In three great *Reports* he incorporated his solution to several immediate problems in larger plans for American society.

| **Hamilton's Reports**   The *Report Relative to Public Credit* boldly proposed that the national debt be paid in full through a complicated process known as "funding." Current holders would exchange their IOU's at par for interest-bearing bonds. Hamilton asserted that the public debt would prove a "public blessing." His *Report on a National Bank* early in 1791 explained why. The nation's economic development required stronger currency and banking facilities. Hamilton proposed a new federally chartered banking corporation, drawing its capital both from the Treasury and from private investors. The new "Bank of the United States," governed by privately elected directors and others chosen by the government, would serve both public and private needs. It would stimulate commerce and manufactures by lending money to private businessmen. The bank would as well hold the government's deposits, pay its bills, and accept its receipts, but the institution's most important service was to issue the paper money of the nation. In itself, paper money was considered a cheap, untrustworthy currency, but the Bank's paper would have something solid to back it up. Its holders could, if they so wished, have the government give them in place of it an equivalent amount in the securities that were part of the new funding scheme. And the public's knowledge that the currency would be so exchanged would make for willingness to use

Paul Revere, the patriot silversmith, made this silver punch bowl to honor General William Shepard for defeating the Massachusetts farmers' rebellion led by Daniel Shays. (*Courtesy, Yale University Art Gallery*)

it. Hamilton was planning to convert the national debt of a gold-poor country into a powerful engine for mobilizing its economy.

Later in 1791 Hamilton issued the last of the major *Reports,* on manufactures. The Secretary acknowledged that agriculture was currently the most important single economic activity, but he saw no conflict between agriculture and industry. The two complemented each other; both together would benefit the nation. Noting the beginnings of the factory system in Britain, Hamilton observed that the new system of manufacture employed every class of people in productive labor, even women and children. Hamilton especially favored the employment of women in factories, believing that in a predominantly agricultural society men would be needed, and would prefer, to work the land. He viewed women as the most readily available pool of wage labor. The United States with its magnificent resources was potentially a great industrial nation, but to compete with other nations would require government aid. To protect "infant industries" until they could compete successfully, the government must impose high tariffs that would raise the price of foreign manufactures. It should also offer

premiums for the production of needed goods and new inventions. Above all, the proposed bank must lend capital to entrepreneurs.

Hamilton's three *Reports* together outlined an economic revolution. Through the energetic use of the national government, the country might be transformed: bustling cities, humming factories, and busy arteries of communication and transport would erupt from the quiet American landscape of prosperous farms and trackless forests.

Hamilton's friends submitted bills to Congress implementing the recommendations of his reports. But the program, so bold in its projections, aroused fierce opposition. Said one observer, "Faction glows within like a coalpit." Hamilton's vision threatened to violate the character of the nation as some Americans saw it, a land of small farms and the simple social relations of the countryside. Many also feared the expansion of federal powers his program required. They imagined that Hamilton's schemes would create an all-powerful centralized government that would become the source of graft and corruption. In the new nation, as in Britain, liberty and republican virtue would then degenerate into tyranny and licentiousness. Especially fearful were the Virginia leaders—James Madison, now a leading member of the House of Representatives, and Thomas Jefferson, Washington's Secretary of State.

Jefferson deplored the industrial and urban society that Hamilton eagerly anticipated. Having witnessed European urban life, Jefferson was convinced that "the mobs of great cities" were "sores" on the social body, and that when people "get piled up one upon another as in Europe, they shall become corrupt as in Europe." Farmers, he insisted, were God's "Chosen People, if ever he had a chosen people," and they along with solid urban holders of some modest amount of property could be relied on to support the common good. The Virginia leaders also believed that Hamilton and his supporters wanted to create a plutocracy, a government of the rich. Jefferson feared both the rich and the mob; the Hamiltonians, it seemed, feared only the mob.

Hamilton's bill to fund the public debt aroused Madison, who quickly became the leader of the forces arrayed against Hamilton. Madison spoke as a southerner, aware that four-fifths of the unpaid securities and state debts were northern. Yet his attack was a principled one. He did not oppose funding in itself, he declared; rather, he believed that Hamilton's scheme unduly benefited speculators. Under Hamilton's plan these people would receive the full face value of their holdings, while original possessors would get nothing. Even now, Madison and his supporters asserted, advance news that the government would assume the state debts had been leaked by people in high places, and speculators were traveling through the South buying up securities from gullible farmers.

For many weeks the funding bill remained blocked. The particular sticking point was the provision that the federal government would assume the payment of the states' debts. Then one morning in July, Jefferson bumped into Hamilton on the steps of the President's house. The Secretary of the Treasury told the Secretary of State that the deadlock in Congress was endangering the Union. Could Jefferson do anything to help? The next day the two cabinet officers met with Madison, and a deal was arranged. The national capital would be moved from New York to Philadelphia. Then, in ten years, it would be permanently located in the South

between Virginia and Maryland, even though one northerner argued that, "It is the opinion of all the Eastern states, that the climate of the Potomac is not only unhealthy, but destructive to northern constitutions." In return, Madison and his friends would cease to oppose assumption. The following month the funding measure passed Congress.

Next on the agenda was a national bank. The bill would charter a Bank of the United States for twenty years with a capital of $10 million, one-fifth to be subscribed by the federal government and the remainder by private investors. Philadelphia was to be the bank's home office, but it might establish branches in other cities.

Over the opposition of Madison, Congress passed the bill chartering the Bank and sent it to the President for his signature. Washington was stumped. His fellow Virginian, Madison, had raised doubts in his mind as to whether the Constitution allowed Congress to charter such a bank. Might this not be an unwarranted extension of federal powers? The President asked for the opinions of his Cabinet. Both Jefferson and Attorney General Edmund Randolph replied that by no stretch of its meaning did the Constitution authorize a federally chartered bank. Hamilton took the opposite view. In a masterly application of what came to be called the principle of "broad construction" of the Constitution, he argued that since a bank was necessary to the collecting of taxes, the regulating of trade, and other functions explicitly conferred on Congress in that great document, its constitutionality was "implied," if not specified. Convinced by Hamilton's logic, Washington signed the bill into law. On July 4, 1791, the stock of the Bank was put up for sale. In a few hours the whole $8 million reserved to private investors was sold out and hundreds of eager capitalists had to be turned down.

The third of Hamilton's *Reports* was not enacted into law in his own day. It stood, however, as an eloquent defense of a high tariff that would become an inspiration to later generations of protectionists. Meanwhile, other items of Hamiltonian legislation also became law. In 1791 Congress passed the Whiskey Tax, imposing an excise on distilled liquors to help pay interest on the funded debt. In 1792 it passed the Coinage Act, establishing the dollar as the United States currency unit, dividing it into smaller coins, and making it equivalent to a specified amount of gold or silver.

| Hamiltonians vs. Jeffersonians | As Congress and the American people debated the Hamiltonian program, two distinct and conflicting positions began to emerge. One had as its principal spokesmen Jefferson and his chief congressional lieutenant, Madison. On the other side were Hamilton and his followers, including John Adams, and, increasingly, President Washington himself.

The Jeffersonians favored state over national power and agriculture over industry, trade, and banking. They advocated a limited government and "strict construction" of the Constitution, a refusal to believe that the Constitution granted to any branch of government the slightest particle of power beyond what the words of the document specifically and explicitly stated. They claimed to have faith in the people and to distrust the rich and powerful. Many were southerners, deeply attached to their local communities, which they did not want to come under the domination of a powerful central government. But the Jeffersonian party would also win support among the farmers of the Middle and New England states and the artisans of the towns. Increasingly this group called itself the Democratic Republicans, a label they adopted to contrast their political views with the supposedly more "monarchical" ones of their Federalist opponents.

The Hamiltonians favored an ever stronger federal government, if necessary at the expense of the states. They believed that the nation's future lay in industry, not in agriculture alone. Generally speaking, they accepted republicanism as best suited to the American genius, but they did not trust majority rule as much as did their opponents, and they hoped to attract the support of the rich and the powerful to the new national government by making their interests coincide with those of the government. The Federalists could count on strong support within the major commercial towns, including such southern ports as Charleston. As defenders of order and stability they could also count on those people who were by temperament conservative. One group that often favored the Federalist position was the defenders of the established Congregational church in New England. On the other side were to be found the Baptists, Methodists, and other dissenting groups, which tended to be Democratic Republican.

Foreign Affairs

| The French Revolution (1789) | No sooner had the new government under the Constitution begun its work in New York than Europe went into a colossal political convulsion. In France, the colonies' ally in the war for independence, the American struggle for liberty had been deeply influential. "Enlightened" men and women recognized a larger significance in the event, and it strengthened their resolve to reform the Bourbon monarchy, custodian of the privilege and inequality that for centuries had shackled the French people. In August 1788 the French king, faced with a severe financial crisis partly induced by France's recent aid to the American revolutionaries, called into session the Estates General, representative of the clergy, nobility, and middle class, expecting that body to give him the taxes he needed, and then adjourn. But instead groups of reformers quickly took over. In a matter of a few months they had converted the Estates General into a revolutionary body that began to replace the entire old regime and convert the nation into a constitutional monarchy based on respect for human rights and on wide popular political participation. On July 14, 1789, a Paris mob attacked the Bastille, the prison that had become a notorious symbol of oppression, tore down the walls, and freed the prisoners.

The early response in the United States to the electrifying events in France was almost universally favorable. When the Marquis de Lafayette, who had helped lead the early stages of the Revolution, sent Washington the key to the Bastille, the President hung the key prominently in the presidential mansion. He later wrote Gouverneur Morris that he hoped the disorders in France would "terminate very much in favor of the rights of man." If such a reserved and inherently conservative man as Washington could applaud the French uprising, the followers of Jefferson were still more enthusiastic. Many Republicans, in imitation of French egalitarianism, adopted the title "Citizen" or "Citizeness" in place of "Mister" or "Mistress." In Hingham, Massachusetts, a Republican wearing a French cockade in his hat was mobbed after attending a church service, and

> the hat fell from the gallery and the Federalists over benches, pews, etc., ran and caught it, from which they dismounted the [cock]ade. This was followed by clinching, swearing, and even by blows. The screechings of old women heightened the scene. Here was in view justices, lawyers, and even grand juries, all clinched by collars, hair, and cheeks, until at last the Jacobins were thrust out of the house, some with no hats, others with bloody cheeks, and nearly all with dishevelled polls [heads].

Others began to abandon knee breeches and adopt the long trousers worn by the Paris artisans and the French reformers. Republicans considered the French Revolution the beginning of a new age. As Jefferson wrote, "the liberty of the whole earth" depended on the contest in France.

In time the initial consensus among Americans disintegrated. Increasingly the French radical leaders, called Jacobins, denounced the church and organized religion. In 1791 King Louis XVI fled Paris with his family, but was caught and thrown into prison. By this time many enemies of the Revolution, including a large part of the French clergy and nobility, had been either driven from the country or hustled off to jail. Soon after, the Revolutionary leaders began a reign of terror against all opponents of their policies, even the moderate reformers. In 1793 a revolutionary tribunal proclaimed a "war of all peoples against all kings." The tribunal then pronounced the death sentence on Louis XVI, and the sentence was promptly carried out. In October his queen, Marie Antoinette, was also sent to the guillotine. In Boston a parade "eight citizens deep" offered a "Peace Offering to Liberty and Equality." But as time passed the excesses of the French revolutionaries shocked many Americans.

Soon radical French leaders proclaimed a crusade against conservative regimes elsewhere in Europe in the name of "liberty, equality, fraternity." Before long, France was at war with Austria, England, Prussia, and Spain. Surrounded as it was with enemies, France sought aid from its ally, the United States. Jefferson thought France's struggle "the most sacred cause that ever man was engaged in" but did not want the U.S. to go to war. Under the Treaty of 1778 the Americans were bound to protect France's West Indies colonies against any enemy. England was certain to use her powerful fleet to blockade and, if possible, take these possessions. The United States now faced the serious prospect of war with Great Britain.

Many Americans would have welcomed such a war. Britain still limited American commerce with her own West Indies possessions. She still occupied western garrisons on American soil. She still stirred up the Indians of the Northwest to discourage American settlement west of the mountains. Now that Britain was locked in combat with revolutionary France, she seemed the special enemy of liberty and freedom. And in 1793 the British began to seize American vessels engaged in trade with the French West Indies and to throw their crews into foul dungeons.

Among the followers of Hamilton, however, France represented all that was chaotic, disorderly, irreligious. That country, exclaimed Fisher Ames, was "an open hell, still ringing with agonies and blasphemies, still smoking with sufferings and crimes." Britain the Hamiltonians perceived as a bulwark of sanity and moderation, and they thought her victory in the struggle to be essential for world order. Another consideration weighed heavily in Federalist calculations. The whole Hamiltonian fiscal program depended on international trade, and in 1793 the United States, like the colonies for over a century before, traded primarily with Britain. Any wartime disruption of this trade would dry up revenues, injure the new national government, and thwart the Federalist economic program.

| Citizen Genêt Meanwhile, the French Republic had dispatched Citizen Edmond Genêt as diplomatic minister to the United States to do what he could to make trouble for Great Britain. Arriving in Charleston early in 1793, Genêt immediately set to work recruiting Americans in his nation's cause. Even before presenting his formal credentials to Washington and Secretary of State Jefferson in Philadelphia, he had commissioned Americans as privateers to prey on British commerce, and opened negotiations with several American frontier leaders to attack Spanish Florida and Louisiana.

Citizen Genêt, who came to America to stir up controversy against Britain, remained to live as a country gentleman in Orange County, New York. *(From the Emmet Collection, Manuscript Division, New York Public Library)*

Despite these highhanded actions, American friends of France cheered Genêt as he made a triumphal procession to the capital. "I live in a round of parties," he wrote, "Old Man Washington can't forgive my success."

By this time Washington, supported by Hamilton and Jefferson, had decided to proclaim American neutrality. In April 1793 the President issued a proclamation declaring the intent of the United States "to pursue a conduct friendly and impartial toward the French and British" and warning that individuals aiding the belligerents would be liable to prosecution in federal courts. Genêt learned of this seeming repudiation of the 1778 treaty but, convinced by his recent experience that Americans were fervent partisans of the French, he determined to ignore it. Hinting that the United States might acquire Canada by aiding the French cause, Genêt commissioned several land speculators as officers in the French Army at the Mississippi. Though at first a hero of the Jeffersonians, Genêt finally offended even the friends of the French Republic. So outrageous were his actions that Jefferson wrote Madison that the French minister would "sink the Republican interest" if the Republicans did not "abandon him." Reprimanded by President Washington and informed that his acts infringed upon American sovereignty, Genêt promised to cease his activities, but then he immediately set about arming yet another vessel as a privateer. Warned not to continue, he threatened to appeal to the American people over the head of Washington. The administration decided it had had enough. In August the United States government demanded Genêt's recall. Washington informed the Congress that the French envoy's conduct threatened "war abroad and discord and anarchy at home." By this time the Jacobins were in power in France. Genêt, who did not belong to this group, most certainly would have been beheaded had he been forced to return to France. The administration allowed him to stay in the United States, but refused to deal with him any further. He soon married the daughter of a member of the politically prominent Clinton family and settled into the quiet life of a country gentleman.

Settlement with Great Britain

While Americans rioted in the streets for or against Genêt, the United States was moving toward a settlement of sorts with Great Britain. Late in 1793 Jefferson, whose sympathies lay increasingly with France, resigned as Secretary of State. Edmund Randolph, another Virginian, succeeded him. Early in 1794 Washington sent Chief Justice John Jay to England as special envoy. John Adams wrote to Jefferson: "The President has sent Mr. Jay to try if he can to find a way to reconcile our honour with Peace. I have no great Faith in very brilliant Success; but hope he may have enough to keep us out of war." Jay, a staunch Federalist, knew that it would be difficult to get an agreement with Great Britain that would be popular. He was right.

The Jay Treaty (1795) The British made much of the American emissary. He in turn bowed to the Queen and kissed her hand, an act that outraged ardent Republicans. One journalist wrote:

John Jay, ah, the arch traitor—seize him, drown him, hang him, burn him, flay him alive! Men of America, he betrayed you with a kiss! As soon as he set foot on the soil of England he kissed the

Queen's hand . . . and with this kiss betrayed away the rights of man and the liberty of America.

The British did not want war with the United States, but neither did they want to adopt any policy that promised to weaken their war effort against France. They drove a hard bargain. In the agreement that Jay carried back from London, the British promised finally to surrender the military posts they had illegally occupied since 1783. Other disagreements, including disputes over the pre-Revolutionary debts owed Englishmen, a boundary dispute with Canada in the Northwest, and the recent British ship seizures, were referred to British-American arbitration commissions. This device of an arbitration commission was an important diplomatic innovation, and in future years the two countries would make much use of it. Left unsettled were such longstanding American complaints as British incitements of Indians in the West and restrictive trade practices in the British West Indies colonies. On the question of British right to limit neutral trade in wartime, Jay retreated from the original American principle "free ships make free goods"—that a nation at war could not seize the goods carried in a neutral ship trading with the enemy nation—and agreed that the British could seize French or other enemy property found aboard American ships.

Jay returned to the United States to find his fellow Americans in no mood to swallow this ungenerous agreement. In the summer of 1794 General Anthony Wayne had smashed the Indians at the Battle of Fallen Timbers in northwestern Ohio. "Mad Anthony" forced the tribes to sign the Treaty of Greenville surrendering all of Ohio and a large part of Indiana to the Americans. Few concerned themselves with Indian rights, but one congressman made an impassioned plea:

> Do these natives hold a land we have an indubitable right to claim? Are we so contracted in territory that we stand in immediate need of immeasurable tracts of wilderness? We are told we have purchased it! Is a keg or two of whiskey, a couple of bundles of laced coats, and a few packages of blankets, an equivalent for a region as great as a kingdom? Is a treaty signed by the scratches of the drunken chief of two tribes to be binding on the chiefs of a hundred tribes? No. They have as much right to their hunting-grounds as we have to our cities or our farms.

Jay's negotiations were greeted everywhere with outrage. One ardent Republican,

unable to contain his feelings, inscribed on his fence: "Damn John Jay! damn every one that won't damn John Jay!! damn every one that won't put lights in his windows and sit up all night damning John Jay!!!" When Republicans met in taverns they toasted "A perpetual harvest to America; but clip't wings, lame legs, the pip, and an empty crop to all Jays." Jay himself ruefully remarked that he could have traveled across the nation by the light of his burning effigies.

Hamilton and other Federalists nonetheless marshaled their forces and wrote articles supporting the agreement as the best that could be obtained. Federalist Congressman Fisher Ames argued that if it were not approved the British and Indians would attack the frontier settlements: "I can fancy that I listen to the yells of savage vengeance, and the shrieks of torture." Washington put his prestige behind the treaty, earning for his efforts the contempt of the Republicans. Jefferson remarked: "Curse on his virtues; they have undone the country." But in June 1795 the Senate by a close vote confirmed the Treaty. Republican Nathaniel Ames wrote: "The Treaty fish swallowed, tail foremost, by Congress." A Congressman named Andrew

John Jay, by Gilbert Stuart. Jay's Treaty of 1795 settled most of the disputes with Britain left over from the Confederation period, but was very unpopular at home. *(Courtesy, National Gallery of Art, Washington, D.C. Lent by Mrs. Peter Jay)*

Jackson thought Washington should be impeached for signing such a "cowardly treaty." One Republican wrote in his diary of his disappointment with the President: "Better his hand had been cut off when his glory was at its height, before he blasted all his laurels." A Federalist woman wrote to a friend that Congress was quiet for the moment, but "what the Demoniaks of Congress may bring forward to excite new commotions on the subject we shall soon know."

Whatever its inadequacies, the Jay Treaty settled most of the disputes with Britain left over from the Confederation period. But difficulties with Spain remained. Then, in 1795, the Spanish government and the United States signed the Pinckney Treaty. This agreement granted Americans rights of free navigation on the Mississippi, restraints on the Florida Indians, and the "right of deposit" for their goods in New Orleans for a period of three years. Although the three-year provision implied possible trouble for the future, the nation greeted the Pinckney Treaty with great enthusiasm and the Senate ratified it unanimously. The treaty ended temporarily the threat that western regions of the United States, dependent on unimpeded use of the Mississippi River, might secede from the Union.

The Whiskey Rebellion

Although the federal government now possessed augmented powers under the new Constitution and the prestige that the national hero, George Washington, brought as its president, it was nonetheless a most fragile polity beset by enormous pressures. No one was certain what to expect from a republic. History told of dangers from mob rule, and the frightening drama of the revolution in France seemed to be confirming that view. Renewed war between France and Great Britain pointed up American weakness. Different American regions, political factions, and ethnic groups had their own interests, and looming over all were the diverging concerns of the rich and the poor, the agrarians and the developing commercial elites, the varying class and economic groups of a sprawling new nation.

The new government's great initiative to

The tarring and feathering of an excise officer during the Whiskey Rebellion (*Courtesy, Brown Brothers*)

unite this variegated republic was Secretary of the Treasury Alexander Hamilton's financial plan. One cornerstone of that policy was an excise tax on alcoholic beverages. This would provide revenues to fund the national debt and to finance the government—including, many feared, its military capacity.

Whiskey was the cash crop of western Pennsylvania. Readily transportable and salable, corn liquor stored much better than the grain from whence it came. It gurgled and jostled in jugs and barrels swaying across the mountains on the backs of mules to slake the thirst of easterners with coins in their pockets. Westerners, even when they hungered for the word of God, continued to thirst for the "old Monongahela rye." The evangelical religion so strong in western Pennsylvania had not yet come out against the drinking cup. A local observer wrote of the back country habits:

> The use of whiskey was universal. The quality was good, the taste pleasant, its effect agreeable. Storekeepers kept liquor on their counters and sold it in their stores, and the women customers used it as well as the men. Farmers kept barrels of it in their cellars. . . . It was good for fevers, it was good for a decline, it was good for ague, it was good for snake-bites. It made one warm in winter and cool in summer. It was used at all gatherings. Bottles of it were set out on the table at christenings and wakes. . . . Ministers drank it. . . . Rev. Father McGirr's drink was whiskey-punch, of which it is said he could drink with any of his day without giving scandal.

Westerners did not like the excise tax. They objected, as one petition phrased it, to "a duty for drinking our grain more than eating it." They objected to the appointment of excisemen with their right of entering private property and inspecting stills. And they especially objected to the federal court's trying cases against those who refused to pay the exciseman's levy. These trials required expensive and disruptive jaunts across the mountains to federal court at Philadelphia. The West, cut off from the Mississippi trade by the Spanish, and from most trade other than in alcohol by the expense of carrying goods over the mountains, was desperately short of currency. The drain of excise payments was a burden on the region's economy. Pennsylvanians had to wonder why the government in Philadelphia (then the nation's capital) could not open the Mississippi to them rather than spending its time and effort on collecting this hugely unpopular tax.

The backcountry was not strong on being governed. These western farmers, particularly the Scotch-Irish Presbyterians, had little faith in anyone's governance but their own. They were soon passing resolutions not merely calling for an end to the tax, but overtly threatening excisemen and even those who cooperated with them by paying the tax. Soon barns began to be fired, gristmills damaged, excisemen attacked. "Tom the Tinker's men," it was claimed, were everywhere "mending" stills. This became the local expression for shooting holes in stills whose owners had paid the tax.

The West was not united on the issue. Battle spread between the small and the large whiskey producers, as the more prosperous distillers began to realize that this specie-draining tax would eventually drive the small producers out of business, leaving the more substantial men with a lucrative monopoly. Wealthy men feared as well that this excise rebellion could ignite into a war against property. In 1794 this almost came true, as the backwoods farmers marched on Pittsburgh, threatening to burn to the ground that symbol of the advance of commercial capitalism. Only adroit maneuverings by several Pittsburgh leaders persuaded the farmers that they ran too large a risk of retribution if they fired the city.

Something had to be done about the sporadic rioting in the West. A finding that the courts had been obstructed in carrying out the excise law provided the federal government with grounds for intervention. Hamilton, eager for a show of force that would establish the precedent of federal military power, led the administration in a vast overreaction. Washington himself for a time directed a larger force than he had ever at one time commanded during the Revolution. Disorganized militia, about 13,000 strong, slogged through endless mud during a rainy November in search of a rebellion. Hamilton marched with the army from start to finish but was not away from his desk overly long; the army remained in the West about three weeks before arresting a few men and marching back to Philadelphia for heroes' welcomes. A grand jury in 1795 indicted over thirty men for treason. Of these but two were convicted. Both were mentally incompetent, and Washington pardoned them.

Despite the element of comedy within the rebellion—a sense that it had perhaps resulted from a bit too much of the spirits at issue—the episode possesses considerable importance for the political and constitutional development of the United States. A direct result of the insurrection was the forcing out of the last Jeffersonian, Edmund Randolph, who had succeeded Jefferson as secretary of state. Never again, except in moments of wartime emergency and then as a deliberate departure from the norm, would any president strive for a nonpartisan rather than a party government. The events of the rebellion had brought successes for both sides in the quarrel. The precedent of national power that Hamilton and Washington considered necessary for the future success of the American

experiment was firmly established: without firing a shot, they had won something they had succeeded in defining as a war. What the farmers failed to achieve by rioting they got from the political activity that followed: in 1802 the new Jeffersonian government repealed the hated excise tax. Americans remained by all accounts the hardest-drinking people in the world for two more generations until a new wave of evangelism from the West brought fundamental changes in American values, and millions of Americans forgot the "old Monongahela rye" and denounced "Demon rum."

John Adams's Presidency

Political Parties

In 1796 the nation faced its first contested presidential election. By this time American voters had a choice between two distinct parties. As yet, little of the machinery of party politics or campaigns had appeared, but throughout the nation people had begun to call themselves either Federalists or Republicans and their opponents by stronger and ruder names.

The division of the country into these two opposing political camps disturbed many Americans. The founders of the Republic, including the authors of the Constitution, had not envisioned political parties. The voters, they believed, should choose for office the best, most public-spirited men. Partisan organizations appeared to be dangerous instruments of selfish men that impeded, rather than advanced, expression of the general will. Many Americans of the 1790s regarded parties as symptomatic of a disease within the body politic. Even the ambitious men engaged in creating the factions thought that they were, at best, necessary evils. "If I could not go to heaven but with a party," Jefferson once wrote, "I would not go there at all."

Such fears were, in part, the legacy of revolutionary thought, particularly the tendency to see an embattled republic surrounded by foreign foes and beset with domestic dangers.

These beliefs actually contributed to the party spirit and the frenzied political temper of the 1790s. The distrust of party, the belief that party politics expressed corruption and conspiracy, made Americans of each faction look on the other side as polluting the virtu-

ous republic: and so each faction deepened its own partisan emotion. Public men, Jefferson wrote a friend, no longer seemed "to separate political and personal differences. Men who have been intimate all their lives, cross the street to avoid meeting, and turn their heads another way, lest they should be obliged to touch their hats." Name-calling and violence became commonplace, especially in the newly emerging party press. The extreme Federalist William Cobbett described Republicans as "cut-throats who walk in rags and sleep amidst filth and vermin." Some New Yorkers threw stones at Alexander Hamilton. Even Washington himself became the target of vicious remarks: in Virginia his opponents toasted "a speedy death to President Washington."

Washington's official family felt the strains. Jefferson the arch-Republican ceased to talk to Hamilton, the arch-Federalist even before Jefferson's resignation from the Cabinet. In 1795 Hamilton, too, left official life and went back to the practice of law in New York. Neither man, however, abandoned politics. From Monticello, the classical mansion he designed on a hill overlooking the Blue Ridge Mountains, Jefferson continued to advise by letter his friends and political allies in Philadelphia and around the nation. Hamilton also remained active politically and would exert great influence in the administration that followed Washington's.

Washington, no doubt, could have held the presidency for life had he so desired. But he was weary of politics and anxious to return to Mount Vernon; he looked forward, he said, to sitting down to dinner alone with his wife,

Washington retired to Mount Vernon, his plantation in Virginia. He was buried there upon his death on December 14, 1799. (*Courtesy, New York Public Library, Ashton, Lenox and Tilden Foundations*)

Martha. He refused to accept a third term, and with the help of Madison and Hamilton he prepared a final address to his fellow citizens.

Washington's Farewell Address (never presented orally but printed in the *Daily American Advertiser,* a Philadelphia newspaper) devoted more attention to domestic than to foreign matters. The retiring president deplored the state of political conflict that had arisen and warned Americans against disunity, whether sectional or political. He also cautioned the nation to be wary of permanent alliances with foreign nations. He did not advocate isolation from international affairs; he merely recommended that the country be guided by its own essentially modest interests and not become too closely tied to the grander designs of other nations.

As Washington prepared to return to Virginia, political conflict remained fierce. As yet there were no national nominating con- ventions as we now know them. Instead, both Federalist and Republican leaders merely agreed among themselves on who should run.

The Election of 1796   The choice of the Federalists was Vice-President John Adams. Less extreme than the "high Federalists" such as Hamilton, he was, nevertheless, peppery and opinionated as well as learned and public-spirited, and he craved the nation's highest office. Of the vice-presidency he told his wife Abigail, "My country has in its wisdom contrived for me the most insignificant office that ever the invention of man contrived or his imagination conceived." Adams had been in the forefront of America's struggle for nationhood ever since the 1770s. Now he considered France the chief threat to his country's peace and order. The Republicans turned to their acknowledged chief, Jefferson. Tall, loose-jointed, red-haired, the former Secretary of State was as hostile to the British and as friendly to the French as ever. Britain, he believed, was determined to subjugate the United States economically and he thought that under Hamilton's auspices the British had come to dominate the American government.

In this election, with the "god-like Washington" out of the fray, intrigues, maneuverings, libels and attacks were numerous. The Republican press assailed Adams as a monarchist who, if elected, would enslave the American people. The Federalist press accused Jefferson of being a lackey of the French and claimed that as governor of Virginia during the Revolution he had fled his capital in a "cowardly" escape from the British. A particularly unpleasant incident of the campaign was the airing of a scandal involving Hamilton.

In 1791 the Secretary of the Treasury had begun a liaison with Maria Reynolds, the estranged wife of James Reynolds, an unscrupulous speculator and political fixer. Soon after his meetings with Mrs. Reynolds her husband appeared, claimed that his heart was "Burst with Greef," and demanded money to repair it. Over the next few months the Secretary gave Reynolds a thousand dollars to shut him up.

But Reynolds would not be quiet. In 1792 he told all to a group of Republican congressmen, including James Monroe, and in addition he claimed that Hamilton had made money by swindling the government. The shocked congressmen confronted the Secretary with their information. Hamilton confessed to the romance, but denied any financial wrongdoing. The congressmen seemed satisfied, and pledged to keep the Reynolds matter to themselves.

They did not. In 1796 the story leaked to John Beckley, a man who held the same role in the Republican Party as the chairman of a national political committee does today. Beckley had the story published as a pamphlet in time to provide some edifying reading for the voters.

Meanwhile, the new French Minister in

President John Adams, by E. F. Andrews. **Washington's vice-president won a close election in 1796 to become America's second president.** *(Courtesy, The New-York Historical Society, New York City)*

the United States, Citizen Adet, was angry at the Federalist administration for coming to terms with the British and he joined the fracas. In November 1796 he published in the American newspapers a set of proclamations announcing that France would suspend diplomatic relations with the United States and come down hard on neutral shipping. The blame for this new policy, he declared, lay with the Federalists' pro-British policies.

When the electors' ballots were counted, Adams had gained seventy-one electoral ballots to Jefferson's sixty-eight, with Thomas Pinckney—an ally of Hamilton—coming in third. Under the existing provisions of the Constitution, John Adams became the second president of the United States, and Jefferson the vice-president. Two political enemies—a Federalist and a Democratic Republican—were now yoked together. Besides partisan politics President Adams would face a complex set of problems, especially in foreign relations.

| **Trouble with Britain** The United States by now had become a major international trader, its ships calling in virtually every port in the world. The reason for this growth was the great European war. As the British Royal Navy swept French and Spanish vessels off the high seas, France and her allies depended increasingly on the most important maritime neutral, the United States, to carry goods to and from their colonies. By 1796 American merchants were bringing in millions of dollars' worth of molasses, rum, sugar, and other products from French and Spanish possessions in the New World, landing them at New York, Baltimore, Charleston, or Philadelphia and then sending them, marked as American exports, to France, Spain, or some other part of continental Europe. They were also pouring into the French and Spanish colonies European goods that Britain's enemies feared to carry on their own vessels.

This wartime trade rained dollars, pounds, doubloons, and gilders on American merchants. Great mansions arose in Salem, Boston, Newburyport, Charleston, and the other centers of foreign trade. Every harbor along the Atlantic coast was dotted with the white sails and black hulls of the brigs, sloops, barges, and full-rigged ships engaged in world trade, while on the shore the streets were crowded with clerks, stevedores, porters, teamsters, and jack-tars hurrying about their business of moving the world's goods and making money.

The British looked on aghast. The good fortune of the United States clearly came at their expense. Not only were the Americans helping their enemies evade the British blockade of Europe and of French and Spanish America, but they were also taking over business formerly handled by British merchants. And the expanding American merchant marine was luring many of Britain's best seamen. Hundreds of experienced British merchant seamen preferred the high wages and clean ships of the Americans to their own fare, and were deserting. At Norfolk, Virginia, the entire crew of a British merchant vessel quit in a body and signed on a departing American ship. Even sailors from the Royal Navy were escaping its harsh discipline to join the American merchant fleet. The new nation was profiting marvelously by England's troubles.

For a while after the Jay Treaty, the British left American ships and seamen alone. But then, in 1796, when marine manpower shortages began to hurt, they resorted to impressment. Whenever a British man-of-war stopped an American merchant vessel to inspect her cargo for goods going to France, a British naval officer lined the men up on deck. Back and forth he went, asking each to speak up and identify himself. Often anyone with an English, Irish, or Scottish accent was assumed to be a British subject and removed to serve in the Royal Navy. The *American Daily Advertiser* fumed: "Are our sailors to be maltreated, our ships plundered and our flag defied with impunity?" "Some of these unfortunate people," wrote one angry ship captain, "are American born, and have wives and children, whose existence, perhaps, depends on the welfare of a husband in slavery—a father in chains!"

| **Trouble with France** The French were no better. The French Directory, as the ruling body was called between 1795 and 1799, considered Adams's victory an unfriendly act on the part of the American people. In 1797 the French government ordered that every impressed United States citizen captured aboard a British vessel be hanged; if any single item of British make was found aboard an American ship, the vessel was to be confiscated. The French gave the United States minister his

In the undeclared naval war with France, the American frigate *Constellation* captured the French ship *L'Insurgent*, February, 1799. *(Courtesy, The Peabody Museum of Salem)*

walking papers, in effect cutting off diplomatic relations.

Knowing that the United States was ill prepared to go to war, Adams decided to negotiate and appointed three commissioners, Elbridge Gerry, Charles Cotesworth Pinckney, and John Marshall, to go to Paris to seek a settlement. At the same time, the administration asked Congress for money to build naval vessels and expand the army. The Republicans fought the administration's request for defense funds. Representative Albert Gallatin of Pennsylvania declared that paying the public debt would be "a much more effective way of securing the respect of foreign nations than . . . building a Navy." Feelings between the two parties grew so bitter that one hot-tempered Republican, an Irish-born congressman from Vermont, Matthew Lyon, spat in the eye of his Federalist colleague, Roger Griswold of Connecticut. A few days later Griswold attacked the Vermonter with a cane. Lyon defended himself with a pair of fire tongs and wrestled his assailant to the floor before other members of Congress separated them. Threatened with expulsion, Lyon cried, "Let me have at him!"

The XYZ Affair   In October 1797 the three American emissaries arrived in Paris prepared to negotiate with the French foreign minister, Talleyrand. Over several weeks they were forced to talk to three French officials whom they later identified only as X, Y, and Z. The Americans, these gentlemen informed Marshall, Gerry, and Pinckney, would have to apologize for some recent anti-French statements of President Adams; they would have to promise a loan to France; and they must privately pay money to Talleyrand and members of the Directory. The American envoys were not naive about how diplomacy was conducted in Europe, but they refused to pay bribes before the French agreed to a settlement, and broke off the talks. Said Pinckney, "No, no, not a sixpence!" Soon after, they reported to Adams on what had transpired during their mission.

In 1798 the American government published the entire "XYZ" correspondence. A popular slogan was "Millions for defense, but not one cent for tribute." Whatever the worldly American emissaries felt, the American people were shocked by the French government's seeming contempt for the United States. Overnight all but the most ardent Republicans became anti-French. In theaters, taverns, concert halls, Americans sang patriotic songs and demanded to hear "Yankee Doodle" and the "President's March." They drowned out with hisses and groans any attempt by die-hard Republicans to respond to this with the French revolutionary anthem, "The Marseillaise." One Federalist wrote a new chorus to the patriotic favorite "Yankee Doodle":

> Yankee Doodle, mind the tune,
> Yankee Doodle dandy,
> If French men come with naked bun,
> We'll strike 'em hard and handy.

Congress appropriated money for forty naval vessels, and for trebling the size of the army. Congress also ended commerce with France, ordered the suspension of the Franco-American treaty of 1778, and created the Navy Department. Shortly thereafter, a full-scale though undeclared naval war broke out on the Atlantic, with American frigates and French vessels exchanging broadside volleys and French privateers attacking United States merchant vessels within sight of the American coast.

| Alien and Sedition Acts (1798) | In this time of intense political excitement, Federalists found it impossible to regard their opponents' |

views as legitimate expressions of dissent. As yet, few Americans fully accepted the legitimacy of a party system and so Federalists (like Republicans) found the opposing party to be treacherous by its very existence. And the French Revolution went so far beyond the American Revolution in attacking traditional social institutions that conservatives saw chaos, anarchy, and atheism in it. In this mood a Federalist-dominated Congress passed four measures, called collectively the Alien and Sedition Acts of 1798, designed to curb opposition and prevent internal subversion.

The Naturalization Act extended from five to fourteen years the period of residence required for citizenship. The Alien Act gave the President the power to deport any alien suspected of "treasonable or secret" intentions. The Alien Enemies Act gave him the authority in time of war to arrest or banish from the country any citizen of an enemy power.

These first three measures were all aimed at foreigners. The Sedition Act was directed at Americans, and especially at opponents of the administration. Under its terms any resident of the United States who sought to prevent the execution of federal law, to stop a federal official from performing his duties, or to start any riot, "insurrection," or "unlawful assembly" could be fined or imprisoned. Anyone convicted of publishing "any false, scandalous and malicious writing" against Congress, the President, or the government could be fined or sentenced to prison for two years. A New Jersey man, watching a salute fired to honor President Adams on a visit there, remarked that he would have liked to see the cannon wadding "lodged in the President's backsides." For that observation he was fined $100.

Using his powers under the Alien and Sedition Acts, Secretary of State Timothy Pickering began a series of prosecutions of Republican newspaper editors and political leaders. The owners of four leading Republican newspapers were indicted and three Republican editors were convicted of violating the Sedition Act. Pickering also charged "Spitting Lyon," the excitable Congressman from Vermont, with libel against President Adams. In the President Lyon saw

> every consideration of public welfare swallowed up in a continual grasp for power, an unbounded thirst for ridiculous pomp, foolish adulation and selfish avarice; men of real merit daily turned out of office for no other cause but independency of spirit . . . men of firmness, merit, years, abilities and experience discarded in their applications for office, for fear they possess that independence, and men of meanness preferred, for the ease with which they can take up and advocate opinions, the consequences of which they know but little of.

The Irish-born Lyon—once an indentured servant and later one of Ethan Allen's Green Mountain Boys who captured Fort Ticonderoga during the Revolution—was convicted, fined a thousand dollars, and hustled off to jail for four months. He was, however, re-elected to Congress from his jail cell.

The prosecutions under the Sedition Act damaged Adams and the Federalists badly.

Many fair-minded Americans considered the acts violations of the freedom of speech and press guaranteed by the Bill of Rights. Others saw them as totally unwarranted at a time when the country was not in mortal danger. Before long, opponents of the measures and the prosecutions were holding meetings throughout the Middle states, the South, and the West and sending petitions of protest to Congress. Great rolls of paper containing thousands of names were soon deposited on the desks of the House and Senate clerks. A mass meeting in Woodford County, Kentucky, declared: "That for the servants of the people to tell those who created them that they shall not, at their peril, examine into the conduct of [their] servants for the abuse of power is tyranny!"

| **Kentucky and Virginia Resolutions** | No Americans were more disturbed by the Federalist repressions than the leaders of the Republican

Party, Jefferson and Madison. Both regarded the Alien and Sedition Acts not only as a violation of freedom, but also as granting excessive power to the federal government over the states. Jefferson and Madison each secretly drafted a set of resolutions against the Federalist laws; friends steered Jefferson's through the Kentucky legislature, and allies took Madison's through Virginia's. The Kentucky Resolution argued that "when the federal government exercises powers not specifically delegated by the Constitution, each state has equal right to judge for itself as well as of infractions as of the mode of redress." The Virginia Resolution claimed that when the federal government acts contrary to the Constitution the states "have the right and are in duty bound to interpose for arresting the progress of the evil."

Later the Kentucky legislators added the provision that "a nullification of those sovereignties, of all unauthorized acts done under the color of that instrument [the Constitution] is the rightful remedy." Neither Kentucky nor Virginia went so far as to nullify the Alien and Sedition Acts, but in 1832 South Carolina would draw on this precedent to nullify a federal tariff.

Together the Kentucky and Virginia Resolutions stated that the federal government was a compact of states for certain limited purposes. Under the Constitution the national government did not possess the sort of powers it was seeking to exercise under the Alien and Sedition Acts. Such measures were, accordingly, "altogether void and of no force." The two Republican leaders then attacked the Sedition Act as contrary to the Bill of Rights.

In later years Americans would remember the Virginia and Kentucky Resolutions primarily as assertions of states' rights in opposition to federal power, but in their own day they seemed manifestos of freedom. Though followed by a new wave of meetings and petitions from around the country, they accomplished little. The Federalists were too well entrenched in Congress, and a committee of the House rejected the complaints. The Alien and Sedition Acts, the committee majority declared, were both wise and constitutional. When Albert Gallatin and other Republicans attacked the committee report, Federalists in Congress drowned them out by loud talking, laughter, hissing, and coughing.

| **Adams Compromises with France** | Despite his loss of popularity, Adams and his party were still in firm control, and the President could

have gotten Congress to declare war on France. Instead, in 1799, without consulting the Cabinet, Adams announced that he intended to send another mission to France to resume negotiations of outstanding differences.

When the American delegation arrived in Paris, they encountered a changed situation. The leader of France now was First Consul Napoleon Bonaparte. His brilliant generalship had reversed sagging French military fortunes. Now, flushed with new victories, the French were reluctant to grant the Americans the indemnities they wanted for "spoliations" of their commerce. But Napoleon was not entirely unreasonable. He agreed to end the naval war and attacks on American commerce; he also agreed to release the United States from its obligations to France under the Treaty of 1778. The American envoys were disappointed, but seeing no possibility of better terms accepted this convention of 1800. Many Federalists thought it a cowardly surrender. The President disagreed—the negotiations, he believed, were "the most disinterested, the most determined, and the most successful" of his whole career. But they cost him a second term.

The Election of 1800

The political campaign of 1800 was one of the most momentous in the nation's history and in the evolution of modern political democracy. For the first time power passed peaceably and constitutionally from one political party to another.

The rhetoric was by no means peaceable. The Republicans attacked the President once again as pro-British, a monarchist, a spendthrift who had burdened the country with enormous debts. Jefferson, the Federalist press charged, was an atheist who placed scientific reason above the teachings of the Bible. Elect him President, they said, and religion would vanish and infidelity flourish. The man was a "voluptuary" who, it was alleged, had fathered mulatto children by a female slave. If the American people elevated such a man to the nation's highest office, it could expect "the just vengeance of heaven." The nation would suffer every calamity: "dwellings in flames, hoary hairs bathed in blood, female chastity violated, children writhing on the pike and halberd."

A split among the Federalists seriously undermined the party's prospects. By this time, Adams had concluded that he must get rid of Hamilton's influence within his official family, and in 1800 he fired Secretary of State Pickering and Secretary of War James McHenry. Hamilton considered this a declaration of war. Before long he was scheming with other high Federalists to replace Adams with Charles Cotesworth Pinckney of South Carolina, one of the three emissaries to France in the X, Y, Z affair. Adams remained the party's candidate, but a much weakened one. And as the incumbent he bore the brunt of Jeffersonian Republican attacks on the Alien and Sedition Acts and Federalist fiscal policies.

The New Capital   One item in the Republican indictment of their opponents was the extravagant cost of the new national capital under construction on the Potomac River. Actually, by the time the government moved from Philadelphia, the federal city was still more a plan than a reality. The scheme drawn up by a Frenchman, Major Pierre L'Enfant, was magnificent in its broad streets, its malls, plazas, and circles; but it had given place to a more modest and achievable plan. The government had begun construction of the President's house in 1792, and shortly thereafter the Capitol began to rise. The third building to appear was a tavern.

The first government officials arrived from Philadelphia in June 1800. On November 1, President Adams and his family moved into the president's house. Abigail Adams confided to a friend her first impressions of her new home:

> Washington, 21 November, 1800.
> . . . I arrived here on Sunday last, and without meeting with any accident worth noticing, except losing ourselves when we left Baltimore, and going eight or nine miles on the Frederick road, by which means we were obliged to go the other eight through woods, where we wandered two hours without finding a guide, or the path. Fortunately, a straggling black came up with us, and we engaged him as a guide, to extricate us out of our difficulty; but woods are all you see, from Baltimore until you reach [Washington]. . . .
> The President's house is upon a grand and superb scale, requiring about thirty servants to attend and keep the apartments in proper order, and perform the ordinary business of the house and stables; an establishment very well proportioned to the President's salary. The lighting the apartments, from the kitchen to parlours and chambers, is a tax indeed; and the fires we are obliged to keep to secure us from daily agues is another very cheering comfort. . . . If they will put me up some bells, and let me have wood enough to keep fires, I design to be pleased. I could content myself almost anywhere three months; but, surrounded with forests, can you believe that wood is not to be had, because people cannot be found to cut and cart it! Briesler entered into a contract with a man to supply him with wood. A small part, a few cords only, has he been able to get. Most of that was expended to dry the walls of the house before we came in, and yesterday the man told him it was impossible for him to procure it to be cut and carted. He has had recourse to coals; but we cannot get grates made and set. We have, indeed, come into *a new country*.

The new city was little more than a paper community. Besides the Capitol, the tavern, and the President's house (it would not be called the White House until the early 1900s) Washington, D.C. consisted of some boarding houses, a few huts for construction workers, and not much else. Streets had been laid out, but these muddy or dusty tracks were lined, not with residences or stores, but with

Pierre L'Enfant's plan for the city of Washington. The basic plan with its circles and broad converging streets was retained. *(Courtesy, Stokes Collection, The New York Public Library)*

virgin forest. Even the President's new home was only half complete. Nothing was lacking in the new federal city, Gouverneur Morris observed, but "houses, cellars, kitchens, well informed men, amiable women, and other little trifles of this kind."

| Aaron Burr   Under the existing provisions of the Constitution, the electors who would place a president and vice-president in this raw new city did not vote separately for each office. Every elector cast two ballots, and the person with the highest vote total was declared president while the runner-up became vice-president. The Republican caucus in Congress had designated Jefferson as the party's presidential and Aaron Burr as its vice-presidential candi-

dates, but in the actual voting all the Republican electors voted for both equally. When the votes were counted, therefore, Jefferson and Burr were tied for first place. This situation threw the choice of president into the House of Representatives, where the members of each state would cast a single collective vote and for election a candidate needed the vote of a majority of states.

The nation now faced a peculiar problem. The Federalists did not control enough states to reelect President Adams, but they could deny the presidency to anyone else. It was not likely that they would block a choice, since that would paralyze the nation, but they were capable of excluding Jefferson and substituting Burr.

The Federalists found Burr preferable to

Jefferson. The New Yorker was an aristocrat, a friend of banks and Hamiltonian funding, and a believer in a strong executive. He also had the reputation of being corrupt, ambitious, cynical, and unscrupulous, but under the circumstances that was to the good: he could be counted on to make whatever arrangements with the Federalists they desired. The choice of Burr would also be sure to upset and confound the Republicans.

Federalist leaders nonetheless recoiled from this choice. Hamilton despised Burr, who he believed, would "employ the rogues of all parties to overrule the good men of all parties." Jefferson, though "tinctured with fanaticism nor even mindful of truth," had some "pretension to character." Hamilton advised voting for the Virginian if he would give the Federalists guarantees that he would uphold the Federalist fiscal system, remove no Federalist from office except those of Cabinet rank, sustain the Army and Navy intact, and maintain the principles of neutrality in foreign affairs established by the two Federalist presidents. Burr was meanwhile refusing to treat directly with the Federalists, since that would have so outraged his fellow Republicans that they would have denied him all support. The election was deadlocked.

In the end, Jefferson gave the Federalists some indirect assurances and he was declared elected. The nation could now resume as a going political concern. Jefferson's inaugural speech declared that "Every difference of opinion is not a difference of principle."

The Revolution of 1800

Jefferson's election has been called the "revolution of 1800." The apprehensive Federalists would not have disagreed. Not only had they lost the presidency; they had also been swept from power in Congress. What would follow the advent of the "Jacobins"? There was still hope: the judiciary might be saved. Hours before leaving office President Adams appointed a flock of Federalists to new judgeships and other legal posts created by the Judiciary Act of 1801. These "midnight judges" might be able to stop the Republicans from upsetting the economic and political arrangements of the country.

Adams had earlier appointed John Marshall to be Chief Justice of the United States. The President did not rank this appointment as one of the contributions of his administration, yet it would turn out to be the most significant of all.

Points To Think About

1. Students of government have credited American political parties with making the constitutional system work. It is therefore no small irony that the Founding Fathers detested the very idea of political parties and hoped to create a political system in which the "spirit of party" would wither away. Their feelings go back to pre-revolutionary days. As colonists, Americans had come to associate British parties with corruption. Eighteenth-century British parties, in fact, often were corrupt. They were organized by means of family ties and patronage. And the Crown, because it had at its disposal a vast number of political offices, was frequently able to use the "spirit of party" to control Parliament. Colonists, in turn, often blamed their own troubles on these same corrupt parties.

In *The Federalist*, Number 10, Madison wrote that the great diversity of interest groups in the new country would prevent the formation of large parties. In fact, it did not. Diversity did, however, help determine the character of the parties that arose. The need to achieve a majority in the elec-

toral college forced American parties to become broad coalitions that could then appeal to a broad range of interests. So the United States got parties, but they were very different from the more ideologically cohesive parties that developed in nineteenth-century Europe.

2. The Alien and Sedition Laws of 1798 seriously jeopardized the Bill of Rights. They were in fact an incident in the unending struggle to reconcile the nation's legitimate need to protect itself with its commitment to safeguarding the rights of citizens—rights which include that of altering the forms of government itself if they so desire. The Alien and Sedition Laws, furthermore, provoked in the Virginia and Kentucky Resolutions a political reaction that, in the long run, proved just as dangerous to the safety of the constitutional system. The Resolutions opened a mare's nest of disputation about the rights of states in the federal union. Federalists at the Hartford Convention and, still later, secessionists in the South would

repeat the arguments first put forward in the Resolutions.

The American constitutional system is based on the idea of balance. It seeks to balance the states against the national government, the branches of government against each other, the rights of the individual against the power of the government. Push it too far in any one direction, and the response may be an extreme motion in some other direction.

3. What happened to the Federalists once their party disintegrated? Some remained in office, especially in Connecticut and Massachusetts. Others, like John Quincy Adams, went to the Republicans and continued in public life. Still others folded their tents and stole away, a few reappearing in sulky memoirs.

Among the most interesting of the Federalists are those who sought nongovernmental means of furthering their social and political goals. Clyde Griffen has written a fascinating account of this last group who became *Their Brother's Keeper* by establishing a series of benevolent societies. Their societies, like the American Bible Society, the American Tract Society, and the American Anti-Slavery Society, formed a "benevolent empire." The goal was to shore up the social order, temper the excesses of democracy, and raise the moral tone of the nation. The societies, which quickly became very large, encouraged people to observe the Sabbath, avoid drunkenness and unseemly language, attend church regularly, and practice the other traditional Christian virtues. They organized Sunday Schools, financed ministers in the developing West, distributed millions of pamphlets and tracts, opposed the delivery of mail on Sundays, and otherwise sought to raise the moral tone of society.

Suggested Readings

Recent works include David Szatmary, *Shays' Rebellion: The Making of an Agrarian Insurrection* (1980), Jay Fliegelman, *Prodigals and Pilgrims: The American Revolution Against Patriarchal Authority 1750–1800* (1982), and Richard Beeman, Stephen Botein, and Edward C. Carter, eds., *Beyond Confederation: Origins of the Constitution and American National Identity* (1987).

In *Securing the Revolution: Ideology in American Politics, 1789-1815* (1972), Richard Buel, Jr., studies the efforts of revolutionary leaders to consolidate their achievements after the adoption of the Constitution. James Thomas Flexner has abridged his four-volume biography into one: *Washington: The Indispensable Man* (1974). See also Marcus Cunliffe's *George Washington: Man and Monument* (1958). Forrest McDonald's *Alexander Hamilton* (1979) is an admiring and penetrating work.

Lance Banning, *The Jeffersonian Persuasion* (1978) traces Republican thought in the 1790s. American legal history has been enhanced by Morton J. Horwitz's *The Transformation of American Law, 1780–1860* (1977); he examines the process by which law, having been rigid in the eighteenth century, became dynamic in the nineteenth. Alexander DeConde is standard on *The Quasi-War: Politics and Diplomacy of the Undeclared War with France, 1797–1801* (1966). Leonard D. White's *The Federalists* (1948) stresses the administrative achievements of the new government. Like everything else that Richard Hofstadter wrote, *The Idea of a Party System* (1973) is illuminating and graceful.

FORREST McDONALD

Countless Americans, having fixed their loyalty during colonial days upon some particular colony, had kept that loyalty after the colony became a state. Virginians remained loyal to Virginia; the people of Massachusetts continued to identify themselves with that New England commonwealth. Americans, moreover, believed that their economic interests would be best served by the governments closest and most familiar to them. It was, after all, out of fear of centralized power, and particularly of centralized taxing power, that Americans had rebelled against the government of Great Britain. In establishing the Constitution, which greatly strengthened the central government of the United States, the Founding Fathers therefore had to overcome a good deal of popular suspicion.

There were also serious problems in political theory to be overcome. When the Americans declared their independence from Britain, they had committed themselves to a republican form of government—a government in which there are no hereditary rulers and all power is derived from "the public." This does not mean they believed in democracy. They thought that democracy always led to mob rule, instability, and tyranny; indeed, though in most states only white adult property-holding males could vote and had full legal rights, the Founders thought the existing American political forms, as established by the Revolutionary state constitutions, were already too democratic. Their remedy was to set up a central government strong enough to check the power of the state governments, and thus to turn the United States into a single large republic containing the smaller state republics. But in doing this they were acting against much of the political theory of the time. Eighteenth-century political theory held that governmental power—sovereignty—could not be divided; yet they proposed to divide it between the federal and state governments. Theory held that republics could succeed only in small territories; yet the United States was an enormous country. It was assumed that republics could work only if their people were virtuous; yet the Founding Fathers believed that individuals were, for the most part, not virtuous but selfish. And it was generally believed that republics could exist only if property were fairly evenly distributed; yet the Founders knew that inequality of wealth naturally develops in any free society. Their decision to establish a huge federal republic was bold in its departure from conventional political thinking.

What the Founding Fathers did was to accept the fact of human selfishness—the appetite for power and the appetite for property—and to set up a political system in which selfishness would cancel out selfishness. The Constitution gave the central government enough powers to prevent individual states from pursuing policies harmful to the rest of the country. The states retained enough strength to prevent the central government from becoming dictatorial. This "federal" system, together with the division of power at the national level among president, Congress, and the courts, would make it difficult for any one interest group in the country to seize control of the whole machinery of government for its own selfish purposes. The very size of the national republic would be advantageous, for it would include so many different groups of people that no single group could impose its will on all others.

The Constitution established the nation's governmental system, but it left open the question of what kind of economic system the country would have. The Founders took human greed for granted and regarded private property rights as sacred, but that did not mean that they advocated the development of capitalism. The essence of capitalism is a particular attitude toward private property: that it should be put to work for the creation of more property, and that to allow it to lie idle is wasteful, even sinful. This was not the attitude of most Americans. Property, as they saw it, was to be used for comfort, enjoyment, and a livelihood. The

A Capitalist Constitution?

distinction can be illustrated with a personal example. I own twenty-odd acres of land, a truck, and a tractor. If I used that property to produce crops for market, it would be capital. Instead, I use it for my personal pleasure, and thus it is not capital. Though Americans did raise crops or animals for market, the attitudes of most were closer to mine than to those of a capitalist.

EUGENE GENOVESE

Could a republic survive over so large a territory, with no ancient government and institutions to hold it together, and with so many of its citizens inclined to give their loyalty not to the nation but to states and localities? Its survival required that its central government be strong enough to impose some measure of will against state and local communities. Such a government the Articles of Confederation did not provide. The Constitution did so. The Articles may have pleased those who, however democratic and noble in spirit, wished for nothing more than a collection of free, placid, small communities. For Americans who wanted to see how much a vast, energetic, and unified republic could do toward building up its economy, its culture, and its civic life, and exploring the possibilities of freedom, only the stronger government that the Constitution established would do.

Politics in the early years of the republic was marked by a violence of words that would suggest that the harshest class struggle was taking place. Followers of Jefferson accused the Federalists of monarchism, of arrogance, of planning through Hamilton's policies to set up a monied aristocracy; Hamiltonians accused the party of Jefferson of anarchism, atheism, a taste for rule by the mob.

As the years passed, it was in considerable measure the agricultural policies of the Jeffersonians—policies consistent with a vision of free and equal farmers—that aided the growth of American business and industry. Jefferson's purchase of the Louisiana territory in 1803 opened a gigantic land for settlement. The Jeffersonian commitment to holding land prices low contributed to the rapid settling of the West by farmers in the decades that followed. Many of these farmers, as it turned out, would have something more in mind than living a simple virtuous life on their own homesteads, growing food only for their own subsistence. They would want to grow big crops for sale and profit—in other words, to be capitalists. And as they filled the West, they provided a vast market that encouraged the textile industry in the East, the manufacture there of agricultural implements and machinery, and the production of a widening array of other goods; and the commerce between the regions brought roads, canals, railroads, and marketing facilities. American business owed much to the creation of this home market, the greatest in world history, which itself arose on the basis of democratic landholding and would have been unthinkable without a democratic politics.

The Jeffersonians and their successors, however, included one element whose relation to capitalism was uneasy. Southern slaveholders were engaged like other Americans in the production of crops for profit on the market. But capitalism supposes a market of workers free to sell their labor-power. The slave system shaped a deeply reactionary ruling class with a world view radically different from that of the developing business civilization of the North. Before long, the Northern business classes would face a struggle to the death with unyielding slaveowners, the most formidable class enemy that had yet confronted American capitalism.

Lewis and Clark holding a council with the Indians. Their expedition was prompted by President Jefferson's vision of an America stretching from "the Western ocean . . . to the Atlantic." This drawing is from the 1812 edition of Patrick Gass's *Journal*, one of the first authentic accounts of the expedition. *(Courtesy, Scribner's Archives)*

CHAPTER 7

Independence Confirmed 1800–1816

THE LEWIS AND CLARK EXPEDITION

Thomas Jefferson wrote eloquently of independence, religious liberty, the education of a free people—as had other men; but Jefferson's words inspired a new nation, a bill of rights, a system of education. The expedition of Meriwether Lewis and William Clark from 1804 to 1806, exploring the Missouri River, the Rocky Mountains, and the Columbia River basin, was a bold Jeffersonian vision become a great historical event.

Jefferson's vision of the West was even grander and more complex than that of Columbus. Like the great Genoese, he saw the westward passage as a way to the riches of the East. Commerce might move "possibly with single portage, from the Western ocean . . . to the Atlantic." To this ancient dream Jefferson added the prospect of more immediate riches: the "great supplies of furs and pelts" that were then flowing only into English coffers, not American. It meant even more to Jefferson's philosophy that much of the West could become a vast, peaceful garden filling with the sturdy yeomen he expected to be the embodiments of republican virtue. The West could also be a garden for Indians weaned from their hunting ways by the advance of trade that would "place within their reach those things which will contribute more to their domestic comfort than the possession of extensive, but uncultivated wilds." The more rugged West of the great rivers and mountains would exhibit treasures of natural history. Mammoths, Jefferson suspected, might still roam the lands farther west. Perhaps the llama ranged this far north. For years, Jefferson had encouraged all who would listen to explore the great West for science, for country, for riches.

Except for slightly underestimating the number of men who would be needed (thirty to fifty in various stages of the expedition), and with no idea that an Indian woman, her infant son, and a giant Newfoundland dog named Scammon would go along as well, Jefferson got exactly the expedition and the results he had envisioned. The exploration extended his Indian diplomacy, his commercial policies, and his diplomatic goals while furiously gathering together every piece of information about geography, plants, animals, and minerals that could be gained by observation or collection of specimens and fossils. Seven men kept diaries; every moment when they were not exploring, negotiating, or being ill the two leaders spent in taking detailed field notes and reworking them into coherent accounts, complete with drawings, maps, and lexicons for Thomas Jefferson and the world.

Meriwether Lewis and William Clark were, like Jefferson, amateurs. Though soldiers, neither had been a professional military man, Lewis being on leave from the army to serve as Jefferson's secretary and Clark having resigned some time before. Nor were they professional scientists or explorers: once Jefferson appointed them, they had to scramble for a rapid education in geography and mapmaking, celestial navigation, mineralogy, and medicine to keep an expedition alive for two years. Lewis sought the counsel of America's most distinguished physician, Dr. Benjamin Rush of Philadelphia, who supplied him with a little information and a large supply of "Rush's Thunderbolts," his famous, violently purgative pills, which Lewis and Clark used for all ailments.

The expedition went from St. Louis to the mouth of the Columbia River and back, through incredibly difficult country, with elementary equipment. The first leg, up the Missouri with a winter's stop in an Indian village, was brutally hard work: poling, pulling, and portaging a string of boats up a huge river whose powerful current undermined banks at each bend, created mudslides, and sent vast jams of tree trunks cascading downriver to knock over the expedition's boats. The second leg, over the mountaintops through high barren badlands, was the hardest part of all. The trip down the Columbia River system was least eventful. The explorers eventually realized that they had gone the long way around and correctly plotted the shortest and fastest route home through the mountains. On the return trip they proved that there was no route, even with portages, where small boats could practically be carried over the Continental divide and relaunched on the Western rivers. Rather, there was a set of mountains and valleys between, which required a substantial trans-shipment. The way west would not be direct or easy: the three-century-old hope of finding a "Northwest Passage" had to be forgotten, at least for a time.

The expedition studied dozens of Indian tribes, arranging trade agreements, asserting the government's influence, presenting gifts, recording manners and customs, seeking geographical information. Of the Shoshones, Lewis wrote in his diary about their varying treatment of men and women:

> They seldom correct their children particularly the boys who soon become masters of their own acts. They give as a reason that it cows and breaks the sperit of the boy to whip him, and that he never recovers his independence of mind after he is grown. They treat their women but with little rispect, and compel them to perform every species of drudgery. they collect the wild fruits and roots, attend to the horses or assist in that duty, cook, dress the skins and make all their apparel, collect wood and make their fires, arrange and form their lodges, and when they travel pack the horses and take charge of all the baggage; in short the man dose little else except attend his horses hunt and fish. the man considers himself degraded if he is compelled to walk any distance; and if he is so unfortunately poor as only to possess two horses he rides the best himself and leavs the woman or women if he has more than one, to transport their baggage and children on the other, and to walk if the horse is unable to carry the additional weight of their persons. The chastity of their women is not held in high estimation, and the husband will for a trifle barter the companion of his bed for a night or longer if he conceives the reward adequate.

Lewis and Clark identified 300 new plant and animal species or subspecies, collecting bones, fossils, and seeds. The homely names they gave the new species—since neither man knew Latin—have not survived in the naturalist literature; but creatures like *Salmo clarkii*, the beautiful cutthroat trout named for Clark, and *Asyndesmus lesis*, Lewis's woodpecker, attest to the ichthyologists' and ornothologists' appreciation of their works. The *Notebooks* and *Journals* of the expedition have been fundamental sources for naturalists, geographers, anthropologists, and historians.

The rigors of the journey produced much illness and hardship, yet only one man lost his life—from a ruptured appendix that in those days would have killed him even had he been in Philadelphia. The only serious injury was to Lewis himself, when one of his own men accidentally shot him in the backside. (Lewis made few mistakes, but going hunting for food with a one-eyed sergeant was certainly one of them.) There were only one or two small scrapes with Indians, although it took firm diplomacy and carefully manned swivel guns, small portable cannons, to prevent a few rough encounters from becoming dangerous. Clark's slave, York, the one black on the expedition, was the wonder of dozens of Indian tribes. The Indians would actually pay to touch his hair or run their fingers over his skin to see whether the dark color would come off. One of the interpreters—a Frenchman named Charbonneau who had been hired in St. Louis because he knew the Sioux dialects—persuaded Lewis to allow him to take his Indian wife, Sacajawea, and their two-month-old baby on the roughest part of the trip from the upper Missouri over the mountains to the Pacific. Apparently, her knowledge of the Shoshonean dialects, which neither her husband nor any of the other interpreters commanded, persuaded the captain to agree. When they finally made contact with the mountain Indians, the first party of braves they met had as its chief her brother, whom she had not seen since she had been abducted from his hunting party as a small child. No novelist could have gotten away with such an unlikely plot.

Jefferson had made his proposal for the expedition to Congress before Talleyrand offered to sell the United States the Louisiana Territory; the President had planned to grasp the trade of the West with stations on territory both unknown and unowned. By the time the expedition set out from St. Louis, Louisiana was American territory. But the Oregon country beyond the Great Divide was not. It belonged perhaps to Great Britain or maybe to Spain. Yet Lewis, once back at St. Louis, wrote of "possessions" west of the mountains, and Jefferson himself by January 1807 was referring to "our country, from the Missisipi [*sic*] to the Pacific." He supported John Jacob Astor's efforts to create an American fur empire that would crowd the British out of the market. In the ensuing race for the strategic mouth of the Columbia River, Astor moved his men across the trail that Lewis and Clark had blazed, while the British pushed southwest from Canada. In July 1811, when the great British explorer and entrepreneur David Thompson pushed his way to the Columbia and canoed to its mouth, he beheld the American flag flying from the parapets of four-month-old Fort Astoria. Lewis and Clark's expedition would, in the end, make Jefferson's largest vision—a continental United States—the future.

Jefferson's Inauguration

At noon on a blustery March day, Jefferson took the oath of office and became the third president of the United States. He had come to Washington the previous November and had spent the winter at Conrad and Mc-Munn's boardinghouse, where for $15 a

Thomas Jefferson, inaugurated as third President of the United States in March 1801. *(Portrait by Rembrandt Peale, 1800, White House Collection)*

week he dined and roomed unostentatiously. The inauguration ceremonies were brief and austere, as befitted a party that made a point of republican simplicity. Jefferson's expensive velvet suit failed to arrive, and he walked in plain garb to the still uncompleted Capitol. "I have this morning witnessed one of the most interesting scenes a free people can ever witness," a Philadelphian wrote to her sister-in-law. "The changes of administration, which in every government and in every age have most generally been epochs of confusion, villainy and bloodshed, in this our happy country take place without any species of distraction, or disorder."

In the crowded Senate chamber, Jefferson swore to defend the Constitution and faith-

fully discharge the duties of his office. Then, almost inaudibly, he delivered his inaugural address. Jefferson's address expressed the philosophy of the men who had fought the Federalists for over a decade. It confirmed the Republicans' dedication to freedom of religion and the press. It endorsed the encouragement of agriculture, and of commerce as its handmaid. The federal government, the new President declared, must conduct its business economically and attempt to pay off its debts. The state governments were "the surest bulwarks against anti-republican tendencies." But besides making these predictable Republican pronouncements, Jefferson sought to calm the fears of Federalists. The nation, he declared, must avoid "entangling alliances": this was a signal that the Republicans would accept the recent termination of the 1778 French alliance. They would also avoid extreme partisanship. Now that the great contest of 1800 was over, all Americans "will, of course, arrange themselves under the will of the law, and unite in common efforts for the common good." Minority rights would be protected, and no one would suffer persecution: "We are all Republicans, we are all Federalists. . . . Let us, then, with courage and confidence pursue our own Federal and Republican principles, our attachment to union and representative government."

So softly did the fresh-minted Chief Executive speak that few in the crowded room could hear what he said. But printed copies of the speech were available, and ushers distributed these to the assembled dignitaries. That evening, the president returned to Conrad and McMunn's to dine as usual. When he entered the dining room, a lady among the paying guests offered him a chair. Jefferson declined the offer and went to his usual place at the foot of the table, far from the warming fire. A simpler age of American manners had begun.

The United States in 1801

▌The People On New Year's Day, 1801, one journalist wrote, "Here ends the 18th century. The 19th begins with a fine clear morning wind at S.W.; and the political horizon affords as fine a prospect under Jefferson's administration, with returning harmony with France—with the irresistible

propagation of the Rights of Man, the eradication of hierarchy, oppression, superstition and tyranny over the world. . . ."

In the twenty-five years since the opening gun of the Revolution the country's population had grown from about 2.5 to 5.3 million; but the nation's white population remained overwhelmingly British in origin and Protestant in religion. Germans were found in eastern Pennsylvania, in the Shenandoah Valley, and along the Mohawk River in New York. The Hudson Valley contained many Dutchmen, and the guttural sound of Dutch could still be heard in Albany. Scattered here and there, primarily in the towns, were small enclaves of Jews and Huguenot French, as well as a handful of Irish Catholics. The largest non-British group by far was the blacks, who numbered over a million, almost all south of Pennsylvania and almost all slaves. But the Revolution and difficulties of postwar readjustment had discouraged both immigration and the slave trade. The vast majority of the slaves were native-born Americans.

Americans were a young people. Half the population was under seventeen years old. Households were large; almost one-fourth of all families had seven or more people living under one roof. This placed a heavy burden on families, and especially on women, who spent many of their best, most vigorous years bearing and rearing children.

The United States in 1801 was a nation of farms and villages. Only 300,000 Americans lived in communities of even 2500 people—fewer than seven percent of the total.

| The Cities

Of these, the largest, the most cosmopolitan, and most gracious was Philadelphia, with almost 70,000 inhabitants. Penn's town was also the most modern in the nation. Most American city-dwellers drew their water from wells or cisterns or bought it from vendors. They relied on hogs to consume the garbage dumped on the street. They were forced to tramp streets usually ankle-deep in either dust or mud, depending on the season. Not so Philadelphians: the city of Brotherly Love, after cholera and yellow fever epidemics in the 1790s, piped water from the Schuylkill River; its streets, paved with cobblestones, were regularly cleaned.

Boston, with 25,000 inhabitants, had fallen behind New York and Baltimore in population since colonial days. Nevertheless, it remained the commercial, financial, and intellectual capital of New England. With its narrow streets and crowded wharves, it had not much changed since the 1770s. The city government was still the same as in the seventeenth century: its affairs were in the hands of "selectmen" chosen at the town meeting. Although Boston's elite was no longer composed of dour Puritan gentlemen, the Federalist merchants, ministers, and lawyers who now formed the town's upper crust retained much of the old Puritan self-confidence and respect for learning. The Bostonian George Cabot was expressing the unshakable conviction of his class when he declared that his native city possessed "more wisdom and virtues than any other part of the world."

Two hundred miles to the south of Boston was New York, on Manhattan Island. In 1801 the city was still partly Dutch. Many houses sat gable-end to the street, as in Amsterdam, and were faced with the characteristically Dutch yellow brick. Even more than Boston and Philadelphia, New York thrived on commerce; most of its 60,000 inhabitants were crowded into the southeastern corner of the island, adjacent to the docks and warehouses. The rich resources of New York port—its accessibility in winter, its many landing spots, its deep water—would soon catapult the city into the nation's most populous.

Baltimore was a comparatively new city that had not acquired official municipal status until 1797. The outlet for much of the Chesapeake tobacco crop, it also tapped the flour, wheat, and farming provisions of the Pennsylvania backcountry through the Susquehanna River. The city's aggressive merchants had pioneered a lucrative trade to Bremen, Germany, and had attracted in return a substantial number of German artisans.

Charleston, the capital of South Carolina, was in some ways the most colorful of all. It was both a major port and a summer resort where rice planters from the malaria-ridden coastal lowlands went during the "fever season" to protect their health. Built in brick and stone, the city was ruled by a planter and merchant elite who combined republican principles with the aristocratic arts of good living, polite letters, fine manners, and elegant hospitality. These avowed republicans could not live without slaves. Of the 18,000 people who packed the little port, 6,000 were blacks; they helped keep its streets clean, its markets stocked, and its wharves busy.

Any observer of Charleston between 1790 and 1800 would have noticed a particularly promising development: a new crop, cotton, was being loaded aboard ships in the harbor by black stevedores. With the perfection of the cotton gin by the Connecticut Yankee Eli

Whitney, green-seed cotton had become a profitable crop in the interior of the Carolinas and Georgia. The South's one major Atlantic port was feeling the invigorating economic effects of the thousands of bales it shipped to Liverpool and Glasgow to feed the new textile factories of Great Britain.

All the nation's cities were coastal communities; only overseas trade employed enough people to create cities. The one potential exception in view was the small town of Pittsburgh, situated where the Allegheny and Monongahela rivers join to form the great Ohio. With about two thousand inhabitants in 1800, it had become a supplier of manufactured goods to the burgeoning West, producing iron, glass, textiles, and vessels for the river trade. As early as 1800 an English visitor reported the town covered with a pall of smoke from the numerous coal fires that fueled the iron foundries and glassworks. By 1810 one expert estimated Pittsburgh's trade at $1 million a year.

The Farms

The great majority of Americans depended for their livelihood in some fashion on the soil. A few thousand belonged to the great landed families, many of them living in the coastal regions of the Chesapeake, the Carolinas, and Georgia, or in the Hudson Valley of New York. Many were either tenants or slaves of such families. The overwhelming majority of the nation's million-odd blacks in 1800 were slaves cultivating rice, tobacco, or corn, and now cotton as well. A majority of white male Americans owned the ground they tilled.

A typical American yeoman and his family worked hard for what they had. Animals had to be watered, their stables cleaned. Plowing in the spring, weeding and cultivating in the summer, and harvesting in fall all required heavy labor. The women cooked, cleaned, spun, made preserves, and took care of flocks of young children. Clearing new land on the frontier required the backbreaking labor of girdling trees, clearing underbrush, and breaking virgin sod. The pioneer farmer of Vermont, western New York, or the newly opened Ohio or Alabama country was lucky if he could add more than four or five usable acres to his farm a year. Even then it took many years before the frontier farmer's land was fully cleared of stumps and he could plow a straight furrow. Meanwhile, his family lived in a primitive one-room log house with a sleeping attic above. Techniques of planting and harvesting had not advanced much beyond medieval practices. American plows in 1800 were heavy wooden contraptions pulled by oxen or mules. Farmers still used the scythe to harvest grain and threshed it with a hand flail made of two sticks joined by a leather thong.

Yet the yeoman family enjoyed a rough abundance. Since the soil was rich, the American farm family ate well and produced more than it consumed. Travelers through the nation's rural regions remarked on signs of prosperity. One Englishman reported of the Connecticut countryside during Jefferson's presidency that it "had the appearance of wealth, numerous broods of poultry straying about, with sheep and cattle grazing in great numbers in the fields." Travelers who accepted the hospitality of local yeomen, rather than brave the fare of notoriously bad country inns, reported on the abundance of everything served. Breakfast tables were loaded down with boiled fish, beefsteak, ham sausages, hotbreads, and cheese.

One country boy remembered this period:

> My father was A Farmer and by the help of his trusty rifle Kept the family in wild meat such as bear, Elk, Deer, and wild Turkey.
>
> How well I Remember the old Hunting stories he used to tell us boys I will try and give you a sketch of a hunting expedition my father and three other men took on one of the head branches of the licking River they killed 16 Bear and A Number Deer they took their horses with them and they would tye one horse and the others wouldn't leave him they would then dig out troughs and pack the meat their horses couldn't carry home in Pack saddles they would pack the Meat in them troughs and split out puncheons and cover the meat with them and pin them down to keep the wolves from eating their meat till they took their first loads home and go back after it. They used the fat bear meat to cook the Deer meat with.

"My farm," said a yeoman of Jeffersonian times,

> gave me and my family a good living on the produce of it; and left me, one year with another, one hundred and fifty dollars, for I have never spent more than ten dollars a year, which was for salt, nails, and the like. Nothing to wear, eat, or drink was purchased, as my farm provided all. With this saving, I put money to interest, bought cattle, fatted and sold them, and made great profit.

Profit—the very word is like a bell! The era of the commercial farm lay in the future.

Now the typical farm family was an isolated social unit. Except in southern New England, where the imprint of the old town system of colonial days remained, the rural American lived in a house widely separated by fields and virgin forest from his nearest neighbor. In rural New England a traveler in the early 1800s observed that "there is scarcely a poor owner of a miserable log hut, who lives on the border of the stage road, but has a newspaper left at his door." One traveler noted how a small New Hampshire town hungered for news: "It was entertaining to see the eagerness of the people on our arrival to get a sight of the last newspaper from Boston. They flocked to the post-office and the inn, and formed a variety of groups round those who were fortunate to possess themselves of a paper." In 1801 there were 200 newspapers in the nation; by the 1830s there would be more than 1200.

Almanacs urged farmers to buy and read books. One author claimed that the farmer sees "his barns, granaries, and cellars, all well filled by his own industry and frugality; his farm affording him all the comforts and necessaries of life, enables him to spend the long and tedious winter evenings with his family round a good fire and a clean hearth, where he may read THEOLOGY, GEOGRAPHY, HISTORY, &C. and edify and entertain them...." The *Farmer's Almanack* paid tribute to another almanac-writer, Benjamin Franklin, by recommending "The life of Dr. Franklin," (published in 1794) "for the amusement of winter evenings."

Some young men left the farm to attend school. A student in Philadelphia wrote a letter to his parents in Allegheny County:

> I now take up my pen to write, but what to say I know not, sinking into debt and no prospect of making any thing to relieve myself. I continue to teach a gentleman's sons the Greek and Latin languages, for which I receive one hundred dollars per year, but this is far from being sufficient to answer my demands. Teaching is out of the question here, for the teachers are almost equal to the scholars so that you might as easily pick up a vacant lot within the precincts of the city, as an unoccupied school. . . . Last summer I bought two pair of nanking pantaloons and a light vest, the whole amounting to $7.60, and this is all I have got since I left home. If I should leave this place, one thing will be in my favour, that is I shall not be burthened with clothes. . . .

Communication was made easier by an improvement in postal service and roads. In the 1790s there were seventy-five post offices in the entire nation, connected by 1,875 miles of post roads. But by the War of 1812 there were 2,610 post offices and over 39,000 miles of roads. Illiteracy and high postal rates (8 cents per letter, 12½ cents for a letter sent over 100 miles) still worked to isolate much of the rural population.

Farm women suffered acutely from the isolation of their lives. They frequently lacked the close network of female kin and friends from which New England women drew comfort and companionship. It is likely that among the yeomanry, as on the frontier, the power of the husband within the family remained greater than in the more settled regions of the Northeast, if only because family life and household production remained pretty much one and the same and the husband assumed the leadership of both. Yeoman women also found themselves further removed from the comforts and distractions that the growing markets of the Northeast could provide women as consumers. One lonely woman in Ohio lamented: "Tis strange to us to see company. I expect the sun may rise and set a hundred times before I shall see another human that does not belong to the family." Ribbons and mirrors remained rare; cookstoves and shoes might have to be ordered from New England. And although husbands and wives frequently worked as close collaborators in daily life—bringing in the harvest, or even delivering children—the lines between male and female spheres remained tightly drawn. When men got together to raise a house, the women would likely work together to produce meals for a large throng or they would quilt.

When rural Americans did gather with neighbors and friends, it was often to engage in rough-and-tumble sports that could turn brutal. Wrestling included kicking, biting, punching, and eye-gouging. "I saw more than one man, who wanted an eye," noted an Easterner as he crossed the border into Kentucky. Country people, especially on the frontier, "baited" bulls and bears—that is, set large dogs to attack them while rooting for either attacker or defender—or they bet on the outcome of cockfights. Whether at taverns or at religious camp meetings, at dances and "hoedowns" or in the home, Americans consumed vast quantities of whiskey, rum, and brandy. Women drank punch or "toddies" made of these. One popular ditty went:

Hail Columbia, happy land,
If you ain't drunk, I'll be damned.

Foreign travelers often noted that New Englanders, were more "steady" than westerners and southerners. But in every section there were sober, well-bred, well-informed men and women who read books, displayed good manners, enjoyed themselves sedately playing cards or attending sewing and husking bees. Politics consumed attention throughout the country. Nevertheless, it would take years of good roads, steady cultivation of the land, and growth of towns before the rudeness of the country lessened along with its isolation.

A WOMAN'S PLACE IN JEFFERSONIAN AMERICA: INFANTS IN CHURCH. *This vignette, composed of letters to the editor of the* Independent Mechanic *(1811), ultimately reveals enormous male condescension towards women. But perhaps in Ms. Sarah Touchstone, who is not blameless, the "Friend to Females" has met his match.*

Mr. Editor,

I know of no subject which deserves more to be noticed, than that of women taking their infants to church. No woman will expose her bare bosom to a gaping multitude of men; and this she is necessitated to do frequently, in order to pacify her babe. Indeed, often it is the case, that when the minister in the sacred desk, is in the most solemn, affecting, and interesting part of his discourse; and when too his audience are loath to hear the sound of a footstep, fearful that they may lose the train of his reasoning, and when the whole congregation are in the most respectful silence, that the ears of all are stunned, the imaginations confused, and the soul tortured by cries and screeches of an infant. What, I ask, is more vexatious? What can be more painful? . . . Besides, other evil consequences flow from it: many an infant receives a death-cold, from their being wrapped up warm in church, and after service are exposed to the damp dews of night and chilling blasts. That mother who possesses a tender feeling for her babe will not sport with its health. May this short notice be received as friendly advice from one who is a

FRIEND TO FEMALES

Independent Mechanic, December 21, 1811

Mr. Editor:

I would beg leave through the medium of your paper, to address a few lines to answer to a morose old jockey who came out in your last in the character of "A FRIEND TO FEMALES."

I cannot say that I thank the gentleman for his pretended friendly advice; and as no person can like their church better than I do, I must attend as often as my family affairs will permit. After having paid this tribute of my God, I feel as happy through the week as possible. I feel as if I had something very heavy taken from my breast. I am sure that my son (God bless his little dimpled cheeks!) never disturbed any one of the congregation, although he is my companion at the house of God. Even while I am writing, it is smiling in my face as if it knew its injured mother busied in vindicating her wrongs. . . .

"Expose her bosom to a gaping multitude of men." A gaping multitude of men, did he say? Yes; and I am sorry to be under the disagreeable necessity of joining with him in the assertion; for how many deluded wretches are there, who only enter the house of the Lord to gape, and put female modesty to the blush, by their rude behaviour. If they came there to hear the word of God, they would not be gaping at the mother's naked bosom. He says— "when the minister is in the most interesting part of his discourse, the ears of the congregation are stunned by the cries and screeches of an infant" a most wonderful *infant,* that can stun the ears of a whole congregation with its weak and unfinished organs, and prevent him from hearing the preacher! Upon my word, I never heard such absurdity in my life.

SARAH TOUCHSTONE

Independent Mechanic, December 28, 1811

Mr. Editor:

In your No. 39, a writer, under the signature of *"Sarah Touchstone,"* has given full latitude to that most mischievous weapon, which all women possess, (the *Tongue*) assisted by pen and paper—and has beset me on all sides; but as it is beneath the dignity of man to quarrel with a woman, or to suffer his gentle passion to be ruffled by their passionate observations, I shall answer *Sarah* with becoming lenity and forbearance. . . .

"A most wonderful infant" says Sarah, "that can *stun* the ears of a whole congregation with its unfinished organs." Yes, *Sarah,* an infant can do it, and frequently has done it. The screeches of a sucking babe, is a sound the most unpleasant to hear; for, as the organs are unfinished, the noise possesses the less harmony, and consequently, pierces the soul quicker. The cries of a babe operates upon the mind equally as bad as the filing of a saw. . . .

I have also asserted, *Sarah,* that mothers expose their children to the nightly dews and northern blasts, and thereby endanger their health; and you have told me, that the mother provides against these things. This, *Sarah,* is impossible, particularly at night, and for this very obvious reason: The early part of the evening may be serene and calm, and before the worship is over, the storm sets in; it rains, it hails, it snows, it blows; and the infant's frame, too tender to endure the dreadful storm, becomes chilled; it withers, and it dies. Alas! poor babe it falls, a victim to the mother's pride. . . .

A FRIEND TO FEMALES

Independent Mechanic, January 4, 1812

❙ Monticello   Thomas Jefferson's country estate, Monticello, illustrates its master's inventiveness as well as America's response to a new environment. Jefferson began building his "little mountain" home near Charlottesville in 1768 on land which his father had owned. The site overlooks the Blue Ridge Mountains in the west and the Virginia plains to the east, vistas which had intrigued Jefferson since childhood. Unable to find a competent architect in the colonies, the resourceful Virginian studied a few books, drew his own plans, and supervised most of its forty-one years of construction. Although he combined currently popular styles—laid out as an Italian villa, Monticello also has a Greek portico, a Roman dome, and colonial detail—Jefferson relied principally upon Andrea Palladio, the architect who had created the "Georgian" style in England. Taken together, Monticello's diverse design did much to launch the "classical revival," which swept the United States during the early nineteenth century.

If stylish, the thirty-five-room manor did not lack substance. Jefferson's originality focused upon graceful use, not just symmetrical display. Most colonial estates grouped carriage house, kitchen, stable, laundry, and smokehouse in separate buildings removed from the main house. For convenience and efficiency, Jefferson moved these functional areas indoors, connected to the living quarters. He built them under terraces which

Thomas Jefferson's home, Monticello, near Charlottesville, Virginia. *(Virginia State Travel Service)*

flank Monticello on either side and open away from the inside. This innovation was soon copied throughout the South. Between the two basements, this Enlightenment figure constructed separate storage rooms for wine, beer, hard cider, and rum.

Monticello is noted for its gadgetry. A pair of glass doors between the main hall and a drawing room opens simultaneously when only one is pushed—Jefferson had installed a series of gears under the floor, much like a modern bicycle-pedal system. The planter-architect set European "alcove beds" into the walls throughout the house, but added an ingenious variation in his own suite: one side of the bed opens onto his study, the other side onto his bedroom. Apparently frustrated by its perverse obscurity, Jefferson connected the weathervane on the roof of Monti-

cello to a dial on the ceiling of the portico so he could read the wind without going outside. A pulley arrangement carried a used bottle of wine to the cellar and retrieved a cooled one.

Style, contraptions, and even its history mark Monticello as uniquely American. In 1781 a platoon of British soldiers led by Captain McLeod raided the house in hopes of capturing its owner, then governor of Virginia; Jefferson narrowly escaped down the mountainside. After a life of political and diplomatic service to the nation, he retired from the presidency in 1809 and returned to the just-completed house. Despite spiraling financial debts, aggravated by the costs of Monticello's upkeep, Jefferson was able to live in the house until his death on July 4, 1826, thanks to loans from friends. The plantation itself never profited its owner, partly because the man who believed that "all men are created equal" could never come to terms with, or even exploit, the slavery that barely supported him amid the quiet splendors of the mansion.

The Republicans in Power

| Thomas
| Jefferson

Jefferson, the new President, was informal in manners and dress to an extent that shocked strait-laced contemporaries. Senator William Plumer of New Hampshire, calling at the presidential mansion, mistook him for a servant. Other visitors, noting his carelessly tied long red hair, his less-than-immaculate linen, his toeless carpet slippers, and his tall, loose-jointed frame, believed that he lacked the dignity required of his office.

Yet the new Chief Executive was one of the most cultivated men of his day. He read French, Italian, Latin, and Greek, played the violin skillfully, corresponded with many of the outstanding thinkers of Europe, was an imaginative and creative architect and inventor, and in science had considerable talent and range.

The combination of informality and restless intellect represents not only Jefferson's private taste and style but his idea of what the citizen of an enlightened republic should be: free of artificialities of manner, free to cultivate talent and put it to public service. Citizenship of this kind, so Jeffersonianism supposed, could best express itself in a relatively simple and stable environment: a farm, a city without poverty, a nation without dictatorial government. And so Jefferson set out to cut and simplify.

He simplified the manners of his office. In place of the formal receptions of the era of Washington and Adams, he substituted gatherings where scholars, scientists, and interesting men of affairs exchanged ideas over madeira and nuts. He dropped his predecessors' practice of appearing before Congress to present his State of the Union addresses, and sent written messages instead.

| Limited
| Government

Jefferson simplified the government. He and his Treasury Secretary Albert Gallatin opposed any rise in the federal debt, and they managed to cut military spending to a third of what it had been under the Federalists. The army was reduced to just 3000 regulars and 172 officers. The five frigates built during Adams's administration were all rendered inactive; in their place the Jeffersonians created a navy of gunboats fit only for coastal service. The President also closed the American legations in Holland and Prussia. The new administration could not abolish the Bank of the United States before its charter expired in 1811, but under Gallatin the government sold its Bank stock at a profit and ceased to play any further banking role.

If government as Jefferson conceived of it had little business regulating finances, and little use for a large military establishment, it certainly had no taste for enforcing political loyalty. He allowed the Sedition Act to lapse; there would be no more criminal prosecutions for attacking the government.

Jefferson's republic would have a virtuous simplicity. He would have shuddered at the size and scope of twentieth-century governments; but he would have shuddered also at twentieth-century business or twentieth-century cities. It is curious that the Federalists, less egalitarian than Jefferson, actually had a concept that comes closer to the reality of modern democratic societies. They planned for a more active economy than Jefferson seems to have envisioned, and their government policies would draw the country's labor and resources more closely together and put them more vigorously to work for the increase of prosperity.

Jefferson advocated the very sort of limited government that Hamilton in *The Federalist* had warned against: "a government at a distance and out of sight." The national government, Jefferson declared in his first message to Congress, was "charged with the external and mutual relations only of these states." It was the states that had "principal care of our persons, our property, and our reputation." The national government had become "too complicated, too expensive"; offices and officers had "multiplied unnecessarily and sometimes injuriously to the service they were meant to promote." As means to his

THE PRESIDENTS
TUNE: Yankee Doodle

George Washington, first president, by Adams was succeeded,
Thomas Jefferson was next, the people's cause he pleaded,
James Madison, he then came forth, to give John Bull a peeling,
James Monroe was next to go in the era of good feeling.

'Twas John Q. Adams then came in and, after, Andrew Jackson,
He licked the British at New Orleans with much great satisfaction,
Van Buren then was next to chair then Harrison and Tyler—
The latter made the Whigs so mad they almost burst their b'iler.

We next elected James K. Polk, the worse that then did vex us
Was, should we fight with Mexico and take in Lone Star Texas?
Then Taylor was our leader, but soon had to forsake it,
For Millard Fillmore filled it more, Frank Pierce then said, "I'll take it."

James Buchanan next popped right in and Lincoln then was chosen,
He found the problems of the day were anything but frozen.
And Johnson had a rougher time, the Senate would impeach him,
But as it took a two-thirds vote, they lacked one vote to reach him.

---

goal, Jefferson's administration sought economy, limited federal powers, and decentralization.

More immediately Jefferson sought to weed out of the federal bureaucracy those Federalists who had taken too partisan a role in the political battles preceding 1801. Most of these were officeholders whom the President could remove at will; but at least one, Supreme Court Justice Chase, had life tenure and could be gotten rid of only by a process of impeachment by the House and trial and conviction by the Senate. In 1805 a Republican House of Representatives did impeach Chase on charges of high crimes and misdemeanors, but the Senate failed to remove him from office.

| *Marbury* v. *Madison*

Far more significant in its ultimate result was the Jefferson Administration's attempt to undo the effects of the 1801 Judiciary Act. Under that measure Adams, just before leaving office, had appointed a flock of Federalist judges and law officials with lifetime tenure; his purpose had clearly been to retain Federalist control in at least one branch of government and, as the Republicans saw it, prevent the new administration from carrying out the will of the people. Hoping to frustrate this goal, Secretary of State Madison refused to deliver several newly appointed officials their commissions. Though appointed under different circumstances, William Marbury sued the Secretary, charging that his action was illegal under the Judiciary Act of 1789. By the provisions of that measure, Marbury's lawyers argued, the Supreme Court could compel a federal official to issue a commission whether he wished to or not.

In 1803 the case came before the United States Supreme Court, Chief Justice John Marshall presiding. Marshall was a Virginian, but not of the political stamp of his fellow Virginians Jefferson and Madison. A Federalist, he deplored the Republican preference for a small national government. He also wanted a strong Supreme Court. Yet Marshall and the Court held, in *Marbury* v. *Madison*, that the Court could not compel Madison to deliver a commission to Marbury, since that portion of the Judiciary Act of 1789 that would have made Madison issue the commission was unconstitutional and therefore unenforceable. The Supreme Court, it seems, was surrendering a little power that it might have claimed and exercised. But it was

BROTHERLY LOVE AMONG THE FOUNDING FATHERS

John Adams on Thomas Jefferson:	*"[He has] a mind, soured, yet seeking for popularity, and eaten to a honeycomb with ambition, yet weak, confused, uninformed, and ignorant."*
—on Alexander Hamilton:	*"This man is stark mad, or I am." "[Consider] the profligacy of his life; his fornications, adulteries and his incests."*
—on Benjamin Franklin:	*"His whole life has been one continued insult to good manners and to decency. . . . From five complete years of experience of Dr. Franklin . . . I can have no dependence on his word. . . . I wish will all my soul he was out of public service."*
Thomas Jefferson on Adams:	*"[He is] distrustful, obstinate, excessively vain, and takes no counsel from anyone."*
—on Hamilton:	*"I will not suffer my retirement to be clouded by the slanders of a man whose history, from the moment at which history can stoop to notice him, is a tissue of machinations against the liberty of the country which not only has received and given him bread, but heaped its honors on his head."*
Alexander Hamilton on Jefferson:	*"A man of profound ambition and violent passions . . . the most intriguing man in the United States . . . the intriguing incendiary, the aspiring turbulent competitor . . . prone to projects which are incompatible with the principles of stable and systematic government."*
—on Adams:	*". . . disgusting egotism . . . distempered jealousy . . . ungovernable indiscretion." ". . . vanity without bounds."*

—With thanks to Robert C. Alberts

doing so at great gain. *Marbury* v. *Madison* immeasurably strengthened the Supreme Court, for it announced and won wide acceptance of the principle of judicial review, the principle that the Court could decide whether a piece of federal legislation was constitutional. Although the idea of judicial review had been asserted before *Marbury* v. *Madison*, that case provided the first occasion for the Supreme Court to define and exercise the right.

The Louisiana Purchase In 1803 the United States acquired the province of Louisiana from France and thereby almost doubled its size. Louisiana was a gigantic wedge of territory stretching from the Gulf of Mexico in the South to some-where in the present-day Dakotas in the North, and from the Mississippi in the East to the Rocky Mountains in the West. Its exact boundaries were unclear, its richness and strategic value unquestioned.

Spain had owned the province until ceding it to France in 1801. Tentative reports of the transfer alarmed Jefferson. The President looked forward to an "empire for liberty" consisting of American farmlands stretching over much of North America. So long as weak Spain controlled the sparsely settled province, he could afford to wait until it dropped into the American lap. But if powerful France now possessed it, who knew whether the United States would ever be able to absorb it? Besides, Louisiana included the port of New Orleans. Whoever controlled this port controlled the trade and commercial outlet for much of the western United States. Hoping to prevent final consummation of the arrangement between Spain and France or at least to acquire some port on the Gulf coast, Jefferson dispatched Robert Livingston to Paris.

Meanwhile, the French were beginning to lose interest in the territory. For a time Napoleon had hoped to fit Louisiana into a great French colonial empire that would also include the valuable Caribbean sugar island of Hispaniola. He first had to recapture the western part of Hispaniola from the blacks who in the 1790s had risen up against French masters there and established the Republic of Haiti. Napoleon sent an army of thirty thousand men, headed by his brother-in-law, to subdue the Haitians under their brilliant leader Toussaint L'Ouverture. The task was impossible. Eventually the French captured L'Ouverture by treachery, but not before their army had been virtually wiped out by a combination of enemy action and tropical disease. Napoleon decided to abandon his dream of a restored French empire in the New World.

It was this new situation that Livingston confronted when he arrived in Paris. France no longer cared much about Louisiana; and Napoleon, facing the prospect of a renewed war in Europe, was certain that he could not keep it from falling into British hands. On the American side, the situation had also changed. In October 1802 Spain, still in legal possession of New Orleans, decided to withdraw the right of deposit the Pinckney Treaty of 1795 had granted to Americans. Once more, the whole American interior was bottled up and this time, so it seemed, France was behind it.

Jefferson now dispatched James Monroe to France with new orders. He should try to get New Orleans from the French, or at least to acquire from Spain part of the Gulf Coast panhandle of West Florida. Either would give the United States an outlet for southern trade. Two days after Monroe joined Livingston in the French capital, they learned a prodigious piece of news: Napoleon would sell not only New Orleans but all of Louisiana! The price: 60 million francs, and up to 20 million francs in settlement of all American claims against France for the "spoliations" of the 1790s. The offer flabbergasted the envoys. They were not authorized to negotiate

such an arrangement, but it was far too good to turn down, and they eagerly accepted. In short order, the signed document was on its way to Washington for Congress and the President to confirm.

It may seem surprising that any American should have questioned such an extraordinary bargain, but many did. One prominent Federalist denounced the purchase as "a miserable calamitous business"—the new nation would now be so gigantic that it would fall apart. Other Federalists were unhappy that the United States had promised to grant citizenship to all the French and Spanish inhabitants of Louisiana. Even Jefferson worried that by buying Louisiana he had exceeded the authority of the federal government under the Constitution, and for a while he supported a constitutional amendment authorizing the purchase. In the end neither side's scruples or reservations could compete with the reality of the most successful land deal in history. On October 20, 1803, the Senate confirmed the treaty, and two months later the United States took formal possession of the province. For a total of $15 million the United States had acquired a region almost equal in area to the whole of western Europe.

Lewis and Clark did immensely valuable work on their expedition to the new territory. They established friendly relations with many Indian tribes. They learned of valuable beaver streams and of many fur-bearing animals. They discovered several usable passes through the Rockies, which they recorded on a map published in 1814. Jefferson sent several other expeditions to the West, the most successful being that led by Lieutenant Zebulon Pike. That explorer traveled the Colorado country, where he gave his name to a high peak of the Rockies west of present-day Denver, and crossed over into Spanish-held New Mexico. His report, published long before that of Lewis and Clark, made him famous and helped to open up the Rocky Mountains to fur trappers.

To the west and the north the vast domain touched Spanish and British territory, but exactly where nobody really knew. The Spaniards suspected that the United States had designs on their possessions in New Mexico and Texas. Years before, they had secretly entered into a financial arrangement with James Wilkinson, a Kentucky adventurer, to act as their spy and agent in the American camp. Wilkinson remained in their pay while

UNITED STATES
SHOWING
TERRITORIAL EXPANSION

PUBLISHED BY
THE UNIVERSAL COMPANY
123 LIBERTY STREET
NEW YORK
Copyright 1915 by THE UNIVERSAL CO., N. Y.

William Sidney Mount, *Early American Farmhouse.* *(Courtesy, Metropolitan Museum of Art)*

rising to brigadier general in the United States Army and to the post of military commander of the new Louisiana Territory. In this strategic position he advised his employers how to thwart American plans. At one point he even suggested that they arrest Lewis and Clark.

Another prominent American, Vice-President Aaron Burr, was fishing in the same troubled western waters.

❙ Burr Again Burr was a complex man. Witty, charming, and intelligent, he was also ambitious and devious; this son of a Presbyterian minister, this grandson of Jonathan Edwards, this former theology student became a notorious womanizer. John Quincy Adams, the future president, noted of Burr that with his "ambition of military fame, ambition of conquest over female virtue was the duplicate ruling passion

of his life." In 1804 he killed Alexander Hamilton in a duel at Weehawken, New Jersey. As one bit of unfriendly doggerel put it,

> Oh Burr, oh Burr, what hast thou done,
> Thou hast shooted dead great Hamilton!
> You hid behind a bunch of thistle,
> And shooted him dead with a great hoss pistol!

The duel was the culmination of longstanding animosity between the two men.

A year later, Burr, according to Wilkinson, was deeply involved in a scheme to detach Louisiana from the United States, join it together with Texas and other parts of Spanish Mexico, and create a new nation. But Wilkinson decided in the end that it was more profitable to stay in Spain's employ than to continue with this chancy venture. In November 1806 he wrote to Jefferson, warning that Burr intended to detach the West from the United States. At the same time he asked the Spanish Viceroy in Mexico to send him $200,000 in appreciation of his refusal to join Burr in dismembering New Spain.

Jefferson ordered Burr's arrest. Burr quickly set out for Pensacola in Spanish Florida, probably intending to escape to Europe. But he was captured and brought to Richmond, Virginia, where he was tried for treason, Wilkinson serving as an important witness against him. The prosecution produced much damaging evidence against Burr. But the former vice-president had the support of the presiding judge, Chief Justice Marshall; when the jury returned the verdict of "not proved," Marshall changed it to "not guilty."

The government refused to drop the matter. Soon after, it obtained Burr's indictment on another treason charge. This time Marshall granted him bail pending trial and rather than face another legal battle, Burr fled to Europe. He remained abroad for four years, and then returned to live a scandalous life in New York City. In his seventies he fathered two illegitimate children, and at the age of eighty he was sued for divorce on the grounds of adultery.

Aaron Burr's schemes to detach the West from the United States led to indictments for treason, charges which he managed to escape.
(Courtesy, The New-York Historical Society, New York City)

France and England—Again

European Entanglements In early 1802 England and France ended their long, exhausting war. It now looked as if the American people would be spared the ordeal they had faced ever since war between the world's two most powerful nations had erupted in 1793. No longer would American commerce be the defenseless prey both of the Royal Navy and of French revenue cutters and port officials. Peace lasted all of fourteen months. By May 1803 Britain was once more at war with France. Austria, and Russia, while Sweden soon joined Britain, and Spain allied itself to imperial France. Once again, America found itself caught between the British hammer and the French anvil.

The Royal Navy immediately resumed its practice of impressing seamen aboard American vessels, claiming that they were deserters from the British fleet. The procedure itself was an insult to American honor; and the British in fact seized numbers of American citizens and forced them into the Royal Navy.

Outside American harbors, British ships waited for American merchant vessels, stopped them, sent an officer aboard, and took crewmen. Britain also reversed its former policy and refused any longer to allow Americans the "broken voyage," a practice by which Americans had brought French goods under the protection of American neutrality by shipping them through American ports. Britain's primary purpose was not to injure American commerce but to hurt the French economy and frustrate the French war effort.

Responding to the British blockade of the French-held continent of Europe, Napoleon issued in 1806 the Berlin Decree, ordering the seizure of any vessel carrying British goods. The following year he directed French privateers to stop all ships, including neutral ones, suspected of carrying enemy cargo. The Berlin Decree set off a round of British countermeasures, followed by still further French retaliation. It began to seem that no American ship would be able to leave port or approach European shores without facing confiscation.

The American response to these indignities and harassments was mixed. Since Britain was now violating American sovereign rights even more flagrantly than France, Britain was the object of an enraged American patriotism. Continuing problems with the Indian tribes in the Northwest further aggravated anti-British feeling. Not all Americans, however, agreed that strong measures were called for. Especially in the Atlantic ports, many citizens were willing to accept harassment. For despite it, American commerce was flourishing in a war-stricken world. So pressing was the need for shipping space that ocean freight rates shot upward. Insurance costs were also high and there was always the risk of confiscation, but profits were unprecedented. Between 1803 and 1807 American exports, much of them in tropical goods from the French and Spanish New World colonies, leaped from $56 million to $108 million, and the American merchant marine grew from 950,000 tons to almost 1.3 million. Why not accept the situation, asked the merchants of Boston, Salem, Providence, New York, Philadelphia, and other ports?

Pressures for War

Still, even the most materialistic citizens could forget their immediate interests in the heat of anger at some indignity committed by the British or French. One such incident took place in the early summer of 1807.

On June 22, the *Chesapeake*, a brand-new Navy frigate commanded by Commodore James Barron, left Norfolk, Virginia, for a Mediterranean cruise. Aboard were several deserters from the Royal Navy. When the *Chesapeake* was only a few miles at sea, it was overtaken by H.M.S. *Leopard*, part of the British squadron patrolling off Hampton Roads. The British captain ordered Barron to heave to and allow a naval party to board to

The attack on the U.S.S. *Chesapeake* by H.M.S. *Leopard* on June 22, 1807, set off a furor among Americans, but Jefferson avoided armed conflict through diplomacy and passage of the Embargo Act. *(Courtesy, The Mariners Museum, Newport News, Virginia)*

look for deserters. This was the first time the British had attempted impressment off an American man-of-war, and Barron refused. But the *Chesapeake's* guns were not yet mounted, and the ship could not defend itself. After repeated murderous broadsides from the *Leopard*, Barron struck his colors; the British removed four deserters and departed. The *Chesapeake* limped back to port with three dead, eighteen wounded, and a tale certain to inflame every American patriot.

The American public screamed for war against "perfidious Albion." "The country," Jefferson noted, "had never been in such a state of excitement since the battle of Lexington." But the President, although he could undoubtedly have obtained a declaration of war from Congress, wished to avoid armed conflict. He was not a pacifist, but he deplored the expensive armies and navies war required; armies and navies and big treasury budgets were Federalist, not Republican, playthings. In accordance with his distaste for a large military, Jefferson had so reduced American forces that war was virtually out of the question. And the United States, he believed, still had at its disposal some powerful unused weapons short of war.

Diplomatic pressure was one of these, and Jefferson immediately dispatched a message to Britain demanding disavowal of the attack, reparations for lives lost and damage inflicted, the recall of the British admiral responsible for the *Leopard's* action, and an end to the impressment policy. He also ordered all British ships out of United States territorial waters and stepped up preparations for defense in case the British forced the nation's hand.

The British response to American diplomatic demands was unsatisfactory. The Foreign Secretary, George Canning, attacked Jefferson for his retaliatory acts and quibbled about reparations for American losses. He also defended the British admiral responsible for the *Leopard's* attack, although he agreed to remove him.

Jefferson now invoked his last peaceable weapon. American trade, the President believed, was essential to both the major belligerents. Both needed American wheat, provisions, and lumber, and the French relied on the United States to carry their Caribbean products. During the imperial crisis before 1775, Americans had forced Britain to back down by boycotting British goods. In all likelihood, Jefferson thought, they would once more yield to commercial pressure if it were applied firmly. In any case, it should be tried before more drastic measures.

The Embargo and Non-Intercourse Acts   Under the President's prodding, Congress passed the Embargo Act of 1807. The law prohibited American ships from sailing for foreign ports. Coastal vessels would have to post bond that would insure that they did not turn east and cross the open sea to Europe, or south to the West Indies. Only ships engaged in public business were to be exempted from the export embargo.

The Embargo Act was temporarily popular in the South and the West. But to the trading centers of the Northeast it seemed a disaster. Almost overnight the glittering trade bubble that had lasted since 1793 burst. Ships rode at anchor, their sails furled, while worms riddled their wooden hulls. Once-busy waterfront streets stood emptied of their milling crowds of seamen, teamsters, tavern-keepers, and stevedores. Wrote John Lambert,

> When I arrived at New York in November [1807], the port was filled with shipping, and the wharfs were crowded with commodities of every description. Bales of cotton, wool, and merchandise; barrels of potash, rice, flour, and salt provisions; hogsheads of sugar, chests of tea, puncheons of rum, and pipes of wine. . . . All was noise and bustle . . . But on my return . . . the following April, what a contrast was presented to my view! . . . The coffee-house slip, the wharfs and quays along South-street, presented no longer the bustle and activity that had prevailed there five months before. The port, indeed, was full of shipping; but they were dismantled and laid up. Their decks were cleared, their hatches fastened down, and scarcely a sailor was to be found on board. Not a box, bale, cask, barrel or package, was to be seen upon the wharfs.

New Yorkers and New Englanders did what they could to evade the new law. Some referred to it as the "Dambargo." Many coastal traders, once out of sight of land, crossed the Atlantic. Jefferson had given the state governors the right to issue special permits for specific reasons. Now the merchants prevailed on the governors to grant permits for almost any excuse. Many New England merchants faced with ruin chose more legal and constructive alternatives: during this period many transferred large amounts of capital from overseas trade to domestic manufactures.

When New England farmers tried to transport their produce across the border to Canada, Jefferson declared them in rebellion and ordered troops to the scene. Pitched battles followed between farmers and militia. Republicans in Congress subsequently passed a series of enforcement acts every bit as repressive as the Alien and Sedition Acts.

Overall, the embargo did not have much effect on the European belligerents. It hurt British workingmen and French colonists, but the ruling classes in both Britain and France were scarcely affected. British manufacturers, meanwhile, could continue to send their goods in their own vessels to compete with American products in the United States. "It was," wrote a critic of the embargo, "as if a flea had tried to stop a dogfight by threatening suicide." At home the embargo produced economic hardship and bitterness. In demanding the subordination of economic self-interest to peace, Jefferson had overestimated the patience and patriotism of his fellow citizens.

So loud became the domestic outcry against the Embargo Act that Congress in 1809 replaced it with the Non-Intercourse Act, permitting exports to every nation except England and France. These two offenders could now neither buy from the United States nor sell to her. If either of the two powers reversed its hostile policies toward the United States, this country could resume trade with it. The man who would administer the new law was not Jefferson but his successor, James Madison.

James Madison Takes Over

No one else had been so instrumental as Madison in fostering and shaping the federal Constitution. After the inauguration of the national government, it had been Madison who led the forces against Hamilton and, in alliance with his good friend Thomas Jefferson, helped to create the Republican Party. In 1801, Jefferson selected him as his Secretary of State and he served with distinction in that office.

Many Republicans viewed Madison as Jefferson's natural successor—but not all. Opposed to him was a group of militant Republicans called the "Tertium Quids," who considered both Jefferson and Madison to be too friendly to Federalist principles. The leading voice of the Quids was John Randolph of Roanoke, an eloquent defender of lost causes and an irresponsible verbal brawler. The Quids tried to deny Madison the nomination, but with Jefferson's support the party caucus in Congress endorsed him. The Federalists were now clearly the minority party, and Madison easily defeated their candidate, Charles Cotesworth Pinckney of XYZ fame.

Physically, the new President was not a commanding figure. Small and wizened, he spoke in a barely audible voice and often seemed bored. The First Lady, the former Dolley Todd, helped to offset her husband's

James Madison, inaugurated as president in 1809, faced growing pressure from the "War Hawks" and others to act against Britain and finally declared war in June 1812. *(Portrait by Gilbert Stuart, Courtesy, Bowdoin College Museum of Fine Arts, Brunswick, Maine)*

dour demeanor. Buxom, pink-cheeked, and charming, Mrs. Madison was a vivacious hostess whose parties and receptions seemed to the social set a vast improvement over the widowed Jefferson's bachelor dinners. Washington was still a city of magnificent distances, as an early observer of its raw, unfilled spaces called it; the presidential mansion was still not complete. But at least the capital now had a social focus it had lacked before.

The new Non-Intercourse Act created difficulties for Madison. Ships leaving American ports were not supposed to touch at French or British ports, but it quickly became clear that there was no way of guaranteeing they would obey the law. The British, in particular, scorned it; it promised to cause them little harm, and they could see little reason to settle the pending *Chesapeake* claims or satisfy American commercial demands.

Not every Englishman took a hard line against the United States. The British minister in Washington, David Erskine, wanted to placate the Americans and told Madison that the British intended to modify their harsh policy toward American trade. On this basis, the President issued a proclamation reopening trade with Great Britain while retaining the restrictions on France. Soon after, Foreign Secretary Canning learned of his minister's indiscretion and disavowed it. The President thereupon reimposed the Non-Intercourse arrangement on Britain.

| **Macon's Bill No. 2**

Dissatisfaction with the Non-Intercourse Act forced Congress into a new tack against the belligerents. In May 1810 it passed Macon's Bill No. 2. This measure was surely one of the most devious in American history. It allowed the President to reopen trade immediately with both Britain and France. In the event that either of the two warring powers modified its trade policies toward the United States before March 1811, the President might reimpose the trade prohibition upon the other. In effect, the United States was offering to ally itself economically against whichever nation was the slower in according it its commercial rights.

An embarrassing and costly blunder was soon forthcoming. In August of 1810, when Napoleon learned of the terms of Macon's Bill, he instructed his foreign minister, Cadore, to inform the Americans that his commercial decrees would be revoked as of November 1, provided that the United States invoke nonintercourse against the British. (Napoleon had larceny in his heart: even as he issued these instructions he prepared to seize any American vessels that might appear in France.) Cadore, in a manner reminiscent of Erskine, took the liberty of informing the United States that the French decrees had actually been cancelled. Once again, Madison responded without checking: he reopened trade with France and declared that trade with Britain would be closed the following February, unless Britain should revoke its Orders in Council before that time. The British replied by once again stationing their warships outside New York harbor and stepping up their campaign of impressing American seamen. Vessels that eluded British capture were confiscated by Napoleon as soon as they reached France.

| **The War Hawks**

Among the victors in the 1810 elections to Congress were a group of young men, mostly from the West and South, who were unwilling to temporize. These "War Hawks" were led by Henry Clay of Kentucky, a young Congressman with a rare eloquence and an unusual power to charm voters and fellow politicians alike. Although this was his first term in the House of Representatives, the magnetic Clay was elected Speaker. He quickly placed young men of like mind in key House posts. Peter Porter of western New York became chairman of the Foreign Relations Committee, where he had the support of such fellow War Hawks as John C. Calhoun of South Carolina, Felix Grundy of Tennessee, and Joseph Desha of Kentucky.

The War Hawks felt keenly the indignities inflicted by the British, a feeling unmodified by concerns in the Northeast for profitable transAtlantic commerce. England's "aggression, and her injuries and insults to us," proclaimed Clay, were "atrocious"—far more so than those of France. Besides, British assaults on American shipping were responsible for low crop prices in the West since they interfered with sales of these crops abroad. Many Westerners, moreover, blamed the British for recent Indian troubles; British agents had instigated the uprising of the Shawnee chief Tecumseh and his brother, "the Prophet." The Kentucky *Gazette* had

Tecumseh saving white prisoners. Despite his martial intentions, he was known for his revulsion at senseless cruelty. *(Courtesy, Henry E. Huntington Library and Art Gallery)*

complained that "British intrigue and British gold, it seems, has greater influence with [the Indians] of late than American justice and benevolence."

In fact, for some time the government had been carrying on military campaigns against western Indians, who had sometimes attacked settlers. In 1793 General "Mad" Anthony Wayne had decisively defeated 2000 Indian warriors at the Battle of Fallen Timbers. In subsequent years Tecumseh forged an alliance of Indians against the whites. He spoke to his braves:

> Since the days when the white race first came in contact with the red men, there has been a continual series of aggressions. The hunting grounds are fast disappearing, and they are driving the red men farther and farther to the west. The mere presence of the white men is a source of evil. . . . His whiskey destroys the bravery of our warriors, and his lust corrupts the virtue of our women. The only

hope . . . is a war of extermination against the paleface.

"Brush from your eyelids the sleep of slavery," he exhorted them, "and strike for vengeance and your country."

On November 7, 1811, General William Henry Harrison beat off Tecumseh's braves at Tippecanoe.

The War Hawks also had an appetite for land. For years the United States had disputed with Spain the boundary of West Florida. That narrow province stretched westward along the Gulf coast from the main Florida peninsula, cutting off much of the American Southwest from the sea. Spain, now an ally of England, held the province loosely. If war broke out, it could certainly be wrenched easily from her feeble hands. And there was Canada. One Congressman declared that "the Author of Nature has marked our limits in the south, by the Gulf of Mexico;

and on the north, by the regions of eternal frost." Congressman John Randolph accused the War Hawks of having "like the whippor-will, but one monotonous tone—Canada! Canada! Canada!"

While the War Hawks and their supporters naturally thought of attacking and taking the exposed colonies of both Spain and England in the event of war, conquest was not their chief purpose. They were nationalists and patriots of the Revolution's memory who hated British arrogance and yearned to avenge the humiliations Britain had recently inflicted. For twenty years, they argued, Britain had refused to treat the United States as a sovereign nation. The effort to preserve peace at any price was making America once more a British colony. "What are we not to lose by peace?" Clay asked rhetorically. His answer: "Commerce, character, a nation's best treasure, honor! I prefer," orated Clay,

the troubled ocean of war, demanded by the honor and independence of this country, with all its calamities and desolation, to the tranquil and pu-trescent pool of ignominious peace.

Madison, concerned with maintaining American agricultural markets in Europe, was soon adopting a tougher policy toward England. In 1811 he asked Congress to vote money to build up the army and navy. In the spring of that year, the U.S.S. *President* encountered the British sloop-of-war *Little Belt*. Although the results were actually inconclusive—the powerful *President* gave the *Little Belt* a drubbing, but failed to sink the weaker British vessel—Americans considered the results ample revenge for the *Chesapeake* attack of four years before.

For months in early 1812 the prospect of war hovered while both the Chief Executive and Congress dithered. In April 1812 a student in Philadelphia wrote to his parents, who lived on a farm near Pittsburgh: "I would be glad if you would write to me as soon as possible, and let me know how you stand affected in this great war that is about to take place. They are beginning to enlist men here; the embargo has put an effectual stop to all trading, and it is likely that a great number of those who are out of employment will join the army." The Republicans had by now come to assume that war was inevitable, but when it came to voting money in preparation for it, their fear of extravagance got in the way of their common sense. Little had been

done to authorize the building of new ships, and appropriations for the army remained inadequate. How the country intended to defend its commerce, and pursue an aggressive policy toward Florida and Canada, nobody made clear.

In the end, war came by mistake. Early in 1812, the British finally decided to modify their commercial policies. On June 23 the British government announced that the notorious Orders in Council that had so offended the United States would be lifted. It was too late. Before the news arrived, Madison impatiently had asked for a declaration of war. On June 4, the House voted in favor by 79 to 49; two weeks later the Senate followed, 19 to 13. The vote revealed a disunited nation. If the way congressmen voted is taken as indicative, southern New England, as well as much of New York, New Jersey, and Maryland, opposed the war. Would they continue to resist once the fighting had begun?

A Republican paper in Boston tried to rally support for the war:

Since war is the word, let us strain every nerve
To save our America, her glory increase;
So, shoulder your firelock, your country preserve,
For the hotter the war, boys, the quicker the peace.

A clergyman in New York was more insistent in his Sunday sermon:

A nation may be treated by another as to justify . . . a declaration of war. . . . Suppose that one man should presume to enjoin his will upon another equally free,—suppose he should say to him, You shall neither buy nor sell at such or such a market;—or, finding him on the highway, going to or returning from market, he should forcibly take away his property and injure his person:—or suppose that, seeing him in the pursuit of some profitable business, he should tell him, You shall pursue that business no longer; perhaps because he is in it himself and wishes to monopolize the profits; or possibly, because he is so circumstanced as not to be able to engage in it, and therefore grudges his neighbor the advantage. Can you then for a moment hesitate as to the duty of the citizen thus insulted!—thus injured! . . . The application to nations is perfectly convenient. . . .

—Either she must tamely and dastardly submit to the dictates and oppressions of imperious Britain, and so make, at once, a surrender of her rights, and an acknowledgment that she is no longer free; or, in the noble spirit of '76, call together her patriotic sons—vest them with authority—furnish them with arms, and say to them, Go,—go by sea and land,—go vindicate my rights, avenge my wrongs, and maintain my LIBERTY, the bounteous gift of heaven, and the invaluable price of your fathers' blood.

The War of 1812

"Mr. Madison's War" By almost any measure, the War of 1812 was mismanaged. The government that was making war had done little to prepare for it, and for three years the Americans lumbered from one encounter to another. One of the government's chief problems was the financing of such an expensive enterprise. Unready for heavy taxes, Americans expected to pay for the war through borrowing. Yet in 1811 the Republicans had refused to recharter the Bank of the United States, and it had died.

The country presented a logistical nightmare. To move troops and supplies over such enormous distances would be next to impossible. Roads were few and poor. The steamboat had been introduced on the Hudson in 1807, but steamboat travel on the Mississippi and the Great Lakes was in its infancy in 1812. The armed forces were unready. Only 7,000 men were immediately available for service, and most of these were scattered in small frontier posts. The state militias were a potential pool of manpower, but most militiamen were poorly trained and led. The best of the state forces were those of New England. "I know," one young Maine man explained typically to his mother upon enlisting:

> I sacrifice my time, and my ease, and expose my morals to be corrupted by the licentiousness of a camp, my health to be impaired by fatiguing marches and the chilly cold of a more northern clime, and my life to danger . . . [but] I am satisfied that the essential rights of my country have been trampled on and are at stake and that the war in consequence thereof is a righteous and necessary war, and that it ought to be spiritedly supported by every man in America.

But the Yankee governors refused to allow their soldiers to be called into federal service unless their own states were threatened with invasion.

And the country was disunited. Many Federalists thought the war a mistake. The governor of Massachusetts called for a fast day to atone for making war "against the nation from which we are descended. . . ." It was "Mr. Madison's war," a Republican venture, not a national one. Particularly in New England, the home of High Federalism, the war also seemed likely to produce a commercial

THE WAR OF 1812
The Northern Frontier 1812-1814
□ Battles
→ American movements
→ British movements

disaster. Inevitably, Yankees said, theirs would be the commerce swept off the seas by the Royal Navy.

Strong leadership might have overcome many of these difficulties, but Madison was a better philosopher and congressional manager than war leader. Almost all the high military officers were elderly gentlemen who had not commanded troops against a trained European army since the Revolution.

| **Canadian Campaigns**

Oblivious to these weaknesses, the Americans began the fighting with an invasion of Canada led by General William Hull, commanding 2,000 regulars. Henry Clay had declaimed: "I trust I shall not be deemed presumptuous when I state that I verily believe that the militia of Kentucky are alone competent to place Montreal and upper Canada at [our] feet." Launched from Detroit, far to the west of Canada's chief population centers, the invasion was seriously misconceived. It required extended supply lines, and to protect these long lines the Americans had to control Lake Erie. But without a naval force on the lake they could not do so.

Nevertheless, the campaign at first seemed to be succeeding. Hull crossed the Detroit River into Canada unopposed. He immediately issued a proclamation that if the Canadian militia remained at home they had nothing to fear from the Americans. In a matter of days half of them had deserted the British and returned to their farms.

The British now expected an immediate attack across the river from Detroit on Fort Malden, which was garrisoned by only a few hundred regulars, some Indians, and the remaining militia. But the Americans delayed. By the time Hull's forces mounted their guns against the British, the American garrison at Michilimackinac to the east had surrendered. Certain that his supply lines were now endangered, Hull withdrew across the river and locked himself up in Detroit. On August 17 he surrendered to the British commander.

Prospects of taking Canada now appeared bleak. If the American invasion prong in the West, where the people were enthusiastic supporters of the war, had failed, what could be expected in the hostile East?

From New York, a part of that state's militia crossed the Niagara to attack the British and Canadian forces. They scored some early successes, but then were pinned down. They could have been rescued and the operation saved, but the remaining New York militia refused to cross the Niagara. Without reinforcements, 900 Americans were captured at Queenston Heights.

The third prong of the invasion was no more successful than the first two. This attack, aimed at Montreal, was at least strategically sound. That city was the heart of British power in North America, and its capture would have been a disaster to England. But the Americans delayed their operations and gave the British many months to prepare. By the time the militia moved northward against a well-entrenched enemy, the autumn was far advanced. The ill-equipped American troops slogged their way through mud and drenching cold rain, sleeping without tents on the soggy ground with dripping blankets. When the American troops reached the Canadian border, many refused to cross. After fighting a few skirmishes, their commander ordered a retreat to Plattsburg, New York. There the militia made camp amid mud and snow; many contracted pneumonia. "The very woods," an army surgeon reported, "[ring] with coughing and groaning." Shortly afterward the invasion force dispersed. Eighteen-twelve had ended with Canada still firmly in British hands and American morale in the cellar.

| **The Naval War**

The naval war was going better. Although the British far outmanned and outgunned the Americans at sea, they were also stretched thin, and suffered from overconfidence. The Americans, they were certain, could not match the Royal Navy in battle or do serious damage to their merchant shipping. They were wrong. Many American merchant captains had secured "letters of marque" commissioning their vessels as privateers. Over the next two and a half years, these ships attacked British commerce in the West Indies, off the east coast of the United States, and even in the waters around the British Isles. While many privateers were captured, others took rich prizes. The success of the small American navy, though less significant in material terms, was important for national morale. The American frigates proved to be remarkably effective in single-ship combat.

In August 1812 the U.S.S. *Constitution*, commanded by Isaac Hull, sighted the Brit-

We have met the enemy and they are ours: Two Ships, two Brigs one Schooner & one Sloop.

Yours, with great respect and esteem

O H Perry.

Oliver Hazard Perry's dispatch to General Harrison on his victory at Lake Erie reflected the pride of the Americans on finally winning a naval battle.

ish frigate *Guerrière* in the mid-North Atlantic. The *Guerrière* was a slightly smaller vessel with a lighter broadside; part of her crew, moreover, consisted of impressed Americans who had to be allowed to go below rather than fight their own countrymen. The British captain tried evasive maneuvers, but Hull was able to bring his ship within fifty yards of the enemy. For two hours he poured deadly broadsides into the British ship, leaving it a wreck. The *Guerrière* struck her colors. Both sides had fought well and bravely, but the performance of the inexperienced Americans was exceptional. American sailors had fought with greater spirit than American infantry.

This victory was only the first of several such single-ship combats that helped redeem the honor of American arms. Several weeks later the *United States*, under Stephen Decatur, encountered H.M.S. *Macedonian* and in a bloody battle sank her. At the end of the year the *Constitution* defeated H.M.S. *Java* in a two-hour engagement.

Chagrined by their losses, the British began to reinforce their American squadron by drawing off vessels needed elsewhere. The British Navy began to improve its performance. Bit by bit its blockade of the American Atlantic coast became tighter and more effective, confirming all the fears of Northeasterners that war would destroy American commerce. The Americans soon lost control of their own coasts and shortly would be unable to repel British troop landings when they came.

The fate of one American privateer, cruising the ocean for prey, was not unusual; as one sailor told it:

> On the 25th of January, 1814, being just one month after we sailed from Portsmouth, at 5 o'clock in the morning, the word was passed from the lookout above, 'Sail, oh!' We bore away, and made sail for the strange vessel. She was a large man-of-war brig, and by her model and rig, we judged her to be an English one. We speedily hauled upon the wind and made all sail, endeavoring to show the enemy a clear pair of heels; . . . . We felicitated ourselves for some time with the hope of escape, but it was a delusive hope. . . . The chaser still gained upon us. We were in the neighborhood of Porto Rico, and we still hoped to keep clear of the brig until darkness came on, and under its cover to escape into the harbor. We lightened our schooner by throwing overboard all our guns, most of our provisions and water, all our small arms, irons, caboose, &c. We sawed down our plank shires, started out the wedges of our masts, and kept our sails continually wet. But all would not do, for at 5 P.M. the brig had neared us sufficiently to commence firing on us with her bowguns. The brig kept up a steady fire upon us till 7 o'clock; but as we were low in the water, they did not often strike us. At 7 o'clock, all hope of escape departed from the captain. He mounted up into the main rigging, and hailing the brig, announced our surrender.

Further Defeats in Canada

Another major attack on Canada came in 1813. In April, 8,500 troops gathered at the eastern end of Lake Ontario under the command of Henry Dearborn. On April 25, 1,700 men of this force sailed off to attack the Canadians at the western end of the lake and two days later arrived before York (now Toronto). The town was defended by only 800 soldiers and some Indians. The British had prepared a surprise in the form of a giant underground mine jammed with high explosives, but the mine went off at the wrong time, killing as many British troops as Americans. Dismayed and outnumbered, the British commander now withdrew. After occupying York for four days, the Americans looted it and burned the parliament buildings—acts for which their country would pay dearly the following year. American troops then departed for the mouth of the Niagara to attack Fort George. By this time the aging Dearborn was too exhausted to lead the expedition, and he turned his command over to the vigorous Winfield Scott. Soon to join the expedition was an equally aggressive young naval officer, twenty-seven-year-old Oliver Hazard Perry.

The force was transported across Lake Ontario, and successfully completed a difficult amphibious landing before Fort George. The troops, led by Scott and Perry, scrambled ashore with their heavy equipment and secured a foothold while still more men came ashore. Supported by the guns of the flotilla, the invasion force drove off the British counterattack. The British commander now withdrew from Fort George and retreated to Beaver Dams. Scott was all for pursuing the enemy and destroying his army completely, but was overruled by his superior in the Niagara theater of operations. When the Americans were finally allowed to set off after the defeated British, Scott remained behind. The results were disastrous. The British commander surprised the Americans in their sleep, captured their leaders, and drove them back to Beaver Dams.

The British had now regained the initiative, and advanced on the American base with their small force of Indians and redcoats. The Indian auxiliaries encountered a large group of Americans under Lieutenant Colonel Charles Boerstler, and attacked. Boerstler held the Indians off until a party of British regulars approached under a flag of truce. Lieutenant James Fitzgibbon, the young British officer in charge, told the American commander that he was being closely followed by the main British army of fifteen hundred regulars and seven hundred Indians. The Americans, Fitzgibbon argued, could not possibly withstand the attack of

this force, and in all likelihood the British would not then be able to restrain the bloodthirsty Indians; the American commander should surrender now and save his men from massacre. Boerstler accepted the lieutenant's advice, laid down his arms, and waited for the main British party to arrive. It never did. Boerstler had surrendered his unit of 500 men to a force only half its size.

The setback on the Niagara frontier was matched by a major defeat before Montreal. Advancing on the Canadian city, the forces from the United States ran into stiff opposition and abandoned the invasion. Soon afterward, the British captured Fort Niagara. They also took Buffalo and burned the city to the ground.

The Battle of Lake Erie In July 1813 six British warships arrived at Lake Erie, and Captain Perry, commanding the hastily-built American fleet there, sent an urgent plea for men: "Think of my situation: the enemy in sight, the vessels under my command more than sufficient, and ready to make sail. . . ." But when the men came, he complained that they were "a motley set, blacks, soldiers, and boys. . . ." His commanding officer wrote back: "I regret that you are not pleased with the men sent you . . . , a part of them are not surpassed by any men we have in the fleet; and I have yet to learn that the color of the skin, or the cut and trimmings of the coat, can affect a man's qualifications or usefulness."

On September 10, 1813, Perry and his "motley set" (about one-fourth of whom were black) defeated the British fleet in a bloody three-hour battle. On the back of an envelope, Perry scrawled a now-famous message to General Harrison: "We have met the enemy and they are ours." Lake Erie was now in American hands, and the British were forced to abandon Detroit. A month later, Harrison overtook a retreating party of British and Indians and at the Battle of the Thames in Canada defeated them decisively. The chieftain Tecumseh was one of those who fell on the British side. Soon afterward, Tecumseh's federation of tribes collapsed and most of Britain's Indian allies deserted her cause.

By 1814 the British navy had established a clear superiority in the Atlantic and in American coastal waters. The Royal Navy could with impunity sail up the Chesapeake Bay, attack merchant ships, and bombard strategic towns and military positions.

Amplifying British successes were American disunity and the Madison administration's blunders. Hard-pressed New England was riddled with disloyalty. Yankees had not wanted war and felt little inducement to support it now that it was proving so expensive. Hoping to rescue something from the calamity, they became the chief suppliers of commodities to the British army in Canada. Madison sought to cut off this dangerous trade and induced Congress to pass an embargo bill in December 1813 restricting all exports from the United States. The effects were disastrous. American exports plummeted and prices increased sharply. The Treasury found that it could not borrow the money it needed to for military operations, and was forced to the edge of bankruptcy. In April 1814 Congress repealed this measure.

Meanwhile the gloomy military situation promised to get worse. In the spring of 1814, Napoleon's empire collapsed and the conqueror of Europe went into exile on the island of Elba. Until then, the British had been conducting a series of holding operations in America on both land and sea. Now, with France out of the war, all the vast resources of the Royal Navy and the seasoned veterans of the European fighting would be free to teach the pesky Americans a lesson.

In early May, the first detachments of British troops began to arrive in Quebec from Europe. Their mission, as explained in orders to the British commandant in Canada, Sir George Prevost, would be to drive the troops of the American republic out of Canada and recover the American Northwest, and thereby to secure Canada's safety.

Winfield Scott attacked first. At Chippewa and Lundy's Lane, American regular troops fought effectively and gallantly against the best the British had to offer. The campaign ended in a draw, but Scott and Brown had frustrated British goals in the Northwest.

British Offensives

The British soon resumed the offensive. In late summer they set out for Plattsburgh, New York, near Lake Champlain. The British plan, as during the Revolution, was to split the United States in two along the line of Lake Champlain and the Hudson Valley. By September Prevost's army, the largest yet seen in America, was at Plattsburgh's gates.

There, however, the American commander was the scrappy John Wool. Though outnumbered almost three to one, Wool put up such a fight along the approaches to Plattsburgh that Prevost paused and called on Captain George Downie, in command of the British fleet on the lake, to come to his aid: together the navy and army would pound the Americans into submission and advance on New York City to complete their mission.

It was not to be. Standing between Prevost and the fulfillment of his scheme was the United States naval squadron commanded by Captain Thomas Macdonough. Macdonough's little fleet consisted of four moderate-sized vessels and ten tiny gunboats, but in firepower it just about matched Downie's squadron.

Downie attacked the Americans. His first shot hit the deck of Macdonough's flagship, the *Saratoga*, and destroyed the coop of the sailors' champion gamecock. The bird was unhurt and immediately flew to a gun carriage where, its feathers ruffled, it crowed defiance at the enemy. The men laughed and cheered; it seemed a good omen.

For over two hours the opposing fleets poured solid and grapeshot into each other. Macdonough himself was knocked unconscious three times. At last the British surrendered. Macdonough brought the defeated British officers aboard the *Saratoga*, complimented them on their bravery, and refused to accept their swords. Shortly afterward he dispatched a message to the Secretary of the Navy that "the Almighty has been pleased to grant us a signal victory on Lake Champlain."

And a signal victory it was. When Prevost learned of Macdonough's triumph, he decided he could not continue; with the enemy in command on the water, his flanks were exposed. Instead of resuming the assault, he marched his men back to Canada. Another invasion threat was over.

The Burning of Washington

A second British invasion prong was meeting with greater success. On August 19, 1814, Sir George Cockburn landed with 4,000 men between Baltimore and Washington, and set out for the nation's capital. A hastily organized defense force of militia, sailors, and a few regulars sought to stop the British at Bladensburg, but the inexperienced Americans could not hold against sea-

In August 1814, the British captured and burned the city of Washington, including the President's house, the Capitol, the Treasury, and the War Office. (*Courtesy, The New-York Historical Society, New York City*)

soned veterans and many fell into British hands. Later that afternoon, after learning of the defeat, Madison and his Cabinet left the city to avoid capture. His wife, the resourceful Dolley, had already removed the sterling silver and other valuables from the presidential mansion. At 8 p.m. the British entered the city. At the White House British officers ate the President's dinner abandoned in Madison's flight. The next morning they burned the public buildings, including the President's house, the Capitol, the Treasury, and the War Office. The following day they left the smoldering capital, having avenged the burning of York. A British soldier recalled the "beautiful spectacle" of the burning of Washington:

The blazing of houses, ships, and stores, the report of exploding magazines, and the crash of falling roofs [informed him and his troops] as they proceeded, of what was going forward. You can conceive nothing finer than the sight which met them as they drew near to the town. The sky was brilliantly illumined by the different conflagrations; and a dark red light was thrown upon the road, sufficient to permit each man to view distinctly his comrade's face. A storm began and the flashes of lightning seemed to vie in brilliancy, with the flames which burst from the roofs of burning houses, while the thunder drowned the noise of crumbling walls, and was only interrupted by the occasional roar of

cannon, and of large depots of gunpowder, as they one by one exploded.

The President [James Madison] had hurried back to his own house, that he might prepare a feast for the entertainment of his officers, when they should return victorious. For the truth of these details, I will not be answerable; but this much I know, that the feast was actually prepared, though, instead of being devoured by American officers, it went to satisfy the less delicate appetites of a party of English soldiers. When the detachment, sent out to destroy Mr. Madison's house, entered his dining parlour, they found a dinner-table spread, and covers laid for forty guests. Several kinds of wine, in handsome cut-glass decanters, were cooling on the side-board; plate holders stood by the fireplace, filled with dishes and plates; knives, forks, and spoons, were arranged for immediate use; in short, every thing was ready for the entertainment of a ceremonious party. Such were the arrangements in the dining room; whilst in the kitchen were others answerable to them in every respect. Spits, loaded with joints of various sorts, turned before the fire; pots, sauce-pans, and other culinary utensils, stood upon the grate; and all other requisites for an elegant and substantial repast, were exactly in a state which indicated that they had been lately and precipitately abandoned.

You will readily imagine, that these preparations were beheld, by a party of hungry soldiers, with no indifferent eye. An elegant dinner, even though considerably over-dressed, was a luxury to which few of them, at least for some time back, had been accustomed; and which, after the dangers and fatigues of the day, appeared peculiarly inviting. They sat down to it, therefore, not indeed in the most orderly manner, but with countenances which would not have disgraced a party of aldermen at a civic feast; and having satisfied their appetites with fewer complaints than would have probably escaped their rival *gourmands,* and partaken pretty freely of the wines, they finished by setting fire to the house which had so liberally entertained them.

In early September the British, arriving by land and sea, moved on Baltimore. They broke through the Americans' first line of defense and drew to within a mile and a half of the city. At this point the British commander decided to call on the British flotilla offshore to bombard the city, to help soften it up for his final assault. All through the day and night of September 13 the British fired rockets, big guns, and mortars at Forts McHenry and Covington, but could not silence them. Watching the attack was a Baltimore lawyer, Francis Scott Key. Deeply moved by the defenders' stout resistance, he wrote a poem, "The Star-Spangled Banner," commemorating the event. The British failure to reduce the harbor defenses discouraged further action, and they withdrew. The city was safe.

Baltimore's escape was, of course, a welcome event, but it could not wipe out the memory of Washington's capture and the general ineptness of the American war effort. In the wake of the Chesapeake invasions defeatism swept across the nation.

The fall and winter of 1814-15 was also a

THE WAR OF 1812
The Southwest 1812-1815

◻ Battles
⇢ American movements
➡ British movements

THE WAR OF 1812
Chesapeake Bay 1814

⇢ British movements

O say can you see, ~~through~~ by the dawn's early light,
what so proudly we hail'd at the twilight's last gleaming,
Whose broad stripes & bright stars through the perilous fight
O'er the ramparts we watch'd, were so gallantly streaming?
And the rocket's red glare, the bomb bursting in air,
Gave proof through the night that our flag was still there,
O say does that star spangled banner yet wave
O'er the land of the free & the home of the brave?

Francis Scott Key's "The Star-Spangled Banner": detail of the national anthem written during the War of 1812.

time of political crisis. Massachusetts elected representatives to meet with delegates from other New England states at Hartford, Connecticut, to consider defense problems and to discuss the possibility of revising the federal Constitution. Behind this action were the profound disgust of New Englanders with the war and their feeling that their section was suffering unduly in the conflict. At Hartford the militants intended to consider either seceding from the war or seceding from the Union itself, but by the time the convention met in December they were outnumbered. New Hampshire and Vermont refused to send delegations at all; and the delegates from Connecticut and Rhode Island proved to be more moderate than anyone expected. The Convention did not call for dissolution of the Union. It urged amendments to the Constitution that would reduce the power of the West and the South and require that declarations of war, non-intercourse acts, and admission of new states all receive a two-thirds vote of Congress to be adopted. But the resolutions in the end amounted to little more than a protest.

The Treaty of Ghent   As early as November 1813 the British and American governments, partly at the urging of the Russian Czar, had agreed to meet to discuss peace terms. Neither government was happy about the war both had sought to avoid; now, even while fighting continued, they began to arrange for its end.

Negotiations conducted at Ghent in Belgium moved slowly. The British hoped that before long their armies would occupy large stretches of the United States and they could use this territory as leverage for extracting favorable terms. Perhaps they might even get their long-held wish to create an Indian state in the Northwest, cutting the Americans off from the interior of the continent. The American negotiators, Henry Clay, John Quincy Adams, and Albert Gallatin, rejected any scheme to slice up their country and insisted on the abandonment of the impressment of sailors from American ships.

At first, neither side would budge. During the last half of 1814 the British began to realize that, though they could win victories, they could not count on totally defeating the stubborn Americans. Then, too, Britain and Russia began to clash at the Congress of Vienna called to sort out the complex affairs of Europe after Napoleon's defeat. Under the circumstances, war with the United States now seemed an unimportant sideshow that should be ended as soon as possible. The Americans, too, were anxious to bring matters to a conclusion, and abandoned their demand for an explicit elimination of impressment.

On Christmas eve, 1814, the commissioners at Ghent finally signed a peace treaty. This agreement merely restored the situation as it had existed before the war. Said John Quincy Adams, "We have obtained nothing but peace." Commissioners from both nations would meet to settle a dispute over the boundary between the United States and Canada, a dispute that had resulted from imperfections in the geographical knowledge available in 1783. The war had been nearly pointless, and it would not be the last such in American history.

New Orleans

Yet the war went on. News of the Treaty of Ghent did not reach the United States for many weeks, and by that time hundreds of men had died in unnecessary battles. The greatest of these was the Battle of New Orleans, which created a national hero, helped destroy what remained of the Federalist Party, and restored the nation's battered self-respect. The hero was General Andrew Jackson of Tennessee, a roughhewn, self-made planter, lawyer, and soldier.

| **General Andrew Jackson** | Born in South Carolina, Jackson had gone to Tennessee when that future |

Born in South Carolina, Jackson had gone to Tennessee when that future state was still the western district of North Carolina. He had served his adopted state in Congress and as a judge. In 1813-14 he led the Tennessee militia against the Creek Indians in Mississippi Territory following the massacre of 250 whites at Fort Mims. At Horseshoe Bend, Jackson surprised the Creeks and defeated them in a fierce battle. For his services the government made him a major general in the army and commander of the Seventh Military District with headquarters at Mobile.

While at Mobile, Jackson learned that the British, as part of their final push to crush the Americans, intended to attack New Orleans with another army of European veterans. Though weak with fatigue and dysentery, "Old Hickory" hurried to the city to prepare its defenses. A flood of directives—to obstruct the roads and bayous leading to the city, to build fortifications, and to strengthen the existing ones—flowed from his headquarters. Militia and volunteers from Kentucky, Tennessee, and Mississippi made up the core of Jackson's army, and he recruited additional troops from among the Creoles (people of French or Spanish origin) and black freemen of New Orleans.

To the governor of Louisiana Jackson wrote:

> Our country has been invaded. . . . She wants Soldiers to fight her battles. The free men of colour in yur city are inured to the Southern climate and would make excellent Soldiers. They will not remain quiet spectators of the interesting contest. They must be for, or against us—distrust them, and you make them your enemies, place confidence in them, and yhou engage them by every dear and honorable tie to the interest of the country who extends to them equal rights and priviledges with white men.

To the army paymaster who questioned equal pay for the black troops Jackson wrote: "Be pleased to keep to yourself your opinions upon the policy of making payments of the troops with the necessary muster rolls without inquiring whether the troops are white, black or tea." Jackson also agreed to accept the services of a group of river pirates led by Jean Lafitte, a colorful rogue in trouble with the governor of Louisiana.

On the morning of December 23, 1814, redcoats newly arrived from the West Indies began to disembark fifteen miles southeast of New Orleans, after a cold trip across Lake Borgne in open boats. Jackson quickly learned of the landings. A more cautious general might have waited to see whether this was the main attack or a mere feint. But Jackson immediately turned to his officers and declared: "Gentlemen, the British are below; we must fight them tonight!"

With 2,000 men he advanced on the British force of some 1,600 that was waiting for further reinforcements before advancing against the city. Jackson achieved complete surprise and gave the redcoats a serious drubbing. The British line held, however, and Jackson withdrew to a line between the river and a swamp.

Here, just as the commissioners were signing the peace treaty at Ghent, Jackson and his men prepared to face the British assault behind breastworks of cotton bales and earth. Both sides were being reinforced. The British were also getting a new commander: Sir Edward Pakenham, brother-in-law of the Duke of Wellington and an experienced officer of the Peninsular War in Spain.

Pakenham moved his army to within a few hundred yards of Jackson's force in preparation for a morning assault. All night long, American raiders made sorties against the British, doing little harm, but keeping the redcoats from getting any sleep. The next morning, with the battlefield enveloped in ground fog, the British advanced on Jackson's men hidden behind their breastworks. For a while they made headway against the firearms and artillery to their front, but shelling on their flank by the U.S.S. *Louisiana* from the river proved more than flesh could bear, and the advance stopped.

For the next three days the two armies confronted each other across a field strewn with dead and dying. On the morning of December 31, the British attacked again and the battle became an artillery duel, with Lafitte's pirates doing especially effective work with their big guns. For almost five hours the cannon boomed, until the discouraged British ceased their attack. Once more both sides brought up reinforcements. When Pakenham was ready to resume the attempt to reach New Orleans, he had close to 10,000 men, far more than Jackson.

On the morning of January 8, 1815, Pakenham asked his veterans for the last time to brave the American defenses. Once more, the attack failed. As the redcoats trudged across the ground in front of the American position, their ranks were shredded by grapeshot and arms fire. Some reached the American lines, but then a counterattack threw them back. Many British officers were hit, and Pakenham himself died on the field. Before dying, the British general ordered a subordinate, General John Lambert, to throw in reserves for a final push; but seeing the hopelessness of the situation, Lambert refused. Instead, he ordered his men to fall back to Lake Borgne. The battle was over.

An ecstatic newspaper writer could hardly contain himself in his dispatch:

> Glory be to GOD, that the barbarians have been defeated and that at *Orleans* the intended plunder-

The Red Fox, **James Hope.** *(Courtesy, Museum of Fine Arts, Boston)*

ers have found their grave!—Glory to *Jackson, Carroll* and *Coffee,* and the hardy and gallant *Tennesseeans, Kentuckians* and *Louisianians* who "seized opportunity by the forelock" to *"demonstrate"* what freemen can do in defence of their altars and firesides. Glory to the *militia,* that the "soldiers of *Wellington,"* the boastful conquerors of the legions of *France,* have shrunk from the *liberty-directed* bullets of the high-souled sons of the west! Sons of freedom—saviors of *Orleans*—benefactors of your country and avengers of its wrongs, all hail! Hail glorious people—worthy, thrice worthy, to enjoy the blessings which heaven in bounteous profusion has heaped on your country! Never may its luxuriant soil be trodden unrevenged by insolent foreigners in arms!

Who would not be an American? Long live the republic! All hail! last asylum of oppressed humanity! Peace is signed in the arms of victory!

| **Victory after Defeat** | The victory was amazing. Over 2,000 British troops had died or been wounded, |

it was said, against American casualties of twenty-one. Soon after the smoke cleared, Jackson and his jubilant staff passed along the lines of cheering troops to the stirring strains of "Hail Columbia" played by the army band. Even if it had all been a mistake, it was a glorious moment for the young nation.

A mismanaged war that had humiliated Americans now became a matter of great national pride. Overnight new confidence suffused the nation. Americans had taken on the greatest power in the world, and in the end had defeated the best it could throw at them. No longer would the nations of Europe treat the United States with the contempt they had been showing. American nationalists managed the incredible feat of puffing a disastrous war into an epic victory. The country had finally and unquestionably confirmed the formal independence achieved in 1783.

The war had momentous political consequences. The Federalists had bet on the wrong side, Britain. If not for New Orleans and the exhilaration that made a bungled national enterprise seem a triumph, Federalist

opposition to the war might have been rewarded with public favor, but Jackson's victory placed the stigma of traitor on every Federalist who had praised England and attacked the administration. In the presidential contest of 1816, the Republican James Monroe overwhelmed the Federalist candidate, Rufus King of New York, carrying every state in the Union except Massachusetts, Connecticut, and Delaware. Thereafter, although they continued to muster some isolated support, the Federalists were finished.

Meanwhile, a strange thing happened: the Republicans became Federalists. In his annual message in 1815, Madison asked Congress to pass a protective tariff, charter a second Bank of the United States, and appropriate funds for the construction of roads and canals—"internal improvements," as they came to be known. Led by Clay, Calhoun, and other converts to nationalism, Congress obliged. In 1816 it passed a tariff affording at least modest protection to American industry, and established the Second Bank of the United States with an even larger capitalization than that of the First. Madison, having changed his mind, vetoed the bill for internal improvements on the grounds that federal funding of them was of dubious constitutionality; but his successors thought differently and thereafter federal subsidies would help the nation overcome its vast distances.

Finally, there was Andrew Jackson. New Orleans had created America's first folk hero since George Washington. Congress struck a gold medal in Jackson's honor and confirmed his rank of major general with the munificent salary of $2400 a year. Before long, a biographer was busy writing a life of the general for an eager public. At this point Jackson might have chosen a life of ease at the Hermitage, his plantation near Nashville, amidst the plaudits of his fellow citizens. His future took a different course. Before many months had passed, Americans would hear from him again.

Points To Think About

1. The Hartford Convention, an ill-fated endeavor to advance Federalist ideas, showed how short-lived a political principle can be. The New England Federalists had been, so long as their own party was in power, among the most fervent advocates of a strong central government. Once

power passed to their political opponents, however, their devotion to Federalist principles began to wane. By 1814, Jeffersonian policies—from the Embargo and Non-Intercourse Acts to the declaration of war against England—had convinced them of the merits of the states' rights position that Jefferson had propounded in the Kentucky Resolution. Meanwhile, of course, Jefferson and Madison had become staunch advocates of national authority.

So the arguments over the powers of the national government balanced against the states continued, but the Jeffersonians and Federalists had switched sides. This state of affairs invites cynicism, but there is an element of reason in it. Power is always dangerous. Naturally enough, it is those who happen to be not in power who recognize the dangers clearly. That awareness gradually fades as they begin to exercise it themselves. And it is then given to their opponents to ring the alarm. That is as it should be.

2. As Federalists explored states' rights, the Republicans underwent a kind of "conversion" to Federalist principles. The Louisiana Purchase far exceeded the proper limits of national authority by Jefferson's own admission. Nonetheless he went through with it. Then the war convinced the Republicans of the need for a national bank, for a sound military establishment, and even for a tariff high enough to protect American industry.

Republicans learned most of these lessons the hard way. They had to see just how dangerous it was to conduct governmental finance without a bank, or challenge a powerful foe without an adequate army or navy. The Republicans had combined two antithetical passions. They distrusted government and wished to limit its scope as much as possible, but they were also intense nationalists who wished to see their country grown and become more and more powerful. Their nationalism proved the stronger of the two passions.

Suggested Readings

Recent scholarship on the years 1800 to 1816 includes Drew McCoy, *The Last of the Fathers: James Madison and the Republican Legacy* (1989), Pierre Berton, *The Invasion of Canada* (1980), Noble E. Cunningham, Jr., *In Pursuit of Reason: The Life of Thomas Jefferson* (1987), J. C. A. Stagg, *Mr. Madison's War: Politics, Diplomacy, and Warfare in the Early Republic, 1783–1830* (1983), and James P. Ronda, *Lewis and Clark Among the Indians* (1984).

On Lewis and Clark read the geographer John Logan Allen, *Passage Through the Garden: Lewis and Clark and the Image of the American Northwest* (1968). Dumas Malone presents *Jefferson and His Times* (1948–1981) in six magnificent volumes. Merrill Peterson's is a one-volume biography, *Thomas Jefferson and the New Nation* (1970). Forrest McDonald's *The Presidency of Thomas Jefferson* (1976) complements Fawn M. Brodie's *Thomas Jefferson: An Intimate History* (1974). Gore Vidal's *Burr: A Novel* (1973) presents the controversial Aaron as a gentleman and portrays the vulgarities and hypocrisies of the society that surrounded him. Also sympathetic is Milton Lomask's biography, *Aaron Burr* (1983).

Nancy Cott's *The Bonds of Womanhood: "Woman's Sphere" in New England, 1780–1835* is a perceptive study of women's experience. For an interpretation of child-rearing practices see Philip Greven, *The Protestant Temperament: Patterns of Child-Rearing, Religious Experience, and The Self in Early America* (1982).

Lance Banning emphasizes Whig ideology in *The Jeffersonian Persuasion* (1978). Also useful on politics are Noble E. Cunningham, Jr., *The Process of Government under Jefferson* (1978), Marshall Smelser, *The Democratic Republic, 1800–1815* (1968), David Hackett Fischer, *The Revolution of American Conservatism* (1965), and James M. Banner, *To The Hartford Convention: The Federalists and the Origins of Party Politics in Massachusetts, 1789–1815* (1970).

Alexander DeConde surveys the Louisiana Purchase in *This Affair of Louisiana* (1976) while Reginald Horsman fights *The War of 1812* (1969). James Sterling Young draws a superb picture of *The Washington Community* (1968).

☆ ☆ DEBATE ☆ ☆ ☆

FORREST McDONALD

The most striking achievement of the United States during its early history was that both the country and its form of government survived. Under the circumstances, those were by no means trivial feats. The western world—Europe and the Americas—was almost continually at war throughout the period. Of the score and more of nations that came into existence in what has been called the Age of Democratic Revolutions, the United States alone produced a stable constitutional government. Forming such a government was not a simple task. Yet the Constitution strengthened the national republic and Alexander Hamilton's realistic policies would promote that strength and enhance the national wealth. When the War of 1812 taught the Republican Party the value of Hamilton's policies, the nation's economic future was secure.

Hamilton wanted the United States to become a great nation, but believed that was impossible so long as Americans retained their local loyalties and their lack of ambition. Americans, he said, worked less than any other people on earth. Money, rather than land and family connections, should be the measure of the value of things. For money is the greatest of equalizers, being blind to class, religion, and inherited social position. If Americans became accustomed to measuring achievement in dollars and cents, the nation would suddenly bustle with energy, and the United States would be on its way to becoming the richest, freest, and most powerful nation in the history of the world. That was the Hamiltonian vision for America.

As the first Secretary of the Treasury, Hamilton proposed a series of measures that transformed the Revolutionary War debts from a crushing burden into a means of stimulating the entire economy. With Hamilton's urging Congress provided that the debt be "paid" in government bonds. These, amounting to perhaps a quarter as much as that of all the farm land in this nation of farmers, furnished most of the country's money supply, for they could pass from hand to hand like any other currency. The bonds were also used for financing a huge expansion of commercial, banking, and manufacturing activity.

But an older American republic of small farms and Southern slaveholders remained. Many Americans could fear the Hamiltonian program for reasons of self-interest. They could also cling on principle to that conservatism that had brought about the Revolution, the moral conviction that the slow and self-sufficient ways of farmers are preferable to the more energetic programs of ambitious governments. Jefferson was a conservative of this sort, however radical he was in his egalitarianism and in his faith in reason as an instrument of progress. Jefferson would later refer to his election and the triumph of his party as the Revolution of 1800, but in a sense it was more properly counterrevolutionary. The Republicans tried hard to do away with the system Hamilton and the Federalists had created. Republicans established policies that would ultimately pay off the federal debt, for it was the existence of the debt that had been Hamilton's justification for the government bonds with which he had stimulated the development of capitalism. The Republicans also abolished domestic taxes, reduced the army and navy to shadow forces, and cut back on the size and authority of the federal government the Hamiltonians had expanded. To do all that was to defy precedent. It went counter to the nature of government to pay its debts, restrict its power to coerce, reduce its authority.

The Republicans might have succeeded but for their unrealistic attitude toward the French Revolution. Following the course that violent revolutions almost invariably follow, it led to anarchy and bloodshed and ultimately to a military dictatorship and far more bloodshed. But the Jeffersonians could never bring themselves to favor the British.

How Much Democracy?

EUGENE D. GENOVESE

Hamiltonian Federalists had neither world enough nor time. Their grand scheme could not be consolidated without a long period in power, and their opponents increasingly had the votes. (It was not for nothing that Federalist conservatives had no use for democracy and swallowed it choking on every bit.) The election of 1800 was no revolution. But power did pass from one party to another without bloodshed, policies were overturned, and the people did firmly decide that American development was to follow a more rather than less democratic path. Those were not trivial matters.

Professor McDonald claims that Jeffersonians began as agrarians, as the particular defenders of agricultural work and life. He is wrong. In a nation almost entirely rural, it would have been even beyond the reach of political paranoia to argue for the rural life as though it were endangered. Jefferson does at one point in his *Notes on Virginia* describe city mobs as "sores" on the body politic, but his remark is not aimed against cities in themselves: the very same passage observes with pride that in American towns citizens have sufficient property to maintain their independence and virtue. What Jeffersonians did argue for was democracy—not absolute social or political equality but at least a widespread distribution of rights, privileges, and power. When Republicans lauded agrarian virtues and stood by the rights of the small farmer, they were merely standing by the common American citizen in his usual role, which was that of a farm worker. Professor McDonald is right in asserting that Jeffersonians were ready to buy into capitalism. But this meant no betrayal of agrarianism, a doctrine that they had never adhered to anyway. Business, industry, cities did not especially disturb them, and so neither did capitalism disturb them so long as capital acculumlation was not monopolistic and the result of special favors of the government. But that is the problem, and the Jeffersonians recognized it at the time. Money is not the equalizer that Professor McDonald claims it to be, as the merest glance at monied societies with their enormous spread of wealth and poverty will reveal. When the Jeffersonians first fought the Hamiltonian program, they did so recognizing that its implications were profoundly inegalitarian. When they came around to Hamiltonian measures, correctly perceiving that the country needed the more energetic economy that only the federal government could evoke, they were surrendering something of their democratic principles in the face of an immediate national need.

Professor McDonald correctly makes much of the lesson the Republicans learned from the War of 1812. The war proved "sorry enough" and "a disgrace" for the United States, which clearly got beaten. (And so the claim that the United States had never lost a war—fed to generations of Americans until the end of the war in Vietnam—has been not only a silly boast but untrue.) The nation's miserable performance in the War of 1812 demonstrated the need for a stronger government and more energetic policies than the Republicans had previously been willing to accept. But if the Jeffersonians had represented millions of farmers determined to have nothing to do with capitalist enterprise, not even to tolerate its existence, and wishing nothing more for their country than that the United States be a simple land of small farms and graceful plantations, it would have taken more than a blundering war to turn things around.

John Gast's rendition of **Manifest Destiny** shows Indians and wild animals skulking off before the advance of westward expansion embodied in Columbia's stringing telegraph wires across the continent. (*Courtesy, Library of Congress, ca. 1862*).

CHAPTER 8

Nationalism and Sectionalism 1816–1828

THE WESTWARD MOVEMENT

For almost 200 years American society had grown in the corridor between the Atlantic Ocean and the Appalachian Mountains. Mountain ranges, Indian tribes, and conflict among European powers had discouraged Americans from pushing into the West. Even those who crossed some of the eastern mountains found the inviting valleys angling south through Pennsylvania, Virginia, and the Carolinas far more tempting than scaling the next ridges toward an uncertain domicile in the western plains. Then, after about 1795, with the Revolution won, the Indian tribes dispersed, the European grasp on the West weakened, and the price of good eastern land mounting, a vast folk migration began. Only briefly interrupted by wars and depressions, it relentlessly populated the continent. The land seemed suddenly and permanently to have tilted, shaking its human burden westward in a long rough tumble toward the Pacific.

The return of peace on the frontier after the War of 1812 and rising prices worldwide for agricultural products sent the migration. The continent lay before Americans, wrote Henry Adams, "like an uncovered ore bed." In 1810 only one American in seven lived west of the Appalachians; in 1820 it was one in four. Before the land fever subsided, five new states had entered the Union—Indiana (1816), Mississippi (1817), Illinois (1818), Alabama (1819), Missouri (1821)—and they made the West a new force to be reckoned with in national affairs.

Settlers traveled by wagon, flatboat, horse, even on foot. The road west was often scarcely a road at all, but a slightly widened trail full of ruts and stumps so that for a passenger in the unsprung wagons "the pain of riding exceeded the fatigue of walking." Americans of the early nineteenth century were hungry for internal improvements, for turnpikes, canals, and finally railroads.

Often, in the stretches that were to be one day a land of motels, fast-food stands, and gas stations, the travelers saw all around them nothing but a forest of tall hardwood trees, dark, sinister, and gloomy. Settlers gloated over the mighty fires that followed a boisterous log-rolling, when perhaps hundreds of trees, felled after back-breaking labor, vanished into smoke, fire, and ash.

Yet the farmers preferred the forests to the prairies, endless meadows of tall grass sweeping across northern Indiana and Illinois. Americans, much as they might curse the trees they had to girdle, cut, and burn, hard as they might work to let in sunshine so that crops could grow, believed that hardwood forests indicated fertile soil. The prairies (actually richer soil where thick grass strangled most other vegetation) evoked, as one traveler noted, "a certain indescribable sensation of loneliness." Rich as prairie soil was, settlers discovered that to farm this land meant first to break the thick, heavy sod. In the early part of the century, when plows were still small and primitive, it was murderous labor.

In addition to doing back-breaking agricultural labor, a man with implements no more sophisticated than an axe and chisel would make "gates, carts, barrows, plow frames, ox yokes, wooden shovels, hay forks, troughs, benches, woodhorses, tool handles, stirring paddles, rakes, mortars, flails, cradles for mowing, swingling knives, flax brakes, and many other articles." More talented woodworkers frequently made their own wagons and furniture as well. And of course everyone, with neighbors helping to raise the logs, built his own house.

Women worked equally hard or harder, raising vegetables and herbs, making soap, butter, and other household articles, and carrying out every step of the manufacture of clothing, from spinning to sewing. This labor, combined with housekeeping and childbearing, tolled heavily. Many women appeared old at thirty, and men widowed two and three times were common.

Homes in the West were far from comfortable or healthy. Clouds of flies and mosquitoes, drafty cabins, primitive sanitation, and animal waste around most cabins were probably more hazardous to life than the better-known dangers of hostile Indians or prairie fires. New Englanders traveled west singing:

Come all ye Yankee farmers who wish to change your lot,
Who've spunk enough to travel beyond your native spot,
And leave behind the village where Ma and Pa do stay,
Come follow me and settle in Michigania.

But others who had been there chanted:

Don't go to Michigan, that land of ills;
The word means ague [usually malaria], fever, and chills.

The reward was worth the travail. At the end of the journey and the settlement lay independence and wealth as nineteenth-century Americans understood it: the ownership of productive agricultural land. The true pioneer stage passed rapidly; mills, towns, canals, newspapers, churches, cloth imported from the East, hardware, glass, even pianos eased and elevated the crude life of the frontier, and families rapidly moved from the backwoods to the front pews.

But for a moment, and only for a moment, the frontier was just what legend says it was. One observer caught the flavor of raw western politics:

I have just witnessed a strange thing—a Kentucky election—and am disposed to give you an account of it. An election in Kentucky lasts three days, and during that

Conestoga wagons brought many settlers from east to west. A journey of 600 miles took about ninety days. *(Courtesy, Scribner's Archives)*

period whisky and apple toddy flow through our cities and villages like the Euphrates through ancient Babylon. I must do Lexington the justice to say that matters were conducted here with tolerable propriety; but in Frankfort, a place which I had the curiosity to visit on the last day of the election, Jacksonism and drunkenness stalked triumphant—"an unclean pair of lubberly giants." A number of runners, each with a whisky bottle poking its long neck from his pocket, were busily employed bribing voters, and each party kept half a dozen bullies under pay, genuine specimens of Kentucky alligatorism, to flog every poor fellow who should attempt to vote illegally. A half a hundred of mortar would scarcely fill up the chinks of the skulls that were broken on that occasion. I barely escaped myself.

And a vivid frontier imagination spoke in words attributed to Davy Crockett of western Tennessee. "I'm fresh from the backwoods," he is said to have boasted, "half alligator, a little touched with the snapping turtle; can wade the Mississippi, leap the Ohio, ride upon a streak of lightning . . . hug a bear too close for comfort. . . ."

Postwar Nationalism

With the end of the War of 1812, Americans turned their attention not only westward but also to pressing national problems.

| **Era of Good Feelings** After many years of political bickering, an interlude of one-party politics followed the war. However divisive the War of 1812 had been, its ending brought a general sentiment of patriotism along with an awareness of weaknesses that had made the conduct of the war so difficult. A consensus grew in favor of some unified political solution to the nation's problems. For a time it was common for voters to call themselves Jeffersonian Republicans, and politics became no more than a contest of personalities within a politics of national harmony. To a people brought up with an eighteenth-century view of political parties as self-serving, divisive instruments, this actually seemed healthy. The "demon of party," a newspaper editor noted in 1817, had been exorcised for good.

To preside over this superficially placid era, voters in 1816 elected James Monroe as President. Like his Virginia predecessors, he had spent his life serving his country. At eighteen he had been wounded in the Revolutionary War. He later served as Minister to France, governor of Virginia, Minister to England, and secretary of state. (From 1813 to 1815 he frequently doubled as secretary of war.) Monroe was sixty years old when he became President. Dignified in appearance, cautious in manner, he provided a link with the heroic past. At a time when most men wore trousers, he still dressed in old-fashioned knee breeches and silk stockings. On ceremonial occasions he wore a faded Revolutionary uniform—a fitting costume for the last Revolutionary veteran in the White House.

| **President Monroe's Grand Tour** | As President, Monroe sought to create "a union of parties in support of our republican government." |

His choice of Cabinet members reflected this goal: he tried to pick Republicans from every section of the country. The secretary of state, John Quincy Adams, was a New Englander. Georgian William H. Crawford stayed on in the Treasury Department. Unable to find a westerner for Secretary of War, Monroe finally picked young John C. Calhoun of South Carolina. William Wirt, a Baltimore lawyer, became Attorney General. Restrained by their loyalty to the President, these political rivals served Monroe well. He also worked hard to gain the confidence of prominent Federalists. Harrison Gray Otis was deeply touched when the "Old Sachem" not only invited him to the White House for dinner, but "drank a glass of wine with me to make friends."

In pursuit of national unity, Monroe set out shortly after his election on a tour of the northern and eastern states. Paying his own travel costs, he followed the seaboard north to Portland, Maine, then headed westward, going as far as Detroit—a three-and-one-half month journey by carriage and steamboat. It was a triumphal procession. Everywhere crowds gathered to honor this "last of the Revolutionary farmers." The high point came at Boston, where over forty thousand turned out to welcome the President. At a public dinner, local Federalists and Republicans sat down together for the first time in years.

James Monroe, elected in 1816, sought to unify the states and parties, and established an "Era of Good Feelings." *(Portrait by Gilbert Stuart, Courtesy, The Metropolitan Museum of Art, Bequest of Seth Low, 1929)*

Monroe's visit, a staunch Federalist editor reported, had established an "Era of Good Feelings." Newspapers throughout the country soon picked up the phrase. For a time, despite bickering on the state and local levels, it seemed appropriate. Overall during this period, before economic crisis in 1819, the country was peaceful and prosperous. In 1820 Monroe was reelected without opposition; only one negative vote in the electoral college prevented his election from being, like Washington's, unanimous. An Ohio newspaper observed that "In most of the States the elections occur with great quietness, too great, perhaps, for the general safety of the Republic."

Government and the Economy

Monroe's presidency expressed the nationalism of sentiment that followed the end of the War of 1812. It was also a time of economic nationalism. Instructed perhaps by the War of 1812 that the country could not get by with the strictly limited central government that the Republicans had once favored, President Madison in 1815 had recommended an energetic governmental program for the nurturing of the economy. At the very time the Federalist Party was withering, the Republicans were adopting the policy the Federalists had once championed. Congress responded by rechartering a national bank, voting funds for internal improvements, and enacting a protective tariff. "Our two great parties," said the retired President John Adams, "have crossed over the valley and taken possession of each other's mountain."

| **Transportation —"Let us conquer space"** | During the War of 1812, the nation's transportation network had proved no more adequate to wartime demands than its banking |

system. With coastal shipping choked off by the British blockade and canals still in their infancy, the burden fell almost entirely on the roads. In a few places in the East turnpikes had been built, but they deteriorated quickly under heavy use. Most roads were hardly more than broad country paths through the forest, filled with ruts and stumps, impassable in wet weather. In one instance, it took a wagon drawn by four horses seventy-five days to travel from Massachusetts to South Carolina. Such delays produced serious food shortages in some cities.

Poor roads had severely hampered the American military effort. General William Henry Harrison reported in 1812 that his advance on Detroit could not begin "until the frost shall become so severe as to enable us to use the rivers and the margins of . . . Lake [Erie] for the transportation of the baggage and artillery upon the ice. To get them forward through a swampy wilderness of near two hundred miles in wagons or on pack horses . . . is absolutely impossible." Harrison estimated that overland hauls required "two wagons with forage [for the horses] for each one that it loaded with provisions and other articles."

Recognition that the country needed a better transportation system was one element in the governmental and economic nationalism to which President Madison turned from his

After Samuel Slater began the use of power-driven spinning machines around 1790, spinning and weaving mills rapidly spread in New England and the Carolinas.

earlier philosophy of limited government. He called for a system of roads and canals "executed under national authority." He recommended a constitutional amendment that would eliminate continuing doubts over the federal government's authority to finance such projects. Representative John C. Calhoun of South Carolina, then a vigorous young nationalist, brushed aside constitutional objections. Sheer size and poor communication, he warned the House—in words that would later haunt him—exposed the country to that "greatest of all calamities," disunion. "Let us, then, bind the Republic together with a perfect system of roads and canals. Let us conquer space." Calhoun proposed setting aside, as a fund for internal improvements, the government's share of the profits from the new Bank of the United States. In 1817 Congress narrowly approved Calhoun's plan, only to have Madison veto it on constitutional grounds. The states and private enterprise would have to finance most internal improvements.

Manufactures American manufacturers found their most severe trial not during wartime but with the return of peace. Before 1807 Americans had imported most manufactured goods from Europe, but Jefferson's embargo and the war had stimulated the growth of domestic industries. In New England and the Carolinas, mills were spinning and weaving cotton; a new iron industry flourished at Pittsburgh; Kentuckians began making local hemp into bagging. British manufacturers moved quickly in 1816 to crush these new rivals. They dumped vast quantities of goods on the American market at cut-rate prices, in order, a spokesman explained, "to stifle in the cradle those rising manufacturers in the United States, which war had forced into existence, contrary to the natural course of things." To protect these "infant" industries, President Madison proposed increased tariff duties on competing imports, which would push up their price. Congress was receptive, since nearly every section of the country had an interest to be protected. Southerners, who had the least to gain, supported higher duties on political and patriotic grounds. Within a few years, a series of threatening events would cause many southerners to reexamine their jubilant support of economic nationalism.

The Bank of the United States When the charter of the first Bank of the United States expired in 1811, the state banks had gone wild. The number increased from eighty-eight to over two hundred. In making loans and paying debts, they issued huge quantities of bank notes, which thereupon circulated as regular currency. A bank note was, in effect, a piece of paper carrying a bank's promise that upon request the bank would give to the bearer of the note an amount of money in specie (gold or silver) equal in value to the sum printed on the note. A holder of a bank note for, say, $1.00 could believe that while the note was not itself a real dollar, it was virtually an equivalent since it could be exchanged for a specie dollar: and so storekeepers and other merchants were willing to accept bank notes from customers.

As long as there was plenty of reliable specie in the banks—enough to cover a comfortable portion if not all of the bank notes in circulation in case many holders of notes got hungry for metallic money—the notes were a useful currency. A bank's ability to issue them allowed it to make more loans, pay more debts, and in general nourish more business than it could do if its activities were restricted to what its holdings in specie alone could accomplish. But if the bank notes got far out of proportion to the specie on which they were supposed to be based, the public would cease to trust them as currency, they would depreciate in value, and business would suffer from the uncertainty. And that is what happened as the state banks multiplied and carried out their transactions with no national bank to steady them, pouring out paper notes in pursuit of quick gain. The mass of confusing, depreciated paper money worried businessmen and pleased counterfeiters. The lack of a national currency such as a Bank of the United States could have issued made it difficult to carry on business among different parts of the country.

Then wartime borrowing overwhelmed this shaky system. By the summer of 1814 every bank outside of New England had suspended the practice of paying specie to holders of notes who demanded it. The country's credit practically vanished. And after the war the federal government, to accommodate settlers in the West, offered for sale vast tracts of public land. The government's terms were generous: the minimum purchase was 160 acres, and the purchaser had four years to complete payment. Much of the land was purchased with credit supplied by state banks. Land sales, then, were inviting more bad currency into circulation.

In response to the crisis in banking, Congress in 1816 chartered a second Bank of the United States, with headquarters at Philadelphia. It was capitalized at $35 million, of which the government put up $5 million. The President was to appoint five "government directors," and the domestic stockholders were to elect the other members of the

twenty-five member board: foreign stockholders were not allowed to vote. The Bank was to serve as a repository of government funds and could establish branches as the directors saw fit. It could issue its own bank notes and thereby provide a more stable currency than the state banks were issuing. And it had the informal power to regulate the activities of state banks. A decision to be cautious in lending to them, or to refuse weak notes in payment of debts owed to the national bank, could force the state banks to act more cautiously themselves.

Judicial Nationalism: The Marshall Court

During the years 1819-24, the Supreme Court, in a series of important cases decided under Chief Justice John Marshall, aided in strengthening the constitutional authority of

As Chief Justice of the United States, Marshall wrote decisions that helped strengthen the federal government. *(Portrait by J. W. Jarvis, Courtesy, Richard Coke Marshall Collection, Frick Art Reference Library)*

the federal government, which had already been strengthening its political presence through its postwar economic policies. The Court also shrank the power of the states over corporations, institutions that, along with the federal government, would assume a larger and larger role in the development of the American economy.

Leading Constitutional Decisions   In *Dartmouth College v. Woodward* (1819) the Court ruled that Article I, Section 10, of the Constitution—"no state shall pass any law impairing the obligation of contracts"—protected charters of incorporation from legislative interference. Dartmouth College had been granted a charter in 1769 by King George III. In 1816 the New Hampshire legislature, in an effort to make the college more democratic, tried to replace the self-governing trustees with a board appointed by the state governor. The campus was in an uproar. One student wrote:

> Such a state of [affairs] necessarily discomposes the mind, and unfits it for steady and quiet reflection. . . . You may easily suppose that it is impossible to sit down cooly & composedly [to] books, when you are alarmed every minute by a report, that the library is in danger or that a mob is about collecting or that we are all about to [be] fined & imprisoned.

The trustees retained Daniel Webster, a Dartmouth alumnus and eloquent orator, to fight their case. Webster's theatrics ("It is . . .

a small school," he plaintively told the Justices, "and yet there are those who love it.") and his arguments proved effective. Dartmouth's charter, wrote Marshall, was a contractual relationship between the Crown and the College. The state of New Hampshire was a continuation of the Crown; the obligations of contract remained unchanged. So long as the trustees did not abuse their powers, the state could not interfere without violating the contract clause. Coming at a time when private corporations were rapidly gaining favor in transportation, finance, and manufacturing, this defense of contracts made it more difficult for the states to control corporate activity.

In *McCulloch v. Maryland* (1819) the Court confirmed the broad construction of the Constitution that Alexander Hamilton had defended thirty years before during arguments over the first Bank of the United States. This case dealt with assaults on the second Bank, which through careless management and its favoritism to big business had aroused bitter opposition. Several states, Maryland among them, had placed high taxes on the Bank's branches within their borders. The cashier of the Baltimore branch, James McCulloch, refused to pay the tax and Maryland brought suit. In his opinion, Marshall upheld the constitutionality of the Bank. The creation of such an institution, he admitted, was not among the powers listed in the Constitution. But Congress also possessed "incidental or implied powers." "Let the end be legitimate," wrote Marshall, "let it be within the scope of the Constitution, and all means which are appropriate, which are plainly adapted to that end, which are not prohibited, but consistent with the letter and spirit of the Constitution, are constitutional." He found that the financial powers of the national legislature gave it the implied power to charter a national bank that would aid Congress in exercising its authority over finance. Maryland's tax, which attempted to destroy a lawful agency of the federal government, was therefore unconstitutional: "the power to tax . . . is the power to destroy." Champions of states' rights angrily denounced this opinion, which would stretch the Constitution beyond its literal statements and have it implicitly grant large powers to the federal government.

Marshall's opinion two years later in *Co-hens v. Virginia* further distressed states' rights advocates. At issue here was the right of a state to limit appeals to the United States Supreme Court from its own courts. The Cohens had been convicted of selling lottery tickets under a Virginia law that prohibited appeals from such a conviction. Asserting that the case involved a "federal question," they turned to the Supreme Court for relief. Counsel for Virginia denied the Court's right of judicial review, claiming that the state's legitimate authority was under attack. The Chief Justice disagreed. He maintained that Virginia had surrendered some of her powers when she joined the Union. The right of the Supreme Court to review cases involving "federal questions" was absolutely essential if the operation of the Constitution was to be uniform throughout the country. Otherwise, the federal government would be prostrate "at the feet of every state in the Union." With this opinion Marshall solidly fixed the Supreme Court as the final arbiter of all constitutional questions.

Gibbons v. Ogden (1824), Marshall's last great decision, gave force to the clauses of the Constitution that had empowered Congress "to regulate commerce with foreign nations, and among the several states." Early in the nineteenth century a number of states had begun awarding monopolies to the operators of the new steamboats. In 1808 New York gave Robert Fulton and Robert Livingston an exclusive right to operate steamboats on the state's waters. It also awarded Aaron Ogden an exclusive franchise to run steamboats on the Hudson River between New York and New Jersey. When Thomas Gibbons began a rival service on this route (the captain of his boat was a young man named Cornelius Vanderbilt), Ogden brought suit to restrain his competitor. When the New York courts upheld the monopoly, Gibbons appealed to the Supreme Court. Once again Marshall championed federal supremacy. A narrow construction of the Constitution, he declared at the outset, "would cripple the government, and render it unequal to the objects for which it is declared to be instituted, and to which the powers given, as fairly understood, render it competent." New York's law was unconstitutional because it conflicted with a 1793 act of Congress regulating the coastwise trade. Congress's power to regulate commerce, "like all others vested in

Congress, is complete in itself, may be exercised to its utmost extent, and acknowledges no limitations, other than those prescribed in the Constitution."

For once the public sided with Marshall. New Yorkers, who detested the steamboat monopolies, hailed the Chief Justice's decision. "Yesterday," a newspaper reported, "the steamboat *United States*, Capt. Bunker, from New Haven, entered New York in triumph, with streamers flying, and a large company of passengers exulting in the decision . . . against the New York monopoly. She fired a salute which was loudly returned by huzzas from the wharves." In a few years

steamboat navigation spread to lakes and rivers throughout the country.

A few years later Marshall could not prevent the removal of the Cherokee Indians from Georgia. He also ducked a case involving the rights of free blacks. Yet his nationalism ultimately helped to free the slaves. For over thirty years Marshall had argued that the United States was a consolidated nation rather than merely a compact of sovereign states. In 1861, when Abraham Lincoln called for troops, thousands of young men took up arms to defend the national Union Marshall's decisions had done so much to define.

Mississippi River Plantation Scene. The opening of the fertile Black Belt in Alabama and Mississippi after the War of 1812 increased both cotton production and the need for slaves. *(Courtesy, Minnesota Historical Society)*

The Panic of 1819

By 1820 the good feelings of the postwar years had begun to wear thin. As the memory of war faded and the Republican Party, lacking the discipline of electoral competition, declined as a national organization, the various sections of the country began looking to their own interests. Among the reasons for the end of the harmony of the postwar years were a resurgence of jealousies among the sections and a revival of slavery that would put slave owners to quarreling with opponents of the institution and its expansion into the western territories. An early agent in disrupting the smooth politics of the time was the Panic of 1819, a financial collapse of the greatest magnitude the nation had yet known. The panic was the result of a buoyant but unhealthy expansion of the American economy during the years immediately after the wars, an expansion that economic dislocations in Europe had encouraged.

In 1816 and 1817 Europe had suffered widespread crop failures. These created a large and high-priced market for American rice, corn, wheat, and meat. British cotton textile manufacturers, moreover, having done without American cotton for three years, had accumulated a great backlog of demand for it. The price of cotton, which had fluctuated around fifteen cents a pound before the war, now rose to twenty-five and thirty cents.

Americans responded to this boom in typical American fashion. On the one hand, they grossly overexpanded production, especially of cotton: in the years 1816-1819 annual production of cotton more than doubled over that of 1814. The production of other American staples likewise increased rapidly, though not so spectacularly as that of cotton. On the other hand, Americans by the thousand succumbed in these prosperous times to what had been, since colonial days, practically a national disease: speculation in land.

| **Speculation and Collapse** Instead of paying attention first to farming and profiting from the inflation while they could, vast numbers of people put every spare cent into land. To accommodate demand, the federal government after the war threw vast tracts of public land on the market. Auctions at the district land offices attracted eager crowds, including squatters hoping to buy the lots they had already occupied and speculators seeking choice tracts for resale at inflated prices. In spite of efforts by speculators to stifle competitive bidding, prices at the sales frequently soared well above the minimum $2 an acre (reduced to $1.25 in 1820). Fertile bottom land near Huntsville, Alabama, brought $70 to $78 an acre in the spring of 1818. Total annual sales of public land rose from less than $3 million in 1815 to over $13 million in 1818. Much of this land was purchased with credit supplied by the steadily increasing numbers of state banks, of which Hezekiah Niles wrote in 1816, "Wherever there is a church, a blacksmith's shop and a tavern seems a proper site for one of them." A Scotsman travelling in the Ohio Valley described the scene:

> The recent history of banking in these western States, is probably unrivalled. Such a system of knavery could only be developed in a country where avarice and credulity are prominent features of character. About four years ago, the passion for acquiring unearned gains rose to a great height; banking institutions were created in abundance. The designing amongst lawyers, doctors, tavern-keepers, farmers, grocers, shoemakers, tailors, &c. entered into the project, and subscribed for stock. . . . To deposit much capital was out of their power; nor was it any part of their plan. Their main object was to extract it from the community. A common provision in charters, stipulated, that the property of each partner was not liable, in security, to a greater amount than the sum he had subscribed. This exempted the banks from the natural inconveniences that might be occasioned by the insolvencies and elopements of members. When it was found, that a few of them could not redeem their bills, the faith of the people was shaken. A run on the paper shops commenced. . . .

The new Bank of the United States not only made little effort at first to check this speculation, but itself proved a major source of credit expansion. For a while it exchanged Bank stock for IOUs instead of specie. Supervision over Bank branches was notoriously lax. Those in the South and West greatly overexpanded their loans and their issues of bank notes. The officers of the Baltimore branch engaged in embezzlement. By 1818 the Bank had loaned out over $41 million. Some of it was invested in canals, turnpikes, and farm improvements; much more, however, went for speculative ventures in urban real estate, cotton futures, and western land. Indebtedness mounted, but as long as prices and rents increased, farmers and speculators would hope to meet their obligations.

Suddenly the economy collapsed. With the return of good harvests abroad in the fall of 1818, demand for American grain fell sharply. At the same time, British manufacturers finally reduced their imports of American cotton: prices for the South's great staple dropped by over one half in 1819. Planters and farmers who had borrowed heavily to expand production could not repay their loans.

This reversal left the Bank of the United States in desperate straits. Its liabilities exceeded its specie reserves by a ratio of ten to one, double the limit allowed by law. The Bank then called in the loans of state banks, which forced them in turn to call in their loans. A wave of bank failures followed, most of them in the South and West; money disappeared and credit dried up, spreading economic distress throughout the country. Speculators who had purchased public land were stuck with it. Agricultural prices sank so low that many farmers resorted to barter. Merchants sold their stock at high losses or declared bankruptcy. In Philadelphia County alone, over 1,800 people went to prison for debt during 1819. Thousands were thrown out of work: in Pittsburgh, thirty percent of the population went back to the country. A traveler remarked on "great numbers of strangers lately camped in the open field near Baltimore, depending on the contributions of the charitable for subsistence." Americans for the first time confronted a nationwide depression—the "Panic of 1819."

| **The Bank of the United States** | The economic crisis provoked a heated debate over both the causes of the depression and appropriate measures of relief. |

Stephen Girard, a Philadelphia financier, blamed the state banks, which "with their fictitious capital have acted imprudently." The state banks, anxious to conceal their own shortcomings, criticized the national Bank. Many, including President James Monroe, lamented the postwar spirit of extravagance and speculation, and called for a return to republican ways. Advocates of a protective tariff pointed to the nation's dependence on European trade, and urged Americans to produce more of the manufactured goods they consumed. Congress rejected a higher tariff and a bill to abolish federal imprisonment for debt, but did agree in 1821 to allow people who had purchased public lands on credit ad-

ditional time to pay. Real debtor relief came mainly from the states. Several passed "stay" laws delaying foreclosure for debt. Cities set up soup kitchens, and churches collected funds for the relief of paupers.

Out of the confused debate on the depression, the Bank of the United States emerged as the chief scapegoat. Charges of fraud and mismanagement filled the air. The old Southern agrarians, Thomas Jefferson among them, condemned the Bank and the federal government for creating a "paper bubble" and hoped the shock of depression would restore the country to its sound, paper-free past. These critics likened the Bank to a monster, foreclosing everything in its path. "I know towns, yea cities," charged one westerner:

> where this bank already appears as an engrossing proprietor. All the flourishing cities of the West are mortgaged to this money power. . . . they are in the jaws of a monster! A lump of butter in the mouth of a dog! One gulp, one swallow, and all is gone!

Many of these accusations were unfair. Fraud and mismanagement there had been, but the Bank was not responsible for fluctuations in the world market or for the public's compulsion for speculation. If the Bank had been inconsistent in dealing with the state banks, so had politicians and the public. But these considerations made little impression on a people mired in debt and depression. The economy recovered in the early 1820s, but by this time the reputation of the Bank among certain constituencies had deteriorated beyond repair. It is ironic that the recovery would owe much to the Bank and its new president, Nicholas Biddle.

Biddle, a wealthy Philadelphian, took over the Bank in 1823 and immediately set about putting its affairs in order. One reform was to increase the BUS's specie reserve, the amount of hard currency it kept on hand. Since all of the holders of the Bank's notes could not have shown up to demand redemption in specie at the same time, even in the case of another panic, this policy effectively meant that the paper money issued by the Bank was "as good as gold." Biddle also reformed the BUS's policies with respect to the notes issued by other banks. Most state-chartered banks had little specie reserve for their notes. When those notes were presented to the BUS for redemption, as they routinely were, Biddle could either demand payment in specie from the bank of issue or refrain from doing so. This was an enormously important power because it enabled Biddle and the other BUS directors to control how much currency was in circulation. That was critical for the simple reason that there was far too little gold and silver available to support a growing economy. The nation's gross national product, the total amount of goods and services produced, was perhaps fifty times greater than the amount of gold and silver. Without paper money the economy would have come to a halt. And it was Biddle and the BUS which largely determined how much money would circulate.

For the most part, historians agree, Biddle exercised these enormous powers wisely. He restrained the worst excesses of local banks that otherwise would have flooded the nation with virtually worthless paper. Biddle also made money for the BUS's stockholders, but many of them, dissatisfied with dividends that averaged about 7% per year during the 1820s, protested that he paid too much attention to the national interest and not enough to theirs. On the other hand, the Bank's private ownership was a source of suspicion because it meant that state-chartered banks had to submit to the regulations of a competitor. Many of these private owners, moreover, were foreigners. Another potential problem was Biddle's practice of making loans on especially favorable terms to important politicians and newspaper editors. The Bank had many enemies, and charges of corruption would dog its career throughout Biddle's tenure in office.

A Resurgent Sectionalism

The changing interests of different parts of the nation soon expressed themselves in disputes over the tariff, internal improvements, and land policy. The South produced cotton for export, obtaining manufactured goods from the North and West as well as from Europe. The tariff pushed up the retail price of European products in this country and thereby allowed northern manufacturers to raise their prices, too, or forced foreign products out of the American market. Compelled to purchase at higher prices, southern planters feared also that Europe would retaliate against U.S. tariffs by putting high duties on southern agricultural goods. Southerners quickly regretted their support for the Tariff of 1816. The disastrous decline in cotton prices after 1819, which cut the planters' purchasing power, made the tariff still more burdensome. In 1820 southerners in Congress barely defeated a bid to raise import duties again.

Internal Improvements Sectional jealousies thwarted plans for a national system of internal improvements. New England, for example, did not favor building roads that, by connecting rival ports with the West, would injure Boston. New York and Pennsylvania longed for the national government to construct such routes; but finally, having put extravagant sums into their own roads and canals, they lost their enthusiasm for federal projects. Southern support for federal improvements faded rapidly. Such expenditures, increasing the need for revenue, would justify the hated tariff, and federal internal improvements implied a broad construction of the Constitution which could as easily allow the federal government to interfere with slavery.

Only the West consistently demanded a federal system of internal improvements. A shortage of capital and a vast expanse of territory made that section perpetually hungry for government assistance. Several times Congress responded by appropriating funds for western roads, but a series of presidential vetoes blocked these expenditures, and this forced state governments and private corporations in the Northwest to join in financing an extensive network of turnpikes and canals.

Public Land Policy The older sections also differed from the West on public land policy. But land sales were a major source of federal revenues and the seaboard states favored high prices. Northern manufacturers also hoped that such prices would discourage their workingmen from going west. Carolina planters feared that their worn-out cotton lands could not compete with the virgin soil of the Southwest. The West craved cheap land.

Spokesmen like Thomas Hart Benton believed that keeping prices low would encourage "a race of virtuous and independent farmers, the true supporters of their country." These noble freeholders would carry America and its democracy across the continent.

On this issue, sectional rivalries worked in the West's favor: the South usually voted for cheap land to gain western support for its own special interests. In 1820 Congress reduced the minimum purchasable tract from 160 to 80 acres and the minimum price from $2 to $1.25 an acre. An act of 1830 gave special rights to the "squatter" who occupied public land he did not own; he could now purchase his tract prior to public sale at the minimum price, regardless of its market value.

The Revival of Slavery

In the North the libertarian ideology of the American Revolution, along with the larger drift of the eighteenth century toward rationalism and humanitarianism, had led numbers of Americans to believe slavery was in decline. Beginning with Pennsylvania in 1780, the northern states had provided for the abolition of slavery; Massachusetts abruptly outlawed the practice in 1783. In 1787 Congress had prohibited slavery in the Northwest Territory. Even in the South, humanitarian sentiments weakened the institution. Virginia and North Carolina passed laws easing the way for slaveholders to free their human property. A southern President, Thomas Jefferson, urged Congress in 1806 to withdraw American citizens "from all further participation in those violations of human rights which have been so long continued upon the unoffending inhabitants of Africa."

The South's depressed economy in the years after the American Revolution reinforced the ideological objections to slavery. Soil exhaustion and a glutted world market injured Virginia's and Maryland's tobacco economy. Many planters switched to wheat, a crop that required fewer slaves to cultivate. Indigo, an important slave-grown crop in upland South Carolina and Georgia, ceased to be profitable when Britain withdrew her bounty to producers during the Revolution. Prices for slaves generally declined, and the wartime ban on slave imports continued in most states.

Cotton Gins Planters anxiously experimented with new crops, especially cotton. Samuel Crompton's spinning-mule, James Hargreave's spinning-jenny, and Richard Arkwright's spinning-frame and water-frame, as well as other innovations in manufacturing, had dramatically lowered the cost of spinning and weaving cotton fiber into cloth, stimulating a worldwide demand for cotton goods. The appetites of English manufacturers for raw cotton became insatiable. As early as 1786 planters in lowland South Carolina and Georgia began to experiment with growing the silky, long-fibered sea-island cotton. It proved much superior to the short-staple upland variety that had been produced in small quantities for many years. When the cotton bolls were passed between two close-set rollers, the smooth black seeds of the sea-island variety popped right out; the same roller gin crushed the sticky green seeds of the upland variety, making it unmarketable. But sea-island cotton would grow only in the warm, humid lowlands of the coast. Large-scale cotton cultivation awaited a successful process to remove the seeds from short-staple cotton.

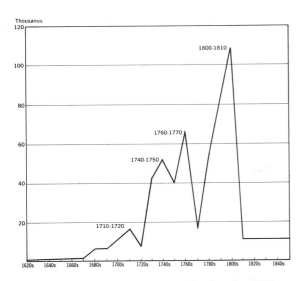

Importation of slaves into America by decade, 1620s–1840s. SOURCE: *Adapted from Robert Fogel and Stanley Engerman, Time on the Cross (1974).*

Eli Whitney's cotton gin created a cotton boom in the South—and a doubling of the number of slaves by 1820. *(Courtesy, The Smithsonian Institution)*

| **Eli Whitney**   A Connecticut Yankee came to the South's rescue. In 1793 young Eli Whitney, fresh out of Yale and unemployed, came South to work as a tutor. On the way this nimble son of a three-hundred-pound Scots peddler stopped to see his friend Phineas Miller, the overseer at "Mulberry Grove" near Savannah, the plantation of Catherine Greene, widow of General Nathanael Greene. There he turned to inventing a machine to clean the cotton of its seed. In just six months he had perfected his "absurdly simple contrivance." The cotton was fed into a hopper. A toothed roller caught the fibers of the cotton boll and pulled them through a slotted iron guard, its slits wide enough to admit the teeth and the cotton fibers caught on them, but too narrow to let the seeds through. A revolving brush then swept the cotton from the roller's teeth. One man could operate a small gin; larger ones could operate by horse or water power. Whitney and his friend quickly formed a partnership to manufacture their gins. "It makes the labor fifty times less," the inventor observed proudly, "without throwing any class of people out of business."

Whitney's statement hid a cruel irony. The agricultural depression, by throwing slaves out of work, might ultimately have ended slavery. The cotton gin fastened slavery on the South. Rival manufacturers and local artisans quickly copied Whitney's design. Cotton cultivation spread rapidly through upland South Carolina and Georgia. By 1820 the United States was producing 335,000 bales of cotton (a bale weighed about 500 pounds), as opposed to 10,000 bales in 1793. The opening of the rich Black Belt of Alabama and Mississippi after the War of 1812 pushed the crop above one million bales by 1835. The cotton boom created an unprecedented demand for slaves. In 1803 South Carolina reopened its foreign slave trade. Before the federal ban went into effect in 1808, nearly 40,000 Africans had entered Charleston. Between 1790 and 1820 the slave population of the South more than doubled, from 657,000 to more than 1,509,000. Such a massive growth would have political repercussions.

The career of Eli Whitney held another irony for the South. This imaginative inventor went from the cotton gin to the manufacture of arms, and in that line he was instrumental in developing the principle of interchangeable parts. The principle was a major contribution to the Industrial Revolution. And industrialism, so it can be argued, met the South on the battlefields of the Civil War and defeated the slave system the cotton gin had revived.

The Missouri Controversy

| **The Tallmadge Amendment (1819)**   Saturday, February 13, 1819, was a dull day in Washington. The Senate was not meeting and the House was occupied with a proposal to reduce the number of officers in the army. Late in the day the Representatives took up a routine bill for Missouri statehood. Without warning, James Tallmadge, Jr., of New York, offered an amendment to prohibit the further introduction of slavery into Missouri and gradually to emancipate slave children born there. An "interesting and pretty wide debate" on Tallmadge's amendment began at

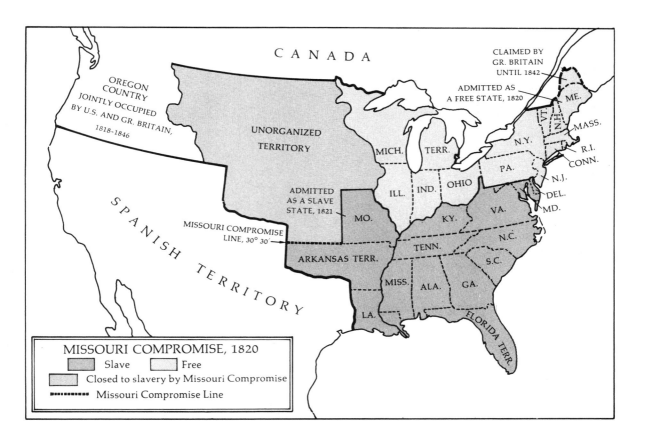

MISSOURI COMPROMISE, 1820
- Slave
- Free
- Closed to slavery by Missouri Compromise
- Missouri Compromise Line

once. For the next two and a half years the question of slavery in Missouri—which Thomas Jefferson likened to "a fire bell in the night"—paralyzed Congress. "This momentous question, . . ." the seventy-six-year-old ex-President wrote, "awakened and filled me with terror. I considered it at once as the knell of the Union."

Prior to 1819 new states had entered the Union without much controversy over slavery. The Northwest Ordinance had prohibited slavery in the territory north of the Ohio River. North Carolina and Georgia ceded to the federal government most of the area south of the Ohio, with the stipulation that slavery should be permitted. Before 1820 new slave and free states entered in equal numbers: Louisiana, Mississippi, and Alabama balanced Ohio, Indiana, and Illinois. In 1819 there were eleven slave and eleven free states. The admission of Missouri threatened to upset this delicate balance.

New Englanders had watched with dismay the march of settlement westward; some hoped to preserve their section's influence by checking the expansion of slavery into new territory, and thereby making it their economic and political ally. Federalists had long attributed the triumph of the Republican Party to "slave representation," charging that the Constitution's "three-fifths" clause gave the slave states a disproportionate influence in national politics. Advocates of the tariff and internal improvements looked increasingly on slaveholders as the opponents of their special interests. But at bottom the opposition of slavery compounded two quite differing ideas: the conviction that human bondage violated the ethos of the Revolution and the republic; and, especially as time passed, the nineteenth-century humanitarian impulse to abolish or mitigate suffering by means of social reform. If the growth of slavery were to be halted, said a New Hampshire Congressman, it would be necessary "to fight the first battle at the water's edge."

Federalist leaders such as Senator Rufus King of New York aimed at reinvigorating their party with an appeal against slavery's expansion. They allied with a faction of Northern Republicans under Governor De Witt Clinton of New York, who resented the southern leadership of the party. Antislavery activists like former Chief Justice John Jay added their support. For a time congressional politics took on a distinct sectional alignment, pitting North against South as morality, politics, and self-interest intersected after Tallmadge introduced his amendment.

The House passed Tallmadge's amendment during 1819, but the Senate rejected it. Congress adjourned without reaching an agreement, and Missouri remained a territory. A year later, when a bill for Missouri statehood was again introduced in the House, Congressman John W. Taylor of New York offered an amendment excluding slavery from the new state. The bill, with Taylor's amendment, easily passed the House, where the North had a sizable majority. But once again the Senate said no. Antislavery forces branded slavery a "monstrous institution" and accused slaveholders of seeking to turn the country west of the Mississippi into a market for human flesh. Southerners talked openly of disunion if the amendment should pass. Said a senator from Georgia, "You are kindling a fire which all the waters of the ocean cannot extinguish; it can be extinguished only in blood!" Missourians threatened to organize a state government without congressional approval.

The Missouri Compromise At this point a compromise emerged. Massachusetts had agreed to the creation of a new state, Maine, out of her northern counties, provided Congress acted by March 4, 1820. The free states hoped to admit Maine before the deadline. The Senate decided to tie Maine to Missouri. It added to the Maine statehood bill then before Congress a section admitting Missouri without restrictions on slavery. In order to make this bill more acceptable to the northern-dominated House, Senator Jesse B. Thomas of Illinois offered his famous amendment prohibiting slavery "forever" in the rest of the Louisiana Purchase territory north of latitude 36° 30' (the southern boundary of Missouri). In this form the Maine-Missouri bill went to the House, where, after much wrangling, Speaker Henry Clay secured its passage on March 2. On the key question of excluding slavery in Missouri the vote was extremely close—the motion lost by 90 to 87, with four northern Congressmen absent. The vote was traumatic for southerners, who increasingly drew into

themselves and lived in a closed society. One northerner observed:

> I believe some years ago there was an openness in the minds of the people, in which they saw the iniquity of slavery, but I believe since the discussion of the Missouri question in Congress, the prejudices of slaveholders have increased against the advocates of liberty. . . .

In the summer of 1820 a convention met at St. Louis and drew up a constitution for Missouri. As expected, this document sanctioned slavery. It also required the legislature to pass laws "to prevent free Negroes and mulattoes from coming to, and settling in, this state." In November 1820, when the Missouri constitution went before Congress for approval, northerners objected to this clause. They pointed out that the United States Constitution provided that "the Citizens of each State shall be entitled to all Privileges and Immunities of Citizens in the several States." A number of northern states recognized Negroes as citizens. This clause would prevent them from settling or even traveling in Missouri. This complicated issue of black citizenship precipitated another lengthy debate over Missouri's admission to the Union.

Missourians were upset over this latest setback. Whatever the constitutionality of the exclusion clause, they pointed out, several states—North and South—had similar laws. Once again Henry Clay arranged a compromise. He proposed a resolution admitting Missouri on an equal footing with the original states, upon the "fundamental condition" that the objectionable clause should never be construed to authorize the passage of any law denying to the citizens of any state the privileges and immunities to which they were entitled under the Constitution. In 1821 Congress agreed to this empty resolution. Missouri made the meaningless promise and officially entered the Union. The state legislature in 1825 and in 1847 violated the agreement by enacting laws that barred free blacks from entering the state.

Denmark Vesey In the summer of 1822 the white South was shaken by the discovery of an alleged conspiracy led by Denmark Vesey, a free black carpenter who had closely followed the Missouri debates. It was said that he had recruited hundreds of slaves in Charleston, South Carolina, to rise up at midnight, kill the whites, and fire the city. A slave revealed the plot to authorities only a few days before the apparent time of the uprising, and a special court sentenced thirty-five blacks to death. The executions were a public spectacle: at a mass hanging on July 26 several of the condemned twisted in an "agony of strangulation," because of "some bad arrangement in preparing the ropes—some of which were too long, others not properly adjusted so as to choke effectually the sufferers to death, but so as to give them the power of utterance, whilst their feet could touch the ground. . . ." Afterward, the authorities left the bodies dangling for hours as an example to other blacks.

Slaves and slaveholders everywhere trembled. The court report noted Vesey's careful reading of the Missouri debates. The involvement of so many trusted family servants was especially disturbing to whites. South Carolina Governor Thomas Bennett had often left his family in the care of Rolla, his beloved personal slave. Yet Rolla was listed among the archconspirators.

Southern lawmakers moved at once to prevent a repetition of the Vesey Conspiracy. They tightened their slave codes and outlawed the distribution of antislavery propaganda. Southerners resisted all further discussion of slavery in the United States Congress. The South Carolina legislature forbade the entry of free blacks into the state. Free black seamen who violated the law were jailed until their ships left port. When the British government protested these detentions and a federal judge ruled the law unconstitutional, the South Carolina Senate defiantly replied that "the duty of the state to guard against insubordination or insurrection" was "paramount to all *laws*, all *treaties*, all *constitutions*. It arises from the supreme and permanent law of nature, the law of self-preservation; and will never by this state be renounced, compromised, controlled or participated with any power whatever." Neighboring states quickly passed similar statutes. Henceforth, the South bristled at every criticism of what came to be called its "peculiar institution."

The *Charleston Times* called blacks "the anarchists and the domestic enemy; the common enemy of civilized society, and the barbarians who would, if they could, become the destroyers of our race."

A "gentleman" of Mobile, Alabama, worried about a rising black population in urban areas, declared: "The cities is no place for the niggers. They get strange notions in their heads, and grow discontented. They ought, every one of them, to be sent back to the plantations."

In the period that followed the angry arguments- over Missouri, and in the reaction to the Vesey conspiracy, criticism of slavery virtually ceased in the South. Proslavery theorists—South Carolina's John C. Calhoun among them—who might earlier have labeled slavery a "necessary evil," began to defend it as a "positive good." Blacks, they contended, could not prosper as freedmen, and the South would be abandoned without black labor to work the cotton fields and rice swamps. Protected by benevolent masters from the burdens of sickness, unemployment, and old age, the slaves, they claimed, were better off than industrial workers in the North or in Europe.

Soon northerners would spread accounts of cruel slave-owners. True stories like this one would gradually awaken the moral sense of the nation:

> I now entered on my fifteenth year—a sad epoch in the life of a slave girl. My master began to whisper foul words in my ear. Young as I was, I could not remain ignorant of their import. I tried to treat them with indifference or contempt. The master's age, my extreme youth, and the fear that his conduct would be reported to my grandmother, made him bear this treatment for many months. He was a crafty man, and resorted to many means to accomplish his purposes. He peopled my young mind with unclean images, such as only a vile monster could think of. I turned from him with disgust and hatred. But he was my master. I was compelled to live under the same roof with him—where I saw a man forty years my senior daily violating the most sacred commandments of nature. He told me I was his property; that I must be subject to his will in all things. My soul revolted against the mean tyranny. But where could I turn for protection? No matter whether the slave girl be as black as ebony or as fair as her mistress. In either case, there is no shadow of law to protect her from insult, from violence, or even from death; all these are inflicted by fiends who bear the shape of men. The mistress, who ought to protect the helpless victim, has no other feelings towards her but those of jealousy and rage. The degradation, the wrongs, the vices, that grow out of slavery, are more than I can describe.

Viewing the growing intransigence of the South on slavery as well as the hardening antislavery feeling in the North, most politicians resolved to mute the slavery issue in the future. For a time they succeeded, in part because the division of the Louisiana Purchase territory into slave and free soil removed the question of slavery expansion from national politics for twenty-five years. In the South during the 1830s a slave rebellion in Virginia and persisting strong fears of uprisings elsewhere continued to disturb slave owners, who closed their hearts and minds of the issue of slavery's morality. Beginning in 1846, with the acquisition of new territory, the furious political struggle over slavery revived. Just as John Quincy Adams had predicted, the Missouri Controversy turned out to be "a mere preamble—a title-page to a great tragic volume."

| **Exit Monroe**   The Monroe administration had attempted to drift with the apparently calm current of nationalism that followed the return of peace in 1815.

But instead, Monroe found himself presiding over the breakup of the old Republican Party. In the 1824 election, four candidates would take the field. Sectional interests tore apart the facade of national unity and the Missouri debates raised the question of the survival of the Union.

The belief that political parties were incompatible with a republican government was incorrect. The country needed not some bland national unity but articulate argument, a political system that would allow the open expression of all the passions and uncertainties that the rapid alteration of American life called forth. And the country needed not only argument but the whole business of politicking: log-rolling, pork-barreling, compromising. The Monroe administration, in domestic politics at least, was a noble failure in its attempt to sustain a politics without party conflict. In foreign affairs, however, it achieved remarkable success.

John Quincy Adams and American Continentalism

For the United States, a fortunate feature of the Louisiana Purchase was that no one knew the exact boundaries. When Robert Livingston, one of the American negotiators, pressed the French minister Talleyrand on this point, he replied: "I can give you no direction; you have made a noble bargain for yourselves, and I suppose you will make the most of it." John Quincy Adams, President Monroe's secretary of state, did just that. In important boundary treaties Adams expanded the nation's frontiers into a continental realm.

Few men have been better equipped to guide American diplomacy than John Quincy Adams. In 1778, at age eleven, he had accompanied his father, John Adams, to France. By the time he was thirty he had served as American minister to the Netherlands and to Prussia. Then, in 1801, Massachusetts elected him to the United States Senate as a Federalist. To the distress of his party, Adams proceeded to side frequently with the rival Jeffersonians. When he voted for the hated Embargo, the Federalist-dominated state legislature evicted the "scoundrel" from his seat. Under President Madison he acted as American minister to Russia and to England, and helped negotiate the Treaty of Ghent. In 1817 Monroe named him secretary of state.

| **Expansionism**   Adams took great pride in his country's military and diplomatic victories during these years. The law of nature had intended "our proper dominion to be the continent of North America." It was our national mission to expand westward to the Pacific and north and south as well. Adams disliked European colonialism, with its commercial monopolies and its pretentious claims to "fragments of territory . . . fifteen hundred miles beyond the sea, worthless and burdensome to their owners . . . ." As secretary of state, Adams deliberately sought to make an "American Continental Empire."

One step toward it was taken in 1817. By a mutual agreement between the United States and Great Britain, both nations signed notes limiting their naval forces on the Great Lakes. This arrangement, known as the Rush-Bagot agreement, was formalized by acting Secretary of State Richard Rush and the British minister Charles Bagot.

But controversy still lingered with Britain over the Northwest boundary. The treaty of 1783 had described the boundary line as running from the northwesternmost point of the Lake of the Woods due west to the Mississippi River—an impossible line, since the Mississippi actually arose 150 miles south of

As Secretary of State under Monroe, John Quincy Adams negotiated key treaties in seeking to build an "American Continental Empire." *(Stuart and Sully Portrait, Courtesy, Fogg Art Museum, Harvard University)*

the Lake of the Woods. The Louisiana Purchase had compounded the error by creating a northern boundary running all the way to the Rocky Mountains. Britain had repeatedly sought to set the boundary far enough south for access to the Mississippi.

Captain Robert Gray had first claimed the Oregon country for the United States in 1792, when he discovered the Columbia River. The explorations of Lewis and Clark fired American interest in the area; John Jacob Astor's company established a fur-trading post there in 1811. The United States, Great Britain, Spain, and Russia each had claims in this region. During the War of 1812 British forces seized Astor's post, which they renamed Fort George. Britain retained this fort until 1818, when Lord Castlereagh, the Foreign Secretary, ordered it returned to the United States.

The Treaty of 1818 with Britain Castlereagh intended this conciliatory gesture as looking to a reconciliation between Britain and the United States. Britain, absorbed by events in Europe, dared not risk a further quarrel with the United States. The War of 1812, moreover, had shown clearly how exposed was

Canada's position—only American military blundering had saved it. Canada had become a hostage for Anglo-American peace. Castlereagh next invited the United States to send commissioners to London for the purpose of settling all the differences between the two countries. At these negotiations the American envoys, acting under Adams's instructions, secured important gains for the United States. The Treaty of 1818—which one expert has called the most important treaty in the history of Canadian-American relations—granted the republic permanent rights to fish off the coasts of Newfoundland and Labrador. On the northwest boundary the United States refused to budge, and Britain agreed to draw it at 49° north latitude (approximately the line of 1783) as far as the Rocky Mountains. Adams's stubbornness had saved for the United States a strip of land more valuable than he could have realized: it contains the rich Mesabi iron range of northern Michigan and Minnesota. West of the Rockies, neither side would yield its claim. As a stopgap, they agreed to joint occupation of the Oregon country, a compromise that lasted until the 1840s.

The Treaty of 1819 with Spain Adams inherited an even more complicated set of problems with Spain. The Spanish government had never accepted the American claim that west Florida was part of the Louisiana Purchase, nor had the border between Louisiana and Texas ever been determined. Beyond Texas, the western boundary of the Louisiana Purchase remained undefined. Spain still hoped to salvage part of this vast area, and to retain its claim to the Oregon country. The biggest dispute concerned Florida.

The United States had tried for years to acquire this strategic area, which stood out on the map like a pistol pointing at New Orleans, the vital outlet for the Mississippi River. Spain's grasp on the peninsula steadily loosened after the War of 1812. The Napoleonic conflict in Europe and revolutions in Spanish America had exhausted its strength. When President Monroe ordered American forces to occupy Amelia Island, Spain in 1817 decided to offer Florida to the United States in return for a favorable boundary west of the Mississippi and an American pledge not to recognize the provinces of Spanish America that had revolted.

The two sides were still far apart in negoti-

SHOOTING PIGEONS *by James Fenimore Cooper*

Amidst the hurly-burly of national politics, the environmental splendors of the United States were already under attack. James Fenimore Cooper (1789–1851), born in upstate New York, wrote the Leather-stocking Tales, *a series of five novels about life on the American frontier. The series takes its name from its hero, a woodsman who is variously called Natty Bumppo, Deerslayer, Hawkeye, Pathfinder, Leather-stocking, and the "trapper."*

This excerpt, taken from Pioneers (1823), *describes a pigeon hunt. The passage furnishes one of the earliest lessons in environmentalism to be found in American literature. Cooper perceived the limits of the seemingly inexhaustible American landscape.*

If the heavens were alive with pigeons, the whole village seemed equally in motion with men, women, and children. Every species of fire-arms, from the French ducking-gun with a barrel near six feet in length, to the common horseman's pistol, was to be seen in the hands of the men and boys; while bows and arrows, some made of the simple stick of a walnut sapling, and others in a rude imitation of the ancient cross-bows, were carried by many of the latter.

The houses and the signs of life apparent in the village, drove the alarmed birds from the direct line of their flight, toward the mountains, along the sides and near the bases of which they were glancing in dense masses, equally wonderful by the rapidity of their motion, and their incredible numbers. . . .

Across the inclined plane which fell from the steep ascent of the mountain to the banks of the Susquehanna, ran the highway, on either side of which a clearing of many acres had been made at a very early day. Over those clearings, and up the eastern mountain, and along the dangerous path that was cut into its side, the different individuals posted themselves, and in a few moments that attack commenced.

Among the sportsmen was the tall, gaunt form of Leather-stocking, walking over the field, with his rifle hanging on his arm, his dogs at his heels; the latter now scenting the dead or wounded birds, that were beginning to tumble from the flocks, and then crouching under the legs of their master, as if they participated in his feelings at this wasteful and unsportsmanlike execution.

The reports of the fire-arms became rapid, whole volleys rising from the plain, as flocks of more than ordinary numbers darted over the opening, shadowing the field like a cloud; and then the light smoke of a single piece would issue from among the leafless bushes on the mountain, as death was hurled on the retreat of the affrighted birds, who were rising from a volley, in a vain effort to escape. Arrows, and missiles of every kind, were in the midst of the flocks; and so numerous were the birds, and so low did they take their flight, that even long poles, in the hands of those on the sides of the mountain, were used to strike them to the earth. . . .

Among the relics of the old military excursions, that occasionally are discovered throughout the different districts of the western part of New-York, there had been found . . . a small swivel, which would carry a ball of a pound weight. . . . This miniature cannon had been released from the rust, and being mounted on little wheels, was now in a state for actual service. For several years it was the sole organ for extraordinary rejoicings used in those mountains. On the mornings of the Fourths of July, it would be heard ringing among the hills. . . .

"An't the woods his work as well as the pigeons? Use, but don't waste. Wasn't the woods made for the beasts and birds to harbor in? And when man wanted their flesh, their skins, or their feathers, there's the place to seek them. But I'll go to the hut with my own game, for I wouldn't touch one of the harmless things that cover the ground here, looking up with their eyes on me, as if they only wanted tongues to say their thoughts."

With this sentiment in his mouth, Leather-stocking threw his rifle over his arm, and followed by his dogs, stepped across the clearing with great caution, taking care not to tread on one of the wounded birds in his path. He soon entered the bushes on the margin of the lake, and was hid from view.

ations at Washington when General Jackson took matters into his own hands. Old Hickory had been sent to the Florida frontier with orders to adopt all "necessary measures" to halt Indian raids into American territory. Jackson, interpreting his orders broadly, advanced into Florida in 1818 with 3,000 soldiers, pushed back the Seminole Indians, and seized the towns of St. Marks and Pensacola. For good measure, he tried and executed two British subjects who had been inciting the Indians. Jackson's acts embarrassed the Monroe Administration; Secretary of War John Calhoun wanted Jackson court-martialed, but Adams defended Jackson's conduct. The secretary of state urged that the occupation of the towns continue until Spain should send a force sufficient to pacify the Indians. Monroe agreed, and Spain received an ultimatum: either place a force in Florida adequate to maintain order or cede it to the United States.

These bold strokes got the negotiations moving. After weeks of hard bargaining, the two sides agreed, and Adams and the Spanish minister, Luis de Onís, signed the Adams-Onís treaty of 1819. Spain ceded Florida to the United States. Nothing was said about the recognition of the rebellious Spanish colonies. In return for fixing the Texas boundary at the Sabine River, Adams secured a magnificent transcontinental settlement from Spain, including title to all Spanish territory north of latitude 42° between the Continental Divide and the Pacific Ocean. Adams reckoned that the four nay votes on the treaty in the Senate included two Clay men, one enemy of Jackson, and one suffering from "some maggot in his brain." With this treaty Adams had at last achieved his "Continental Empire" and a place in history as a brilliant secretary of state.

The Monroe Doctrine

The boldest assertion of American nationalism in this period came from President James Monroe. His annual message in December 1823 laid down two important principles: that "the American continents, by the free and independent condition which they have assumed and maintain, are henceforth not to be considered as subjects for future colonization by any European power"; and that the United States would consider any attempt by the European powers "to extend their political system to any portion of this hemisphere as dangerous to our peace and safety." In later years these two maxims, known as "noncolonization" and "non-interference," came to be called together the Monroe Doctrine. No other presidential statement, with the possible exception of Washington's Farewell Address, has won such acceptance from the American people. On the hundredth anniversary of Monroe's message, Mary Baker Eddy, the founder of Christian Science, spoke for millions when she said: "I believe in the Monroe Doctrine, in our Constitution, and in the laws of God."

The principles Monroe expounded in 1823 were not original. From the first Americans had sought refuge in the New World in order to escape the Old. Out of the Revolutionary experience inevitably flowed the belief that the New World should isolate itself from the alliances, the quarrels, and the colonizing schemes of the European powers. Washington gave this idea its classic expression in his Farewell Address, and Jefferson echoed it in his warning against subordinating American affairs to those of Europe. In 1823 Monroe and Secretary of State John Quincy Adams shaped these broad beliefs into an official statement.

Adams had for years sought an excuse to forbid further European colonization in the Western Hemisphere. Russia unexpectedly gave him the opportunity. Russian explorers had long before laid claim to the northwest coast of America. By 1812 the Russian-American Company had extended its trading operations southward within only a few miles of San Francisco. Suddenly, in 1821, Czar Alexander I issued an imperial decree conferring upon this company exclusive trading rights down to 51° north latitude and forbidding all foreign vessels to come near the coast. In July 1823 Adams flatly told the Russian minister at Washington that the United States would assert the principle "that the American continents are no longer subjects for *any* new European colonial establishments."

Here was the genesis of the Monroe Doctrine; President Monroe inserted almost these very words into his annual message six months later.

The warning against European interference within the hemisphere attacked a more fundamental European threat to American interests.

Spain's colonies in Central and South America had been struggling for independence for some time. When Spain tried to regain her American provinces by force, full-scale war broke out. For six years, beginning in 1814, the revolutionists, led by Simón Bolívar and San Martin, liberated one colony after another. The United States sympathized with these heroic struggles and granted belligerent status to the rebellious colonies, enabling them to buy supplies in this country. But Monroe, and especially Adams, hesitated to recognize the new revolutionary governments until Britain did. The British government twice refused American invitations to do this jointly. Finally, the United States decided to act alone, extending formal recognition in 1822 to Mexico, Colombia, Chile, Peru, and the Provinces of Rio de la Plata, present day Argentina. Having taken this bold step, the Monroe Administration was naturally alarmed at the prospect of intervention.

Great Britain shared this concern, for the Spanish-American revolts had opened a whole continent to British trade. When rumors of possible intervention by other European powers reached George Canning, the British foreign secretary, in 1823, he decided to seek American cooperation in opposing such a scheme. Canning proposed a treaty or exchange of notes between the two countries expressing joint opposition to any attempt to restore Spain's lost colonies by force; he still refused, however, to agree to immediate British recognition of the former colonies.

Monroe almost accepted Canning's offer. Former Presidents Jefferson and Madison both advised acceptance, as did all the Cabinet—except the secretary of state. "It would be more candid as well as more dignified," Adams argued, "to avow our principles explicitly . . . , than to come in as a cock-boat in the wake of the British man-of-war." At this point in 1823 Monroe drafted the famous declaration in his annual message opposing further intervention by the European powers in the Western Hemisphere. At Adams's insistence, Monroe inserted a statement dis-

avowing American interference "in the wars of the European powers in matters relating to themselves." And Adams publicly admitted that it was the power of the British navy that had enabled the United States to throw down its audacious challenge to the rest of Europe.

Americans cheered the President's message. The young republic's challenge to the "crowned conspirators" of Europe, boasted one newspaper editor, would be read with "a revolting stare of astonishment." Europe scoffed at the message, labeling it "blustering," "haughty," "arrogant." It had little effect on the actions of the continental powers. Russia, a major object of the non-colonization clause, had already decided to limit its territorial claims in North America to the area north of latitude 54° 40'. Late in 1823 Canning, tired of waiting for American agreement on a joint statement, had served an ultimatum on France. A French newspaper derided Monroe for assuming

> the tone of a powerful monarch, whose armies and fleets are ready to march. . . . Mr. Monroe is the temporary President of a Republic situated on the east coast of North America. This republic is bounded on the south by the possessions of the King of Spain, and on the north by those of the King of England. Its independence was only recognized forty years ago; by what right then would the two Americas today be under its immediate sway from Hudson's Bay to Cape Horn?

By the time Monroe issued his warning, the immediate danger of interference had already vanished. During the next twenty years Britain and France both violated the Doctrine with impunity. Not until the late nineteenth century, when the United States had become a major power, did the Old World respect the new hemisphere.

Yet Monroe's message had an important future. Against an Old World order founded on a doctrine asserting the absolute rights of sovereigns and empires, Monroe championed a new order founded on the right of peoples to determine their own destiny. Only later, by a series of corollaries, did Monroe's successors turn his Doctrine into an instrument for United States meddling in Latin American affairs. "From a candid but commendable United States gesture against European interference," a Mexican diplomat observed bitterly, "the Doctrine was turned into a ruthless axiom utilized by Washington administrations to suit the interests of . . . 'Yankee Imperialism.'"

The Election of 1824

From 1796 to 1816 meetings of the congressional members of each party had nominated their own presidential candidates. In 1820, when President Monroe ran unopposed, the Republicans did not even bother with a caucus nomination. By 1824 that party, lacking an organized opposition, had dissolved into a series of warring factions. One newspaper editor remarked upon hearing "so great a buzz about the person who should succeed Monroe." President Monroe wisely declined to pick his successor from among the several Republicans battling for the nomination.

The "Old Republicans," of the caucus devoted to states' rights and economy, pushed William H. Crawford of Georgia as their candidate for President. Others attacked the caucus as undemocratic. A Baltimore newspaper joked about it: "The poor little political bird of ominous note and plumage, denominated a CAUCUS, was hatched in Washington on Saturday last.... The sickly thing is to be

In the election of 1824, Henry Clay's program called the "American System" was, in effect, the nation's first campaign platform. (*Courtesy, National Archives*)

fed, cherished, pampered for a week, when it is fondly hoped it will be enabled to cry the name of Crawford, Crawford, Crawford." Crawford is an obscure figure today, but to his contemporaries he was a "plain *giant* of a man." Like many young men of his day, he had parlayed a successful law practice into a distinguished career. He married a wealthy heiress, spent a few years in the state legislature, and then went to Washington as a senator. Crawford later served as minister to France and secretary of war, and had, since 1816, been secretary of the treasury. He used this last post to pack government offices with his supporters. In 1823, just when his position seemed impregnable, illness struck him. Medical experts bled him twenty-three times within three weeks. Crawford never fully recovered, but his partisans continued to put his name forward. They called a caucus of congressional Republicans, and with only a third of the eligible members present, nominated Crawford for the presidency. The other candidates promptly repudiated the caucus as undemocratic, and accused Crawford of trying "to ride into power on 'King Caucus.'" The nomination ruined any chances Crawford may have had.

As an alternative to the congressional caucus, the other candidates accepted nominations from state legislatures and public meetings. A Tennessee newspaper likened the process to a horse race, with each state entering its own "nag." The result was what one political wit called a contest between "Hasbeens," "Cantbees," "Mightbees," and "Wouldabeens."

Several New England states endorsed John Quincy Adams, Monroe's capable secretary of state. South Carolina had supported John C. Calhoun, but he dropped out when Pennsylvania Republicans failed to nominate him. The young Carolinian accepted the vice-presidential spot instead and easily won that office.

| **Henry Clay's American System** | Henry Clay had been charting a course toward the White House for a decade. |

Born in Virginia, he had migrated to Kentucky, where he became a highly successful criminal lawyer—so successful, according to legend, that no person who hired Clay to defend him was ever hanged. After a stint in the state legislature he went on to Congress, a perfect environment then for a man with his quick mind, engaging personality, and fondness for drinking and gambling. In 1811 his colleagues made him Speaker of the House. After the war Clay became a vigorous advocate of internal improvements, a national bank, and a protective tariff. He hoped that this program, which he called the "American System," would win support in every part of the country. This was, for practical purposes, the nation's first campaign platform. Clay had not anticipated rising sectional jealousies. "I will be opposed," he wrote gloomily before the election, "because I think that the interests of all parts of the Union should be taken care of. . . ." Clay cherished a sweeping national vision: "This government is to last, I trust, forever," he said, "We may at least hope it will endure until the wave of population, cultivation and intelligence shall have washed the Rocky Mountains. . . ."

Clay's rival for the western vote was Andrew Jackson, a latecomer to the race. Jackson's victories over the Creek Indians at Horseshoe Bend and the British at New Orleans had made him a national hero. "I cannot believe that killing 2,500 Englishmen at New Orleans qualifies for the various, difficult and complicated duties of the Chief Magistracy," said Clay. Jackson's arrogant conduct during the Seminole campaign in 1818 only increased his popularity. In spite of brief terms in both houses of Congress, Old Hickory was not associated in the public mind with the grimy politics of Washington; he was a "plain farmer," his backers claimed, fresh from the people. In the uncertain politics of the time, his lack of experience in public affairs probably worked to his advantage. While the other candidates discussed the tariff or internal improvements, the Jackson people, observed John Quincy Adams resentfully, had only to shout "8th of January and the Battle of New Orleans" to win votes.

The House of Representatives, 1821. As provided in the Constitution, the House elected John Quincy Adams President in 1824 after none of the four candidates had received a majority in the electoral college. *(Courtesy, Library of Congress)*

When the ballots were counted in November, the Old Hero had received by far the largest popular count—43 percent against 31 for Adams, his closest rival. But none of the candidates had a clear majority in the electoral college; there were 99 votes for Jackson, 84 for Adams, 41 for Crawford, and 37 for Clay. As the Constitution provides, the House of Representatives was required to select the chief executive from among the three men with the largest number of electoral votes. Each state would cast one ballot, determined by majority vote of its delegation.

Everyone now looked to Clay, whose fourth-place finish had eliminated him from the contest. As Speaker he had enormous influence in the House, and the managers and friends of the three candidates besieged him with arguments and deals. Clay carefully considered their words and his own political fortunes before making up his mind. He easily eliminated Crawford; the Georgian was physically unfit to assume the burden of the presidency.

Clay was inclined to dismiss Jackson as a "military chieftain" with no moral, intellectual, or other attributes worth the name. And the General was a dangerous rival for the western vote; it was to Clay's future political advantage to exclude him from the contest. This left John Quincy Adams. The two men had quarreled in the past, but Adams was unquestionably qualified for the presidency, and he alone shared Clay's faith in a strong national government. After consulting with friends, Clay threw all his support behind the Secretary of State. By a bare majority, John Quincy Adams was elected President.

At first Jackson took the news of his defeat gracefully. Then, three days after the election, Adams announced his intention to appoint Clay as secretary of state. The warm and impulsive Clay contrasted with the dour Adams, making them strange political bedfellows. Working together in Belgium on the treaty to end the War of 1812, Adams wrote in his diary: "Just before rising I heard Mr. Clay's company retiring. . . . I had left him . . . at cards. They parted as I was about to rise." But the appointment was made, and the cry of "corrupt bargain" went up at once.

Senator John Randolph of Virginia ranted against the "Black George" and "black-leg" Clay, who later challenged the eccentric Randolph to a duel. When their initial exchange of shots on the banks of the Potomac missed their targets, Clay insisted on another round and put a bullet through Randolph's coat while his opponent shot into the air. That was all there was to the duel, but the political damage had been done.

"So you see," wrote Jackson bitterly, "the *Judas* of the West has closed the contract and will receive the thirty pieces of silver." Had there been a deal? No evidence, then or later, has ever clarified the matter. Adams insisted that the Kentuckian was the best man for the job. Clay presumably could have made the same deal with any of the other candidates. Politically, the appointment drove the Jacksonians and the Calhoun men into immediate opposition, and put the new administration on the defensive. Jackson, heretofore a hesitant candidate, set out for Tennessee in full cry: "The people have been cheated," he charged. ". . . The corruptions and intrigues at Washington [have] defeated the will of the people." The campaign of 1828 was under way before John Quincy Adams had settled into the White House.

The Second President Adams

John Quincy Adams, a biographer once remarked, "was not among America's more lovable figures." By his own description, he was reserved, stubborn, and independent. "It is a question," an observer wondered, "whether he ever laughed in his life." A reporter at the Ghent peace conference termed him "a bulldog among spaniels." When he was secretary of state, these qualities served Adams well; once he was in the White House, they quickly became his undoing.

Instead of seeking to overcome his liabilities by building a political machine in the federal bureaucracy and developing a popular program, Adams did precisely the reverse. In the interest of conciliation, he appointed political opponents to his Cabinet and retained outspoken critics in government of-

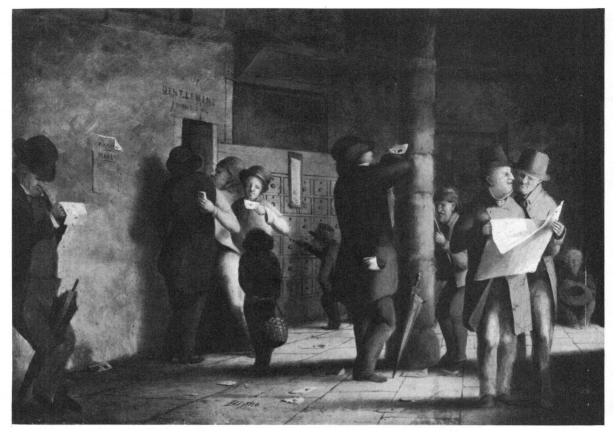

Patrons discussing politics and much besides in David Gilmour Blythe, *In the Pittsburgh Post Office.*
Courtesy, Museum of Fine Arts, Boston

fices instead of making room for his own backers. Above all, he scorned public opinion. The great object of government, Adams believed, was to improve the condition of mankind. It was the President's duty to give direction to the national government, and the people's to follow. Even when proposing a popular measure, Adams made no effort to dramatize it: instead of making a straightforward statement urging Congress to pass a federal bankruptcy law, Adams recommended "the amelioration in some form or modification of the diversified and often oppressive codes relating to insolvency." In 1828 the Jacksonians revived a popular campaign slogan: "John Quincy Adams who can write and Andrew Jackson who can fight."

Adams spelled out a nationalistic program for the country. Now that America's independence had been secured and her borders enlarged, he would strengthen the country internally with a nationally planned and financed system of roads and canals, a national university, a naval academy, government-supported astronomical observatories and expeditions to map the country, and a department of the interior to regulate the use of natural resources. Adams expected to finance this program by selling public lands.

It was not the right time for a nationalist in the White House, particularly one lacking the political skill to rally support. Westerners wanted free public land, not sales at high prices for revenue. Southerners increasingly feared that a powerful federal government would interfere with slavery. The Old Republicans accused the President of trying to revive the Federalist policies of his father. "The cub," John Randolph remarked, "is a greater bear than the old one." The Jacksonian press derided Adams's proposals: his reference to astronomical observatories as "light-houses of the skies" became a national joke. Congress rejected every one of the President's recommendations.

At every turn, Adams's integrity and his belief in national authority landed him in trouble. In 1825, for example, he refused to enforce a fraudulent treaty dispossessing the Creek Indians of their tribal lands in Georgia. Governor George Troup of Georgia, anxious to open these rich cotton lands to settlement, sent surveyors into the Indian country anyway. A confrontation between the United States and Georgia threatened. A new treaty averted a clash: the Creeks agreed to cede all their lands and move west. Adams's stand had been honorable, but unpopular. Southerners condemned his challenge to state authority; westerners objected to his defense of the Indians.

The failure of Adams's domestic program had profound consequences for the country. A vast system of roads and canals, coming at a time when the forces of sectionalism were gaining strength, might have tied the nation together and prevented the disintegration of the Union. Instead, as Adams predicted, "the clanking chain of the slave" was riveted "into perpetuity" and "the invaluable inheritance of the public lands" was wasted "in boundless bribery to the West."

The Panama Congress

Adams's presidency was never to reward with success the skills and brilliance he brought to it. His chief effort in foreign policy went no farther than his domestic programs.

In 1824, Simón Bolívar, the "Liberator" of Spanish America, proposed a conference to be held in Panama. He hoped to bind the former Spanish colonies into a confederation to protect the hemisphere against Europe's Quadruple Alliance. Mexico and Colombia, rebuffed in earlier efforts to obtain individual treaties of alliance with the United States, added the Republic of the North to the list of participants. All hoped to bring the United States into a hemispheric alliance that would make the Monroe Doctrine Pan-American. Their invitations reached Washington early in 1825, just as John Quincy Adams was entering the White House.

| **Pan-Americanism** | Secretary of State Henry Clay welcomed the idea of an inter-American conference. He had ardently supported the cause of Latin American independence. Clay envisioned an "American System" of republics, led by the United States, standing against the despotism of the Old World. The irrepressible Clay had scarcely been able to contain himself on the House of Representatives floor:

> Within this vast region we behold the most sublime and interesting objects of creation; the loftiest mountains, the most majestic rivers in the world; the richest mines of the precious metals, and the choicest productions of the earth. We behold there a spectacle still more interesting and sublime—the glorious spectacle of eighteen millions of people, struggling to burst their chains and to be free.

Adams himself, as Monroe's secretary of state, had rejected all proposals for collective security with the Latin American republics. At Clay's urging, however, he asked Congress to confirm the appointment of two delegates to the Panama meeting. It was the time, he decided, to extend "the most cordial feelings of fraternal friendship" to our sister republics. Adams hoped to advance throughout the hemisphere fundamental principles of commercial reciprocity, neutral rights, freedom of the seas, and resistance to European colonization.

Adams's request met unexpected opposition in Congress. Led by Vice-President Calhoun and supporters of Andrew Jackson, the faction within the Republican Party that was going to call itself the Democrats, vigorously attacked the administration. They accused Adams and Clay of seeking to fasten the United States to a hemispheric alliance, in plain violation of President Washington's warning against foreign entanglements. Opposition senators bombarded the President with questions and requests for additional documents. The debates soon turned ugly. At one point John Randolph of Roanoke insinuated that Clay had procured the American invitation to further his own interests: "This Panama mission is a Kentucky cuckoo's egg, laid in a Spanish-American nest," he told the Senate. Southerners had a further objection to the Panama meeting. Delegates from Haiti were expected at the conference, and the question of recognizing the black republic might arise. Recognition of Haiti, warned a Georgia Senator, would "strengthen and invigorate" the determination of these black revolutionaries, whose hands still reeked "in the blood" of their murdered masters, "to spread the doctrines of insurrection" to the United States.

Adams defended his proposal. Times and circumstances, he argued, had changed since Washington's day; the United States had trebled its territory, population, and wealth and must act with a breadth of vision befitting a great nation, said this devoted nationalist. After months of debate and delay, Congress finally approved the President's choice of delegates and appropriated funds for the mission. Adams had scored a major triumph—the only one of his presidency.

The triumph was empty. One of the American delegates died on his way to the conference; the other arrived too late. The meeting itself was a fiasco. One delegate went into a dithyramb of oratory:

> An entire world is about to witness our labours. . . . Our names are about to be written either in immortal praise or in eternal opprobrium. Let us raise ourselves above a thousand millions of inhabitants, and may a noble pride inspire us, likening us to God himself on that day, when He gave the first laws to the Universe.

But only four Latin American nations sent representatives. They signed a treaty of mutual defense and alliance, and quickly adjourned from fever-ridden Panama City, planning to meet again in Mexico early in 1827. By that time Bolívar had lost interest in the idea of a hemispheric confederation, and the conference never reconvened.

At home, the issue of Haiti quickened the sectional controversy that had flared in the debates over the Missouri Compromise. Southerners once again envisioned the federal government moving against their "peculiar institution." Adams's proposal gave his political enemies their first opportunity to attack the President and his secretary of state. Once again John Quincy Adams was ahead of his time; the American people in 1826 were looking West, not South. Not for another fifty years would the United States take an interest in the concept of Pan-Americanism.

His administration a failure in both domestic and foreign affairs, Adams gave up all hope of reelection. His subsequent career was unique for an American President: In 1830 he was elected to the House of Representatives. "No election or appointment conferred upon me ever gave me so much pleasure," said Congressman Adams. A spokesman for the antislavery forces and a model of integrity, he served until his death in 1848 at the age of eighty-one.

Points To Think About

1. Prior to 1820, many prominent southerners, such as Thomas Jefferson and Henry Clay, had maintained that gradual emancipation was both necessary and desirable. Slavery, many in the South believed, was an evil. Even its staunchest defenders tended to argue merely that the evil was a necessary one.

After 1820 the white southern climate of opinion started to shift. Gradual emancipation began to have difficulty obtaining a hearing. And defenders of slavery shifted to the offensive. Slavery was good, they held, for both slaveholders and the slave. It was a school in which Africans learned Christianity, English, and civilized manners. It benefited the slave. Eighteen-twenty also marked the beginning of the end of the free discussion of the issue in the South. And this may have been the worst positive evil of the argument. It had the effect of cutting the South off from the rest of the nation.

The argument that slavery was a positive good went with a growing sectionalism in the white South. White southerners began to contrast their section's needs with those of the rest of the country. One result was a sort of neo-Jeffersonianism. Southerners like John C. Calhoun became apostles of limited government and states' rights. What Calhoun and his colleagues abandoned were Jefferson's insistence on equality, his fervent nationalism, and his commitment to civil liberties. The Jeffersonian legacy in the South, in short, was unraveling. Calhoun took only those strands which were of use in defending slavery, his section's "peculiar institution."

2.   The Northeast as well as the South could succumb to national self-interest. But, and it is a crucial but, New Englanders and representatives of the Middle Atlantic states could pass their sectionalism off as nationalism. The issue of internal improvements provides a clear case in point. The Northeast and Middle Atlantic states shared with the Middle Western states a desire for improved roads and canals, and later for railroads. To pay for them they advocated high tariffs. Not so coincidently the tariffs would also protect northern manufacturing interests even as the internal improvements would bind West and Northeast ever closer. The South consistently stood in the way. It was a comparatively simple matter for northerners to cast their proposals in language thick with references to future national glory and to castigate southerners with putting narrow sectional interests before the nation's good. Southerners could contest the rhetoric, but to little avail.

Over the long run, this state of affairs gave the North a distinct rhetorical and, ultimately, a moral advantage over the South.

Suggested Readings

Some newer books on this period are Mary M. W. Hargreaves, *The Presidency of John Quincy Adams* (1985), Randolph B. Campbell, *An Empire for Slavery: The Peculiar Institution in Texas, 1821–1825* (1989), David B. Davis, *The Problem of Slavery in the Age of Revolution, 1770–1823* (1975), Ralph Ketcham, *Presidents Above Party: The First American Presidency, 1789–1829)* (1984), and Francis M. Stites, *John Marshall* (1981).

See the *History of the Westward Movement* (1978) by Frederick W. Merk and Ray Allen Billington's *Westward Expansion* (rev. 1974). On population shifts, there are Richard H. Easterlin, *Population, Labor Force, and Long Swings in Economic Growth* (1968) and Robert Riegel and R. G. Athearn, *America Moves West* (1964). A beautiful book on the American frontier is Annette Kolodny's *The Land Before Her: Fantasy and Experience on the American Frontiers* (1984). Good books on politics and diplomacy are Harry Ammon, *James Madison* (1971), Dexter Perkins, *A History of the Monroe Doctrine* (1955), Samuel F. Bemis, *John Quincy Adams and the Union* (1956), and Glover Moore, *The Missouri Compromise* (1953). Leonard Baker depicts *John Marshall: A Life in Law* (1974).

☆ ☆ DEBATE ☆ ☆ ☆

FORREST McDONALD

The leading public entertainment in the United States is politics, but it is a form of entertainment that we tend to confuse with reality. Accordingly, we are often inclined to regard past political events as the measure of what was then happening. Seen in that light, the 1820s were a rather humdrum time: a noisy to-do over slavery, a couple of fairly interesting presidential elections, a few Supreme Court decisions of note, a great deal of talk about tariffs, and otherwise ho-hum. But in actuality profound and decisive changes were taking place outside politics that would promote increasing sectional conflicts.

The most obvious of the changes were technological and economic. The proliferation of steamboats on inland waterways, in conjunction with the construction of many miles of canals and turnpike roads, set off a transportation revolution that would be an endlessly repeated feature of American life. The transportation revolution, in turn, drastically reduced shipping costs for farmers in the interior and redirected the attention of merchants and producers on the northeastern seaboard away from Europe and toward the hinterland. The South alone would continue to be dependent upon European markets.

The polarization of interests was intensified by the emergence, in the late twenties, of capitalistic manufacturing in New England, the production of textiles in mechanized, steam-powered factories. Earlier, textiles had been produced by hand in the home and in small shops. For that earlier system, slave labor, could have been far cheaper than free labor; under the factory system it was the other way around. This was particularly ominous to slaveholders in the upper South, for there were more slaves there than could be profitably employed in raising tobacco, and none of the other great staple crops could be grown in the region. When manufacturing as an alternative outlet for slave labor ceased to be viable, the economic decay of the area became inevitable.

Less visible and less tangible but not less important political changes were taking place as well. There was a changing of the guard, dramatically symbolized by the death on July 4, 1826—the fiftieth anniversary of the Declaration of Independence—of John Adams and Thomas Jefferson. The Revolutionary generation had been a race of giants, men who were intensely practical but also immensely learned. Steeped in the Greek and Roman classics, versed in Renaissance humanism, learned in English legal and constitutional history, enriched by the Scottish Enlightenment, they represented a continuum and in some ways the climax of the best in a tradition that had extended over the course of two thousand years. They were the products of a unique set of circumstances, and American society had now become so vulgarized that it would never be able to produce their likes again. The ablest of the public men in the era after the 1820s—John Marshall, Henry Clay, John C. Calhoun, John Quincy Adams, Daniel Webster, Joseph Story, Nicholas Biddle—were towering figures compared to their contemporaries, but apart from Adams and Marshall, who were long-lived holdovers from the earlier era, not even these rare men were on a par with the Founders; and the public arena was soon to be overrun by pygmies. Indeed, the very unattractiveness of political life after the 1820s provided powerful stimulus to economic development, for it diverted the ablest Americans away from government and into private economic activity. Contrary to Professor Genovese's praise of the political system, this decline in the quality of leadership was as important in shaping the American destiny as any of the great technological and economic changes.

Nationalism or Sectionalism?

EUGENE D. GENOVESE

From the first days of the republic, if not well before, American society encompassed an assortment of geographically grounded differences that nonetheless pointed toward national unity: settled, older regions against newer ones; cities against the countryside; capital-lending areas against debtor regions; manufacturing districts against agricultural. These divisions gave rise to conflicts of interest, to local, state, or regional pride and prejudices, to suspicions and hostilities. But in the North, these conflicts rested upon the solid foundations of a property system and constitutional polity that well represented the common interests of a coalescing nation. And they took place within a developing economy that steadily integrated the parts into the whole by the extension of markets and a superb system of transportation.

The South was another matter. It too had its sections and its sectionalisms: upper South and lower; black belt and upcountry; pro-tariff hemp and sugar areas and anti-tariff cotton areas; genteel tidewater communities and rough-and-tumble frontier communities; economically dynamic regions and economically stagnant or declining regions; and more. But slave property distinguished the entire South. The nonslaveholding majority of whites was caught in the web of the larger social system of slavery. Hence, while the South fought out internal sectional battles within each state and between states and regions, it increasingly closed ranks against the threat to its social system that was being mounted from without and, in muted ways, even from within.

The sectionalism that divided free from slave society had a much different character from the sectionalism that existed within the North. Differences among Northerners were never likely to provoke war. The division between the Northern and the Southern property systems, to the contrary, was likely to provoke war no matter how sensible and restrained the statesman on either side tried to be.

The republic, then, was from its earliest days dividing itself into distinct sections, but Professor McDonald speaks as though the sections, their economies, their mutual antagonism just happened, each section developing out of its own pre-established nature. He does not recognize how intensely political and ideological the whole process was. Hamiltonianism was possibly an inevitable expression of nascent capitalism and industrialism, but it was also certainly a conscious stimulant to both, and for a time Hamiltonianism had to argue against its politically powerful Jeffersonian opponent. Southern slaveholding culture was intensely aware of its needs, determined to give itself a satisfying ideology and character—it even tried to import medieval tournaments—and its defensive political assault against Northern politicians was quite purposeful. And politics, which had so much to do with shaping each of the sections and putting them at verbal war with each other, did a remarkable job of staving off actual war. From the Constitution to the Missouri Compromise, then to the nullification crisis and beyond, Congress, the executive, and the courts, as well as the political parties and their leaders, sought to compromise on slavery. But each compromise proved more fragile than the one before, as two societies, one slave and one free, expanded at a quickening rate within a single nation-state that could not reconcile them.

Professor McDonald's denigration of politics and exultation of economics is an instance of that peculiar contradictory "conservatism" that he presents with considerable eloquence throughout these debates. Like others in his political camp, he perceives of the industrious, hardworking entrepreneur as a being: free-willed and able to reshape the world. But then he and his fellow conservatives will not grant to this American society, so plenteous in imagination and will, the ability to impose any measure of social and economic justice through the instrumentality of government.

Asher Durand conveys Andrew Jackson's willfulness by giving attention to his angular nose and jaw; even his swept-back hair stands at attention. (*Historical Pictures Service, Chicago*)

The Jacksonian Era 1828–1840

ANDREW JACKSON'S INAUGURAL

Washington, D.C., was a cheerless place in the winter of 1828–29, after Andrew Jackson's presidential victory. Even the victors were gloomy: Rachel, the President-elect's wife, had just died, and with their leader in mourning, Democrats avoided putting on too boisterous a display of pleasure over their triumph. The weather was dreadful: "snow storm after snow storm—the river frozen up, and the poor suffering the extremity of cold and hunger," wrote Margaret Bayard Smith, a resident who has left us the most vivid account of Washington in the winter of Jackson's inauguration.

One Washingtonian suggested in a letter to the local newspaper that celebrants make the inaugural ball "a means of producing a fund for the relief of the poor [by] dispensing with the usual decorations and expensive accompaniments of such a fete." In response to reports that people had frozen to death, Congress did authorize giving fifty cords of wood to the poor.

Jackson decreed a sober and dignified inauguration: he would have no military parades, no pre-inaugural festivities. Like Jefferson, he would walk to the Capitol to take the oath, then proceed to the White House on horseback. Margaret Smith approved Jackson's "avoidance of all parade—it is *true* greatness, which needs not the aid of ornament and pomp," but wished that "the good old gentleman might indulge himself with a carriage." But some 20,000 people of every class and from every section of the country flooded into the Capitol to witness the inauguration of the "people's President." It was "like the inundation of the northern barbarians into Rome," wrote one haughty Washingtonian, "save that the tumultuous tide came in from [all points] of the compass."

The sun finally shone on March 4, and tens of thousands of citizens gathered for the oath-taking. The spectacle reflected the fondest hopes of ardent Democrats. People "without distinction of rank" stood "silent, orderly and tranquil" to glimpse Jackson—who could be picked out from the crowd around him because he alone wore no hat—a servant of the sovereign people:

"There, there, that is he," exclaimed different voices. "Which?" asked others. "He with the white head" was the reply. "Ah," exclaimed others, "there is the old man and his gray hair, there is the old veteran, there is Jackson."

Jackson, in a low voice that only a handful of the massed thousands could have heard, delivered his inaugural address, which John Quincy Adams described as "short, written with some eloquence, and remarkable chiefly for a significant threat of reform." Then, in a scramble of people that suggested to some the mobs of the French Revolution, but to a modern observer would seem reasonably orderly, farmers, politicians, women, children, carts, wagons, horses, and carriages followed the silver-haired hero down Pennsylvania Avenue to the White House. Once there they jammed inside hoping to pump the President's hand and share his offering of ice cream, cake, lemonade, and orange punch that had been intended only for the eligible social elite of Washington.

It was a physical impossibility. Ladies fainted from the press; in the grab for refreshments glasses and china broke, people's clothing got ripped, fights broke out; strong men had to cordon off the frail President to prevent injury by exuberant well-wishers. Margaret Smith put the incident in the worst possible light:

> The *Majesty of the People* had disappeared, and a rabble, a mob, of boys, negros, women, children, scrambling, fighting, romping. What a pity, what a pity! No arrangements had been made, no police officers placed on duty and the whole house had been inundated by the rabble mob. We came too late. The President, after having been *literally* nearly pressed to death and almost suffocated and torn to pieces by the people in their eagerness to shake hands with Old Hickory, had retreated through the back way or south front and had escaped to his lodgings at Gadsby's. Cut glass and china to the amount of several thousand dollars had been broken in the struggle to get the refreshments, punch and other articles had been carried out in tubs and buckets, but had it been in hogsheads it would have been insufficient, ice-creams, and cake and lemonade. . . . Ladies fainted, men were seen with bloody noses and such a scene of confusion took place as is impossible to describe,—those who got in could not get out by the door again, but had to scramble out of windows.

In reality, alert servants began carrying tubs of rum punch onto the lawn to thin the crowd inside the house. The event passed off with nothing worse than mudprints on the furniture (anything to catch a glimpse of Old Hickory) and broken plates and cups. It was not a party anyone would want to repeat, but neither was it the first scene of a social revolution.

The product of happenstance, of poor planning, the White House party spoke as much of the American people's instinctive good-natured sense of order as it did of their new sense that the White House and the President belonged at last to them. While several aristocratically inclined observers saw the reign of "King Mob" in the inauguration, the *Washington National Intelligencer* commented editorially on the general good order of the crowds:

> What particularly gratifies us, and does credit to the character of our people, is, that, amidst all the excitement and bustle of the occasion, the whole day and night of the Inauguration passed off without the slightest interruption of the public peace and order, that we have heard of. At the mansion of the president, the Sovereign People were a little uproarious, but it was in any thing but a malicious spirit.

A new, but not a revolutionary, political age had begun.

The representative of that new age illustrates, however, the elusive nature of

American democracy. Of humble origins, Jackson was nonetheless by this time clearly a member of the patrician class: a slaveholder, a commander of troops, the master of a large and gracious estate. Even his simple manners, which had the politically useful look of democracy, could as easily present itself as the plain direct demeanor appropriate to a military aristocracy. Americans have thought themselves committed to democracy. They have also wisely or absentmindedly failed to establish any rigorous test of what properly constitutes a democracy or its leadership.

The Election of 1828

The election of 1828 was a landmark in American politics. For the first time in nearly twenty years two vigorous parties contested for the presidency. Responding to this stimulus, the voters turned out in unprecedented numbers to elect Andrew Jackson President of the United States.

The Second Party System
A second two-party system was forming, in which each of the parties would appeal more directly for wide popular support than had the old Federalist and Republican parties. They would in time set up extensive local organizations for winning an electorate and holding its loyalty. The new party system rested in part on legal changes that broadened the popular base of government: the gradual removal of qualifications for voting, and the trend among the states toward popular election of public officials and presidential electors in place of the earlier practice of leaving the choice to state legislatures. The new party system was a way of capturing this larger voting public.

In choosing John Quincy Adams over Jackson in 1824, the House of Representatives had unwittingly made for the new era of partisan politics. In the next four years the followers of Adams and Clay, working for federal policies that would actively promote the nation's economy, began to call themselves National Republicans; their opponents kept the name Democratic Republicans (soon shortened to Democrats). Because the House had selected Adams over General Jackson—who had received the greater number of popular and electoral votes—under circumstances that suggested to many people the existence of a "corrupt bargain," Jackson became an even stronger political figure than before. He captured the imagination of the public and infused new glamour into national politics.

After his defeat, Jackson allied with Senator Martin Van Buren of New York, a highly skilled political manager, to create the new Democratic Party. At its core were the original Jackson men, those who had supported him in 1824. These included voters in every part of the country except New England, and opportunistic politicians eager to profit from this enthusiasm for the "Old Hero." They were joined after the election by the followers of John C. Calhoun, whose own path to the presidency the alliance between Adams and Clay had blocked. Between 1826 and 1828, Van Buren brought into the party the southern Old Republicans, who had formerly supported Crawford. United in their opposition to the policies of Adams and Clay that gave the federal government a larger role in organizing the economy, the new coalition worked in Congress to block the administration's programs.

Election of 1828
While the Jacksonians maneuvered in Congress, they also began to build the necessary organization to boost Old Hickory into the White House. Most states had adopted the system, still in use today, that gives all the state's electoral votes to the presidential candidate who wins the state's popular vote instead of allotting to other candidates a share of the electoral votes that corresponds to their share of the popular vote. Since a winning of a majority of the popular vote brought so rich a reward, parties wanted a state machinery that could mobilize voters throughout the state. Van Buren thoroughly organized the Democratic Party. He established central committees in Washington and Nashville. The committees worked closely with influential state leaders, who in turn organized Hickory Clubs at the local level. A string of newspapers favorable to Jackson appeared across the country. Jackson

remained at home in Tennessee, posing as the innocent victim of a "corrupt bargain." Yet he supervised every detail of the campaign. In order to hold together his fragile coalition, he avoided taking a stand on the issues. When asked for his position on the tariff, Jackson replied ambiguously that he favored a "middle and just course." When Van Buren quoted Jackson's comment on the tariff at a New York rally, one man in the audience cheered the remark and then asked his neighbor: "On which side of the tariff question was it?" Meantime, Adams steadfastly refused to electioneer in his own behalf. Too late, his friends tried to erect an organization similar to the Democrats'.

In 1828, as in 1824, more was made of personalities than of issues. The campaign itself was unbelievably dirty. No charge seemed too base. Jackson was portrayed as a frontier ruffian, a gambler, the son of "a COMMON PROSTITUTE [who] ... married a MULATTO MAN." A "coffin hand-bill" charged the general with the cold-blooded murder of six militiamen during the Creek Campaign of 1814. A rhymester wrote:

All six militia men were shot;
And O! it seems to me
A dreadful deed—a bloody act
of needless cruelty.

Indignant Jacksonians replied that the six were deserters who had been executed after a proper court-martial.

Jackson's wife, Rachel, was not spared. The two had met while Rachel was separated from her first husband. In 1791, believing that her husband had obtained a divorce, she had married Jackson. Not until some time later did the couple learn that the divorce had not become final. The earlier marriage was formally dissolved in September 1793, after which Rachel and Andrew recited their wedding vows a second time. Rumors of this technical adultery circulated for years. During the campaign a Cincinnati newspaper published the story. "Ought a convicted ad-ultress and her paramour husband to be placed in the highest offices of this free and christian land?" fumed the editor. A pro-Jackson paper in the same city called the assertion a "BASE, WANTON AND MALIGNANT FALSEHOOD." But when his beloved Rachel, sick and shamed by the "wormwood and gall" of ugly publicity, died suddenly in December 1828, Jackson blamed his political opponents. "May God Almighty forgive her murderers," he cried at her funeral, "as I know she forgave them. I never can." And he never did.

Jacksonians countered with some mud-slinging of their own. It was said that President Adams, while minister to Russia, had procured an American girl for Czar Alexander I. Adams's wife was reported to have had premarital relations with her husband. Stories of the president's "aristocratic" receptions at the White House and his use of public funds to buy "gambling devices" (actually a chess set and a billiard table) circulated widely. The puritanical Adams was so offended by these stories that he refused to attend his successor's inauguration.

Jackson's victory in November 1828 was a triumph both for the Old Hero and for the Democrats' fresh style of political appeal. Over three times as many voters turned out as in 1824. The general received fifty-six percent of the popular vote, a margin unequaled in any other presidential election during the nineteenth century. Jackson the southwestener, to all appearances a reflection of the democratic way of the West and a spokesman for inland interests however ill-defined, swept the South and West. Adams carried his native New England along with Delaware and New Jersey, and shared with his rival New York and Maryland, which had not instituted the system of awarding the state's entire electoral vote to the popular winner. Exuberant Jacksonians hailed the election results as a revolution, a triumph of "democracy" over "aristocracy." The following January, after burying his wife, a broken-hearted Andrew Jackson set out for Washington.

The "Rise" of the Common Man?

For years history books uncritically accepted the idea that popular democracy arrived with Jackson's election. They pictured him as the champion of frontier democracy, battling the forces of privilege and corruption. During his presidency the common man won the right to vote and took politics out of the hands of the elite. Socially and economically, too, the

Jacksonian Era brought greater equality. With Jackson's election, according to one historian, "a new day dawned in American history. The democratic philosophy of Thomas Jefferson became a reality."

Recent studies have substantially modified this view. Historians now realize that the political power of the common man had been increasing for decades. Even in colonial times, the franchise had been quite open in some places. The Revolutionary ideology and the fierce political contests of the Jeffersonian Era opened still wider the door to popular participation in politics. The new western states adopted constitutions that gave the vote to all adult white males and made most public offices elective. Many of the older states, concerned about the loss of population to the West, followed their example. By Jackson's time only two states, Delaware and South Carolina, still left to their legislatures the selection of presidential electors. The Jacksonians shrewdly developed techniques to win this broader electorate. But the most notable political innovation of the Jackson period, the national convention, a democratic way of capturing popular sentiment throughout the nation, was invented not by Democrats but by the Anti-Masonic Party. The Anti-Masons were a short-lived party opposing the fraternal order of Freemasonry, which had aroused suspicion with its secrets and its tight loyalties.

| **How Much Democracy?**   Although foreigners like Alexis de Tocqueville considered Jacksonian America remarkably egalitarian, recent historians have painted a less glowing picture. Two million blacks were held as slaves. For most women, free blacks, Irish-Catholic immigrants, and many others, social and economic equality did not exist. Such important economic developments as the rise of the factory system and the transportation revolution were not affected much by Jackson's presidency. The most careful studies of social mobility indicate an increasingly less egalitarian society, with urban elites growing in wealth while industrialism and mass immigration created new lower classes.

And yet people at the time believed that Jackson's eminence was linked to the "rise of the common man." Millions of Americans—for diverse and often conflicting reasons—could readily identify with him. It was a "Go Ahead" era, remarked one observer; "the whole continent presents a scene of *scrambling* and roars with greedy hurry." And some saw in Jackson the egalitarian spirit of the nation; he was a child of the frontier, self-made, independent, and democratic. They gloried in his success and hoped to imitate it. Others, looking back romantically to what they thought of as a simpler agrarian society, perceived Jackson as a simple and noble embodiment of that earlier time. As a big loser in the Panic of 1819, he appealed to hard-pressed debtors in the West and South. His opposition to the older entrenched banking system got him support from businessmen who wanted banks that would extend credit more freely.

| **"Andy" Jackson**   Jackson had been born in 1767 in the Waxhaws, a wooded frontier area on the border between North and South Carolina. He had lost both brothers and his widowed mother during the Revolution, in which young Andrew served briefly as a horseman. For a time he seemed destined to be "the most roaring, rollicking, game-cocking, horse-racing, card-playing, mischievous fellow" in the neighborhood until, fired with ambition, he began reading law. In 1788, after completing his studies, he moved to Tennessee to take a position of public prosecutor.

This developing country was the ideal place for an eager young attorney. Jackson speculated avidly in land, slaves, and horses. As a public prosecutor, he usually sided with the creditors, executing numerous writs against debtors. In 1796 he was elected to Congress from Tennessee. Albert Gallatin would remember him as "a tall, lanky, uncouth-looking personage . . . [hair] down his back tied with an eel skin. . . . manners of a rough backwoodsman." After three years in Washington he returned to Tennessee, where he served as a superior court judge, once again siding with the land barons. Near Nashville he acquired a fine plantation, the "Hermitage," and many slaves. Although success had polished his rough edges, Jackson never lost his "roaring, rollicking" character; he was wounded three times in duels.

Jackson in his early years, in 1804, repeatedly published an exceeding cruel advertisement for the return of a runaway slave:

FIFTY DOLLARS REWARD
Eloped from the subscriber, living near Nashville, on the 25th of June last, a Mulatto Man Slave, about thirty years old, six feet and an inch high,

The Verdict of the People, by George Caleb Bingham. Americans of the 1830s widely linked Andrew Jackson with the rise of the common man, though both the number of voters and the number of elective offices had been increasing for decades. *(Courtesy, Collection of the Boatmen's National Bank of St. Louis)*

stout made and active, talks sensible, stops in his walk, and have a remarkable large foot. . . . The above reward will be given any person that will take him, and deliver him to me, or secure him to jail, so that I can get him. If taken out of the state, the above reward, and all reasonable expenses paid—and ten dollars extra, for every hundred lashes any person will give him, to the amount of three hundred.

ANDREW JACKSON
Near Nashville
State of Tennessee

During the War of 1812 Jackson, already an experienced Indian fighter, led a victorious campaign against the Creeks in Alabama. When the theater of war shifted South in 1814, the desperate politicians at Washington called Jackson to save New Orleans. His famous victory over "the conquerors of Europe" electrified the country. He was the nation's savior, its greatest hero since George Washington. His rough handling of the Florida Indians and their British allies in 1818 was wildly popular on the frontier.

Jackson lost heavily in the Panic of 1819. In its wake a group of his wealthy friends, alarmed by the growing demand for debtor relief in Tennessee, decided to use Jackson's immense popularity to protect their assets. They began touting him as the "people's candidate" for President—this man who had recently brought suit against 129 people who owed him money. His candidacy caught fire. For what people believed about Jackson was more important than the facts. And no one understood this better than Jackson as he campaigned for the presidency in 1828.

Though Jackson was a large landowner and by some standards an aristocrat, he did have perhaps more democratic sentiments than any previous President. He had a westerner's inherent distrust of entrenched status and dictatorial government. In his youth he had been of fairly moderate means and could continue to think of himself as a man of the people. And so if Jackson did not come to the presidency with any clearly articulated set of democratic policies, he did have styles and tastes that accorded with popular policies other politicians devised.

| **The Spoils System** | Arriving in Washington, Jackson found the government offices filled with bu- |

reaucrats, many of them supporters of the men who had slandered his beloved Rachel. As an astute politician, Jackson recognized the value of rewarding his partisans with government jobs. He agreed with his New York lieutenant, William Marcy, that "to the victors belong the spoils." And Jackson firmly believed that no one had "any more intrinsic right to official station than another." Men who held office too long were "apt to acquire a habit of looking with indifference upon the public interests, and of tolerating conduct from which an unpracticed man would revolt." In his first annual message, Jackson therefore recommended that appointments be limited to four years. Congress balked, but Jackson "rotated" officeholders anyway, insisting: "The duties of all public officers are, or at least admit of being made, so plain and simple that men of intelligence may readily qualify themselves for their performance." In eight years Jackson replaced about twenty percent of the government's employees, sometimes with due cause. Jefferson had removed roughly the same proportion. But it was the Jacksonians, with their spirited defense of the common man, who fixed firmly upon American politics the spoils system and rotation in office.

Van Buren vs. Calhoun

The coalition that elected Andrew Jackson in 1828 was too broad and diverse to be stable. Immediately after the election a struggle broke out between two of its major figures, Martin Van Buren and John C. Calhoun. The clash between these two intensely ambitious men was inevitable.

Usually dressed in black, Calhoun with his great eyes glowing looked as though his face were consumed by inner fires. Having already suffered one setback in his quest for the White House, Calhoun accepted another vice-presidential term in 1828, with the firm expectation of succeeding Jackson in the presidency.

Calhoun met his equal in Martin Van Buren. This shrewd New Yorker was one of the nation's first professional politicians. Starting as a lawyer in his hometown of Kinderhook, Van Buren had climbed the political ladder rung by rung: county surrogate, state senator, state attorney general, United States senator. He fashioned a powerful political machine in New York, known as the "Albany Regency," which dispensed patronage, subsidized friendly newspapers, ran campaigns, and set the party line. Van Buren usually worked behind the scenes, trying to mold a consensus toward his own ends.

Whenever possible, he avoided controversial commitments. He had managed "to be on circuit" in 1820 when a meeting was called at Albany to endorse the prohibition of slavery in Missouri; he was accompanying "a friend on a visit to the Congressional Cemetery" during a key vote on the tariff in 1827. Enemies considered Van Buren devious, opportunistic, hypocritical; admirers nicknamed him the "Red Fox" and the "Little Magician."

In 1824 Van Buren led William H. Crawford's unsuccessful presidential campaign. Having been burned once, he determined to choose a winner in 1828. He helped to bring the Old Republicans into the Jackson camp and worked tirelessly for the general's election. To assure New York's pivotal vote, Van Buren resigned his Senate seat to run for governor, thus adding his popular name to the Jackson ticket.

Jackson rewarded Van Buren's efforts by making him secretary of state. Otherwise, the new Cabinet was undistinguished. Jackson had no intention of calling on it for advice or of allowing powerful figures like Calhoun to undermine his own power. Instead, he relied on an informal circle of political cronies, who came to be called the "Kitchen Cabinet." Be-

Martin Van Buren of New York was one of the country's first professional politicians. His loyalty to the President won him the chance to succeed Jackson in that office. *(Scribner's Archives)*

sides old Tennessee friends like Major William B. Lewis, who actually roomed at the White House, this group included several newspaper editors and, before long, Van Buren, who took up horsemanship in order to accompany the President on his morning rides.

| **The Peggy Eaton Affair** | Calhoun fretted over these signs of Van Buren's grow-

ing influence. The vice-president had hoped to control the Cabinet appointments, and especially to make a South Carolinian secretary of war. But Jackson appointed to that position another old Tennessee friend, John H. Eaton. Calhoun was humiliated, and to reassert his power, he set out to force Eaton from the Cabinet. An opportunity soon appeared. The secretary of war had recently married the notorious Peggy O'Neale Timberlake, a Washington tavern-keeper's daughter with a dubious reputation. Eaton had lived with her while she was married to John Timberlake, a navy officer, and it was said that he even used his influence to have Timberlake sent to sea. After

Timberlake's death, Eaton married Peggy with Jackson's blessing. Washington society hummed with scandal. An English diplomat described one of Mrs. Eaton's antagonists in the "Ladies' War" as having "worn the enamel off of her teeth by the slander of her tongue." The other Cabinet wives, led by the aristocratic Mrs. Calhoun, refused to receive Peggy socially. All Washington was soon afflicted by this "Eaton malaria," a drawing-room disease.

The President, recalling the slander heaped on his own wife, was sympathetic to the Eatons. "I tell you," roared the Old General, "I had rather have live vermin on my back than the tongue of one of these Washington women on my reputation." Jackson had a tendency to personalize issues, to make them death struggles with a hated foe. Calhoun, he announced, was trying "to weaken me . . . and open the way to his preferment

John C. Calhoun. As vice-president, Calhoun worked against Jackson, especially during the controversy over a state's right to nullify a federal law that infringed on its sovereignty. *(In the Collection of the Corcoran Galley of Art)*

on my ruin." He summoned a special Cabinet meeting to examine the evidence, then pronounced Peggy "chaste as a virgin," and demanded that she be treated with respect. When most of the Cabinet refused, further meetings were suspended. Only Van Buren, long a widower, accepted Mrs. Eaton as a respectable lady.

This petty struggle dragged on into 1831. Finally, to break the deadlock, Van Buren and Eaton offered their resignations. This calculated gesture gave Jackson a chance to reorganize his Cabinet. He asked the other secretaries to resign and replaced them with loyal followers. As a reward, Jackson nominated the faithful Van Buren to be minister to England. In December, when Congress reconvened, Calhoun plotted revenge. A tie vote in the Senate allowed him, as vice-president, to cast the deciding vote, and he gleefully spiked Van Buren's nomination. "It will

kill him dead, sir, kill him dead," Calhoun gloated. "He will never kick, sir, never kick." But others agreed with Missouri Senator Thomas Hart Benton, who replied, "You have broken a minister, and elected a vice-president."

Benton was right. The breach between Jackson and Calhoun widened steadily. The President had suspected for some time that it was Calhoun who had urged Monroe's Cabinet in 1818 to censure Jackson's Florida raid. During the Peggy Eaton controversy Calhoun's old enemy, William H. Crawford, provided proof. Hastily, the vice-president published a pamphlet defending his stand and disclosing the feuds within the Administration. When Jackson saw it, his well-known temper flared. "They have cut their own throats," he said of Calhoun and his allies. Van Buren's triumph was complete. He would be Jackson's successor.

Jackson and States' Rights

For years Van Buren had worked to build a political alliance between North and South, stressing principles of laissez-faire and states' rights. He sought particularly to avoid conflicts over the slavery issue, fearing the rise of an antislavery party in the North, and to find a compromise on the tariff, since Pennsylvania Democrats desired a protective tariff—a tariff high enough that it would protect American manufactured goods by pushing the price of imported goods beyond the level at which they could compete—while southern party voters demanded free trade. (Conscience, or some change in his politics, would later turn Van Buren to the antislavery cause he had once avoided. In 1848 he was the presidential candidate of the Free Soil Party, which urged the banning of slavery from the western territories.) Calhoun who also advocated states' rights and limited government, had as much taste for confrontation as did Van Buren for compromise. He wanted to face down the North with southern demands on slavery and the tariff. The South Carolinian, increasingly the champion of southern rights, believed that only a party dominated by southerners could protect the South. During Jackson's first term, he and his followers worked in Congress to create an alliance between South and West based on a

program of cheap land for the West and a tariff kept low in the interest of the South. The political maneuvering soon provoked a great national debate on the nature of the federal Union.

| Public Lands   Late in 1829 Senator Samuel A. Foote of Connecticut proposed a resolution of inquiry into limiting the sale of public lands. Senator Benton of Missouri promptly denounced Foote's resolution as a plot by eastern manufacturers to prevent their workers from migrating to the West. Robert Y. Hayne, a debonair young senator from South Carolina, supported Benton and spoke vigorously in favor of a cheap land policy. Continued large revenues from land sales, he warned, would be used to create a powerful and tyrannical government; they would be "a fund for corruption—fatal to the sovereignty and independence of the states. . . ."

| Webster vs.   Daniel Webster of Massa-
| Hayne   chusetts rose to answer
                       both Benton and Hayne.
The New Englander was one of the great orators and constitutional lawyers of the day. Deliberately goading Hayne, Webster

claimed that the South Carolinian's appeals to state sovereignty were equivalent to preaching disunion. In January 1830 Hayne, with Calhoun's coaching, rose to the challenge. He vigorously defended the right of a state to nullify a federal law that violated "the sovereignty and independence of the states." New Englanders, he reminded Webster pointedly, had been "not unwilling to adopt" this same doctrine at Hartford in 1814, "when they believed themselves to be the victims of unconstitutional legislation."

The next day, before a packed gallery, Webster answered Hayne. The people, Webster contended, and not the states, had formed the Constitution. They, and not the individual states, were sovereign. If each of the states could defy the laws of Congress at will, the Union would be a mere "rope of sand." The Union was "a copious fountain of national, social, and personal happiness," and the individual states and sections should subordinate their selfish interests to the common good. Webster closed with a moving appeal, later memorized by successive generations of school children: "Liberty *and* Union, now and forever, one and inseparable!"

| **Jackson vs. Calhoun**

Webster had voiced the feelings of a generation of Americans who believed that "while the Union lasts we have high, exciting, gratifying prospects spread out before us—for us and our children." Did Andrew Jackson share this vision? The President's answer came a few weeks later, at a Jefferson Day dinner. The exponents of nullification planned to use the celebration to advertise their views. Jackson, forewarned of their intentions, had prepared his toast in advance. When his turn came the President, glaring at Calhoun, raised his glass and declared: "Our Federal Union—it must be preserved." The boisterous crowd stood in deathly silence. The diminutive Van Buren had climbed onto a chair so as not to miss a moment of his triumph. Calhoun, his hand trembling so "that a little of the amber fluid trickled down the side" of his glass, replied: "The Union—next to our liberties the most dear." But there was no mistaking the President's words; despite his sympathy for states' rights, he would not countenance nullification. Calhoun was further discredited. Most southerners and westerners scurried back to the banner of Jackson and Van Buren.

Jackson tried to balance the powers of the federal government and the rights of the states. In 1830, anxious to reassure the strict constructionists in the party, he vetoed a bill providing federal aid for the construction of a turnpike from Maysville to Lexington, Kentucky. This road lay entirely within a single state, and Jackson doubted the constitutionality of federally funding projects of a "purely local character." But well-publicized vetoes like this were the exception; at other times Jackson approved substantial amounts of federal aid for building roads and canals. During his presidency, appropriations for this purpose averaged over $1.3 million annually, nearly double that under Adams.

The Nullification Crisis

| **South Carolina**

South Carolina had once been rich. The mucky swamps of its low country were ideally suited for growing rice. After the invention of Whitney's gin, the Carolina upcountry became a major cultivator of cotton and for a time the little state produced half the nation's crop. Flushed with prosperity, South Carolinians shared fully in the nationalistic fervor of the early republic. Native sons like Pinckney, Calhoun, and Cheves served ably in the nation's councils.

Abruptly in 1819, the state's economic fortunes slid into decline. Falling world prices for cotton, coupled with increased competition from the newer states to the Southwest that could produce it more cheaply, wrecked the South Carolina cotton planters' economy. Their worn-out soils could not stand against those in the fertile Black Belt of Alabama and Mississippi. Facing ruin, South Carolinians migrated westward by the thousands.

| **The Tariff**

Those who remained increasingly fixed their frustration and anger on the protective tariff. Only the necessities of national defense had prompted men like Calhoun to accept the tariff of 1816. When Congress began raising duties to protective levels, they objected an-

The Nullification Crisis threatened to tear the Union apart. This 1833 cartoon supporting Jackson portrays the South Carolina resolution as leading to civil war and despotism. *(Courtesy, The New York Public Library, Astor, Lenox and Tilden Foundations)*

grily. Resentful at being deprived of the cheaper prices that foreign manufactured goods would have carried without the tariffs, South Carolinians also warned that foreign governments might retaliate by imposing high tariffs on American exports, such as cotton. In 1830 Congressman George McDuffie of South Carolina charged that higher prices ultimately cost the southern planter the equivalent of forty out of every one hundred bales of cotton produced. Although McDuffie and others exaggerated the tariff's pernicious effect on their economy, there is no question but that protective duties did contribute to hard times in South Carolina.

In 1824 representatives from the manufacturing, grain, and wool states pushed through a bill increasing duties on a wide variety of items. Flushed with victory, protectionists held a grand convention at Harrisburg, Pennsylvania, to map out a campaign for still higher duties. In the 1828 session of Congress northern protectionists resorted to a trading of votes and programs that goes by the term logrolling. They persuaded members representing Missouri lead miners, Kentucky hemp raisers, Vermont wool growers, and Louisiana sugar planters to support higher rates on manufactured articles in exchange for protective duties on their own constituents' products. To save themselves, southerners hit upon a scheme that would make the tariff obnoxious to New England manufacturers by increasing the price the New Englanders would have to pay for raw materials. Southerners in Congress would vote with northern producers to raise the duties on raw materials like wool, flax, and molasses, expecting manufacturing interests to vote with the South against the whole bill. This stratagem was a bit too clever. New England manufacturers were prepared to submit to the inconvenience of high tariffs on raw materials in exchange for the benefits of adequate protection for their finished goods. Their legislators accepted the whole bill, saddling the South with the highest tariff rates between the Revolution and the Civil War.

Angry southerners damned this "Tariff of Abominations" and threatened to boycott goods from the tariff states. Some began dressing in clothes of homespun, scorning northern broadcloth. Immediately after the tariff bill passed, the South Carolina delegation in Congress met at the home of Senator Robert Y. Hayne to plot resistance. In the fall of 1828 Vice President John C. Calhoun, bending to the changing opinion in his native state, set to work writing his famous *Exposition and Protest* developing the doctrine of nullification, which held that a state could prevent the exercise of a federal law within its borders.

By now Calhoun was revealing himself to be a relentlessly combative political philosopher, singleminded in his commitment to the doctrine of state sovereignty. The British traveler Harriet Martineau would describe the gaunt South Carolinian as

the cast-iron man, who looks as if he had never been born and never could be extinguished. . . . His mind has long since lost all power of communicating with any other. I know of no man who lives in such utter intellectual solitude. He meets men, and harangues them by the fireside as in the Senate; he is wrought like a piece of machinery.

Must South Carolina submit to the federal government? No, Calhoun insisted, and here, rather than on the tariff issue itself, his argument had its most ominous implications.

Prior to the formation of the Constitution, Calhoun observed, the states had been independent and sovereign. They had created the federal government and endowed it with strictly limited powers. A state therefore had the "right" to "interpose" its original sovereignty against the "despotism of the many," the sheer weight of a national majority. Thus a state could call a state convention and nullify any act of Congress that exceeded the authority granted by the Constitution.

Under the Constitution, Calhoun argued, Congress might tax for purposes of raising revenue, but not to protect domestic industry against foreign competition. The Tariff of 1828 was therefore "unconstitutional, unequal, and oppressive." It made southerners "the serfs of the system—out of whose labor is raised, not only the money paid into the Treasury, but the funds out of which are drawn the rich rewards of the manufacturer and his associates in interest."

| Racial Fears In 1828 Calhoun's remedy seemed too drastic for the many Carolinians who still turned hopefully to Jackson. In the meantime, the nullifiers worked to strengthen their cause. They were aided by a deepening of racial fear in South Carolina, a state where in some areas black slaves outnumbered whites by a ratio of eight to one. Denmark Vesey's revolt in their own state in 1822 and Nat Turner's rebellion of 1831 in Virginia left white South Carolinians fearful for their property and their very lives. They blamed these unsettling events on the small but noisy antislavery movement. The bitter Missouri Controversy had awakened slaveholders everywhere to the potential threat that the federal government posed to their peculiar institution. And so even those whites who had not suffered by the fall in cotton prices embraced the doctrine of nullification as offering a constitutional protection against the growing abolitionist movement.

By 1832 nullifiers like George McDuffie were spoiling for a fight. "South Carolina," he told Congress in a typical speech:

is oppressed (a thump). A tyrant majority sucks her life blood from her (a dreadful thump). Yes sir (a pause), yes, sir, a tyrant (a thump) majority unappeasable (horrid scream), has persecuted and persecutes us (a stamp on the floor). We appeal to them (low and quick), but we appeal in vain (loud and quick). We turn to our brethren of the North (low, with a shaking of the head), and pray them to protect us (a thump), but we t-u-r-n in v-a-i-n (prolonged, and a thump). They heap coals of fire on our heads (with immense rapidity)—they give us burden on burden; they tax us more and more (very rapid, slam-bang, slam—a hideous noise). We turn to our brethren of the South (slow with a solemn, thoughtful air). We work with them; we fight with them; we vote with them; we petition with them (common voice and manner); but the tyrant majority has no ears, no eyes, no form (quick), deaf (long pause), sightless (pause), inexorable (slow, slow). Despairing (a thump), we resort to the rights (a pause) which God (a pause) and nature [have] given us (thump, thump, thump). . . .

The Ordinance of Nullification

By 1832 Jackson and his party, faced with an impending election, were determined to reform the "Tariff of Abominations." John Quincy Adams, newly elected to the House of Representatives and already the chair of the Committee on Manufacturing, would help. Adams realized that the tariff was a sectional rather than a party issue and accepted the political necessity of moderating the rates. So he cooperated with the administration in framing a bill which essentially repealed the increases of 1828 and restored the rates of the Tariff of 1824. Jackson happily signed a bill that provided a real measure of protection to northern manufacturers and also met the legitimate complaints of the South, or so he thought. John C. Calhoun did not agree. He had resigned as vice president to lead the anti-protection battle in the Senate and was determined to press the issue even after the Tariff of 1832 was passed.

In October, after a hard-fought contest, the nullification party elected an overwhelming majority to the South Carolina legislature. The governor immediately called the legislature into session, whereupon it authorized a state convention and a special election of delegates. On November 19, 1832, 136 nullifiers and 26 unionists met at Columbia, the state capital. The convention passed an Ordinance of Nullification declaring the Tariffs of 1828 and 1832 unconstitutional, and null and void in South Carolina. The collection of duties by the federal government after February 1, 1833, was forbidden, unless Congress lowered the tariff to twelve percent. Any attempt by Washington to coerce the state, warned the Ordinance, would be "inconsistent with the longer continuance of South Carolina in the Union." The legislature, at its regular session in December, took steps to implement the Ordinance and appropriated money to buy arms and raise an army.

The nullifiers soon discovered that they had penned themselves in. At home, a determined band of unionists prepared to resist their fellow Carolinians by force: both sides were soon drilling volunteers in cities and towns across the state. Neighboring slave states sympathized with South Carolina, but condemned her "reckless precipitancy." President Jackson appeared determined to uphold national authority. He reinforced federal installations in Charleston harbor and ordered General Winfield Scott to take charge of military preparations. His famous Nullification Proclamation of December 10, 1832, squarely repudiated nullification. American nationhood, Jackson asserted, had existed before the states; the federal Constitution only made more workable a preexisting Union. Under these circumstances, "to say that any state may at pleasure secede from the Union is to say that the United States is not a nation." The power of nullification was "*incompatible with the existence of the Union, contradicted expressly by the letter of the Constitution, unauthorized by its spirit, inconsistent with every principle on which it was founded, and destructive of the great object for which it was formed*." Disunion by armed force, Jackson concluded, was "*treason,*" in the face of which he, as President, could not "avoid the performance of his duty." On a trip to New York City, greeted enthusiastically by a corps of state militia, Jackson announced "*Nullification will never take root* HERE."

| **The Compromise Tariff of 1833** | At the same time that he brandished the stick, Jackson held out a carrot to the nullifiers. |

He urged Congress to lower the tariff, limiting protection to articles essential to the nation's defense. In order to avoid a premature clash of arms, he removed federal troops from the Charleston Citadel to the forts in the harbor. Yet he also secured a Force Bill from Congress early in 1833, authorizing the collection of import duties from ships offshore and reaffirming his power to call up the state militias and to use the army and navy. Old Hickory had completely outmaneuvered the Carolina radicals. As the "Fatal First" approached, they prudently decided to delay enforcing nullification until Congress completed its deliberations on the tariff. Early in March 1833, Congress passed the Compromise Tariff, which provided that rates on protected articles would be lowered in gradual stages to twenty percent in mid-1842. Even though the new rates were nearly double what the nullification ordinance had demanded, South Carolinians accepted the compromise figure

with relief. The convention promptly rescinded the Ordinance of Nullification; then, as a symbolic gesture, it declared the "Force Bill" null and void.

South Carolina had lost. The passage of the Compromise Tariff was a signal triumph for nationalism and majority rule. Nullification as a principle had been thoroughly discredited. In the process, South Carolinians had learned an unforgettable lesson: successful resistance to northern "tyranny" demanded the cooperation of the other slave states.

Georgia and Indian Removal

The Indian Removal Act   In one instance, Jackson actually encouraged a state to defy federal authority. He speeded the removal of Indians from lands under settlement by whites by encour-

aging Georgia to ignore a Supreme Court decision favorable to Indian rights.

Since Jefferson's time the government had been forcing the Indian tribes to sell their lands and migrate westward. In 1830 the

The Trail of Tears, by Robert Lindneux. Jackson disregarded the Supreme Court ruling that the Cherokees of Georgia had a right to their land. Many perished when they moved west on "the trail of tears." *(Courtesy, Woolaroc Museum)*

President urged Congress to set apart "an ample district west of the Mississippi" for their permanent use. Here the "aborigines" might learn "the arts of civilization" and form "an interesting commonwealth, destined to perpetuate the race and to attest the humanity and justice of this government." Senators like Theodore Frelinghuysen of New Jersey courageously defended the Indians' right of "immemorial possession, as the original tenants of the soil," but the Indian Removal Act passed anyway. In the following years many Indian nations, recognizing the futility of resistance, signed over their lands and moved west, some of them prodded by the United States Army.

Although disunited and demoralized by defeat, some Indians did not peacefully acquiesce in the march westward. In Illinois portions of the Sac and Fox tribes, led by Chief Black Hawk, refused to leave their rich ancestral lands. Black Hawk initially hoped that, if his people remained peaceful, they would be permitted to keep their farming communities and live alongside the incoming whites. But hunger and incessant military pressure finally forced Black Hawk into war. It was a one-sided fight. In the final battle of the Black Hawk War, the Bad Axe Massacre of 1832, United States troops and militiamen killed all but 150 of the original thousand Indian men, women, and children. In the South, the Seminole War that lasted from 1835 to 1838 was even bloodier. Many Seminole tribesmen, led by Chief Osceola, refused to leave Florida. Accompanied by runaway blacks, they retreated into the swamps. Jackson sent troops, but the Indians conducted a skillful guerrilla war in the impenetrable Everglades. It took several years and $14 million to subdue Osceola's warriors.

Americans had traditionally argued that the white man's "superior" civilization justified dispossessing the wandering "savages" of their ancestral lands. Andrew Jackson's attitude toward Indians had long been contemptible. As a major in the Battle of Horseshoe Bend in 1814, he had participated in a needless slaughter of Creek Indians seeking to escape by swimming a river. In 1817 he had written to President Monroe that "I have long viewed treaties with the Indians an absurdity not to be reconciled to the principles of our government." In the case of the Cherokees, Choctaws, and Chickasaws, even the shabbiest of rationalization collapsed. They

were all settled peoples, skilled in the ways of agriculture. In spite of this, the government bribed, intimidated, and lied to force the Choctaws and Chickasaws of Mississippi and Alabama to move to the Indian Country (the present state of Oklahoma). Even these tactics failed to move the Cherokees of Georgia. They adopted a written constitution and declared themselves an independent nation. In response the Georgia legislature, ignoring federal treaties recognizing Cherokee nationhood, extended state jurisdiction over them and prepared to seize their lands. One spokesman argued in the Indians' behalf:

> Do the obligations of justice change with the color of the skin? As the tide of our population has rolled on, we have added purchase to purchase [of Indian lands]. The confiding Indian listened to our professions of friendship: we called him brother, and he believed us. Millions after millions he has yielded to our importunity, until we have acquired more than can be cultivated in centuries—and yet we crave more. We have crowded the tribes upon a few miserable acres on our southern frontier; it is all that is left to them of their once boundless forests: and still, like the horse-leech, our cupidity cries, 'give! give!'

Hiring William Wirt, the former federal attorney general, to represent them, the Cherokees appealed to the Supreme Court for an injunction restraining Georgia from carrying out this seizure. Chief Justice Marshall, in an 1831 decision, *Cherokee Nation v. Georgia*, ruled that the Cherokees were a "domestic dependent nation" possessing unquestioned right to their lands. A year later, in *Worcester v. Georgia*, the Court held that the Cherokee nation was a distinct political community, within which "the laws of Georgia can have no force." The United States, the Court's decision implied, was duty-bound to keep intruders from the Indian lands.

"The Trial of Tears" Both Jackson and Georgia ignored the Court's ruling as well as the opposition of such powerful senators as Henry Clay and Daniel Webster and such congressman as the frontiersman Davy Crockett of the President's native Tennessee. Informed of the *Worcester* opinion, Jackson reputedly said: "John Marshall has made his decision, now let him enforce it." Georgia continued to harass the Cherokees, declaring their tribe "extinguished." In 1835 a corrupt faction was bribed into signing a treaty, and General Winfield Scott began the Indians' systematic removal. Scott threatened:

> The full moon of May is already on the wane, and before another has passed away, every Cherokee man, woman, and child must be in motion to join their brethren in the far west. . . . My troops already occupy many positions in the country that you are to abandon; thousands and thousands are approaching from every quarter, to render resistance and escape alike hopeless. Will you, then, by resistance, compel us to resort to arms? God forbid! Or will you, by flight, seek to hide yourselves in mountains and forests, and thus oblige us to hunt you down? I am an old warrior, and have been present at many a scene of slaughter; but spare me, I beseech you, the horror of witnessing the destruction of the Cherokees.

The general built some two dozen log stockades around the tribe's home. In May 1838 some 7000 soldiers captured nearly 15,000 Cherokees and imprisoned them in the camps, where several hundred died. On October 1 thirteen separate groups began an 800-mile migration, chiefly on foot and without shelter. Heavy rain and cold weather decimated the tribe: at least 3000 Indians died of exposure and disease. One tribesman remembered of "The Trail of Tears":

> One each day, and all are gone. Looks like maybe all be dead before we get to new Indian country, but always we keep marching on. Women cry and make sad wails. Children cry, and many men cry, and all look sad when friends die, but they say nothing and just put heads down and keep on go toward west. . . . She [his mother] speak no more; we bury her and go on.

The Choctaws had been forced out of Mississippi in the dead of winter, "thinly clad and without moccasins." In 1838 the government forcibly removed the Pottawattomies from Indiana. They began the trek west "under a blazing noonday sun, amidst clouds of dust, marching in a line, surrounded by soldiers who were hurrying their steps. Next came the baggage wagons, in which numerous invalids, children, and women, too weak to walk, were crammed." Dozens died along this "Trail of Death." The resettlement of these farming Indians west of the Mississippi River created bitter resentment among the Plains tribes who hunted there. The government was soon forced to send troops to the West to separate the warring tribes.

The Second Bank of the United States

Andrew Jackson brought with him to the White House a westerner's instinctive dislike of monopolies and entrenched privilege, and a vague distrust of banks and paper money. Beyond this, however, he had few ideas about economics; political needs shaped his tariff and internal improvement policies. But in his first message to Congress he sharply criticized the Bank of the United States for its failure to establish "a uniform and sound currency." He urged the lawmakers to consider carefully "the constitutionality and expediency" of renewing the Bank's charter at its expiration in 1836.

Nicholas Biddle After a shaky start the second Bank of the United States had prospered, especially under its third president, Nicholas Biddle. Born into a wealthy Philadelphia family, Biddle had displayed a precocious versatility from the start. After graduation from Princeton at the age of fifteen, he traveled widely, served in the diplomatic corps, and wrote the classic account of the Lewis and Clark expedition. Impressed with his knowledge of banking, President Monroe appointed him a director of the Bank; four years later, at the age of thirty-seven, he became its president. The choice was a good one. Biddle understood banking and the function of the Bank in the American economy at a time when few others did.

The Bank marketed government securities and performed other Treasury operations. Its loans stimulated business and facilitated the swift exchange of agricultural staples. And one of its most remarkable services was to make possible for the country a reliable paper currency.

During much of the nineteenth century the only money that the nation considered absolutely sound was specie—gold and silver coin. Americans used much paper money, but many thought paper to be money only if it could be taken to a bank and exchanged for its face value in coin. The National Bank was prepared to repay in specie the notes that it issued, and these therefore constituted a currency that was as sound as it was portable. At

Nicholas Biddle, president of the Second Bank of the United States. (*Courtesy*, The National Portrait Gallery)

the same time the Bank helped to keep the state banks from issuing reckless amounts of paper currency. This it did by periodically requiring them to redeem in specie their notes that it was holding.

Though his direct responsibility was to private stockholders, Biddle's chief concern prior to 1832 seemed always to be the welfare of the country as a whole. He liked to boast that the Bank was "the balance wheel of the banking system."

Biddle's very success proved his undoing. New York bankers chafed at the restraints imposed by a Philadelphia institution. Some people sincerely questioned the constitutionality or the wisdom of making an essentially private bank the depository of the public funds. Many still blamed the Bank for the

Panic of 1819. Advocates of cheap money, most of them state bankers and speculators, objected to the Bank because it restrained the state banks from issuing notes as freely as they wished. At the other extreme partisans of hard money, believing that specie was the only safe currency, condemned all note-issuing banks—the National Bank among them— as instruments of speculation. Advocates of hard money were now employing the populistic rhetoric, spiced with denunciations of privileged wealth, that more often in American history has been the rhetoric of champions of cheap or paper currency. Banknotes, wrote one critic, formed "the foundation of *artificial* inequality of wealth, and, thereby, of *artificial* inequality of power."

The source of Jackson's hostility to the Bank remains obscure. He did not act in response to popular demand or on behalf of state banks. In spite of his well-known suspicion of banks and paper money, Old Hickory had kept his own money in the Bank's Washington and Nashville branches for years. Most likely, his antagonism stemmed from jealousy toward the uncontrolled political power of the Bank and its identification with unfriendly eastern interests. He readily believed the reports that some of the branches had worked against his election in 1828, and reached the conclusion that the Bank was a "hydra of corruption—dangerous to our liberties by its corrupting influence everywhere." He must, he decided, strip the "Monster" of its malign power. Once engaged in the contest, Jackson quickly turned the dispute into another death struggle between himself and a loathed foe.

For a time Biddle tried to placate Jackson, but with no success. He then turned to the President's enemies for support. He extended generous loans to Clay, Webster, and other influential politicians and newspaper editors. In 1832 he reluctantly acquiesced in their plan to seek a recharter well in advance of the expiration date. It was an election year, and the Bank's friends reasoned that Jackson would hesitate before vetoing a recharter bill. If he did veto it, they would have a good issue in the presidential campaign.

The Bank War

The bill renewing the Bank's charter cleared Congress in July 1832, with nearly a third of the Democratic representatives voting in fa-

vor. Jackson was enraged. "The Bank," he told Martin Van Buren, "is trying to kill me, *but I will kill it!*" He was as "fixed in my

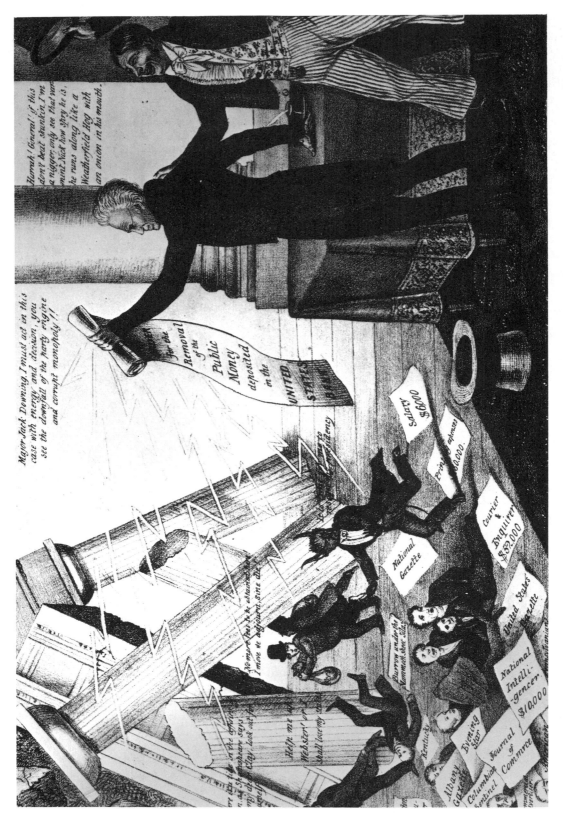

This cartoon supporting President Jackson's withdrawal of federal deposits from the Bank of the United States shows how successful he was in portraying the Bank and its supporters as tools of the rich.

course as firm as the Rocky Mountain.... Providence has a power over me, but frail mortals . . . can have none." He sent the bill back to Congress with a blistering veto message in which he denounced the Bank as "not only unnecessary, but dangerous to the government and country." It enjoyed a virtual "monopoly of foreign and domestic exchange"; it threatened the rights of the states and the liberties of the people; it discriminated against the West. Refusing to be guided by the opinion of the Supreme Court in the *McCulloch* case, Jackson declared the Bank unconstitutional: "The opinion of the judges has no more authority over Congress than the opinion of Congress has over the judges, and on that point the president is independent of both." One-fourth of the Bank's stock was held by foreigners, the veto message observed; the country needed a *"purely American"* institution. Jackson closed with an impassioned attack on the renewal bill as an attempt by "the rich and powerful" to "bend the acts of government to their selfish purposes" and pledged to resist "the advancement of the few at the expense of the many."

| **Jackson vs. the Bank** | The veto message was superb propaganda but poor economics. A developing country like the United States needed a stable currency to encourage foreign investment, not wildcat banking to drive it away. The Bank was not strictly a monopoly. In 1830 it made about one-fifth of the nation's bank loans and had barely one-third of the total bank deposits and specie reserves held by American banks. In his message Jackson completely ignored the important services the Bank provided and offered no effective substitute for them.

At first, Jackson's enemies rejoiced over the message. Biddle compared the President to "a chained panther biting the bars of his cage" and called the veto "a manifesto of anarchy." But in November 1832 Jackson, with Van Buren as his running mate, overwhelmed the National Republican candidate, Henry Clay, by a margin of five to one in the electoral college.

Jackson took his decisive victory as a mandate to destroy the Bank even before its charter expired. As soon as the nullification crisis passed, he set out to remove the government deposits from the bank and place them in selected state banks. By law, it was the secretary of the treasury who had to give the actual order for removing them. When he refused, Jackson "promoted" him to the State Department and named a new treasury secretary. This official, too, refused to do Jackson's bidding, citing the "irresponsible" policies of the state banks. The President then replaced him with Roger B. Taney, formerly the Attorney General. The faithful Taney continued drawing on the government's funds in the Bank to meet current expenses, but he began depositing the incoming receipts in certain state banks. These banks were supposedly chosen for their fiscal soundness, but political considerations were not overlooked. Prior to 1836 over seventy-five percent of the officers in these banks were Democrats. The administration's critics nicknamed them the "pet banks."

As the government's deposits dwindled, Biddle began calling in loans and curtailing the issuing of new notes. In the beginning this contraction was thoroughly justifiable, since the federal deposits had given the notes much of their reliability. But Biddle soon succumbed to opportunistic motives. He continued the contraction into the spring of 1834, in the hope of producing a short recession that would force a recharter of the Bank. "Nothing but the evidence of suffering," he reasoned, would "produce any effect in Congress." As interest rates climbed and credit dried up, the business community begged for relief. All over the country supporters of the Bank organized meetings and flooded Congress with petitions. A Cincinnati man tried a more direct approach: "Damn your—soul," he wrote Jackson, "remove them deposits back again, and recharter the bank or you will certainly be shot in less than two weeks and that by myself!!!"

Old Hickory refused to budge. Told of rumors that a mob threatened to "lay siege to the Capitol until the deposits were restored," he promised to hang the ringleaders "as high as Haman." When a delegation of businessmen visited him seeking relief, he replied coldly: "Go to the Monster, go to Biddle. . . . Biddle has all the money!" In the end Jackson had his way. Biddle was forced to let credit flow more freely, and the economy quickly recovered.

The chief result of the so-called "Biddle depression" was a marked decrease in the Bank's popularity. In 1836, when the old federal charter expired, the Bank received a new one from the state of Pennsylvania. In 1841, after a series of financial reverses, it closed its doors forever. Biddle died three years later, a broken man.

Jackson had destroyed the Bank in the name of sound money and "those habits of economy and simplicity which are so congenial to the character of republicans." But in so doing he removed the most effective restraint on "the stock-jobbers, brokers, and gamblers" he professed to despise. Aided by the government deposits, the "pets" flooded the country with paper banknotes. One traveler commented:

> The greatest annoyance I was subjected to in travelling was in exchanging money. It is impossible to describe the wretched state of the currency—which is all bills issued by private individuals; companies; cities and states; almost all of which are bankrupt; or what amounts to the same thing, they cannot redeem their issues. All the bills are at a discount, varying from ten percent to fifty percent; and such rags of bills, too! And these do not pass out of the state, or frequently, out of the city in which they are issued.... Some of these bills bear a promise to be received in payment of a ride on a railway; all sorts of notes—

An orgy of speculation and inflation followed. Belatedly, between 1834 and 1836, Jackson tried to drive paper money from circulation. He directed the deposit banks not to issue or receive notes worth less than $10. Land officers were instructed not to take small notes in payment for public lands. Jackson secured a law preventing deposit banks from issuing bills valued at under $20. Finally, in 1836, Jackson issued the Specie Circular, which prohibited the purchase of public lands in anything but coin. He acted too late. In 1837 bad money helped to plunge the country into its worst depression to date. Jackson had accused the Second Bank of being beyond federal control, but so were the state banks in which he had deposited federal revenues. One newspaper, reflecting a widespread view, complained that

> President Jackson's 'experiment' has stripped the businessmen of their means, till they can no longer employ their mechanics, while it has enabled the capitalists to . . . *grind the poor at the rate of* 24 PER CENT PER ANNUM.

Boom and Bust Again

On March 4, 1837, Andrew Jackson turned over the presidency to Martin Van Buren. As the Old Hero left the Capitol, the crowds cheered him lustily. For once, remarked Thomas Hart Benton, "the rising was eclipsed by the setting sun." In his inaugural message, Van Buren painted a glowing picture of a "great, happy, and flourishing" country. But even as he spoke, the dark clouds of depression were gathering once again.

Since the early 1820s the American economy had grown steadily. Demand for American agricultural products seemed insatiable: exports of cotton alone increased from 92 million pounds in 1818 to 300 million pounds in 1830. Moving these bulky products to market required the expenditure of immense sums on transportation projects of all kinds. Construction of turnpikes and bridges continued in most parts of the country, and steamboat building became an important industry. The success of the Erie Canal brought a time of canal building, even while more than three thousand miles of railroad were completed in the same period. And the construction boom went far beyond internal improvements: the rapid settlement of the West and the growth of urban areas created a great demand for new homes, barns, stores, and public buildings. Manufacturing industries, particularly cotton textiles, iron, and machinery, also grew rapidly.

The United States had long had a vigorous entrepreneurial tradition. Fathers in Boston during Jacksonian times guided sons on daily walks to the wharves, banks, and counting houses a few blocks from home. Eight-year-old Frank Appleton reported to his bank-president father that he had "laid out 1 cent for 8 marbles and one cent for 2 allies." As teenagers, William and Amos Lawrence kept strict accounts, heeding their parents' advice to record "*every cent* you receive, and *every cent you expend*." Western farms were now becoming more intent on making money by selling parts of their crops than on raising produce for their own consumption. And

Yankee Peddler, by John Whetton Ehninger. Economic activity was feverish in the 1830s, but an excess of speculation helped to bring about a depression by the end of the decade. *(Courtesy, Collection of the Newark Museum)*

westerners and southerners often opposed entrenched financial interests that prevented them from rising on the economic ladder.

But by the middle thirties healthy growth was giving way to feverish speculation. Investors, most of them British, bought enormous quantities of stock in state-owned canal companies and other public works of increasingly doubtful utility and profitability. With labor and materials in short supply, these new construction projects merely drove up wages and prices. Sales of public land—mainly to speculators—rose from only $2,300,000 in 1830 to almost $25,000,000 in 1836. With speculators snapping up everything in sight, urban land values also soared. A farm near Brooklyn that had gone begging at $20,000 in 1831 was sold in 1835 for $102,000. When Chicago was incorporated in 1833, optimists were already buying and selling lots twenty miles from Lake Michigan. All over the West and South, farmers and planters plunged heavily into debt for land and slaves, sometimes borrowing at rates as high as thirty percent.

The Jackson Administration's monetary policies contributed to this orgy of what contemporaries called "overbanking and overtrading." The demise of the Bank of the United States removed an important check on state banks and their number rose from 330 in 1830 to 788 in 1837. Many were purely speculative ventures, deliberately located "out where the wildcats howled" on the assumption that there they could avoid holders of their notes seeking redemption in specie.

Lax state laws permitted these "wildcat banks," as they were called, to issue banknotes without maintaining adequate specie reserves to back them up. The note circulation of state banks soared from $61 million in 1830 to $149 million in 1837. Jackson's war on the Bank, animated by his own distrust of paper money, had made possible a flood of paper. One speculator observed:

> Everyone was imbued with a reckless spirit of speculation. . . . The whole country seemed to be in motion; the most extravagant anticipations prevailed in regard to the settlement of the country, and the rapid growth of cities and towns.

The shifting of government deposits to the "pet" banks and the decision in 1836 to distribute the surplus federal revenue to the states pushed the inflation further. The series of hard-money policies that the Jackson Administration finally decided to take, culminating in the Specie Circular of 1836, came too late.

In 1837 the boom collapsed. The President's order requiring all payments for public lands in gold or silver led banks in the West to draw heavily on eastern banks for coin. In the midst of this specie drain a recession in Britain depressed cotton prices, and British investors called in their loans. On May 10 New York banks suspended specie payments and other banks followed. Prices fell and credit tightened: for speculators the only question, an observer wrote, "was as to the means of escape, and nearest and best route to Texas." Numerous commercial houses and banks failed. In 1838 the economy revived briefly, as states borrowed heavily for internal improvements, but the revival could not be maintained. Fewer and fewer improvements paid their way: the credit of the states was exhausted: the confidence of foreign investors had evaporated: most improvement projects were halted. It was "national pay day," a contemporary wrote. "The nation has been drawing on the future, and the future dishonors the draft."

| Depression   The depression that stretched from 1839 to 1843 was one of the severest in American history. Prices fell by as much as one-half in some places; real estate values and stocks declined even more drastically. The collapse of prices set off a tidal wave of bankruptcies. Under the federal Bankruptcy Act of 1841, some 28,000 debtors freed themselves of nearly a half-billion dollars of debt. Rural areas were hardest hit, but they at least were self-sustaining. In the cities unemployment brought widespread distress. Some wealthier Americans, as always, welcomed the distress of others. Mehitable Goddard of Massachusetts wrote thankfully to her sister that "wages are lower, and of course there is a corresponding improvement in the behavior of this class of people. . . . I do fear nothing but absolute want will compel them to do their duty."

Mobs in New York looted the flour stores in 1837 and similar violence flared elsewhere. Once again municipalities and charitable agencies set up soup kitchens and unemployment offices. Casting about for a more permanent solution to urban unemployment, Horace Greeley advised the unemployed to "go to the Great West, anything rather than remain here." Public land sales had plunged by 1842 to less than six percent of their 1836 peak. With land sales and tariff receipts declining, the federal government, which had been out of debt since 1835 (for the first and only time in its history), began running a new deficit. The states, which had contracted nearly $200 million of debts, were especially hard-pressed. By 1842 eight of them had defaulted, and three had even repudiated part of their debt, thereby ruining American credit with European investors for years to come.

One faction in the Democratic Party favored banks and paper money, wanting the federal government to maintain some active role in managing the economy. Radicals, on the other hand, clung resolutely to hard money and would have the government do little in the economy except discourage banks from issuing paper notes. The Little Magician decided to stick with Jackson's policies. He refused to repeal the Specie Circular. Calling Congress into special session, he blamed the depression on "excessive issues of bank paper" and "reckless speculation." Concerned about the growing strain on the federal Treasury, he asked Congress to authorize the borrowing of $10 million for current expenses. And he specifically recommended passage of a law permitting the federal government to keep its receipts in its own Treasury vaults, which would sever all connections with the nation's banks. Beyond this Van Buren refused to go. It was not the place of government, he insisted, to relieve economic distress. The framers of the Constitution had "wisely judged that the less government interfered with private pursuits the better for the general prosperity." Government assistance to one class would mean using "the property of some for the benefit of others," and it was better "to leave every citizen and every interest to reap under its benign protection the rewards of virtue, industry, and prudence." Many of the states made at least some effort to relieve hunger and unemployment. They could do so with none of the constitutional scruples that inhibited federal officials, for the states possessed power that the national government had not yet assumed for itself. It was later to do so under amendments to the Constitution and interpretations of that document.

In spite of protests against "leaving the people to shift for themselves," most of Van Buren's program became law in 1837. The President's opponents concentrated their fire on the Independent Treasury Bill. This proposal would require customs collectors, postmasters, and other government receivers of funds to hold their receipts until ordered to pay them out. It would also direct the secretary of the treasury to withdraw the government's deposits from the "pet" banks and to place them in special subtreasuries. Opponents charged that the bill would curtail loans and credit, thereby stifling recovery. Van Buren's supporters countered that it would keep the government independent and the currency safe and check unwise expansion of bank notes. A coalition blocked the scheme until 1840, when it finally passed Congress. But the Democratic Party was now the party of depression, and that is never a good omen for an American political regime.

The Democrats and the Whigs

By the end of Andrew Jackson's second term in 1837, the Democratic Party had changed significantly. Gone was the diverse political coalition that had elected the Old Hero in 1828; its leadership now adhered to a fairly definite body of ideas. Government, the Jacksonians believed, should restrict its intervention in the economy to eliminating special privilege and monopoly, leaving a fair field for individual competition. Like Adam Smith, whose *Wealth of Nations* (1776) many of them had read, they believed that the power of the marketplace would best regulate the economy and distribute wealth equitably. Watchful that the rich would use the government for personal advantage, the Jacksonians advocated universal political freedom (for white men) and majority rule. Although recognizing the supremacy of the Union, Jacksonians respected states' rights, holding that the area of federal authority should be kept within narrow bounds.

The party in the late 1830s and 1840s was much influenced by the Locofocos, a powerful Democratic splinter group in New York. These dissidents—who took their name from a type of friction match they had used to light candles when rival Democrats tried to disrupt one of their meetings by turning off the gas lights—opposed monopoly in any form. They denounced banks and corporations, demanding a return to hard money and the abolition of laws allowing limited liability for stockholders. They advocated free trade, labor unions, free public education, and abolition of imprisonment for debt. Some Locofocos also had a racist streak; of Mexicans they wrote in a later campaign song:

General Pierce, he is not fierce,
But full of Yankee game,
For he did go to Mexico
The Hottentots to tame.

Chief Justice Roger Taney The decisions of the Supreme Court in the late 1830s reflected Democratic thinking. During his two terms, Jackson appointed seven associate justices. And when Chief Justice John Marshall died in 1835, the President named Roger B. Taney (pronounced tawny) to succeed him. Under Taney's leadership the Court showed a less rigid respect for private property rights as against the rights of popular majorities, and had more regard for states' rights.

In the *Charles River Bridge* case of 1837 the Court again took up the question posed in the *Dartmouth College* case of whether a state could alter an agreement with a private corporation. The Massachusetts legislature had incorporated the Charles River Bridge Company to operate a toll bridge under a long-term contract. Later it authorized an-

Asher Durand, *Kindred Spirits*. Durand was a leading figure in the ante-bellum Hudson River school of landscape art. *(Courtesy, New York Public Library)*

other corporation to build a toll-free bridge over the Charles River at a point nearby. The first company sought an injunction, contending that the second charter constituted a breach of contract. Taney sided with Massachusetts. The great object of government, he declared, was "to promote the happiness and prosperity of the community." In a collision between the rights of private property and those of the community, the rights of the people came first. The Court could not consent, Taney said, to take away from the states "any portion of that power over their own internal police and improvement, which is so necessary to their well being and prosperity." Although conservatives denounced the decision as a blow to business and the sanctity of contract, the decision was really a liberating one. The young American economy would have been greatly handicapped if established companies had been able to maintain monopolies and choke off competition. Taney's opinion opened the way for a host of developments in industry and transportation.

Two years later, in *Bank of Augusta v. Earle*, the Court enlarged state powers again. Here Taney rejected the claim of a Georgia bank that under the federal Constitution a corporation, like a citizen, could automatically enter another state and engage in business there. Though in the absence of positive legislation a company might do business in another state, said Taney, that state had the power to exclude the corporation if it wished. In the wake of this decision, many states enacted regulatory laws for outside corporations. On the whole, they proved to be socially beneficial, since there was as yet virtually no federal regulation of interstate commerce.

The Democratic appeals for strict economy, equal rights, and the abolition of government favors did appeal to popular sentiments. By the late thirties there was some truth in Jackson's claim that his party represented the "farmers, mechanics, and laborers." It especially attracted people who resented the privileges that established bankers and tariff-protected businessmen seemed to enjoy; people who had been affected adversely by changing patterns of transportation and trade; ordinary people who had been hurt by currency fluctuations and unstable commodity prices. Others supported the Democrats for special reasons. Many southern planters looked to them to protect slavery and southern rights from gov-

ernment interference. Businessmen engaged in international trade favored Jackson's call for a lower tariff. The Democratic Party early recognized and encouraged the aspirations of immigrants, particularly Irish Catholics, who flocked to the Democracy. Opponents of evangelical Protestantism, with its righteous moralizing and aggressive crusading, found refreshing the rough-and-tumble egalitarianism of the Democrats. The party attracted free-thinkers and intellectuals. Many Democratic voters just plain liked Jackson.

Yet Jackson's policies and political success provoked growing opposition. Initially, Old Hickory's opponents lacked cohesion, and political alliances were unsettled. In time they would gather into a party that could compete with the Democrats in the tapping of popular emotions.

One of the first of the forces to oppose Jackson was the Anti-Masonic Party, which after 1826 had gained strong support in New England, New York, and Pennsylvania. Originally a protest movement against the supposedly despotic political and economic power of Masonry, it soon turned into a general protest against inequality and immorality. As a powerful religious and democratic movement, it attracted ambitious young politicians—William Seward, Thaddeus Stevens, Horace Greeley, and Millard Fillmore—who welded it into an effective political party. Because Andrew Jackson was a Mason, and because his party was in power, these leaders made the Democrats the chief target of attack. In 1831 the Anti-Masons held at Baltimore the first nationwide presidential nominating convention in the country, choosing William Wirt as their presidential candidate. He won just seven electoral votes in 1832, splitting the anti-Jackson vote with Henry Clay, the National Republican candidate. After that election, leaders of these two groups began organizing a political force alternative to the Democrats.

They were joined by a motley assortment of former Jacksonians. After the Cabinet reshuffle of 1831, two Calhounites, John Branch of North Carolina and John M. Berrien of Georgia, went home to lead movements against the administration. Jackson's firm rebuke to nullification drove many other southern states' righters into opposition. Then the bank war caused many people to desert the President. The selection of the New Yorker Martin Van Buren as Jackson's successor awakened hostility in the South and West. Even John C. Calhoun cooperated for a time with nationalists like Clay and Webster in opposing administration measures in Congress.

In 1834 James Watson Webb of the New York *Courier and Enquirer* gave the anti-Jackson coalition the title "Whigs." That name had been in use for earlier British opponents of policies of the monarchy, and for rebel colonists in the period of the American Revolution; it was now supposed to define the opponents of the tyrannical "King Andrew."

Use of the name "Whig" by opponents of Jackson and Jacksonianism became widespread in 1834, but the actual formation of a Whig Party varied in time from state to state. It was organized first in the New England and Mid-Atlantic states, later in the West and South. The lack of an effective national organization and conflicts in ideology among the coalitionists hindered the Whigs in 1836. Unable to agree on a common platform or a single presidential candidate, they adopted the strategy of running strong regional candidates in the hope of throwing the election into the House of Representatives. In the South, the Whigs's choice was Hugh Lawson White, a Tennesseean who, like many southern Jacksonians, distrusted Van Buren on the tariff and slavery. Henry Clay denounced the "WHIGS" as merely "ANCIENT TORIES." In the East, they ran Daniel Webster. The candidate in the West was General William Henry Harrison of Ohio, a former governor of Indiana Territory and the hero of the Battle of Tippecanoe. Among them the three Whigs piled up 124 electoral votes, but Van Buren, with Jackson's prestige behind him, had 170, enough to win the election.

| **The Nature of the Growing Whig Party** | During the next four years the Whigs slowly gathered strength and developed a more coherent political |

philosophy. As the Panic of 1837 worsened, people throughout the country flocked to the

new banner, convinced that Van Buren's hard-money policies were somehow responsible for their woes. The Whigs's ambitious economic nationalism attracted new adherents in the South, even while it drove Calhoun and the extreme states' righters back to the Democrats.

The Whigs brought democratic manners and sentiments to an essentially Hamiltonian concept of government and economics. They believed that it was a chief function of government to promote, actively and positively, the national economy. They advocated internal improvements at federal expense, a national banking system, and a protective tariff for industry. As they saw it, a wise government working alongside capital and labor would harmonize the interests of every class and section. As their taunts at "King Andrew" indicated, the Whigs also believed in a strong congressional voice in government and respect for the opinions of the Supreme Court.

There was also a strong strain of evangelical Protestantism in Whiggery, which gave rise to moral and humanitarian reform. Many Whigs still hoped "to Christianize America through politics." They frequently criticized Jackson's Indian policy; and numbers of northern Whigs opposed slavery. Yet Whigs feared the political power of immigrants and Catholics.

The Whigs attracted a substantial following among all classes of society. Many northern merchants, bankers, and industrialists found the Whig philosophy appealing; so did large cotton, tobacco, and sugar planters and their urban business associates in the South. Many farmers, hungry for internal improvements, voted Whig. The party was popular among Protestants and native Americans concerned about the influx of immigrants, particularly Irish and German Catholics. Workingmen in industries hurt by foreign imports, or fearful of immigrant competition for jobs, supported the Whig ticket. With broad support throughout the country, the Whigs looked forward eagerly to the election of 1840.

The Election of 1840

In 1840 the second national party system came of age. The Democratic organization now faced a Whig Party just as skillfully de-

vised for the winning of a large electorate, and the Whigs had picked as their candidate a military hero. Contesting the election in almost every state, they now proceeded to beat the party of Jackson at its own game.

The Democratic convention had little choice but to renominate Van Buren; but it dropped Vice-President Richard M. Johnson, whose private life—he had fathered two daughters by a mulatto mistress—powerfully offended the sensibilities of southerners. Unable to agree on a substitute, the convention left the choice to the voters. The Democratic platform endorsed the Independent Treasury and condemned federally sponsored internal improvements, a national bank, and protective tariffs.

The early front runner for the Whig nomination was Henry Clay. The veteran senator from Kentucky had been the chief spokesman for Whiggery and master of the anti-Jackson forces in Congress. The new professional politicians in the Whig Party, however, had a different strategy in mind. Men like Thurlow Weed of New York wanted a candidate with "availability"—someone inoffensive who could appeal to a broad spectrum of the electorate. Clay was too closely identified with the Bank of the United States, and had too many enemies. The Whigs especially wanted a military hero. Their convention passed over Clay and chose William Henry Harrison. In an attempt to balance the ticket geographically, the Whigs selected as Harrison's running mate John Tyler of Virginia, a states' rights strict constructionist. Because there were divergent views within the party on national issues, the Whigs adjourned without drafting a platform.

The Log Cabin Campaign

Born on a Virginia plantation in 1773, the son of a signer of the Declaration of Independence, Harrison had begun his career in the Old Northwest, first as an army officer, then as governor of Indiana Territory. His rout of Tecumseh's out-

George Caleb Bingham, *Raftsmen Playing Cards*, 1847. (*Courtesy, The Saint Louis Art Museum*)

MOTHERS LOOK OUT FOR YOUR CHILDREN!
ARTISANS, MECHANICS, CITIZENS!

When you leave your family in health, must you be hurried home to mourn a

DREADFUL CASUALITY!

PHILADELPHIANS, your RIGHTS are being invaded! regardless of your interests, or the LIVES OF YOUR LITTLE ONES. THE CAMDEN AND AMBOY, with the assistance of other companies without a Charter, and in VIOLATION OF LAW, as decreed by your Courts, are laying a

LOCOMOTIVE RAIL ROAD!

Through your most Beautiful Streets, to the RUIN of your TRADE, annihilation of your RIGHTS, and regardless of your PROSPERITY and COMFORT. **Will you permit this?** or do you consent to be a

SUBURB OF NEW YORK!!

Rails are now being laid on BROAD STREET to CONNECT the TRENTON RAIL ROAD with the WILMINGTON and BALTIMORE ROAD, under the pretence of constructing a City Passenger Railway from the Navy Yard to Fairmount!!! This is done under the auspices of the CAMDEN AND AMBOY MONOPOLY!

RALLY PEOPLE in the Majesty of your Strength and forbid THIS

OUTRAGE!

This poster is an early example of "Nimby"—not in my backyard. Local residents feared that a busy train line through their neighborhoods would drive down property values. *(Courtesy, New York Public Library)*

numbered Indians at Tippecanoe in 1811 had made him a national hero. As commander in the Northwest during the War of 1812, he won the important Battle of the Thames, finally driving the British and their Indian allies off the soil of the United States. After the war, Harrison spent much time on his farm in Ohio, and also served briefly as a United States senator and as minister to Colombia. Thereafter, however, his career languished and he was serving as a county clerk in 1836 when the Whigs tapped him as one of their presidential candidates. His strong showing at the polls—he got over half the Whig vote—kept him in public view until 1840.

At first, the Democrats professed joy at the Whigs's decision to run "Granny" Harrison (he was sixty-seven) instead of Clay. But when a Democratic newspaper, sneering at Harrison's presumed lack of sophistication, suggested that he would be content with a barrel of hard cider, a log cabin, and a pension of $2000 a year, the Whigs seized on the remark. Mounting an elaborate campaign, they cast Harrison in Jackson's image and portrayed the Whigs as the friends of the people.

In their songs and speeches Whig orators glorified Harrison as a plain, virtuous farmer whose cabin door (he actually owned three thousand acres and lived in a substantial home) was always open to strangers. "Matty" Van Buren, by contrast, was pictured as a bloated aristocrat, squandering the public funds on lavish White House entertainments in the midst of a depression. Why, thundered one Whig orator, this *democratic peacock* had even installed a bathtub at a cost of "thousands of the people's dollars." Taking to the gutter, Davy Crockett observed that "it would be difficult to say, from his personal appearance, whether he was man or woman. . . . Aunt Matty was the perlitest cretur among the wimmen."

The Whigs held parades and rallies, with floats, flags, bands, and endless replicas of log cabins. They paraded fake Indians, to remind the voters of Harrison's record of Indian fighting. Another reminder was their catchy campaign slogan, "Tippecanoe and Tyler Too!" Barrels of cider were everywhere, with sweet cider for the drys and hard for the wets. The E.C. Booz Company of Philadelphia packaged its Old Cabin whiskey in cabin-shaped bottles. Wealthy Whigs dressed in homespun and boasted of their humble upbringing. The party distributed a campaign newspaper, the *Log Cabin,* and countless songbooks in the first musical campaign of American history:

> Tippecanoe has no chariot to ride in,
> No palace of marble has he to reside in,
> No bags of gold eagles, no lots of fine clothes—
> But a log cabin shelters a patriot true,
> 'Tis the home of our hero, bold Tippecanoe!

Another gem from the musical campaign of 1840 purported to give a biography of Van Buren.

> Who never did a noble deed?
> Who of the people took no heed?
> Who is the worst of tyrant's breed?
> > Van Buren!
>
> Who, while but a little boy,
> Was counted crafty, cunning, sly,
> Who with the wily fox could vie?
> > Van Buren!
>
> Who, when an urchin, young at school,
> Would of each classmate make a tool,
> In cheating, who the roost would rule?
> > Van Buren!
>
> Who like the wily serpent clings,
> Who like the pois'nous adder stings,
> Who is more base than basest Kings?
> > Van Buren!
>
> Who rules us with an iron rod,
> Who moves at Satan's beck and nod,
> Who heeds not man, who heeds not God?
> > Van Buren!
>
> Who would his friend, his country sell.
> Do other deeds too base to tell,
> Deserves the lowest place in Hell?
> > Van Buren!

One staunch Democrat, after witnessing the spectacle of 10,000 Whigs celebrating Harrison Day in Cleveland on September 10, 1840, recoiled with disgust:

> I have seen vast assemblages collected together at great labor and cost, not to respond to any principle, or listen to any argument but to drown the voice of reason in shouts of revelry, and lead captive the feelings of the people in a senseless excitement. Hurrah for the newly found hero, annunciations of his poverty or his residence in a Log Cabin and love of hard cider, the hauling of miniature log hen coops and canoes, gourd, shells, and cider barrels through the streets, the rolling of balls, and a display of different colored banners

with unmeaning mottos, doggerel, rhymes, and vulgar pictures, coon skins.

The drinking of hard cider, the nibbling of corn dodder [sic] and imitating the cries of birds and the howl of wild beasts with other mummery and mockery, are disgraceful to the country. It is saying to the people, you are too ignorant for self government, and is a down right insult to the good understanding of the American freeman.

The Whig campaign theme, then, made use of the democratic, populistic posturing that had served the Democrats so well. But it was not merely posturing and strategy. The Hamiltonian program for economic development, a clear antecedent to the program of the Whigs, had seemed aristocratic, but that was partly because of the character of its Federalist architects. The idea of a federal government actively managing a single national economy in the interest of the common good is at bottom entirely democratic, and to that the politics of the twentieth century will attest. The economic nationalism and the populism of the Whigs went together sincerely as well as strategically, and foreshadowed a continuing if rocky alliance of Hamiltonianism and democracy.

The Democrats tried to counter hard cider with hard money, pointing to the newly established Independent Treasury. No one listened. "We could meet the Whigs on the field of argument and beat them without effort," a Democrat lamented. "But when they lay down the weapons of argument and attack us with musical notes, what can we do?" Attracted by the ballyhoo and angry over the depression, nearly eighty percent of the eligible voters went to the polls. Harrison won a clear-cut victory, carrying nineteen out of twenty-six states and fifty-three percent of the two-party vote. Nearly unnoticed in the hullabaloo was the Liberty Party, whose meager 6,225 votes represented an early stirring of antislavery politics in the North.

The election of 1840 established a new pattern in American politics. For the first time a President had been saddled with responsibility for hard times and turned out of office. The carnival atmosphere of the campaign inaugurated a tradition that has persisted in American presidential elections. The public had clearly adopted politics as its favorite spectator sport, and the presidential campaign as its most important national ritual. For the rest of the nineteenth century, Americans in great numbers—usually about eighty percent of the electorate—would vote for a party's presidential candidate.

Points To Think About

1. If Andrew Jackson's presidency represented the symbol rather than the substance of democratic rule, the symbol was nonetheless important and has continued to count for much in American politics. Highly successful politicians are, virtually by definition, highly uncommon men and women. Jackson himself is a good example. He was a member of the slaveholding aristocracy. Yet he presented himself as the embodiment of the common folk. And his successors have felt the necessity to do the same. When Jimmy Carter after his inauguration in 1977 walked up Pennsylvania Avenue instead of riding in the presidential limousine, holding hands with his wife and daughter, he was a twentieth-century Jackson. And Jackson, for his part, had been consciously seeking to revive Jefferson's simplicity of manner.

It is ironic that the chief exemplars of the American preference for the "common touch" should have been aristocrats like Jefferson and Jackson.

Yet the popular insistence that leaders at least maintain the appearance of being one of them is not to be sneered at. It has saved American politics from endless pretentiousness. And a little hypocrisy seems a small price to pay for such a blessing.

2. Andrew Jackson's grasp of the economic issues associated with the question of rechartering the second Bank of the United States was so uncertain that historians have sometimes wondered whether he had any reasons for attacking it. Perhaps, some have speculated, he opposed it simply because it was there. A variant of this theory is somewhat more plausible. As put forward by Rush Welter in his massive study *The American Mind 1820–1860*, this explanation suggests that Jackson objected to the Bank not because it adopted one or another policy but because it had great power.

Jackson was in a number of ways the heir of the Jeffersonian distrust of organized power. Power was, in his mind, antithetical to liberty. So it was not how the Bank used its power that Jackson disliked. It was the simple fact that the Bank had the power to act decisively. Any bank worthy of the name of course had to have such power. That was the whole reason for having a central bank. And so Jackson took on not merely Biddle's bank, but the whole idea of the central banking system.

Jackson's veto was itself, however, an exercise of power. And historians generally agree that Jackson enormously strengthened the office of the presidency. This left him open to some of the same charges he had leveled at the Bank. The heart of the matter is that Jackson, and Jacksonians, could not conceive of legitimate power even though they recognized that no government could exist without it.

3. It is no small irony that the Whigs who organized themselves in opposition to Jackson did so in Jacksonian terms. They attacked his personal fitness for office, but even more they attacked his style of leadership, calling him "King Andrew." Jackson was a very strong President; and he left the office far stronger than it had been when he first assumed it. But Jackson's political style rested on denunciations of power. Thus he left himself open to like denunciations.

The Whigs were happy to turn Jackson's rhetoric against him. Their attack involved questioning the office of the presidency as a potential source of despotism as was, by extension, the national government as a whole. Whigs came to office in 1840 pledged, as Welter puts it, to a "political ethic of self denial." Their political ambitions, expressed in schemes like Henry Clay's American System, made a self-defeating position. They came into power with grand plans putting the government's power to developing the American economy and with a platform based on denials of governmental power.

Suggested Readings

Recent books on the Jackson Era include Lawrence Kohl, *The Politics of Individualism: Parties and the American Character in the Jackson Era* (1989), Merrill D. Peterson, *The Great Triumvirate: Webster, Clay, and Calhoun* (1987), Richard E. Ellis, *The Union at Risk: Jacksonian Democracy, States' Rights, and the Nullification Crisis* (1987), and Daniel B. Cole, *Martin Van Buren and American Political System* (1984).

Edward Pessen's *Jacksonian America* (rev. 1978) is a sharp critique of the traditional view of the Old Hero as the representative of an egalitarian society. Pessen finds little to admire in Jackson and writes of a rigidly stratified society with slight opportunity for mobility. Marvin Meyers's *The Jacksonian Persuasion* (1957) examines certain American ideas and attitudes that attended Jacksonian politics, such as the conviction that the nation, having begun as a virtuous republic, needed a politics of renovation that would recover something of that lost republican austerity. Richard P. McCormick describes *The Second Party System* (1966). Robert V. Remini's *Andrew Jackson* (1966) and subsequent works emphasize the man's administrative skill and the importance of his military campaigns and dealings with the Indians. Michael Paul Rogin's *Fathers and Children: Andrew Jackson and the Subjugation of the American Indian* (1975) is intriguing and debatable psychohistory. Lee Benson's *The Concept of Jacksonian Democracy: New York as a Test Case* (1961) remains provocative. The nullification crisis is the subject of William W. Freehling's *Prelude to Civil War* (1966).

☆ ☆ DEBATE ☆ ☆ ☆

FORREST McDONALD

The framers of the Constitution had distrusted democracy as much as monarchy, fearing that the majority could persecute minorities just as monarchies could oppress the people as a whole. They accordingly set up a government in which power was so divided that no majority, so they hoped, would be likely to have its way completely. But despite the efforts of the framers, American politics became more and more democratic. Democratic politics found its expression in the party system—a system that the Constitution had not provided for.

In the first phase of the development of the party system the Republican party of Thomas Jefferson and James Madison formed to combat the policies of the Hamilton Federalists. Real differences in principles and programs divided the two parties. Hamiltonians wanted a strong national government that would encourage capitalistic enterprise and thereby stimulate economic growth and progress; Republicans sought to reduce the activities of the national government, leave most decisions to state and local governments, and maintain the old agricultural economy. But then the Republicans, in the wake of the War of 1812, virtually adopted the Hamiltonian program, grafting on to it a more democratic rhetoric; and for a few years they were for practical purposes the only party. Then a second party system developed, which pitted Whigs against Jacksonian Democrats. The new party system—the one Americans have had ever since—differed radically from the original: it was organized not around principles and policies, but around power and personalities.

As reconstituted during the Jacksonian age, American political parties came to exist solely for the purpose of winning elections and handing out the offices and other benefits that victory brings. It is true that the parties were supposed to stand for something, the Whigs being for a national bank, a protective tariff, internal improvements, and other nationalist measures associated with the Hamiltonian tradition, and the Jacksonian Democrats calling for states' rights, low tariffs, a more careful limitation of activities on the part of the federal government, and other positions connected with the Jeffersonian tradition. Yet each party, in Jackson's time and after, accommodated members who held to some or all of the principles for which the other party claimed to stand. What the parties did at election time was carry out a sort of ritual substitute for war, each presenting itself as standing between the nation and the disaster that the other party would bring, each offering candidates who for the moment captured the hopes and dreams of a portion of the American public. And so the two party system has done ever since. This mock warfare has had little or nothing to do with what the candidates have actually proposed to do once they get in office.

The party system performed an immensely valuable social function. It provided ordinary Americans with a sense of participation in public affairs; it strengthened their feeling of being part of the nation; and in bringing into the same political camp Americans of differing economic, social, ethnic, and regional identities, it relieved some of the hostilities that arise from these differences. But it also had some grave weaknesses. It kept genuine issues forever out of focus, and thereby prevented Americans from perceiving their fundamental problems and acting on these through government. And the party system tended to turn democracy and capitalism into uneasy partners if not incompatible opposites. Americans, to be sure, were attached to the proposition that if the individual seeks by any legitimate means to grow as wealthy as possible, society as a whole will be enriched. But the Jeffersonian and Jacksonian tradition preserved a habit of denouncing winners in the pursuit of wealth as enemies of the people and an equally nonsensical habit of regarding economic activity as a "zero sum game" in which, as in poker, if one man wins, another must necessarily lose. In modern times these policies have produced a policy of taking money on a large scale from people who earn it and giving it to people who do not earn it.

What Was the Party System?

EUGENE D. GENOVESE

The party system that Professor McDonald describes probably deserves credit for temporarily keeping under control the quarrels and hostilities that finally resulted in secession and Civil War. Parties did bring together people of different interests and regions. Parties and the factions within them chose leaders, and those leaders could talk things out in Congress and elsewhere—arriving, for example, at the compromises that from moment to moment seemed to calm the slavery question. If in the end compromise failed, it was because the interests and the ideologies that clashed over slavery allowed no ultimate reconciliation.

So let us acknowledge that the party system may have kept secession off for a while. That is perhaps the best we can say of it. Professor McDonald has some severe judgments to make of the party system. I think we can still be tougher on it. Providing the occasion for flamboyant political oratory, it spawned speakers and legislators who aroused chauvinistic emotions in themselves and their audiences as they urged the country on its westward march.

During the period of our history from the Era of Good Feelings to the Civil War, the years in which the second party system developed, the United States pushed to the Pacific to round out a continent and positioned itself, more or less self-consciously, to become a world power. It pushed southward, too. It annexed Florida and it carried out a long series of thinly disguised aggressions, interventions, and attempted annexations in the Caribbean and Central America. The westward march took in Texas and plunged into a series of dishonorable and hooligan acts that eventually resulted in the dismemberment of Mexico. Citizens of the United States may not wish to dwell on their nation's having seized half of Mexico's territory after provoking a war and having a President lie about it. Mexicans have longer memories.

The westward march, begun long before the appearance of those disagreeable incidents in the Southwest, has provided much of the stuff of American folklore. And indeed the story of the pioneers and settlers who hacked a modern nation out of a wilderness deserves to rank among the wonders of human history. At its best, and its worst, it displayed ingenuity, vision, heroism. Possibly—some would say probably and others would say certainly—the settlers would have had to take the Indians by violence if they intended to win the continent for western civilization. But along the way sober national leaders, especially among the more conservative Whigs, did advance proposals for more humane, or at least less disgusting, solutions. In the event, the United States, the most democratic, freedom-loving nation in the world, simply took land by force, broke treaty after treaty, lied (possibly to itself) about its intentions and policies, cheated people who often made the terrible mistake of trusting the white man's word, and killed. The job could not have been done more savagely.

The party system did not invent the greed that hungered for land, or the swaggering nationalism that shrilled for expansion and power, or the racism that swept the Indians aside. But it did provide the institutions that encouraged the people to send to our state capitals and to Washington politicians prepared to give voice to our worst emotions and desires. And I disagree with Professor McDonald's suggestion that the political system that grew out of those years has recently encouraged "taking" money from those who have "earned" it and giving it to people who have not. The well-to-do have not "earned" their affluence: it has come to them by the chances and large sweeps of an economy that willfully bestows its favor on one individual and inflicts suffering on another. But it has been typical of our democratic society for Americans at each level of affluence and comfort to congratulate themselves on their success and despise those below them. Political rhetoric encourages flattery and self-flattery, and our nation's major parties have been instruments of that rhetoric.

The Erie Canal at Rochester, New York. Cities prospered all along the canal, which extended from Buffalo, on Lake Erie, to Albany, on the Hudson, opening an economical transportation system from the Great Lakes to the Atlantic. *(Courtesy, New-York Historical Society, New York City)*

Tocqueville's United States 1820–1860

THE ERIE CANAL

The idea of an Erie canal caught George Washington's imagination as early as 1783, when he toured the Mohawk Valley and envisioned "the vast inland navigation of these United States." The patriot poet Joel Barlow in his *The Vision of Columbus* (1787) has the explorer predict the building of a canal "From fair Albania" (Albany) to "the far lakes."

Pushed through the New York legislature in 1817 by Governor DeWitt Clinton's powerful political machine, the Erie Canal project has been called "the most decisive single event in the history of American transportation." It was built largely by immigrant labor. On December 11, 1818, newly-arrived David Richard of Utica wrote to his brother in Wales, "William Thomas and myself are working on the arches under the canal. . . . Wages on the canal are one dollar a day and thirteen to fourteen dollars a month with food and washing and half a pint of whiskey a day." Beginning at Albany on the Hudson, the finished canal wound 363 miles through the Mohawk River Valley to Buffalo, on Lake Erie. Along the way eighty-three locks lifted the boats up and down the 650-foot elevation, and eighteen stone aqueducts carried the canal over rivers and streams.

The Erie Canal was an immediate success. Before its opening, the cost of hauling grain across the Appalachian foothills to New York City had been three times the market value of wheat, six times that of corn, ten times that of oats. Overnight these stifling transportation costs disappeared, as horses pulled hundred-ton barges loaded with freight along "Clinton's Big Ditch" at rates as low as a cent a ton-mile. At the canal's Albany terminus steamboats took over for the comparatively swift and economical trip down the Hudson to New York City. By 1825, when the Erie was completed, toll revenues already exceeded a half-million dollars a year. Soon the canal's entire $7 million cost had been recovered, and state officials ordered the canal widened to accommodate the increased traffic. Towns all along the route from Buffalo to New York City prospered, none more than New York, which became the transportation gateway to the West and the nation's largest port.

Once opened in 1825, the Erie became an essential part of a tourist's itinerary: "The canal is in everybody's mouth," one traveler rather awkwardly expressed it. The bustle and activity, the remarkable circumstances of its construction, its overwhelming success and national importance made it an eighth wonder of the world. The Great Western Canal—one of its more formal names—was but four feet deep and forty feet wide, later deepened to seven feet and widened to seventy. Mule teams on the towpath zipped the fast passenger boats (called packets) along at the canal speed limit of four miles an hour, while freighters made but one and a half to two miles per hour, and log rafts annoyed everyone with their slowness. Yet the trip was not without its excitement. "Commending my soul to God," remarked a first-time rider boarding at Rochester, "and asking His defense from danger, I stepped on board the canalboat and was soon flying towards Utica."

Long trips by water had always been dangerous, and the idea of taking a trip of over 300 miles in complete safety was fascinating. Mock-heroic epics of the dangers of a storm at sea became a standard bit of Erie folklore: the ship pitching, the captain barking orders, the endless verses celebrating each maritime danger.

In a folk song that has survived to the present day, a chorus defines the real danger of a storm on the canal:

> *Oh, the E-ri-e was a-risin'*
> *And the gin was a-gettin' low,*
> *And I scarce do think we'll get a drink*
> *'Till we get to Buffalo.*

But the story ends happily: Buffalo had not run out of gin and the crew got the bawds, the brawls, and the inevitable night in the cooler they had demanded:

> *Oh the girls are in the Police Gazette,*
> *The crew are all in jail,*
> *And I'm the only living sea cook's son*
> *That's left to tell the tale.*

And Buffalo was the "tame" end of the canal. At the other end, in Watervliet near Albany, the notorious "side-cut" area with its twenty-nine saloons in two blocks (with names like The Black Rag and The Tub of Blood), its fights, its large-scale vice, and an occasional body floating in the canal gained the district the title "The Barbary Coast of the East."

The Erie traveler saw a splendid microcosm of young America. The men and women who made the canal work, "part water, part sand, part wind . . . but all canawler," were a colorful lot. The tough Irish workers who had dug the ditch now crewed the boats. The pompous captains, the fierce lock-keepers in endless battle with the crews, the floating showboats, saloons, general stores, and vice dens were famous among travelers, as were the legendary cooks: one "with a bosom like a boxcar," another who "stood six feet in her socks; her hand was like an elephant's ear, her breath would open locks."

These slow boats to Buffalo allowed remarkable freedom for travelers to see the countryside when they were not ducking under the famous low bridges. Even on the packets, a passenger could walk the towpath alongside the boat for

Leila T. Bahmah, *Geese in Flight* (ca. 1850). **The absorbing theme of this painting is movement both man-made and in nature: the geese, the smoke and steam of the riverboat and locomotive, the galloping horse.** *(Courtesy, National Gallery of Art)*

exercise. On the slower boats, poor travelers could step ashore and forage for their food, picking berries and hunting rabbits. And the scenes were grand: bustling ports, ingenious locks and romantic swamps, rivers and streams, and magnificent aqueducts; curious bridges of water allowed ships to pass over such picturesque obstacles. Sometimes the canal cut straight through primeval forests with no hint of man's work but the calm swath of canal and towpath. A British visitor, Mrs. Trollope, the most vinegary of travelers, complained that "From the canal nothing is seen to advantage, and very little is seen at all." But another Englishman, the great novelist Charles Dickens, after criticizing the packet's accommodations vividly recalled: "the exquisite beauty of the opening day, when light came glancing off from everything; the gliding on at night so noiselessly, past frowning hills sullen with dark trees and sometimes angry in one red, burning spot high up, where unseen men lay crouching round a fire; the shining out of the bright stars undisturbed by any noise of wheels or steam or any other sound than the limpid rippling of the water as the boat went on; all these were pure delights."

The New Society

When the French nobleman Alexis de Tocqueville began his tour of the United States in 1831, he imagined that he was looking into the very face of the modern democratic future. His *Democracy in America*, published here in translation in the late 1830s, described a nation of exploding energies, of individualists throwing lifetimes of force and work into the pursuit of achievement. Certainly many immigrants complained about the "go along steam-boat" pace of life in the United States. James Dawson Burn, a British immigrant, wrote that "work, work, work is the everlasting routine of everyday life." Americans were "savagely wild in devouring their work." William Darnley wrote to his wife in Stockport, England, "I can assure you I never worked so hard indeed I would not stop in this country if I thought I must work all my life."

At first skeptical about democracy, Tocqueville nevertheless liked much of what he saw. He was respectfully surprised that American society had managed to enjoy so much liberty amid an equality that he had thought to be an enemy to liberty. And yet he found American individualism flawed. The haste to succeed prevented the slow cultivation of excellence, and the individual American, lacking smaller communities and classes with which to identify, was pitifully submissive to public opinion.

Tocqueville's analysis of early nineteenth-century American individualism does not take adequate account of powerful elements of community and cooperation in neighborhoods, in churches, in voluntary associations and activities. And in describing the American mentality as one of submission to public opinion, he was writing too early to see the full flowering of an American literature of private visions and of brooding inquiry into the deeps of the soul. Nathaniel Hawthorne and Edgar Allan Poe were not far into their careers; the works of Herman Melville and still other seers into the secret heart were yet to come. These writers might have revealed to Tocqueville a side of the American mind that was hauntingly introspective rather than bustlingly aggressive. Tocqueville's portrayal of the energetic American, free to chase after wealth, did not fit the case of Americans condemned to drudgery, struggle, and isolation on farms, or pressed down into the poverty of the growing cities. And of course, as he knew, it did not apply to the black slaves. But Tocqueville offers a starting point for understanding a society that was, by and large, bursting with energy and hope, and committed to democracy, with its conflicting urges toward freedom and toward conformity.

Economic Developments: The Transportation Revolution

In 1808, when Secretary of the Treasury Albert Gallatin proposed his ambitious system of internal improvements at federal expense, it took a New Yorker three days to travel to Boston, ten days to reach Charleston, and nearly six weeks to journey west to St. Louis. The movement of bulky or heavy goods over long distances by land was prohibitively expensive: it cost more to drag a ton of iron overland a few miles than to bring it across the ocean. Farmers and merchants still depended mainly on waterways to move their crops and merchandise. Coastwise shipping was inexpensive but slow. Inland areas were

peculiarly dependent upon river transportation. But this was strictly a one-way affair—downstream. The flatboats that floated down to New Orleans with western produce had to be broken up for lumber, and the boatmen left to get home as best they could. Sectional jealousies and constitutional squabbles prevented the passage of Gallatin's and Clay's plans for internal improvements. Transportation remained haphazard and wasteful. Nonetheless, the fragmented American republic slowly linked itself up into a connected whole.

| Turnpikes   Early American roads were little more than broad, stump-filled paths through the forest. Impassable in wet weather, they were adequate only for local needs. A system of through routes, bringing together the chief commercial centers, was desperately needed. In the 1790s private corporations had begun building turnpikes along the most important routes of travel. These companies financed construction mainly by the sale of stock to investors, and sought profits by collecting tolls from people using the roads. The best turnpikes had a firm stone foundation overlaid with gravel, drainage ditches for run-off, and substantial stone or wooden bridges. The extreme difficulty of moving men and material during the War of 1812 stimulated a boom in turnpike construction. By 1825 these roads crisscrossed New England and the mid-Atlantic states; Pennsylvania alone had about 2400 miles of toll road. In the West and South, where private capital was scarce, state and local governments often financed the turnpikes. The greatest of them all, the National Road, was built by the federal government. Begun in 1811, it ultimately stretched from Cumberland, Maryland, to Vandalia, Illinois. Travelers on this great western highway encountered an endless stream of people on foot, on horseback, in stagecoaches, on one-horse wagons, and driving lumbering teamster wagons.

Few of these turnpikes ever showed a profit to their owners. Maintenance proved a constant drain. The public devoted considerable ingenuity to outwitting toll collectors: short roads popularly known as "shunpikes" frequently circled around the toll gates. The turnpikes, although popular with travelers, failed to provide economical long-distance freight transportation. Even where tolls were low, it was not profitable for heavy wagons with six- and eight-horse teams to make long

Deck Life on the Paragon, one of Fulton's steamboats. *(Courtesy, The Metropolitan Museum of Art, Rogers Fund, 1942)*

Steamboats loaded with bales of cotton were tinderboxes. *(Courtesy, Library of Congress)*

hauls over them. Many of the turnpike companies had failed even before the emergence of competition from canals and railroads.

▌Steamboats   Men had been experimenting worldwide for years with the application of steam power to water transportation, but it remained for Robert Fulton, a young American engineer, to perfect an efficient design. His steamboat, equipped with an English-built engine and paddle wheels, averaged five miles per hour on its first voyage up New York's Hudson River in 1807. Spectators on shore watched in astonishment as it overtook the sluggish sailing vessels and "passed them as if they had been at anchor." Fulton and his partner, Robert R. Livingston, tried to keep exclusive control over their invention, but steam navigation was too important to be monopolized.

By the time the Supreme Court, in *Gibbons v. Ogden* (1824), formally annulled the Fulton-Livingston monopoly in New York, steamboats had been introduced on every major river in the country.

The years from 1820 to 1850 were the age of the steamboat, the first economical inland transportation for both freight and people. On eastern rivers, harbors, and bays, steamboats served primarily as passenger vessels. They were designed for speed and comfort, with razor bows, long narrow hulls, giant paddle wheels amidships, and elegantly furnished cabins. Even larger boats plied the Great Lakes, carrying thousands of immigrants west to Detroit and Chicago. But it was in the fertile valley of the Mississippi that steamboats had their greatest importance. Ingenious shipbuilders quickly adapted them to navigate the western rivers even at low water. Hulls were made broad and shallow, engines and cabins placed on deck, and paddle wheels moved to the stern. Western rivermen boasted that all they needed for successful navigation was a heavy dew. Some of their boats could operate in water as shallow as thirty inches. These ungainly boats brought the West firmly into the national economy.

The floating rafts at last made it economical to ship the bulky exports of the interior to market. Receipts of produce at New Orleans leaped from $12 million in 1820–21 to a peak of $197 million in 1850–51. There larger ships took on the grain and cotton for destinations on the East Coast or in Europe. On their return upstream the steamboats carried consumer goods formerly hauled overland at enormous cost.

The boats were not what Americans of the 1990s would consider fast. One helmsman wrote home to his family: "They can run from New Orleans to Pitsburgh in 16 and 18 days which is 25 hundred miles. They can go down in 8 and 10 days. They can carry 200 passengers each." He added: "Thare are a grate many fish caught in this river. Catfish which way from 10 to 100 pound. Thare are steam packets that carry from 100 to 700 tuns burden each." The very smallness of scale of the steamboats add to their romance, which Mark Twain, himself a Mississippi helmsman, caught in his *Huckleberry Finn* and other stories.

Steamboats were also hazardous. One account of 1851 noted:

> Our steamboats very far exceed in number those of any other country, and the navigation of most of our rivers is dangerous in the extreme. The frequency of explosions upon our Western boats is owing in a great measure to their employing high pressure boilers and engines. The steam is generated with great rapidity by this mode, yet as long as the boat is in motion all is safe, but let a boat under a full head stop suddenly and there is always a danger of explosion; so much so indeed, that old stagers will generally be seen hurrying to the stern as soon as the engineer's bell is heard to command "stop her. . . ." With regard to the frequent losses of boats by fire, these are too often the result of the manner in which they are built and freighted. The cabin is entirely above the deck, built of the lightest material, and always as dry as tinder, from the constant heat beneath. It only wants a full load of cotton to complete the danger. When a boat is fully freighted with this article she appears like a moving mass of cotton bales, no part of her hull being visible except the paddle-boxes.
>
> Around the bows and upon the guards the bales are piled as high as the "hurricane deck." They almost touch the boilers, which are exposed and unprotected upon the forward deck, and generally surrounded by huge piles of wood, not unfrequently in absolute contact with them. A tier of cotton often adorns the hurricane deck itself, and needs but a spark from the smoke-pipe to convert the boat into a fiery furnace, from which the chance of escape is small indeed.

Canals

Knowing the success of the early English canals, landlocked Americans had talked for years of linking the nation's navigable rivers and lakes with artificial waterways. A major obstacle was the inability of private capital to supply the large sums—$25,000 a mile or more—necessary for canal construction. By 1816 only about a hundred miles of canals had been constructed in the United States, most less than two miles long. None had returned a profit to their owners. Then came the Erie Canal.

Peter Cooper's "Tom Thumb," the first locomotive made in America, racing with a horse-car on the Baltimore and Ohio line, 1830. *(Courtesy, New York Public Library)*

The success of the Erie touched off a nationwide boom in canal building. Several eastern states, jealous of New York's position, tried to tap the western market with canals of their own. Pennsylvania's Main Line system over the Allegheny Mountains required a portage railroad—a stairstep of inclined planes by which cable cars carried the canal boats up one side of the highest ridges and down the other. In the West, Ohio and Indiana raced to link the waters of Lake Erie and the Ohio River. Indiana's contribution, the Wabash and Erie Canal, was over 450 miles long. By 1840, when the boom collapsed, the American people had constructed over 3300 miles of canals, at a total cost of $125 million. State governments provided most of this huge capitalization, selling bonds against anticipated revenues. Few states or bondholders recovered even a fraction of their investment. Many of the canals were poorly planned and constructed; maintenance costs were high; ice or low water closed them at certain seasons. Nevertheless, these costly ditches greatly stimulated the economy. They offered the first economical means of transferring the bulky products of the West directly eastward.

Railroads   The nation soon had cheaper, faster, more dependable and profitable overland transportation. Americans had taken an early interest in another English development, the railroad. Construction of a few small tramways began in the United States during the 1820s, and in 1828 the first major railroad, the Baltimore and Ohio, was chartered. Many early railroads ran only short distances, being designed to serve mainly as feeders into nearby rivers and canals, but major eastern cities like Boston and Baltimore, which lacked adequate water connections, promoted longer lines. Merchants of Charleston, South Carolina, anxious to divert upcountry cotton shipments to their wharves, built a railroad to Hamburg on the lower Savannah River. When completed in 1833, it extended 136 miles and was the longest railroad in the world. In these years ingenious American inventors made a number of important technical improvements in the design of locomotives and roadbeds. By 1840 the nation's total railway mileage equaled that of canals, and many lines were competing successfully with canal companies for business.

Railroads, like other forms of transportation, received public aid. Between 1830 and 1843 the national government lowered tariff duties on railroad iron. State legislatures—once again taking the lead in such public assistance—granted tax incentives, required newly chartered banks to invest in railroad stock, extended large grants, and sometimes operated lines directly. Added to the foreign capital that American railroads attracted, government help provided strong impetus to private companies. Almost 9000 miles of track were laid in the 1840s and 22,000 more in the next decade. At the beginning of the Civil War railroads overshadowed all other forms of long-distance transportation in the country.

Economic Developments: Labor and Immigration

The transportation revolution, making the movement of goods vastly easier and cheaper, opened up a large new potential market for manufactured products. But where were the workers to produce these goods?

From colonial times, labor had been in short supply in America. Cheap land was so available that people could work their own land instead of hiring out their labor. In 1800 only ten percent of the white labor force were people who sold their labor. The rest of the working force were farmers, self-employed artisans and mechanics, and independent tradesmen.

Early manufacturers experimented with various ways of overcoming this acute labor scarcity. One was the "domestic" or "putting-out" system. Entrepreneurs furnished raw materials to people who worked in their own homes, making cloth, shoes, and wearing apparel; the entrepreneurs then collected and marketed the finished product. In a predominantly agricultural country, where most people lived in rural areas, this system, though cumbersome, allowed manufacturers to tap a tremendous pool of part-time labor, especially women and children. Other businessmen tried to centralize production, hiring whole families whom they housed in tenements adjacent to their mills. But as factories grew larger, requiring a labor force of hundreds, even thousands, factory owners turned increasingly to the Waltham system.

The Waltham System

This system was the brainchild of Francis Cabot Lowell, an early textile manufacturer. Anxious to recruit young women from New England farms to work in his mill at Waltham, Massachusetts, Lowell built dormitories nearby to house them. In order to counteract the widespread reputation of mills as places of loose morals, he placed these dormitories in charge of respectable widows who maintained rigid rules of conduct. The factory girls typically had to be in their rooms by 10 p.m., to attend church regularly, and to save part of their earnings. A few mills sponsored evening classes and libraries for their workers.

Lowell's plan was an immediate success. Many young women welcomed the chance to get away from the farm for a few years and to earn a little money of their own. In the 1820s and 1830s they flocked by the thousands to New England mill towns like Lowell, Chicopee, and Manchester. Visitors to the textile factories usually praised the Waltham system. After a tour in 1834, Davy Crockett described Lowell's "mile of gals" as "well-dressed, lively, and genteel" and happy in their work. Many of the female workers were not so enthusiastic. They objected to the length of the work day, the low wages, the overcrowded dormitories, and the close supervision of their lives. "Susan" wrote home,

> It makes my feet ache and swell to stand so much. . . . The girls almost all say that when they have worked here a year or two they have to procure shoes a size or two larger than before they came. The right hand, which is the one used in starting and stopping the loom, becomes larger than the left; but in other respects the factory is not detrimental to a young girl's appearance.

Above all, the workers opposed a series of attempts by the mill owners to increase the amount of work—"speed up" and "stretch out"—and reduce the pay. A group of the more experienced workers founded the

---

TIME TABLE OF THE LOWELL MILLS,

Arranged to make the working time throughout the year average 11 hours per day.

TO TAKE EFFECT SEPTEMBER 21st., 1853,

The Standard time being that of the meridian of Lowell, as shown by the Regulator Clock of AMOS SANBORN, Post Office Corner, Central Street.

From March 20th to September 19th, inclusive.

COMMENCE WORK, at 6.30 A. M. LEAVE OFF WORK, at 6.30 P. M., except on Saturday Evenings.
BREAKFAST at 6 A. M. DINNER, at 12 M. Commence Work, after dinner, 12.45 P. M.

From September 20th to March 19th, inclusive.

COMMENCE WORK, at 7.00 A. M. LEAVE OFF WORK, at 7.00 P. M., except on Saturday Evenings.
BREAKFAST at 6.30 A. M. DINNER, at 12.30 P.M. Commence Work, after dinner, 1.15 P. M.

BELLS.

From March 20th to September 19th, inclusive.

Morning Bells.	Dinner Bells.	Evening Bells.
First bell,..........4.30 A. M.	Ring out,..........12.00 M.	Ring out,..........6.30 P. M.
Second, 5.30 A. M. ; Third, 6.20.	Ring in,..........12 35 P. M.	Except on Saturday Evenings.

From September 20th to March 19th, inclusive.

Morning Bells.	Dinner Bells.	Evening Bells.
First bell ....5.00 A. M.	Ring out,..........12.30 P. M.	Ring out at ....7.00 P. M.
Second, 6.00 A. M. ; Third, 6.50.	Ring in,..........1.05 P. M.	Except on Saturday Evenings.

SATURDAY EVENING BELLS.

During APRIL, MAY, JUNE, JULY, and AUGUST, Ring Out, at 6.00 P. M.
The remaining Saturday Evenings in the year, ring out as follows :

SEPTEMBER.	NOVEMBER.	JANUARY.
First Saturday, ring out 6.00 P. M.	Third Saturday ring out 4.00 P. M.	Third Saturday, ring out 4.25 P. M.
Second " " 5.45 "	Fourth " " 3.55 "	Fourth " " 4.35 "
Third " " 5.30 "		**FEBRUARY.**
Fourth " " 5.20 "	**DECEMBER.**	First Saturday, ring out 4.45 P. M.
OCTOBER.	First Saturday, ring out 3.50 P. M.	Second " " 4.55 "
First Saturday, ring out 5.05 P. M.	Second " " 3.55 "	Third " " 5.00 "
Second " " 4.55 "	Third " " 3.55 "	Fourth " " 5.10 "
Third " " 4.45 "	Fourth " " 4.00 "	**MARCH.**
Fourth " " 4.35 "	Fifth " " 4.00 "	First Saturday, ring out 5.25 P. M.
Fifth " " 4.25 "		Second " " 5.30 "
NOVEMBER.	**JANUARY.**	Third " " 5.35 "
First Saturday, ring out 4.15 P. M.	First Saturday, ring out 4.10 P. M.	Fourth " " 5.45 "
Second " " 4.05 "	Second " " 4.15 "	

YARD GATES will be opened at the first stroke of the bells for entering or leaving the Mills.

SPEED GATES commence hoisting three minutes before commencing work.

Penhallow, Printer, Wyman's Exchange, 28 Merrimack St.

Lowell Female Reform Association, essentially one of the first labor unions in the United States. Ultimately, their two large strikes and their appeal to the Massachusetts state legislature failed to accomplish their goals. The rapid increase in the immigration of destitute Irish during the 1840s permitted the owners to turn to a new and more dependent supply of labor.

In their own way, the Lowell mill girls constituted something of an elite labor force. When they struck they claimed the rights of direct heiresses of the Revolution, daughters of the Sons of Liberty.

The events at Lowell in fact had much to do with the status of women in the early nineteenth century. One extraordinarily literate worker at Lowell, Harriet Robinson, remembered:

At this date woman had no property rights. A widow could be left without her share of her husband's property. . . . A woman was not supposed to be capable of spending her own or of using other people's money. In Massachusetts, before 1840, a woman could not legally be treasurer of her own sewing-society, unless some man were responsible for her.

The law took no cognizance of woman as a money-spender. She was a ward, an appendage, a relict. Thus it happened, that if a woman did not choose to marry, or, when left a widow, to re-marry, she had no choice but to enter one of the few employments open to her, or to become a burden on the charity of some relative.

In almost every New England home could be found one or more of these women, sometimes welcome, more often unwelcome, and leading joyless, and in many instances unsatisfactory, lives. The cotton-factory was a great opening to these lonely and dependent women. From a condition approaching pauperism they were at once placed above want; they could earn money, and spend it as they pleased; and could gratify their tastes and desires without restraint, and without rendering an account to anybody. . . .

JOHN STURM, *in an autobiographical fragment, recounts his family's crossing of the Atlantic in 1847. It was an easier voyage than was typical for the time. Usually there were several deaths on a crossing.*

When we set out from home, we went to Mannheim in a wagon, then to Mainz and Koln on the Rhine in a steamboat and then to Antwerp, a seaport, where we lay over several days until a ship was ready.

Our baggage was supposed to be in Koln when we got there, but it was not there. My father looked around for it for several days, but he did not find it. We were told it must have been sent to Antwerp and we would find it there. But to our misfortune and almost to our utter despair, everything was lost.

In Antwerp we waited several days until our ship was ready to go to sea. My father bought food again for use on the ship, because what we had brought from home was all lost. Before we boarded ship, my father hunted for our baggage again, but in vain. So we had nothing but the clothes on our backs. When the ship was ready to go, we had to go along.

The ship was a three-master, the "Carolina." We had many a stormy day. There were many of us on the ship. There was only one kitchen for all the people to cook in for the passengers had to cook, each family for itself. So it happened that each family had a chance to cook only once in two or three days. We had little interest in eating, anyway, as most of the people were sea-sick and had no appetite.

The ship heaved and rolled almost all the time so that we had to hold on to something. Many people never came up on deck at all during the entire journey. The trunks and boxes had to be tied fast so they wouldn't be thrown about. Some of the children were happy and gay, but most of them were not.

One day a pirate ship came toward us and everyone had to come on deck, no doubt to show how many able-bodied men we had.

The sailors had their own kitchen and their own cook. Peas cooked with bacon and beans were their main foods. We also had bacon and black bread, which we almost had to split with an ax. Here a dog would hardly eat it. Some had white bread, which was more appetizing than the black. But in spite of all this, we survived. One child died on the ship. It was buried at sea.

| **European Immigrants** | Nothing had prepared the country for the mass immigration that took place in the first half of the nineteenth century. Previously immigrants had come in trickles. After 1815, especially beginning in the mid-1840s, they came in endless waves, fleeing from economic distress or political turmoil in their homelands. Between 1815 and 1860 4,777,000 immigrants entered the country—more than the entire population of the United States in 1790. The largest number, over 2,000,000, came from Ireland, many to work on the construction of the Erie Canal or the railroads. Germany ranked second as a country of origin, with 1.5 million. Another 750,000 arrived from England, Scotland, and Wales; most of the remainder were from Switzerland and Scandinavia.

These immigrants, many of them illiterate, unskilled, without resources, had little in common with those who had come before the War of 1812. Lacking the knowledge and money to undertake farming on the frontier, and anxious to remain near their fellow countrymen, most of the newcomers did not venture far from the ports of arrival. Crowded into cities, they formed an enormous pool of unskilled labor, ripe for exploitation. Some found jobs in the Pennsylvania coal fields and Illinois lead mines. During the 1840s immigrants rapidly began to replace native farmers' daughters in New England textile and shoe factories. The paternalistic spirit of Lowell vanished. "I regard people just as I regard my machinery," a manufacturer explained in 1855:

> So long as they can do my work for what I choose to pay them, I keep them, getting out of them all I can. What they do or how they fare outside my wall I don't know, nor do I consider it my business to know. They must look out for themselves as I do for myself. When my machines get old and useless, I reject them and get new, and these people are part of my machinery.

Neither the factory system nor the great canal and railroad projects of the period could have come into existence so quickly without this foreign labor. Between 1830 and 1850, immigrants supplied nearly half the increase in the free working force. But exploitation brought poverty, disease, and crime.

Economic Developments: Industrialization

Improved transportation unified the national economy; mass immigration provided the necessary labor force. Only one additional ingredient was yet required for the American economy to take off—a native technology capable of sustaining mass production.

Here again, the nation was at first heavily dependent on Britain. When Robert Fulton designed his steamboat, he had the engine made in England, for no one in the United States could produce such a complex piece of machinery.

| **Inventions** | Why did Americans succeed in winning independence from European technology? It has been suggested that Britain's restriction on the export of textile machinery and even on the emigration of skilled mechanics unwittingly forced Americans to become inventive. But the mere absence of British machines and artisans in this country did not compel investment. Americans still needed a reason to invest. It has also been thought that the chronic shortage of labor compelled Americans to devise labor-saving machinery.

This, again, is unconvincing. But certain facts of American society and culture may explain why technology grew so much more rapidly here than elsewhere. Freedom from traditional class barriers and the absence of guilds—the associations of craftsmen that in Europe had regulated the conditions and techniques of their trades—allowed Americans to experiment. Perhaps also the nation's natural wealth and the spread of prosperity among its citizens enticed Americans to see how the bounty at their disposal could be made even richer through technology. And the inventiveness that flowered amid this freedom and this promise was not for the sake of material gain alone: intellectual curiosity and an urge to invent were then powerful motives, as they have been in other times of technological and scientific experimentation.

During the first half of the nineteenth century, inventions for manufacturing and agriculture multiplied. Besides developing the automated grist mill, Oliver Evans pioneered in the design of the high-pressure steam engine, a distinct improvement over the British

Technological Development, 1750–1860
(Dates refer to patent or first successful use)

Year	Inventor	Contribution	Importance/Description
1787	John Fitch	Steamboat	First successful American steamboat
1793	Eli Whitney	Cotton gin	Simplified process of separating fiber from seeds; helped make cotton a profitable staple of southern agriculture
1798	Eli Whitney	Jig for guiding tools	Facilitated manufacture of interchangeable parts
1802	Oliver Evans	Steam engine	First American steam engine; led to manufacture of high-pressure engines used throughout eastern United States
1813	Richard B. Chenaworth	Cast-iron plow	First iron plow to be made in three separate pieces, thus making possible replacement of parts
1830	Peter Cooper	Railroad locomotive	First steam locomotive built in America
1831	Cyrus McCormick	Reaper	Mechanized harvesting; early model could cut six acres of grain a day
1836	Samuel Colt	Revolver	First successful repeating pistol
1837	John Deere	Steel plow	Steel surface kept soil from sticking; farming thus made easier on rich prairies of Midwest
1839	Charles Goodyear	Vulcanization of rubber	Made rubber much more useful by preventing it from sticking and melting in hot weather
1842	Crawford W. Long	First administered ether in surgery	Reduced pain and risk of shock during operations
1844	Samuel F. B. Morse	Telegraph	Made long-distance communication almost instantaneous
1846	Elias Howe	Sewing machine	First practical machine for automatic sewing
1846	Norbert Rillieux	Vacuum evaporator	Improved method of removing water from sugar cane; revolutionized sugar industry and was later applied to many other products
1847	Richard M. Hoe	Rotary printing press	Printed an entire sheet in one motion, vastly speeded up printing process
1851	William Kelly	"Air-boiling process"	Improved method of converting iron into steel (usually known as Bessemer process because English inventor had more advantageous patent and financial arrangements)
1853	Elisha G. Otis	Passenger elevator	Improved movement in buildings; when later electrified, stimulated development of skyscrapers
1859	Edwin L. Drake	First American oil well	Initiated oil industry in the United States
1859	George M. Pullman	Pullman car	First sleeping-car suitable for long-distance travel

Source: Freedom and Crisis: An American History, Third Edition, *by Allen Weinstein and Frank Otto Gatell.*
Copyright © 1974, 1978, 1981 by Random House, Inc. Reprinted by permission of the publisher.

engines of Newcomen and Watt. Norbert Rillieux, a free black, invented a multiple-effect evaporator to process the sugar cane grown in his native Louisiana. The endless fields stimulated significant improvements in farm machinery. Before Cyrus McCormick invented his reaper in 1831 a man with a sickle could cut approximately one acre of wheat in a day; with a reaper he could harvest ten to twelve. In 1837 John Deere perfected a steel plow capable of turning the tough prairie sod of Iowa and Illinois. In 1860 the United States Patent Office issued 4,589 new patents, a five hundred percent increase over 1820.

While inventions transformed basic industries and with them much of American life, other ingenious tinkerers sought to increase the comforts of the home: the steam radiator for home heating; an immensely important ice-making machine; condensed milk and concentrated coffee (which came in a cube, light, and with sugar), both invented by Gail Borden in the 1850s; the paper window shade; hundreds of different kinds of new stoves and lamps; thousands of household gadgets. A comfortable, efficient home sheltering a happy and sturdy family was an implicit part of the American democratic ideal, and technology rushed to further it.

Along with new inventions came a specifically American development: mass production employing interchangeable parts. This concept had originated in Europe, but an American, Eli Whitney, first applied it successfully. His unsuccessful fight to get a legal monopoly on his cotton gin had impoverished the inventor. Anxious to recoup his fortunes, Whitney struck upon an idea for producing great numbers of muskets quickly. According to this scheme, a factory making muskets would not make each one separately from parts constructed for it alone, but would make every component part in great quantity and then assemble the parts into identical muskets. In time the spread of interchangeable parts made it possible for owners of damaged objects to send away to a factory for the needed part, confident that the new one would precisely substitute for the old. "In short," Whitney wrote federal officials in 1798, "the tools which I contemplate are similar to an engraving on copper plate from which may be taken a great number of impressions exactly alike."

This was a bold proposal at a time when gunsmiths still made muskets one at a time, filing and fitting the individual pieces to mate them into a working mechanism. The government, then fearful of war with France, and highly respectful of Whitney's talents, accepted his audacious offer to manufacture ten thousand muskets in twenty-eight months. Whitney badly underestimated the difficulties of tooling up for this kind of operation; he was several years late in delivering the promised muskets. Gradually, however, his "uniformity system" gained acceptance, and it was applied in dozens of industries. Americans proved especially adept at designing and building the lathes, borers, and calipers necessary for the precision manufacture of parts for clocks, watches, and sewing machines.

On the eve of the Civil War, industrializa-

The American Economy		
	1815 (1820*)	**1860**
U.S. Population	8,419,000*	31,513,000
Northeast	50.4 percent*	36.5
South	30.4	25.6
West	19.2	37.8
Annual Immigration	8,385	153,640
Miles of Railroads	23	30,626
Cotton Production (bales)	209,000	3,841,000
Lumber Production (board feet)	600,000,000	8,000,000,000
Soft Coal Production (tons)	253,000	9,057,000
Comparative GNP per capita	67.6	137.0

McCormick's self-raking reaper was one of the many inventions that transformed American agriculture in the 1800s.

tion was far advanced in the United States. A modern transportation network had been laid down. A sufficient labor force had been assembled. The factory system had largely displaced household manufacture. Several industries—textiles, carpets, shoes, paper— were thoroughly mechanized. The American economy had begun to assume its now familiar shape.

Manufacturing on a mass scale altered American expectations. From colonial days the material environment had been permanent. People lived in the same houses, used the same furniture, employed the same implements, wore the same clothes, and viewed the same scene from youth to old age. Variety was the privilege of the rich. With the growth of manufactures all this changed. The material surroundings of the average American became diversified in ways undreamed of before. Americans were learning to live in a perpetually changing environment. Their surroundings increasingly taught them that the physical world of buildings, vehicles, implements of work could change over and over, as the older, stable, agricultural environments had once taught people that the world never changes much.

The Land and the People: The Northeast and mid–Atlantic

Between 1820 and 1860 manufacturing grew rapidly in the New England and mid-Atlantic states. Both sections boasted readily available capital and labor, and superior transportation. Turnpikes, rivers, the Erie Canal, and safe harbors provided good access to raw materials and markets. Commerce and agriculture, particularly dairy and truck farming, remained important in the region, but southern New England and the Hudson and Delaware river valleys began to resemble the most industrialized areas of Great Britain in their economy and social structure.

Factory Life   The conditions of labor changed fundamentally after 1820, as independent craftsmen, many men, women, and children from farms, and masses of immigrants became wage earners. The widespread adoption of steam power in the 1840s freed factories from their dependence on rural free-flowing streams for their power, and allowed them to be placed near cities. Henceforth workers were completely divorced from the land. The influx of immi-

grant labor worsened wages and working conditions in many industries. Most workers had no protection against long hours, occupational hazards, illness, or unemployment. Apprentice girls could have particularly trying assignments; the best that Lydia Noyes could say to her friend Mary was "we are not required to work before light or after nine at night."

The limited attempts at unionization in this period failed in the face of public hostility and periodic panics that so depressed the economy as to make it impossible for workers on strike to survive. Not until 1842, in the case of *Commonwealth v. Hunt,* did the Massachusetts Supreme Court uphold the legality of trade unions. White southerners could be as shocked at the condition of northern "free" labor as some northerners were at slavery. Free labor, wrote George Fitzhugh of Virginia,

is more cruel, in leaving the laborer to take care of himself and family out of the pittance which skill or capital have allowed him to retain. When the day's labor is ended, he is free, but he is overburdened with the cares of family and household, which make his freedom an empty and delusive mockery. . . . The Negro slave is free, too, when the labors of the day are over, and free in mind as well as body; for the master provides food, raiment, house, fuel, and everything else necessary for the physical well-being of himself and family.

Cities

Industrialism, immigration, and the expanding transportation system brought a more rapid growth of cities than has occurred at any other time in American history, before or since. In 1820 only 6.1 percent of the population lived in urban areas (that is, places of 2500 or more inhabitants). On the other hand, Pittsburgh in the same year was so heavily industrialized that, according to one traveler, "It is surrounded . . . with a dense black smoke which, bursting forth in volume from the foundries, forges, glasshouses, and the chimneys of all the factories and houses, falls in flakes of soot upon the dwellings and persons of the inhabitants. It is, therefore, the dirtiest town in the United States." By 1860

close to 20 percent of the people were city dwellers. On the eve of the Civil War there were fifteen cities (nine of them in the Northeast) with populations in excess of 50,000. Philadelphia exceeded 500,000 and New York passed 1,000,000.

The cities were hopelessly ill-equipped to deal with these numbers of people. Municipal water and sewage systems were in their infancy. Pigs roamed city streets, the only effective street cleaners. Housing was always in short supply. Many people lived in tiny apartments; often a whole family, and perhaps a few boarders, were crowded into the same room. The poorest lived in unfinished cellars. In 1849 a Boston doctor found "one cellar . . . occupied nightly as a sleeping-apartment for thirty-nine persons. In another, the tide had risen so high that it was necessary to approach the bedside of a patient by means of a plank which was laid from one stool to another; while the dead body of an infant was actually sailing about the room in its coffin."

New York's Crystal Palace Exhibition of 1853 recorded the accomplishments of Americans and symbolized the vitality of its cities. *(Courtesy, Eno Collection, New York Public Library)*

Cities festered in filth, overcrowding, and poverty. Cholera epidemics in 1832 and 1849 killed thousands. A canal boat helmsman wrote in 1834: "I am at present stearing the canal boat 'Emigrant' which runs from Cincinnati to Dayton which is 65 mils. I went to Santlewes [St. Louis] last sumer and staed thare one month. The collary [cholera] was thare very bad and in Cincinnati. Thare was not many cases on the canal but in town thare ware 80 and 100 of a day."

Fires were an everyday occurrence, sometimes leveling whole sections of cities. Crime, ranging from prostitution to burglary and murder, flourished everywhere, even on New York City's Broadway, where according to one contemporary "whores and blackguards made up about two-thirds of the throng." In response the business and middle classes created or expanded such institutions as the police force. Slowly, grudgingly, but inevitably cities ran up debts to finance water and sewer systems, street lights, schools, and parks.

Cities alternately repelled and fascinated Americans. Moralists condemned them as sinful. Native Protestants shuddered at the rapid growth of ethnic ghettos, where immigrants retained their old customs, languages, and Catholic religion. Americans now confronted contrasts between wealth and poverty that their republic in its egalitarian origins had never imagined. Still, people came to the cities in ever-increasing numbers—to visit, to work, to seek their fortunes. For those who could find steady employment, urban life with its shops, newspapers, amusements, and parks had many fascinations. New York's Crystal Palace Exposition of 1853, a visitor observed, reflected on a smaller scale the essential characteristics of the city as a whole: "What a wilderness of objects! Statues and statuettes, silks and satins, china and glass, furniture of all descriptions, and for all uses. What bright colors! What never ending glitter! What crowds of people!"

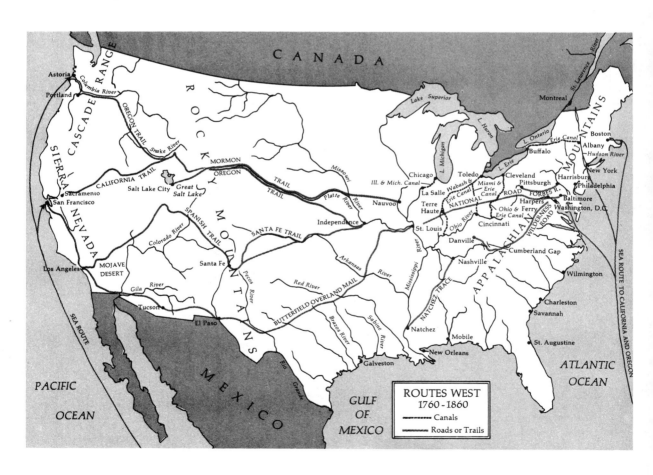

The Land and the People: The Midwest and Northwest

| **Farming** At the beginning of the nineteenth century eastern and European travelers were amazed at the fertility of western farms. One visitor to the Ohio River Valley in 1818 wrote:

> I believe I saw more peaches and apples rotting on the ground than would sink the British fleet. I was at plantations in Ohio where they no more knew the number of their hogs than myself. . . . And they have such flocks of turkies, geese, ducks, and hens, as would surprise you. . . . The poorest family has a cow or two and some sheep . . . and adorns the table three times a day like a wedding dinner—tea, coffee, beef, fowls, pigs, eggs, pickles, good bread; and their favorite beverage is whiskey, or peach brandy.

Between 1820 and 1860 the American economy showed a growing regional specialization. While manufacturing expanded in the Northeast and the South continued to cultivate staple crops for agriculture, the Northwest turned increasingly to commercial agriculture. The growth of industry, and the resulting rise of cities in the Northeast and in Europe, created a steadily expanding market for farm products. The upper Mississippi and Ohio valleys, with their fertile soil and vast tracts of public land, were in an ideal position to meet this need, especially after canals and railroads made it possible to ship large quantities of meat and grain directly eastward. The Northwest became the nation's breadbasket, supplying food for northern cities and southern plantations.

With every decade the centers of production for wheat, corn, cattle, hogs, and sheep shifted westward, as settlers opened the prairies to cultivation. Many of these newcomers had abandoned the thin soils of New England for places like Indiana and Michigan, where wheat yields were several times greater per acre. Farmers from the upper South flocked into the southern counties of Ohio, Illinois, and Indiana and gave that region a distinctively southern character. Sizable numbers of English, German, and Scandinavian immigrants migrated west, fanning out through the rich farmlands of Iowa, Illinois, Minnesota, and Wisconsin. On the eve of the Civil War the population of the Northwest, which had numbered less than one million in 1820, exceeded nine million.

Farms in the Northwest tended to be small—about 200 acres on the average. Most farmers owned their own land, relying for labor on their families, on hired help, and increasingly on machines. Wheat, always in demand, was the cash crop; and mechanical drills, harvesters, and threshers permitted an enormous increase in production throughout the period.

In the 1840s and 1850s wheat dominated farming in the upper Mississippi Valley almost as completely as cotton dominated agriculture in the lower South. Wheat and flour became important export items in the Fifties, undermining slightly the dominant position of cotton in American foreign trade. Western farmers also grew much corn and oats, but primarily as feed for livestock. The demands of eastern cities and southern planters assured a ready market and good prices for the beef, pork, and mutton of the prairies. Before railroads came to the Ohio Valley, cattle were driven overland to market; most hogs were slaughtered and packed locally. Frequently they were "stuck," or cut in the throat—often the pioneer woman's job. Then women and children took out and washed the various innards, saving the bladder to inflate and use as a football. So much pork was processed at Cincinnati that the city became known for a time as "Porkopolis." Later, increasing numbers of livestock were shipped east by rail to city markets for slaughter.

| **Cities** While the Northwest remained primarily agrarian, the region's cities grew swiftly. Older communities like St. Louis, Cincinnati, and Louisville all expanded rapidly in this period. Even more spectacular was the progress of new cities like Milwaukee, Indianapolis, and especially Chicago. In 1833 Chicago consisted "of about 150 wood houses . . . ," wrote one resident. "This is already a place of considerable trade, supplying salt, tea, coffee, sugar, and clothing to a large tract of country to the south and west." People then regarded Chicago "as the germ of an immense city." The Windy City had barely 17,000 people when Cyrus McCormick moved his reaper factory there in 1847: thirteen years later the population numbered 109,000. Yet the city remained a raw and uncomfortable place. Its mud was the subject

for endless tales. Signs read "No Bottom," "Road to China," or "Man Lost." A story was told of a man who saw a hat in the mud; picking it up, he saw a man's face underneath. "Say, stranger, you're stuck in the mud! Can I give you a hand to pull you out?" "Oh, no, thanks," replied the face, "I'm riding a good horse. He's got me out of the worst spots." These western cities served principally as extensions of the rural economy, processing, shipping, and marketing agricultural products. Their mills and packing houses led the country in 1850 in the production of lumber, flour and meal, liquor and meat. The cities were also the site of the growing farm-machinery industry.

The expansion of urban markets had a powerful effect on sectional alignments. Between 1820 and 1860, western farmers came increasingly to depend on eastern cities to purchase their produce, while the industrial Northeast, in turn, found a growing market for its manufactures in the western states. An economic bond was being forged between the two sections that would undermine the old alliance between the West and the South.

The Land and the People: The South

The antebellum southern economy was surprisingly diverse. Cotton was "King," but corn was actually the South's most widely grown crop. Many planters in Virginia and Maryland, their soil exhausted after prolonged tobacco cultivation, shifted to raising wheat or cattle. Rice grew in the swampy low country of South Carolina and Georgia. Southern Louisiana produced another exotic crop, sugar. Cotton, the South's major cash crop, was cultivated throughout the lower South. The center of cotton production moved steadily westward after 1820, the inevitable result of overplanting and soil exhaustion. Just before the Civil War over a fourth of the 4.3 million bales grown in the United States came from west of the Mississippi River. Southern industry was limited primarily to the processing of locally grown timber, tobacco, and grain, but a start had been made in the manufacture of cotton goods, machinery, and iron. A number of important cities—Baltimore, Richmond, New Orleans, St. Louis, Charleston, Mobile—dotted the South's navigable perimeter. One visitor to South Carolina admitted that the state's frontiersmen were no match for Yankee peddlers:

> As the value of the lands and the wealth of the inhabitants decrease, while you journey toward the back country, so also does the intelligence of the people. I never met in my whole life with so many white persons who could not read nor write, who had never taken a newspaper, who had never travelled fifty miles from home, or who had never been to the house of God, or heard a sentence read from his Holy Word, as I found in a single season in South Carolina. Many of them could not discern between the right hand and the left. What wonder then that the hosts of Yankee pedlers until driven out by the sumptuary laws, fattened upon the land! "What do you think I gave for that?" asked an ignorant planter in Sumpter district, while pointing to a Connecticut wooden clock which stood upon a shelf in the corner of the room. "I don't know," was my answer, "twenty dollars, or very likely twenty-five!" "*Twenty-five dollars, stranger!*" replied the planter; "why, what do you mean? Come, guess fair and I'll tell you *true!*" I answered again that twenty-five dollars was a high price for such a clock, as I had often seen them sold for a quarter of that sum. The man was astonished. "Stranger" said he, "I gave one hundred and forty-four dollars for that clock, and thought I got it cheap at that! Let me tell you how it was. We had always used sun-dials hereabout, till twelve or fourteen years ago, when a man came along with clocks to sell. I thought at first I wouldn't buy one, but after haggling about the price for a while, he agreed to take sixteen dollars less than what he asked, for his selling price was one hundred and sixty dollars; and as I had just sold my cotton at thirty-four cents, I concluded to strike a bargain. It's a powerful clock, but I reckon I gave a heap of money for it!"

> In fact, during those years when the staples of Carolina sold for nearly thrice their intrinsic value, and wealth flowed in an uninterrupted stream through every channel of industry, the plantations of the South became the legitimate plunder of Yankee shrewdness. It was no meeting of Greek with Greek in the contest of wits, but a perfect inrush of shrewd, disciplined tacticians in the art of knavery, upon a stupid and ignorant population.

Contrary to popular myth, the South was not inhabited solely by rich planters, impoverished "white trash," and enslaved blacks.

In 1860 the bulk of the South's 5.5 million whites lived on small farms not unlike those in the North. Most farmers owned their land, cultivating it with their own hands or the help of a few slaves. With the exception of rice and sugar, these yeoman farmers raised the same crops as did the planters. Many of them also grazed cattle. Outside of the older states of Virginia and the Carolinas, many small farmers moved upward into the planter class. They had little in common with poor whites—the "crackers" or "white trash"—who eked out a meager existence in the sterile sand hills or pine barrens. These unfortunate people existed under miserable living conditions and suffered the ravages of malaria, hookworm, and pellagra.

The Planters The actual number of planters was small. The federal census of 1860—defining a planter as a person owning at least twenty slaves—counted 46,274. Most of these owned up to fifty slaves and 500 to 800 acres. They were hardworking businessmen with field work to supervise, laborers to oversee, books to balance. And their wives seldom conformed to the southern-belle stereotype. Managing a large household required energy and intelligence, as well as graceful manners. Home was more likely to be a modest frame cottage than a Tara or a Mount Vernon. At the apex of southern society were the large planters. Although few in number—only 1700 people owned as many as a hundred slaves in 1850—these planter aristocrats cast a giant shadow over the region. Their wealth gave them considerable social and political influence. Living in palatial mansions or elegant townhouses, surrounded by vast fields and liveried servants, they represented the ideal to which other white southerners aspired before the Civil War.

In spite of this diversity, the South possessed a distinctive flavor. The great majority of southern whites were Protestant and Anglo-Saxon or Scotch-Irish. The economy was colonial: southerners raised staple crops for export and imported finished goods. Before the Revolution the South had traded mainly with England, but in the first half of the nineteenth century southern trade, lacking local capital for financing merchant shipping, came increasingly under the control of northerners, and particularly under the dominance of the port of New York. Above all, there was slavery, a uniquely southern institution that exerted a powerful influence over the region.

Although the number of great planters was small, slaveholding was remarkably widespread throughout the white South. Fewer than forty percent (38.7 percent) of the farmers in the Cotton South owned no slaves in 1850. This number increased to almost half (47.9 percent) by 1860, largely because the rapidly increasing cost of purchasing a slave priced many small farmers out of the market. But the important point is that on the eve of the Civil War most white farmers in the cotton-growing portions of the region were themselves slaveholders. And this understates the whites' stake in the South's peculiar institution. Many who did not own slaves rented their services to those who did. Others served as overseers on plantations, usually in the hope that several successive good harvests would earn them enough to buy a small farm and slaves of their own. Still other white southerners had sold their own slaves, prompted to do so by the windfall profits they could realize. All of these non-slaveholders had as pervasive ties to the institution of slavery as did the planters themselves. Further, the presence of millions of blacks gave whites of all classes something in common—a determination to keep the South a white man's country. Race consciousness helped to unify the white South.

The Slaves Slaves worked everywhere in the antebellum South: as common laborers, skilled craftsmen, and servants; in factories, mines, and foundries; on riverboats, wharves, and railroads; in hotels, stores, and private homes. A Charleston census of 1848 listed forty-six occupations that employed slaves. Most, of course, worked as field hands. Over half belonged to planters who owned twenty or more slaves. These large units were especially common in the newer states of the lower South, where the work was harder and the conditions more brutal than in the older slave states.

On farms of less than ten slaves, the slaves usually worked alongside their masters, who directly supervised their labor. Male slaves frequently performed the same tasks as the farmer and female slaves the same tasks as his wife, though in the busiest seasons all

$200 Reward.

RANAWAY from the subscriber, on the night of Thursday, the 30th of Sepember,

FIVE NEGRO SLAVES,

To-wit : one Negro man, his wife, and three children.

The man is a black negro, full height, very erect, his face a little thin. He is about forty years of age, and calls himself *Washington Reed*, and is known by the name of Washington. He is probably well dressed, possibly takes with him an ivory headed cane, and is of good address. Several of his teeth are gone.

Mary, his wife, is about thirty years of age, a bright mulatto woman, and quite stout and strong.

The oldest of the children is a boy, of the name of FIELDING, twelve years of age, a dark mulatto, with heavy eyelids. He probably wore a new cloth cap.

MATILDA, the second child, is a girl, six years of age, rather a dark mulatto, but a bright and smart looking child.

MALCOLM, the youngest, is a boy, four years old, a lighter mulatto than the last, and about equally as bright. He probably also wore a cloth cap. If examined, he will be found to have a swelling at the navel.

Washington and Mary have lived at or near St. Louis, with the subscriber, for about 15 years.

It is supposed that they are making their way to Chicago, and that a white man accompanies them, that they will travel chiefly at night, and most probably in a covered wagon.

A reward of $150 will be paid for their apprehension, so that I can get them, if taken within one hundred miles of St. Louis, and $200 if taken beyond that, and secured so that I can get them, and other reasonable additional charges, if delivered to the subscriber, or to THOMAS ALLEN, Esq., at St. Louis, Mo. The above negroes, for the last few years, have been in possession of Thomas Allen, Esq., of St. Louis.

WM. RUSSELL.

ST. LOUIS, Oct. 1, 1847.

slaves were likely to work in the fields together. On plantations slaves were organized in two ways. Rice planters preferred the task system, allotting individual slaves a particular task for the day. Cotton and tobacco planters favored the gang system, dividing the slaves into work parties under the supervision of an overseer or trusted Negro driver. The plantation routine followed the seasons in a monotonous cycle. Both men and women worked in the fields, plowing and planting in the spring, weeding in the summer, harvesting in the fall. In winter and in slack times, they dug ditches, repaired fences, and sawed wood. Although masters of large plantations usually worked their female slaves as hard as their male slaves, and assigned them to most tasks in the fields, they frequently observed gender distinctions in the organization of labor. Above all, they were likely to organize slaves into work gangs according to gender so that female field hands would work with other female field hands, frequently under the supervision of a male slave. Masters rarely assigned supervisory positions in field work to female slaves. The young and the el-

derly tended livestock or cared for the small children. Field hands labored from sunrise to sunset, with a rest at midday. They usually had Sunday off and received a week's vacation at Christmas. For many slaves these holidays, with their occasional feasts, dances, and visits to neighboring plantations, provided relief from the hardship of their daily lives. And in religious meetings the slaves created an "invisible" church. On Sunday nights they would go into the woods to sing, dance, shout, and pray.

Most slaves lived in rude cabins. Some masters encouraged their bondsmen to marry and live as families; others left the matter to the slaves or assigned them arbitrarily to a mate. The owner provided food, clothing, and medical care. The typical slave's ration consisted of cornmeal, fatback, and molasses; but many slaves varied this boring and unhealthful diet by raising their own vegetables or fishing.

Household servants and city slaves enjoyed a somewhat easier life than field hands. And many slaveholders hired out their bondsmen as servants, laborers, and mechanics, sometimes for extended periods. This practice of hiring out was especially common in the upper South and in the cities, where there was frequently a surplus of slaves. Many hired slaves became quasi-free, though the practice of hiring out normally brought more advantages to male than to female slaves. Although female slaves might be hired out as house servants, especially as cooks or nursemaids, their position did not give them much excuse for free movement in the society. Slave women, much like free white women, tended to be confined within households. Masters almost never offered slave women training in such skilled crafts as carpentry or blacksmithing. But the slave men who held those positions received an unusual opportunity to learn to read, to accumulate some money of their own, and, above all, to have an excuse to circulate fairly freely in society. The pool of slave craftsmen provided runaways and participants in revolts in disproportion to its numbers. Women, who did not belong to that pool, were less likely than men to run away or to engage directly in revolts.

Slaves had little motivation to work hard. Although some worked willingly for kindly masters, others delighted in "first-rate tricks to dodge work." Planters combined close supervision with a system of incentives—praise, additional rations, extra holidays—in an attempt to make their slaves work efficiently; but often they found it necessary to resort to whipping, deprivation of privileges, and other punishments to keep them in line. "The only principle that can maintain slavery," one comment went, "tis the principle of fear." Masters who maintained a rigid discipline probably had the least trouble in the long run. Those who found employing a lash distasteful—and there were many—might see their plantation go to ruin. Yet punishment too severe could bring the injury or loss of a prime male or fertile female, and no owner would want that. And of course there were cases of affection or respect. Some owners allowed their slaves to acquire property or taught them to read and write.

Slave men lacked many of the powers that free men could draw upon to maintain their control of women, notably the legal powers assigned to husbands and property owners. Yet slave women, as women, remained vulnerable to particular hardships such as sexual exploitation on the part of white men and be-

ing separated from their children. Slave women's reproductive capacities also afforded them some marginal advantages. Since masters were eager to increase the numbers of their slaves through reproduction—and the slaves of the United States were the only self-reproducing slave population in the New World—they were likely to accord women who claimed to be pregnant some release from work. But overall, slave women did not benefit from the idealization of womanhood that whites cultivated for themselves.

Was slavery profitable to the planters? Not all the evidence is in, but apparently it was. Investments in new plantations in the lower South consistently yielded a return upon capital sufficient to attract outside funds, an indication that a well-managed cotton plantation on good soil was at least as profitable as alternative forms of investment. Slaveholders in the less productive regions of the upper South exported their surplus slaves profitably to the Cotton Belt. For the South as a whole slavery was probably less economically beneficial. Four million blacks were kept in the strictest poverty, when as free property owners they could have provided a rich market for the products of southern agriculture and industry, and as free workers they could have constituted a versatile and energetic work force. Slavery caused white southerners to concentrate their resources in staple agriculture at the expense of industry and transportation. The human effects of slavery were, of course, horrible; it stifled the intellectual and creative energies of generations of black Americans.

Race Control   Slavery was more than a labor system; it was also a means of race control. The southern states enacted elaborate slave codes touching virtually all of black life. Slave marriages and divorces had no legal validity. Slaves were forbidden to leave their plantations without a pass, to be out after curfew, to congregate in groups unless a white man was present, to carry arms, or to strike a white person. They could not own property or testify in court against whites. Punishment for most crimes was left to the master, who was given immunity from prosecution should a slave die under "moderate" correction. Death was the penalty for rebellion or plotting to rebel. To enforce these codes, the white males mounted regular patrols, which traveled the neighborhood at night in search of arms or runaways. Members were chosen at militia muster and all members of the community—slaveholders and non-slaveholders alike—were supposed to take their turn.

Enslaved blacks faced the constant task of adjusting to the condition of bondage. Rebellion was rare; outright resistance was suicidal. When Nat Turner, a slave preacher, led a band of armed followers on a bloody rampage through Southampton County, Virginia, in 1831, killing sixty men, women, and children, terrified whites retaliated by slaughtering at least one hundred blacks. The South was on edge for months afterward. No one knew when this black fury, like some smothered volcano, would erupt again. Individual acts of resistance, such as arson, running away, or even suicide, were not uncommon. Instead of confronting their masters directly, blacks developed various stratagems of accommodation and subtle resistance. They became particularly adept at malingering, breaking tools, and otherwise obstructing the workings of a system in which they were not free participants.

The black family may have been a more cohesive unit than historians and sociologists once believed. If plantation records contain instances of families being broken up, these same sources reveal many others in which they remained intact over several generations. And even when spouses and children were sent to other areas, black people retained a powerful sense of family. After emancipation, thousands of blacks wandered across the South in search of relatives and loved ones.

A treasury of folklore demonstrates the extent to which slaves retained a sense of identity. Slaves blended African and New World materials into their own culture. Black spirituals were a form of religious music unique in sound and feeling but expressive of profoundly Christian themes of sorrow and hope. Spirituals could also be a commentary on the system in which the slave was imprisoned. One song, ostensibly about Biblical Samson, expressed the wish that "if I had my way, I'd tear this building down." "Field hollers" and work songs combated the boredom of mindless field labor and provided the coordination and timing essential to people working under close and difficult conditions:

> Massa in the great house, counting out
>   his money,
> Oh, shuck that corn and throw it in the barn.
> Mistis in the parlor, eating bread and honey.
> Oh, shuck that corn and throw it in the barn.

And in their quarters, conducting prayer meetings of their own, often in defiance of the law, the slaves created forms of preaching, of worship, of social union that would give structure to black society not only under slavery but in the dangerous century of freedom that followed emancipation.

Points To Think About

1. The shortage of skilled craftsmen and the relative isolation of many farming settlements meant that the average American needed to be a jack-of-all-trades. He had to know some carpentry, some masonry, something about shoemaking, and so forth. But he did not have to master any of the trades completely. America lived by the rule of thumb. Virtually nothing the average American needed to do required precise measurement or exact work.

As Elting Morison points out in his *From Know How To No Where*, the canals were the first projects that required modern engineering skills. Canals called for a very high level of workmanship. If their walls were not of a precise thickness, for example, they would leak; the water level would fall; and the boats would be unable to move. This is, in fact, what happened with most of the country's early canals.

The Erie presented enormous technical challenges. Gratings had to be measured exactly, new kinds of locks designed and built, and all had to be constructed to last for generations. The rule of thumb would not suffice. So the first generation of American engineers learned their profession on the job. For the next thirty years, the graduates of the Erie Canal would build the nation's canals, railroads, and machines.

In this sense the Erie had an enormous impact on American economic development quite apart from the improvement in transportation and shipping it brought. The Erie not only opened up the West but also provided the opportunity for Americans to learn the skills that rapid industrialization would require. In the long run, this may have been as important as the link between the Great Lakes and the Atlantic.

2. Historians, until recently, thought of slavery as an institution that, on the one hand, destroyed the African culture the slaves had brought with them and, on the other, prevented them from fully assimilating the white American culture. Slaves, for example, were not permitted to marry or learn to read. The rise of black consciousness in the 1960s prompted historians to reexamine the question, and their research now supports a sharply different view. Slaves did manage to hold on to at least some of their African heritage, and, more importantly, managed to build a distinctive Afro-American culture of their own despite the many obstacles the institution of slavery put in their way. Slaves formed stable families, developed their own religious institutions, produced a rich musical tradition, and invented their own language—a colorful and expressive variant of standard English that employed a number of African expressions and rhythms of speech.

One prominent black historian, John Blassingame, has developed a typology of male slave personality that can help us understand how blacks adapted to life on the plantations. The plantation, Blassingame reminds us, was more than just a big house, where the planter and his family lived, and cotton fields. It also included a slaves' quarters where blacks lived without any continuous white supervision. Black culture developed in the quarters. And it was developed by the kind of typical slave Blassingame nicknames "Jack." Unlike the shuffling, grinning "Sambo" who continually abased himself before whites and the rebellious "Nat" (named after Nat Turner) who either ran away or revolted, "Jack" accepted slavery as something he could not change but insisted on a measure of human dignity. "Jack" was normally quiet and obedient, but he expected the slave owner to treat him decently. He refused to accept cruel treatment or uncalled-for punishment. And he demanded that his family rights be respected. Blassingame's work is part of a continuing effort by scholars to demonstrate that, terrible as the institution was, even slavery did not crush the human spirit of black Americans.

Suggested Readings

Some recent studies include David Hawke, *Nuts and Bolts of the Past: A History of American Technology, 1776–1860* (1988), David J. Jeremy, *Transatlantic Industrial Revolution: The Diffusion of Textile Technology Between Britain and America, 1790–1830* (1981),Thomas Dublin, *Farm to Factory: Women's Letters, 1830–1860* (1981), Barbara Tucker, *Samuel Slater and the Origins of the American Textile Industry, 1790–1860* (1984), and Thomas C. Cochran, *Frontiers of Change: Early Industrialism in America* (1981).

Other good studies of economic development are Stuart Bruchey's *Roots of Economic Growth, 1607–1861: An Essay in Social Causation* (1968), Thomas C. Cochran's *200 Years of American Business* (1977), and George Rogers Taylor's *The Transportation Revolution, 1815–1860 (1951)*. The emergence of a market economy is discussed in W. Elliot Brownlee, *Dynamics of Ascent* (1974). The economic changes under way in the pre-Civil War era are covered in Cochran's *Frontiers of Change: Early Industrialism in America* (1981) and Paul Gates's *The Farmer's Age: Agriculture, 1815–1860* (1960). Ronald E. Shaw studied the Erie Canal in *Erie Water West* (1966). Anthony Wallace's *Rockdale* (1978) is an important study of an early textile community near Philadelphia, while Hannah Josephson treats both employer and employees in *Golden Threads: New England Mill Girls and Magnates* (1949).

The classic work on the United States of the 1830s is Alexis de Tocqueville's *Democracy in America* (1832). Although a French nobleman, Tocqueville was prepared to view the growth of popular institutions sympathetically. He defined a clash between free and strong individuality, which he believed was nurtured in a civilization of class distinctions, and a democratic tendency to submerge individuality within mass public opinion. He found that special conditions in this country made for a reconciliation of liberty and democracy.

FORREST McDONALD

The United States did not merely survive in the early nineteenth century; it thrived. By 1840 its territory, swelled with the acquisition of Louisiana and Florida, was double what it had been in 1790, and some of its citizens were looking hungrily toward California, Oregon, and Texas. Its population had grown even faster, from less than four million to more than seventeen million. Its economic growth was greater yet, its annual exports increasing nearly sevenfold, from $20 million to $132 million. Attending this phenomenal growth were a pair of institutions, capitalism and democracy, which made the young republic a beacon light for the world.

Capitalism was largely a matter of casting off shackles that had restrained economic endeavors from early times. Ancient religion had taught the nonsense that the love of money is the root of all evil, and for many dreary centuries a government-ridden, tradition-ridden, and priest-ridden western civilization was in paralysis and poverty because law and institutional inflexibility had discouraged and hampered the ambitious or flatly prohibited them from winning a profit. The American commitment to capitalism was based on an understanding that the desire for private profit quickens effort and inventiveness and can therefore be the wellspring of great public good. The principle was as simple as it was profound: that the free exchange of goods for private profit can better serve the material needs of society than can government planning, community spirit, or love of mankind. Into the bargain, Americans embraced a new, broadened concept of freedom: that people should be free to sell their time, their talents, and their labor as they alone see fit, and in exchange should take their chances on survival.

But all of this describes for the most part only the North, and only portions of the Northern population. The Southerners continued to follow the life patterns of their Scots, Irish, and Welsh ancestors as adapted in the new continent. The vast majority of white Southerners owned no slaves, did a little farming, and raised animals for cash. The minority who were slaveholders lived well or moderately so on the yields of their plantations. What the two major elements of white society had in common was a disinclination for a life given over to work and money. They had no prejudice against work if they could force slaves or animals to do it for them, but they were not disposed to do it themselves. The herdsmen simply let their animals roam the woods—anybody's woods, for the open range system that prevailed throughout the South prevented landowners from fencing any land except that with crops growing on it—and rounded them up for slaughter from time to time. Planters exploited the labor of the slaves—though even the slaves did not usually work especially hard, and their material standards of living were higher than those of most agricultural workers in Europe, Asia or Africa. Southerners, like Yankees, sought the material things of this world, but for use and enjoyment, not for Yankee-style accumulation. They preferred a leisure ethic as opposed to the Yankees' work ethic. They were generally indolent unless roused to war (which they loved) or to some other form of violent amusement.

Not all Americans were either Yankees or Southerners, of course. Most people in the Middle states from New York and Pennsylvania westward avoided the two extremes. As long as they remained neutral between the extremes, the United States could remain a house divided yet not divided against itself, and the nation could continue to thrive and grow. If the middle should embrace either side, and if enough loud and shrill voices began to cry that the house must be all one or all the other, the vibrant young republic would be torn asunder. In 1840, however, that sinister prospect seemed remote.

American Capitalism

EUGENE D. GENOVESE

Many commentators at home and abroad looked to a brilliant future for the new republic. Its tough, free, enterprising people, its extraordinary natural resources, the sheer size of its open spaces gave reason to expect that its history would be a happy one. Yet a country so short of capital and labor would surely take several centuries to develop into an important power. Probably few if any of the nation's optimistic observers would have predicted as fast a growth of the economy of the United States as actually happened. What was the place of capitalism in that growth?

It is the freedom that the modern world has given to the desire for profit, Professor McDonald suggests, that is the reason for the productivity and wealth of modern times; and capitalism, of course, worships profit. But in fact much more than the profit motive has found expression in recent centuries and moved populations to work and invent in such a way as to add to the world's wealth. Scientific curiosity, an inventor's delight in designing a new machine, even a simple dedication to work itself: all these, by themselves or mixed in with an ambition for personal gain, have made an increase in production. And the profit motive by itself has no interest in getting out a good product if it can make a flimsy one for greater margin of profit. The best motives for good workmanship operate in socialist nations as well as capitalistic ones. A successful capitalist may be an honest and dedicated worker; but capitalism and work are opposite and antagonistic to each other in basic motive. What the modern age has provided in the service of industrialism is not greed—which Professor McDonald quite correctly associates with capitalism—but a new way of looking at the world as not fixed but changeable in response to inventive effort. And it is that perception of the world, and not capitalism, that was the most creative component of nineteenth-century American civilization and provided a beacon for the world.

There was one fact about the remarkable expansion in the American economy that should have been an embarrassment to capitalism and to democracy both. The economic miracle arose on the strength of an export crop. Without that crop the American economy would have moved forward much more slowly. The crop was cotton. Its producers were hundreds of thousands, then millions, of laborers who did not enjoy the political rights that democracy demands, and did not possess that liberty to sell their labor-power on the market that capitalism proclaims. These laborers were black slaves. They or their forebears had been part of the massive forced migration from Africa—part of the millions who had been shipped into the plantation colonies by a greedy European capitalism. What they might have had to say about the American system of free enterprise, if anyone had thought to ask them, we must leave to our imaginations.

What did the slave plantations contribute to the American economy? The sale of cotton to Britain and Europe gave to Americans the financial credit with which to buy the industrial commodities and technology the country had to have for a modern economy. Southern cotton constituted the raw material for the Northern textile industry. Northern factories profited from orders from the South for clothing and for agricultural implements. Farmers migrated to the Northwest, which was supplying the South as well as the Northeast with food. An impressive meat-packing industry rose in Cincinnati, and before long the Northwest had a far-flung warehousing and shipping network and was demanding a national transportation system, the building of which would be another great industrial project. Since the South itself, like other plantation societies, did not develop its own financial and commercial facilities at as great a rate as that of its agricultural growth, northern bankers, insurance agents, and assorted middlemen did a splendid business; they thereby siphoned off much of the profits of the cotton trade to the advantage of the northern free states. Meanwhile, European capital was flowing into the country, attracted by the robust young economy and nourishing it further.

Elizabeth Cady Stanton. *(Courtesy, American Antiquarian Society)*

Lucretia Mott. *(Courtesy, Library of Congress)*

Stanton and Amelia Bloomer shown wearing the daring loose "bloomers"—long full Turkish trousers of black broadcloth with a short skirt and Spanish cloak. *(Seneca Falls Lily)*

The Logic of Democracy 1820–1860

THE WOMEN'S DECLARATION: SENECA FALLS, NEW YORK, JULY 19–20, 1848

The World Anti-Slavery Convention, held in London in 1840, was an even more important event in the women's rights movement than in the antislavery movement. American women, who had gained their first access to public platforms in antislavery activity, were horrified when their idols, the heroes of Great Britain's successful abolition of slavery in the empire, and particularly the many clergymen present, refused to allow them their seats as delegates to the conference. Lucretia Mott, who had long exercised a public role both in Quaker and in antislavery affairs, was particularly incensed. Her straightforward anger, her willingness to argue with the men, and especially her preaching in a Unitarian Church in London "opened to me a new world of thoughts," Elizabeth Cady Stanton would recall. One of Stanton's thoughts was of organizing for women's rights. "As Mrs. Mott and I walked away arm in arm, commenting on the incidents of the day, we resolved to hold a convention as soon as we returned home, and form a society to advocate the rights of women."

Eight years elapsed before this resolve bore fruit in the Seneca Falls Women's Rights Convention. The barriers had been many. Elizabeth Cady Stanton was newly married in 1840, and in the subsequent eight years she settled in three different locations, bore three children, and assumed all the other cares of a busy middle-class household. She needed further maturation and confidence to move on to a public stage. Lucretia Mott was unusual in having had so many opportunities, largely because of her Quaker environment, to speak in public and organize meetings. Stanton cautiously worked for a New York State law that would give married women control of their inherited wealth, but she remained quite timid, fearing the social disapproval that befell women who spoke in public on any subject, much less women's rights. Finally in 1848, with Lucretia Mott planning a visit to relatives in the Seneca Falls area, the two women made a last minute decision to hold a small local convention, which they advertised only in the Seneca Falls newspapers.

The results were a surprise to the organizers, the participants, and particularly the press and pulpit whose subsequent attacks gave the conference much of its historical importance. Three hundred people—including forty men—attended this meeting. Overwhelmed by the response, the women had Lucretia's husband James preside. In two days of orderly meetings, the Convention heard a series of well-prepared speeches, adopted a Declaration of Sentiments and a set of resolutions, and planned a set of further meetings that flowered into one of the major reform movements of American history.

What made the Seneca Falls Convention special and powerful was its Declaration of Sentiments. Written by Elizabeth Cady Stanton and modeled after Jefferson's Declaration of Independence, the document aligned women's rights with American ideology, challenging the nation to be true to its tradition. It also avoided the thicket of religious arguments about the role of women that had bedeviled the World Anti-Slavery Convention and was a major part of the anti-feminist argument then as now. The Declaration (reprinted here) is both a good summary of the sources of the women's rights movement and is still capable of provoking at least some of the controversy that it stirred in the years before the Civil War.

Declaration of Sentiments

When, in the course of human events, it becomes necessary for one portion of the family of man to assume among the people of the earth a position different from that which they have hitherto occupied, but one to which the laws of nature and of nature's God entitle them, a decent respect to the opinions of mankind requires that they should declare the causes that impel them to such a course.

We hold these truths to be self-evident: that all men and women are created equal; that they are endowed by their Creator with certain inalienable rights; that among these are life, liberty, and the pursuit of happiness; that to secure these rights governments are instituted, deriving their just powers from the consent of the governed. Whenever any form of government becomes destructive of these ends, it is the right of those who suffer from it to refuse allegiance to it, and to insist upon the institution of a new government, laying its foundation on such principles, and organizing its powers in such form, as to them shall seem most likely to effect their happiness. Prudence, indeed, will dictate that governments long established should not be changed for light and transient causes; and accordingly all experience hath shown that mankind are more disposed to suffer, while evils are sufferable, than to right themselves by abolishing the forms to which they were accustomed. But when a long train of abuses and usurpations, pursuing invariably the same object evinces a design to reduce them under absolute despotism, it is their duty to throw off such government, and to provide new guards for their future security. Such has been the patient sufferance of the women under this government, and such is now the necessity which constrains them to demand the equal station to which they are entitled.

The history of mankind is a history of repeated injuries and usurpations on the part of man toward woman, having in direct object the establishment of an absolute tyranny over her. To prove this, let facts be submitted to a candid world.

He has compelled her to submit to laws, in the formation of which she had no voice.

He has withheld from her rights which are given to the most ignorant and degraded men—both natives and foreigners.

Having deprived her of this first right of a citizen, the elective franchise, thereby leaving her without representation in the halls of legislation, he has oppressed her on all sides.

He has made her, if married, in the eye of the law, civilly dead.

He has taken from her all right in property, even to the wages she earns.

He has made her, morally, an irresponsible being, as she can commit many crimes with impunity, provided they be done in the presence of her husband. In the covenant of marriage, she is compelled to promise obedience to her husband, he becoming, to all intents and purposes, her master—the law giving him power to deprive her of her liberty, and to administer chastisement.

He has so framed the laws of divorce, as to what shall be the proper causes, and in case of separation, to whom the guardianship of the children shall be given, as to be wholly regardless of the happiness of women—the law, in all cases, going upon a false supposition of the supremacy of man, and giving all power into his hands.

After depriving her of all rights as a married woman, if single, and the owner of property, he has taxed her to support a government which recognizes her only when her property can be made profitable to it.

He has monopolized nearly all the profitable employments, and from those she is permitted to follow, she receives but a scanty remuneration. He closes against her all the avenues to wealth and distinction which he considers most honorable to himself. As a teacher of theology, medicine, or law, she is not known.

He has denied her the facilities for obtaining a thorough education, all colleges being closed against her.

He allows her in Church, as well as State, but a subordinate position, claiming Apostolic authority for her exclusion from the ministry, and, with some exceptions, from any public participation in the affairs of the Church.

He has created a false public sentiment by giving to the world a different code of morals for men and women, by which moral delinquencies which exclude women from society, are not only tolerated, but deemed of little account in man.

He has usurped the prerogative of Jehovah himself, claiming it as his right to assign for her a sphere of action, when that belongs to her conscience and to her God.

He has endeavored, in every way that he could, to destroy her confidence in her own powers, to lessen her self-respect, and to make her willing to lead a dependent and abject life.

A Reforming Spirit: Political and Economic Radicalism

During the first half of the nineteenth century, new social forces broke in upon the American villages, farms, and regions that had once existed in near isolation, practicing slow, traditional ways of work and life. Poverty, disease, and illiteracy became more concentrated and apparent as cities grew. The transportation revolution broke down barriers of distance and isolation, uprooting established communities and existing markets. Increasing reliance on machines turned independent craftsmen and sturdy farmers into wage earners. The tempo of life had speeded up. An English watchmaker who emigrated to New York in 1832 wrote in his diary: "My employers have brought me so much work that I have scarce anytime for reading [as he evidently had had in England]." An Irish moulder was shocked by his first visit to an American foundry:

> I peered into the semi-darkness and saw men, bare-headed and almost nude racing back and forth, handling between trips small wooden hammers most dextrously. I asked . . . a bystander what was going on inside, and was told it was a foundry. The information made me gasp. I had never seen a foundry like it. Mechanics, and for that matter all others in the old country never worked so exhausting a way as these men did. . . . The American moulders seemed desirous of doing all the work required as if it were the last day of their lives.

A few Americans questioned the very foundations of capitalism. Some turned to religious or social experiments designed to reform society. A large number, however, aimed at correcting specific problems. Reformers disagreed on goals and methods. But they shared frustration at disorder in society, apprehension about loss of consensus and community, and fear that morality was declining. These pessimistic motives for reform combined with an optimistic motive: a faith in the ultimate perfectibility of the world in general and American society in particular. A vigorous and many-sided movement for reform gained energy in the 1830s and continued to the Civil War.

| **The Early Labor Movement** | The American labor movement had its origins in the economic upheavals of the Jacksonian era. In dozens of cities, craftsmen and artisans organized associations and sponsored strikes for better hours and wages. A few citywide federated unions and one national federation—the National Trades' Union—existed until hostile judges and the economic cataclysm of 1837 dragged them under. Labor also entered politics. In the early 1830s, for example, New York City workingmen organized politically to seek improved working conditions, free public education, abolition of imprisonment for debt, and an end to chartered banks and other monopolies. Most of their demands were eminently practical; some of their leaders were not.

Frances Wright and Robert Dale Owen attracted a considerable following in New York. "Fanny" Wright's avowals of atheism and her intemperate attacks on organized religion caused one conservative newspaper to brand her "the great Red Harlot of Infidelity"; Owen advocated birth-control measures to alleviate the miseries of the poor. Their chief remedy for society's ills, however, was to make the state guardian of all children, providing them with food, clothing, board, and education. Only then could they enter a highly competitive world on an equal footing. Opponents immediately denounced state guardianship as an infringement on parental rights and a covert attack on marriage. The question of endorsing it split the ranks of New York workingmen.

George Henry Evans had another remedy for unemployment and poverty: "Let us . . . emancipate the white laborer, *by restoring his natural right to the soil.*" As early as 1834, Evans advocated free land grants to actual settlers and a limitation on the holdings of any one person. Adopting the motto "Vote yourself a farm," he tried for years to convince Eastern workingmen that their happiness and independence could be found only in agriculture. In 1862, six years after Evans's death, Congress passed the Homestead Act, offering free grants of Western land. Workingmen did not have the capital, the knowledge, or the desire to go west and take up farming; and so the Homestead Act did not succeed in making independence and prosperity available to the whole nation. But the Act, an important component of the Republican scheme for nurturing the economy under governmental leadership, was a nineteenth-century foreshadowing of more daring twentieth-century social reforms.

A Reforming Spirit: Religious Movements

| **The Second Great Awakening** | During the first part of the nineteenth century, America experienced a second "Great Awakening" of religious enthusiasm. Relying on the excitement of revival meetings, a wide variety of evangelical sects sought to turn the masses toward spiritual regeneration. Evangelists like Charles G. Finney rejected the harsh traditional Calvinist view of original sin and predestination and preached that any good Christian could attain eternal salvation. Their teachings generally involved a literal interpretation of the Bible. Many emphasized the Second Coming of Christ and believed that God's Kingdom would establish itself on earth. This religious resurgence reflected distinctly American values and attitudes. Its intensely democratic message stressed individual free will and immediate salvation; it breathed optimism; it brought religion to the people in language they could understand. These common people wanted sermons devoid of "literary quibbles and philosophical

Shaker Society Meeting. During worship members were sometimes "seized with a mighty trembling, with violent agitations of the body, running and walking on the floor, with singing, shouting, and leaping for joy." *(Courtesy, American Antiquarian Society)*

speculations." As one spiritual put it to music, every person wanted to "see bright angels stand waiting to receive me."

The characteristic doctrine of the Second Great Awakening was perfectionism, the idea that human beings could achieve not merely salvation, but could overcome sin altogether. Perfectionism's Scriptural basis lay in the New Testament account of Jesus telling his disciples that they were to "be perfect, even as your Heavenly Father is perfect." Charles Grandison Finney, the most successful of the revivalists of the day, read this text literally. Jesus did not tell his followers to try to be perfect, he reasoned. He told them to be perfect. Since he had, Finney argued that he must also have supplied the means for them to do so. There must be a special form of divine assistance, a special grace, available to the converted, which would enable them to transcend their sinful natures and achieve

moral perfection. Here was a doctrine matched to the contemporary American belief that this truly was a New World and that Americans could avoid the ills of the Old. Like the first Great Awakening of a century before, the new evangelicalism was more than a religious movement. And the spirit of perfectionism animated the many reform movements of the era.

The Second Great Awakening has been called "a women's awakening." Although men certainly responded to the religious enthusiasm, women far outnumbered them among converts and played a decisive role in leading men either back to established churches, or into new ones. Historians have shown that male conversions frequently followed the conversion of one or more female members of the family. Mothers often proved especially influential in converting their sons and husbands. But the most characteristic

RELIGIOUS ECSTASY ON THE FRONTIER *The renowned evangelical preacher Lorenzo Dow early in the nineteenth century*

had heard about a singularity called the *jerks* or *jerking exercise* which appeared first near Knoxville, Tennessee, in August last, to the great alarm of the people. . . .

When I arrived in sight of that town, I saw hundreds of people collected in little bodies; and observing no place appointed for meeting, before I spoke to any, I got on a log, and gave out a hymn; which caused them to assemble round, in solemn attentive silence: I observed several involuntary motions in the course of the meeting, which I considered as a specimen of the jerks.

Thus I got on to meeting; and after taking a cup of tea gratis, I began to speak to a vast audience, and I observed about thirty to have the *jerks,* though they strove to keep still as they could; these emotions were involuntary and irresistible, as any unprejudiced eye might discern.

Hence to Mary's-ville, where I spoke to about fifteen hundred, and many appeared to feel the word, but about fifty felt the jerks; at night, I lodged with one of the Nicholites, a kind of Quakers who do not feel free to wear coloured cloaths; I spoke to a number of people at his house that night. Whilst at tea, I observed his daughter, (who sat opposite to me at the table), to have the jerks, and dropped the teacup from her hand, in the violent agitation: I said to her, "young woman, what is the matter?" she replied, "I have got the jerks." I asked her how long she had it? she observed, "a few days," and that it had been the means of the awakening and conversion of her soul, by stirring her up to serious consideration about her careless state, &c.

Soon after I spoke again in Knoxville, to hundreds more than could get into the Court house, the Governor being present; about one hundred and fifty appeared to have the jerking exercise, amongst whom was a circuit preacher, who had opposed them a little before, but he now had them powerfully; and I believe that he would have fallen over three times had not the auditory been so crowded that he could not, unless he fell perpendicularly.

After meeting, I rode eighteen miles, to hold meeting at night: The people of this settlement were mostly Quakers: and they had said, (as I was informed) the Methodists and Presbyterians have the jerks, because they *sing* and *pray* so much, but we are still peaceable people, wherefore we do not have them: However, about twenty of them came to meeting, to hear one, as was said, somewhat in a Quaker line; but their usual stillness and silence was interrupted; for about a dozen of them had the jerks as keen and powerful as any I had seen, so as to have occasioned a kind of grunt or groan when they would jerk. It appears, that many have undervalued the great revival, and attempted to account for it altogether on natural principles; therefore it seems to me, (from the best judgment I can form), that GOD hath seen proper to take this method, to convince people that he will work in a way to shew his power; and had sent the *jerks* as a sign of the times, partly in judgment for the people's unbelief, and yet as a mercy to convict people of divine realities.

converts were adolescent girls. An affirmation, or reaffirmation, of religious belief and commitment seems to have offered young women a powerful sense of identity and purpose at a time in which their brothers and male peers could look forward to identifying themselves with jobs or careers, while women were expected to prepare for a life of secluded domesticity.

Religious enthusiasm rapidly increased the membership of most Protestant denominations, Methodists and Baptists increasing the fastest. But new sects also arose. Each new prophet, interpreter, or mystic found followers willing to join in anticipating the literal fulfillment of even the most outlandish prophecies. For a time the poor farming district of upstate New York burned with religious emotions. "Enthusiastic" sects, sects cultivating emotion—among them Adventists and Universalists—flourished in this "burned-over district," as it was called: whatever the ultimate derivation of the phrase, it came to signify a region seared by fires of religious enthusiasm.

Some of the fervent young religious movements of the early 1800s encouraged believers to join together in exclusive communities of the faithful. The more distinctive the tenets of their faith, leaders reasoned, the more necessary the intensive instruction and supervision that community living made possible. This often led to communal property-holding and cooperative economic enterprise. Many of the religious communities barely survived the death of their founders; others, such as the Shaker Society, lasted a century or more.

The Shakers and the Mormons The Shaker faith, brought to this country by Ann Lee in 1774, received its name from one of its most distinctive practices, a sacred dance during which the members "shook" their bodies free of sin through their fingertips. "Mother Ann," as she was called, believed that she had received direct revelations from God and, since she preached millennialism—that is, the imminent coming of the millennium, the period of Christ's rule on earth—she saw no need for the Shakers to have children. The members therefore practiced celibacy. After reaching a membership of some six thousand in the 1830s, the Shakers gradually died out. Their furniture and housing arrangements, which were simplicity itself, are their best-remembered achievements.

By far the most important of the religious communitarians were the Mormons. Mormonism strikingly elaborated the new theology of free will, direct revelation, universal salvation, the expectation of Christ's imminent return, and the establishment of a millennial Kingdom.

In 1830, at the age of twenty-five, Joseph Smith of Palmyra, New York, published the *Book of Mormon*. He had transcribed it, he claimed, from gold plates that had lain undisturbed in a nearby hillside for more than a thousand years. The angel Moroni had directed him to the spot where the plates were buried. Using two magic "seeing stones" fixed in silver bows, Smith translated the ancient script into a readable text. The book was a curious mixture of Old Testament theology, popular history, and social beliefs of the times.

One young man recalled the accounts of the doings of Smith and his followers.

> It was adjoining one of the farms where the farce of walking on the water was enacted. It was in haying time and the Cornwalls were mowing near the river and they discovered tracks through the brush to its bank. The boys made an examination which developed a plank bridge just under the water which extended across a level branch of the river to its opposite side. The planks were supported by legs driven into the ground, upon which they were supported, and a tall straight tree was plainly visible in its line. The mowers procured a saw and weakened the third plank so that no one could step upon it without going into the river to its bottom. That night from a good vantage point the boys watched for its development. After dark on came Smith with a number of his proselytes to see walking on the water verified. Smith stepped forth with confidence and turned to address his hearers, telling them that this performance was wholly a matter of faith and that their faith for its success was as necessary as was his own, and continuing we will all thus continue our faith—and walking onward until coming to the weakened legs, down went the prophet breast deep into the river. He clambered out of the water with the answer that their faith had weakened and that this alone was not sufficient to support him on the water.

Jemimah Wilkinson, the "Universal Friend" of Penn Yan, New York, also took followers to water, but she asked them if any doubted that she could walk on it. When no one spoke, she left saying that it would therefore not be necessary to perform the miracle.

Although Mormonism borrowed freely from the convictions and practices of evangelical Protestantism, it offered a simple alternative to the confusing proliferation of Christian sects. By extending salvation to all adherents and clerical status to each adult white male, and by stressing the sanctity of secular accomplishments and the need for a community of "saints" (the church's official name was and is "The Church of Jesus Christ of Latter-Day Saints"), the new faith tapped the energies and talents of the unsuccessful and the neglected. In Joseph Smith, a prophet at the top of the church hierarchy who received instructions or revelations directly from God, Mormonism provided theological truths and authoritarian leadership to whoever craved practical and spiritual guidance.

After converting a small group of relatives and friends, Smith moved his flock to Ohio and then to Missouri in an attempt to establish a commonwealth of believers. In each place, nonbelievers persecuted the Mormons and drove them from their lands. In 1839 Smith led his followers to Illinois. After securing political authority from state officials, he founded a city, called Nauvoo, which became a self-sufficient religious community. The success of Nauvoo, which grew to fifteen thousand inhabitants by 1844, as well as its voting power in state elections, brought the envy and hostility of outsiders. Smith's increasingly eccentric behavior (he declared himself a candidate for President in 1844) also generated unfavorable publicity. When a disgruntled Mormon confirmed that Smith and other members of the church's elite practiced polygamy, state officials arrested Smith and his brother. Soon after their confinement at Carthage, a mob of disbanded militia murdered them both.

When the harassment and violence continued, Brigham Young, Smith's successor to the presidency of the church, led the Mormons on the long difficult exodus from Illinois to uninhabited Mexican territory beyond the Rocky Mountains. Under Young's stern but effective leadership, the Mormons established a thriving agricultural community near the Great Salt Lake. Believers recall a miracle that saved that first band. After a desperate winter, the Mormons had planted a small crop and irrigated it by hand, a backbreaking task. Then, just as harvest time approached, a horde of locusts swept down upon the fields. Near despair as they watched the insects devouring the only food available for the next winter, the Mormons suddenly heard the calls of hundreds of seagulls. The mysterious visitors, a thousand miles away from any ocean, ate the locusts and saved the community. The event freshened the vision of a new Zion. By 1877, the year of Young's death, the commonwealth numbered some 350 settlements with a total population of 140,000.

Organized like a medieval kingdom, the church collected from each individual an annual tithe in goods, labor, or money, and channeled this surplus into projects that benefited everyone. Banning or discouraging the use of tea, coffee, tobacco, liquor, fashionable clothing, and elegant furniture, the church curtailed wasteful spending and assured the development of an industrious community. This mixture of collectivism and private enterprise saved the community from the worst evils of uncontrolled capitalism and prevented Utah from becoming dependent on imports from the industrial East.

Although the Mormons wished to be self-sufficient and independent, they also considered themselves Americans and asked for Utah's admission to the Union. Congress, however, balked at the Mormon practice of polygamy, which the Republican Party had linked to slavery. In fact, only a small percentage of the community participated in this patriarchal institution; but most of the American public thought that Brigham Young's twenty-seven wives and fifty-six children were typical, and they considered polygamy to be a form of "Oriental" debauchery. In 1890 the church formally renounced polygamy. Mormonism was retreating from the attempt to establish a society operating in entire accordance with religious principles and communal ideals. Mormons continued however to integrate themselves tightly into the life of their church and community. Congress admitted Utah to the Union in 1896.

| Millennialism   Not content with establishing an earthly paradise, some Americans looked to the fulfillment in their own time of the New Testament prophecy of Christ's Second Coming. The foremost exponent of millennialism was William Miller, a hard-working farmer in upstate New York who became caught up in a revival shortly after the War of 1812 and spent the rest of his life pondering religious questions. A literal interpretation of the Bible led him to a graphic belief in the Second Coming or Advent, which he calculated would occur in about 1843. Aided by the widespread economic distress of the late 1830s, Miller made crowds of converts throughout New England with his vivid sermons depicting the glory of the Advent, the joy of those who would be saved, the suffering of the unrepentant. In a single year he gave 627 hour-and-a-half lectures before eager audiences, often of a thousand or more. Ministerial disciples with a knack for publicity spread Miller's views over an even wider area.

Miller spoke lines like these throughout the 1830s:

Ah! what means that noise? Can it be thunder? Too long—too loud and shrill—more like a thousand trumpets sounding an onset. It shakes the earth. . . . See how it reels. How dreadful! How strange! The very clouds are bright with glory. . . . See, the heavens do shake, the vivid clouds, so full of fire, are driven apart by this last blast, and rolling up themselves, stand back aghast—And O, my soul, what do I see? A great white throne, and One upon it. . . . Before him are thousands and thousands and thousands of wingèd seraphim, ready to do his will. The last trumpet sounds—the earth now heaves a throb for the last time, and in this last great throe her bowels burst, and from her sprang a thousand thousand, and ten thousand times ten thousand immortal beings into active life. . . . I saw them pass through the long vista of the parted cloud, and stand before the throne. . . . The air now become stagnated with heat; while the dismal howlings of those human beings who were left upon the earth, and the horrid yells of the damned spirits . . . filled my soul with horror not easily described.

Miller hesitated to give his frantic followers a definite date, promising only that deliverance would come soon, in God's appointed time. As 1843—the Last Year—passed, March of 1844 came to be accepted as the crucial month. (A little girl told her mother, "I want to die this summer—I don't want to live next year and *be burnt up*.") Finally, when nothing happened, a weary and discouraged Miller frankly admitted his mistake, explaining that he had done his best. But his lieutenants were not yet ready to quit. They chose October 22, 1844, as the new "Advent Day" and talked Miller into accepting it. Excitement mounted higher than before as extensive preparations were made to enter God's Kingdom. The faithful made themselves white "ascension robes" and neglected nearly all secular business. Voting in the fall elections was very light in some districts. Crowds blocked the streets near Boston's Millennial Tabernacle, forcing the mayor to close the building.

On the night of October 21, Millerites gathered on hilltops to meet the new world together. No provisions were made for eating or sleeping, and many suffered as the night and the next day and then another night passed; in some places severe thunderstorms added to their terror. Some claimed to have seen a jeweled crown in the sky. In western New York, an earthquake intensified the expectation. A few Adventists committed suicide—one man leaped over Niagara Falls. The day of the "Great Delusion" effectively ended the Adventist movement, although isolated Adventist sects continued to flourish.

The Fox Sisters

Various forms of spiritualism, or attempts to contact the spirit world, were another manifestation of the desire to break down all barriers between this world and the next. Mesmerism, electro-biology, clairvoyance, phrenology, magnetism—each had its following. New York farmer John Fox had two remarkable young daughters, Maggie and Katie. Wherever they went in their home, mysterious rapping sounds were heard. Eventually the girls and their mother worked out a system of communication with the presumably otherworldly source of the rappings. Soon the neighbors flocked in to observe these conversations with the spirit world. The Fox home in this year 1848 set off a mania of spiritualist excitement. With an older sister acting as manager, the Fox girls began holding exhibitions—at the insistence of the spirits, of course—and quickly developed into professional fee-charging mediums.

With the wide publicity given the Fox sisters, mediums rapidly appeared all over the country, and spiritualist circles developed in nearly every town and village. They refined their techniques as they went along; the Foxes' managing sister, for instance, discovered that total darkness could produce many more manifestations of the spirits' presence. Table-moving, spirit-writing, and cold, ghostly hands soon supplemented the mystic rappings, and within a few years all the now-familiar paraphernalia of spiritualism were in use. The spiritualist excitement filled for thousands of people a need to become more comfortable with the mysteries of death and immortality. A number of intellectuals saw in spiritualism a replacement for traditional Christianity—a proof of the existence of a supernatural world for a scientific age that could not accept revelation resting only on faith. Even when the Fox sisters some years later admitted that their whole career had been a fraud (the rappings had from the first been produced by the joints of their toes), many spiritualists remained undeterred.

Methodism

The most powerful evangelical movement, more orthodox than these other religions of excitement, had begun in the eighteenth century. John Wesley had led within the Church of England a revival movement that after his death produced a separate denomination, the

Methodist church. Methodists believed in free will. In its early days especially, Methodism had a strong element of emotional revivalism; but it also preached a rigorous piety and a morality of self-discipline, industry, thrift, and good works. Methodism was powerfully attractive, in Great Britain to the working classes and to the poor, and in this country to people on the frontier. It is said that in both nations it had something to do with the bringing of an ordered moral life to previously disordered sections of society. While the Methodist church did have an organization, in its first period it did not stress the role of bishops or of a highly trained ministry. That made it possible for Methodism here to develop a distinctive and effective system in which preachers, many with little, if any, formal religious education, would travel about on the frontier, bringing a sustaining Methodism to the families and communities at which they stopped.

Each preacher worked a "circuit" or route that covered a particular area. Francis Asbury, who had come to this country in 1771 and was influential in the beginnings of Methodism here, was an early and influential traveling preacher. The typical circuit rider went by horseback, depended on friendly settlers for food and shelter, and was much a part of the frontier environment: the evangelist Peter Cartwright could thrash a rowdy who tried to disrupt a Methodist meeting.

Cartwright would hold his revivals outside in a grove because the local church could not hold the crowds he attracted. Of his own conversion at such a camp meeting he recalled:

> The people crowded to this meeting from far and near. They came in their large wagons, with victuals mostly prepared. The women slept in the wagons, and the men under them. Many stayed on the ground night and day for a number of nights and days together. Others were provided for among the neighbors around. The power of God was wonderfully displayed; scores of sinners fell under the preaching, like men slain in mighty battle; Christians shouted aloud for joy.
>
> To this meeting I repaired, a guilty, wretched sinner. On the Saturday evening of said meeting, I went, with weeping multitudes, and bowed before the stand, and earnestly prayed for mercy. In the midst of a solemn struggle of soul, an impression was made on my mind, as though a voice said to me, "Thy sins are all forgiven thee." Divine light flashed all round me, unspeakable joy sprung up in my soul. I rose to my feet, opened my eyes, and it really seemed as if I was in heaven; the trees, the leaves on them, and everything seemed, and I really thought were, praising God.

The Methodists divided their territory into regions, each holding an annual conference that heard reports, appointed new preachers, and assigned circuits. As the frontier became heavily populated, large circuits—some had been hundreds of miles long—were replaced by smaller ones, and by about the middle of the nineteenth century these had given way to settled parishes. By that time the Methodist church had become the largest Protestant denomination in the country.

A Reforming Spirit: Secular Communitarianism

Dozens of experimental communities built upon a trust in human perfectibility sprouted up in the nineteenth century, some of them later succumbing to selfishness, quarrels, or loss of interest.

| New Harmony Robert Owen, a famous English socialist whose model factory town at New Lanark, Scotland, inspired many American utopians, organized his own communal experiment at New Harmony, Indiana. Owen believed that the American West provided the unspoiled and egalitarian location that a new social system required, and in 1825 he collected a mixed group of followers whom he intended to transform into a prosperous, self-governing community. Stressing cooperation and common ownership of property, Owen hoped to eliminate selfishness and want. Quarrels and dissatisfaction finally forced Owen to abandon his misnamed experiment. Such experiments, his son Robert Dale Owen later concluded, were bound to fail in a country where cheap land and high wages fostered individualism and discouraged cooperative action.

A Philadelphia Anabaptist Immersion During a Storm, by Pavel Svinin. *(Courtesy, Metropolitan Museum of Art, Rogers Fund, 1942)*

❘ Brook Farm Brook Farm, a New England community, existed for a few years in the 1840s. Most of its members, such as Margaret Fuller, Nathaniel Hawthorne, and its founder George Ripley, were New England intellectuals; and it was influenced by Transcendentalism, a moral and spiritual doctrine to which numbers of New England writers and social critics adhered. Transcendentalism was an American variant of the idealist philosophy that teaches that the world of material objects as we see them is really no more than an expression of mind or consciousness. Transcendentalists believed that since it is mind rather than the objective and physical world that is the ultimate reality, the mind ought to draw into itself and cultivate its own powers. Transcendentalist intellectuals opposed slavery and other institutions that they perceived as getting in the way of individual and collective perfection. Brook Farm aimed at combining manual and intellectual work; this, its members hoped, would develop and enrich the inner self. Brook Farm—much of it destroyed by a major fire—is remembered for the high and not always practical intellectuality of its life, though residents did operate a successful experimental school.

❘ The Oneida Community John Humphrey Noyes, whose social ideas rested on perfectionism, founded a community at Oneida in upstate New York. Residents operated thriving manufactures, but the community was better known for its sexual arrangements. Wishing to substitute cooperativeness for competitive individualism, Noyes prohibited "special love" and instead established "complex marriage," a system in which every member resident was considered married to every other of the opposite sex. Like the Shakers, the communitarians at Oneida were seeking to control sexuality. They wished to break down the idea that any woman "belonged" to any man or that any child was the exclusive "property" of the biological parents. So where the Shakers practiced strict abstinence, Noyes and his followers engaged in what they called "sexual communion." This involved sexual intercourse, but not male climax, unless the community had previously decided on the desirability of the woman becoming pregnant.

Sexual communion involved the regular rotation of sexual partners. And it entailed the use of communal nurseries to raise children. Women had sexual equality with the men and shared in the work; the entire community had responsibility for the children. The community had a prosperous and successful existence, derived from making Oneida silverplate and carrying on other successful business enterprises. Later in the century it abandoned complex marriage in the face of attacks from moral critics.

A Reforming Spirit: Social Reform

Some shared the communitarians' basic optimism that the United States was still a plastic society, not yet set in its ways, and therefore malleable to the reformers' efforts. Prison reformers, for example, often thought that the new penitentiary would all but eradicate crime. Others came to reform out of a deep pessimism. They believed that American society was in an advanced state of collapse and that only the most radical reform could halt the decay they saw all about them. At the top of their list of danger signals was the decline, as they saw it, of religion in American public life. Actually, Americans in the Jacksonian era were much more likely to belong to a church and to attend it faithfully than their parents and grandparents of the Revolutionary era had been. But, as people followed the frontier westward, they left their churches behind and many feared that the Ohio and Mississippi Valleys would develop as pagan enclaves. Or worse. Many Protestants worried that the Catholic presence in St. Louis, a holdover from the French exploration of the Mississippi, might presage the loss of the interior of the continent to Romanism, as Catholicism was often called. Other Americans were leaving their homes not for the frontier but for the rapidly growing cities. Some, like Rochester, New York, were brand new "boom" towns. Others, like New York City, were already well established. All seemed to threaten the central role of the church in people's lives. No longer was the church the essential institution it had been, and still was, in village life. No longer did the pastor exert personal influence over everyone's public behavior. In the cities houses of prostitution operated seven days a week. Taverns served all comers. And the city's anonymity weakened old forms of social control, such as one's neighbors' disapproval of certain kinds of behavior. Large scale immigration, especially of Irish and German Catholics, further undermined the old supremacy of Protestant morality.

Still another danger sign was the crime which accompanied urban growth. Colonial America had had comparatively little street crime, but the Jacksonian era saw the emergence of packs of young toughs, gangs who roamed the streets and made travel after dark a risky undertaking. Almost as disturbing as crime was the growth of a highly visible underclass of the propertyless and homeless. Middle- and upper-class Americans were horrified to discover young children, often called street arabs, sleeping in alleyways, begging for food, and selling themselves into prostitution. American society seemed about to collapse, and reformers of all sorts set themselves the task of shoring up the social order. Such organizations as the Bible Society, the American Tract Society, and the Home Missionary Society worked to instill religious principles in the population or portions of it; meanwhile, revivalists like Charles G. Finney preached to crowds. Other reformers worked for education, women's rights, improvement of prisons, care of the insane, temperance in drinking, total abstinence from drink, or the abolition of war. The best known of the reform movements, of course, were those opposed to slavery. Some opponents of slavery wished to colonize former slaves in Africa; some

The DRUNKARD'S PROGRESS,

OR THE DIRECT ROAD TO POVERTY WRETCHEDNESS & RUIN.

Designed and Published by J.W.Barber, *New Haven. Com. Sept. 1826.*

Woe unto them that rise up early in the morning that they may follow Strong Drink . . . Isa. 5 C. 11v.

Woe unto them that are mighty to drink wine, and men of strength to mingle Strong Drink . . . Isaiah 5 C.22v.

Who hath woe? Who hath sorrow? Who hath contentions? Who hath wounds without cause? . . . They that tarry long at the wine. Prov. 23

The drunkard shall come to poverty. Proverbs. 23. Chap. 21 v. *The wages of Sin is Death* Romans. 6. Chap. 23 v

The MORNING DRAM.

The GROG SHOP.

The CONFIRMED DRUNKARD.

CONCLUDING SCENE.

The Beginning of Sorrow, Neglect of Business, Idleness, Languor, Loss of Appetite, Dulness and Heaviness, a love of Strong Drink increasing.

Bad Company, Profaneness, Cursing and Swearing, Quarreling & Fighting, Gambling, Obscenity, Ridicule and Hatred of Religion. The Gate of Hell.

Beastly Intoxication, Loss of Character, Loss of Natural Affection, Family Suffering, Brutality, Misery, Disease, Mortgages, Sheriffs, Writs &c.

Poverty, Wretchedness, a Curse and Burden upon Society, Want, Beggary, Pauperism, Death.

An 1826 caricature depicting the evils of drink. (*Courtesy, The New-York Historical Society, New York City*)

wanted to keep slavery from being permitted in the Western territory; others, the most militant, called for abolition of slavery in the South. For all its varieties and conflicts of objectives, much of the reformist activity in the United States was of a single mind in its restless morality, its conviction that the world can be improved and that we are under obligation to set ourselves to improving it.

Personal experience motivated such reformers as Southern abolitionists Angelina and Sarah Grimké and the black abolitionist Frederick Douglass. Others, especially those associated with the Bible societies and the American Tract Society, came from an elite. Fearing that social disorder would grow worse unless the masses were inculcated with proper values, they took it upon themselves to serve as the moral stewards of the nation. "The gospel is the most economical police on earth," said a leader of the Home Missionary Society. The religious enthusiasm of the 1830s inspired such men as the antislavery activist Theodore Dwight Weld and the temperance advocate Neal Dow. And the prevalent belief in moral perfectionism sharpened the conviction of many reformers. The abolitionist editor William Lloyd Garri-

son, for example, became so obsessed with the need to maintain moral purity that he publicly burned a copy of the Constitution, symbolically dissociating himself from a document contaminated by slavery.

| Temperance   From colonial days Americans had been heavy drinkers. When Thomas Jefferson returned from France in 1789, he brought back over three hundred bottles of wine. Less affluent New Englanders settled for rum, which the Puritans distilled from West Indian molasses. Before the advent of canals and railroads, farmers often sent their corn to market distilled in a jug or barrel: whiskey cost less than corn to ship over long distances and found a ready market. In many places it was safer to drink than water. An early nineteenth-century traveler in Ohio found the use of ardent spirits near universal: "A house could not be raised, a field of wheat cut down, nor could there be a log rolling, a husking, a quilting, a wedding, a sheepwashing, or a funeral without the aid of alcohol." Concerned particularly over the harm that drink could do to the family, reformers mounted a determined attack on "Demon Rum."

The temperance crusade seemed, superficially at least, to be one of the most successful reforms. Using techniques borrowed from religious revivals and mass politics, temperance workers distributed leaflets, held "cold water parades," and organized lecture circuits of reformed drunkards who made emotional appeals for converts to sign temperance pledges.

One former drinker confessed:

> I began Backsliding to the drinking of Eggnog. I went to a house raising never thinking satan would tempt me But they had the curse of the nation there and they took sugar, milk, and Eggs and stirred into the whiskey and begged me to Drink of it and I was green enough to submit and drank too much I crawled away and lay down, trying to hide the Disgrace. Poor old mother wept bitter tears when she heard of my Downfall and begged me to repent But all to no purpose for I was young and stubborn. I kept going on from bad to worse. Drinking fighting gambling playing the fiddle for dances and a great many other things.

In the late 1830s a million people belonged to temperance societies. Timothy Shay Arthur's lurid account of the evils of drink, *Ten Nights in a Bar-room, and What I Saw There* (1845), ranked just behind *Uncle Tom's Cabin* as the bestseller of the 1850s. A book of etiquette of the period instructed a lady to write to a young man fond of liquor: "Under ordinary circumstances, I would be delighted to go to the opera with you. I regret to add, however, that I have undoubted evidence that you are becoming addicted to the use of the wine-cup. With an earnest prayer for your reformation, ere it be too late, I beg you to consider our intimacy at an end."

Yet in spite of the impressive numbers of pledges obtained, moral suasion had obvious limitations. Pledges of abstinence did not affect hard-core drinkers who did not care to sign, and the pledges represented no more than the good intentions of those who did. The fervent converts of one day could be staggering out of the taverns the next.

As growing numbers of immigrants entered the country, the Germans bringing their tradition of beer and the Irish their taste for hard liquor, temperance crusaders grew more fearful. Many women's rights activists also joined the cause. Feminists argued that women, as the victims of the behavior of drunken men, were the chief sufferers. Amelia Bloomer answered the claim that women had no business speaking out on this matter:

> None of woman's business, when she is subject to poverty and degradation and made an outcast from respectable society! None of woman's business, when her starving naked babes are compelled to suffer the horrors of the winter's blast! . . . In the name of all that is sacred, what is woman's business if this be no concern of hers?

Slowly, moral appeals gave way to political action. Under the leadership of Neal Dow, Maine in 1851 passed the nation's first statewide prohibition statute. In the next decade over a dozen states followed Maine's lead, although not all of these measures remained on the books.

Public Schools Like temperance, educational reform appealed to Americans who believed that dangerous influences and moral decay were spreading throughout the land or those who more cheerfully thought that their age was a time of universal progress. Horace Mann, the first Massachusetts superintendent of education and a crusader for state-financed education, warned that "the unrestrained passions of men are not only homicidal, but suicidal; and a community without a conscience would soon extinguish itself." How could individuals and society be saved? Universal education—entailing moral guidance and firm discipline—must become the responsibility of the state. Mann and his supporters in the common school movement also argued that leaving education in the hands of families, or preserving it as a luxury of the elite, threatened the nation's political and economic stability. Public schools would encourage social mobility and lessen class differences by providing rich and poor with a common educational background as a basis for the pursuit of future careers. The schools would also prepare Americans for the exercise of intelligent, informed citizenship. "In a republic," Mann wrote, "ignorance is a crime":

> If we do not prepare children to become good citizens—if we do not develop their capacities, if we do not enrich their minds with knowledge, imbue their hearts with the love of truth and duty, and a reverence for all things sacred and holy, then our republic must go down to destruction, as others have gone before it; and mankind must sweep through another vast cycle of sin and suffering, before the dawn of a better era. . . .

Coupled with the growing civic interest in free schools, these arguments produced results.

In 1800 there were no public school systems outside New England; by 1850 every state had at least some public elementary and secondary schools. Northern states surpassed Southern in the percentage of white children enrolled. Several states made appropriations for schools to educate the deaf and the blind. Public schools required a new, more practical curriculum, in place of the traditional, classical one designed for an elite. The study of Greek and Latin or of classical authors would be of limited value for future generations of farmers and mechanics. McGuffey's *Reader* and Webster's *Speller,* whose short lessons simultaneously taught useful skills and proper moral habits, became standard classroom texts, and teachers added exercises in geography, United States history, and science. Gradually, the look of the classroom changed—maps, globes, and blackboards all made their appearance.

Institutions of higher education also proliferated. New kinds of schools opened: technical schools such as Rensselaer Polytechnic Institute in New York; state universities in most Western states; hundreds of denominational colleges, and some "colleges"—more correctly, advanced academies and seminaries—for women. Women's education presented a special problem and challenge to the reform movement; since the end of the eighteenth century there had been a growing sentiment among both men and women in favor of education for women. But few of those who sought to educate women wanted to train them for the professions or otherwise give them a schooling identical to men's. Women were to be educated for enlightened republican motherhood, and to be suitable companions to educated husbands. Female educators such as Emma Willard who founded Troy Seminary, and Mary Lyon, who founded Mount Holyoke Seminary, justified women's schooling with the claim that educated women would enhance the home. But increasingly, some female educators, notably Catharine Beecher—daughter of Lyman Beecher and sister of Harriet Beecher Stowe—also stressed the importance of educating women as primary school teachers, especially single women who would have to earn their livings. The teaching profession, which was distinctly moving toward femini-

zation by the middle of the century, was viewed as an appropriate extension of women's primary domestic role.

Throughout higher education the content of schooling changed. Older universities modified their curricula, reducing the heavy dose of theology and the classics in favor of modern languages, political economy, and the sciences. Several added professional programs in law, medicine, and engineering. A number of Western colleges adopted the unusual concept of student self-help through manual labor. Founded by radical reformers, these schools, such as Oberlin in Ohio (also the first to be coeducational) and Knox in Illinois, became centers of both educational experimentation and antislavery activism.

In taking over from the family the primary obligation for schooling, the state was doing what it was coming to do also for other dependent members of society. Formerly, responsibility for them, too, had gone to the family or to local authorities; but as an increasing density of population intensified social problems, reformers began seeking better solutions. To the Christian cult of perfectionism these humanitarians added a growing belief in the power of environment to shape human character. The result, in the words of one historian, was "the discovery of the asylum."

| **Reform of Prisons and Asylums** | At the urging of reformers, most states rewrote their colonial penal codes, abolishing imprisonment for debt and restricting the application of the death penalty to murderers. For lesser offenses, imprisonment took the place of such brutal corporal punishments as whipping, dunking, and branding. To house and rehabilitate prisoners, the states began to build modern prisons. (Connecticut had formerly housed felons in an abandoned copper mine.) New York, with the construction of its prison at Auburn in 1821, inaugurated the system of individual confinement by night and group labor by day. Under the theory that isolation would promote moral reflection (in fact it often promoted suicide), Pennsylvania's new penitentiary (1829) provided for strict solitary confinement of prisoners at all times. Alexis de Tocqueville concluded that, while the Pennsylvania system made "the deepest impression on the soul of the convict," the Auburn system was "more con-

formable to the habits of man in society, and on this account effects a greater number of reformations." States also created special correctional facilities for juveniles, and for minor criminals such as drunks and vagrants.

Before 1840, victims of mental illness had been cared for privately—in locked rooms, cages, or outhouses—or else confined to jails and poorhouses. A Massachusetts schoolteacher, Dorothea Dix, undertook an investigation of the problem in her native state. Armed with the facts, she prepared a memorial to the legislature. Pledging to "tell what I have seen," she described graphically "the *present* state of insane persons confined within the Commonwealth, in *cages, closets, cellars, stalls, pens! chained, naked, beaten with rods, and lashed into obedience!*" The lawmakers, shocked by her descriptions, voted funds in 1843 to enlarge the state hospital for the insane. During the next decade Miss Dix traveled over thirty thousand miles in behalf of her cause. As a result, nearly every state made some provision for the care and treatment of the indigent insane.

| **Women's Rights** | The career of Dorothea Dix illustrates nicely the general plight of free

women in the mid-nineteenth century. Intelligent, educated, and an expert in her field, Dix was obliged, in the interests of maintaining a "womanly dignity," to work mainly behind the scenes, rarely speaking in public herself. The only professions open to upperclass and middle-class women at that time were those of teacher, missionary, and writer; women of other classes worked in factories or as laundresses, seamstresses, or servants.

The era seemed in many ways to be relegating women to a life of privacy and domesticity. From the beginning of the nineteenth century, but especially following 1820 and particularly in the Northeast, home was becoming separate from income-earning work. A major reason was that the development of commerce and cities, followed by the development of modern industry, created workplaces physically as well as socially distant from dwellings. Men went out to work; women, or a large proportion of them, stayed home. This separation of home from "work"—a word that is often confined to efforts that earn money—reinforced the nineteenth century ideals of domesticity and true

womanhood, which suggested that human life is divided into a public male sphere based on competitive values and a private female sphere of nurture and morality. In the home under a woman's governance a "man . . . seeks refuge . . . where some of his finest sympathies, tastes, and moral and religious feelings—are formed and nourished." So declared a New Hampshire minister in 1827. Women were expected to concentrate on housekeeping and child-rearing, leaving public affairs to men. A woman, wrote one male observer,

cannot too studiously shun the gaze of the multitude. The strife and tumults of the senate-house and the platform are too much even for her eye to rest upon, much more for her voice to mingle in. Her chastity is her tower of strength, her modesty and gentleness are her charm, and her ability to meet the high claims of her family and dependents, the noblest power she can exhibit to the admiration of the world.

Dorothea Dix's crusade on behalf of victims of mental illness led most states to make provisions for the indigent insane. *(Courtesy, Library of Congress)*

I'll Be No Submissive Wife. This song of 1835, a foretaste of the women's movement, went into many editions.

I'll be no submissive wife
No, not I; not I.
I'll not be a slave for life
No, not I; no, not I.

Think you on a wedding day
That I said, as others say
Love and honor and obey
Love and honor and obey?
No no no no no no no
No no no, not I.

I to dullness don't incline
No, not I; no, not I.
Go to bed at half-past nine
No, not I; no, not I.

Should a humdrum husband say
That at home I ought to stay
Do you think that I'll obey,
Do you think that I'll obey?
No no no no no no no
No no no, not I.

Public opinion and economic circumstance were embodied in the law, which regarded women as perpetual minors. Married women had almost no rights over their property or children; they could not sue in their own name. They could not even sign contracts. This advice, given a daughter by her father upon her marriage, speaks volumes about the position of women in 1838:

> Now that you are married, do not always expect the lover. Be more than ever anxious to please, study his interest, make it yours. If any little domestic care troubles you, such as indifferent servants &tc let it not ruffle your temper. Is it not better to endure this than wear him by not being amiable? . . . Be only what you seemed to be when first you won his love. Be more cautious of wounding the feelings of a husband than you were ever anxious to please the lover. If you are fond of any amusement he does not approve & cannot share, give it up— you will find your reward in so doing. You are to keep him happy & cheerful & to make sacrifices if necessary without murmuring. You may see faults in him that in your fondness you never dreamed of. Be as blind to them as you can. If by gentleness & love you cannot alter them, then conform yourself to your circumstances, for reproaches never will do good. Better feel the secret pain than let him fear you love him less than when you thought him faultless.

Divorces were rarely granted and usually thought to be the wife's fault. The Civil War diarist Mary Chesnut wrote: "there is no slave . . . like a wife."

All this could have encouraged women to stay away from reform movements, which aggressively entered the public sphere that sentimentality claimed to be the domain of males; and many women undoubtedly drew that lesson. But the idea central to the nineteenth-century exclusion of women from public life, the belief that they possessed a superior intuition into morality and a superior urge to nurture the sick and helpless, was to provide in time an argument for their entrance into the public sphere. If morality is the special province of women, they must have important things to say about issues that were at once public and moral, such as the dangers of alcohol, or matters concerning the protection of the weak and the ill.

Women engaged in a long struggle to assert their right to speak in public, to organize, and eventually to vote on behalf of moral issues. They made slow but solid progress. In their effort they relied particularly upon the bonds and networks that they had established with other women—the "bonds of sisterhood." These female networks supported a wide variety of female associations providing charity to the needy, raising funds for the education of ministers, combating slavery, working for various moral reforms that included temperance and the elimination of prostitution, and giving support to mothers seeking to set their children on the right path. Although many reform associations, such as those contributing to the abolitionist and the temperance movements, remained firmly under male leadership throughout the first half of the nineteenth century, female reformers supplied much of the dedication.

The cause of women's rights soon became a movement in itself. Lucy Stone, an antislavery and women's-rights activist who retained her maiden name after marriage, refused to pay taxes since she was not represented in the government. Some women even rejected their long, immobilizing skirts in favor of the less constricting "Bloomer" costume. The Bloomer costume now seems tame, compared to present-day women's clothing. It consisted of a tunic that fell to mid-calf worn over a pair of ample bloomers that covered the legs and were gathered tightly at the ankle. But in its time and place, it earned the women who wore it ridicule, hostility, and a showering of rotten eggs and tomatoes. Even those most determined advocates of women's rights, Susan B. Anthony and Elizabeth Cady Stanton, eventually gave it up with heartfelt relief. Women reformers proved especially active in defense of the personal rights of other women whom they perceived as oppressed or exploited by the familial and sexual demands of men. Susan B. Anthony helped a woman kidnap her child from her husband's custody—idealization of motherhood notwithstanding, fathers usually got custody of children. Other women worked for temperance to protect women from the beatings and domestic violence of drunken husbands. A group of women in New York—objecting to the double standard that allowed men to have sex outside marriage while denying it to women—started a society to reform the city's prostitutes.

Numbers of middle-class women who took up feminist causes had begun by becoming involved in other social reforms. As women extended their interests outside the home, met together, assumed leadership, and became adept at public speaking, they soon came to recognize the status in which women were kept. "In striving to strike the [black man's] irons off, we found most surely, that *we* were manacled ourselves," wrote Abby Kelley, a women's rights leader. But if the antislavery cause helped launch the women's rights movement, it also contributed to its temporary demise. Even many sympathetic men abandoned feminist causes when they threatened to divert or divide the antislavery crusade. Led by Lucretia Mott, Elizabeth Cady Stanton, and Susan B. Anthony, women held conventions (the Seneca Falls, New York, meeting in 1848 had been the first) and brought their concerns before the public. They asked for full rights to hold property and leave bequests, for educational and economic opportunities, and for the right to vote. But despite the feminists' energy and intelligence, fundamental changes in popular attitudes, occupational choice, legal status, and political participation came slowly. The "cult of true womanhood," emphasizing the frailty and purity of women, remained strong.

One of the chief successes of the early women's movement lay in its sympathy for another unemancipated group, that of black slaves. One stunning former slave, who stood at a towering six feet, was Sojourner Truth, born Isabella in New York in 1797. A domestic servant for many years following New York's emancipation law of 1827 and illiterate until her death, she was nonetheless a commanding orator in the cause of both abolition and women's rights. An Ohio feminist presiding over the 1851 women's rights convention recorded her inspiring talk:

Every eye was fixed on this almost Amazon form, which stood nearly six feet high, head erect, and eyes piercing the upper air like one in a dream. At her first word there was a profound hush. She spoke in deep tones, which, though not loud, reached every ear in the house, and away through the throng at the doors and windows.

"Wall, chilern, whar dar is so much racket dar must be somethin' out o' kilter. I tink dat 'twixt de niggers of de Souf and de womin at de Norf, all talkin' 'bout rights, de white men will be in a fix pretty soon. But what's all dis here talkin' 'bout?

"Dat man ober dar say dat womin needs to be helped into carriages, and lifted ober ditches, and to hab de best place everywhar. Nobody eber helps me into carriages, or ober mud-puddles, or gibs me any best place!" And raising herself to her full height, and her voice to a pitch like rolling thunder, she asked, "And a'n't I a woman? Look at me! Look at my arm! (and she bared her right arm to the shoulder, showing her tremendous muscular power). I have ploughed, and planted, and gathered into barns, and no man could head me! And a'n't I a woman? I could work as much and eat as much as a man—when I could get it—and bear de lash as well! And a'n't I a woman? I have borne thirteen chilern, and seen 'em mos' all sold off to slavery, and when I cried out with my mother's grief, none but Jesus heard me! And a'n't I a woman? . . .

"Den dat little man in black dar, he say women can't have as much rights as men, 'cause Christ wan't a woman! Whar did your Christ come from?" Rolling thunder couldn't have stilled that crowd, as did those deep, wonderful tones, as she stood there with outstretched arms and eyes of fire. Raising her voice still louder, she repeated, "Whar did your Christ come from? From God and a woman! Man had nothin' to do wid Him." Oh, what a rebuke that was to that little man.

| Anti-Catholicism

The conviction that American society has special democratic and moral traditions to preserve and protect has led more than once to movements to rid the country of something or somebody. A case in point is the rapid growth of anti-Catholic sentiment after 1830. Before then American Catholics had been too few in number to attract much attention. Over the next thirty years, mass immigration, especially from Ireland and Germany, swelled the Catholic proportion of the total population from one in fifty to one in ten. Many native-born Protestants believed that the newcomers posed a direct threat to America's democratic heritage. In part this conviction grew out of their understanding of history.

The American Revolution, in their eyes, was an extension of the Protestant Reformation, particularly of Luther's doctrine of the primacy of individual conscience. The Reformation, they thought, had been a struggle for liberty against an oppressive, autocratic perversion of true Christianity. Their own Revolution had carried the struggle into the political domain. So the rapid increase in the Catholic population caused many to worry for the nation's commitment to a republican form of government. This concern grew as American Catholics made it clear that they did not necessarily accept the separation of church and state mandated by the First Amendment to the Constitution. Not only would the pope denounce this as one of several "American heresies," but American bishops and other Catholic clergy aggressively campaigned in New York City and Lowell, Massachusetts, and elsewhere for public funds for parochial schools. Such prominent men as Lyman Beecher, the celebrated preacher, and inventor Samuel F.B. Morse pointed to these Catholic demands and warned against "papal puppets working to inflame and divide the nation, break the bond of our union, and throw down our free institutions." Militant Protestants formed societies aimed at converting "Papists to Christianity" (these had little success), stoutly resisted all suggestions of public aid to parochial schools (sometimes with success, sometimes not), and demanded curbs on immigration (entirely without success).

Anti-Catholicism, however, did not spring simply from devotion to the First Amendment or from concern for the purity of the Revolutionary tradition. It also sprang from distaste for the immigrants themselves. The Irish were stereotyped as drunken brutes. One woman recalled seeing the "poor fellows, strung along the canal, stupid from drink . . . they are for the most part covered with mud, where they have rolled when drunk." The Germans also affronted the growing anti-liquor feelings of many native-born Protestants with their insistence on incorporating the use of beer, sometimes to excess, even into such otherwise innocent activities as Sunday picnics. Protestant nativists also drew upon centuries of anti-Catholic propaganda. Zealots composed and circulated fictitious stories of convent life replete with sex orgies.

The Arts

During Jacksonian times and just after, the United States at last achieved cultural independence of Europe in literature, painting, and architecture. The newly popular lyceums and public lectures furnished native talent with an audience. In 1860 knowledgeable Europeans would no longer ask, as one English literary wit had in 1820, "In the four quarters of the globe, who reads an American book? Or goes to an American play? Or looks at an American picture or statue?"

Speaking at Harvard in 1837, the philosopher Ralph Waldo Emerson attacked "the timid, imitative, and tame" in American cre-

Sunny Morning on the Hudson River by Thomas Cole. *(Courtesy, Museum of Fine Arts, Boston)*

ative life. Americans, he asserted, must learn to work with their own hands and speak with their own minds. And they were doing so.

American painters abandoned the formal, classical style of the eighteenth century. Influenced by the romantic movement and nationalism, they experimented with more individualistic, democratic, emotional styles of painting. Genre painters like William Sidney Mount and George Caleb Bingham took their studios outdoors to capture revealing incidents of American life. Bingham's "Stump Speaker" and "Country Elections" are miniature essays on Jacksonian politics. Nature painters like Thomas Cole glorified the spectacular qualities of the American landscape. Cole was a leader of the so-called Hudson River School, those painters who captured especially the magnificent Hudson River Valley with its deep woods, its jagged rocks, its sweeping vistas.

American architects also turned from eighteenth-century styles of European origin.

Their search for a pure, simple, democratic architecture led naturally to the Greek Revival, inspired by the buildings of ancient Greece. Among the best examples of this style are Benjamin Latrobe's Bank of the United States at Philadelphia and Robert Mills's Treasury Building at Washington. Responding to the individualistic and romantic impulses of the age, American architects later adopted a variety of styles. By 1850 Philadelphia had an Egyptian jail, a Greek bank, medieval cottages, and Moorish churches, while New York boasted a Jewish synagogue with a Gothic tower.

American Literature

American writers and poets were also influenced by the forces of nationalism. Breaking with the rigid neoclassical writing of the eighteenth century, they sought a literature that was expressive, imaginative, intuitive, filled with "the animating spirit of democracy." Walt Whitman called for a poetry that was one with the spirit of the times and with the country's culture, incarnating its "geography and national life and rivers and lakes." Whitman's *Leaves of Grass* (1855) used free verse and slang words and borrowed freely from music, religion, and politics for its imagery and metaphors. *Leaves of Grass* was American.

Edgar Allan Poe became the master of the short story. Nathaniel Hawthorne brought intensity, depth, and craftsmanship to the American novel. In works like *The Scarlet Letter* (1850) and *The House of the Seven Gables* (1851) he probed the souls of American Puritans and Quakers. Hawthorne looked into dark motives and somber emotions, but looked as well for the innocence and freshness that human nature could contain. Herman Melville aspired to be a "thought-diver." His *Moby Dick* (1851), with its driven Captain Ahab searching for the great white whale, symbolized the human quest for the mysterious forces of the universe.

Then, as now, the mass of Americans preferred a different sort of literature. With the development of more efficient printing techniques, inexpensive books and newspapers circulated widely. The most prolific type of fiction was the sentimental domestic novel. Filled with scenes of domestic joy and sorrow, these novels preached conventional morality and pictured church, home, and family as anchors against life's trials. Novels like Mrs. E. D. E. N. Southworth's *Retribution* and Mary Jane Holmes's *Tempest and Sunshine* were bestsellers for years. Another form of popular culture was the humorous essay, which dated from Benjamin Franklin's *Poor Richard*. It gained new popularity in the 1830s with Seba Smith's *Jack Downing Papers*. Downing was a crackerbox philosopher who commented on current events and poked gentle fun at American foibles. Smith soon had dozens of imitators, among them James Russell Lowell's Hosea Bigelow, Charles F. Browne's Artemus Ward, and Johnson Hooper's Simon Slugs. Plays, minstrel shows, lectures, and public speaking also provided entertainment and education.

The cult of patriotism grew in the early nineteenth century. Holidays were increasingly devoted to skyrocketing oratory, parades, and patriotic enthusiasms. Monuments and statues appeared by the hundreds, and biographies of American heroes sold by the tens of thousands. And along with the cult of patriotism flourished a variety of popular symbols.

Americans adopted a native bird, the eagle. For holidays they chose Washington's Birthday and the Fourth of July. "Uncle Sam," a creation of the War of 1812, soon displaced "Yankee Doodle" as the national prototype. Although not adopted officially as the national anthem until 1913, Francis Scott Key's "Star-Spangled Banner" gradually replaced "My Country 'Tis of Thee." No token of nationalism became more important than the American flag. Originally created in 1777, the stars and stripes had remained chiefly a naval flag until 1834, when the army adopted it as well.

Along with symbols, Americans needed heroes. They turned to the Revolutionary War for material. By Jackson's day the important figures in the War—Francis "Swamp Fox" Marion, Ethan Allen and his Green Mountain Boys, John Paul Jones, the martyred Nathan Hale— were celebrated in song and prose. Jackson himself became an instant hero after the Battle of New Orleans that followed the War of 1812. Above all other na-

Nathaniel Hawthorne. He and the other writers of the period—Poe, Emerson, Melville, Whitman, Thoreau—created a literature that was uniquely American and attracted international attention. *(Courtesy, Essex Institute, Salem, Massachusetts)*

tional heroes was George Washington. Even before his death Washington had attained in the estimation of his countrymen a place above politics and above criticism. Much of the responsibility should go to Mason Locke Weems. In 1800 this itinerant book salesman and evangelist published his *Life of Washington*. Partly fabricated (the cherry tree story started here), the book fulfilled the American public's need for heroes.

Americans were swept up in the outpouring of nationalism. "We were taught every day and in every way," recalled one contemporary, "that ours was the freest, the happiest, and soon to be the greatest and most powerful country in the world. . . . We read it in our books and newspapers, heard it in sermons, speeches, and orations, thanked God for it, in our prayers, and devoutly believed it always." Not even the cult of patriotism, however, would forever quiet the disruptive effects of the slavery question, which burst on the country again in the 1840s.

Points To Think About

1. Historians, long preoccupied with politics, have characterized the period between the "Era of Good Feelings" and the onset of the Civil War as the Age of Jackson. An equally strong case can be made for calling it the Age of Finney—after the leading revivalist of the day, Charles G. Finney. Finney was the George Whitefield of the nineteenth century. His revivals had the same spectacular success. And he used methods which were equally controversial. Finney, for example, often prayed for sinners by name.

Finney's revivals reflected many of the contradictory strains in American culture. On the one hand, he called on his hearers to acknowledge their abject dependence upon the process of conversion, which was a gift from on high. Yet when Finney insisted that he could start a revival with the same likelihood of success that a farmer had when he planted his crops, he appeared to be assuming that the work of conversion could begin by the strenuous labor of a preacher. Finney published a handbook on revivals, in which he spelled out in detail just what a successful preacher should do. Man, Finney preached in defiance of the old Puritan beliefs, could help himself. He could be saved by wanting to be saved. Finney's preaching also reflected the general concern for order. Like the upper-class builders of the benevolent empire, who generously supported his work, he saw religion as a bulwark of the social order. And he encouraged his converts to join established churches. Yet Finney also preached the primacy of the individual conscience. He told his listeners that conversion would mark a radical change in their lives. They should, he urged, reexamine the whole pattern of their lives. Finney always left it for his converts to determine the direction of their new lives for themselves. He did not, that is, attempt to channel the enthusiasm he unleashed.

And so Finney's revivals, despite the conservative cast of much of his preaching, often produced unpredictable results. Theodore Dwight Weld became a radical abolitionist. John Humphrey Noyes became the leading utopian socialist of the period.

2. A revival, Finney used to lament, presupposes a declension (that is, a falling away from religious fervor). Revivals, he believed, should not be necessary. Converts should have been able to maintain the intensity of their first enthusiasm. But of course they did not. Too many were "backsliders" who needed periodically to be recalled to a higher standard.

Finney's complaint went to the heart of American evangelicalism. It had produced a kind of cyclical religion. American Protestants swung between intense fervor and indifference. Finney, like most ministers, wanted instead a steady religiosity. The question was how to produce it. Clearly the revival did not. Although Finney never admitted as much, one reason was that the revival produced such intense experiences that they were impossible to sustain. Something else was needed.

Finney thought he had found the answer in the theological doctrine of perfectionism. Its basis was the New Testament injunction by Christ to the disciples to be "perfect even as your heavenly Father is perfect."

Perfectionism seems a doctrine especially suited to this country in the nineteenth century. Nowhere else were people so ready to believe that anything was possible. Perfectionism mirrors perfectly the tendency in the United States to believe, at one and the same time, that things are going to hell in a handbasket and that they can be dramatically improved in a single stroke. It mirrors, that is, the curious mixture of pessimism and optimism that so much of American life displays. Recall, for a moment, that the same conservative reformers who bemoaned the social chaos of democracy also thought that they had in the asylum a means of ending crime, mental illness, and poverty.

This same combination of pessimism about the present and boundless confidence in the future would also mark the utopian socialists. Their experiments in communal living grew out of their deep dissatisfaction with American society on the one hand, and on the other their faith that they had discovered the blueprint for a perfect tomorrow.

3. Communitarians, Arthur Bestor has observed in a classic article, shared with other Americans a "Patent Office Model of Society." Americans through the first half of the nineteenth century were intensely aware of how new their society was. It was being, in a word, invented, and this sense that a whole nation was being invented encouraged some people to go farther and try to invent perfect societies. The patent office model is an apt designation. Communitarians, like other inventors, sat down with pencil in hand and designed new social forms.

This seemed shockingly naive to European conservatives. They believed that forms like the family or the community were slow historical growths that reflected, in Edmund Burke's phrase, the "accumulated wisdom of the race." The idea of inventing a society seemed preposterous. And to judge from the eventual failure of the communitarian experiments, they were right.

Yet if European conservatives could see the hopeless innocence of drawing up blueprints for a better family, American conservatives could not. They, in fact, shared the very same patent office approach. They were the ones, we should recall, who drew up the blueprints for the penitentiary and insane asylum. They, too, were inventors, and that means that they were not classical conservatives, who do not invent but preserve.

The communitarian experiments failed, and that was an end to them. But while the penitentiaries and other asylums also failed (they did not, that is, rehabilitate the criminal or cure the insane), they were nevertheless widely copied. For all of their shortcomings, they did serve as real models. The reason, according to David Rothman in his *The Discovery of the Asylum*, was that they did succeed in one important respect. They did quarantine and care for people unadaptable to society. Rehabilitation may have failed, but custody remained. And so the asylum was adopted widely.

Suggested Readings

Recent books on topics in this chapter include Barbara Welter, *Godey's Lady's Book: The Women Who Wrote It and the Women Who Read It* (1989), Christine Stansell, *City of Women: Sex and Class in New York, 1789–1860* (1980), Priscilla Brewett, *Shaker Communities, Shaker Lives* (1986), Michael Barkun, *Crucible of the Millennium: The Burned-over District of New York in the 1840's* (1986), Marvin S. Hill, *Quest for Refuge: The Mormon Flight from American Pluralism* (1989), Kennan H. Winn, *Exiles in a Land of Liberty, 1830–1846* (1989) and Richard Rabinowitz, *The Spiritual Self in Everyday Life: The Transformation of Personal Religious Experience in Nineteenth-Century New England* (1989).

R.G. Walters's *American Reformers, 1815–1860* (1978) is a good introduction to the period, while Rowland Berthoff's *An Unsettled People: Social Order and Disorder in American History* (1971) is a stimulating general study. On feminism a good book to begin with is Barbara J. Berg, *The Remembered Gates: Origins of Feminism—Women and the City, 1800–1860* (1977). Other books also tell some of the story of women in this era: Ellen Carol DuBois's *Feminism and Suffrage* (1979), Nancy Cott's *The Bonds of Womanhood: "Women's Sphere in New England," 1780–1835* (1977), and G.J. Barker-Benfield's *The Horrors of the Half-Known Life: Male Attitudes Toward Women and Sexuality in Nineteenth-Century America* (1976). Lewis Perry's *Childhood, Marriage, and Reform* (1980) is thought-provoking.

Rush Welter's *The Mind of America, 1820–1860* (1975), is a good treatment of intellectual history. In *The Discovery of the Asylum: Social Order and Disorder in the New Republic* (1971), David S. Rothman argues that people believed the "asylum"—the orphanage, the penitentiary, the poorhouse—would rehabilitate the individual and provide a model of social organization. On religion see William G. McLoughlin, *Revivals, Awakenings, and Reform* (1978) and *Modern Revivalism: Charles Grandison Finney to Billy Graham* (1959), Paul E. Johnson, *A Shopkeeper's Millennium: Society and Revivals in Rochester, New York, 1815–1837* (1978), and John Boles, *The Great Revival in the South* (1972). Herbert Hovenkamp, *Science and Religion in America, 1800–1860* (1978) is a useful survey of the relation of religious to scientific thought in the early republic.

FORREST McDONALD

"Idle hands," according to the Victorian aphorism, "are the devil's workshop." The saying was conventionally used as a justification for keeping the poor toiling away in factories from dawn to dusk and even longer, but in fact it was the well-to-do who were apt to have leisure to commit mischief. During the 1830s and the 1850s, especially, prosperity was sufficiently widespread in the United States that a goodly number of such people, mainly in cities and towns, could live fairly comfortably without working; and they confirmed the wisdom of the aphorism. Old maids of both sexes, having made thorough botches of their own lives, busily turned their idle hands to silly schemes for remaking other people's lives. So much for the "reforming spirit."

But leisure also makes possible a blossoming of arts and letters, if a people have it in them. Americans had neither taste nor talent for most of the arts. Of painters, sculptors, and architects the nation had none of consequence. No good serious music was to be heard, even in the larger cities, until German immigrants began to arrive in quantity in the 1850s, and opera did not begin to flourish until large-scale Italian immigration commenced later in the century. The one creative art in which Americans did excel was the one in which English-speaking people had ever excelled, the composition of prose literature.

This is not to claim that what American authors wrote was uniformly original or uniformly of high quality. Much of the fruit of the so-called Flowering of New England—the work of such writers as Emerson, Thoreau, and Holmes—was drivel. Much of the fiction written by American authors was both flimsy and imitative. But when Hawthorne and Melville and Poe explored in their work the darker recesses of the soul, the results were writings of depth and power comparable to those of Dostoevski and Dickens.

The impressive thing about American literature during the middle years of the nineteenth century, however, is not so much what Americans wrote but that so many of them read. From the beginning of American nationhood, it had been an unquestioned tenet that the republic could flourish only if the citizenry were literate and informed, and the Northwest Ordinance as well as the state constitutions had committed government to support general public education. The crusade of Horace Mann was a reaffirmation and a revitalization of that early commitment. The yield was by far the highest literacy rate in the world—over ninety percent of the adult white population. And Americans not only could but did read. Newspapers, of course, were their most common fare: there were about 3,000 newspapers by 1860 (three or four times the number in England or France), some having circulations in the scores of thousands. But the newspapers contained more than just news. The New York *Weekly Tribune*, for instance, treated its 200,000 subscribers to full reports of lectures, to serialized novels by Dickens and lesser English writers, to condensations of other books, to poems long and short, and to book reviews. In addition, sales of books were often large and sometimes (as in the case of *Uncle Tom's Cabin*) utterly stupefying. And the impact of Harriet Beecher Stowe's melodrama indicated that the written word could be powerful.

In sum, while the emergence of democracy and capitalism in this country regrettably brought with it the demise of the classical and civic humanist traditions, it also brought about what Jose Ortega y Gasset called "a rise in the historic level." The great masses of the country's ordinary people had achieved not only a large measure of economic security and abundance but also something more precious, free access to information and to the world of ideas. That was unprecedented in human history.

Reform and the Arts: A Link?

EUGENE D. GENOVESE

Reformers can be humorless and unpleasant. Their business is to mind other people's business. It is not so much that they quit smoking, for example, as that, once they do so, they expect everyone else to follow. They are, in short, easy to make fun of. We could have great sport with the persistent efforts of antebellum reformers to bring God's Kingdom to earth—whether or not their neighbors, not to mention God, would have it so. Among their least attractive qualities was the firm conviction that they had special knowledge of God's will and were His chosen instruments.

For all that, this country would have been much worse off without them. The greatest of their antebellum projects was antislavery, and it is largely through their intransigent struggle that the slumbering conscience of the nation was finally aroused against the greatest evil of the nineteenth century. In pursuing their object of abolishing slavery, they displayed, among other splendid qualities, the physical and moral courage to face down lynchings, imprisonment, beatings, and constant assaults on their meetings. If men like Thomas Wentworth Higginson, not to mention John Brown, and women like the Grimké sisters qualify as "old maids of both sexes," then let's hear it for the old maids. And I assume that even Professor McDonald would not sneer so at the gallant efforts of the black abolitionists like Frederick Douglass and Sojourner Truth to free their people.

Among the other campaigns for reform that marked the period, feminism, as it would come to be called, ranked high. The abolitionists, or rather a solid proportion of them, joined the effort to secure rights for women. Northern conservatives, like Southern slaveholders, were shocked to learn that women dared to address abolitionist meetings and that they were often well received by "old maid" men who fought side by side with them in the cause of black freedom. The historical verdict has gone not to those shocked but to those who did the shocking. Honor to them.

A sizable number of these reformers were "intellectuals," broadly defined. By no means were all Northern intellectuals reformers. Hawthorne, for example, opposed the abolitionists as readily as Emerson supported them. The intellectual life of the period, like so much else, demonstrated the deepening chasm between the sections. The literary giants, as Professor McDonald says, were largely Northerners, but even in New England the best literary men—and women like Emily Dickinson, the greatest American poet of her time—appealed to small "highbrow" audiences, while others made money on trashy novels. And the South also had its claims to a thriving literary culture of sorts.

Political writing, including work in political economy and what by the 1850s was coming to be called "sociology," aroused substantial interest. The more philosophical discourses of John C. Calhoun, as well as his more direct political speeches and essays, displayed considerable power. The South boasted the finest political economists in the United States in Jacob N. Cardozo, a luminary of the Jewish community in Charleston, and George Tucker of Virginia, who wrote widely on moral philosophy, the arts, and other subjects besides economics. During the 1820s and 1830s Thomas Cooper, who settled in South Carolina late in life, and Thomas R. Dew of Virginia, had set a high standard in history and political science as well as economics. But to one extent or another, they, as well as other writers like the learned clergymen William Stringfellow and James. H. Thornwell, applied their talent to the defense of slavery, not as a "necessary evil" or a profitable labor system, but as the foundation of a healthy social order. And the South welcomed their ringing defense of slavery. Southern "reformers" had been dispatched—driven out or silenced. The South was not much troubled by "silly" campaigns for reform. Too bad. It would, in a short time, pay dearly for its immunity to the disease of radicalism.

The Battle at the Alamo, 1836. The Mexican "victory" cost Santa Anna 1600 of his best troops and helped Texas win its war of independence. *(Courtesy, Scribner's Archives)*

Slavery and Expansion: The 1840s

THE ALAMO

In nineteenth-century America, no place had a larger reputation for wild living than Texas. Men tired of society could move to the frontier; if the frontier offered too little excitement, room, danger, opportunity, they could go to Texas. The history of Texas justified this reputation. For nearly three centuries Texas had belonged to Spain, but throughout that long period, the Spanish system of colonization—missions, soldiers, conversion of Indians, entrance of settlers—had failed. Hundreds of miles of deserts and mountains separated Texas from the other Spanish lands, and fierce Plains Indians—mainly Comanches and Apaches—did not take kindly to life at the Spanish missions. The land, which Mexico inherited with its independence, lay long ungoverned.

The Alamo was an apt symbol of this history. The mission San Antonio de Valero was founded in 1718, but when Spanish rule of Texas ended with Mexican independence in 1821, the mission itself had been abandoned and there were about 1500 people living in the town. Aside from the Indians there were only about 4000 colonists in all of Texas.

When Mexico became independent, Texas was joined to its state of Coahuila, with a promise that when its population was large enough, it would become a separate Mexican state. The newly-established Mexican government planned to develop Texas by encouraging Americans to settle there and farm, provided they became at least nominal Catholics and Mexican citizens. The plan worked, perhaps too well. By 1831, 20,000 settlers had poured in, most of them from the United States, and the Mexicans envisioned this potentially rich province slipping from them. So they banned further immigration, raised tariffs, restricted trade, and reinforced their military presence.

The situation was further complicated by unstable Mexican politics. Antonio Lopez de Santa Anna, Mexico's most brilliant general, was challenging his own government. The Texans, led by Stephen F. Austin, who had brought 300 families in 1825, petitioned for separate statehood. Then in 1834 Santa Anna proclaimed himself president of Mexico forever and sent its Congress home.

Said Austin: "War is our only resource." Once Santa Anna took control in Mexico City and moved to garrison his northern province, the Texans were ready to fight—but not at first for independence. The men defending the Alamo in the spring of 1836 were unaware that a hundred miles away, at a capital called "Washington-on-the-Brazos," a hastily-called convention had declared Texas's independence.

Texans by and large were fighters, not soldiers. Skilled marksmen, deadly with knives and fists, they loved a good scrap. The slow, boring routine of soldiering was another story. The Texans picked up an army—or several armies—but enlistments were for very short periods, and volunteers, answerable to no one, often outnumbered the loosely disciplined regulars. Men who would risk their lives in a moment in battle would refuse such mundane tasks as building fortifications or digging latrines.

The rebels, including a number of Mexicans living in Texas, managed to defeat Mexican detachments in a few small encounters and took the town of San Antonio from its Mexican commander in house-to-house fighting. Then General Sam Houston, struggling to put together a military strategy and an army to carry it out, ordered them to destroy the Alamo and abandon San Antonio. He sent Jim Bowie, a legendary figure of the tough Southwest frontier, to carry out his orders. Bowie, who had recently turned from land speculation, slave trading, and brawling with his famous knife eight-and-one-half-inches-long, decided, "We will rather die in these ditches than give them up to the enemy."

The Alamo desperately needed reinforcements. It got a few, powerful in legend but not in number. William Barret Travis, a militant advocate for war and now a colonel in the rag-tag Texas army, arrived with thirty of his soldiers to add to Bowie's volunteers. When Bowie fell ill with pneumonia, Travis took command of the beleaguered fort. Davy Crockett arrived from Tennessee with twelve men. Then as now he was the epitome of the American frontiersman, the teller and subject of tall tales. Following his legend right into the West, by some instinct he wound up at the place that would transform his essentially comic career into real and towering heroism. Eventually thirty-two more volunteers arrived from the nearby town of Gonzales. And so it was that, all told, 187 men garrisoned the old mission, when on February 23, 1836, Santa Anna's army of 4,000 began its siege.

With Mexican guns tightly ringing the fort, the Alamo's defenders finally abandoned their hopes for further reinforcements. When Santa Anna sent a messenger offering terms for surrender, Travis answered him with a cannon shot. Tradition has it that Travis called the men together, explained their probable fate, and offered a chance to leave to those who wished it. Drawing a line in the dust with his sword, he stepped across it and asked who would join him and who would leave. All but one man—who got through the Mexican lines and lived to tell the tale—crossed the line. Bowie, from his sickbed, asked to be carried across. Travis wrote a final letter, correctly predicting that "The victory will cost the enemy so dear that it will be worse for him than defeat." After March 3 no one entered or left the fort. The next morning revealed Mexican cannon virtually under the wall. In one more day the cannonade blasted a sizable hole in the old mission's wall. The final assault had begun.

As the Mexican troops advanced, Santa Anna's buglers played the dreaded "El Deguello," a tune that since the days of the Inquisition had signaled "no quarter: death to all enemies."

Before dawn on March 6, the Mexicans—four thousand strong—attacked, almost catching the exhausted defenders by surprise. The first assault with scaling ladders was repulsed with dreadful carnage. A second wave was more successful, actually getting ladders onto the walls, only to have the men driven off by rifle butts, tomahawks, and Bowie knives. Then came the third assault, and there were simply not enough Texans, enough cannon, or enough wall left. Taking incredible losses—one battalion lost 670 of 800 men—the Mexican soldiers poured in with a courage to match that of their adversaries. Abandoning the central plaza of the Alamo, the defenders retreated to the smaller rooms, to kill and then to die in hand-to-hand battle. Crockett and two of his men, according at least to the received romantic version of the story, were found after the battle under a heap of seventeen dead Mexicans. Jim Bowie, confined to a sickbed in the chapel, was one of the last to die. The first two soldiers who burst into the room he dispatched with his brace of singleshot pistols; then he was helpless, too weak to wield his famous knife. One of the few survivors, the wife of an officer, deliberately spared to spread the news of Texan defeat, remembered seeing his body being tossed on the bayonets of a dozen soldiers when the battle ended and the wanton mutilations began. By 8:00 a.m. on March 6, 1836, the siege had ended with all the Alamo's defenders dead.

No question at all: Santa Anna's "victory" in this battle cost him the war. He had lost sixteen hundred of his best troops, with many more wounded. He had lost not only the weeks it took to besiege the fortress, but the weeks his army needed afterward to recover. The Texans, sobered and inspired, declared their independence, settled their quarrels, and gave Sam Houston a chance to build an army.

Santa Anna chased Houston and caught up with him at San Jacinto, an elbow formed by the confluence of a river and a bayou. Houston burned his bridges behind him so that neither his army nor Santa Anna's could retreat. The Texans, shouting as their battlecry "Remember the Alamo!" destroyed the Mexican army in an afternoon. Texas was an independent nation, the Lone Star Republic, until 1845, when it was admitted to the Union as the twenty-eighth state.

The Fall of the Alamo by T. Genlitz. *(Courtesy, Library of Congress)*

America in 1840

In 1840 the future of the young American republic seemed rich with promise. In fifty years the population had increased by over four hundred percent, while the land area had more than doubled. As each region found what it could best manufacture or grow and as transportation improved, the different sections became more interdependent in the making of a richer economy. With two national parties competing for office in every part of the country, the political system worked to bind the country together. The vast majority of Americans remained English in speech, Protestant in religion, lower middle-class in social status, agricultural in occupation; this common social ground, together with the experience of two wars against Britain, made for a shared national loyalty. Each July 4, Americans in every part of the country gathered for elaborate ceremonies glorifying the Union. Alexis de Tocqueville was deeply impressed by one such celebration at Albany, with its dramatic reading of the Declaration of Independence and its parade of Revolutionary veterans "preserved like precious relics, and whom all the citizens honor. . . ."

And yet, even as patriotism and economic interdependence strengthened the Union, one issue threatened the country with disruption. In the 1830s a crusade against slavery arose in the North. During the next decade the slavery question became entangled with the issue of territorial expansion, and that combination gradually eclipsed all other issues. Unable to settle the question peacefully, by 1861 Americans would resort to arms.

The Antislavery Crusade

The roots of the antislavery movement in the United States stretched back to the eighteenth century. Confronted by the powerful forces of rationalism and revolution, many Americans had condemned slavery as incompatible with the egalitarianism of the Declaration of Independence. In 1787 Congress excluded slavery from the area it was organizing north of the Ohio River as the Northwest Territory. That same year the delegates to the Constitutional Convention agreed to a compromise permitting, though not requiring, Congress to abolish the African slave trade in 1808. In the meantime, a number of northern states abolished slavery within their own borders, and abolition societies multiplied even in a few southern states.

Most Americans, although opposed to slavery, rejected the idea of its immediate eradication in the South, a course fraught with serious constitutional, economic, and social difficulties. Many favored a policy of gradual emancipation, to be followed by deportation. With the support of such influential men as Henry Clay and John Marshall, these gradualists in 1817 founded the American Colonization Society. The Society worked to resettle emancipated American blacks in Africa. Free blacks themselves objected to colonization. "We are *natives* of this country," one protested; "we only ask that we be treated as well as *foreigners*." Their opposition gradually undermined the Society's efforts. In 1829 a free black named David Walker published "An Appeal to Blacks," calling for emancipation. The year after this work was published, Walker died under mysterious circumstances.

The Abolition Movement During the early 1830s a small but vocal band of activists began calling for the total and immediate abolition of slavery. Abolitionism became an integral part of the reform ferment of the Jackson era. Slavery, abolitionists believed, was both a national and an individual sin; Americans could not wait for time or circumstance to eradicate it. These abolitionists viewed gradual emancipation and colonization as dead ends. Any large-scale deportation of blacks would have raised both enormous practical obstacles and grave moral difficulties. And southern opposition to gradual emancipation, which stiffened after the invention of the cotton gin, indicated that the opponents of slavery had little to lose by adopting a more radical stance. The victory of the British abolitionist movement in 1833 gave new hope to advocates of immediate emancipation in the

Illustrations of the American Anti-Slavery Almanac for **1840.**

"*Our Peculiar Domestic Institutions.*"

Northern Hospitality—New-York nine months law. [The Slave steps out of the Slave State, and his chains fall. A Free State, with another chain, stands ready to re-enslave him.]

Burning of McIntosh at St. Louis, in April, 1836.

Showing how slavery improves the condition of the female sex.

The Negro Pew, or "Free" Seats for black Christians. | *Mayor of New-York refusing a Carman's license to a colored Man.*

Servility of the Northern States in arresting and returning fugitive Slaves.

Selling a Mother from her Child.

Hunting Slaves with dogs and guns.   A Slave drowned by the dogs.

"*Poor things, 'they can't take care of themselves.'*"

Mothers with young Children at work in the field.

A Woman chained to a Girl, and a Man in irons at work in the field.

Branding Slaves.

Cutting up a Slave in Kentucky.

Paid.   *Unpaid.*

The abolition movement was an integral part of the reform sentiment that began in the 1830s. It emphasized moral suasion rather than legal coercion. (*Courtesy, Library of Congress*)

United States. The president of Harvard, Edward Everett, registered the intensity of these militants' feelings when he responded to criticism of his having allowed a Negro to take the entrance test: "If this boy passes the examination he will be admitted; and if the white students choose to withdraw, all the income of the college will be devoted to his education."

Everett was a good representative of the eastern intellectual wing of the antislavery movement. Very many abolitionists were of a different character, drawing their inspiration from revivalistic religion. Their religion put the matter as bluntly as Everett but in a different vocabulary. Slavery is wrong; being a good Christian means rejecting and resisting it. When enough individuals embrace God's way, the larger society can be purged of evils such as slavery. Slaveholders meanwhile had only to recognize their complicity in sin and renounce it. It was by using the techniques of moral suasion—appealing to the American conscience rather than employing legal coercion—that abolitionists thought to end human bondage in the United States.

Accounts of slaves being sold and families broken made excellent propaganda for the abolitionists. Elwood Harvey wrote:

> [In 1846] we attended a sale of land and other property, near Petersburg, Virginia, and unexpectedly saw slaves sold at public auction. The slaves were told they would not be sold, and were collected in front of the quarters, gazing on the assembled multitude. The land being sold, the auctioneer's loud voice was heard, 'Bring up the *niggers!*' A shade of astonishment and affright passed over their faces, as they stared first at each other, and then at the crowd of purchasers, whose attention was now directed to them. . . .
>
> During the sale, the quarters resounded with cries and lamentations that made my heart ache. A woman was next called by name. She gave her infant one wild embrace before leaving it with an old woman, and hastened mechanically to obey the call; but stopped, threw her arms aloft, screamed, and was unable to move.
>
> One of my companions touched my shoulder and said, "Come, let us leave here; I can bear no more." We left the ground. The man who drove our carriage from Petersburg had two sons who belonged to the estate—small boys. He obtained a promise that they should not be sold. He asked if they were his only children; he answered; 'All that's left of eight.' Three others had been sold to the South, and he would never see or hear from them again.

Garrison and Weld

One person led to abolitionism by perfectionist beliefs was the young William Lloyd Garrison. He had embraced a number of reform causes in the 1820s and worked with the famous Quaker abolitionist Benjamin Lundy before establishing his own antislavery newspaper, the *Liberator*, at Boston in 1831. In unequivocal, though bombastic, language, Garrison preached the cause of immediate abolition with no compensation to slaveholders: "I *will be* as harsh as truth, and as uncompromising as justice. . . . I will not equivocate—I will not excuse—I will not retreat a single inch—AND I WILL BE HEARD." In his obsessive moral purity, he denounced the churches as "cages of unclean birds" for tolerating slavery. Northerners at first dismissed Garrison as a fanatic; only eleven people accepted his invitation to form

William Lloyd Garrison, one of the earliest abolitionists and an organizer of antislavery societies. *(Courtesy, Scribner's Archives)*

the New England Antislavery Society. But the Nat Turner revolt of 1831 made his name familiar throughout the nation, as nervous slaveholders connected the "incendiary publications" of Walker, Garrison, and others with the bloody events in Southampton County, Virginia, in which more than sixty whites were killed. The Georgia Senate offered a $1000 reward for Garrison's arrest and conviction. Newspapers throughout the country began reprinting his fiery editorials, and the stern Massachusetts editor soon became the very personification of abolition.

Abolitionism had other leaders, and much of the movement was outside of New England. Some of Garrison's contemporaries, and a few later historians, considered Theodore Dwight Weld an even more important figure. Like Garrison, Weld had entered the movement because of intense religious convictions about the evils of slavery. After being converted by the famous evangelist Charles G. Finney, he devoted his life to the cause of moral reform. In 1834, while a student at Cincinnati's Lane Theological Seminary, he organized debates on the slavery question.

After eighteen nights of discussion, the students endorsed immediatism—immediate abolition—and rejected colonization. When their antislavery activities aroused opposition among Lane's trustees, Weld and forty others left to attend Oberlin College near Cleveland. Securing funds from two wealthy New York City reformers, Arthur and Lewis Tappan, the Lane rebels made Oberlin a center of abolitionist activity. By employing the techniques and rhetoric of the religious revival, they converted to abolitionism thousands throughout the Old Northwest and nearby areas of New York and Pennsylvania. Weld also joined with his Southern wife, Angelina, and her sister, Sarah Grimké, to write *American Slavery as It Is* (1839). This popular tract, a compilation of southern newspaper accounts revealing the cruelties of slavery, offered documentary evidence to support the abolitionists' moral outrage. "Slaves," they wrote,

> are often hunted with bloodhounds and shot down like beasts, or torn in pieces by dogs . . . they are often suspended by the arms and whipped and beaten till they faint, . . . and sometimes till they die; . . . they are maimed, mutilated and burned to

---

ESSAY ON CIVIL DISOBEDIENCE (1839) *by Henry David Thoreau. Thoreau was ardently opposed both to slavery and the Mexican War.*

How does it become a man to behave toward this American government to-day? I answer, that he cannot without disgrace be associated with it. I cannot for an instant recognize that political organization as *my* government which is the *slave's* government also.

All men recognize the right of revolution: that is, the right to refuse allegiance to, and to resist, the government, when its tyranny or its inefficiency are great and unendurable. But almost all say that such is not the case now. But such was the case, they think, in the Revolution of '75. If one were to tell me that this was a bad government because it taxed certain foreign commodities brought to its ports, it is most probable that I should not make an ado about it, for I can do without them. When a sixth of the population of a nation which has undertaken to be the refuge of liberty are slaves, and a whole country is unjustly overrun and conquered by a foreign army, and subjected to military law, I think that it is not too soon for honest men to rebel and revolutionize. What makes this duty the more urgent is the fact that the country so overrun is not our own, but ours is the invading army.

If the injustice is part of the necessary friction of the machine of government, let it go, let it go: perchance it will wear smooth,—certainly the machine will wear out. If the injustice has a spring, or a pulley, or a rope, or a crank, exclusively for itself, then perhaps you may consider whether the remedy will not be worse than the evil; but if it is of such a nature that it requires you to be the agent of injustice to another, then, I say, break the law. Let your life be a counter friction to stop the machine. What I have to do is to see, at any rate, that I do not lend myself to the wrong which I condemn.

death over slow fires. All these things, and more, and worse, we shall PROVE.

On July 4, 1854, Garrison burned a copy of the Constitution proclaiming "So perish all compromises with tyranny."

The treatment of slaves of course reflected the qualities of their masters. Some were kind. Frederick Douglass was "astonished" at the "goodness" of his mistress, Sophia Auld, "a woman of the kindest heart and finest feelings," who taught him how to read. Others were cruel. One memory of such a master was passed down most graphically to a slave's daughter recalling her memories in the 1930s:

> I remember Mammy told me about one master who almost starved his slaves. Mighty stingy, I reckon he was.
>
> Some of them slaves was so poorly thin they ribs would kinda rustle against each other like corn stalks a-drying in the hot winds.

Another master wrote in his logbook laconically of the death of a slave. The same day he gave his field hands a "general whipping" he tearfully wrote of his "best horse in the South . . . ruined forever."

Initially, the abolitionists' demands for emancipation and an end to racial discrimination angered many people in the North, and during the mid-1830s anti-abolitionist mobs harassed and assaulted prominent abolitionists. A Boston mob dragged Garrison through the streets with a rope around his neck in 1835; two years later a crowd at Alton, Illinois, killed the abolitionist editor Elijah Lovejoy. Often leading citizens—lawyers, doctors, bankers, merchants—directed these actions; they, like many other Americans in the Jackson era, considered mob violence a legitimate means of protecting society, not itself a threat to law and order. Abolitionists thought these gentlemen of property were insensitive outsiders. They pitched their radical message directly to the mass of citizens by means of printed propaganda and traveling speakers.

A drawing of an inside deck of a slave ship. (*Courtesy, American Antiquarian Society*)

A PIRATE/SLAVE SHIP IS BOARDED. *The conditions described aboard this slaver are typical. The importation of slaves from outside the United States ended in 1808.*

On Friday, May 22, [1829] . . . a midshipman entered the cabin and said in a hurried manner that a sail was visible to the northwest on the larboard quarter. We immediately all rushed on deck, glasses were called for and set, and we distinctly saw a large ship of three masts, apparently crossing our course. It was the general opinion that she was either a large slaver or a pirate, or probably both. . . .

At twelve o'clock we were entirely within gunshot, and one of our long bow guns was again fired at her. It struck the water alongside, and then, for the first time, she showed a disposition to stop. While we were preparing a second she hove to, and in a short time we were alongside her.

The first object that struck us was an enormous gun, turning on a swivel, on deck—the constant appendage of a pirate; and the next were large kettles for cooking, on the bows—the usual apparatus of a slaver. Our boat was now hoisted out, and I went on board with the officers. When we mounted her decks we found her full of slaves. She was called the *Veloz,* commanded by Captain José Barbosa, bound to Bahia. She was a very broad-decked ship, with a mainmast, schooner rigged, and behind her foremast was that large, formidable gun, which turned on a broad circle of iron, on deck, and which enabled her to act as a pirate if her slaving speculation failed. She had taken in, on the coast of Africa, 336 males and 226 females, making in all 562, and had been out seventeen days, during which she had thrown overboard 55. The slaves were all inclosed under grated hatchways between decks. The space was so low that they sat between each other's legs and [were] stowed so close together that there was no possibility of their lying down or at all changing their position by night or day. As they belonged to and were shipped on account of different individuals, they were all branded like sheep with the owner's marks of different forms. These were impressed under their breasts or on their arms, and, as the mate informed me with perfect indifference "burnt with the red-hot iron." Over the hatchway stood a ferocious-looking fellow with a scourge of many twisted thongs in his hand, who was the slave driver of the ship, and whenever he heard the slightest noise below, he shook it over them and seemed eager to exercise it. . . .

But the circumstance which struck us most forcibly was how it was possible for such a number of human beings to exist, packed up and wedged together as tight as they could cram, in low cells three feet high, the greater part of which, except that immediately under the grated hatchways, was shut out from light or air, and this when the thermometer, exposed to the open sky, was standing in the shade, on our deck, at 89°. The space between decks was divided into two compartments 3 feet 3 inches high; the size of one was 16 feet by 18 and of the other 40 by 21; into the first were crammed the women and girls, into the second the men and boys: 226 fellow creatures were thus thrust into one space 288 feet square and 336 into another space 800 feet square, giving to the whole an average of 23 inches and to each of the women not more than 13 inches. We also found manacles and fetters of different kinds, but it appears that they had all been taken off before we boarded.

The heat of these horrid places was so great and the odor so offensive that it was quite impossible to enter them, even had there been room. They were measured as above when the slaves had left them. The officers insisted that the poor suffering creatures should be admitted on deck to get air and water. This was opposed by the mate of the slaver, who, from a feeling that they deserved it, declared they would murder them all. The officers, however, persisted, and the poor beings were all turned up together. It is possible to conceive the effect of this eruption—517 fellow creatures of all ages and sexes, some children, some adults, some old men and women, all in a state of total nudity, scrambling out together to taste the luxury of a little fresh air and water. They came swarming up like bees from the aperture of a hive till the whole deck was crowded to suffocation from stem to stern, so that it was impossible to imagine where they could all have come from or how they could have been stowed away. On looking into the places where they had been crammed, there were found some children next the sides of the ship, in the places most remote from light and air; they were lying nearly in a torpid state after the rest had turned out. The little creatures seemed indifferent as to life or death, and when they were carried on deck, many of them could not stand.

After enjoying for a short time the unusual luxury of air, some water was brought; it was then that the extent of their sufferings was exposed in a fearful manner. They all rushed like maniacs towards it. No entreaties or threats or blows could restrain them; they shrieked and struggled and fought with one another for a drop of this precious liquid, as if they grew rabid at the sight of it.

It was not surprising that they should have endured much sickness and loss of life in their short passage. They had sailed from the coast of Africa on the 7th of May and had been out but seventeen days, and they had thrown overboard no less than fifty-five, who had died of dysentery and other complaints in that space of time, though they had left the coast in good health. Indeed, many of the survivors were seen lying about the decks in the last stage of emaciation and in a state of filth and misery not to be looked at. . . .

While expressing my horror at what I saw and exclaiming against the state of this vessel for conveying human beings. I was informed by my friends, who had passed so long a time on the coast of Africa and visited so many ships, that this was one of the best they had seen. The height sometimes between decks was only eighteen inches, so that the unfortunate beings could not turn round or even on their sides, the elevation being less than the breadth of their shoulders; and here they are usually chained to the decks by the neck and legs. . . .

Cinqué was an African chief who aboard a slave ship organized a mutiny that killed most of the Spanish crew. Spain had signed a treaty, however, agreeing not to take part in the slave trade. Cinqué and his cohorts wound up in a Connecticut jail after entering Long Island Sound. Defended by John Quincy Adams, now a congressman, Cinqué was released in 1841. *(Courtesy, National Portrait Galley).*

Southern Counterattack

The rise of militant abolitionism, coupled with the Nat Turner uprising, stimulated another round of soul-searching among southern whites. In 1831–32 the Virginia House of Delegates began a lengthy debate on a plan for the gradual emancipation and deportation of all slaves. The proposal was at last defeated, and this defeat marked a turning point. Thereafter, few southerners would deny that slavery was sanctioned by the Bible and the laws of nature, provided a harmonious solution to the South's racial dilemma, and offered beneficent schooling to the black race.

To shore up their "peculiar institution," southern legislatures enacted tougher slave codes and further curtailed the liberties of free blacks. In many states it was illegal to teach slaves to read and write, and in some they were not allowed to work as typesetters or printers. The repression touched whites as well. Slave-state lawmakers forbade the publication or distribution of antislavery propaganda—sometimes under penalty of death. Public pressure silenced other critics of slavery: several prominent university professors left the South. The antislavery societies that had existed throughout the region quickly disappeared.

The "Gag" Rule   Southerners also sought to stifle criticism from without. Backed by a war chest of over $30,000, abolitionists embarked in 1835 on a campaign to send hundreds of thousands of antislavery pamphlets to all parts of the country. A mob of South Carolinians seized the materials from the Charleston post office and in a huge bonfire burned them, along with effigies of Arthur Tappan and Garrison. Afterward, Postmaster General Amos Kendall, with President Jackson's approval, authorized southern postmasters to censor the mails and stop the flow of antislavery material into the South. Southern politicians urged the House of Representatives not to receive petitions demanding the abolition of slavery in the states or the District of Columbia. Formerly Congress had accepted such memorials and then rejected them as "inexpedient." Following angry debate, the House now approved a modified "gag" rule; henceforth it would receive antislavery petitions but automatically table them without formal consideration.

Repressive tactics rebounded against slaveholders. "Gag" rules, mob attacks, the censorship of mails, and other violations of civil liberties created a reaction that broadened the antislavery movement's appeal. Sounding a note that would grow loud by the 1850s, abolitionists charged that a vast "slave power" conspiracy was threatening the liberty of northern whites as well as southern blacks. Slaveholders and their northern allies, those "gentlemen of property and standing," stood ready to destroy the freedom of all Americans in order to safeguard slavery.

Antislavery Disunity

As they struggled to influence popular opinion, abolitionists promoted one broad organization: the American Antislavery Society, founded in 1833. Garrison, Weld, the Tappan brothers, and the Grimké sisters all belonged to the Society, which claimed as many as thirteen hundred local chapters. Under Weld's direction, the Society's members bombarded Congress with petitions opposing slavery in the District of Columbia and urging an end to the interstate slave trade. The petition campaign attracted widespread support after southern Congressmen obtained their "gag" rule. Former President John Quincy Adams, now a Massachusetts congressman, led the battle to vindicate the historic right of petition. Year after year "Old Man Eloquent," though never an advocate of immediatism, fought to get petitions discussed before the House of Representatives, winning thousands to the antislavery cause in the process. In 1844 Adams finally secured repeal of the "gag" rule. He served in Congress until 1848 when he suffered a stroke in the House and died two days later at the age of eighty-one. American abolitionists also sought closer ties with British reformers, and in 1840 many had attended the World Antislavery Convention in London. Yet the antislavery movement had deep internal divisions. Personality clashes, doctrinal conflicts among different religious denominations, and fundamental differences over strategy splintered the movement.

Tactical Disagreements   The split over strategy and tactics involved conflicting interpretations of American society and the role of abolitionism in American life. Shocked by anti-abolition mob violence, Garrisonians concluded that American society was sick. Slavery was one of the symptoms of moral decay, but there were others—militarism, expansionism, the oppression of women and the poor. Only a total reformation of the nation's ethical values would suffice. Abolitionists, Garrison maintained, must "revolutionize the public sentiment" by an expanded campaign of moral suasion; having done this, they would accomplish the overthrow of slavery. Garrison's opponents in the antislavery movement possessed a broader faith in the possibilities of American society and a narrower vision of reform. When they surveyed the events of the 1830s, they concluded that abolitionism had made considerable progress. Efforts to link the movement too closely with other causes, they believed, risked alienating people who had been converted by the campaign against postal censorship or angered by southern violations of the civil liberties of whites. "Garrisonian fanaticism," so they feared, only endangered the future of abolitionism.

Involvement in the antislavery movement fostered female abolitionists' demands for the equality of their own sex. After Garrison's New England Antislavery Society voted to accept women on equal terms with men, several important male leaders promptly resigned. When female abolitionists found themselves segregated in the gallery at the London World Antislavery Convention of 1840, Garrison and other sympathetic men joined them there. The Garrisonians' active support for the women's cause angered many antislavery activists who charged that feminism would only sidetrack the crusade against slavery.

The Liberty Party   The question of involvement in politics proved even more divisive. The "Log Cabin and Hard Cider" campaign of 1840 expressed the nation's new fascination with mass politics, and many antislavery leaders wanted to get involved. The success of the petition drives and other quasi-political activities offered some hope that electoral politics and antislavery would be joined. Over the strident objections of Garrison, a group of abolitionists formed the Liberty Party in 1840; as their presidential candidate, they selected James G. Birney, a slaveholder turned abolitionist, and they framed a platform calling for the abolition of slavery in America. Lost in the hoopla of the contest between the Whig Harrison and the Democrat Van Buren, the Liberty Party attracted little attention. Birney, in London for the World Antislavery Convention, did not even campaign. In the next presidential election Birney polled almost 65,000 votes. An improvement over 1840, this still represented only 32 out of every 1,000 votes cast in the North. Garrison and his followers consistently opposed the Liberty Party experiment. Political organizations, they argued, implied acceptance of the legitimacy of the existing system, which for them was morally diseased at its root. Retaining his faith in perfectionism and therefore rejecting participation in important institutions and measures, Garrison refused even to vote.

But abolitionists, including even Garrison, were more than simple idealists or frustrated politicians. Most were hard-headed reformers who recognized the need for many types of nonviolent action. They tried, unsuccessfully, to organize a boycott of slave-produced products; they worked to impel churches to denounce slavery; a few helped slaves escape southern bondage on the celebrated "underground railroad." While this institution enjoyed a legend beyond its reality, one Quaker recalled its workings:

> In the winter of 1826–27 fugitives began to come to our house. The roads were always in running order, and the connections were good, the conductors active and zealous, and there was no lack of passengers. Seldom a week passed without our receiving passengers by this mysterious road. We knew not what night or what hour of the night we would be roused from slumber by a gentle rap at the door. Outside in the cold or rain there would be a two-horse wagon loaded with fugitives, perhaps the greater part of them women and children. When they were all safely inside and the door fastened, I would cover the windows, strike a light, and build a good fire. By this time my wife would be up and preparing victuals. The companies varied in number, from two or three fugitives to seventeen.
>
> The pursuit was often very close, and we had to resort to various stratagems in order to elude the pursuers. Sometimes a company of fugitives were scattered and secreted in the neighborhood until the hunters had given up the chase. At other times their route was changed and they were hurried forward with all speed. It was a continual excitement and anxiety to us, but the work was its own reward.

Northern Blacks   By 1850 the quarter of a million blacks who lived in the free states were free in name only. In most places they could not vote, hold office, or testify in court. They were confined to menial jobs and wretched housing. Everywhere law and public opinion combined to exclude or segregate them: in railroad coaches, schools, restaurants, theaters, churches, even cemeteries. Most northerners, including some who condemned slavery, viewed this not as a departure from democratic principles, but as a natural and legitimate response to the presence of the Negro.

A scientific apologist, Dr. Josiah Nott of Mobile, Alabama, published his *Types of Mankind* in 1854, concluding on the basis of head size that blacks were a separate and permanently inferior species fit only for slavery. Other writers contrasted the "security" that slaves enjoyed with the brutal exploitation suffered by northern workingmen. Excluded from the dominant political and social institutions, Northern blacks found in the abolitionist crusade their first opportunity to play a major role in American public life. Their subscriptions kept Garrison's newspaper alive, and Boston blacks protected him from violence. Escaped slaves like Frederick Douglass lectured and wrote of their experiences. Harriet Tubman, an escapee who made nineteen trips into slave country to bring out runaways, had a price of $40,000 on her head. Initially the protégés of white abolitionists, blacks gradually asserted their independence. They founded newspapers and civil-rights organizations of their own and established vigilance committees in northern cities that protected black fugitives from slave-catchers. "Should any wretch enter my dwelling, any pale-faced spectre among ye, to execute this fugitive slave law on me or mine," a black abolitionist warned defiantly in 1850, "I'll seek his life, I'll shed his blood."

Slavery in the Territories

In 1840, the antislavery movement was still struggling for a foothold in American politics. Abolitionist sentiment was vague, sporadic, and moralistic; the slavery interest was concentrated, practical, and testily defensive. Moral suasion had utterly failed to convert southerners, who feared not only a loss of property but a loss of racial mastery. Most northerners scorned the abolition movement as radical and disruptive. The vast majority of southern whites discriminated against free blacks and were content to leave slavery alone where it existed. Northerners may have opposed slavery in the abstract, but few favored actual emancipation unless it was accompanied by colonization, fearing that the free states would be overrun with emancipated blacks. Slavery also had powerful allies among northern businessmen dependent on the success of southern crops. The churches, too, wrestled with the problem of slavery. By the end of the 1840s the Presbyterians, the Methodists, and the Baptists, unable to reach a consensus on slavery at their national meetings, had split into northern and southern organizations.

The United States Constitution itself discouraged abolitionists. Both sides in the slavery controversy recognized that the Constitution perceived slaves as property and that the federal government could not abolish slavery in the states. This was a decision for the people of the states themselves to make. The southern states were happy to uphold a Constitution and a Union that protected slavery. Abiding by the Missouri Compromise, both Whigs and Democrats shunned the potentially divisive slavery issue in order to preserve harmony between their northern and their southern wings.

There was one vast area, however, where the federal government did hold power over slavery. The Constitution authorized the Congress to make "all needful rules and regulations" respecting the territories.

For decades Americans had agreed to an informal division of territory into free and slave soil. The Northwest Ordinance of 1787 had prohibited slavery north of the Ohio River. South of the Ohio, North Carolina and Georgia had ceded western lands to the national government on the specific condition that slavery should be permitted in the states that would eventually be formed from these lands—Tennessee, Alabama, and Mississippi. The Missouri Compromise line of 1820 divided the vast Louisiana Purchase into slave and free soil. These arrangements covered all the existing United States territory, leaving nothing after 1820 for argument in Congress. Abolitionists were left to battle over such narrow issues as the status of slavery in the District of Columbia, where Congress had undisputed authority.

Suddenly in the late 1840s the issue of slavery in the territories came alive. For Congress had to deal with slavery in the regions acquired after the Mexican War. The antislavery movement now had a practical political issue to which it could attach itself. Since the government could determine the status of slavery in the territories, abolitionists could make concrete demands on Congress. And because many northerners had some thought of moving to the fresh land in the territories and did not want those lands dominated by slaveholders, abolitionists could appeal to self-interest as well as to conscience. Beginning in the late 1840s the antislavery movement fixed upon the territorial issue, and for the next fifteen years this question dominated national politics as no issue before or since.

Manifest Destiny

The Whig Party   In March 1841 jubilant Whigs flooded Washington, hungry for government offices. The crush of office-seekers proved tiring for the elderly and infirm William Henry Harrison. A cold contracted while he was doing the White House grocery-shopping soon developed into pneumonia, and on April 4—just a month after the inauguration—he died. Two days later Vice-President John Tyler, summoned hastily from his Virginia plantation, took the presidential oath. Since Harrison was the first President to die in office, questions arose over whether Tyler was actually president or merely the vice-president assuming the duties and responsibilities of the presidency. Tyler insisted that he had become President in every sense of the word. "God and the Constitution" had made Tyler President, a Missourian regretfully declared, "but who made him Vice President?" But Tyler's conduct in support of this claim set an important precedent.

Lean and hawk-nosed, with a Virginian's pride and a streak of obstinacy, the fifty-one-year-old Tyler entered the White House with a distinguished career in Virginia politics behind him. He had started in politics as a states' rights Democrat and he and the Whigs were mismatched from the start. The new president resisted domination by Henry Clay and Daniel Webster, the acknowledged leaders of the party. He had no sympathy for the Whigs's economic nationalism. In September, when he vetoed Clay's bill to reestablish a national bank, the entire Harrison Cabinet resigned except Secretary of State Daniel Webster. He stayed on to conduct negotiations with Great Britain over various outstanding problems, especially the disputed northeastern boundary between Maine and New Brunswick.

Tempers had flared between the United States and Great Britain in 1838 when a small American steamer, the *Caroline*, had been burned by the British when it was caught ferrying supplies to a group of Canadian nationalists on the Niagara River. Two years later Alexander McLeod, a Canadian deputy sheriff, was arrested in New York State for murder in connection with the *Caroline* incident. McLeod was released only after talk of war with Britain filled the newspapers. In 1842, nevertheless, the Secretary of State managed to conclude the Webster-Ashburton Treaty, which settled the Maine boundary and other problems by compromise, and set an example for the friendly resolution of future disputes between Britain and the United States and between this country and Canada. Shortly after the treaty was signed, Webster too left the Cabinet. That resignation completed the break between Tyler and the Whigs, who henceforth referred to the President as "His Accidency."

Tyler appointed a new Cabinet heavy with southern Democrats, and began searching for issues that would win him reelection. For the North he signed the Tariff of 1842, restoring protective duties to roughly the level of 1832. To soothe southern resentment over the tariff, Tyler offered a daring proposal—the annexation of Texas.

Spanish Settlement   After Mexico won its independence from Spain in 1821, the mission era ended and many of the Spanish holdings were taken by large landholders who established *ranchos*, often encompassing thousands of acres. These estates produced a lively cattle-raising economy controlled by men of Spanish descent. Their *vaqueros* began cowboy traditions in the Southwest, many of which would later be adopted by the incoming white settlers. Their chaps, bandannas, and rodeos would become American traditions. The distinctive architecture of the Spanish missions with their red-tiled roofs, whitewashed adobe walls, courtyards, and fountains graced the landscape from San Antonio to San Francisco. The patio barbecue descended from a Spanish custom. The Southwest would retain many Spanish laws regarding water and mining, along with techniques for irrigation, sheep ranching, and orchard planting. Even Spanish laws and customs concerning the disposition of property within families prevailed long after these areas became part of the United States.

The independence of Mexico from Spain did not eliminate the isolation of the Spanish outposts to the north. Isolation gave these settlements much self-sufficiency, but they were receptive to the manufactures that traders from the United States were able to furnish. By 1824 wagons and pack animals were hauling tools, textiles, and weapons over the

Santa Fé Trail, forged by William Becknell in the early 1820s. In the 1830s English-speaking Americans and even Europeans began to drift into California. Some traversed the California trail and competed as successful ranchers alongside the Spanish. The Swiss John Sutter, who would discover gold in California in 1849, settled in Monterey.

The Gold Rush vastly sped up settlement and contributed to the reputation nearby San Francisco was acquiring for gambling, drinking, and prostitution. One letter sent home caught the fever:

People are arriving and departing daily and hourly. I have no doubt 400 people have already arrived from Oregon. They usually camp for a day or so near us, look about, swear at the high prices and disappear in the grand vortex. . . . It is impossible to get at anything like truth, but that the amount of gold in these mountains exceeds any previous calculation I have no doubt. . . .

One miner complained to his wife: "I do not like to be apacking a thousand dollars about in my coat pockets for it has toar my pockets and puld the Coat to peaces." The truth was not so spectacular. Most claims soon petered

Texas land titles were freely issued to colonists, here by Stephen Austin and Baron de Bastrop, representing the Mexican government. (*Courtesy, Southern Pacific Company*)

out, and miners either became wage workers or chased the get-rich-quick rainbow to another site.

Others came to California, having sailed around the southern tip of South America, and established trading enterprises in San Diego and elsewhere. Some of these newcomers married into Spanish families and adopted their religion.

In all these areas, relations with the Mexican government deteriorated. In the wake of a rebellion among California's Mexicans, the influence of the Mexican republic was weakening even among its own California citizens. In New Mexico, Mexicans and Indians rebelled in 1837 against the government, executing the governor and seizing his palace.

Annexation of Texas

The broad plains stretching west and south of the Sabine River had long attracted Americans. Lured by the cheap land, several thousand of them had settled on the grants established by Stephen F. Austin and others by the 1830s. Mexican law required them to become nominal Catholics as well as Mexican citizens; otherwise the colonists enjoyed considerable autonomy and retained their national character. Stephen Austin advised them to "play the turtle, head and feet within your own shell," but differences soon arose between the Texans and the Mexican government. Alarmed by these signs of independence and by the rapid increase in the number of settlers in Texas from the northern republic, 30,000 in 1835, the Mexican government tightened its control and prohibited further immigration. After several armed uprisings, the Texans declared their independence in 1836. The slaughter of the defenders of the Alamo only united them behind General Sam Houston, and led to the rout of the Mexican army at San Jacinto.

The United States had adopted a distinctly unneutral attitude during the Texan war of independence. Money was raised for supplies, and many volunteers swelled the ranks of the Texan army. After independence, the public on both sides of the United States border strongly favored annexation. But since Mexico refused to acknowledge Texan independence, annexation might provoke war. Politicians also feared that incorporating new slave territory into the Union would aggravate the rising antislavery sentiment in the North. President Jackson waited until his last day in office before recognizing the new

Texan republic. His successor, Martin Van Buren, carefully avoided the question of annexation. Texas drifted for several years, developing ever closer ties with Great Britain.

The movement for annexation revived in 1842. Texas President Sam Houston, facing an empty treasury and renewed hostilities with Mexico, made overtures to Washington and found an enthusiastic ally in John Tyler. Annexation was politically expedient, and, like other slaveholders, Tyler was convinced that continued expansion was vital to the slave economy and the southern way of life. After the unsympathetic Webster resigned as secretary of state, Tyler appointed a fellow Virginian, Abel P. Upshur, and ordered him to seek a treaty of annexation.

The move was well timed: Americans dreamed anew of continental empire. Southerners feared that Britain, which had abolished slavery in its possessions in 1833, was working to abolish slavery in Texas. Northern commercial interests sought American control of valuable Pacific coast ports as trading centers, and annexation of Texas would shorten the distance to the Pacific. The idea spread that it was the nation's "manifest destiny" to overspread and civilize the continent. Secretary Upshur, confident that the Senate would approve a treaty, negotiated with Texan representatives. The Transcendentalist author Margaret Fuller wrote in 1845, "It looks as if a great day was coming, and that time one of democracy. Our country will play a leading part. Her eagle will lead the van; but whether to soar upward to the sun or stoop for helpless prey, who dares promise?" After Upshur's death the new secretary of state, John C. Calhoun, completed the arrangements for annexation and submitted the treaty to the Senate.

James Polk: Expansionist

The Senate, however, delayed action until after the 1844 party nominating conventions, at which Texas suddenly emerged as a major political issue. Both leading candidates, Henry Clay and Martin Van Buren, came out against annexation. The Whigs, passing over Tyler, nominated Clay, but the Democrats bypassed Van Buren in favor of an avowed expansionist, James Knox Polk. This political maneuvering and Calhoun's defense of annexation as a proslavery measure doomed the treaty. A combination of Whigs and disappointed Van Buren Democrats killed it. Tyler refused to surrender; he

President James K. Polk. His aggressive actions against New Mexico and California brought about the Mexican War. *(Courtesy, Scribner's Archives)*

sent a message to the House of Representatives three days later proposing to annex Texas by other means.

Tyler had forced the issue of expansion to the center of American politics. Democratic politicians hoped to preserve sectional harmony within their party with a platform promising both the "re-annexation" of Texas and the "re-occupation" of Oregon all the way to 54° 40' latitude. Whigs and Democrats again clamored for votes. In Lowell, Massachusetts: "The Whig Party of this city have got a large flag stretched across one of our streets. The Democratic Party not to be outdone [obtained] a large hickory tree surmounted with a flag staff, making the whole length upwards of 100 feet." One Senator declaimed in favor of 54° 40' or fight: Give up Oregon?

> History, speaking from the sepulchre of the sainted dead, forbids it. The shades of Washington, of Adams, of Henry, and of their immortal compeers, forbid it. The still small voice of Camden and

> Concord forbids it. The holy blood that fell in torrents in the parched fields of Monmouth, and Camden, and the Brandywine, forbids it. . . . In the name of the past, in the name of the unborn millions whose proud fortune it will be to direct the destinies of free America—I protest here, in the face of Heaven and all men, against any dismemberment of our territory—the surrender of our principle—the sacrifice of our honor!

Too late, Clay sensed the public mood and endorsed annexation of Texas "upon just and fair terms." That November, Polk won a narrow victory in the presidential election ("Thank God Clay is defeated and the Republic saved. Amen," wrote a Democratic hatmaker in Connecticut). President Tyler interpreted Polk's victory as a mandate for annexation of Texas. Just before he left office in March 1845, the President got Congress to admit Texas to the Union by a joint resolution, which required only a majority vote in each house, while a treaty would have required approval by two-thirds of the Senate. When Polk entered the White House, annexation was a settled question.

Another of Polk's major objectives was the solution of the Oregon boundary question. Formidable mountain barriers had retarded settlement in the Pacific Northwest until the 1830s, when traders and missionaries began publicizing the area. By 1845 five thousand had migrated there, settling mainly in the fertile Willamette Valley in Oregon. Throughout his campaign, Polk had promised to assert American control over all the Oregon Territory, which the United States and Great Britain had occupied jointly since 1818. Once in power, however, Polk began a search for compromise with Britain.

The British government at first rejected the American idea of putting the line at the 49th parallel, which would place the Columbia River wholly in American hands. Polk then called upon Congress for authority to give the required one year's notice terminating joint occupation. The United States, he announced, would look John Bull "straight in the eye." Congress consented. Polk served the expected notice in April 1846; on both sides of the Atlantic, people talked of war. One newspaper declared: *"Oregon is ours,* and we will keep it, at the price, if need be, of every drop of the nation's blood."

Neither country really wanted a fight. Britain had all but abandoned the area between the Columbia River and the 49th parallel to the advancing wave of settlers. Polk, anticipating war with Mexico at any moment, could no longer afford a quarrel with Britain. He therefore welcomed a British offer to divide Oregon at the 49th parallel. The Senate approved this arrangement, despite angry protests from northwestern Democrats, who charged that Polk and his southern Democratic allies, having acquired Texas, had reneged on their promise to acquire "all of Oregon or none." Their residual bitterness combined with abolitionist sentiment to hamper Polk's conduct of the Mexican War.

Caricature of Davy Crockett. The celebrated Tennessee frontiersman fought for Texas independence. *(Courtesy, American Antiquarian Society)*

The Mexican War

Polk's other objective, acquiring California, was not so easily accomplished. Mexico had no intention of selling the province. The proud Latin republic had broken diplomatic relations with the United States in March 1845, in protest over the decision of the United States to annex Texas. And a controversy had arisen over the question of just what had been annexed. Texans asserted that their republic stretched as far south as the Rio Grande; Mexico insisted that the province's boundary stopped at the Nueces River. Mexico probably had the better case. Polk nevertheless claimed all the disputed area for the United States and used his nation's demands on the Texas boundary to press Mexico to a settlement on California.

Sentiment for expansion was vigorously expressed by Louis O'Sullivan in his *The United States Magazine and Democratic Review* in 1845; note the startling demographic prediction:

> Texas has been absorbed into the Union in the inevitable fulfillment of the general law which is rolling our population westward; the connexion of which with that ratio of growth in population which is destined within a hundred years to swell our numbers to the enormous population of *two hundred and fifty millions* (if not more), is too evident to leave us in doubt of the manifest design of Providence in regard to the occupation of this continent. It was disintegrated from Mexico in the natural course of events, by a process perfectly legitimate on its own part, blameless on ours; and in which all the censures due to wrong, perfidy, and folly, rest on Mexico alone. And possessed as it was by a population which was in truth but a colonial detachment from our own, . . . their incorporation into the Union was not only inevitable, but the most natural, right and proper thing in the world—and it is only astonishing that there should be any among ourselves to say it nay.

The Drift Toward War   In July 1845, Polk ordered General Zachary Taylor, with nearly four thousand troops, to take up a position south of the Nueces. Taylor halted at Corpus Christi, where he remained for several months. At about the same time, the President issued secret orders to naval officers in the Pacific to occupy the California ports in the event of war with Mexico. He worked actively to encourage a Texas-style revolution among settlers. Just in case the dissatisfied settlers from the United States needed any help, the President sent Colonel John C. Frémont and a party of heavily armed engineers on a "scientific expedition" to California.

His weapons now primed and ready, Polk sent John Slidell, a Louisiana politician, to Mexico in November 1845 to negotiate. The President, refusing to compromise on the Rio Grande boundary, offered only to assume payment of claims by United States citizens against the Mexican government in return for its acquiescence. He also authorized Slidell to purchase all or part of Upper California and New Mexico. When two successive Mexican governments refused to risk public disfavor by receiving him, Slidell withdrew. "Be assured," he wrote to the Secretary of State, "that nothing is to be done with these people until they shall have been chastised." Polk had reached the same conclusion. In January 1846 he sent General Taylor's army to the Rio Grande. On the 150-mile march across the coastal plain the soldiers jokingly called their dust-covered comrades "adobes," which later became "dough-boys," a term used for troops in World War I. In late March Taylor and his men took up a fortified position opposite the Mexican City of Matamoros; naval units then blockaded the mouth of the river. For several weeks, nothing happened.

On May 9 Polk decided to ask Congress for a declaration of war against Mexico for failing to pay the claims due citizens of the United States and refusing to receive Slidell. News arrived that very evening of a skirmish with Mexican forces on the north bank of the Rio Grande. Polk at once revised his war message. Mexico, he told Congress, had "invaded our territory and shed American blood upon American soil." Congress, not fully aware of the President's maneuvering, voted overwhelmingly for war. Thousands of volunteers enthusiastically answered the call.

Polk and his Cabinet agreed at the outset that the United States must acquire both New Mexico and Upper California (the present state, as distinct from Lower California, still part of Mexico) and secure the Rio Grande boundary. New Mexico and California took but six months to conquer. During the summer of 1846 Colonel Stephen W. Kearny's "Army of the West" (actually just sixteen hundred men) marched from Fort Leavenworth, Kansas, to Santa Fe, and occu-

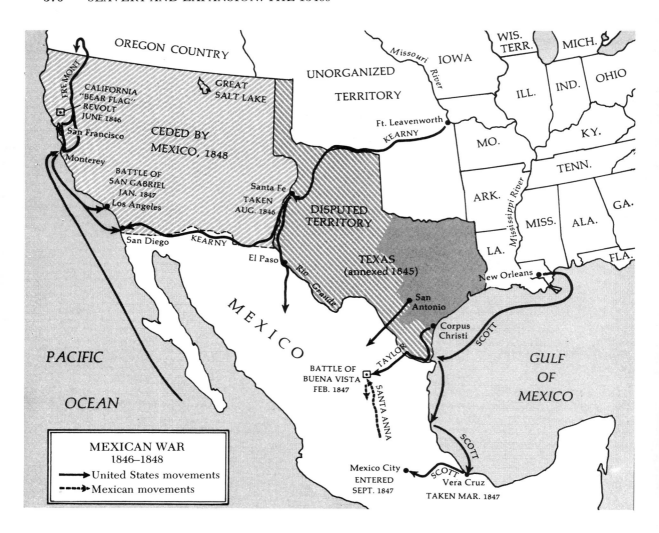

pied it without opposition. Kearny then proceeded with part of his force to aid the navy in the conquest of California. A column of Missouri volunteers under Colonel A. W. Doniphan descended the Rio Grande to El Paso, marched from there into the interior, and in March 1847 occupied Chihuahua.

Polk's objectives in Mexico were unclear. Apparently he hoped that an advance into Mexico would force General Santa Anna into a quick settlement.

Taylor at once pushed the Mexicans back across the Rio Grande and occupied Matamoros. The enthusiasm of the volunteers waned as the summer advanced. One soldier stationed near Matamoros wrote home:

> We had just moved our camp into a corn field newly ploughed, the soil an adhesive clay, and by the time I had in some measure secured my bag-

gage . . . the water was some inches deep, or rather there was a soft adhesive mortar bed, about ankle deep, over the whole camp. The rain and gale were still at their worst, when I began looking about to see the state of the nation. In every direction the tents were overthrown and their contents scattered in the mud. My own company had almost entirely disappeared, a few despairing wretches, groping about in the mud for their arms, were all that were left. The fires were extinguished and desolation reigned throughout the camp.

At another camp, on the Rio Grande, a volunteer reported:

> The water here unless well-qualified with brandy has a very peculiar effect on one. . . . it opens the bowels. . . . Gen. Scott came to see us the other day. He complimented Major Sumner very warmly on our improvement and especially on the extraordinary vigilance of our scouts—who, as he said,

were peering at him from behind every bush as he approached the camp. To those aware of the disease prevalent here, the mistake of the General is ludicrous.

In September, nevertheless, Taylor captured the Mexican stronghold of Monterrey and moved on to Saltillo and Victoria. The following February he repulsed Santa Anna at Buena Vista. "Old Rough and Ready's" victories and Doniphan's occupation of Chihuahua secured his country's possession of Mexico's northern territories.

In the meantime, Polk had decided to bring the stubborn Santa Anna to terms with a strike at Mexico City itself. Polk, hating the Whigs even more than the Mexicans, picked General Winfield Scott to lead the campaign instead of Zachary Taylor, who was already being pushed as a Whig presidential candidate. Landing at Vera Cruz in March 1847, Scott took the city with few United States casualties on his side. One soldier wrote home to his parents:

> On entering the city, I was disappointed at not seeing as many houses in ruins as I had supposed would be the case; but as I continued my stroll, I soon saw the dreadful destruction which our shells occasioned, while solid shot from our batteries had passed entirely through the city, reaching in their flight the quay or mole running into the sea, upon which the affrighted citizens had fled for safety from the bombs. . . .
>
> I went into one of the churches, now converted into a hospital, in which there are upwards of five hundred patients; it was a curious sight thus to see the pallets of the sick placed in the chapels, and the various ornaments of the church, sacred to many eyes, made use of as need required. On looking up at the vaulted ceiling, behold there were several large holes through which the sky was visible; several thirteen-inch shells had dropped through the roofing as if it had been paper, exploding within the body of the church; all around, walls, paintings, and wood-work showed the terrified force of their bursting; the débris was still lying over the floor or swept into piles to make room for beds. . . . Our victory, in its present gain and future results, is very great indeed, and I doubt whether ever as great a one was obtained with less loss to the victors. Scott deserves immense praise.

The Mexican loss of life at Vera Cruz, by their own report, was 1100, mostly by the explosion of shells, while only thirteen United States troops died.

Scott then pushed inland through the mountains, routing Santa Anna at the pass of Cerro Gordo, after a party of engineers under Captain Robert E. Lee had hacked a path through ravines and underbrush to surround the Mexicans. On September 13, Scott's army stormed the fortress of Chapultepec guarding Mexico City. The capital fell the next day.

Treaty of Guadalupe Hidalgo (1848) Polk was by now desperate to end the fighting, and the intense domestic opposition to "Mr. Polk's War." Whig politicians—among them a young Illinois congressman named Abraham Lincoln—charged him with provoking Mexico into war as an excuse for expansion.

In December 1847 Lincoln introduced resolutions requesting Polk to inform Congress as to the "exact spot" where the first "blood of our *citizens* was shed." He declared "that the war with Mexico was unnecessarily and unconstitutionally commenced by the President." Later Lincoln praised a speech by Congressman Alexander Stephens of Georgia, who said that "the principle of waging war against a neighboring people to compel them to sell their country, is not only dishonorable, but disgraceful and infamous." In the Senate, Illinois Democrat Stephen Douglas spoke up for the President, quoting Frederick the Great's maxim, "Take possession first and negotiate afterward." A new senator from Mississippi, Jefferson Davis, who had fought at Buena Vista, said that Mexico was held "by title of conquest." If the country could not agree, said Davis, then "let the sections part."

Outside Congress, other voices of opposition were heard. Antislavery spokesmen like James Russell Lowell accused the President of wanting "bigger pens to cram with slaves." The American Peace Society grew in membership, and Henry David Thoreau counseled civil disobedience. Some critics of the war even longed for the defeat of the United States. As Scott's army approached Mexico City, William Lloyd Garrison thundered in the *Liberator:* "We only hope that, if blood has had to flow, that it has been that of the Americans, and that the next news we shall hear will be that General Scott and his army are in the hands of the Mexicans. . . ."

Especially in the West and in the border states feelings about slavery and the Mexican War were smouldering. In January 1848 one new resident in Kentucky observed an increasingly closed society:

An early daguerreotype of Thomas Wood, a member of Zachary Taylor's staff, leading American troops through the streets of Saltillo, capital of Coahuila province in northern Mexico. *(Courtesy, Yale University Library)*

The man with whom I board (a slave holder) says that all questions that involve the subject of slavery ought not to be discussed in Ky. And I have heard him say that slavery was an evil, yet he says it ought not to be debated in Ky. for it makes the Negroes uneasy & has a tendency to make them try to escape (which by the way) a great many do. . . . A minister to go into the pulpit and preach Anti slavery doctrine, as some do in the East, would be in danger of his life, it would not be allowed—Aye, in our boasted land of *Liberty* one has not the privelege of expressing his opinions—Shame on such actions! Call not this the land where Liberty's broad shield shines over all, while one sixth of her sons & daughters toil & bleed beneath the lash, 'tis a disgrace to the Union—Our Eagle is no longer an emblem of protection, but of Despotism, Tyranny, & Oppression. It lives by plunder, it feasts on innocence—& drinks the life blood of its victims. Does not the present war with Mexico show it. It tears her *limbs* from her body & then because she writhes & offers some resistance, she strikes her beak to its very vitals. I have said more than I intended but not half what I feel.

At the same time "Continental Democrats," party members of extreme expansionist persuasion, were urging the President to take all of Mexico. Polk had previously dispatched Nicholas P. Trist to Mexico as a peace negotiator, and although in late 1847 he called Trist home, the emissary ignored Polk's order and stayed to sign the Treaty of Guadalupe Hidalgo on February 2, 1848. The United States gained the Rio Grande boundary, New Mexico, and California in return for an agreement to assume the claims of its citizens against the Mexican government, and to pay $15 million to Mexico.

Robert Stockton, a hero of the fighting in

California against the Mexicans, revealed traces of antiCatholicism in a speech at a banquet about the war:

> I care not for the beautiful fields and healthful skies of California; I care not for her leagues of land and her mines of silver. The glory of the achievements there, if any glory there be, is in the establishment of the first free press in California; in having built the first school-house in California; in having lighted up the torch of religious toleration, as well as of civil liberty, in California. May the torch grow brighter and brighter, until, from Cape Mendocino to Cape St. Lucas, it illumines the dark path of the victim of religious intolerance and political despotism.

The ratification in 1853 of the Treaty of Guadalupe Hidalgo turned over to the United States approximately 80,000 Mexicans whose citizenship, property rights, and religious freedom the treaty supposedly guaranteed. Mexicans residing within the United States gradually saw their property and influence dwindle as they faced increasing pressure from the flood of Anglo-Americans. The California Land Law of 1851 required that they submit proof of their land ownership. The cost of doing so in taxes, legal fees, and battles with squatters, in combination with the rainfall conditions that made incomes uncertain, gradually took away their land. Violence broke out in northern California in the 1850s and 1860s, and some Mexican Americans, called *Californios*, resorted to banditry. *Bandidos* who roamed the California area spawned legends. In southern California, in the 1870s and 1880s, the *Californios* lost more land to the railroads which nonetheless provided jobs for Hispanics. In New Mexico, the *ricos*, wealthy Mexican landowners and merchants, played an important role in the creation of the territorial government. While remaining separate from the Anglo-Americans, they retained substantial influence into the post-Civil War era. In Texas, the Spanish and Anglo cultures blended after the war into the familiar cowboy traditions of that area as the cattle industry grew phenomenally in response to the demand for beef that increased with the country's population.

The war was over. Writing in 1848 about the Mexican War, a Mexican historian observed: "To explain then in a few words the true origin of the war, it is sufficient to say that the insatiable ambition of the United States, favored by our weakness, caused it." For an apparently small price the United States had rounded out its continental domain, acquiring the present states of California, Nevada, Utah, New Mexico, and Arizona. In Texas as elsewhere in the Southwest the Hispanic and Anglo cultures blended in music, food, and architecture, but a growing Mexican population (70,000 by 1900) faced discrimination at the hands of the non-Hispanic majority. Eventually, however, the cost would prove enormous: the problem of organizing this vast new territory reopened the explosive issue of slavery expansion, ultimately splitting in two the new transcontinental republic.

The Election of 1848

When Congress adopted the Missouri Compromise in 1820 it had also adopted the rule that all territories above 36 degree 30 minute line of longitude would be closed to slavery while all below this "Missouri line" would be open to it. This formula had worked for a quarter of a century, in large measure because both northerners and southerners believed it fairly divided the national domain. The war with Mexico changed this. Most of the land acquired fell below the line. And California, easily the most valuable of the new territories even before the discovery of gold triggered the famous "rush" of 1849, would have been divided into two, were the compromise line used to settle the question of the status of slavery in the former possessions of Mexico. Meanwhile the Polk administration's diplomatic settlement of the Oregon boundary with Britain, although probably the best arrangement the United States could have gotten short of war, also rankled northerners who saw the Mexican War as a conspiracy to advance the power of the slave states.

With this in mind a member of President Polk's own party, a first-term Congressman from Pennsylvania named David Wilmot, introduced his famous proviso in August of 1846 to a military appropriations bill. The Wilmot Proviso would have prohibited slavery from ever being introduced into lands acquired from Mexico. The House, with both northern Whigs and northern Democrats voting in favor, adopted the Proviso. The Senate, where southerners were more powerful, rejected it. Ominously, Congress was now splitting not so much between Whigs and Democrats as between northerners and southerners. But the question of slavery in the territories would not go away. Senator Thomas Hart Benton compared it to the Biblical plague of frogs: "You could not look upon the table but there were frogs, you could not sit down at the banquet but there were frogs, you could not go to the bridal couch and lift the sheets but there were frogs!" So it was with the slavery question, "forever on the table, on the nuptial couch, everywhere!"

Congress would have to act to organize the new territories sooner or later. And each time a bill concerning them came up in the House, that chamber attached the Wilmot Proviso to it guaranteeing its defeat in the Senate. John C. Calhoun, leader of the militant proslavery forces, determined to force an outcome satisfactory to the South and drew up his own set of resolutions that not only rejected the Wilmot Proviso but declared that Congress had no power to bar slavery in any territory. This meant that, in Calhoun's view, even the Missouri Compromise line was an unconstitutional measure although he was willing to continue to abide by it as a practical matter. Calhoun's resolutions became rallying cries throughout the South and, in 1857, the Supreme Court would accept their basic contention in the Dred Scott Case of 1857.

In the midst of this acrimonious and inconclusive struggle the election of 1848 was fought. James Buchanan, a Pennsylvanian with strong southern ties, sought to settle the debate by extending the Missouri Compromise line to the Pacific. Buchanan's main Democratic challenger, Michigan Senator Lewis Cass, had originally supported the Wilmot Proviso, but quickly realized that he could never hope for any southern support unless he took a more conciliatory line. This he found in a proposal he called popular sov-

ereignty. Instead of Congress deciding the question of slavery in the territories, Cass declared, the voters living there should choose for themselves whether they wanted slavery. This proposal had the merit, from Cass's point of view, of appearing to favor both sections. Southerners could take heart that it did not bar slavery from any of the territories while northerners could find comfort that few slaveholders would be foolish enough to move into the territories and risk their valuable property until slavery had already been adopted.

The Democrats decided on Cass and popular sovereignty. A group of disgruntled New York Democrats, angry over Cass's role in preventing the nomination of their own Martin Van Buren in 1844, formed the Free Soil Party with the Little Magician as their standard bearer. They were joined by the so-called "Conscience Whigs," northerners who could not support their own party's nominee, Zachary Taylor, the hero of the Mexican War they had opposed and the owner of a Louisiana plantation. Also joining the Free Soilers were the remnants of the old Liberty Party who found in the slogan "free soil, free speech, free labor and free men" a new rallying cry for their own abolitionist beliefs. The key to Taylor's victory may have been that his position on slavery in the territories was even vaguer than Cass's. If the Michigan Senator's popular sovereignty doctrine blurred the question, Taylor simply ducked it altogether. His southern supporters used the fact that he was himself a slaveholder to reassure that section that he was safe on the issue. At the same time his northern backers, including such stalwarts as Abraham Lincoln, were promising that, if elected, Taylor would accept the Wilmot Proviso. Taylor himself said nothing. So the election of 1848 ended without any clear resolution of the slavery question.

The Compromise of 1850

It was a warring Congress that met in December 1849. It took three weeks and fifty-nine ballots to elect a Speaker of the House. Californians, tired of waiting for Congress, had held a convention at Monterey and drafted a state constitution prohibiting slavery: some

of them simply did not want whites to have to compete with black labor. Without waiting for congressional approval, California chose a governor and legislature. Only one obstacle remained: formal admission to statehood.

On this Congress could not agree. The new

President, Zachary Taylor, decided to intervene in the imbroglio. Although a defender of slavery, Taylor did not regard expansion as necessary for its protection. Like Polk, he considered California and the Southwest as unsuitable for slavery. The President therefore recommended to Congress that California and New Mexico be admitted directly to statehood, bypassing the territorial stage. The residents could then decide the slavery question for themselves without embarrassment to Congress. Southerners, seeing that California had already prohibited slavery and expecting New Mexico to do the same, realized that Taylor's plan was as effective as Wilmot's Proviso in keeping slavery out of this area. When they protested, the old soldier drew a firm line, threatening to use force if necessary to preserve the Union.

Taylor, southerners decided, had betrayed them. California would be the first in what they feared would be a flood of new free states admitted to the Union. Free and slave states had been equal in number, and therefore North and South had enjoyed equal representation in the Senate. Now the South would lose that precarious equality. Northerners would make war upon slavery—an institution, southern spokesmen insisted, "upon which is staked our property, our social organization and our peace and safety." When a call went out in October 1849 for the southern states to send delegates to a convention at Nashville the following June to consider secession, most of these states accepted.

| Clay, Calhoun, and Webster

At this moment, with disunion threatening, an aged Senator Henry Clay offered a compromise that he hoped would settle for good the territorial crisis and other disputed issues between the sections. Clay's plan, introduced in Congress in January 1850, contained five key provisions: immediate admission of free California; organization of the rest of the area acquired from Mexico into two territories, Utah and New Mexico, without restriction on slavery, the matter to be decided by their own constitutions; assumption of the Texan national debt by the federal government; abolition of the slave trade in the District of Columbia; and a tough new fugitive slave law.

The debate on Clay's compromise was the grand twilight for the generation of statesmen

Daniel Webster. He urged both North and South to avoid extreme positions on slavery. *(Courtesy, Scribner's Archives)*

who had guided the nation's destinies since 1812. Twice before, in 1820 and 1833, stirring appeals to love of Union, flag, and Constitution had soothed sectional tensions. During the winter and spring of 1850, Senate veterans tried to revive this tested formula. Day after day, packed galleries followed their speeches.

Clay took the floor first, urging the North not to demand the principle of the Wilmot Proviso—nature would as effectively exclude slavery—and to honor the constitutional obligation to return fugitive slaves. He reminded the South of the many benefits she enjoyed in the Union. The "Great Pacificator" closed his two-day oration with an appeal to both sides to pause at the edge of the cliff, before leaping "into the yawning abyss below." Clay expressed the hope that, should disunion occur, he would not live to see it.

Clay's compromises did not go far enough to satisfy John C. Calhoun. The old Nullifier, his body wracked by tuberculosis, sat defiantly while his speech was read for him. The North, he charged, had taken advantage of tariffs and other federal favors to outstrip the South in population and power. He demanded that the North must not only grant slaveholders equal rights in the territories but pass constitutional guarantees giving the South equal power in the government. The only alternative for the South was secession.

Daniel Webster spoke on March 7, displaying an eloquence reminiscent of his brilliant reply to Hayne two decades before. He pleaded with both sections to show tolerance for the sake of Union. He criticized the abolitionists' ethical absolutism and deplored the agitation over slavery in the territories. The law of nature precluded a slave economy there, he asserted, and no legislation was needed to reenact God's will. He took sharp issue with Calhoun's talk of "peaceable secession": "There can be no such thing as a peaceable secession. Peaceable secession is an utter impossibility." A thousand physical and social ties bound the sections together. Disunion, Webster warned the South pointedly, "must produce such a war as I will not describe, *in its twofold character*"—a hint at the prospect of slave revolts. Much to the anger of abolitionists, who criticized it savagely, Webster's Seventh of March speech did much to rally northern support for compromise.

For all his skill, Clay had miscalculated. Patriotic appeals for Union could not overcome sectional bitterness in 1850. When Clay's package of compromise measures (known as the Omnibus Bill) came to a vote in July, opponents of the individual measures ganged up to defeat it. With his bill and his health in ruins, Clay withdrew into retirement.

| **Stephen A.** | Thirty-four-year-old   Ste-
| **Douglas** | phen A. Douglas assumed

his place in steering the compromise through Congress. Only five feet four, nicknamed "the Little Giant" and "a steam engine in britches," this brash, hard-driving Senator from Illinois devised a new compromise strategy. He introduced Clay's measures separately, relying on sectional blocs and a few swing votes to form majorities for each. The individual bills, one observer remarked, resembled "cats and dogs that had been tied together by their tails for months, scratching and biting." Upon being released "every one of them ran off to his own hole and was quiet."

As Senator from Illinois, Stephen A. Douglas skillfully engineered the Compromise of 1850. *(Courtesy, Scribner's Archives)*

Douglas's strategy worked. The North won admission of free California and a ban on the slave trade in Washington. The South had a more stringent fugitive slave law and a promise that there would be no congressional prohibition of slavery in the New Mexico and Utah territories. The federal government assumed the Texas debt. Two events immeasurably aided Douglas's efforts that hot summer. The unexpected death on July 9 from a digestive disorder of President Taylor, who had obstinately opposed any compromise plan but his own, put in the presidency Millard Fillmore, who supported the measures of Clay and Douglas. And Texas bondholders, who stood to gain handsomely if the federal government purchased their depreciated securities, lobbied for the legislation.

The Compromise of 1850 received an enthusiastic welcome. Celebrations were held in many cities. In Washington, word went out that it was the duty of every patriot to get drunk. Before the next morning dawned, many citizens, including Senators Foote, Douglas, and Webster, had amply proved their patriotism. To many Americans, it now seemed that the slavery question had at last been settled. But in the South there were still 3,204,000 slaves worth over $1 ½ billion—a property many southerners were determined to protect at any cost.

Events soon revealed that the Compromise had settled nothing at all. Deliberate ambiguities embedded in it raised questions instead of comfortably obscuring them. The Utah and New Mexico territories had been organized without congressional restriction on slavery. The Compromise said only that they would be admitted to statehood with or without slavery, as their constitutions prescribed "at the time of their admission." But could the people of these territories now restrict slavery as long as the new lands remained in a territorial status? Opponents of slavery believed that even in the period before they attained statehood, the people of Utah and New Mexico would have the right to decide whether to exclude the practice. Southerners, convinced that slaveholding like any other conventional form of property should be permitted unless prohibited by a state of the Union, insisted that as long as the new lands remained territories, slavery must not be restricted. The critical question of slavery in the territories had merely been evaded. There had been no compromise in 1850, only a fragile truce.

The Plantation. (Courtesy, The Metropolitan Museum of Art)

Points To Think About

1. The Missouri Compromise of 1820 temporarily removed the slavery issue from national politics, but it did not settle the issue permanently. There were many reasons for this, including the world-wide reaction against slavery that characterized the nineteenth century. Closer to home there was the relentless push west. As Americans asserted their "Manifest Destiny" to control the continent, they repeatedly resurrected the slavery question. Each new territorial acquisition threatened to upset the delicate balance of power the compromise had established.

In this way the issue of slavery continuously came up against one of the strongest forces in the United States during the nineteenth-century: nationalism. The balance between slave and free states might have been maintained indefinitely in a country of stable dimensions. But America's "destiny" was to grow, and growth involved ceaseless changes for both slave and free states. Over the long run these changes favored the free states. And, as time passed, the Missouri Compromise became obsolete. The Wilmot Proviso merely signaled this fact.

2. The label of conservative does not closely fit the Whigs, who have been assigned it. To the extent that the Whigs shared a coherent ideology— and American political parties have never prized ideological consistency—it was a commitment to the efficient and rapid development of the country. If a label must be attached, modernizer may be more accurate than conservative. It captures the unconservative Whig commitment to promoting change.

The Whig faith was that the rapid development of the country could be combined with social stability. It was, like the Jacksonian faith in growth without planning, a naive vision.

3. Abolitionism was a remarkably dangerous trade. Elijah Lovejoy had his printing press thrown in a river, and subsequently lost his life as a mob sought to seize a second. Other abolitionists also confronted angry mobs. Most escaped with their lives, but not until suffering harrowing ordeals. Terrifying as they were, some abolitionists seemed to court these dangers. Theodore Dwight Weld was wont to ride into hostile towns, announce an abolitionist meeting, and then attempt to convert to his view the angry crowd who would collect.

This seeking of danger has led some historians to suspect that many abolitionists suffered from a martyr complex. This explanation may hold for one or another individual, but it is hazardous to psychoanalyze historical figures. Psychoanalytic categories, moreover, reflect the personal values of an era in which they are developed. These change over time, and it is unwise to attempt to fit into today's classifications the lives of people long dead. And psychoanalysis deals with the individual psyche. It is misleading to speak of whole groups such as the abolitionists as if they shared a single mental life.

We still need to explain the extraordinary fortitude of the abolitionists. One explanation, first offered in Gilbert H. Barnes's *The Anti-Slavery Impulse,* focuses upon the ties between antislavery activism and revivalism. Weld was a Finney convert, as were many other abolitionists. They adopted the movement against slavery as a vocation, a form of ministry; it was their calling, the work they were intended to do. And, like the early Christians they so often modeled themselves after, they were even willing to suffer martyrdom.

Not all abolitionists, of course, were evangelical converts; some, like William Lloyd Garrison, had no formal connection with any church. Yet Garrison too was an intensely religious person. He too regarded slavery as a sin. There is, in brief, much evidence to suggest that abolitionism is better understood as a religious movement than as a psychic aberration.

Suggested Readings

Recent scholarship on this period includes John Niven, *John C. Calhoun and the Price of Union* (1988), Paul Bergeton, *The Presidency of James K. Polk* (1987), Steve Stowe, *Intimacy and Power in the Old South: Rituals in the Lives of the Planters* (1987), Norma Peterson, *The Presidencies of William Henry Harrison and John Tyler* (1989), Daniel W. Howe, *The Political Culture of the American Whigs* (1980), Blanche Glassman Hersh, *The Slavery of Sex: Feminists and Abolitionists in America* (1978), Jack Bauer, *Zachary Taylor* (1985), and Gavin Wright, *The Political Economy of the Cotton South* (1978).

Eugene D. Genovese's *Roll, Jordan, Roll: The*

World the Slaves Made (1974) is a literary study of slave life before the war. The author discusses the slave family, the black work ethic, slave resistance, miscegenation, and slave language, all within the larger themes of the paternalistic ideology of the southern planter and the accommodation between master and slave. Genovese's *The World the Slaveholders Made* (1969) elaborates on the class structure of southern society. Herbert G. Gutman, in *The Black Family in Slavery and Freedom, 1750–1925* (1976), challenges theories that speak of the disorganization of the black slave family and the lasting effect of that disorganization on black life; instead, he argues, the black family was resilient and adaptive.

It is impossible to escape the debate over a two-volume study by Robert Fogel and Stanley Engerman, *Time on the Cross* (1974). This book by two economists quantifies the southern slave economy to conclude that slaves were productive and efficient, well fed, rarely abused, and enjoying a variety of incentives. Excellent critiques of this argument include Paul A. David et al., *Reckoning with Slavery: A Critical Study in the Quantitative History of American Negro Slavery* (1976) and Herbert G. Gutman, *Slavery and the Numbers Game: A Critique of 'Time on the Cross'* (1978). George M. Fredrickson examines the sources of racist ideas in *The Black Image in the White Mind* (1971). John Blassingame collected *Slave Testimony* (1977) about the slave experience. Vincent Harding's *There Is a River* (1981) examines the black community. In *Slavery and the Annexation of Texas* (1972), Frederick W. Merk studies the Mexican imbroglio from the standpoint of slavery. His *Manifest Destiny and Mission in American History* (1965) is standard. K. Jack Bauer's *The Mexican-American War* (1974) is a recent account while Gene M. Brack's *Mexico Views Manifest Destiny, 1821–1846* (1975) presents the Mexican viewpoint. The politics of sectionalism is the subject of William Brock's *Parties and Political Conscience: American Dilemmas, 1840–1850* (1979).

☆ ☆ DEBATE ☆ ☆ ☆

FORREST McDONALD

For the most part the expansion of the United States across the continent requires neither explanation nor apology. Doing so, as the politicians said, was the nation's manifest destiny: to extend from sea to sea was the logic of a great nation in the making. An enormous expanse of virtually unoccupied land (there was roughly one native for every five square miles) awaited the taking; and the Americans, a restless, energetic, and adventuresome people, simply took it.

But that bald statement of the facts, though accurate, may be misleading: it suggests that the expansion was motivated by the desire for material gain and national pride.

As Henry Adams pointed out a century ago, materialism and idealism were inseparable in this country. Other people looked upon the world as a vale of misery and resigned themselves to it. The American looked at the savage wilderness and saw boundless acres of grain and magnificent cities, in a future world that he and his would make—and he set out to make it. Impelled by this dream, even the humblest immigrant was caught up in the American spirit, "for every stroke of the axe and the hoe made him a capitalist, and made gentlemen of his children."

The other respect in which expansionism was nonmaterialistic had to do with American ideas about the quality of life. Most Americans shared the belief that living on the land was the most desirable kind of existence, breeding independence and strength of character. Most also viewed with horror the prospect that some day America, like Europe, might be plagued with huge industrial centers with their foul air and teeming multitudes of impoverished laborers. Since the time of Jefferson's presidency it had been the policy of the United States government to stave off "progress" toward that kind of world by regularly acquiring new territory. Jefferson bespoke this attitude when he declared, upon receiving news of the Louisiana Purchase, that the acquisition would make it possible for the United States to remain a nation of farmers for a thousand years. (It was a part of the same policy, however, to share the nation's bounty with those who fled from Europe's sorrows. During the 1840s scores of thousands of refugees from Ireland's potato famine were finding their way to the new land, and they would soon be followed by political refugees from the abortive European revolutions of 1848.)

As for the Mexican War, several points may be briefly made. It was the annexation of Texas that led to the conflict. Texas had won its independence from Mexico, even as Mexico, a short time earlier, had won its freedom from Spain; if Mexico's independence was legitimate, so was that of Texas. Again, the United States offered to buy all disputed territory, but Mexico scornfully turned down the prewar offer on the ground that any nation that preferred to purchase rather than fight for what it wanted was too cowardly to win it in a fight. After the war, when the United States compensated Mexico for the territory it had taken, Mexico was not too proud to accept the settlement. And who, in the long term, gained and who lost as a result of the transfer of the great southwest from Mexico to the United States? The lucky ones were those who thereby became citizens of the northern republic. The unlucky were those who had to remain under Mexican rule. No further proof should be needed, I think, than the silent testimony of the millions of immigrants, legal and illegal, who have moved from Mexico to the United States over the course of the years.

How Manifest a Destiny?

EUGENE D. GENOVESE

Professor McDonald, to my great surprise, neglected to call upon the authority of a leading theorist of genius who proclaimed that the conquest of Mexico by the progressive, enterprising United States would be a great favor to the backward, slothful Mexicans. But then, conservatives do not like to quote Karl Marx. With due respect to Marx and to Professor McDonald, I think I detect a trace of Eurocentric racial presumption in this version of "I am doing this to you for your own good."

The primary difference between, say, the *mafia* and gangster nations is that *mafiosi* normally know and admit that they are stealing and murdering. With at least a speck of concern for their immortal souls, they prefer not to commit the sin of lying or, worse, of self-deception. If indeed superior energy, economic and technological advancement, and political and military prowess justify the annexation of Texas and then half of Mexico, then the Soviet Union should have been encouraged to enter Afghanistan a long time ago. And why all the fuss about the Libyan invasion of Chad or the Somalian invasion of the sparsely populated Ogaden region of Ethiopia? The United States is today rich and Mexico poor. The reasons are complex, as I am sure Professor McDonald would agree. Here I only wish to note that if the Mexicans had held on to California and developed those gold mines, as they certainly would have, Mexico might have done a good deal better.

Very well. Let us be blunt in answering the question of the origins of national boundaries. All of northern Mexico, from California to Texas, was ripe for the taking, and we took it. As a conservative United States senator from California said about the Panama Canal during the debates of the 1970s, "We stole it fair and square." The Mexicans fought for their country, and their soldiers and armed civilians showed great courage under superior fire. It is no disgrace for a people to get speedily crushed by a vastly superior military machine.

Americans combined high idealism with the most vulgar material greed in an ideology of expansion that had fateful consequences for the world, and the first consequence descended upon the Americans themselves. Mexico was our nation's forbidden fruit. Even before the annexation of half of our neighbor's territory, northern and southern bandits—capitalists and slaveholders—began to compete for the spoils. The "territorial question"—should the acquired territories be opened to slavery or preserved for Northern economic interests—brought to a climax the long-building confrontation between North and South. As the inhabitants of the United States fell on one another during the ghastly war of 1861–1865, the Mexicans were too busy with their own troubles to take much solace. But St. Paul in his Epistle to the Galatians says of God's justice: "Be not deceived. God is not mocked. For whatsoever a man soweth, that he shall also reap." Nineteenth-century Christian inhabitants of the United States, both North and South, might have gained wisdom had they reflected a bit as their country, having torn Mexico apart, now tore at itself.

This frontispiece of an edition of *Uncle Tom's Cabin* pictures Eliza, in the center, escaping to freedom over the ice to the shores of Ohio. *(Courtesy, The New-York Historical Society, New York City)*

CHAPTER 13

Distant Thunder: The 1850s

UNCLE TOM'S CABIN (1852)

In 1826, when Harriet Beecher was fifteen years old, she had already read much of her father's theological library. She would recall with fondness her "non-resistant" childhood in Massachusetts and Cincinnati and her admiration for her "God-like" father, Lyman Beecher. In Harriet's youth her father became president of Lane Theological Seminary, and she married a young teacher there, Calvin Stowe. Stowe encouraged his wife's first writings for literary magazines, and she supported him during his long encounter with hallucinations and an inability to work. In 1850, Bowdoin College offered Calvin Stowe a professorship. Within a few months of Harriet's arrival in Maine she began to turn her moral attention to matters of a worldly nature. After a chance reading of a southern slave-dealing newspaper, American black slavery arrested her with "an icy hand." Mrs. Stowe began a considerable research into the institution of chattel labor, reading southern defenses of slavery as well as the attacks on it by Theodore Weld and Frederick Douglass, himself an ex-slave.

The Fugitive Slave Law of 1850 angered her into action, and she wrote *Uncle Tom's Cabin* in serial form in 1852. Mrs. Stowe later described the novel as having been "dictated" to her from a source outside of herself. One measure of the novel's power was the number of imitations it generated. More than fifty novels about slavery appeared after 1852, thirty of which were intent on portraying the institution as beneficial. None of these captured Mrs. Stowe's great audience. Sales in book form set publishing records: 300,000 copies the first year, a million in seven years. Adapted for the stage, the story quickly became the nation's most popular play. By 1861, millions of northerners had thrilled over Eliza's dramatic escape and wept for Tom's fortitude under the lash.

The first part of the story is about George Harris and Eliza, his wife, slaves so near white that they can "pass" while escaping from slavery. Mistreated by his master who considers him "uppity," George disguises himself as a gentleman traveler and quits Kentucky thanks to the help of a kindly white southerner. Eliza overhears that the slave foreman, a robust, kindly figure named Tom, is to be sold by his master, and she and her son Harry take flight to join George in Canada. With Harry in her arms Eliza escapes from the slave traders by leaping from ice floe to ice floe across the Ohio River, to the northern underground railroad. Tom the slave is sold to a New Orleans family and makes friends with the saintly Little Eva, who dies of tuberculosis in a scene that has wrung tears from generations of readers. In the end Tom is sold to Simon Legree, a savage drunk who flogs him. Tom dies, like Christ, forgiving his killers.

But Mrs. Stowe cut right to the heart of the matter: it was not fundamentally people who were evil, but the system under which they lived. Given absolute power over their slaves, few masters could resist the temptation to use it. Slavery often dragged down even "good" masters when circumstances occurred beyond their control. At its worst (Simon Legree's domain) the "peculiar institution" brutalized everyone—black and white. It is difficult to measure the exact impact of *Uncle Tom's Cabin*, but after its appearance the northern attitude toward slavery was never quite the same. There was truth in the remark with which President Lincoln allegedly greeted Mrs. Stowe when she visited the White House during the Civil War: "So you're the little lady who wrote the book that made the great war."

Mrs. Stowe was not pursuing slavery with a bludgeon. Her instrument was as delicate as a surgeon's knife, and she operated on the national psyche. The slave was commercial property, and the business of slavery passed through

Scenes from *Uncle Tom's Cabin.* *(Courtesy, The New-York Historical Society, New York City)*

northern as well as southern hands. The trade in human beings, a constant assault on the black family, tore against the fabric of a society woven of Christianity and the family. Mrs. Stowe possessed a firm sense of the uneasiness that many Americans felt over the disrupting tendencies of commerce. Instead of making the slaveowning South a direct contrast with the "free" society of the North, she made it a grotesque extension and intensification of that world. Men "alive to nothing but trade and profit—cool, and unhesitating, and unrelenting as death and the grave roamed the American earth, building things and disrupting and destroying lives." Under slavery, men of commerce could take their avarice to its final meaning: trade in human flesh. Mrs. Stowe originally and correctly subtitled her book *The Man That Was a Thing*, a commodity to be traded on the market. Northerners understood her picture of slavery because it reached the guilt they felt about their own society. Southerners knew this too: their many replies to *Uncle Tom's Cabin* aimed ineffectual blows at northern commercial society. "At present, the North fattens and grows rich upon the South," an Alabama newspaper had complained:

> We purchase all our luxuries and necessities from the North. . . . Our slaves are clothed with Northern manufactured goods, have Northern hats and shoes, work with Northern hoes, ploughs, and other implements. . . . The slaveholder dresses in Northern goods, rides in a Northern saddle. . . . sports his Northern carriage . . . reads Northern books. . . . In Northern vessels his products are carried to market, his cotton is ginned with Northern gins, his sugar is crushed and preserved by Northern machinery; his rivers are navigated by Northern steamboats.

No wonder southerners were so furious. One southern reviewer wrote in ardent denial:

> We have said that Uncle Tom's Cabin is a fiction. It is a fiction throughout; a fiction in form; a fiction in its facts; a fiction in its representations and coloring; a fiction in its statements; a fiction in its sentiments; a fiction in its morals; a fiction in its religion; a fiction in its inferences; a fiction equally with regard to the subjects it is designed to expound, and with respect to the manner of their exposition. It is a fiction, not for the sake of more effectually communicating truth; but for the purpose of more effectually disseminating a slander. It is a fictitious or fanciful representation for the sake of producing fictitious or false impressions. Fiction is its form and falsehood is its end.

The Fugitive Slave Law

President Fillmore had barely signed the Compromise of 1850 into law before the slavery controversy flared anew. It was the Compromise itself that rekindled the quarrel. Among its several provisions was legislation designed to assist slaveholders in recovering their runaway property. This Fugitive Slave Law had been passed in response to southern complaints that the original law of 1793 was weak and ineffectual, putting slaveholders to great personal expense and failing to provide for assistance from federal officers. The new law of 1850 remedied these defects, and did more. It created special commissioners to deal with fugitive-slave cases. These commissioners had only to be convinced of a fugitive slave's identity before granting the owner authority to seize the runaway. They were empowered to call on federal marshals to enforce the law, and to compensate slaveholders who had incurred undue expense. Anyone who aided fugitives or obstructed their arrest was subject to fine and imprisonment. Here was a slaveholder's dream. But to

FUGITIVE SLAVE BILL!

HON. HENRY WILSON

Will address the citizens on

Thursday Evening, April 3,

At the

At 7 o'clock, on the all-engrossing topics of the day—the FUGI-
TIVE SLAVE BILL, the pro-slavery action of the National Government and the general aspect of the Slavery question.

Let every man and woman, without distinction of sect or party,
attend the meeting and bear a testimony against the system which
fills the prisons of a free republic with men whose only crime is a
love of freedom—which strikes down the habeas corpus and trial by
jury, and converts the free soil of Massachusetts into hunting ground
for the Southern kidnappers.

Ashby, March 29, 1851.

White & Potter's Steam Press—4000 Impressions per hour—Spring Lane, Boston.

many northerners it was an outrage. Especially offensive were the sections denying accused fugitive slaves the right to a jury trial,
or even to testify in their own behalf.

Here was not a complicated, constitutional
issue pitting federal against local rule in the
territories. Here was concrete oppression on
northern soil before northern eyes. Northerners had before them the spectacle of fugitive
slaves, handcuffed and guarded, and read of
cases of mistaken identity in the kidnapping
of free blacks. The fugitive slave question
drew together the splintered anti-slavery
movement. Garrisonians, free-soilers, Whigs,
Democrats, blacks: all could agree on it.

Enforcement of the Fugitive Slave Law
sparked several well-publicized acts of resistance. In 1851 a mob of blacks in Boston
burst into a courtroom during the extradition
hearing of a fugitive slave named Shadrach.
While the crowd struggled with the police,
two husky blacks grabbed the startled Shadrach and carried him out of the building.
Shadrach was soon spirited off to Canada.
Later that same year, black and white abolitionists successfully resisted enforcement of
the law at Syracuse, New York, and Christi-
ana, Pennsylvania.

In over eighty percent of the cases brought
under the law, slaveholders successfully recovered their property. But spectacular res-
cues like that of Shadrach confirmed southerners in their conviction that the Fugitive
Slave Law could not be enforced north of the
Mason-Dixon Line. As a result, few southerners made use of the new law. Instead the
South nursed its feeling that the North had
failed to fulfill an essential part of the compromise.

Harriet Tubman

We have had the greatest heroine of the age here,
Harriet Tubman, a black woman, and a fugitive
slave, who had been back eight times secretly and
brought out in all sixty slaves with her, including all
her own family, besides aiding many more in other
ways to escape. Her tales of adventure are beyond
anything in fiction and her ingenuity and generalship are extraordinary. . . . The Slaves call her Moses. She has had a reward of twelve thousand dollars offered for her in Maryland and will probably be
burned alive whenever she is caught, which she
probably will be, first or last, as she is going again.

They never caught Harriet Tubman. She
lived fifty-four years after the famous abolitionist Thomas Wentworth Higginson wrote
these words in 1859. Other accounts credit
her with the escape of two to three hundred
slaves and clothe her with various achievements that suggest a figure out of folklore
rather than history, a black Paul Bunyan or a
female John Henry. The legends identifying
her as "Black Moses" or "Chief Conductor on
the Underground Railroad" merely extend a
real history that is already heroic enough.

No one recorded the birthday of Harriet
Ross, one of eleven children born to a slave
family on the eastern shore of Maryland. But
the child who would become Harriet Tubman was probably born in 1820 or 1821. She
never spent a day in school and never
learned to read or write. Her childhood in
any sense that we would understand the term
ended at the age of five or six. Then her master attempted unsuccessfully to apprentice
her to a weaver. Various efforts to make her
useful about the master's house also proved
unsuccessful, and Harriet became a runaway
for the first time at age seven. She stayed

Herself an escaped slave, Harriet Tubman returned to the South and, risking great danger, repeatedly led groups like the one pictured here north to freedom. *(Courtesy, Sophia Smith Collection, Smith College)*

away four days, hiding in a pigsty and scrapping with the pigs for garbage to eat, until hunger drove her back to the inevitable whipping. Eventually she was sent to the fields, where she became a powerful worker, a match for most of the men. A serious head injury in the early teens left her with a permanent disability which caused her to fall asleep involuntarily for brief periods, even at the height of danger. Her rebellious temperament, combined with this odd malady, set her apart from others in her youth, and she absorbed a brand of millennial slave Christianity. Marriage to a free black, John Tubman, further aroused her questionings about slavery and freedom, but the difficulty of escape and concern for her parents and husband held her back until 1849, when the death of her owner led her to fear being sold into the deep South. Harriet headed north, traveling by night, and with help from some sympathetic whites made her way to Pennsylvania. "I had crossed the line," Harriet Tubman recalled.

> I was *free;* but there was no one to welcome me to the land of freedom. . . . My home, after all, was down in Maryland; because my father, my mother, my brothers, my sisters, and friends were there. But I was free and *they should be free!* I would make a home in the North and bring them there!

And so she did, earning money as best she could to finance such desperate ventures. Joining with the loose network of free blacks and Quakers—out of whose limited activities post-Civil War legend created the "Underground Railroad," complete with "switching station," "conductors," and "brakemen"—and traveling without benefit of maps or signs, she brought back from Maryland first her relatives, then other slaves, and finally her aged parents. Even in December 1860, with political turmoil over slavery at its height, Harriet made her last trip south before the war, returning with seven slaves, one of them an infant child who had to be drugged with paregoric to keep its cries from giving away their hiding places.

Harriet headed south again during wartime, now to serve as a nurse, a scout, and even as a spy for the Union army in South Carolina. Although most of her activities were in caring for runaway slaves and black troops, she seems to have taken an active part in several guerrilla raids behind southern lines:

> And then we saw the lightning and that was the guns; and then we heard the thunder, and that was the big guns; and then we heard the rain falling, and that was the drops of blood falling; and when we came to get in the crops, it was dead men that we reaped.

Harriet Tubman outlived the entire generation of antislavery heroes with whom she had worked, becoming a legendary reminder of the age of runaway slaves and abolitionists. Her home in Auburn, New York, became a place of pilgrimage. Black leaders like Booker T. Washington would visit Harriet and then view John Brown's grave in the Adirondacks. Women suffrage leaders came as well; this had become one of her causes in the postwar years. She founded a Home for the Aged and Indigent in Auburn on land abutting her house, moving to it herself in 1911 when she became too infirm to live alone. She died in 1913 and received, fittingly enough, a soldier's burial, with the local post of the Union army veterans' association, the Grand Army of the Republic, presenting the honors.

Manifest Destiny Again

A new President, Franklin Pierce, would call for further expansion in his inaugural address. "My administration," he boldly proclaimed in 1853, "will not be controlled by any timid forebodings of evil from expansion." True to his word, Pierce dispatched James Gadsden of South Carolina to Mexico with instructions to purchase additional territory. At the very least, Gadsden was to acquire the Gila River region, which lay along the proposed southern railroad route to the Pacific. In addition, he might offer up to $50 million for the northern provinces of Mexico. The Mexican government refused to sell anything more than the Gila River region. Even this small triumph for Gadsden was too much for the Senate. Northern Senators, suspecting a southern plot to expand the domain of slavery, accepted the Gadsden Treaty only after 9,000 square miles, one-sixth of the total, had been cut from the purchase. For the first time in its history, the United States had refused to accept land ceded to it. Despite this minor setback, the hapless Pierce embarked upon a new imperialist venture. This time the object was Cuba, owned by the Spanish.

Yet southerners had long desired to acquire Cuba, with its large and valuable slave population. It would compensate the South for the admission of California as a free state and prevent England from intervening in the island and eliminating slavery. President Polk had tried without success to purchase Cuba from Spain. During 1853 the Pierce Administration lent support to John A. Quitman of Mississippi and others who proposed to "liberate" Cuba by force. When Quitman backed off, Pierce instructed the American Minister in Madrid, Pierre Soulé, to offer Spain as much as $130 million for Cuba.

But Spain indignantly rejected the American offer. A New Orleans newspaper reflected popular feeling:

> The North Americans *will* spread out far beyond their present bounds. They *will* encroach again and again upon their neighbors. New territories *will* be planted, declare their independence, and be annexed! We have New Mexico and California! We *will* have old Mexico and Cuba! The isthmus cannot arrest—nor even the Saint Lawrence!! Time has all of this in her womb.

Soulé then arranged a meeting at Ostend, Belgium, in October 1854, with the American ministers to London and Paris, to consider further action regarding Cuba. Their recommendations to Washington, known as the "Ostend Manifesto," soon found their way into print, to the great embarrassment of the Pierce Administration. Particularly damaging was the statement that, should Spain refuse renewed offers to purchase Cuba, the United States would "by every law, human and Divine, be . . . justified in wresting it from Spain." Both American and European critics denounced the Manifesto. It was "a robber doctrine," "a highwayman's plea." The administration promptly repudiated the Manifesto, whereupon Soulé resigned amidst bitter recriminations. Manifest Destiny had suffered by its association with slavery. Renewed expansion would have to await the return of sectional peace.

The Kansas-Nebraska Act

The settlement of the Oregon boundary controversy and the acquisition of California made the United States a Pacific power. American commerce quickly expanded across the great ocean. In 1844 Caleb Cushing, the first American minister to China, negotiated a treaty granting Americans special trade privileges in that country. A decade later, Commodore Matthew Perry gained a diplomatic and commercial toehold in Japan. The United States sought unsuccessfully in 1854 to annex the Hawaiian Islands, already a cultural outpost of the United States. Forward-looking Americans proclaimed the dawn of a great commercial era in the Pacific.

For shortening the route from Atlantic ports to the Orient and improving communications between the two American coasts, the United States began considering a canal that would link the two oceans. An 1846 treaty with Colombia granted citizens of the United States the right of transit across the Isthmus of Panama, in return for recognition of Colombian sovereignty there. American efforts to control the alternative canal route through Nicaragua aroused protests from Britain, which had bases of its own in the vicinity. In 1850 the two sides compromised their differences in the Clayton-Bulwer Treaty. Each party agreed not to seek exclusive control over the proposed isthmian canal or to colonize the surrounding area. In spite of this official enthusiasm, capitalists showed little interest in the idea of building a canal. Travel across the isthmus remained a primitive affair until 1855, when a railroad replaced muleback and coach as the chief means of transportation.

More attractive was the idea of a trans-continental railroad. Asa Whitney, a New York merchant who had made a fortune in the China trade, labored throughout the 1840s to persuade Congress to finance construction of a railroad from Lake Michigan to the mouth of the Columbia River. This route, although mountainous, had the advantage of passing north of Mexican California. The Treaty of Guadalupe-Hidalgo brought California into the United States, but a new obstacle—sectional rivalry—soon appeared. The South favored a southern route for the railroad, running from New Orleans to California via Texas and the Gila River Valley. The North preferred either Whitney's northern route or a central way, extending from Chicago or St. Louis by way of South Pass to San Francisco. Unable to agree on any one route, Congress in 1853 authorized surveys of all three.

This delay was intolerable to Stephen A. Douglas of Illinois, the foremost advocate of a central route. As chairman of the Senate Committee on Territories, Douglas had pioneered in opening the Mississippi Valley to settlement. A Pacific railroad would help his concept of a great West become a reality. Personal considerations also motivated Douglas. His home town of Chicago, where he had heavy real estate investments, would be the probable eastern terminus of a central railroad. But the land known as Nebraska west of Iowa and Missouri was still unorganized Indian country. Until the region had territorial government, it could not be surveyed and opened for settlement. In this respect, advocates of a southern route had a real advantage: all the area along their route had already been made into states or territories.

Douglas late in 1853 had to find some way to induce southerners in Congress to vote for a bill organizing Nebraska. Southerners had no motive to support a measure that cleared the path for a rival railroad route to the Pacific. And they had absolutely no reason to vote to create what would become another free territory. As part of the Louisiana Purchase, Nebraska had been made "forever" free by the Missouri Compromise of 1820. Senator David Atchinson of Missouri spoke for many southerners when he vowed that he would "sink in hell" before handing Nebraska over to the free-soilers. Douglas therefore decided that he would have to make a concession to the South.

Popular Sovereignty The Illinois Senator offered the repeal of the Missouri Compromise line excluding slavery north of 36° 30′ latitude. His territorial bill, introduced in Congress in January 1854, would create two territories—Kansas and Nebraska. It would specifically repeal the Missouri Compromise restriction on slavery. In its place, Douglas substituted the principle of popular sovereignty, as it was called. The people of the two territories were

HUCKLEBERRY FINN *by Samuel Clemens (Mark Twain). Huck talks about his feelings towards the slave Jim.*

. . . I about made up my mind to pray, and see if I couldn't try to quit being the kind of a boy I was and be better. So I kneeled down. But the words wouldn't come. Why wouldn't they?
. . . I was trying to make my mouth say I would do the right thing and the clean thing, and go and write to that nigger's owner and tell where he was; but deep down in me I knowed it was a lie, and He knowed it. You can't pray a lie—I found out.

So I was full of trouble, full as I could be; and didn't know what to do. At last I had an idea; and I says, I'll go and write the letter—and then see if I can pray. Why, it was astonishing, the way I felt as light as a feather right straight off, and my troubles all gone. So I got a piece of paper and a pencil, all glad and excited, and set down and wrote:

Miss Watson, your runaway nigger Jim is down here two mile below Pikesville, and Mr. Phelps had got him and he will give him up for the reward if you send.

I felt good and all washed clean of sin for the first time I had ever felt so in my life, and I knowed I could pray now. But I didn't do it straight off, but laid the paper down and set there thinking—thinking how good it was all this happened so, and how near I come to being lost and going to hell. And went on thinking. And got to thinking over our trip down the river; and I see Jim before me all the time: in the day and in the night-time, sometimes moonlight, sometimes storms, and we a-floating along, talking and singing and laughing. But somehow I couldn't seem to strike no places to harden me against him, but only the other kind. I'd see him standing my watch on top of his'n, 'stead of calling me, so I could go on sleeping. . . . and at last I struck the time I saved him by telling the men we had small-pox aboard, and he was so grateful, and said I was the best friend old Jim ever had in the world, and the only one he's got now; and then I happened to look around and see that paper.

It was a close place. I took it up, and held it in my hand. I was a-trembling, because I's got to decide, forever, betwixt two things, and I knowed it. I studied a minute, sort of holding my breath, and then says to myself:
"All right, then, I'll go to hell"—and tore it up.

Samuel Clemens (Mark Twain). *(Courtesy, Scribner's Archives)*

free "to form and regulate their domestic institutions in their own way." Thus, to enlist southern support for his railroad, Douglas held out the bait of making Kansas and Nebraska slave states by the operation of popular sovereignty.

As Douglas himself had predicted, the idea of repealing the Missouri Compromise line raised "a hell of a storm." Most northerners regarded the Act of 1820 as an inviolable pledge of freedom. Repeal was part of a slaveholder's plot to make free territory into "a dreary region of despotism, inhabited by masters and slaves." In Congress, many northern Democrats joined their Whig colleagues in opposition. Objections came not only from abolitionists but from moderates who, having accepted the Compromise of 1850, had now lost all confidence in the good faith of the South. Douglas and his co-conspirators, wrote Horace Greeley in the *New York Tribune,* had made "more abolitionists than Garrison . . . could have made in half a century." Slavery, Douglas insisted in response, was an outmoded institution, unsuited by climate and geography to the plains of Kansas. Popular sovereignty would just as effectively bar slavery as would exclusion. After three months of fierce debate Douglas, with the support of President Franklin Pierce, carried his bill.

Passage of the Kansas-Nebraska Act shredded what little had remained of the uneasy truce of 1850. It turned Kansas into a battleground and ruptured the Democratic Party.

By using the scheme of popular sovereignty to open free soil to slavery, Douglas discredited what until then had been an effective instrument for compromise. Rarely in American history had so much been risked for so little. The next year—1855—when Douglas introduced his long-awaited Pacific Railroad bill in Congress, his enemies had their revenge by killing it. At Douglas's death in 1861 his great Pacific railroad, on which he had expended so much energy and prestige, was still bottled up in Congress, a victim of the sectional conflict he had helped to revive.

"Bleeding Kansas"

With the passage of the Kansas-Nebraska Act, the slavery contest moved from the halls of Congress to the plains of Kansas. Both sections attached great importance to the decision over slavery there. Southerners hoped to make Kansas a slave state and thereby to restore to the South the equality of representation in the Senate that the region had lost when California was admitted as a free state. Slavery expansion also had great symbolic importance to southerners. By denying the South's right to expand, the North seemed to be denying southern equality. Southerners reasoned that if they could not take their slaves into the common territories, they would no longer be the equal of northern citizens. Opponents of slavery of course wished to prevent its extension into Kansas. Resistance to the expansion of slavery also had a more unsavory side. Many northerners, especially in the Midwest, were determined to preserve the rich prairie soils for the white race. Here, said David Wilmot, "the sons of toil, of my own race and color, can live without the disgrace which association with Negro slavery brings upon free labor." These same racial prejudices applied to free blacks in the North. Such attitudes increasingly dominated the antislavery movement, and conditioned the public views even of moral opponents of slavery like Abraham Lincoln. The demand for free soil, then, greatly broadened the antislavery movement's appeal at the same time that it diluted the morality of the movement.

| Border War   From the beginning, the contest in Kansas over slavery was mainly the work of outsiders. In the North, groups like the New England Emigrant Aid Company, founded in 1854, subsidized the migration of free-state settlers to Kansas. To protect them, the Company sent new breech-loading rifles known popularly as "Beecher's Bibles," after Harriet's ministerial brother, Henry Ward Beecher, who proclaimed them a greater moral agency in Kansas than the Bible. Bands of Missouri "border ruffians" regularly crossed into neighboring Kansas to aid the proslavery cause. In March 1855, at the first election for a territorial legislature, their votes helped to give the proslavery party a majority. This assembly immediately enacted a slave code for the territory. Free-state settlers, refusing to recognize this legislature, elected one of their own. By late 1855, Kansas had two rival governments, neither of which would recognize the other's laws or participate in its elections.

Orderly government was impossible, and militants on both sides of the slavery question carried on a private war of their own. After proslavery men raided the free-state stronghold of Lawrence, the fanatical John Brown and seven followers (four of them his sons) retaliated at Pottawatomie Creek by bursting in on five sympathizers with slavery slashing and hacking them to death with broadswords. When one of his men urged caution, Brown responded that it was "noth-

John Brown, by John Steuart Curry. Following a raid against the free-state stronghold of Lawrence, Kansas, by proslavery men, Brown and his followers murdered five slavery sympathizers at Pottawatomie Creek. *(Courtesy, Kansas Industrial Development Commission, Topeka, Kansas)*

ing but the word of cowardice." Many settlers had to take sides in self-defense.

The recently established telegraph system, which now made possible swift reports of faraway events, brought the warfare in Kansas extensive press coverage. The antislavery press pictured the sack of Lawrence as an orgy of destruction and killing. In reality, it was a rather tame affair; only one person was killed, and he a proslavery man struck on the head by a falling brick.

Early in 1857 federal troops restored order to Kansas, and the free- and slave-state parties each promptly fell to internal quarreling. Before the year was out, a visitor to Kansas reported that "speculations run high [here], politics seldom named, *money* now seems to be the question." A southerner agreed in letters written home to his sister:

> The Missourians . . . are very sanguine about Kansas being a slave state & I have heard some of them say it *shall* be. Everyone seems bent on the

Almighty Dollar, and as a general thing that seems to be their only thought.

Later he wrote:

> I fear, Sister, that coming here will do no good at last, as I begin to think that this will be made a Free State at last. 'Tis true we have elected Proslavery men to draft a state constitution, but I feel pretty certain, if it is put to the vote of the people, it will be rejected, as I feel pretty confident they have a majority here at this time. The South has ceased all efforts, while the North is redoubling her exertions.

Nevertheless, the territory remained deeply divided, with each side retaining its own government.

The struggle in Kansas forced the slavery issue back into Congress. (The intent of instituting popular sovereignty had been to get the slavery question out of that body.) In 1856 the House of Representatives sent a fact-finding committee to Kansas. Meantime, Congress endlessly debated the Kansas question amid steadily rising tempers. Passion spilled into violence on the floor of the Senate. Senator Charles Sumner of Massachusetts delivered a violent antislavery speech entitled "The Crime Against Kansas." In it he made several personal references to Senator Andrew P. Butler of South Carolina. Butler's nephew, Representative Preston S. Brooks of South Carolina, decided to avenge these insults to an elderly kinsman. Brooks stole up behind Sumner at his Senate desk during a recess and beat him severely over the head with a cane.

The attack, northerners believed, was another example of the domineering insolence of slaveholders. The injured Sumner became a martyr of the antislavery cause. Southerners, although many privately disapproved, publicly applauded Brooks's action and showered him with canes inscribed with slogans like "Use Knock-down Arguments." When Brooks resigned from Congress, his Carolina constituents reelected him. This incident, and the controversy over Bleeding Kansas, further polarized a country already divided.

FILLING IN THE CONTINENT *These excerpts from a letter of Lucia Loraine Williams show that parts of the United States were far removed from the slavery controversy of the 1850s:*

September 16, 1851

Dear Mother,

We have been living in Oregon about two weeks, all of us except little John, and him we left twelve miles this side of Green River. He was killed instantly by falling from a wagon and the wheels running over his head.

After passing the desert and Green River [in present-day Wyoming] we came to a place of feed and laid by a day for the purpose of recruiting [resting] our teams. On the morning of 29 June we started on. John rode on the wagon driven by Edwin Fellows. We had not proceeded more than 2 miles before word came for us to turn back—we did so but found him dead. The oxen had taken fright from a horse that had been tied behind the wagon preceding this, owned by a young man that Mr. Williams had told a few minutes before to leave, and [the runaway team had] turned off the road. Two other teams ran also.

John was sitting in the back of the wagon, but as soon as the cattle commenced to run he went to the front and caught hold of the driver who held him as long as he could, but he was frightened and did not possess presence of mind enough to give him a little send which perhaps would have saved him.

Poor little fellow! We could do nothing for him, he was beyond our reach and O! How suddenly!

One half hour before we had left him in health as lively as a lark, and then to find him so breathless so soon was awful. I cannot describe to you our feelings.

We buried him there by the roadside, on the right side of the road, about ½ mile before we crossed the Fontonelle, a little stream. We had his grave covered with stones to protect it from wild beasts, and a board with his name and age. If any of our friends come through I wish that they would find his grave and if it needs, repair it.

[The letter proceeds to give excerpts from a diary of the trip.]

NEBRASKA

21 May—We had one of the worst storms that I ever read of. It beggars all description— thunder, lightning, hail, rain and wind. Hailstones so large that they knocked a horse onto his knees. The driver got out and held the oxen by the heads for they showed a disposition to run. Most of our things were completely soaked, so the next day we stopped and dried up.

On the 23rd we came to a creek that overflowed its banks, Elm Creek. The water was some 20 feet deep but not very wide. They fell a tree over the creek and packed the loading [across on foot], put our wagons into the water with a rope attached to the tongue, and swam them across.

June 1—Passed the Sioux village. Their wigwams are made of buffalo skins (the Pawnees' were mud). They seemed to be a much wealthier tribe than any that we [had] yet seen. The squaws were in antelope skins ornamented with beads; the men were also clothed with skins or blankets. They owned a great many ponies. On one of the wigwams were several scalps hung out to dry—taken from the Pawnees. They were friendly.

I saw some beautiful bluffs, apparently not more than ½ mile off, and wished to visit them. W consented to go with me but said that it was further than I anticipated. We walked 4 miles, I should judge, crossing chasms and bluffs before we reached the road and after all did not ascend the one we set out for. Camped by the Platte. No wood [to burn], but buffalo chips, which we have used for a long time.

WYOMING

On the 7th we arrived at Fort Laramie, and on the 8th commenced crossing the black hills. Some of them were steep. Laramie Peak to the left covered with snow.

9 June—Crossed the red hills and camped by a lake.

17 June—Traveled over 20 miles and camped by the Devils Hole, or Gate. In the morning two young ladies and myself visited it. The rocks on each side were perpendicular, 400 feet high, and the narrowest place was about 3 feet, where [the] Sweetwater came tumbling through. The road leading to it was crooked and thorny, but we found all kinds of beautiful flowers blooming beside the rocks; it was the most sublime spectacle that I ever witnessed

19 June—[Could] see the Rocky Mountains [at] a distance of some 60 miles. The tops were covered with snow, and from there they looked like fleecy clouds. Camped near two snowbanks in a beautiful valley.

IDAHO

2 July—[During the] night we were awakened by serenaders—five horsemen circled around the carriage singing "Araby's Daughter." It was a beautiful starlight night. We were surrounded by bluffs in a little valley, and on being awakened by their song, seeing their panting steeds and looking around upon the wild country, it seemed as tho we were transported into Arabia. They were beautiful singers from Oregon; said they were exiles from home. They sang "Sweet Home" and several others. Invited us to stay and celebrate the 4th. Said they would make us a barbecue, but we were anxious to get on and the affliction that we had just suffered unfitted us for such a scene.

31 July—Camped on the Snake. Indians came with salmon to sell. I let them have Helen's apron with a needle and thread and bought salmon enough for several meals. I wish you could [have eaten] with us. I certainly never tasted any fowl or fish half so delicious.

OREGON

3 September—Arrived at Milwaukie, and went into a house to live again, the first one that I had been in since we crossed the Missouri. . . .

If a nearby family's dinner in Oregon was typical, the journey was worth it:

Well We had Rosted Ducks . . . And Fat Chickens And Rosted pig and Sausages And green Apl pie And Mince pies and Custard pies And Cakes of difrent kindes [and] Inglish goosburyes And Plums Blue And green gages And Siberian crab Apples And oregon Apples. . . . Like wise Buter And Sturson pikles and Beet pickles And Sauce And Bread and Mashed potatoes and Oister pie And Coffe And Tea to be shore. Now I Must tel you What other preserves that I have. I have peaches And citrons And Sweet Aples, Crab Aples Jelley And Tomatoes And Mince And pairs and Aple Butter. And now I will Tel you of the Rest of My Winter Suplies. I have A plenty of Butter And Milk And a Thousand poundes of Salman And plenty Cabage And Turnips And A Bout A Hundred and Fifty Bushel of potatoes And plenty of dried fruits—Aples and Black Buryes the Best that I evr saw. . . . I never Saw Sutch Black Buryes And Ras Bryes As There Is in this Countrey in All My Life Time. . . . O yes I Have plenty Shougar Laid in For Winter This Year Two. And Salt   (NEW YEAR'S DAY, 1852)

A wayside grave on the route west. *(Courtesy, Library of Congress)*

Political Upheaval

Before 1850 the country's political system had been a bond of union. In both the Whig and the Democratic parties, strong northern and southern wings had worked together in their mutual interest, especially in presidential elections. The dependence of each wing on the other served to override the potentially divisive effect of issues like slavery. Party loyalty was intense. William Pitt Fessenden, a Whig stalwart, declared that he "would vote for a dog, if he was the candidate of my party." The Compromise of 1850 and the Kansas-Nebraska Act drastically altered the system, destroyed one party, disrupted another, and created a new one. A once unifying political system had become sectionalized.

| **The Decline of the Whig Party** | It was the Whigs who felt the strain of slavery first. They had never been as strong organizationally as |

the Democrats, and moreover drew their strength in the North from Yankee Protestants whose sense of moral stewardship made them especially sympathetic to the antislavery cause. The abolitionist and Free Soil

movements made many converts among these "conscience Whigs." At the 1852 Whig Convention the dispute over slavery broke wide open. The two sides even disagreed over the choice of a minister to lead the opening prayer. President Fillmore, the favorite of southern Whigs, had supported the Compromise of 1850, and so northern Whigs opposed him. The northerners backed instead another Mexican War hero, the Virginian General Winfield Scott, and Scott was finally chosen after fifty-three ballots: a southerner whose political strength was in the North. In retaliation, southern Whigs rammed through a platform endorsing the Compromise, including the Fugitive Slave Law.

Saddled with a candidate unpopular in the South and a platform unpopular in the North, the Whigs lost disastrously in 1852. Franklin Pierce of New Hampshire, the Democratic candidate, carried twenty-seven of thirty-one states—the most lopsided election victory since 1820. Surveying the ruins, antislavery Whigs began to seek a new alliance.

Not long afterward, it was the Democrats whom the slavery issue divided. The Kansas-

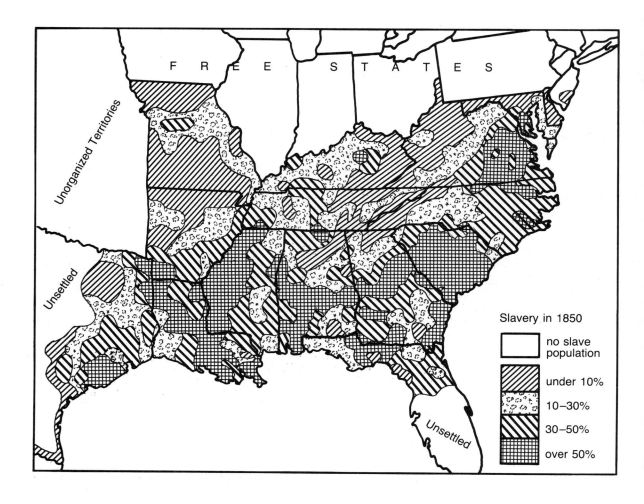

Slavery in 1850

- no slave population
- under 10%
- 10–30%
- 30–50%
- over 50%

Nebraska Act bitterly antagonized Northern antislavery Democrats, and their frustration found expression in the "Appeal of the Independent Democrats," composed in 1854 by Charles Sumner, Salmon P. Chase, and other antislavery Democratic congressmen. The appeal invited all opponents of slavery expansion to form a common front "to rescue the country from the domination of slavery."

This rebellion among antislavery Democrats made for a dramatic restructuring of northern politics. Antislavery politicians—former Whigs, breakaway Democrats, some of the more moderate abolitionists—struggled to create the coalition called for in the appeal. The new organization came formally into existence at a convention held in Ripon, Wisconsin, in February 1854; the delegates adopted a statement of principles proclaiming their opposition to the extension of slavery in the territories. The new party officially adopted the name "Republican" a few months later.

The "Know-Nothing" Party For a time another party, the "Know-Nothings," was also in the field. The flood of Irish and German immigrants after 1840 had alarmed lower-class, old-stock Protestants, who feared that this predominantly Catholic immigration would undermine republican institutions. Those "governed by a head in a foreign land," exclaimed one nativist editor, where "*no genuine liberty, either civil or religious*" exists, must not "control the American Ballot Box." One nativist blamed "the vast influx of immigrants" for lowering wages, raising the price of food and rent, and bringing "a thousand evils . . . [on] the working class." The newcomers were also charged with corrupting the nation's morals. According to another nativist, they brought "grog shops like the frogs of Egypt upon us." The visit of a special papal envoy to the United States in 1853 triggered a series of riots in Cincinnati, Pittsburgh, and elsewhere. A mob in Charlestown, Massachusetts, burned a Catholic convent to the ground. In 1849 Charles B. Allen of New York had formed a secret "patriotic" society, the Order of the Star-Spangled Banner, anti-Catholic and anti-foreign. Party members, when questioned by outsiders, customarily answered, "I know nothing." For a few years the society remained an obscure local organization, but in 1854, hoping to capitalize on the breakup of the old party alignments, nativists went political and formed the American, or "Know-Nothing" Party.

For a time the Know-Nothings demonstrated much political strength, capturing several state governorships and seventy-five seats in Congress. They were strongest in the Northeast and the border states. The Know-Nothings soon discovered, however, that as a bisectional party, they enjoyed no more immunity from the disruptive influence of the slavery question than the other parties. After a quarrel at the 1855 national convention, the party disintegrated. Most Northern Know-Nothings went into the new Republican Party, which had been actively soliciting the nativists with pledges of "No Popery and Slavery."

| **The Republican Party** | The 1856 Republican Convention resembled a revival meeting. "There is but a slight quantity of li- |

quor consumed," a journalist reported, "very little profane swearing is heard, and everything is managed with excessive and intense propriety." The platform condemned slavery as a "relic of barbarism" and reaffirmed the "right and duty" of Congress to prohibit it in the territories. Immigrants wary of competition in the labor market from slaves, "all vote the Republican ticket," one newspaper observed, "as faithfully as they hew wood and draw water." For president the Republicans nominated forty-three-year-old John C. Frémont, the dashing "Pathfinder" of Western exploration. The Democrats bypassed President Pierce and Stephen A. Douglas, who were too closely identified with the Kansas-Nebraska Act, in favor of sixty-five-year-old James Buchanan of Pennsylvania. Buchanan was a veteran politician and diplomat who,

happily, had been out of the country during the Kansas-Nebraska struggle. A third candidate, ex-President Millard Fillmore, was nominated by the still-existing Southern wing of the Know-Nothing Party.

The election itself was not a three-cornered affair, but rather two separate contests—one between Buchanan and Frémont in the North, the other between Buchanan and Fillmore in the South. As the only really national candidate, Buchanan benefited from the fear that a clear-cut sectional victory would split the Union. In November he won, carrying all the slave states but one, and gaining Pennsylvania, New Jersey, Indiana, Illinois, and California. In the other eleven free states, Frémont made a clean sweep—an impressive showing for a new party.

A Frémont campaign song demonstrated the vitality of the new Republican Party:

The Freemont Train has got along,
Just jump aboard ye foes of wrong,
Our train is bound for Washington
It carries Freedom's bravest son.
CHORUS:
Clear the track, filibusters,
Now's no time for threats and blusters
Clear the track (or) ere you dream on't,
You'll be 'neath the car of Fremont.

Now don't you see we've just the man
To meet the foe?—for he who can
Brave torrents wild and mountain snows
Will fear no Brooks nor Southern blows.

So jump aboard the Fremont train
And soon the Capital we'll gain;
Then we'll rejoice there's one in power
Who never will to slavery cower.

And a Buchanan song pointed to the intractibility of the South:

Come Democrats and listen,
While I sing to you a song,
Tis all about the Nigger Worshippers,
And it will not take me long.

Fremont is on their platform,
And their principles endorse,
To worship Niggers night and morn,
And ride the Wooly Horse.

Free speech, free niggers, and Fremont,
Now seems to be the go . . .
But these crazy Nigger Worshippers
The Union would destroy.

For there's balm in Gilead
We hear the people say
With Buchanan and with Breckenridge
We will surely win the day.

The real winner in 1856 was sectionalism: with the exception of Ohio, all eleven Frémont states were farther north than any of the twenty Buchanan states. No longer was the national political system a bond of union. Another of the cords holding the country together had snapped.

The Triumph of Sectional Politics

❚ Dred Scott   After 1848 the slavery question, like some evil curse, transformed everything it touched. It divided churches, shattered political parties, turned Congress into a battleground, and ruined presidential careers. Only one institution—the Supreme Court—had remained unchanged. Pressure had been building on the Court for a definitive judgment regarding slavery in the territories. In 1857, in the case of *Dred Scott v. Sanford,* the Court's majority, sympathetic to the South, abandoned judicial impartiality in the hope of settling this nagging question once and for all. The justices assumed that respect for the Court would insure acceptance of its decision by all sides. Rarely had American public figures so misgauged the popular temper: rather than settling the slavery question, the *Dred Scott* decision pushed the country forward on the road to civil war.

The case involved a Missouri slave, Dred Scott, who had sojourned with his master for several years in Illinois and in Minnesota Territory. Upon returning to Missouri, Scott sued for his freedom, contending that he had been emancipated by virtue of his residence on free soil. Chief Justice Roger B. Taney, speaking for a majority of the Supreme Court, rejected his claim on three grounds: as a Negro he could not be a citizen, and therefore had no right to bring suit in the federal courts; as a resident of Missouri he did not fall within the law of Illinois prohibiting slavery; and his sojourn in the Minnesota Territory had not emancipated him, for the provision of the Missouri Compromise prohibiting slavery north of 36° 30′ was unconstitutional. Congress, Taney declared, had no right to deprive citizens of their property in the territories without "due process of law," and he was defining slaves as property.

On nearly every point the Chief Justice's opinion was either plainly wrong or open to serious dispute. To declare that Negroes in general, and hence even free blacks, were non-citizens who, as Taney said, had "no rights [that whites] were bound to respect" defied American history. Free blacks had always been recognized as citizens in at least some northern states, and therefore did have the right to sue in the federal courts. In rejecting the principle that the status one state granted to an individual held for that person in another state, Taney ignored several earlier decisions in which Missouri courts had recognized the claim to freedom of slaves who had sojourned in free territory. The supreme authority of Congress over the territories had previously been upheld no less than three times by the Taney Court itself.

Dred Scott. The Supreme Court's decision in the Scott case—denying both the right of a slave to sue for freedom and the right of a territory to exclude slavery within its boundaries—further inflamed the antislavery factions. (*Courtesy, The Missouri Historical Society*)

Taney's pronouncement that it was unconstitutional for Congress to exclude slavery in the territories provoked a storm of criticism in the North. Republicans dismissed the decision as part of the "slavepower conspiracy." According to Horace Greeley's *New York Tribune,* it was entitled "to just so much moral weight as would be the judgment of a majority of those congregated in any Washington bar-room." The decision also embarrassed northern Democrats such as Stephen A. Douglas. They had fixed their hopes on the doctrine of popular sovereignty. But if Congress could not exclude slavery in the territories, then neither could it bestow on the people of a territory the authority to do so. Southerners, of course, hailed the *Dred Scott* decision as a vindication of their claim that slavery could not be excluded from the territories prior to statehood. By striking down popular sovereignty, the Supreme Court had destroyed just about the last device for sectional compromise. Meanwhile, events in Kansas deepened sectional division still further.

The Lecompton Constitution

In 1857 the proslavery faction in Kansas held a convention at Lecompton, drafted a constitution recognizing slavery, and applied for statehood. Although a clear majority of the territory's residents opposed the Lecompton Constitution, President Buchanan accepted it and asked Congress to admit Kansas to statehood. The President took this fateful step out of fear that a rejection of Lecompton would antagonize southern Democrats.

Buchanan's action outraged Stephen Douglas, who had proposed popular sovereignty as a democratic solution to the question of slavery in Kansas. Bucking the administration, he denounced the "Lecompton fraud" as a travesty on popular sovereignty and joined with Republican congressmen in opposing it. Douglas's opposition to Lecompton offended southerners and probably ruined his presidential prospects. After a struggle, Congress in 1858 sent the Lecompton Constitution back to the people of Kansas to be voted on again. This time a fair election was held, and Kansas rejected the "Lecompton fraud" by a margin of 11,300 to 1,788. Kansas remained a territory until after the Civil War had begun.

Buchanan's attempt to ram the Lecompton Constitution through Congress, coming so soon after the Kansas-Nebraska Act, broke the northern wing of the Democratic Party. Few northern Democrats who supported him on Kansas survived the 1858 mid-term elections. From this point on and for about a century thereafter, the white South was to identify with the Democratic Party.

The Republicans were now just as surely the party of the North or much of it. Within the party antislavery sentiment was coalescing with northern economic nationalism.

Numbers of American statesmen, among them Hamilton, John Quincy Adams, and Henry Clay, had wished to make the national government an active partner in the shaping and strengthening of a unified American economy. But economic nationalist programs differed in detail. Adams would have kept a high price on public lands in the West and applied the revenues to his ambitious governmental programs for the enriching of the economy and culture. For a time, northeastern business interests also had wanted the price of public lands to remain high, for they feared that cheap land would drain away eastern labor to the West. But now industrialists could think differently: immigration was supplying labor for northern industry and a prosperous West could be a customer for northeastern manufactured goods. So northerners of varying economic condition, land-hungry farmers along with ambitious businessmen, could unite behind a nationalist program that would have the government nurture northern industry, turn government land over to western settlers, and finance transportation connecting the Northeast to the West.

This economic nationalism had much common ground with the antislavery movement. Northerners wishing to settle in the West did not want the new lands dominated by the slave powers. Northern industrialists were at war politically with southern slaveholders who opposed protective tariffs. The Republican conviction that Congress had the authority to prohibit slavery in the territories blended with a larger belief in strong federal government, the kind that could legislate an active and continental economic program. Perhaps northerners who championed a vigorous program of economic development could even detect a cultural identity between their economic and their antislavery convictions, believing that industriousness and progress were the way of the free-labor North while indolence was the way of the southern slaveholding class.

In any event, Republicans sponsored legislation in Congress favoring free homesteads for settlers, agricultural colleges financed by grants of land, government-aided internal improvements, and a protective tariff. Southern Democrats blocked each of these measures. By obstructing the dynamic economic forces then at work in the North and Midwest, the South pressed these two sections to work together.

Northern politics, like the northern economy, was now moving along an east-west axis. And the Republican program for the economy, like the Republican opposition to slavery, had the more generous view of how the republic could conduct its life, for the party was really looking beyond the localism of states' rights and proposing a cooperative commonwealth in which the resources of the entire nation would be put to the common welfare.

The Emergence of Lincoln

The Lincoln-Douglas Debates   The earliest principal contender for the Republican nomination in 1860 was William Seward. As governor of New York for four years and senator for twelve, he enjoyed a national reputation. But suddenly, in 1858, a new potential candidate appeared. Throughout that summer, newspapers carried reports of a series of debates between Stephen A. Douglas and a little-known Illinois lawyer and former congressman named Abraham Lincoln. The occasion was the contest for Douglas's seat in the Senate. Political feelings in the 1850s ran so strong that one debate, at Galesburg, drew many horse drawn floats; one carried thirty-two young women, one for each state, dressed in white, and a thirty-third in black labeled "Kansas" carrying a banner, "THEY WON'T LET ME IN."

One woman who lived into the 1930s remembered the "electricity crackling in the air" and claimed Douglas remarked that if Lincoln thought so much of the Negro he imagined Abe would like one for a wife. Replied Lincoln in his slow drawl: "No, I do not want a negro for a wife, neither do I want one for my slave."

When the debates were over, Lincoln had lost the election but had become a figure to be reckoned with in the Republican Party. "You are like Byron," a friend wrote, "who woke up one morning and found himself famous."

The Supreme Court's *Dred Scott* decision, which in effect denied to the people of a territory the right to exclude slavery within its boundaries, had placed Douglas in a difficult situation. The "Little Giant" was the fore-

most advocate of popular sovereignty. If he accepted the Court's decision, he would probably lose the election in Illinois, where free-soil sentiment was strong. But if he reaffirmed the right of settlers to decide the slavery question for themselves, he would lose the support of southerners, which he desper-

Abraham Lincoln lost the 1858 election for senator of Illinois to Stephen A. Douglas, but beat Douglas and two other candidates to become President of the increasingly divided nation in 1860.

ately needed if he hoped to win the Democratic presidential nomination in 1860.

A popular song of the time, referring both to the Compromise of 1850 and popular sovereignty, pointed to the difficulty of Douglas' position:

Once we had a Compromise,
A check to Slavery's wrong,
Douglas crushed the golden prize,
To help himself along,
Then the North and then the West,
Arose with giant power,
Pierce succumbed to the South's behest,
But Douglas had to cower.
    Hi! Douglas! Sly Douglas!
    A Senator would be.

According to legend, Lincoln took advantage of Douglas's predicament to further his own political ends. At Freeport he asked Douglas whether, in light of Taney's opinion, the people could still exclude slavery from a territory. Douglas replied that they could, merely by withholding the police regulations and local laws that slavery needed in order to exist. The Freeport formula, summed up in the phrase "unfriendly legislation," supposedly assured Douglas's reelection to the Senate, but would cost him the support of southerners in 1860. Lincoln, so the legend goes, had thus with superhuman foresight sacrificed the short-run of a Senate seat in the interests of winning the big prize in 1860.

This story, like so many pieces of Lincoln lore, is more fiction than fact. In reality Douglas had announced his doctrine of "unfriendly legislation" months before the Freeport debate. And by the time of his confrontation with Lincoln, popular sovereignty was no longer a major issue. The real issue between the two men—and the one Lincoln strove to develop—was the ultimate one of the morality of slavery. Here Lincoln and Douglas differed fundamentally.

Douglas did not regard the question of slavery in the territories as a moral issue. He believed that blacks, whatever their status, would never achieve equality with whites. Whether they were subordinated as slaves, therefore, or merely as second-class citizens was not a matter of great concern for him, certainly not an issue worth breaking up the country over. Douglas disliked slavery; but what to do about it, he thought, should remain a local decision. Southerners had chosen to keep it. Northerners had decided to get rid of it. In the territories Douglas would let the local residents decide by popular sovereignty. He would never try to impose a single national policy on the slavery question. This position accorded with his friendly way with the voters: "I live with constituents," he once proudly asserted, "drink with them, lodge with them, pray with them, laugh, hunt, dance, and work with them. I eat their corn dodgers and fried bacon." He wanted them all to like him and, like Henry Clay before, wanted desperately to be President, thinking a middle ground the safest route to victory in national politics. But by temporizing in an era of polarization, he would lose both poles of the electorate.

For Lincoln slavery was a profound moral wrong. Although political considerations and respect for constitutional guarantees to slaveholders often impelled Lincoln to compromise his moral views in public, he never deserted them. Lincoln could never say, as Douglas said, that he did not care whether slavery was "voted up or voted down."

Lincoln differed from Douglas on another point: he insisted that slavery, as a national problem, required a national policy. Lincoln would not interfere with slavery where it existed; but he would not allow it to expand. Lincoln believed that the Founding Fathers, recognizing slavery as a wrong, had placed restrictions on it designed to produce its eventual extinction. Douglas and the Democrats, by refusing to recognize the moral wrong, had provided constitutional sanctions for slavery and made possible its expansion.

In 1858, Douglas narrowly won reelection to the Senate. But it was Lincoln who had sensed and shared the growing moral and emotional concern over the slavery issue in the North. This would prove critical in the election of 1860.

As the election year approached, North and South ceased even to pretend to any interest in compromise. In 1859 Senator Jefferson Davis of Mississippi introduced resolutions in Congress designed to get the Democratic Party to support the extreme southern position on slavery in the territories. These upheld the constitutional right of slaveholders to go into territories and called for the creation of a federal slave code for those areas. Senate Democrats finally adopted the Davis resolutions, over the vigorous objections of Stephen Douglas. At about the same time some southerners launched a movement to revive the African slave trade. This proposal had no chance of success, even among southerners; its main purpose, successfully

Thomas Cole, *The Oxbow*. *(Courtesy, The Metropolitan Museum of Art)*

achieved, was to irritate northern sensibilities. During the 1850s several northern state legislatures had defied the Fugitive Slave Act by passing "personal liberty" laws. Most of these prohibited state officers from aiding federal officials in their efforts to reclaim fugitives. In 1854 the Wisconsin supreme court had carried defiance of the federal government a step farther by declaring the Fugitive Slave Act of 1850 unconstitutional. Eventu-ally the United States Supreme Court overturned this judgment, whereupon the Wisconsin legislature, taking a line from the Kentucky Resolves of 1798, declared the Court's action to be "an act of undelegated power, void, and of no force." But going beyond these acts of North and South in prefiguring sectional war was John Brown's raid at Harpers Ferry, Virginia.

Points To Think About

1.   As the late Edmund Wilson argued in *Patriotic Gore, Uncle Tom's Cabin* is a far better novel than it is credited with being. The book is filled with melodramatic episodes and sentimental death-bed scenes—both likely to strike present day readers as excessive. But the novel is also blessed with a remarkable cast of characters. Harriet Beecher Stowe created evil slaveholders and saintly slaves. Yet she also portrayed kind, well-intentioned masters and rascally slaves. She created a whole range of human types. Even Uncle Tom himself is believable, because Mrs. Stowe insists that he was not a typical slave but an extraordinarily heroic and saintly man. Mrs. Stowe continually emphasized the distinction between slaveholders and the institution of slavery. There were, she insisted, good masters. There were even contented slaves. But slavery, as an institution, of-

ten forced even kind masters to be cruel. The novel opens with such a master forced to sell his slaves to meet his debts. He had been used to thinking of them as people, but they were also his property. The novel's greatest source of strength, perhaps, was evangelical pietism. Mrs. Stowe was the daughter of Lyman Beecher, who, next to Charles G. Finney was the most famous preacher of his day. Her husband was also a minister, as were several brothers. Her Uncle Tom stands, throughout the whole novel, as the embodiment of true piety. He is neither servile nor cringing, as the present day use of the term might suggest. He is gentle and always willing to turn the other cheek because that is his Christian duty. And the novel of which he is the central figure is a moving reflection on sin and redemption.

2. The politics of the 1850s had both a highly moral and an amoral character. Most public issues, such as internal improvements, concern questions that are serious enough, but do not raise questions of good or evil. Slavery, however, did raise questions of good and evil. And so the politics of the 1850s forced contemporaries to make moral judgments about public issues. And historians have had to make similar judgments. So it is disconcerting to find that the Republican Party, so good in its opposition to slavery, also harbored much hostility to immigrants. And the same Democratic Party that welcomed immigrants and defended their rights also contained many defenders of slavery.

The key to the Republican mentality, many historians believe, lies in evangelical Christianity. Republicans brought a fervent Protestant conscience to politics. It made them deeply suspicious of Catholic immigrants, whose aptitude for self-government they doubted. And it made them deeply susceptible to moral arguments against the sin of slavery. Hence their approach to these issues is less contradictory than it may have first seemed.

Suggested Readings

The newest books bearing on the 1850s include William E. Gienapp, *The Origins of the Republican Party, 1852–1856* (1987), Deborah White, *Ar'n't I a Woman? Female Slaves in the Plantation South* (1985), Elizabeth Fox-Genovese, *Within the Plantation Household: Black and White Women of the Old South* (1988); and Eugene D. Genovese, *Freedom and Progress in Southern Conservative Thought,* 1820–1860 (1991).

The politics of the 1850s is increasingly well covered. Notably, see Michael F. Holt, *The Political Crisis of the 1850s* (1976), David M. Potter, *The Impending Crisis: 1848–1861* (1976), Gerald W. Wolf, *The Kansas-Nebraska Bill: Party, Section, and the Coming of the Civil War* (1977), Don E. Fehrenbacher, *The Dred Scott Case* (1978), and Eric Foner, *Free Soil, Free Labor, Free Men: The Ideology of the Republican Party Before the Civil War* (1970). Holt argues, in an extremely stimulating study that deemphasizes the role of slavery in the development of sections, that voters could not discern substantial differences between the old parties in the fifties (the "second American party system" of the Whigs and Democrats), and that as a result there was a crisis in confidence in political institutions. Roger Brown, *Modernization* (1976), demonstrates that by the mid-nineteenth century the North was modernizing while the South was not. Other important studies are George B. Forgie, *Patricide in the House Divided: A Psychological Interpretation of Lincoln and His Age* (1979), and Drew Gilpin Faust, *A Sacred Circle: The Dilemma of the Intellectual in the Old South, 1840–1860* (1978). Stephen B. Oates's biography of John Brown is entitled *To Purge This Land With Blood* (1970).

The best discussion of *Uncle Tom's Cabin* appears in the opening pages of Edmund Wilson's *Patriotic Gore* (1961). Milton Rugoff's family history is entitled *The Beechers* (1981).

☆ ☆ DEBATE ☆ ☆ ☆

FORREST McDONALD

Scholars have argued endlessly about the causes of the Civil War, but the argument usually ignores the longer-range course of history. It fails to consider that the Americans' ancestors in Great Britain had been at war with one another, off and on, from ancient times through the eighteenth century, even though none of the supposed causes of the American Civil War had then been present. It also fails to consider that every modern nation-state had at least one civil war, and most had several, before diverse peoples could be brought to give their allegiance to a single government: civil war is part of the price of nationhood. It is better, therefore, to view the coming of the Civil War as part of an ongoing process rather than as a departure requiring special explanation.

Culturally, Yankees and southerners remained worlds apart, as they had been since the arrival of the first colonists. Yankees were dedicated to work and achievement; southerners preferred to have others work for them, or else let it go undone. Yankees were realistic, southerners romantic. Yankees were shrewdly calculating: they schemed, bargained, negotiated, put success ahead of scruple. Southerners were hot-blooded: they dreamed, bragged, fought, put honor ahead of money. Yankee life was oriented toward the community and the marketplace, southern toward the family and the land. Perhaps most importantly, eternal salvation was, to the Yankee, a community matter, whereas to the southerner it was intensely personal.

The political issues were complex. Constitutionally, to be sure, the question was clear: it was whether the Constitution had established a political union of the American people and a national government superior to the state governments, as the North maintained, or a compact among states that retained final authority, as the South insisted. But people on each side had taken each position more than once in the past, responding according to whether it was they or their enemies who controlled the government, and people on both sides had more than once flirted with nullification and secession. What was genuinely at stake, therefore, was not the nature of the federal Union but the uses to which the powers of the federal government were to be put. And on that crucial question the positions of the two societies had come to be polarized during the three decades since Andrew Jackson became President.

The South advocated a system of free trade among nations and a domestic policy that did not invite much governmental interference in the economy; and through its dominance of the Democratic party, it largely succeeded in creating such a system and establishing such a policy during the 1840s and 1850s. Meanwhile, ever-larger portions of the North, and ultimately almost all of it, advocated high tariffs and active governmental interference to promote economic development; and though the North lacked the political clout until 1858 to enact that program on the federal level, it increasingly employed the power of state governments toward that end. The surge of the Republican party to power in the House elections of 1858 and its victory in the elections of 1860 indicated the triumph on the federal level of the northern system of political economy.

Most portentously, what was at issue was whether social relations should be fixed or free. The South was defending a way of life in which birth, law, custom, and a stable social structure determined relations among people. The North was defending the idea that a man's status and wealth, his place and his privileges, should be determined by what he did on this earth, and not by what his ancestors had done before him. The southern way was as old as man, and was in fact all that man had ever known. The northern was a radical experiment, not yet a century old, but one that had already wrought astonishing changes. The southern cause was supported by the record of history, the northern by the promise of the future.

The Civil War: Causes?

EUGENE D. GENOVESE

Professor McDonald presents the conflict between North and South as a conflict of cultures. It was that. But it was also a conflict of ideologies, and, as Professor McDonald demonstrates, a conflict of economies. What I do not perceive in his analysis is any perception of the absolute centrality of slavery to all that divided the two sections.

The South was not just another society that tolerated slavery; it was a slave society. The distinctive features of southern culture were the products of slavery—more precisely, of the relationship between master and slave. The slaveholders were very much a breed apart, with contradictory qualities rooted in the condition of being outright owners of human flesh. They had their virtues, which even some of their harshest critics admired: graciousness, generosity, tolerance of human foibles, physical courage, a strong sense of personal and family honor. These were the proud virtues of people who, as masters, could afford and were expected to show a certain confident kindness toward others, and as masters shunned any conduct suggestive of weakness or smallness. And the slaveholders had their vices, which their warmest admirers conceded: hot tempers, a frightening penchant for violence, an inability to allow contradiction on any matter that touched their honor, and a fearful habit of defining their honor to include everything and anything. These were the proud vices of masters. If slaveholders despised the virtues northern culture admired and practiced, it was precisely because they were slaveholders. The diligent money-making of the North seemed to them mean, beneath the dignity of masters.

It is true that the majority of southern whites owned no slaves; the South was nonetheless a slave society. A much smaller percentage of citizens of the United States today owns capital; yet few if any would argue that the United States is therefore not capitalist. Capitalism, like slavery and all other systems in which one class dominates another, defines itself by its ruling class. And the slaveholders did face constant challenge from the small white farmers and the middle classes. There was always the danger that white southerners without slaves would begin to look on slavery as giving too much wealth and power to the planter class at the expense of the rest of the South. The slaveholders' push for secession from the Union was at least partially the result of their fear of political opposition, an opposition that could even turn against slavery itself. For the moment, though, white southerners who owned no slaves were loyal enough to the planters' regime: they raised no powerful anti-slavery movement before the war came and, with significant exceptions, fought bravely for the Confederacy during the war.

One reason that nonslaveholders supported, or at least did not actually oppose, the slaveowners' regime was their fear of the black population, and of what it might do if it were ever free. But this fear, while important, has been much exaggerated. That small farmers in the plantation areas were related to slaveholders by blood was additional reason for their good will toward the slave system. Then, too, they suffered no direct exploitation by the slaveholders, and only the most knowledgeable could glimpse the ways in which slavery as a whole oppressed them. Their small surpluses of food or cotton had to be sold to the wealthy planters or marketed through them: the planters were able to offer friendship and services. These and other relationships strengthened the ties between planters and other whites and lessened the antagonisms. Probably, too, nonslaveholders shared a little of the pride of the planters: if they were not masters, they could at least see themselves as participating in the masters' domination of the slaves.

John Brown. *(Courtesy, Library of Congress)*

CHAPTER 14

"A Great Civil War" 1860–1865

JOHN BROWN'S RAID

In the summer of 1859, the nation seemed still capable of veering off the collision course on which its sections were hurtling. Then John Brown, his bloody work in Kansas still fresh in the minds of millions, shocked the country with a bold desperate stroke in western Virginia.

Brown, whom William Lloyd Garrison described as a "tall, spare, farmer-like man, with head disproportionately small, and that inflexible mouth," had gone in July 1859 to Harpers Ferry, about sixty miles northwest of Washington, D.C., at the confluence of the Potomac and Shenandoah rivers. Renting a farm near the town and using funds supplied by several abolitionists, he accumulated 198 rifles, a load of pistols he could not use because he had purchased the wrong firing caps for them, and 950 cast-iron pikes with which to arm slaves. He had gathered an army of sixteen whites and five blacks. On the evening of October 16, Brown's little band set out to capture the town and its federal arsenal. No slaves voluntarily joined them, and the townspeople, militia from the county, and then United States Marines led by Robert E. Lee besieged them. Within thirty-six hours, Brown and his army were captured. Ten of them died, including two of Brown's own sons. That was all there was to the raid, a total failure and, had people accepted it as a failure, a demonstration of the impossibility of starting a vast slave insurrection.

That was all there was to the raid, but not all there was to John Brown. "He is the gamest man I ever saw," admitted the governor of Virginia, who came to question the wounded captive. Brown replied to every questioner at his interrogation and at his trial with crisp assurance borne of clarity of purpose. His many letters after his conviction breathed saintly dedication to the biblical injunction to remember them that are in bonds as bound with them. Brown never wavered, showed no fear, no vindictiveness toward his captors, no selfish purposes at all. He awed his enemies and captured the respect of much of the North for a deed that few would actually have condoned. He transparently but consistently lied about his purposes in making the raid, as he was evasive to the point of dishonesty about his role in the Pottawatomie Massacre in 1856, when in retaliation against a proslavery group Brown and a small band had murdered five proslavery settlers near Pottawatomie Creek, Kansas. "It was all so thin," Robert Penn Warren observed of Brown's argument before the court, "that it should not have deceived a child, but it deceived a generation."

John Brown's favorite saying was that "without the shedding of blood there is no remission of sin." When his eldest son, John, Jr., was less than ten years old, he had kept a record of the son's sins. One day the elder Brown removed his own shirt, handed the boy the whip and ordered him to "lay it on." "I dared not refuse to obey," John, Jr., would remember, "but at first I did not strike hard. 'Harder!' he said, 'harder, harder!' until he *received the balance of the account*." The son would also remember the "drops of blood showing on his back." It was only years later that John, Jr., began to think that he understood this bizarre event. It was, he decided, a "practical illustration" of the doctrine of atonement. "I was then too obtuse to perceive how Justice could be satisfied by inflicting penalty upon the back of the innocent instead of the guilty."

In 1856 on Pottawatomie Creek in Kansas, and in 1859 at Harpers Ferry, John Brown offered an entire nation a "practical illustration" of the doctrine of atonement that he had derived from his family heritage and from "the ponderous volumes of Jonathan Edwards' sermons which father owned." John Brown, a lifelong failure, a bankrupt, sometime thief, eccentric, fanatic, liar, perhaps insane, would take upon his own back the nation's giant sin, would remove the debt that a society gone morally and politically bankrupt with slavery could not discharge.

Harper's Ferry, Virginia, the site of John Brown's raid. (*Courtesy, Stokes Collection, The New York Public Library*)

Brown's acts struck terror in the South, aroused many fears and uncertainties in the North, yet played upon the deepest chords of the Puritan conscience. Herman Melville later called Brown the "meteor" of the Civil War. Brown's behavior facing execution, which impressed even his captors, caught the imagination of Americans who accepted the doctrine of atonement, voiced most eloquently in Lincoln's Second Inaugural Address.

There is something blasphemous in Brown's reading of Christianity: the Son of God, not the son of Owen Brown, atones for mankind's sins. His last words, sent out to the world as he mounted the wagon that would carry him to the gallows, burn both with prophecy and with his disappointment at the realization that his own killings had not been enough.

> I, John Brown am now quite *certain* that the crimes of this *guilty land: will* never be purged *away;* but with Blood. I had as I now think: *vainly* flattered myself that without *very much* bloodshed it might be done.

Yet many northerners could easily link Brown with Christ. Ralph Waldo Emerson predicted that Brown "will make the gallows as glorious as the cross." Union troops sang:

> John Brown's body lies a moldering in the grave.
> John Brown's body lies a moldering in the grave.
> John Brown's body lies a moldering in the grave.
> His truth is marching on.

To the same melody runs *The Battle Hymn of the Republic*. Its composer, Julia Ward Howe, was the wife of Samuel Gridley Howe, one of the "Secret Six" who had supplied Brown with arms and money. One stanza reads:

> In the beauty of the lilies Christ was born across the sea,
> With a glory in his bosom that transfigures you and me,
> As he died to make men holy, let us die to make men free,
> While God is marching on.

The Election of 1860

The Democrats Meet in Charleston

Four months after John Brown's execution, the Democrats began their national convention at Charleston, South Carolina. The choice of the convention site was unfortunate; Charleston was a tinderbox of southern radicalism. For the Democrats, 1860 was the climax of the intra-party struggle between the dominant southern faction and the northerners, whose spokesman was Stephen Douglas. Ever since the split over Lecompton, both sides had been spoiling for a confrontation over the question of slavery in the territories. Most southern delegates came to Charleston pledged to the adoption of the Davis Resolutions. When the convention rejected their inclusion on the platform, delegates from eight southern states left. The convention then adjourned for several weeks, reassembling at Baltimore on June 18, where the fight immediately resumed. This time delegates from eleven southern states (all the future states of the Confederacy) walked out. The remaining delegates nominated Douglas for president on a platform endorsing popular sovereignty. The bolters met in another hall and nominated John Breckinridge of Kentucky for President. Their platform upheld the Davis Resolutions. The split between the Democrats was complete.

A number of factors brought this fatal action by the southern Democrats, which virtually assured a Republican victory in November. A few hotheads sought deliberately to split the party, precisely in order to produce the Republican victory that would, they anticipated, precipitate secession. Some delegates hoped merely to force the election into the House of Representatives. The Democrats had met amidst extreme excitement, and many delegates were simply swept away by the violent speeches of "fire-eaters," a term applied to agitators like William Yancey of Alabama. They bolted without fully considering the consequences. Right up to November, many of the bolters assumed that somehow the party would come back together.

Between the two Democratic conventions another party had met at Baltimore. This was the Constitutional Union Party, composed mainly of old Whigs from both sections and of southern Know-Nothings. These conservatives joined in their general concern for the safety of the Union. For President, they nominated John Bell of Tennessee, a Whig and a large slaveholder, although not an extreme advocate of southern rights. As their platform, the Constitutional Unionists settled for a vague pledge to uphold the Constitution and the Union.

| **The Republicans Convene in Chicago** | The Republican convention opened at Chicago on May 16. The Republican strategy in 1860 was simple: to win the White |

House the party had only to win the same states Frémont had carried in 1856, plus just 34 additional electoral votes. This meant carrying Pennsylvania (27 votes) and either Illinois (11), Indiana (13), or New Jersey (7). All these states adjoined the South and were less hostile to slavery than was the upper North. And each of these four states had special concerns such as the tariff or internal improvements.

The Republican platform had these states in mind. It treated the slavery question cautiously. The delegates reaffirmed Republican opposition to the expansion of slavery, but promised to leave slavery alone where it existed. The platform pledged support for a protective tariff, a Pacific railroad, and a homestead law.

This same concern for the swing states gov-erned the choice of a candidate. William Seward was considered extreme on the slavery question, and the party's congressional and local candidates in the states in question did not want to run with him. After reviewing the other contenders, the party pros settled on Abraham Lincoln as the man most "available": he resided in the important state of Illinois, was a moderate on slavery, had never been identified with nativism, and had made fewer enemies than his rivals. Lincoln also benefited from the shrewd tactics of his managers, who packed the galleries at the convention hall by distributing counterfeit tickets, and stationed men around the floor to begin noisy demonstrations on a prearranged signal.

In 1860 the national political system effectively failed to operate. There were two campaigns that year. In the North the contest was between Lincoln and Douglas: Bell and Breckinridge were also on the ballot, but neither had much support. In the South Breckinridge divided votes with Bell, though Douglas was also on the ballot. Lincoln, Bell, and Breckinridge adhered to the tradition of staying close to home and letting supporters do the campaigning. On the real issue of the campaign—the possible dissolution of the Union—Lincoln and Breckinridge remained silent. Stephen Douglas campaigned hard and heroically throughout the country—at some risk to his personal safety in the South—in an attempt to break down the barriers between the two sections.

On election day each of the hard-line candidates won in his own section. Lincoln carried all the northern states except New Jersey; Breckinridge captured eleven slave states. Douglas ran well in the North, but carried only Missouri and three electoral votes in New Jersey. Bell, whose popular vote was the smallest, took Virginia, Kentucky, and Tennessee. In the country as a whole Lincoln won only 39 per cent of the popular vote, but his votes were concentrated in the populous North. As a result, he had a clear victory in the electoral college—180 votes against a total of 112 for his three opponents. Lincoln carried all but three of the northern states by majorities. He would have won even if the opposition to him had been united. The Republican victory in November might not alone have ruptured the Union. Conservatives within the Republican Party hoped to appease the upper South with a pol-

THE NATIONAL GAME. THREE "OUTS" AND ONE "RUN".
ABRAHAM WINNING THE BALL.

This cartoon employs a setting from the new game of baseball to argue that Lincoln won the 1860 election because he stood for equal rights and free territory. *(Courtesy, The New-York Historical Society, New York City)*

icy of popular sovereignty instead of outright opposition to admission of any of the territories as slave states. But a single event of 1859 stuck in the craw of southerners, the act of a madman or a saint—John Brown's nightmare attack at Harpers Ferry.

Secession

Appropriately, South Carolina led the way toward secession. As soon as Lincoln's election was certain, the South Carolina legislature called for a state convention. On December 20, 1860, the convention met at Charleston and unanimously declared "that the Union now subsisting between South Carolina and other States of America is hereby dissolved." Similar declarations followed in rapid succession in Alabama, Georgia, Florida, Mississippi, and Louisiana. The smooth course of secession was upset only in Texas, where crusty old Governor Sam Houston, a staunch Unionist, refused to summon a special session of the legislature. The lawmakers met anyway, and called an election of delegates and a convention without Houston's authorization.

Up to this point, the secession process had moved forward with electrifying speed. Moderates like Stephen Douglas had tried to avert the catastrophe. Even before the election, looking to one observer like a "way worn backwoods traveler," he had gone south to reason with the secessionists. But there was no reason. Too much blood had been shed in Kansas, too much madness exhibited at Harper's Ferry. In the space of forty-two days, seven states, stretching from South Carolina to Texas, had seceded from the Union. On February 4, 1861, however, the secessionist tide broke momentarily when the voters of Virginia elected a majority of convention delegates opposed to immediate secession. Subsequently the electorate in four other upper South states—Tennessee, North Carolina, Arkansas, and Missouri— voted in effect against secession. The three remaining slave states—Kentucky, Maryland, and Delaware—did not even call conventions. Having stronger ties to the North and smaller ratios of blacks in its population, the upper South was hesitant to secede. For the moment, the lower South was isolated.

Nonetheless, at Montgomery, Alabama, on February 7, 1861, delegates from the seven states proceeded to adopt a provisional constitution for the Confederate States of America. It was modeled closely on the United States Constitution, but several modifications safeguarded state sovereignty and slavery. The Confederate Constitution reserved to the states the power of amendment and even permitted them to impeach Confederate officials under certain circumstances. It guaranteed the property rights of slaveholders both in the existing states and in any future territory the Confederacy might acquire. To lead the new government the delegates chose Jefferson Davis of Mississippi as provisional president and Alexander H. Stephens of Georgia as vice-president.

A Compact of States

Declarations issued by the various state conventions spelled out the reasons for secession. South Carolina's was typical. The United States Constitution, the declaration began, was a compact among sovereign states for the purpose of establishing "a government with defined objects and powers." Like all compacts, this one bound the contracting parties to certain mutual obligations. The failure of one of the parties to perform these obligations, in whole or in part, released the other from its bond. The northern states, continued the South Carolina declaration, had refused to fulfill their constitutional obligation to return fugitive slaves. They had denounced slavery as "sinful" and tolerated abolition societies "designed to disturb the peace and steal the property of the citizens of other states." They had encouraged "servile insurrection"—a reference to John Brown. At last, a sectional party "hostile to slavery" had captured control of the federal government. This party was dedicated not merely to excluding slavery from the "common territory," but to slavery's ultimate extinction. The actions of Brown and the writings of Harriet Beecher Stowe and others incorrectly convinced many southerners that abolitionists had triumphed in the North.

We can now see that even on their own terms southerners were wrong: slavery would have remained far safer in the Union than out of it. Democrats and southerners still had a majority in both houses of Congress. Lincoln could not have acted without their approval. Even had the South eventually lost all control of the government, important constitutional guarantees protected slavery in the states where it existed and Republicans had pledged themselves not to interfere with it there. Lincoln even expressed his willingness early in 1861 to support a constitutional amendment to that effect. If the southern states had remained in the Union, the Republicans could never have put through a constitutional amendment abolishing slavery. Only an act of war could do this. Secession united a North previously divided on the question of slavery and doomed the peculiar institution.

Secession as the founders of the Confederacy viewed it was not an act of revolution but a defense of a traditional order. It was, they argued, a return to the system of independent states out of which the Constitution had come, a resumption by individual states of the exercise of a sovereignty they had never surrendered to the United States. The object was to preserve a social system and to protect a form of property, the holding of slaves. Yet secessionists would not have described themselves as repudiating the modern world. Their society, so they thought, was one of freedom—for white people—and of enlightened republican government.

Southerners of this sort would associate the case for slavery with the case for secession,

An old northern textbook map depicting the tree of Slavery (God's curse) branching out across the South and into Missouri, and the tree of Liberty (God's blessing) branching out across the rest of the nation. The traditional dividing line between North and South was the Mason-Dixon line, a 1769 survey of the Pennsylvania-Maryland border by Charles Mason and Jeremiah Dixon.

claiming that both slaveholding and states' rights were old institutions strongly founded in law. But the two issues were in fact quite separate. In previous years northern opponents of slavery had proposed that free states refuse cooperation with a national government that protected slavery; and in 1860 some sympathizers with slavery were also supporters of the Union. Earlier in the century political and constitutional quarrels had taken place over whether it was the Union or the states that possessed sovereignty. The argument looked back to the process of ratification, in which each state had held a convention to decide whether that state should adhere to the Constitution. Nineteenth-century champions of state sovereignty concluded from this that ratification had been by individual states, each state retaining sovereignty and the right of independence. They believed that sovereignty belonged also to the states formed after ratification.

Northern Reactions The opposite argument started with the proposition that at the time of the American Revolution it had been the whole people who asserted sovereignty, rebelling against the false claim of the British throne to be sovereign over British America. Thereafter that same whole and undivided sovereign people, following the Confederation period, had voted for the Constitution, the states providing no more than convenient administrative units for the conduct of the vote. If the states at the time of ratification had been that—administrative units within the nation—they would not later present themselves as being sovereign and having been so in the eighteenth century. Americans who thought this way could believe that in opposing southern secession they were opposing an illegal rebellion by a part of the people against the whole people.

In 1860 and 1861 reasoning of that kind, in this age that took seriously such philosophical inquiries, must have been in the minds of unionists. Even a citizen convinced of the legal right of secession might be a unionist out of patriotism toward the Union or a recognition of its economic and strategic benefits. In their appeals to southerners to stay by the United States, unionists could keep away from the slavery issue, on which they could not have made converts, and instead could make use of the self-interest, the patriotism,

President and Mrs. Jefferson Davis. In February 1861, the first seven Confederate States of America—there were to be eleven in all— elected Davis as President. *(Courtesy, Confederate Museum, Richmond, Virginia)*

or the constitutional arguments that might even draw slaveholders to the Union.

By early winter 1861 Lincoln was on his way to Washington. The seven states of the deep South had seceded and formed themselves into the Confederate States of America, with Montgomery, Alabama, as their capital. The crisis was the greatest since the Revolution. Washington was astir with worry and excitement.

The nation's capital, tucked between the slave states of Virginia and Maryland, was a largely southern city. For decades southern politicians, or "northern men with southern principles," had dominated the political, business, and social life of the capital. The city still had hundreds of slaves in its population, although since the 1850 Compromise the slave pens and auction blocks had gone. Now, in the country's greatest crisis, the southern sympathies of many Washingtonians were visible everywhere. At the city's many bars the imbibers of "toddies" and "flips" announced that Lincoln would never be inaugurated: proud "southrons" would not allow it. At the government executive departments young clerks wore "secession cockades" much as we wear campaign buttons in presidential election years.

Unionists who found themselves in the capital during the secession winter were apprehensive. The young Henry Adams, who had come to Washington as private secretary to his father, Congressman Charles Francis Adams of Massachusetts, thought the southerners "demented." Confident of independence, they were already cultivating the good will of their future Yankee customers. Senator Stephen Douglas, waiting for Congress to begin its session, talked darkly of the "slave power" conspiracy that had connived at defeating him for President and was now intent on breaking up the Union. Other unionists were charging that the conspirators could be found in President Buchanan's cabinet itself. Cabinet members Howell Cobb of Georgia, Jacob Thompson of Mississippi, and John B. Floyd of Virginia, they said, were providing the Confederacy with guns and ammunition from federal arsenals and threatening the weak-willed Buchanan that if he tried to move against the secessionists he would be either assassinated or impeached.

Indeed, from the unionist view it looked at first as if the seventy-year-old James Buchanan had been terrified into inaction. The Democratic president had proclaimed secession illegal and declared the Union "perpetual." But he denied that the federal government had any constitutional authority to force the return of seceded states, and he feared that any attempt at coercion would make the situation worse. Buchanan attributed the whole trouble to fanatical abolitionists and to the menace the free-soil movement posed for the South. The President hoped for some new compromise that would still the issue of slavery as had the arrangements of 1820 and 1850.

Efforts at compromise were not wanting. The issue needing resolution was that of whether or to what extent the territories should be open to slavery. Early in 1861 the Washington Peace Convention, a gathering of statesmen under the chairmanship of former President John Tyler, looked for a solution. Congress also debated. A plan pressed by Senator John J. Crittenden of Kentucky would extend the Missouri Compromise line to the Pacific and add a constitutional amendment protecting slavery wherever it existed. But the extremists dominating politics in the cotton states would probably have turned down the plan, and the Republican party could not have abandoned its principle of opposing slavery in the territories.

While attempts at compromise were unsuccessful, neither secession nor war appeared anything like a certainty. Republican and Democratic upholders of the sovereignty of the United States perceived secession as an impulsive and irrational act that the South could decide to reverse. War, or at any rate a prolonged one, must have been almost unthinkable. While many, and perhaps almost all, northern statesmen along with some southerners would have agreed that secession was unconstitutional, it was not clear that the federal government had the constitutional means to prevent it by force: President Buchanan denied that the government did. Nor could supporters of the Union have any confidence that the northern people could summon the will to march against the seceded states. For President-elect Lincoln and prospective members of his cabinet, the problem was to find a political solution to the crisis.

The Problem of the Forts

Lincoln in his inaugural address told the South that he would enforce the Fugitive Slave Law and support a constitutional amendment protecting slavery where it already existed. But he did not modify his position on free soil in the territories; and he condemned secession, pledging to "hold, occupy and possess" all Union property within the regions that had announced their secession.

By February 1861 the issue was largely symbolic, but not the less critical for that. Throughout the lower South federal forts, customs houses, and post offices had fallen into the hands of the Confederate or state authorities soon after secession. But two key posts held out, Fort Pickens at Pensacola, Florida, and Fort Sumter in Charleston harbor. For the Confederates to concede these to the United States meant accepting the intolerable presence of a "foreign" power in the new southern nation's domain. For the Union to surrender them would be acquiescence in southern independence. The Pickens problem was not acute, since in Florida authorities were for the moment willing to tolerate the presence of the forces of the United States. Fiery Charleston was a different story.

Fort Sumter   As the citizens of the southern port went about their business, they were aware of the drama at their doorsteps. Across the harbor they could see the Stars and Stripes flying defiantly over Sumter, while on Morris Island and at the city's main fortifications uniformed men loyal to the new Confederacy rushed here and there moving big guns, ammunition, and powder.

For weeks South Carolina officials had been negotiating with both the Washington authorities and Major Robert Anderson, the garrison commander, for evacuation of the fort. Anderson had holed up at Sumter when he concluded that his small force was inadequate to occupy all three federal strong points in the harbor, but from that grim, gray bastion he refused to depart. Soon after the new year Buchanan, his resolve stiffened by four new Unionist cabinet members, dispatched the *Star of the West*, an unarmed steamer, to reinforce Anderson with men and supplies. The Charleston authorities ordered their guns to let loose at the vessel. Anderson came within an eyelash of returning the fire to protect the ship, but before he could, it turned back.

Lincoln inherited the Sumter problem from his predecessor. He sought advice from his cabinet members and other statesmen. William Seward of New York, his Secretary of State, startled him with the suggestion that the administration bring the country together by getting into a war with Europe. On April 4, 1861, the President announced the send-

ing of a squadron for the relief of Fort Sumter. The ships would carry only food. If the secessionists allowed them through, the federal government would make no attempt to send men or ammunitions to Anderson.

News of Lincoln's intentions infuriated the Confederate authorities in Montgomery, who believed that the Republican President had assured them he would evacuate Sumter. Convinced that they could not avoid a clash without seeming to be weak, they reluctantly ordered that Sumter be reduced by attack before the promised reinforcement could arrive.

The hotheads at Charleston, the moral and intellectual capital of "Secessia," rejoiced. Happiest of all, perhaps, was the venerable Edmund Ruffin, long a leading figure among writers on southern agronomy. Now a silver-haired man of sixty-seven, Ruffin had been among the staunchest defenders of southern rights and had long advocated secession. When his own state of Virginia proved slow to take up the northern challenge he came to fire-eating Charleston and, despite his age, joined the Palmetto Guard of the South Carolina infantry. When the order to attack Sumter was given early on the morning of April 12, the elderly gentleman was positioned at the great Columbiad cannon pointing at the federal fort. Later Ruffin would insist that he had fired the first shot of the war. In reality his shot was preceded by a mortar barrage. But it was to him that the symbolic honor went.

The bombardment lasted for a respectable period for the outnumbered Union force. During the first hour Abner Doubleday, second-in-command, wrote, "It was determined not to return their fire until after breakfast. I remained in bed." Anderson, his food and gunpowder low, finally sent word that he was ready to surrender. The next day the flag of the Union was lowered and the Palmetto banner of South Carolina raised. No soldier was killed or seriously injured. But by seceding and by firing the first shot, the Confederacy brought together in defense of the Union a North that might not have chosen to fight the South on the question of slavery alone.

The War Strategies

The attack on the fort began the Civil War. In the absence of Congress, President Lincoln issued a proclamation requesting 75,000 volunteers for the suppressing of "combinations too powerful to be suppressed by the ordinary course of judicial proceedings." Upon its reassembling that summer, Congress gave legality to this proclamation along with other actions that Lincoln had taken in the military emergency.

Lincoln's call for troops confronted the upper South states with an unwelcome choice: to fight against the South or to fight against the Union. Virginia, North Carolina. Tennessee, and Arkansas joined the Confederacy. Four slave states remained: Delaware, Maryland, Kentucky, and Missouri. Only Delaware stayed peaceably in the Union. In the other three states opinion was divided. President Lincoln used force to aid the Union cause in strategic Maryland. When a mob favoring the South attacked federal soldiers in Baltimore and cut the rail line between that city and Washington, he sent troops to subdue the disorder and arrest potential secessionists. Kentucky, birthplace of both Lincoln and Jefferson Davis, declared its neutrality, but within months Union and Confederate troops had entered the state. It and Missouri became the scene of guerrilla warfare, as supporters of both sides fought for control of the state government. Although the Confederacy claimed these two states, both remained in the old nation. Later in the Civil War, the federal government arranged to make into a separate state West Virginia, the Northwestern region of Virginia where slaves were few and Unionist sentiment was strong.

Two basic facts dictated the North's military strategy: restoring the Union required subduing the South; and a war of conquest required vast material and human resources. These the North possessed in abundance. Its population in 1860 numbered twenty million, while the South had barely nine million, 40 percent of whom were slaves. Nine-

tenths of the country's manufacturing capacity was situated in the North, which also had two-thirds of the railroad mileage. Most of the nation's merchant shipping and financial resources were in northern hands.

Recognizing these advantages, General Winfield Scott mapped out the basic northern strategy right after Sumter's fall. He proposed starving the South by a blockade of her ports; driving down the Mississippi River, which would divide the Confederacy in two; sending in armies of invasion that would break the southern nation into bits. northerners expected a short war, but once the reality of a long war sank in, they closely followed Scott's strategy.

The Confederacy's crucial disadvantage was economic, though it also suffered from a deep moral isolation in a world that increasingly repudiated slavery as a loathsome and retrograde remnant of a benighted past. Having few mills, factories, and foundries, the South began the war with a stockpile of captured or imported equipment. In spite of heroic efforts toward industrial self-sufficiency, the South could never replace equipment as rapidly as it wore out. With imports cut off, the Confederacy would gradually die of economic starvation.

Yet the South at the beginning of the war was not in a weak position. For while the Confederacy could not have won a head-on conflict with the North, it did not have to. Against the North's enormous task of conquering a vast territory, the rebels needed to do no more than demonstrate to the northern people and to Europe, by one military strategy or another, that the old Union was no longer a single, workable nation. A few decisive southern victories might have done that.

Resources of the Union and the Confederacy, 1861

	Union	*Confederacy*
Population	23,000,000	8,700,000*
Real and personal property	$11,000,000,000	$5,370,000,000
Banking capital	$330,000,000	$27,000,000
Capital investment	$850,000,000	$95,000,000
Manufacturing establishments	110,000	18,000
Value of production (annual)	$1,500,000,000	$155,000,000
Industrial workers	1,300,000	110,000
Railroad mileage	22,000	9,000

*40 percent were slaves (3,500,000)

Source: From Freedom and Crisis: An American History, *Third Edition, by Allen Weinstein and Frank Otto Gatell. Copyright © 1974, 1978, 1981 by Random House, Inc. Reprinted by permission of the publisher.*

Instead the South fought a mostly defensive war, keeping the Confederate armies close to home base. That revealed itself ultimately as a losing strategy because it made for a long war that expended the South's limited supplies and troops.

The South made other mistakes. Unwilling to see their black slaves as men, southerners never effectively used this vast source of manpower. Only in the closing months of the war would the Confederate Congress at last authorize using slaves in the army—too late to affect the outcome. Equally damaging to the South's cause was its naive faith in the power of "King Cotton." Convinced that Britain could not long do without southern cotton, the new Confederate government in 1861 forbade all exports of this, the South's only major source of foreign credit. Starving British textile makers, Richmond thought, would force Britain to intervene in the Confederacy's behalf. But British manufacturers, expecting war in America, had stockpiled cotton. By the time the South realized its error, the northern blockade had closed tight. For the rest of the war the South's "white gold" rotted on the wharves while southerners starved.

Classic War in the East; Decisive War in the West

The American Civil War, like other wars, was shaped as much by geography as by generals. The placing of the Confederate capital at Richmond, only one hundred miles from Washington, focused the fighting in the East in a narrow theater between and around the capitals. Here in northern Virginia rival armies marched and countermarched for four years, as each side sought to protect its capital and threaten that of its rival. The dramatic battles fought here—such as Chancellorsville and Gettysburg—constitute the classic war so celebrated in Civil War legend. It is often overlooked that after four years of bloodshed neither side had accomplished its objective—destruction of the enemy's capital.

Robert E. Lee, who led the Confederacy's northern Virginia troops and would become the South's most prominent general, had been no enthusiast for secession. Family tradition opposed it: his father, "Lighthorse Harry" Lee, had been a Revolutionary War hero, and his mother's family had also played an honorable role in the founding of the United States. His wife was the great granddaughter of Martha Washington, and Lee had grown up in Alexandria, Virginia, surrounded by mementos of George Washington, upon whom he modeled his life. Educated at West Point, Lee spent all his adult life in the United States Army, distinguishing himself in the Mexican War, serving as the superintendent of West Point, and achieving some eminence as an army engineer. When secession came, the Lincoln administration sounded him out about taking command of the Union army. Lee, who only days before had accepted promotion to colonel, saw no choice but to resign his commission rather than to face the responsibility of leading troops against his native state. In the end he was a Virginian. When after 1865 the Confederacy was no more, he could find it relatively easy to resume his loyalty to the Union and to urge other southerners to follow his lead. Perhaps he was never a southern nationalist, only a Virginian in a bad season.

While the preoccupation of the two warring governments was with the territory between their capitals, the decisive theater of the Civil War was in the West. Here nature had formed a series of southerly-flowing rivers—the Cumberland, the Tennessee, the Mississippi—that thrust into the heart of the Confederacy. Union strategists recognized early the value of these rivers for rapid movement of men and supplies, and acted to secure control of them. It was here, and in Sherman's later invasion of the deep South from the West, that the North won and the South lost the Civil War.

Both governments were totally unprepared for war in April 1861. Guns and ammunition were in short supply. Few officers on either side had commanded large bodies of men. The hastily-formed volunteer regiments lacked even the rudiments of military training. Such units wore gaudy, impractical uniforms and adopted flamboyant names.

These amateur armies had their first taste of war in July 1861. Pressured by a public demand to take Richmond at once, Union General Irvin McDowell led his ill-trained army into northern Virginia, followed by carriages full of Washingtonians out to see the show. At Bull Run (or Manassas Junction), the Union troops met an equally ill-prepared army under General P.G.T. Beauregard. For some time the two armies fought with a courage beyond their experience. After early reverses, Confederates rallied behind General Thomas Jackson—"Stonewall," as he would soon be known because of an incident in which he and his troops stood as firm as a stone wall—and broke the Union advance. Retreat became chaos as green troops struggled with panic-stricken civilians along the roads to Washington. McDowell's army simply fell apart; soldiers threw down their guns, canteens, coats, and ran. "One Southerner is equal to five Yankees," pronounced southern newspapers. But the Confederate soldiers, nearly as disorganized, did not pursue, although Jackson boasted that with 5000 men he could have finished the job.

Bull Run awakened the North to reality. Lincoln gave the command to General George B. McClellan, a cautious soldier but brilliant organizer, who set about shaping the Army of the Potomac into a real fighting machine. As McClellan trained his troops, critical events were taking place in the West. Union attention here focused on the rivers, where Confederate strong points barred an advance southward.

Western Campaigns

In February 1862 an army under General Ulysses S. Grant, supported by a fleet of iron-clad gunboats, pushed up the Tennessee River and captured Fort Henry. Union forces crossed over immediately and besieged Fort Donelson on the Cumberland. Grant took this fort, too, and fired the North's imagination with his demand for "immediate and unconditional surrender."

Confederate troops struck back hard at Grant's army in April at Shiloh, on the Tennessee River near the northern border of Mississippi. Catching Grant off guard, they nearly pushed his troops back into the river. All day long the battle raged. "From right to left, everywhere," an Illinois soldier was to write, "it was one never ending, terrible roar, with no prospect of stopping." General Sherman was wounded twice, in his hand and shoulder, and a ball of shot passed through his hat; he also had several horses shot from under him during the day. At nightfall Union reinforcements turned the battle. The human cost at Shiloh was appalling—nearly 23,000 casualties. A civil war soldier wrote "a private knows nothing but what he sees come to pass." But that could be immense. "O it was too shocking too horrible," wrote a Confederate soldier. "God Grant that I may never be the partaker of such scenes again. . . . When released from this I shall ever be an advocate of peace."

The results of Shiloh were decisive. The Confederacy had lost its supreme bid to regain western Tennessee. Other Union forces opened the upper Mississippi as far as Memphis. That same April of 1862 the Confederacy suffered one of its greatest losses when Admiral David Farragut captured New Orleans, the South's biggest seaport. By midsummer the South's hold on the Mississippi was limited to a narrow stretch of river between Vicksburg, Mississippi, and Port Hudson, Louisiana. A New York soldier stationed in Louisiana wrote of the insensitivity the carnage had wrought:

> What hardened wretches we have become. The word came, 'Eph. Hammond is dead, hurry up and make a box for him.' He was one of the best-liked men in the regiment. Yet not a tear was shed, and before his body was cold he was buried in the ground. We will talk about him more or less for a day or two and then forget all about him. That is what less than a year has done to us.

Blockade

While the North was pressing in on the Confederacy in the West, it was also pushing in from the sea. The blockade included the stopping of foreign merchant ships and the confiscation of nonmilitary goods that they were carrying to the Confederacy. In a regular war between independent countries such seizures would have been contrary to international law, and the United States faced complaints from Europe. But the South, the federal government responded in effect, was not an independent nation at war, to which citizens from neutral countries could have the right to ship non-

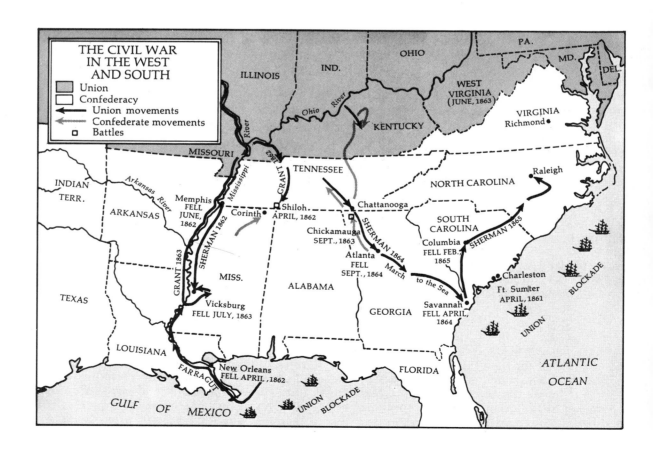

THE CIVIL WAR IN THE WEST AND SOUTH

military provisions. It was instead a rebellious part of the United States, and the legitimate national government therefore had the authority to exclude commerce from southern ports. For a time the Union had to face the possibility that Great Britain or France, not displeased at a weakening of the United States and eager to resume full trade with the cotton South, might recognize the Confederacy as a separate nation. British recognition would give a tremendous lift to southern morale and injure that of the North. And in recognizing the Confederacy as an independent country the British would have grounds for challenging the federal blockade for not following the rules that international law dictated in war between sovereign nations. France might recognize the Confederacy in return for southern support of Napoleon III's plan to install a French puppet, Austrian Archduke Maximilian, on a specially created Mexican throne. But when federal troops in September 1862 stopped the rebel invasion at the Battle of Antietam (or Sharpsburg, as the southerners called it), Great Britain decided to put off recognition of the Confederacy. The blockade was safe from direct foreign interference.

The southern navy could not successfully take on the Union fleet. For one day in 1862 in a battle off Hampton Roads, Virginia, the Confederate vessel *Merrimac* did much damage to Union naval forces. In a great technological innovation, the ship had been covered with iron plates, and against them northern naval guns had little effect. The next day the North set its own ironclad *Monitor* against the *Merrimac*, rendering it harmless. One southerner confided to his diary on May 20: the port of Norfolk, Virginia,

> has been evacuated by the Confederate troops and the Merrimack has been destroyed. There ends for the present all hope of a southern navy. The loss of Norfolk involves that of the Navy yard at Portsmouth with its dry dock and ship building facilities. Yet, I believe, the destruction of the Merrimack produced a deeper mortification in the South than all the other losses that attended it. There had been among the people the most exaggerated expectations.

Later in the war northern commerce suffered from the raids of the Confederate ship *Alabama*, built in Britain by a private company. Charles Francis Adams, the United States minister to that nation, protested to the British government for its failure to stop the

construction and after the war the United States would win compensation from Britain for losses the ship had inflicted. The Union navy finally sank the *Alabama*. Confederate privateers could attack merchant ships, but were no threat to the northern navy. While the blockade could not keep the Confederacy from the sea trade, it was effective enough to deprive Confederate society of much that it needed for smooth functioning.

| Eastern Campaigns

In the East, General McClellan in 1862 drilled his Army of the Potomac for months, all the while ignoring the public clamor for action. (An exasperated Lincoln once said he would like to borrow McClellan's army if the general did not intend to use it.) Prodded by the President, he finally proposed in the spring of 1862 a bold plan to take Richmond from the rear. Instead of fighting his way overland, McClellan would make an amphibious landing on the James River Peninsula; from there he could march up the Peninsula and seize the Confederate capital. Lincoln approved, provided McClellan left enough men behind to protect Washington.

McClellan embarked in March 1862, without leaving the promised covering force. When Lincoln discovered this, he recalled part of the Army of the Potomac. This nearly immobilized the cautious McClellan, who consistently overestimated Confederate strength: he in fact still had 90,000 men to the enemy's 70,000. The slowness of his progress up the Peninsula gave the Confederate troops, commanded by Lee, time to organize. In a series of battles known as the Seven Days, Lee hammered at McClellan's army and threw it back. In August McClellan began a slow withdrawal from the Peninsula. Command of the Army of the Potomac passed to General John Pope.

Sensing an opportunity to strike before the federal army could regroup, Lee took the offensive. On August 30 he smashed Pope's army at the second battle of Bull Run, then swung north into Maryland. But a copy of his battle plans fell into the hands of McClellan, whom Lincoln had hurriedly recalled to command. On September 17, McClellan engaged the invading Confederates at Antietam Creek. After the bloodiest single day's battle of the entire war—24,000 dead and wounded—Lee withdrew unpursued. Tac-

Robert E. Lee, native son of Virginia, brilliant military strategist, and leader of the Confederate forces. *(Courtesy, Library of Congress)*

Twice during the winter of 1862–63, federal generals renewed the offensive against Richmond, each time with disastrous results. In December General Ambrose Burnside, a handsome West Pointer remembered for his legendary growth of side whiskers, and now in command in place of McClellan, was soundly defeated at Fredericksburg. At Chancellorsville in the spring of 1863, Lee and Jackson caught the army of Burnside's successor, General Joseph Hooker, straddling the Rappahannock River, and cut it to pieces. Lee paid a fearful price—"Stonewall" Jackson was mortally wounded, shot down by his own men in the confusion of battle as they waged hopeless frontal assaults against entrenched Union forces. After two years the northern drive on Richmond was back where it had started—on the Potomac.

| **Vicksburg and Gettysburg** At this point, in the summer of 1863, two battles put the North on the way to final victory in the war. Ulysses S. Grant struck in the West. For months his troops had besieged Vicksburg, the last Confederate stronghold on the Mississippi River. Situated high on a hill above the river, with bayous on both flanks, the city seemed impregnable. After repeated failures to dislodge the Confederate defenders, Grant hit on a bold plan. Abandoning his supply base, he slipped around the city on the Louisiana side, marched downstream, and crossed below Vicksburg. With dazzling speed, he moved inland to Jackson, cutting Vicksburg's rail link with the Confederacy, then turned west to lock up the city from the land side. Cut off, Vicksburg surrendered on July 4, 1863. Grant had reopened the Mississippi and split the Confederacy in two, leaving the trans-Mississippi region isolated. Mrs. Lincoln could not tolerate General Grant. "He is a butcher and is not fit to be at the head of army. He loses two men to the enemy's one. . . . He would depopulate the North."

"But he has been very successful in the Field," quietly argued the President.

In the East, just a day before Grant's victory at Vicksburg, the Union army at Gettysburg had won what was to become the most famous battle of the war. Gettysburg was the devastating outcome of a daring Confederate attempt begun in June, when Lee marched his army north again in search of a decisive

tically the battle had been a draw, but measured against Confederate expectations it was a crushing defeat. Clara Barton, the northern nurse, evoked the sorrow and scope of the battle:

> Antietam! With its eight miles of camping armies, face to face; 160,000 men to spring up at dawn like the old Scot from the heather! Its miles of artillery shaking the earth like a chain of Etnas! Its ten hours of uninterrupted battle! Its thunder and its fire! The sharp unflinching order—'Hold the Bridge, boys—always the Bridge.' At length, the quiet! The pale moonlight on its cooling guns! The weary men—the dying and the dead!

Although Lee had failed at Antietam, he was still unbeatable on his home ground.

General William Tecumseh Sherman, second to Ulysses S. Grant among northern generals, marched through Georgia in 1864. His army, burning and looting, left a wide path of destruction in its wake. (*Courtesy, Library of Congress*)

Immigrants or citizens in the Union army celebrated their experiences in their native languages:

Viva Grant! Viva Grant! ciudadanos,
que cinco años la guerra sostuvo,
y un ejército enorme mantuvo
en defensa de la libertad.
　Y después de sangrientos combates,
do murieron valientes soldados;
fueron libres aquellos estados
que jamás pretendían la igualdad.

Dios te salve, caudillo del Norte!
Yo saludo tu sacra bandera,
que en el mundo flamea por doquiera,
ofreciendo la paz y la unión.
　También México ensalza tu nombre
porque fuiste con el indulgente,
fuiste siempre y serás el valiente
que defiende la Constitución.

• • •

Ich in Gettysburg mit schlug,
Half erringen jenen Sieg,
Und die Kosten auch mit trug,
Wenn ich auch keinen Nickel krieg.
Hancock führte an, du sagst,
Im gefecht ein grosser Mann,
Ob ich für ihn stimm', du fragst?
Nein, o nein, das geht nicht an.
Damals trug er Union Blau,
Jetzt liebt er Rebellen Grau.

victory. The South needed one. It was in trouble in the West, and the Union blockade was withering the southern economy.

Lee's army moved quickly out of the Blue Ridge Mountains into Maryland. Hooker followed, keeping to the east in order to protect Washington. As Lee drove into Pennsylvania, a nervous Lincoln replaced the timid Hooker with George G. Meade. Respectful of General Meade's abilities, Lee concentrated his forces at Gettysburg. Rushing forward, Meade collided with him at that Pennsylvania town, and on July 1, 2, and 3 they fought the greatest single battle of the war.

Lee struck first, before Meade could concentrate his army, and on July 1 nearly drove the Federals from the field. During the night Union troops arrived in strength and dug in. On the next two days Lee attacked at both flanks and the center of the Union line in a to-

tal effort to crush the Army of the Potomac. "Where the line stood the ground was covered in blue," a Georgia soldier recalled. "I could have walked on them [the corpses of Union soldiers] without putting my feet on the ground." But nothing quite worked. The climax came on July 3 when 15,000 Confederate troops under General George Pickett made a gallant frontal assault on the Union center on—appropriately—Cemetery Ridge. On Pickett's men came, "an ocean of armed men . . . magnificent, grim, irresistible," as Union gunners fired triple loads of iron shot into their ranks. A few Confederate soldiers reached the Ridge; then suddenly Union reinforcements poured into the breach. The surviving Confederate troops retreated, leaving many of their number dead. The battle was over. On July 4, while a rainstorm washed the blood from the grass, the Confederate army withdrew. Meade, as paralyzed as his predecessors, did not pursue. Lee had lost 20,000 men—a third of his army. The Confederacy's offensive power was broken forever.

An excited New York *Tribune* ran its account of Gettysburg under seventeen headlines

THE GREAT VICTORY.

_____

The Rebel Army Totally Defeated.

_____

ITS REMAINS DRIVEN INTO THE MOUNTAINS.

_____

It is There Surrounded and Hemmed in.

_____

Its Retreat Across the Potomac River Cut Off.

_____

TWENTY THOUSAND PRISONERS CAPTURED

_____

One Hundred and Eighteen Guns Taken.

_____

THE REBEL GENERAL LONGSTREET KILLED

_____

DETAILS OF THE THREE DAYS' FIGHTING.

_____

The Most Terrific Combat on Record

_____

Desperate Charges by the Rebel Troops Massed.

_____

OUR TROOPS STAND FIRM AS A ROCK.

_____

The Rebel Assaults Repeatedly Repulsed.

_____

Their Solid Ranks Dashed into Fragments.

_____

STILL THE UNION ARMY STAND FIRM.

_____

The Rebels Pause—Waver—Break and Scatter

_____

A great and Glorious Victory for the Potomac Army.

| **Grant Takes Command** | In 1864 the Union organized for final victory. Lincoln called Grant to Washington and put him in overall command of federal armies. Grant outlined a coordinated Union campaign. In the East he would lead the Army of the Potomac against Lee. From the West William T. Sherman, a trusted subordinate, would press into Georgia.

Grant pushed south in May. In a region of Virginia known as the Wilderness, his army, larger than Lee's, drove relentlessly forward. Repeatedly Lee checked Grant's advance, but the Army of the Potomac did not retreat. After each battle Grant slipped around the Confederate right flank and continued south, never giving Lee the initiative. The brilliant Virginian had no chance to organize one of those counterstrokes that had disrupted previous federal offensives. By the end of June the Confederate troops were bottled up around Richmond. There followed months of siege warfare suggestive of World War I, as Grant gradually squeezed Lee's Army of Northern Virginia.

Simultaneously with Grant's offensive, Sherman began an advance from Tennessee into Georgia. Joseph E. Johnston conducted a skillful retreat, and the invaders did not reach Atlanta until September. At this point Sherman changed the rules. Leaving sufficient troops behind to deal with Johnston, he marched off across Georgia, allowing his men to burn and loot as they went. By marching a federal army unmolested through the heart of the Confederacy, living off the land as it went, he aimed to demonstrate to southerners the futility of continued resistance. Sherman's army reached Savannah in December, leaving a fifty-mile-wide path of destruction in its wake. From there, Sherman slashed northward through the Carolinas, while Johnston tailed him, powerless to intervene. A southerner, Fanny Andrews, wrote:

I used to have some Christian feeling towards Yankees, but now that they have invaded our country and killed so many of our men and desecrated so many homes, I can't believe that when Christ said 'Love your enemies,' he meant Yankees. In another generation or two, this beautiful country of ours will have lost its distinctive civilization and become no better than a nation of Yankee shopkeepers.

Eliza Andrews of Georgia wrote of the "Burnt Country":

The blood-soaked battlefield at Gettysburg after the fighting of July 1, 1863. *(Courtesy, Scribner's Archives)*

December 24, 1864.—About three miles from Sparta [Georgia] we struck the "Burnt Country," as it is well named by the natives, and then I could better understand the wrath and desperation of these poor people. I almost felt as if I should like to hang a Yankee myself. The fields were trampled down and the road was lined with carcasses of horses, hogs, and cattle that the invaders, unable either to consume or to carry away with them, had wantonly shot down, to starve out the people and prevent them from making their crops. The stench in some places was unbearable. . . . The dwellings that were standing all showed signs of pillage, and on every plantation we saw charred remains while here and there lone chimney-stacks, "Sherman's sentinels" told of homes laid in ashes. The infamous wretches! Hay ricks and fodder stacks were demolished, corn-cribs were empty, and every bale of cotton that could be found was burnt by the savages. I saw no grain of any sort, except little patches they had spilled when feeding their horses and there was not even a chicken left in the country to eat.

The Confederacy's end came swiftly in the spring of 1865. With his last supply line threatened, Lee abandoned Richmond. Explosions set off by retreating rebels left the city a "sea of flames." A Union soldier described "a canopy of dense smoke" hanging over the city "lighted up now and then by the bursting shells from the numerous arsenals throughout the city." Grant caught up with him at Appomattox Court House, and on April 9 Lee surrendered his proud but exhausted Army of northern Virginia. Johnston surrendered to Sherman a few days later and the war was over.

Life in the Confederacy

During the rush of enthusiasm following Sumter many southerners rejoiced at the prospect of glory and independence. "I feel as tho' I could live poetry," exclaimed Mrs. Catherine Edmonston, mistress of a North Carolina plantation. But among the South's white population thousands wondered whether their section had not made a colossal mistake.

Even slaveholders had their doubts. One Mississippi planter anticipated the defeat of the Confederacy and saw the time "when the northern soldier would tread her cotton fields, when the slave should be made *free* and the proud southerner stricken to the dust in his presence."

Still more skeptical were large groups of people who owned no slaves. In the mountain backbone that split the older from the newer South, Unionist sentiment smoldered. Virginia's western counties would carry their dissent so far as to secede from "Secessia" and form the state of West Virginia. In eastern Tennessee, western North Carolina, and Kentucky—that state never seceded anyway—thousands of young men joined the Union army. Dissent from the rebellion was not confined to the Appalachian plateau. Wherever small farmers tilled their acres with the sole help of their families or a few hired hands, the Union found favor. In places like northern Louisiana, Alabama, and Mis-

Slaves planting sweet potatoes on James Hopkinson's plantation, Edisto Island, South Carolina, 1862. Though there were no major uprisings, the old slave system began to disintegrate by late 1863 as blacks refused to work for their old masters or simply left the plantations. (*Courtesy, The New-York Historical Society, New York City*)

sissippi, however, Unionist sentiment was more difficult to act on than in the mountains.

For many years after the Civil War southerners with a nostalgic affection for the Confederacy would speak of how loyal slaves had been to their southern masters. When southern white men were off fighting Yankees and blacks had a chance to revolt, they remained at their jobs, providing the Confederacy with its food and manufactured goods. This romantic image of contented and loyal slaves is only partly accurate. The experience of the Pryor family of Georgia furnishes an example. In 1861 Shepard G. Pryor went off to fight, leaving his wife in charge of his farm and his thirteen slaves. Mrs. Pryor chose as her overseer a white man who had no control over the slaves. Eventually she made a crucial decision to appoint one of her slaves, Will, as overseer. The choice was fateful for the Pryors' corner of the slave system. For a while Will performed as his mistress wished, and he successfully managed the 1862 crop harvest. But soon Will was hiding slave runaways and in general refusing to cooperate with the slave system. The authorities finally arrested him for sheltering slave fugitives. By late 1863 the slave system was disintegrating in many parts of the South. Nowhere was there a major slave uprising, but black people were helping to pull the system apart in other ways. Whenever rumors spread of Yankee troops nearby the slaves of the neighborhood would desert the plantations in droves. Many of those who remained became disobedient and refused to work. One elderly slave was overjoyed when freedom came. She "dropped her hoe" and shouted at her mistress: "I'm free! Ain't got to work for you no more! You can't [sell me] now!"

| **Economic Problems** | Life in the Confederacy after the early months of enthusiasm was difficult for everybody. The southern economy was not suited for swift adaptation to war production. Most southern railroads were short lines; the rail system consisted of eleven different gauges, which meant that a railroad car fitted for one gauge would have to confine itself to

---

ONE SOUTHERNER'S DIARY ENTRIES, *for 1861 and 1865, tell the course of war:*

Saturday, July 13, 1861   Events transcending in importance anything that has ever happened within the recollection of any living person in *our* country, have occurred since I have written last in my Journal. Since then *War* has been declared. Our ministers sent North to negotiate terms of peace have been treated with cool indifference. Our forts are still retained with the exception of Sumter. *There* the ever memorable victory was achieved which added fresh laurels to the glory of the gallant little state of South Carolina. Never shall I forget the state of intense excitement which pervaded the city of Augusta when it was announced that the fight was going on down at Sumter. Pa went down to Charleston just in time to witness from the top of the Charleston Hotel, the whole proceeding of the bombardment. It is needless to account the gallant achievement of Wigfall and others or to note the additional honour acquired by Gen Beauregard. . . .

*   *   *

Wednesday, March 29, 1865   I know I will regret hereafter that I have made no record of time and events which are fraught with so much interest, record of events which are hourly making history—but I cannot. I shrink from the task. At times I feel as if I was drifting on, on, ever onward to be at last dashed against some rock and I shut my eyes and almost wish it was over, the shock encountered and I prepared to know what destiny awaits me. I am tired, oh so tired of this war. I want to breathe free. I feel the restraint of the blockade and as port after port becomes blockaded, I feel shut up, pent up and am irresistibly reminded of the old story of the iron shroud contracting more and more each hour, each moment. I live too fast. A strange contradiction, yet true. A life of emotion, quick rapid succession of startling events will wear upon the constitution and weaken the physical nature. I may perhaps be glad hereafter that I have lived through this war but now the height of my ambition is to be *quiet*. . . .

some portion of the tracks; and there was not enough railway equipment. The South in 1861 did only a fifth of the whole nation's manufacturing, and it lacked the knowledge and technology necessary for quick growth. By the award of generous contracts, the Confederate and state governments gave their encouragement to industries such as textiles and iron, and by the end of the war Atlanta had become a considerable industrial center. But some manufacturers had to be satisfied with makeshifts, such as lard in place of grease and cloths soaked in linseed oil as a substitute for machine belts. The Confederacy had to import much of its arms and civilian goods, slipping a large portion of them through the Union blockade. To support itself the Confederate government turned to "tithing in kind," collecting from farmers one-tenth of their produce in certain crops, and printed great amounts of paper money that worsened inflation. Shortages and, by the last years of the war, invasion and the sense of defeat were the lot of the rebel population.

The price of flour in Richmond more than doubled in the first year of the war. Soap, made from scarce animal fat, went up a thousand percent in price. Imported coffee, selling for twelve cents a pound before the war, went to five dollars by 1863. In late December 1863 some Richmond prices in Confederate money were: apples, $65 to $75 a barrel; onions, $30 a barrel; Irish potatoes, $6 to $9 a bushel; sugar, $3.50 a pound; and eggs, $3 a dozen. Worst of all to one young soldier stationed at the Confederate capital was the price of whiskey. "It would cost about fifty Dollars to get tight here," he wrote his family in 1863.

At times essential commodities were unavailable at any price. Shortages were more common in the cities, swollen with war refugees and soldiers, than in the countryside. One southern woman, Margaret Preston, wrote in her diary:

April 3d, 1862: . . .
Darkness seems gathering over the southern land; disaster follows disaster; where is it all to end? My very soul is sick of carnage. I loathe the word —*War*. It is destroying and paralyzing all before it. Our schools are closed—all the able-bodied men gone—stores shut up, or only here and there one open; goods not to be bought, or so exorbitant that we are obliged to do without.

Sept. 4th: The worst has happened—our fearful suspense is over: Willy, the gentle, tender-hearted, brave boy, lies in a soldier's grave on the Plains of Manassas! This has been a day of weeping and of woe to this household. I did not know how I loved the dear boy. My heart is wrung with grief to think that his sweet face, his genial smile, his sympathetic heart are gone. My eyes ache with weeping. . . . Oh! his precious stricken Father! God support him to bear the blow! . . . Alas! the beloved son has been five days in his grave. My poor husband! Oh! if he were only here, to groan out his anguish on my bosom. I can't write more.

In the spring of 1863, three hundred Richmond women, some brandishing revolvers and others bowie knives, attacked the city's business district demanding affordable food. The riot soon got out of hand and the women looted the jewelry and clothing stores before they were stopped. And even in the country districts food and clothing shortages provoked direct action. In 1863 fourteen women armed with "guns, pistols, knives, and tongues" attacked a mill near Thomasville, Georgia, and seized a large supply of flour.

War transformed the lives of southern white women. They were often fiery Confederate patriots. It has been said that young southern belles, by favoring army volunteers and shunning young men who avoided the war, were the most effective recruiters for the Confederate army. Southern women of the middle and upper classes had always managed large households. As the war progressed, their administrative skills were put to running the plantations and businesses their husbands had left behind. Wives of ordinary farmers, too, took over managerial duties. The Confederate Treasury hired hundreds of women clerks. Women found jobs in the South's factories or worked in Confederate hospitals. Few of these gains lasted beyond the war, but they demonstrated what women were capable of and foreshadowed expanded opportunities in later generations.

States' rights, the doctrine upon which the Confederacy had been founded, was no help in wartime. Several governors, notably Joseph E. Brown of Georgia and Zebulon Vance of North Carolina, showed a narrow jealousy of every exercise of Confederate power. They developed revenue programs of their own and obstructed Confederate tax collections in their states. They retained control of state troops and even prevented them from leaving the state. In Georgia, men who wished to escape Confederate service could do so by enlisting in the state militia. Governor Vance hoarded food and supplies for North Carolina troops that Lee's starving army at Richmond desperately needed.

Ultimately the Confederate government resorted to measures of centralization that amounted to a revolution within a revolution. Davis declared martial law in "disloyal" areas. The Confederate Congress authorized the first thorough military draft on the North American continent. Richmond took an increasingly active role in the southern economy, impressing food supplies from farmers, building factories to produce critical war materials, commandeering space on blockade runners for essential imports. In 1865 the Confederate government reached the ultimate measure of centralization when it got authority to take black men into the army.

Life in the Union

Initially the northern economy faltered as businessmen, fearful of disruption and disorder, sought to call in debts. In many northern cities, especially New York, Chicago, and Cincinnati, the loss of southern customers disrupted the economy. Some economic historians claim that on the whole the Civil War slowed economic growth. Yet the newspapers of the day suggest that, after the middle of 1862, the Union experienced an economic boom. The draining of men into the military left shortages of labor. On some farms women filled in. The North, however, had more machines than the South with which to replace manpower; during the years from 1860 to 1865 the McCormick Reaper Company received more orders for its harvesting machines than it could fill. The continuing influx of immigrants, almost half a million during the war years, relieved labor shortages in the cities. The demand for war supplies invigorated the northern economy, already fitted for manufacturing. Factories hummed and wages rose. Farmers benefited from the increase in demand in food. The effect of the war on the economy of the North was quite the opposite from the effect in the South, where invasion unsettled the normal pattern of production and trade and the blockade broke commerce with Europe.

Still, the Union had an inflation rate only slightly less staggering than that of the Confederacy. The policy of financing the war by a combination of heavy borrowing and paper money was a cause; so was the scarcity of labor that machines and immigrants only partially offset. And the wartime prosperity bestowed itself unevenly. While consumer prices had risen by 1865 between seventy-five and a hundred percent, the wages of skilled workers went up during the same period about sixty percent, and those of common laborers rose just under fifty percent. Meanwhile the business and professional classes crowded Broadway in New York, Michigan Avenue in Chicago and Pennsylvania Avenue in Cincinnati, buying at the fashionable shops, attending the theaters, and dining at the fancy restaurants. Some of these people were profiteers who had made a good thing out of the swelling orders from the War and Navy Departments and the flow of greenback currency. Charging the government high prices for desperately needed supplies, some profiteers also provided uniforms and shoes that disintegrated at the first heavy rain, powder that would not explode, and beef, pork, and flour that were inedible.

In the Army

The Civil War sorely tested the American traditions of individualism and provincialism. In the beginning men on both sides enlisted in local regiments raised by the state governors. Each regiment wore its own uniform and many elected their own officers, a practice that discouraged strict discipline. Gradually all this changed. The national governments took over many duties of recruitment and the appointment of officers. Standardized uniforms were introduced. Drill and discipline tightened. The sons of a raw-boned democracy slowly adjusted to become cogs in a larger machine. At the same time

Prisoners from the Front, by Winslow Homer. Union and Confederate soldiers respected each other's fighting abilities, but prison conditions for those captured were brutal. *(Courtesy, The Metropolitan Museum of Art. Gift of Mrs. Frank B. Porter, 1922.)*

they accustomed themselves to a world beyond their own communities. Their care and feeding became increasingly the responsibility of central governments or national organizations like the United States Sanitary Commission, a forerunner of the Red Cross. Along with the Union victory, the experience of army life could contribute to the nationalist element in American civilization that has struggled to maintain itself against the pull of loyalty to region, state, or locality.

At the same time that the armies were taking American farmboys and town dwellers away from their familiar surroundings, they were also pulling in thousands of immigrants. The Union army especially spoke with many tongues, and in that sense represented what American cities were and would increasingly become in the years after the victory of the Union. But one common experience was firsthand observation of former ill-treated slaves. One northerner wrote in his diary:

> Some of them were scarred from head to foot where they had been whipped. One man's back

was nearly all one scar, as if the skin had been chopped up and left to heal in ridges. Another had scars on the back of his neck, and from that all the way to his heels every little ways; but that was not such a sight as the one with the great solid mass of ridges, from his shoulders to his hips. That beat all the antislavery sermons ever yet preached.

Patriotic Gore Of about two million federal troops, 360,000 died. Among the more than one million who at some time served in the Confederate military, about 250,000 never came back. Only one in three of these died of battle wounds; the others succumbed to disease or accident. There were also about a half million wounded, many of them severely maimed.

During the Civil War, a conflict more dangerous for participants than many wars that had preceded and that have followed, infantry weapons became highly destructive while infantry tactics continued to follow older concepts. Many soldiers carried rifles rather than smooth-bore muskets. These hurled a lead ball for hundreds of yards with deadly accuracy. Yet until the very end of the war commanders on both sides frequently ordered their men to charge the enemy across open fields as if the older, less accurate musket opposed them. Toward the end of the war attackers had to face the fast-firing breechloaders with which more and more soldiers were being equipped.

If a man were wounded his chance for survival was not very good. Nothing was known about infectious bacteria, and military surgeons performed operations without sanitary precautions. Soldiers contracted gangrene and other deadly infections. Though anesthetics were known, doctors did not always have them on hand, and shock, followed by death, was often the consequence of major surgery. Long delays occurred in getting the casualties to medical aid stations or hospitals. Following the battle of Seven Pines in mid-1862, wounded federal soldiers were carried to the rear for shipment to the hospitals around Washington. The trains were slow to arrive, a sensitive observer noted, and the men

> lay by the hundreds on either side of the railway track . . . exposed to the drenching rain . . . shivering from the cold, calling for water, food, and dressings . . . the most heart-rending spectacle. Many died from exposure, others prayed for death to release them from their anguish.

Soldiers soon lost their sense of the romance of war. A North Carolina volunteer wrote home in 1862:

> The dirt of a camp life knocks all its poetry into a cocked hat. . . . We had no tents after the 6th of August, but slept on the ground, in the woods or open fields, without regard to the weather. . . . I learned to eat fat bacon raw, and to like it. . . . Without time to wash our clothes or our persons, and sleeping on the ground all huddled together, the whole army became lousy more or less with body lice.

In every part of the battlefront were mosquitoes, lice, and biting flies, which helps to explain the high incidence of malaria and other diseases. Heat in the deep South and cold, particularly in the mountain areas and the upper South, afflicted the soldiers. Wool uniforms were standard year-round issue and soldiers of both armies simply shed as much as they could during the summer. If northern troops were often overdressed, rebels were often half naked. As the Union blockade took hold and internal transport broke down, Confederate soldiers found it difficult to get replacements for worn or torn uniforms. Many ended up wearing homemade garments sent by relatives and friends. Others relied on captured Yankee shoes and other clothes. Especially serious was the shortage of boots and shoes. In the last winter of the war the troops accompanying General J. B. Hood on his campaign through Tennessee often marched barefoot through snow and sleet. The path of Hood's army, it was said, was marked by a trail of blood.

Few Union soldiers went hungry, but the diet of salt pork, bread, and coffee undermined health. The Confederate soldier's standard diet consisted of bacon, cornmeal, and coffee—when he could get them. Coffee, an imported item that had run the Union blockade, went quickly; the bacon lasted longer, but it, too, was often in short supply and southern troops supplemented their meat rations with cuts of mule, horse, racoon, and bear. Sometimes Confederates were reduced to consuming little more than parched corn. Chewing the grains, reported one southern soldier, was "hard work"; it made "the jaws ache and the gums so sore as to cause unendurable pain."

During the Civil War, as during the Revolution, both sides required the mobilization of society as a whole in the service of the war effort. But the Civil War reflected social and economic changes that would also influence the nature of the civilian contribution. The nursing of soldiers acquired a far more organized and professional character. Under the auspices of the United States Sanitary Commission, Dorothea Dix organized nursing services for the Union side. In the early months of the war, Ladies Aid Societies sprang up throughout the North to provide volunteer services for soldiers, including sewing, assembling food, clothing, and supplies, and providing communication between soldiers and their families. These societies eventually joined in a unified national institution. But, as Clara Barton wrote, they fell far short of their goal. After the Battle of the Wilderness, she attended the wounded in Fredericksburg:

> I saw, crowded into one old sunken hotel, lying helpless upon its bare, wet, bloody floors, 500 fainting men hold up their cold, bloodless, dingy hands, as I passed, and beg me in Heaven's name for a cracker to keep them from starving (and I had none); or to give them a cup that they might have

something to drink water from, if they could get it (and I had no cup, and could get none).

In the South, comparable societies remained local, volunteer efforts. Southern women nursed the wounded soldiers of the Confederacy in what were frequently makeshift hospitals. The growing professionalization of the federal government during the war years resulted in the hiring of the first female government clerks.

At the beginning of the war, North and South had relied on volunteers and militia. In time, both sides resorted to a draft. The Union conscription law permitted a draftee to find a substitute. He could also make a payment in place of service; that feature drew charges that the law favored the wealthy. In neither North nor South was conscription popular. In 1863 an antidraft riot broke out among the Irish in New York City. The rioters lynched several blacks and burned a black orphanage, and federal troops had to be called. But volunteers continued to come in; the large bounty the Union offered was an inducement, as was the threat of the draft. And in time, as black soldiers proved themselves on the battlefield, according to one account, attitudes in New York changed:

> Eight months ago the African race in this City were literally hunted down like wild beasts. They were shot down in cold blood, or stoned to death, or hung to the trees or to the lamp-posts. . . . How astonishingly has all this been changed! The same men who could not have shown themselves in the most obscure street in the City without peril of instant death, even though in the most suppliant attitude, now march in solid platoons, with shouldered muskets, slung knapsacks, and buckled cartridge boxes down through the gayest avenues and busiest thoroughfares to the pealing strains of martial music, and everywhere are saluted with waving handkerchiefs, with descending flowers, and with the acclimations and plaudits of countless beholders.

While it was not until the South was badly in need of additional troops at almost the end of the war that the Confederacy contemplated the recruitment of blacks, the Union was accepting them as early as 1862. Earlier Lincoln's government had held back, fearing that the presence of black soldiers would seem to indicate that the war was not only for restoration of the Union but for the abolition of slavery. The acceptance of black volunteers, from both the North and the South, came at the urging of black leaders and white abolitionists, and by the end of the war, blacks composed about a tenth of the army and a fourth of the navy. For most of the war, black privates got three dollars a month less than whites. Some were relegated to labor units. Some Confederate commanders declared a policy of putting black prisoners into slavery or of killing them. But in combat the black soldiers won the respect of their officers, both northern and southern, and helped to discredit further the remnants of the slave system. As one officer wrote of his black comrades:

> No officer in this regiment now doubts that the key to the successful prosecution of this war lies in the unlimited employment of black troops. Their superiority lies simply in the fact that they know the country, while white troops do not, and, moreover, that they have peculiarities of temperament, position, and motive which belong to them alone. Instead of leaving their homes and families to fight they are fighting for their homes and families, and they show the resolution and the sagacity which a personal purpose gives.

Not all northerners were so kindly disposed toward blacks. One New England soldier said only "I'm fightin' for $14 a month and the Union."

The War and Civil Liberties

In the extraordinary danger that the nation faced at the time of the war, free civil institutions continued in the North and for the most part in the border states. Lincoln's government did not attempt in any major and consistent way to put those institutions aside. But it was conscious that disruption or demoralization among the people in the regions loyal to the Union could bring to the Confederates the victory that they were not far from achieving.

Lincoln suspended the writ of *habeas corpus*—the power of a court to have a prisoner brought before it—in cases in which an individual was suspected of illegal disruptions of the war effort. The suspension meant that the federal government could hold people for long periods without trial. Despite protests, Lincoln in the autumn of 1862 issued a proclamation subjecting to martial law and to trial in military tribunals anyone who discouraged others from enlisting or committed any disloyal act. The War Department in the course of the conflict arrested at least thirteen thousand people, most of whom never came to trial.

The chief northern political opponents of the conduct of the war were the Peace Democrats, or Copperheads, as supporters of the war called them. The most prominent of the Peace Democrats was Clement Vallandigham of Ohio, who insisted that the war was strengthening the central government at the expense of civil liberties. Vallandigham called for "the Constitution as it is, the Union as it was." In 1862 he was defeated for reelection to Congress. He continued his attacks on the war and after General Ambrose Burnside arrested him in 1863, a military tribunal sentenced him to prison for its duration. The affair was an assault on the constitutional right of free speech; protest was widespread, and the situation was a political danger to the administration. To deflect the issue, Lincoln by use of his executive power banished Vallandigham to the Confederacy. But the Ohioan returned to the North and kept up his criticisms. The administration now left him alone. Vallandigham tried to get the Supreme Court to consider his claim that the government had acted unconstitutionally. The Court in 1864 ruled in *ex parte Vallandigham* that it had no jurisdiction over the proceedings of military tribunals. In 1866, however, the Supreme Court did find the methods of the war administration to have been unconstitutional. In *ex parte Milligan* the Court held that martial law and the subjection of civilians to military trials were illegal when the civil courts were open and in full operation.

Emancipation

At the beginning of the war the federal government was careful to insist that it was fighting only to preserve the Union and not to free the slaves. The war, said a resolution adopted by Congress, was not for "overthrowing or interfering with the rights or established institutions" of the seceded states. The government wanted to convince those proslavery southerners who were prepared to be sympathetic to the Unionist cause that the institution of slavery was not in danger. But it is reasonable to suppose that something beyond mere political strategy lay behind the caution of the President and Congress about interfering with slavery. Neither Lincoln nor most of the national legislators had been abolitionists; and however distasteful slavery may have been to much of the government, the slave system was so firmly established, and so hedged with legal protections, that even opponents might have had doubts about the sudden military abolition of slavery. Politicians and statesmen, like the rest of humankind, are hesitant to imagine any workable society that is far different from whatever one they are accustomed to. It took time and the events of the war to make the government see the tangible possibility of wiping out slavery at a stroke.

General John C. Frémont issued a military order freeing the slaves in Missouri, but Lincoln modified Frémont's order. He did, however, ask Congress in 1862 to grant federal funds to any state adopting a scheme of emancipation. Though Congress did not respond, it declared in the Second Confiscation Act of 1862 that wherever the Union army was in control, all slaves owned by rebels would be free. The Act was both a substantial measure and a somewhat limited one. It did not apply to slaves held by southern Unionists. But the Second Confiscation Act signified that Union politicians were losing their timidity about abolishing slavery, and the very existence of the Act must have provided a certain momentum toward abolition. Abolitionists meanwhile were urging a wider policy of emancipation. Such a policy, moreover, could have desirable diplomatic effects. The apparent success of the South in maintaining its independence, and the advantage that European countries might gain from a dividing of the United States, raised the danger that they might recognize the Confederacy as

Lincoln and his son, Robert Todd. *(Courtesy, Library of Congress)*

a sovereign nation, which would greatly weaken the Union effort. Lincoln believed that if European nations could see the war as a struggle not merely between Union and secession but between freedom and slavery, they would be less likely to recognize the slave republic. And while Lincoln had not been an abolitionist, he had been a free soiler and a moral opponent of slavery. Surely his conscience welcomed the decision toward which political considerations were pushing him.

| The Emancipation Proclamation | The Union victory of Antietam gave Lincoln the opportunity to issue in |

The Emancipation Proclamation The Union victory of Antietam gave Lincoln the opportunity to issue in September 1862 a preliminary Emancipation Proclamation, announcing that as of January 1, 1863, all slaves in those regions still in rebellion on that date would be free. Lincoln was offering to secessionists an alternative to loss of their slaves: they could voluntarily bring their communities back into the Union. The Emancipation Proclamation itself, issued on January 1, carried out the terms of the preliminary proclamation: it declared that all slaves in areas still in rebellion were "then, thenceforward, and forever free." Lincoln was drawing on the power he possessed as Commander-in-Chief; the Proclamation was essentially a military order, on somewhat the same principle as the instructions an officer might give his troops for the treatment of citizens and property. The Emancipation Proclamation, like the Second Confiscation Act, was of sharply limited scope; it freed no slaves immediately because it did not apply to the border states or to regions already under Union control. But it was understood at the time, as it has been understood ever since, as the great symbolic moral action of the war, a public statement, in however confined a form, that the war was now for freedom. After the preliminary Proclamation the military had begun seriously taking in black volunteers. It was a logical consequence of the events of the Civil War that in 1865 the nation adopted the Thirteenth Amendment outlawing slavery.

Congress contained a variety of opinions on racial matters. At one extreme were several Democrats reluctant to make changes in existing institutions. At the other extreme, as the war progressed, was a small but important group of Republicans who wanted the strongest possible policy of abolition and of protection for the rights of the freed slaves. Within this faction ideas emerged for going beyond emancipation and bringing about changes in the social and economic condition of black Americans. Congress in the course of the war repealed a law prohibiting blacks from carrying the mail and a ban on testimony of black witnesses in federal court, outlawed slavery in the territories, and established a scheme for emancipation in the District of Columbia that would provide compensation to the slaveholders. Blacks were allowed in places from which they had once been excluded: the congressional visitors gallery, lectures at the Smithsonian Institution. Some states got rid of a number of discriminating laws. The country was taking some halting steps beyond emancipation and toward equality or at least a concept of justice.

Politics and Legislation

The successful waging of the war required that Lincoln have as much popular support as he could get. In his 1864 reelection campaign he ran not as a Republican but as the candidate of a coalition of Republicans and Democratic supporters of the war, which called itself the Union Party. The vice-presidential candidate of the party was Andrew Johnson, a Tennessee Democrat who had remained loyal to the Union. The presidential candidate of the regular Democratic party was General McClellan. McClellan, who had been commander of the Union armies, was loyal to the war effort, and in effect he rejected his party's pronouncement that the war was a failure. By the time of the campaign and election the war had been going so successfully for the North that Lincoln's victory was assured.

While the winning of the war was the most important objective for the Republicans, they were committed also to an entire political, social, and economic policy within which the emancipation of the slaves and the preservation of the Union were elements. Before the Civil War much of the antislavery movement had also wanted a more vigorous national government working for the achievement of an advanced industrial and agricultural economy. Some Americans had possessed a vision of what a powerful American economy and society might be: an industrialized Northeast trading its manufactured goods for the produce of a great agricultural West. The federal government, these people believed, should stimulate eastern manufactures through a protective tariff, populate the agrarian West by giving government lands to settlers, and

M. B. Leisser, *Libby Prison, Richmond, Virginia* (*Courtesy, Museum of Fine Arts, Boston*)

tie together the two regions by a railroad system built with federal aid. Northern politicians who thought this way could wish to exclude slavery from the territories not only because they genuinely disliked slavery on moral grounds but also because they desired that the western lands be reserved for free American farmers. And in the years before the Civil War they clashed with the South on other political issues: the southern cotton interest opposed a protective tariff, wanting instead to bring manufactured goods more cheaply from Europe, and resisted the construction of a northern railroad from East to West, holding out for a southern route. It is fitting that political circumstances put the Republicans in command of the war for the saving of the Union; for the Union came to mean strong central government presiding over a vast and economically progressive nation, while secession would have broken the country into weaker republics. It is fitting

also that the Republicans became the champions of federally enforced emancipation.

Wartime Legislation In 1861, just before Lincoln's inauguration, Congress passed the Morrill Tariff, a protectionist measure putting duties to the levels they had been at in 1846; and later the national legislature raised duties higher. The war put a strain on the system of banking and currency. In response, Congress reformed the system in a way that agreed with the Republican concept of strong government in the service of a national economy. The National Banking Acts of 1863 and 1864 provided that, in return for investing one-third of their capital in federal banks, private banks could issue national bank notes that would serve as paper money: these could be in amounts up to ninety percent of the market value of the securities the banks had purchased from the government. The notes of state banks, which had circulated as a form of money, were unstable and injured the economy; in order to suppress them, Congress later placed a ten percent tax on the notes of all institutions that did not take part in the national bank system.

The Republican idea of supplying federal lands for settlers triumphed in the Homestead Act of 1862. A settler who filed a claim to a quarter-section of one hundred and sixty acres of federal land and lived on it for five years would get ownership of it after payment of a small fee. The act permitted single women as well as men to file a claim. In practice, women alone, or even women with children, had great difficulty in sustaining their claims. Men needed the assistance of a woman as much as women needed the assistance of a man, but when men and women settled together in a family unit, the man invariably held title to the claim and officially directed its operation. Nor did the law permit married couples to file claims. Later in the century considerable amounts of the land went to timber and mining companies that had employees put in claims for homesteads. But at the time of the adoption of the act, there was some expectation that it would pull

labor from the East to the free lands; and in face of the labor shortage that the war was bringing about, Congress authorized immigration of contract workers from Europe and the Orient, permitting employers who paid the laborers' passage to deduct that cost from the pay.

Congress made another use of federal lands. The Morrill Land Grant Act of 1862 offered lands to states that in return would finance colleges offering schooling in agriculture, engineering, and military science. It was a less dramatic measure than others of these wartime years, but a significant one: it made the national government a partner to modern technical education.

The absence of legislators from the deep South made it easier for Congress during the war to adopt a scheme for a transcontinental railway running through the middle of the country, from Omaha to California. Southerners would have fought for a more southern road. During the 1860s the national legislature granted to railroad developers thirty million acres of federal land and made them large loans. It was one of the first of many extensive projects in which the government has joined with business.

Points To Think About

1. Who was John Brown? And what did he hope to accomplish? According to Brown's own account, the raid was designed to demonstrate to the South the necessity of emancipation. He and his small band would seize the arsenal. They would arm nearby slaves and lead them into the hills. From there they would stage periodic raids. Slaveholders would be forced to recognize that they could not crush Brown's guerrillas and so could not protect their slave property. They would be forced to turn to emancipation. That was the idea. It explains Brown's famous remark that he once fancied slavery could be ended without the shedding of "very much" blood. Once Brown took the arsenal, however, he made no move to put the rest of his plan into effect. He simply stayed at Harpers Ferry. It was as if he were waiting to be captured. When Virginian forces arrived, Brown fought as though eager to die in battle. Instead he was wounded, captured, and held for trial. His remarkable composure during and after his trial also

suggested to some that he was seeking death. What did motivate this unusual man?

We know that Brown was intensely religious, that he had learned from his father to shoulder heavy responsibilities and that, until the panic of 1837, he had been a moderately successful businessman as well as the conscientious father of a large family. Brown went bankrupt in the panic and never again managed to succeed in business. For fifteen years he struggled through one unhappy enterprise after another. Meanwhile he had to feed his family. Brown's first wife died, and one of his children accidentally scalded another to death. Brown's life during these years, in fact, reads like the Book of Job.

It may be that Brown found in antislavery militancy a sense of redemption. It certainly redeemed him from having to continue his unavailing efforts to reestablish himself in business. And it released him from the terrible responsibilities of caring for his family. Brown had taken these responsibilities very seriously and the frustration of being unable to meet them for so long a time might have been more than he could bear.

However all of that may be, it is striking that once embarked upon his abolitionist activities Brown was downright reckless with the lives of his sons and sons-in-law. In the failure of his raid on Harpers Ferry he found a success so vast that it made up for all his other failures. His manner of death made him a martyr in the North. And this did what all of his years of business activity could not. It moved wealthy supporters to step forward and guarantee the decent living for his family.

John Brown may have been both madman and saint. And he may also have been a victim of the American competitive system, who found in religious fanaticism a way of escaping from the rat-race.

2. Did states have a right to secede? The South, of course, claimed and the federal government denied that right.

The two positions, though irreconcilable, were at least clear. They remained clear through the first several years of the fighting. The North sought to impose a total blockade on all shipping entering or leaving southern ports—an act contrary to international law if the South was a separate nation, but permissible if it was only a rebellious province. Hence the Lincoln Administration continued to argue that secession was not possible under the Constitution and that the southern states were still legally part of the Union. southerners, for their part, continued to argue the opposite.

Yet as the prospects of a northern victory grew brighter, the constitutional waters grew muddier. The North intended to exact certain concessions from the southern states before letting them back into the Union. But if, as the North argued, the South had never legally left the Union, there was no need to readmit it. Nor was there a legal basis for demanding concession. The southern states, though their citizens had been in rebellion, had remained states in the Union, completely entitled to resume their old seats in Congress and their other constitutional privileges. It would be, curiously enough, the southern doctrine of secession that at the end of the war left the South in the worse legal position. If the South had in fact seceded, if it had been for these four years of carnage an independent republic, then after its surrender, it would be no more than a conquered land, subject to the conqueror.

Northern politicians devised doctrines that would describe what the southern states had done and would entitle the North to reconstruct them as the price of their readmission. Plainly, the North wished to treat the Confederate states as if they had seceded, even though the claim of the North during the war had been that secession was legally impossible and nonexistent. Southerners were quick to seize upon the obvious contradictions between the new formulations and the North's original view.

Lincoln, for his part, avoided elaborate constitutional theorizing. The southern states, he held, had disrupted the normal relations between themselves and the Union. The task was to "restore" those normal relations.

The legal issues never were sorted out. Instead the nation adopted the Thirteenth, Fourteenth, and Fifteenth Amendments. They at least make it clear that secession would be unconstitutional in the future.

3. Lee's strategy of defending Virginia before all else was one of the fatal flaws in the Confederate military strategy. The South could have fought a defensive, guerrilla war of attrition of the sort Washington had waged against the British. But Washington's strategy, which was designed not to defeat the British in open battle but to prevent them from gaining secure control of the countryside, required him to sacrifice a good deal of territory including such prizes as New York and, for a time, Philadelphia. In the Civil War a similar strategy would have involved sacrificing much of Virginia including, in all probability, Richmond. It would, in fact, have run against the very reason people like Lee supported the Confederacy in the first place. His goal, after all, was the preservation of Virginia, and it led him to try to defend every inch of her soil. Despite Lee's tactical brilliance, it was a strategy doomed to defeat in the long run because it involved too many open battles with the stronger Union forces.

Lee's strategy, moreover, faithfully reflected the spirit of secession; its failure mirrored the failure of the Confederacy as a whole. The secessionists were dedicated to their individual states. The resulting states' rights philosophy made it impossible for them to make the kinds of national decisions waging a successful war requires. The very ideas that had led to secession also led, in the long run, to a northern victory.

4. The predominant public image of Lincoln is that of the Great Emancipator. But the Emancipation Proclamation did not free the slaves. The Thirteenth Amendment did that. What the Proclamation did was provide the states still in rebellion (portions of several had been recaptured) with one hundred days to return peacefully to the Union. The penalty was that those remaining in the Confederacy would suffer the loss of their slaves. But first the Union armies had to reconquer the territory. So it is accurate to say that the Proclamation did not really free anyone.

Lincoln's Proclamation, then, signaled a crucial change in the Union's war aims. It had begun the war with the simple intent of putting down the rebellion (as it saw secession). Lincoln made it clear he would respect the "peculiar institution" wher-ever it legally existed. But as the war dragged on, and the toll of dead and wounded rose ever higher, Lincoln—and the Union—came to think of the war as a great moral crusade. By the time of his second inaugural address (one of the few master-pieces by an American president), Lincoln had come to view the terrible suffering of the war as a punishment from God for the national sin of slav-ery. The war was no longer simply to restore the union. Now it was also to free the slaves. The Emancipation Proclamation was a turning point in this process.

Suggested Readings

Among recent works on the Civil War era are Richard Beringer et al., *Why the South Lost the Civil War* (1980), Philip Paludan, *"A People's Contest": The Union and the Civil War* (1988), Frederick Blue, *Salmon P. Chase* (1987), Gerard Linderman, *Embattled Courage: The Experience of Combat in the American Civil War* (1987), John M. Priest, *Antietam* (1989), and Drew Faust, *The Creation of Confederate Nationalism* (1988).

A standard work on the era is James G. Randall and David Donald, *The Civil War and Reconstruction* (revised 1973). James McPherson presents an excellent guide to the period in *Ordeal by Fire: The Civil War and Reconstruction* (1982), while all of Bruce Catton's books make beautiful reading. Emory L. Thomas analyzes *The Confederate Nation* (1979). For biographies of the Union and Confederate leaders, see Stephen B. Oates's *With Malice Toward None* (1978) and Clement Eaton's *Jefferson Davis* (1977). Two major books on the response of intellectuals to the war are George Fredrickson, *The Inner Civil War: northern Intellectuals and the Crisis of the Union* (1965) and Daniel Aaron, *The Unwritten War: American Writers and the Civil War* (1973). Robert Manson Myers, ed., *The Children of Pride: A True Story of Georgia and the Civil War* (1972), presents history in the first person; this collection of the letters of a Georgia planter's family gives us its religious sentiments and attitudes toward human property, the day-to-day demands of running a plantation, and the dissolution of a way of life.

FORREST McDONALD

Slavery was an abomination, and one way or another it had to go. That is self-evident. It is not self-evident that only a great civil war could have eliminated it. The conscience and the whole social structure of the nineteenth century were pressing it toward obsolescence. Nor, in the early days of the war, was the Union fighting for the abolition of slavery. On a completely different issue, the South was mainly in the right. That is the issue of nationalism.

Southern public opinion held that each of the seceding states had the legal right to leave the Union. For this belief the South had a good case. It is at least as defensible to claim, as secessionists argued, that the Constitution had been a pact among sovereign republics, each retaining the right to withdraw from the pact, as it is to insist, with Unionists, that a single American nation had ratified the Constitution. But this question is secondary.

The more important point is that at the time of secession a working majority of the public and the new Confederacy (that public, to be sure, excluded the slaves) wished to be separate from the North, either state by state or as a republic embracing all the seceding states. Southern culture was separate from that of the North; and distinctiveness of culture is a splendid basis of nationhood.

Ours is a time when the peoples of Africa and Asia enjoy the dignity of their independence from their former imperial masters, who now acknowledge the justice of that independence. It is a time for celebrating the new freedom of eastern Europe from Soviet domination, and the increasing self-assertion of republics and ethnicities that had been included within the monstrosity that is the Soviet Union. Our century therefore has an obligation to respect the southern struggle for the rights of free and independent nationality, in the conflict that southerners have liked to call not the Civil War but the War Betweeen the States. That the southern culture fighting for its nationhood contained slavery is not in itself sufficient ground for rejecting southern independence, unless every claimant to nationhood be examined for noxious elements in its culture: an examination to which few countries would find it wise to submit.

I am not contending that southern independence would have been a good. I like the United States as it is or could be, and see it as a more creative and productive entity than its two separate segments could have been. But this is to speak only of the utilitarian benefits that came of the northern victory, and I must say that these benefits have been gained at the expense of a certain justice.

Union vs Secession ☆ ☆ ☆

EUGENE D. GENOVESE

It is a mistake common among champions of nationalism to use the concepts "freedom" and "right" as though they could apply not only to individuals but to regions, cultures, or peoples. Freedom, if it has any meaning, is something that an individual possesses. The same is true of rights. And there is not a shred of reason to believe that the "freedom" of a nation, or an ethnic group, or a region to express its collective self reinforces the freedom of individuals. It is just as likely that a great number of individuals within the group or nation concerned will surrender their intelligence, their judgment, their independence of character—in short, their real freedom—to group emotions, while minorities will suffer from the bigotry of the "free" majority.

Our defender of secession invites us to celebrate the new assertiveness of the republics and ethnic nationalities within the Soviet Union. It should, in fact, trouble any friend of freedom to observe how little interest in individual freedom the secessionist ethnicities within the Union of Soviet Republics are displaying, at least in their public rhetoric. The disintegration of a repressive ideology and bureaucracy that for seven decades had betrayed the original promise of socialism raised great hopes. Instead, the newly-revived nationalities rejoice in their new freedom to hate their ethnic rivals.

All this applies specifically to the case of the secessionist South. It took an invasion from the outside to free the slaves. Even for a century after the victory of the Union, the white South possessed sufficient cohesion—or, if you will, collective "freedom"—to suppress the rights of black southerners. Another invasion from the outside, this time in the form of Supreme Court decisions, civil rights laws, and when necessary federal troops, has been needed to break the collective repression that white southerners had maintained, and the free whites themselves from the massive conformity that had enslaved their minds.

What emerged victorious from the Civil War, of course, was another assertive nationality, that of the United States, now clearly and unbreakably united. That country has since displayed its own brand of strident and bullying nationalism, bullying both toward its own dissenting citizens and toward whatever nations abroad have refused to accept its hegemony. But the United States is big enough, and ethnically diverse enough, to lack on a countrywide scale the vicious, snarling parochialism that would continue in southern (and, for that matter, northern) communities, a parochialism that manifests itself today in the countless ethnic and regional nationalisms that infest the globe.

Professor McDonald has argued that even though the South contained slavery, southern secession had some justification. I would make a counterproposal: that even had the South not contained slavery, southern secession would have had no justification.

Louisiana was one of five southern states to have a majority of black voters after the Civil War. A total of 133 black legislators served in the state from 1868 to 1896. *(Courtesy, Louisiana State Museum)*

CHAPTER 15

"Been in the Storm So Long": Emancipation and Reconstruction

THE NEW ORLEANS RACE RIOT OF 1866

Resentment had been building in New Orleans during 1866, the first year after
the victory of the Union and four since wartime federal occupation of the city.
Sympathizers with the triumphant cause of Union were to hold a political
convention on July 30. Blacks would mix with whites at Mechanic's Hall to
demand humiliating measures against the proud former Confederacy, now
fallen but allowed under President Andrew Johnson's lenient policy to
organize white supremacist state governments like that of Louisiana. Three
weeks before the convention, an ex-rebel advised his Unionist friend not to
attend the gathering, indicating that no one there would be left alive. On the
morning of Monday the 30th, business in New Orleans gunshops was brisk.

At noon a parade of blacks marched up Burgundy Street in support of the
convention. Shots were fired and fights broke out, but the parade continued
until it stopped in front of Mechanic's Hall. There another fight started and
whites fired shots into the crowd of blacks. Some were armed and returned fire.
Outnumbered, the marching crowd broke and scattered, many entering the
convention building, where delegates and visitors, black and white, sat waiting
for others to arrive. The fire alarm bell rang and police descended on the hall.
Pistols fired indiscriminately through the windows. Abetted by the mob, police
broke open the doors, rushed to the top of the steps leading into the convention
room, and fired their weapons into the crowded delegates. The massacre
spread over many blocks. Whites assaulted blacks openly on the streets. The
riot continued until 3:00 p.m., when federal troops arrived. By the end of the
disturbance, an estimated thirty-four black and three white Unionists were
dead and 119 blacks and seventeen whites wounded.

In the aftermath of the riot, federal troops stepped in. General Philip
Sheridan, who had been in Texas at the time of the riot, returned to New
Orleans to take charge of the situation. Sheridan later testified to Congress
that the events at Mechanic's Hall had been a massacre on the part of the
police, with no attempt on the part of the civil authorities to intervene. The

Republican majority on the congressional committee concluded that the riot had been a police action for which no responsible person had been arrested. An army board of investigators judged that "[anyone] examining the evidence must come to the conclusion that the massacre resulted from a prearranged and preconcerted programme."

The fury of the rioters in New Orleans was the product of years of war and more particularly the long federal occupation of the city. General Ben Butler's "General Order 28," which came to be known as the "Woman Order," had infuriated the whole South and outraged genteel Europeans. Aimed at the many New Orleans women who showed hostility to federal troops, this order stated that "When any female shall, by word, gesture, or movement, insult or show contempt for any officer or soldier of the United States, she shall be held liable to be treated as a woman of the town plying her vocation." Radicals and white supremacists both would be continuing during Reconstruction the struggle for the city that had begun in the time of Butler.

The year of the riot was also that of the founding of the first Ku Klux Klan. The New Orleans massacre was preceded by the Memphis riot in May 1866, when forty-six blacks, including three women and two children, were killed. Racism permeated the South. But was the New Orleans riot attributable purely to racial hatred? The North was also steeped in racism. What distinguished the violence in New Orleans was its connection to an ongoing struggle, in Louisiana, in much of the rest of the defeated Confederacy, and in the national government, over what kind of power and society were to prevail in the South. Was the South to pass back into the hands of the former slave-owning aristocracy and its friends among the plain folk; or would southern blacks win racial equality? Even the white South was divided. There were white Unionists, who during the war had stayed loyal to the old United States. And they too were split: some were conservatives capable of joining with the Democrats; others were committed to political equality for the black population, or at least opportunistically allied with the Radicals. In New Orleans, the struggle between Radicals and defenders of the old order was very much a struggle for control of the police.

In 1868 the state, now submissive to a federal Radical plan insuring that ex-secessionists would not dominate politics, elected a Radical governor and was readmitted to the Union. The Radical state government thereupon put the New Orleans police under a state board of commissioners, to which the governor appointed a majority of blacks. The police recruited veterans of both armed forces of the Civil War. In 1870 a white-supremacist organization, the White League, seized control of the city after an essentially military engagement against the police. Once again, intervention by the federal military was necessary. But in 1877, competing parties formed separate state governments. The Democratic gubernatorial claimant used members of the White League to occupy police stations, and organized a police force under his board of commissioners. The Radicals, with the support of the old police and the federal military, now held only the state house. The settlement of the disputed national presidential election of 1876 meant that radical Reconstruction was going to be abandoned. The police came under local control.

| **Emancipation** | "I have vowed," declared |

Emancipation and Reconstruction   "I have vowed," declared a southerner toward the war's end, "that if I should have children—the first ingredient of the first principle of their education shall be uncompromising hatred & contempt of the Yankee."

Hatred crackled and seared among white southerners in the first postwar days, amidst other compounds of emotion: sadness, resignation, relief, doubtless in a few cases a renascent loyalty to the Union. The feelings of the freed slaves are easy to imagine: their joy and exaltation at the dizzying prospect of freedom have been documented. "I'm free as a frog!" one exultant former slave exclaimed. The southern land, meanwhile, was in a physical disruption to match the broiling emotions of the more irreconciled of its inhabitants.

Wherever travelers went in the months following Appomattox they saw abandoned fields, twisted rails, and burned structures. People in creaking wagons drove their gaunt mules for miles to find fords across bridgeless streams. For decades to come, men hobbling on one leg or with empty sleeves would be common sights throughout Dixie. In 1866 the state of Mississippi would spend a fifth of its revenues on artificial arms and legs for Confederate veterans. The defeat of the Confederacy had also wiped out millions of dollars of bank capital and made all Confederate money worthless. But most unsettling of all the changes the war had brought was the end of slavery. For generations it had been the foundation on which the entire southern economy rested. Now that it was gone, what would take its place?

Many former slaves remained on farms and plantations, but others had departed. Some had gone to the towns where life seemed more interesting than in the sleepy countryside. Others took to the road to test their new freedom. Many others went traveling to seek out lost relatives and friends separated years ago by the migration of white masters or by the domestic slave trade. Eventually most would return to the land somewhere in the South.

Lincoln and most other northerners had entered the Civil War determined only to preserve the Union. Southerners, believing they saw larger and more menacing aims on the part of the North, had been as determined to protect their independence. The Emancipation Proclamation gave the Union a moral purpose and confirmed the fears of many white southerners that victory for the Union would mean social revolution. It was the leveling of the southern social and racial hierarchy as much as it was the leveling of Atlanta that caused bitterness among southerners after Appomattox.

Together, the ending of slavery and the social dislocations of defeat prepared the South for the very thing that white southerners had dreaded and most northern Unionists had been careful not to intend. The South was ripe for social revolution. That revolution, in fact, had already come in the sheer numbers of black southerners free and in motion across the countryside. What form that revolution would take, how long it might endure: all this in 1865 was a matter of endless and unpredictable possibility. Would liberty fulfill itself, as black southerners wanted, in the independence that comes of owning a plot of land? Would liberty amount to the freedom defined by northern capital: freedom on the part of workers, black and white, to sell their labor to the highest bidder with the least security to fall back on? What form would black family life take on: the patriarchy of the white family or the community of affection that had developed in slave quarters? Would blacks achieve social equality and integration with whites? What were white southerners going to think about black freedom, now that they had to think about it? Such questions would have been unimaginable two or three years earlier as immediate practical considerations. Unplanned conditions now made them inescapable. Too many memories survived like those of Della Garlic, a field hand on a Louisiana plantation in 1861. Born in Virginia and sold three times, she recalled:

> Dem days was hell. Babies was snatched from dere mother's breas' an' sold to speculators. Chilluns was separated from sisters an' brothers an' never saw each other ag'in. Course dey cry; you think dey not cry when dey was sold lak cattle? . . . Folks a mile away could hear dem awful whippings. Dey was a turrible part of livin'. . . .

In the end, social revolution was not to endure. That failure has defined the character of American social and political life ever since.

The Black Family   The country roads in the early days after Appomattox, crowded with newly freed slaves seeking lost loved ones, speak of the violence the slave system had done to the

Store for freedmen, Beaufort, South Carolina. The Freedmen's Bureau coordinated relief efforts and tried to ease the transition from slavery to freedom. *(Courtesy, National Archives)*

black family. Protecting their absolute right to their property, slaveholders had refused to give formal and legal recognition to slave marriages. Masters had often found it in their interest, however, to encourage slave unions, for the children they produced and because family responsibility would restrain rebelliousness. Yet when the economics of plantation life demanded it, husbands would be separated from wives, wives sold away from husbands, and children parted from mothers and fathers. Advertisements, angry or pathetic, were placed in newspapers by blacks following the war:

> Information Wanted, of Caroline Dodson, who was sold from Nashville, Nov. 1st, 1862, by James Lumsden to Warwick, (a trader then in human beings), who carried her to Atlanta, Georgia, and she was last heard of in the sale pen of Robert Clarke, (human trader in that place), from which she was sold. Any information of her whereabouts will be thankfully received and rewarded by her mother. Lucinda Lowery, Nashville.

It is logical to suppose that in the absence of socially protected marriage, the mother would assume the primary parental role. Historians have described the slave family as matriarchal. That view is under question. Evidence indicates the presence within the slave community of males who performed the tasks of husband and father: providing their families with game or fish as dietary supplements, fashioning articles of furniture, passing along to a child some memory from an earlier time and a different land, and, when possible, protecting a wife or child against an abusive overseer or master.

But beyond these elements of similarity between black and white fatherhood, little division of responsibilities along gender lines existed within slave quarters. The necessities of plantation agriculture assured, for example, that the great majority of slave men and women worked alongside one another in the fields. Slave parents, faced with the problem of bringing children to maturity safely, rarely observed Victorian distinctions in sex roles. Both parents taught their children survival, the subtle art of accommodation to the plantation system. And even within the unimaginably racist conditions of the slave system, whites might accept from a slave woman a degree of aggressiveness in defense of her children that they would not tolerate from black fathers.

Unable under the conditions of slavery to enjoy a secure and stable nuclear family life, blacks established an enlarged community of relations, stretching from one plantation to the next, of "brothers" and "sisters," "aunts" and "uncles" who took up family responsibilities. When the opportunity presented itself after the war, the freed slaves rejoined their immediate biological families and sought legitimacy and protection in legally recognized marriages. The Freedmen's Bureau, a new federal agency designed to ease the slave's transition to freedom, presided over many of these unions and made them a matter of public record. But the black society of Reconstruction and for decades afterwards contained a compound of nuclear and neighborhood family.

For blacks, gaining control of their own families was perhaps the most important immediate consequence of freedom. But emancipation also worked to alter relations within the black family. Slavery had flattened, though not entirely, the differences between men's roles and the roles of women; emancipation made possible a differentiation between roles that the larger society endorsed. Black males most often went to work for whites in various jobs as they had done before the war, but now for hire. They generally preferred, however, that their wives not work for the white man, and many black females wished to create a conventional household and give their energies to raising children. In the years immediately following the war, white southern landowners complained of the scarcity of black women and children available for field work or domestic employment. For black men and women emancipation was supposed to mean at least the freedom whites enjoyed to organize a household.

Freed women when they stepped out from their homes encountered barriers already set up for the rest of their sex. Black women who had to seek employment complained to Freedmen's Bureau officials that they received wages lower than men were getting for the same work. Bureau policy required husbands to sign contracts for the labor of their wives. Though black men acquired more and more political liberty throughout the Reconstruction era, especially the right to vote and hold office, black women like their white sisters remained outside the political system. The experience of sexual equality that had belonged to slavery was being swallowed in theories of male primacy that came with freedom.

The black family, meanwhile, thrived in freedom. By 1870 a large majority of black children were growing up in households of two parents. Relations between the sexes, while not so nearly equal as under slavery, were not so sharply defined and as hierarchical as conventional morality might have demanded. Blacks, in any event, now had a stable home foundation on which to build wider forms of community and political organization.

| **Building the Black Community** | From the earliest days of Reconstruction, there emerged into full public view an institution that |

had maintained a powerful place in slave society and among antebellum free blacks. Evangelical Protestantism spoke to the condition of American blacks. Most slave states had made it illegal to educate slaves. But the incomparable vocabulary of the King James Bible was available. Illiterate blacks could learn the cadences by ear; free blacks with schooling could read it, as could slaves who had learned to read despite the prohibitions. A story of ancient Jews whose lot seemed close to that of the slaves; a language of bondage, flight, and deliverance, of suffering endured, rendered into prayer and devotion and in time ended: all was magnificent material for preaching and for hymns. With religion came a ministry of slaves and free blacks. During Reconstruction, blacks pressed for separate churches, nurturing their own congregations already established. The black ministry gained political leadership to supplement its spiritual role, taking a place within the black community that it would still occupy during the civil rights struggles of the 1950s and 1960s.

Side by side with the ministers in a position of leadership stood the teachers, now at liberty openly to instruct other blacks and to enlarge their own education. Ex-slaves and black southerners who had been free even in slavery times now joined with black and white teachers who had come from the North to serve in the new time of emancipation. Schools flourished: vast numbers of tiny schools run on a shoestring, a few more affluent, the whole process receiving the countenance and aid, however meager, of the Freedmen's Bureau. The teachers might be passing on the fragments of learning they had snatched and hoarded in the days of slavery; pupils, eager for a schooling that Americans in general have traditionally prized as a means of success and a good in itself, might have the ambition to become teachers. The halting eloquence to be found among the papers of newly schooled Reconstruction blacks has its counterpart in the letters of immigrants, trying in their freshly acquired English to explain their place and hopes in their adopted country.

Even before the end of the war, black southerners in regions under control of federal troops were meeting in committees or larger conventions to provide a voice for their community.

Enormously impressive to black southerners was the coming of black soldiers to the South:

> We march through these fine thoroughfares where once the slave was forbid being out after nine P.M., or to puff a 'regalia,' or to walk with a cane, or to ride in a carriage! Negro soldiers!—with banners floating. . . . [walking] fearlessly and boldly through the streets of a southern city . . . without being required to take off his cap at every step, or give all the sidewalks to those lordly princes of the sunny south, the planters' sons!

The main insistence was on political and legal rights. More generally, such meetings appear to have had as their objective the establishment of an organized and articulate presence in American society. Underlying this purpose was a fear that even the more enlightened of white Americans were likely to treat the freed slaves as no more than wards and recipients of white benevolence. That was not going to be to the liking of blacks who had won for themselves an education, whether pieced together in defiance of laws forbidding literacy schooling for slaves or acquired in the precarious margins of southern society allowed to free blacks before the war. Blacks made more particular demands during the early days of Reconstruction for the right to vote, to serve on juries, to exercise the other freedoms of Americans. These demands too can perhaps best be understood as reflecting the determination to be an active rather than a passive component of the nation. The plan of Reconstruction imposed by Congress later in the decade would succeed, if only for a moment, because there existed among southern blacks a roughly hewn political structure, a stratum of educated leaders, and a political will. These could respond to the congressional program for bringing the freed slaves into the nation's public life.

Political Reconstruction

Reorganizing the Union The Confederate surrender opened a difficult constitutional question about the status of the defeated states. Did the former rebel states have the right, as members of the Union, to come straight back to Congress and resume their old political life under the Constitution? Would the government have no authority to set conditions that they would have to meet before they resumed their seats in the House and Senate? If so, Congress would lack the power to force on the South whatever reforms might be necessary for the protection of the freed slaves and the prevention of any future disloyalty. Republicans who favored a coercive policy toward the South argued that by the act of secession the Confederate states had forfeited their status of statehood and reverted to the condition of territories. If they were no longer states, they were not entitled to the rights of states and could not be subject to the will of the federal government.

The Union victory might actually give the South a stronger presence in the House of Representatives than the region had enjoyed before the war. The Constitution had provided that in counting the population of a state for determining how many members it was to have in the House, three-fifths of the slaves in the state were to be counted in. But if slavery no longer existed and the blacks were legally free, the whole black population rather than three-fifths of it would be counted within the population of the state, and the South would gain about twenty seats in the

House of Representatives. And if former Confederate states should succeed in finding methods denying full freedom for the black populace, the South would be getting extra seats without even having to give up its oppression of the black race.

Overshadowing all these issues was the question of the future status of the black people. By eradicating slavery, the country unwittingly confronted long-delayed questions regarding the civil and political status of blacks. Would the ballot and citizenship be conferred on them?

Such questions had to be worked out amid a legacy of bitterness and frustration created by the war. White southerners found themselves in the unique position of being the only Americans to know defeat in wartime, their region burned and bare, their economy a shambles. The abolition of slavery also threatened white racial domination. The North had not suffered the physical and economic devastation experienced by the South. Even its human losses were proportionally less. But northerners had sacrificed to preserve the Union. They needed to know that their expenditures had gone for something, that their principles had been vindicated. They expected a measure of symbolic satisfaction from the South as well as physical surrender.

| Lincoln's Reconstruction Plan | In the efforts during the war to settle on some scheme for restoration of the rebel states to the Union, President Lincoln generally favored policies that would make few demands on the South. He had originally hoped for a speedy end to the war and a rapid resumption of antebellum political ties. Although the prolonged struggle on the battlefield made that impossible, the President continued to advocate a moderate postwar Reconstruction. Lincoln had not been an advocate of black equality. He always approached racial issues cautiously. He had hoped that the process of emancipation would be gradual and under the direction of officials of the former slave states. Believing that the colonization of blacks outside the United States was the ideal solution, Lincoln's Administration sponsored efforts to resettle blacks in the Caribbean and Central America. And Lincoln was a cagey politician. An ex-Whig himself, he may have had it in mind that moder-

ate policies attractive to southern former Whigs might draw them to the Republican Party.

In December 1863 Lincoln outlined a formal plan for Confederate areas coming under Union control. It clearly contemplated swift restoration, with no penalties for ex-rebels beyond loss of their slaves. It did not anticipate black participation in Reconstruction. Under Lincoln's "ten percent plan," whenever a total of whites equal to one-tenth the number who had voted in 1860 took an oath of future loyalty to the United States and its laws—which included the abolition of slavery—they could form a new state government. Before the war ended Lincoln had recognized "ten percent" governments in Arkansas, Tennessee, Virginia, and Louisiana. But Congress refused to admit representatives from these states, and their votes were not counted in the 1864 presidential election. Lincoln agreed that Congress should take some role in the reconciliation process, but he always sought to keep restoration under presidential leadership.

The national legislators were looking for a plan more firmly insuring that the new southern governments would remain loyal. The Wade-Davis Bill of 1864 required that, before a formerly seceded state could form a government, fifty percent of the adult white males in that state would have to take an oath of loyalty to the Union. The state could then hold a constitutional convention to make a new government for itself. But voting for delegates to that convention would be limited to people who had taken an oath that they had never supported the secession. The state must outlaw slavery. The plan was not to go into effect until the war had ended. Thinking the Wade-Davis Bill too severe and an invasion of presidential responsibility for reconstruction, Lincoln vetoed it. Supporters of the bill responded with a manifesto calling Lincoln's veto an "outrage on the legislative authority."

Neither Lincoln's plan nor that of the Wade-Davis Bill provided for blacks to be given the vote. But some Republicans in Congress wished for a program of reconstruction that would grant a wide range of rights to the freedmen and guarantee protection of these rights. Legislators of this kind wanted the national government to have strong control over former rebel states, so that their legal and social systems could be thoroughly

Charleston, South Carolina. At the war's end, much of the South lay in ruins. *(Courtesy, Library of Congress)*

reshaped and white southerners would not get the chance to bring back the old slavery system in a new form.

During the final year of the war President Lincoln appeared to be moving somewhat toward a more active and progressive solution to the race question. In March 1864 he came out in favor of granting the vote to "very intelligent" black people and black Union soldiers. He pressed for the Thirteenth Amendment outlawing slavery. A month before his death Lincoln signed the bill creating a Freedmen's Bureau to aid the ex-slaves in their transition to freedom.

In the end, Reconstruction was to be in hands other than Lincoln's. But in the spring of 1865 the President and the Union public did have a brief period to savor victory.

Lincoln's Last Days   On April 4 Lincoln went to Richmond to view the Confederate capital now evacuated by the government of Jefferson Davis. Accompanied by his son and a mili-

tary escort, he walked up Main Street to the Confederate executive mansion. Black men and women crowded around the presidential party and sang and shouted. When he entered the Confederate President's house and took a seat in Davis's chair, the Union troops, black and white, cheered. Later the President toured the captured city that for four bloody years had been the supreme goal of Union armies. Like many other large southern towns Richmond was in ruins: it was blackened by a fire set accidentally by the Confederate authorities before they withdrew.

Lincoln returned to Washington on April 9, the day Lee surrendered to Grant at Appomattox Court House. The news reached Washington the next day and the government declared a holiday for its employees. On the tenth, throngs gathered on the streets of the capital. The crowds eventually converged on the White House, where Lincoln was working at his desk. They interrupted him several times by their shouts for a speech until he finally made an appearance. He would deliver some appropriate remarks the following evening, he said, but for the moment he would just order the bands to play "Dixie." The Confederate anthem, he noted, was now the lawful property of the Union.

The next evening the President came to the upper window of the White House as he had promised and made some graceful remarks. "We meet this evening . . . in gladness of heart" he began, and then went on to deliver a thoughtful address, his last, on the problems to come. If the crowd had wanted a rousing cock-crow of triumph, it was disappointed. At least one man in the audience, however, found himself deeply moved, but to rage and anger. John Wilkes Booth was a Marylander, an actor from a distinguished theatrical family. The defeat of the South had sent him into despair.

On the evening of April 14 the President, accompanied by his wife and several friends, went to see the comedy *Our American Cousin* at Ford's Theater. The President's party arrived late but quickly settled down to enjoy the story of a shrewd comic American visiting his English relatives. During the third act the sounds of a muffled shot and a scuffle came from the President's box. Suddenly a tall figure leaped from the box to the stage and shouted *Sic semper tyrannis!* (thus ever to tyrants), the motto of Virginia. Before he could be stopped Booth escaped into the night.

They carried the unconscious President to a house nearby and placed him on a bed. While high officials and family members gathered around, the doctors examined him. The bullet had entered the rear of his head and lodged near his eye. Nothing could be done. He died at 7:22 A.M.

Andrew Johnson

Like other Vice-Presidents in American history, Andrew Johnson was selected without much consideration that he might become President. A self-educated tailor from East Tennessee and a strong Jacksonian Democrat, Johnson had been in 1861 the only southern senator to support the Union. After Tennessee fell to Union troops, Lincoln made him war governor, a task he performed with vigor and courage. In 1864 the Republican Party, seeking to broaden itself into a Union party, turned naturally to Johnson, an ex-Democrat and a southern Unionist, to be Lincoln's running mate. Then suddenly, on April 14, 1865, he was the President.

Johnson, a President without a party, had to deal with a Republican Congress. And Johnson was a southern white supremacist, willing and perhaps happy to accept emancipation and some rights for black Americans but cooperative with southerners who wished to place strict controls over the black population. This brought him into conflict not only with the increasingly strong band of radical Republicans in Congress but with moderates as well. Courageous and stubborn but belligerent and lacking in political tact, Johnson both endured and to an extent brought on himself one of the most troubled presidential administrations in American history.

Johnson wanted an easy restoration of the seceded states. There was not yet any clearly defined program that would instruct a rebel state in how it must go about reorganizing itself so as to be accepted back into the Union, and Johnson did not wait for Congress to reconvene (it was out of session until December) before dealing with the problem. He announced at once a program of restoration similar to Lincoln's. He too offered pardon to ex-rebels pledging future loyalty. He asked only that the reorganized state governments nullify their ordinances of secession, repudiate their Confederate debts, and ratify the Thirteenth Amendment.

Johnson's assumption of primary responsibility for Reconstruction policy was bound to alienate Republicans in Congress. His leniency toward the South angered radicals. Southerners, moreover, took a course that aroused northern resentment. They elected to state office and to Congress prominent ex-rebels, including Vice-President Alexander Stephens and numerous generals. Some of the reorganized state governments refused to repudiate their Confederate debts or nullify their secession ordinances. A number of them passed "black codes" defining the rights of emancipated slaves in ways that severely restricted their freedom. Some blacks had abused the privileges of freedom in the aftermath of war. A Union soldier mildly upbraided a former slave: "Don't you think you did wrong, Dick, to take your mistress' horse?" "Well, I do' know, sah; I didn't take the best one." Far worse cases, including a few atrocities, are a matter of reliable record. The South, however, would rise again.

A typical black code might bar blacks from jury duty and from testifying in court against whites; it might forbid them to take up any occupation except agriculture or to rent land on their own; some subjected unemployed blacks to arrest and forced labor. The character of the "restored" governments and the "black codes" seemed to indicate that southerners remained rebels at heart. "Nigger life's cheap now," a white Tennesseean soon observed. "When a white man feels aggrieved at anything a nigger's done, he just shoots him and puts an end to it." The Freedmen's Bureau Commissioner in Mississippi and Louisiana wrote:

> I hear the people talk in such a way as to indicate that they are yet unable to conceive of the negro as possessing any rights at all. . . . To kill a negro they do not deem murder; to debauch a negro woman they do not think fornication; to take the property away from a negro they do not consider robbery. The people boast that when they get freedmen affairs in their own hands, to use the classic expression, 'the niggers will catch hell.'

Andrew Johnson's attempt to assume primary responsibility for Reconstruction after Lincoln's death alienated Congress, while his leniency toward the South increasingly angered northern voters.

Congressional Reconstruction

When Congress met in December 1865, it refused to seat newly elected southern representatives, but disagreed on what to do next. Radicals demanded a thoroughgoing political and economic shakeup of the South. Moderate Republicans wanted only minimal guarantees of legal protection for the ex-slaves. "To have refused the Negroes the simplest rights granted to every other inhabitant, native or foreigner, would be outrageous," declared Senator John Sherman of Ohio, a moderate leader. The emancipated slave, warned another Senator, would "be tyrannized over, abused, and virtually reenslaved without some legislation by the nation for his protection."

At this point moderates still dominated Republican policy. But they too wanted to insure the civil rights of black southerners. In 1866 Congress passed a bill giving to a Freedmen's Bureau the power to try by military commission anyone charged with depriving freedmen of their civil rights. It also put through a bill that gave the freedmen citizenship and civil rights. Johnson vetoed both bills as unconstitutional extensions of federal power. Congress thereupon enacted the civil rights measure over his veto, passed a revised bill for a Freedmen's Bureau, and overrode Johnson's veto of it.

Congress's establishment of the Freedmen's Bureau departed from normal government policy by addressing various aspects of people's lives that had normally been left to private initiative. The Bureau was essentially responsible for protecting blacks against reenslavement in the unsettled conditions of the southern states.

Black students learning geography. *(Courtesy, Hampton Institute)*

| The Fourteenth Amendment | The national legislature soon offered Johnson and the South another chance. It framed an elaborate Fourteenth Amendment covering a range of issues and gave each of the state governments favored by Johnson the opportunity to return to Congress if it should ratify.

The Fourteenth Amendment declared "all persons"—the lawmakers were thinking particularly of black Americans—"born or naturalized in the United States, and subject to the jurisdiction thereof, are citizens of the United States and of the State wherein they reside." The Amendment prohibited the states from violating the "privileges or immunities of citizens of the United States," depriving "any person of life, liberty, or property, without due process of law," or denying "to any person within its jurisdiction the equal protection of the laws." It barred from public office anyone who, having taken a federal or state oath of office to protect the Constitution of the United States, afterward engaged in rebellion against the nation. The provision was aimed at high-ranking Confederate officials who before the Civil War had served in federal or state office. A two-thirds vote of the Senate and the House of Representatives could relieve any individual of that disability. The Amendment prohibited the states and the nation from paying any debt incurred in rebellion against the country. The Amendment did not directly extend the right to vote. It attempted instead to entice the states to give the vote to blacks. It provided that a state would lose seats in the House of Representatives insofar as it denied to some of its adult male population the right to vote for federal and state officials.

A state ratifying the Amendment could expect to be granted readmission without further reform. Implicit in the offer was penalty for rejection: restoration would begin anew, with Congress dictating terms. Had it not been for Johnson, the South might have ratified. But Johnson refused to bend. On his advice all the southern states except his Tennessee rejected the amendment. Tennessee ratified and was readmitted to the Union.

The other ten, said James A. Garfield, had "flung back into our teeth the magnanimous offer of a generous nation."

The break between the President and Congress was now complete. In the fall of 1866 Johnson stumped the North encouraging the defeat at the polls of leading Republican Congressmen. The tour was a disaster for the President personally and politically. Forgetting that he was no longer a Tennessee stump-speaker, Johnson engaged in undignified arguments with hecklers and even suggested hanging leading Radicals. In November the Republicans swept the elections, winning over a two-thirds majority in both houses of Congress. Reconstruction would begin anew, under the leadership of such Radicals as the Massachusetts Senator Charles Sumner and Representative Thaddeus Stevens of Pennsylvania.

Radical Reconstruction

The situation when Congress met in December 1866 was very different from that a year earlier. Events during 1866 had conspired to bring together moderate and Radical Republicans, at least temporarily. A majority in Congress now agreed on the necessity of creating new southern state governments on the basis of black suffrage and excluding ex-rebels. Arming blacks with the ballot, Republicans hoped, would give them a weapon against white Democratic oppression and build up a strong Republican Party in the South.

The Military Reconstruction Act of 1867 set the terms of the congressional program. It divided the South into five military districts. Military governors in each were to register voters, including blacks but not whites who had held public office before the Civil War and then supported the Confederacy. The governors would thereupon call elections for new constitutional conventions. These conventions had to write black suffrage into the new state constitutions. Once the voters had approved these constitutions and the Fourteenth Amendment, the states might apply to Congress for readmission. If the constitution met approval, the state would be readmitted to the Union and its representatives seated. Three other Reconstruction Acts followed the first.

Reconstruction had something in common with the economic policy of the Republican Party and with the party's defense of the Union during the Civil War. It represented that commitment to strong and active central government toward which Republicans tended. In the enforcement of civil rights, the legal establishment of universal male suffrage, and the work of the Freedmen's Bureau, the federal government for the first time in its history was lending its resources, or some of them, to a political and social revolution.

To southern whites haunted by the old antebellum fear of slave insurrection, Radical Reconstruction seemed a nightmare come true. With their traditional leaders barred from office and illiterate ex-slaves enfranchised, they predicted a grim era of black rule. One southern newspaper warned in 1869:

> That the State has been cursed and almost ruined by a class of 'carpet bag' vultures from the North, aided by degenerate and too often corrupt natives, is patent to anybody who opens his eyes. . . . The day of reckoning will come. Mark what we say! Let every man watch how he connects himself even innocently with those who have so outraged the State and the people.

Changing Interpretations of Reconstruction   The earliest critics of Reconstruction condemned it as a rape of southern society. Political opportunism and hatred of the South, so such critics argued, had motivated the Radical Republican policies: military rule, black suffrage, and violation of the spirit, if not the letter, of the Constitution. Accounts sympathetic to the white South stressed the corruption of Reconstruction state regimes, the unruliness—by which some of them may have meant the claims to equality—of former slaves, the greed of northern "carpetbaggers," and the treachery of southern "scalawags." Reconstruction was a "blackout of honest government." In this view, the lifting of Radical rule by the white "redeemers" represented a return to constitutional government and to proper racial relations in the South.

By the 1930s historians were becoming in-

Massachusetts Senator Charles Sumner and Pennsylvania Representative Thaddeus Stevens, leaders of Radical Reconstruction. *(Courtesy, Library of Congress)*

creasingly interested in explaining events by economic causes. That brought a new way of interpreting Reconstruction. Now writers looked back to the days before the Civil War when southerners had opposed such measures favorable to northern business as the protective tariff, which would force the South to buy its manufactured goods from the North rather than at cheaper European prices. Scholars now perceived the Radical Republicans as representatives of northeastern business interests. These interests had feared that a speedily reconstructed South might regain its political power and overturn the control of the national government acquired by northern business during the war years, when southern seats in Congress were empty. Idealistic rhetoric, according to economic interpretation, masked the sordid economic motives of the business-dominated Republican party: exploitation of the South and advancement of industrial over agrarian interests.

More recently, a generation influenced by the civil rights struggles of the 1950s and 1960s has taken up these findings and begun describing Reconstruction as another phase in the black American search for justice. Radical Republicans, this analysis insists, represented the last moment of abolitionist idealism; the Radicals tried to provide national protection for the rights of the freed people and to extend some measure of social and economic assistance. Not particularly vindictive and not the tools of a capitalist conspiracy, congressional Republicans, moderates as well as Radicals, undertook their actions only after they realized the extent of white southern stubbornness and presidential obstructionism. And their measures were not especially severe, particularly when compared to the postwar policies of other victorious nations. The national government committed only a small number of troops to military Reconstruction, and the whole process lasted only a few years in most states. This recent idea of Reconstruction would hold that if any fault is to be found with the policy, it is not for being too severe toward the defeated South but for not being thorough enough to win the black race full and permanent equality and justice.

Reconstruction and the South

The Road to Freedom In 1870 Congress brought the right to vote under federal control. The Fifteenth Amendment declared that a citizen's right to vote "shall not be denied or abridged . . . on account of race, color, or previous condition of servitude." The Amendment applied to black males in the North—much of the North had not allowed black Americans to vote—as well as to former slaves in the South. Most of the black vote went to Republicans, and some northern supporters of the Amendment may have been mainly concerned with strengthening the Republican Party. But others risked a white backlash to guarantee suffrage to the black man.

The vote that was granted to black males was denied to both black and white females. White women leaders of the movement for women's rights were incensed. Before the war, they had worked within the abolitionist movement and then supported the Republican cause. In 1866, Susan B. Anthony, Elizabeth Cady Stanton, Lucy Stone, and Lucretia Mott organized the American Equal Rights Association (AERA) to support suffrage for both white women and blacks. The refusal to grant women the vote angered them, and some even asserted that white women were better fitted to vote than black men. In the ensuing dispute about priorities, the AERA split into two groups. Lucy Stone and Henry Blackwell formed the American Woman Suffrage Association, which accepted the refusal to grant women the vote in order not to jeopardize the vote for black men. Susan B. Anthony and Elizabeth Cady Stanton organized the more militant National Woman Suffrage Association. Bitter about what they took to be betrayal by male Republican leaders, they warned that women could not trust men, refused to support the freedmen's right to the vote, and even used racist arguments to defend the greater importance of giving the vote to white women. Although their racism declined after the passage of the Fifteenth Amendment, it left a disturbing legacy to the women's movement.

In most southern states, Reconstruction lasted for only a few years. In states with large white majorities, conservatives regained political control rather quickly. Virginia was "redeemed" in 1869, Tennessee and North Carolina in 1870. Georgia fell under conservative rule in 1872, Alabama, Texas, and Arkansas in 1874, and Mississippi in 1876. In only three states—Louisiana, Florida and South Carolina—did Radical Republican government last a full decade, and they were all "redeemed" in 1877. Congress hastened the process of redemption through a generous policy of restoring the right to hold public office to former rebels deprived of it under terms of the Fourteenth Amendment. And a look at Reconstruction in action reveals something quite different from the dreadful years of corruption, disorder, and tyranny that postwar southern lamentings and subsequent legend have described.

Even in those states where blacks made up a majority of the voters, they did not dominate the reconstructed state governments. They formed a majority in one state constitutional convention, that of South Carolina, exactly one half the membership in the Louisiana convention, and a minority in eight others. After the new governments were formed, blacks never held a majority in both houses of a state legislature. No state had an elected black governor; only two black senators and fourteen black representatives were elected to the national Congress. At the local level, blacks never enjoyed a proportionate share of offices. In the constitutional conventions and in legislatures, blacks rarely pressed for equal access to public facilities.

Nor were the Reconstruction governments particularly incompetent or corrupt. Much of the leadership of Republican regimes fell to native whites or to northerners who had resettled in the South after the war. Most of the local whites—known derisively as "scalawags"—were ex-Whigs seeking to reenter politics. The northerners—nicknamed "carpetbaggers"—defy easy characterization. Many were former Union soldiers attracted by the South's climate and cheap land. Some undoubtedly were profiteers; others, like Governor Adelbert Ames of Mississippi and Governor Daniel Chamberlain of South Carolina, were idealists. Any discussion of corruption must be measured against the records of previous white southern administrations and against the sorry performance of several northern governments during this era. On the whole, Reconstruction governments made substantial progress toward postwar recovery and social reform. They drafted

BLACKS *recalling slavery decades later had a wide spectrum of memories:*

Might as well tell the truth. Had just as good a time when I was a slave as when I was free. Had all the hog meat and milk and everything else to eat.
—HARDY MILLER

De white folks wuz good ter us, an' we loved 'em. But we wanted ter be free 'cause de Lawd done make us all free.
—TOM WILCOX

There was no such thing as being good to slaves. Many white people were better than others, but a slave belonged to his master, and there was no way to get out of it.
—THOMAS LEWIS

I thought slavery wuz right. I felt that this wuz the way things had to go—the way they were fixed to go. I wuz satisfied. The white folks treated me all right. My young missus loved me, and I loved her. She whupped me sometimes—I think, just for fun, sometimes.
—JOE HIGH

Some colored people say slavery was better, because they had no responsibility. It is true, they were fed, clothed, and sheltered, but I'm like the man that said, "Give me freedom or give me death!"
—BELLE CARUTHERS

progressive new constitutions, reapportioned legislatures to give back-country districts equitable representation, expanded social services, improved roads, encouraged railroad construction, and established the South's first substantial public school system. Much of the so-called extravagance of Reconstruction legislatures merely represented expenditures for public services that previous regimes had neglected.

| **Humanitarian Efforts** | During the Reconstruction years, the national government provided some assistance to the freed people in the South. The

Freedmen's Bureau coordinated relief activities and tried to ease the difficult transition from slavery to freedom. The Bureau found employment opportunities, supervised labor contracts, and attempted to safeguard the legal rights of black people. Critics at the time generally indicted the Bureau for doing too much to assist blacks. Later historians have found quite the opposite. Many well-meaning officials were overly paternalistic; others displayed outright prejudice toward black people; some encouraged freedmen to enter into exploitive labor contracts; the agency did too little to enlarge opportunities for the former slaves. Yet the Bureau represented a notable though mild and temporary expansion of the social role of the federal government. One freedman observed:

Perhaps some *will* get an education in a little while. I *knows* de *next generation will.* But . . . we has been kep down *a hundred years* and *I* think it will take *a hundred years to get us back again.*

Another ex-slave recalled sending his children to school:

We had no idea that we should see them return home alive in the evening. Big white boys and half-grown men used to pelt them with stones and run them down with open knives, both to and from school. Sometimes they come home bruised, stabbed, beaten half to death, and sometimes quite dead. My own son himself was often thus beaten. He has on his forehead today a scar over his right eye which sadly tells the story of his trying experience in those days in his efforts to get an education. I was wounded in the war, trying to get my freedom, and he over his eye, trying to get an education.

Private philanthropic and religious groups also tried to aid freed people. Various churches, especially the Congregationalists and the Quakers, sent both money and volunteers to the South. Educational institutions related to the churches gave many black children and adults their first opportunity to learn to read and write. Blacks rushed to make use of the new schools, where northern female schoolteachers took an especially important role. Teachers like Laura Towne have left poignant records of their experiences in the South during Reconstruction. Their devotion to the people they were teaching mingled with their commitment to inculcating them with northern, middle-class values. Church groups also helped establish black colleges and industrial schools, and the

Freedmen's Bureau extended some financial assistance to missionary schools, including Howard University in Washington, D.C.

Many northern black churchmen and educators journeyed south to spread the gospel and the primer among the ex-slaves. Former slaves themselves put up school houses and paid for teachers, established churches, organized conventions to lobby for equal rights and the ballot, and opened savings banks. A black convention speaker in New Orleans in 1865 explained:

> If we are men—as our friends contend we are—we are able to attend to our own business. There is no man in the world so perfectly identified with our own interest as to understand it better than we do ourselves. . . . We need friends, it is true; but we do not need tutors. The age of guardianship is past forever. We now think for ourselves, and we shall act for ourselves.

The Land Question

The blacks were legally free and had the vote. But they lacked the one essential basis of independence and equality: land or an equivalent property. Both races in the postwar South recognized the importance of the land question. "The way we can best take care of ourselves is to have land and turn it and till it by our labor," contended a delegation of freed people in 1865. This is exactly what former slaveholders feared most, and they determined early on to prevent blacks from owning land. Without access to employment except on white-owned land, all the ballots and education in the world would be worthless. "They who own the real estate of a country control its vote," warned one observer. It is this as much as anything else that explains the successful overthrow of Reconstruction in the South.

A few antislavery activists had wanted to provide land for emancipated slaves. As early as 1862 Congress passed legislation confiscating plantations of Confederate sympathizers, and it was proposed to resettle blacks on them. But the Lincoln Administration showed little interest. In 1865 General William T. Sherman temporarily allotted small tracts of confiscated land along the South Atlantic coast to thousands of homeless ex-slaves. After the war Representative Thaddeus Stevens of Pennsylvania advocated breaking up the large southern plantations and allocating them in forty acre tracts to freed people. "Forty acres and a mule" became a byword among landless ex-slaves.

This was as close as anyone came to providing a new life for the blacks to move into when they moved out of slavery. Andrew Johnson restored confiscated lands to their previous owners and evicted the black tenants. Few northerners supported Stevens's plan to confiscate private property, even from slaveholders. Congress soundly defeated his watered-down confiscation plan in 1866, though it did set aside certain public lands in the South for purchase by freed people. This scheme failed badly, however, because the land available was inferior, and because few ex-slaves had the capital to buy land and farm equipment.

In many areas, the first system to develop in the absence of slavery was that of wage labor. Guided and prodded by agents of the Freedmen's Bureau, blacks signed contracts to work for so much a month and were provided with cabins, often in the former plantation slave quarters, and sometimes with food. Yet work in the fields at the white man's bidding, on the white man's land, under the immediate supervision of a white overseer seemed far too much like old slavery in a new guise. Many blacks would have none of it and sabotaged the arrangement. One way was to collect wages during the planting and cultivating months and then decamp just before the crucial harvest, which left the owner with the problem of gathering in the cotton or tobacco without a work force.

Sharecropping The specific reason for the rejection of the gang labor system was that it suggested the organization of field work under slavery. But in looking for some alternative, the freed slaves were acting in keeping with an American tradition that identified personal independence with the possession of property. One estimate has a fifth of black farm workers owning land by the 1880s. For most, conventional ownership was not an immediate option. Sporadic attempts, soon after the defeat of the rebels, to seize the land of planters met with resistance by the federal government. An alternative, however inadequate, gave the black family an opportunity to work independently on a plot of ground. The black newspaper in New Orleans predicted: "A kind of general serfdom and humiliation is about to take the place of slavery. . . ."

The land and labor system finally devised in the postwar South was sharecropping. In this form of tenancy the black worker contributed labor and perhaps the use of some tools and a mule, and received from the landlord some land to farm. At harvest time the cropper got to keep from one-half to two-thirds of the crop, the remaining portion going to the landowner.

The system had some advantages. Blacks now had some personal freedom; there was no overseer to supervise their work. Instead of living in the old slave quarters, moreover, each black family could reside apart on its own rented piece of land. Some blacks simply raised the slave cabin from the old quarters and removed it to their own farm. Blacks could now decide how to spend their money. And they could arrange their own family division of labor.

The sharecropper system was a poor substitute for landowning. Sharecroppers, like other tenants, had little incentive to improve the land they farmed. Since they did not own it, they could not expect to be the beneficiaries. The credit system that grew up alongside sharecropping was its worst element. Tenants often could not wait until harvest to buy the things they needed during the year. Storekeepers sold them cloth, tools, knickknacks, and even food on credit, taking out a lien, a kind of mortgage, on the crop as security until harvest time in the fall. Then, when the crop was sold, the storekeeper subtracted the debt from the cropper's share. Those caught in this crop-lien process might not ever see any cash once the storekeeper and the landlord had taken their shares. Goods bought on credit were far more expensive than those bought with cash. The system also allowed many opportunities for fraud. Storekeepers, themselves under considerable economic pressure, kept the accounts and sometimes juggled the books to make sure that the sharecropper remained permanently in debt. Such a tenant remained tied to the storekeeper as a perpetual customer, unable legally to deal with any other storekeeper until the debt was discharged. Some scholars have seen this debt peonage as the virtual reenslavement of the South's black population. It

---

A SHARECROPPING CONTRACT

This contract made and entered into between A. T. Mial of one part and Fenner Powell of the other part both of the County of Wake and State of North Carolina—

Witnesseth—That the Said Fenner Powell hath bargained and agreed with the Said Mial to work as a cropper for the year 1886 on Said Mial's land on the land now occupied by Said Powell on the west Side of Poplar Creek and a point on the east Side of Said Creek and both South and North of the Mial road, leading to Raleigh, That the Said Fenner Powell agrees to work faithfully and dilligently without any unnecessary loss of time, to do all manner of work on Said farm as may be directed by Said Mial, And to be respectful in manners and deportment to Said Mial. And the Said Mial agrees on his part to furnish mule and feed for the same and all plantation tools and Seed to plant the crop free of charge, and to give the Said Powell One half of all crops raised and housed by Said Powell on Said land except the cotton seed. The Said Mial agrees to advance as provisio to Said Powell fifty pound of bacon and two sacks of meal pr month and occasionally Some flour to be paid out of his the Said Powell's part of the crop or from any other advance that may be made to Said Powell by Said Mial. As witness our hands and seals this the 16th day of January A.D. 1886

Witness

W. S. Mial [signed]

A. T. Mial [signed]   [Seal]

        his
Fenner X Powell   [Seal]
      mark

certainly destroyed any chance that share-cropping could become a way-station to land ownership for any sizable number of former slaves.

As pursuers of the nineteenth-century American ideal of small property ownership, the ex-slaves had been from the beginning cousins to the middling and poor whites of the South. In Reconstruction days as before, landowning was common among whites who had possessed no slaves or few. In this respect much better off than the newly freed black population, the white plain folk in this time of uncertainty and open possibility had reason for antagonism to the planters who had led them on a fruitless war for the maintenance of a slaveholding system in which they had largely not shared. But no politics of cooperation materialized between blacks and whites. Racist psychology dominated, and instead of seeing blacks as fellow victims of planter hegemony, poor whites would soon come to view the Negroes as upstart competitors for the scraps and tatters of poverty. This gave added cause for the violence that blacks even a century later have suffered from their white neighhors.

As regional impoverishment continued throughout the remainder of the nineteenth century, increasing numbers of whites were ground down into sharecropping. All in all, racial animosity never gave way to a politics of class, but by the late 1880s there were to be some feeble beginnings of just such a politics. Tentative alliances between a few poor blacks and poor whites form a remarkable though faltering episode of late nineteenth-century southern history.

Impeachment of President Johnson

Although his policies had clearly been rejected, President Johnson continued to resist Radical Reconstruction by every possible means. Using the authority he possessed as commander-in-chief, he issued orders curtailing the powers of the military commanders in the South. He also removed from office people friendly to radical policies. Congress responded in 1867 and 1868 by trying to trim the President's powers so as to reduce his capacity for harm. In particular it passed the Tenure of Office Act, which forbade him to dismiss federal officials without the consent of the Senate. Another law required him to issue all orders to the army through its commanding general, U. S. Grant.

There had been talk among radicals for some time of removing Johnson from office. Under the Constitution a President could be removed only for "treason, bribery, or other high crimes and misdemeanors." Johnson had committed none of these. His only real offense was to refuse to cooperate in legislative policies that Congress and the public had approved. This might indicate bad political judgment, but it was not a crime.

Then Johnson, always his own worst enemy, blundered. In August 1867 he suspended Secretary of War Edwin M. Stanton, a close ally of the Radicals. There followed a comic opera in which Stanton barricaded himself in his office while his successor stood outside begging him to vacate. Outraged at Johnson's defiance, and convinced that he intended to destroy Radical Reconstruction, the House of Representatives in February 1868 impeached the President—that is, charged him with misconduct. Johnson stood accused of a number of doubtful offenses such as delivering "inflammatory and scandalous" speeches, but especially the offense of dismissing Stanton. Impeachment meant that Johnson now had to go on trial before the Senate, which would decide whether to remove him from the presidency. For three months the Senate sat as a court, listening to arguments from attorneys for both sides. Johnson's lawyers argued that a President could be removed only for violation of criminal law; counsel for the House contended that Johnson had exceeded his presidential authority and therefore provided adequate grounds for removal. Suspense mounted as it became clear that Republican senators were divided over the question of Johnson's guilt. In the end, seven Republicans broke with their colleagues and voted with Democrats against conviction. As a result the Senate fell one vote short of the required two-thirds needed to remove the President from office.

Johnson's impeachment and trial were the product of nerves stretched to the limit after three years of feuding. So convinced were many northerners that Johnson had joined

Facsimile of a ticket to Andrew Johnson's impeachment trial. Though Johnson was guilty of no crime other than continued resistance to Radical Reconstruction, a switch of a single Senate vote would have removed him from office. *(Courtesy, Library of Congress)*

with unrepentant rebels to undo the results of the war that they sanctioned any means to drive him from office. Johnson's conviction—especially on such flimsy grounds—might have damaged permanently the role of the President in the American political system.

The End of Reconstruction

Reconstruction remained, at least in fragments, into the 1870s. After white organizations, among them the Ku Klux Klan, began threatening and committing violence on black citizens for exercising their newly acquired rights, the national legislature in the early 1870s put through several Force Acts that aimed at restraining the terrorist groups. The administration of Ulysses S. Grant, elected President in 1868 as the candidate of the Republican Party, broke the Klan by the end of 1871. In 1875 Congress passed a Civil Rights Act—which in 1883 the Supreme Court was to find unconstitutional—that required states to provide equality to blacks in public places and prohibited the exclusion of blacks from jury duty. For a while into the 1870s, some southern states had Reconstruction governments that represented black as well as white voters. And in 1876 there were still a few federal soldiers in the South whose

object was to defend the rights of the black community. But by that year American politics had been turning away from Reconstruction for some time.

In 1868 Grant, as a war hero, had won a solid victory over Democratic presidential candidate Horatio Seymour of New York. In the next years Democrats made politically effective attacks on Reconstruction policy, winning voters unsure of the wisdom of Radical Reconstruction or unfriendly to the rights black people were gaining. Some Republicans were also challenging the party's southern programs. In 1872 Congress lifted from many former rebels the penalties prescribed in the Fourteenth Amendment and passed an Amnesty Act pardoning most of the remainder. Democrats and a faction of Republicans put up newspaperman Horace Greeley as a presidential candidate. Grant won reelection, but his administration suffered from a number of political scandals that suggested widespread corruption. Crédit Mobilier, a dummy corporation formed by an inner circle of Union Pacific Railroad shareholders, extorted wealth from the company and distributed bribes to prominent congressmen. In the elections of 1874 the Democratic Party won control of the House of Representatives and cut into Republican strength in the Senate.

The Reconstruction governments in the South were facing both political opposition and violence from citizens who wanted whites to be in control of southern society. White Democrats formed terrorist organizations, disrupted Republican gatherings, and threatened blacks. The federal government, tiring of Reconstruction, did little to stop all this.

| **The Compromise of 1877** | Finally, in the events that followed the presidential contest of 1876 between Republican candidate Rutherford B. Hayes of Ohio and Democrat Samuel J. Tilden of New York, the Republican Party ended Reconstruction and abandoned black southerners and their rights. After the general election, which chose the presidential electors who were to cast the actual vote for President, charges of irregularities had arisen concerning procedures in three southern states, South Carolina, Florida, and Louisiana. There the election boards that had counted the popular presidential vote, giving it in each case to the Republicans, were un-

der the control of Republican Reconstruction forces; Democrats suggested that the vote in each state had actually gone for the Democrats. Both parties also claimed one disputed electoral vote in Oregon. Unless the Republican claims could stand in each of the four states, the majority in the whole electoral college would be Democratic and Tilden would be the next President. Democrats and Republicans worked out a scheme for a commission that was to decide among the disputed electors; it was supposed to be balanced between Democratic and Republican members, with one other member who would be independent of either party in his decisions. When it came to appear that this member, a justice on the Supreme Court, was going to decide in all cases in favor of the Republicans, Democrats believed that they were about to have the election taken away from them. After the dispute had lasted for months, during which there was talk of civil war, the parties came to a solution. In return for a Democratic agreement not to oppose the selection of Hayes electors, Republicans agreed that a Republican Presidential administration would not only remove the remaining federal troops from the South but also give political patronage to white southerners and be friendly to economic legislation beneficial to southern states. Hayes, who had expressed concern for the rights of black southerners, presided over the end of a policy that by 1877 no longer had political support. The Republican effort to protect civil rights in the South in a major way had ceased.

Points To Think About

1. Historians have long speculated over how Lincoln would have approached the problem of postwar reconstruction. And in so doing they are merely following the lead of his contemporaries, most of whom claimed their own proposals reflected Lincoln's plans. The real question may be: did Lincoln have any plans?

It seems probable that he did, but Lincoln confided them to no one. In this matter, as in most others, he kept his own counsel. The result is that, following the assassination, people have tried to infer his postwar plans from his wartime programs. This is a very dubious enterprise. The reason is that Lincoln sought throughout the war to shorten it by enticing the seceding states back into the

Union. The generous terms he offered were contingent on their willingness to lay down their arms. And so they should be seen as the carrot Lincoln used alongside the military stick. That they should not be seen as likely precedents for his postwar plans is suggested by this logic. Leniency was held out as a reward for voluntarily returning to the Union. None of the Confederate states earned that reward. That means that Lincoln, by his own terms, was free to deal with them as harshly as circumstances might demand. All this is technically true, and indicates Lincoln's essential conservatism. Yet there is a contrary truth to the Proclamation. Lincoln knew what it implied, and so did the white South in its angry formal public reaction to the Proclamation. It was, by implication and beneath its limited surface, a declaration of war against slavery. We also have Lincoln's reaction to the Wade-Davis Bill to go by. He objected not so much to its rigor as that it would tie his hands in advance. Lincoln wanted to be free to deal with a defeated South as circumstances might suggest.

All in all it seems that we will never know what Lincoln would have proposed. But the disastrous course of Johnson's attempts at reconstruction will always tempt us to speculate on what Lincoln might have done had he lived.

2.   Reconstruction has, until recently, been almost universally seen as a failure. And it is certainly true that it left many vital problems unresolved. After more than a century blacks are still second-class citizens. They still are denied equal opportunity. They still suffer discrimination. What went wrong? The obvious answer is: plenty.

After the war President Johnson decided not to summon a special session of Congress. This was a disastrous mistake because Congress would be highly critical of plans adopted in its absence, no matter how wise. It was a mistake too because Johnson, as a southerner himself, could not give even the appearance of leniency without creating the suspicion on the part of northerners that they were being cheated of the fruits of victory. And it was a mistake because it gave the South the false

impression that, if it followed Johnson's lead, all would be well.

By the time Congress met, in December of 1865, northern public opinion was convinced: by issuing wholesale pardons, Johnson had betrayed the nation. The South was trying to reinstitute slavery by passing the notorious black codes; and only the Congress could be trusted to safeguard the rights of the slave and preserve the fruits of victory. Southern opinion, meanwhile, was convinced that the southern states had already met every reasonable demand and should be readmitted as quickly as possible. Under these circumstances, Congressional Reconstruction began. There were two further handicaps. Republicans in Congress were unwilling to break up the plantation system because respect for property rights was too basic to their ideology. And northerners, while determined to give the former slaves some protection, were themselves racist. The limits of their sympathies for black people were quickly reached.

All things considered, we might better marvel that Reconstruction accomplished so much instead of so little. The race question ran too deep to be resolved in so short a time. The South's economy was in a shambles. The task would perhaps have been impossible under the best circumstances. The schools and roads built, the hundreds and thousands fed, the protection given to life and property were not negligible achievements.

Suggested Readings

Recent books on Reconstruction start with Eric Foner's volume of that title (1988). Kenneth Stampp's *The Era of Reconstruction, 1865–1877* (1965) is also thorough on the Reconstruction years. An important study of the consequences of freedom for blacks is Leon F. Litwack's *Been in the Storm So Long: The Aftermath of Slavery* (1979). Michael Les Benedict, *The Impeachment and Trial of Andrew Johnson* (1973) is a superior analysis of the divisions and alignments within the Reconstruction Congress and its relationships with the President, whom the author depicts unfavorably. C. Vann Woodward's *Reunion and Reaction* (1951) is a collection of essays that takes as its theme the South's distinctive heritage. See also

John Hope Franklin, *Reconstruction After the Civil War* (1961), William Gillette, *Retreat from Reconstruction* (1980), Eric McKitrick, *Andrew Johnson and Reconstruction* (1965), and Allen W. Trelease, *White Terror: The Ku Klux Klan Conspiracy and Southern Reconstruction* (1971). See also William E. Nelson, *The Fourteenth Amendment* (1988), and Richard Current, *Those Terrible Carpetbaggers* (1988).

On the Freedmen's Bureau see George R. Bentley, *A History of the Freedmen's Bureau* (1955) and William S. McFeely, *Yankee Step-Father: General O. O. Howard and the Freedmen's Bureau* (1968). A good state study is Joe Gray Taylor's *Louisiana Reconstructed, 1863–1877* (1974).

FORREST McDONALD

The economic consequences of the Civil War and Reconstruction were enormous, most of them flowing from policies of government. Congress increased the tariff from a modest seventeen percent to a highly protective forty-seven percent, and thereby gave a large stimulus to manufacturing; it granted tens of millions of acres of federal land to subsidize the building of railroads; it granted more lands for "land-grant colleges" to provide agricultural and mechanical training and offer extension services. What was most significant was a dramatic change in the pattern of capital accumulation in the United States. Southern capital had been concentrated almost exclusively in slavery and land; and when slavery was abolished, wiping out more than $2 billion of capital in human form, nearly that amount of capital in the form of plantations was also flushed down the drain.

In the North capital was created on a scale that matched its destruction in the South. This took the form of greenback currency and United States government bonds, which represented obligations of the government but also represented an unprecedented concentration of purely liquid capital in private hands. As a result of these various developments, the ultimate triumph of urban capitalism was assured. The rural, agricultural America was not dead, but it did not own the future. The future belonged to the city—which meant merchants, industrialists, and financiers, and if they could win a share, the urban workingmen.

Constitutionally, the results were likewise significant, though they were not nearly so profound as they might have been had the radicals not slackened. State sovereignty as a doctrine was discredited, and the government in Washington increased greatly in authority and in the scope of its powers. The most significant long-range change was the emergence of the Supreme Court as the final arbiter of what the states could and could not do—and, after Congressional radicalism had run its course, as the most energetic branch of the federal government. In the entire period before the war the Court had declared only two acts of Congress unconstitutional, and on both occasions the decisions aroused powerful opposition that threatened the very existence of the Court. During the first decade after the war the Court struck down more than a dozen congressional acts and many state laws, and it virtually nullified the Fourteenth and Fifteenth Amendments, yet almost no one protested.

The ideologues who brought about most important result of all, the abolition of slavery, failed to understand and accommodate in the polity of emancipation a basic conservative principle. The greatest burden the freedmen had to bear was psychological: they had been enculturated into a mentality of dependence and were suddenly thrust into a position of responsibility for their own welfare. In ancient times the Lord had required the Children of Israel to wander the desert for forty years, until none was alive among them who could remember slavery, before He delivered them unto the Promised Land. In 1865 the government of the United States delivered unto an accursed land a people who could remember nothing but slavery; and the efforts of the Freedmen's Bureau to help them learn to cope with the awesome responsibilities of freedom were pathetically inadequate.

And instead of encouraging blacks to fill the millions of jobs created by the technological revolution that was just getting under way, Congress continued an unrestricted immigration policy and even passed a contract labor law, under which industrialists could recruit cheap European labor. Within a generation the vast majority of people in the region, black and white alike, had fallen into the peonage of sharecropping.

Lincoln was right: the nation could not continue to exist half slave and half free, and slavery had to be abolished. But the cost was enormous, and the scars were indelible.

Reconstruction

EUGENE D. GENOVESE

By the Civil War the northern hostility to slavery had made its broadest connections with the other beliefs and habits that characterized the northern culture Professor McDonald speaks of. Slavery came to be identified with economic backwardness, political reaction, and social disorder—with all that was slow and untidy and offensive to the Yankee morality that demanded work and progress. The ideology of the marketplace had a vision of boundless expansion—of enterprise and riches, of liberty and democracy, of free land and booming manufacturers, of a continent to be filled with farms and factories.

On the more immediate social results of the war Professor McDonald is right on one particular: that the efforts of the Freedman's Bureau were inadequate to protect the liberated blacks and bring them fully into the technological future that was being prepared. He does not tell why or in what ways the Bureau acted inadequately. The United States, as daring for the time as it had been in freeing the slaves, had no satisfactory vision of what to do next. It was too racist to make a central project of the integration of blacks into the rest of society. And its notions of the rights of property and the limits of government restrained it from undertaking a program large enough to bring political, economic, and social justice to the Freedmen. It recoiled, for example, from any major redistribution of land of the former slaveholders into the hands of the slaves who had worked it; and that hesitancy meant a failure to make more widespread the property holding that the nation so revered.

An adherence to the property rights of the ex-slaveholders succeeded in preventing the wide and healthy spread of the institution of property. For decades even the enemies of slavery had not known how to attack the institution: slaves had been, after all, property and therefore according to the American mind the absolute possession of their owners. Now once again, the American reverence for property was getting in the way of any intelligent thinking about how property could best serve the common good. Neither the Freedmen's Bureau nor the rest of the northern establishment was able to see how vigorous a social existence the black Americans had developed under slavery, an existence that with government aid could have been made the basis for full social equality. Down to this day, Americans have repeated the mistake. Believing themselves to be staunch defenders of property, they have protected the property of the well-to-do at the expense of imaginative consideration of the better social uses to which property might be put.

During the last decade or two many historians have told us much about that antebellum black society. Among the oppressed peoples of modern times none has surpassed in courage and resourcefulness the blacks who struggled for survival during and after slavery. Despite laws that denied them the right to marry and have legitimate families, despite every attempt to impose upon them a religion that taught submission to the will of their masters, despite the whip and separation from loved ones, despite countless abuses and indignities, they created a powerful religious and family life of their own, which sustained their sense of humanity, justice, and deliverance—which kept alive their determination to be free. In the 1860s they became free, or free according to law, but soon afterwards their liberators became interested in other things, abandoned them to the nation's powerful white racist majority, and therein blighted the promise that even as slaves blacks had implicitly, perhaps unconsciously, made to themselves to live as a free community.

Appendixes

Succeeding in History Courses
by John McClymer

STUDYING HISTORY AND STUDYING FOR EXAMS

The instructor who designed this course hopes you will take advantage of the opportunity to learn about the American past. Your own objectives in taking the course may be somewhat different. You may be taking it because it fulfills some requirement for graduation or because it fits into your schedule or, perish the thought, because it seems less objectionable than the alternative you could be taking.

In a better world, these differences between your objectives and those of the course would not matter. The studying you do to perform well on exams and papers would involve your learning a fair amount of history. And so your grade would certify that you had indeed left the course with a more informed and thoughtful understanding of the American past than you had when you entered it. Unhappily, in the world we must actually live in, the connection between studying history and studying for exams in history is not necessarily so clear or straightforward.

The hard fact is that many students manage to prepare themselves for mid-terms and finals without permanently adding to their understanding. There they sit, yellow hi-liting pens in hand, plodding through the assigned chapters. Grim-faced, they underline every declarative sentence in sight. Then they trace and retrace their tracks trying to commit every yellowed fact to memory. As the time of the test draws near, they choke back that first faint feeling of panic by trying to guess the likeliest question. The instructor is never, they say to themselves, going to ask us to identify George Washington. But what about Silas Deane? And Pinckney? No, wait. There were TWO Pinckneys! That means there is almost certainly going to be a question about ONE of them. So it is that some students devote more energy to Thomas and Charles Cotesworth Pinckney than they do to George Washington. By such tactics they may get ready for the exam, but sabotage their chance of gaining any insight into American history.

Life does afford worse tragedies. This one, however, is remediable. And this appendix can help. It is designed to help you do well in the course, and to help you learn some history. It is, in fact, dedicated to the proposition that the easiest and most satisfying way to succeed in a history course is to learn some history. It makes very little sense, after all is said and done, to spend your time trying to keep the Pinckneys straight or running down a fact or two about Silas Deane. What will it profit you? You may pick up a few points on the short answer section of the exam, but those few points are a small reward for hours of studying. And, in the meantime, your essay on Washington as a political leader was distinctly mediocre. Clearly something is wrong.

That something is that studying for exams is a poor way of learning history. On the other hand, studying history is an excellent way of preparing for exams. If you had, for example, thought about American relations with France during John Adams' presidency, you would very probably remember who Charles C. Pinckney was. And you would scarcely have had to memorize anything.

The object of this essay is to persuade you to make some changes in the way you study. The first is to conserve your yellow pens. All that hi-liting simply lowers the resale value of the book. If you underline everything you read, you will wind up with a book of underlinings. There may be some psychological comfort in that. All of that yellow does provide visible evidence that you read the material. Unfortunately, it will not leave you with a useful guide to what to review. You have hi-lited too much.

A second drawback follows from the first. You have created a democracy of facts. All names, dates, and events are equally yellow. The Pinckneys and Silas Deane, in other words, have just become as noteworthy as George Washington or John Adams. You need, more than anything else, some way of determining what is important.

The next step may prove harder. You will have to give up trying to learn history by rote. A certain amount of memorizing may be unavoidable in a survey course, but ultimately it is the enemy of understanding. That is because many people use it as an alternative to thinking. Have you ever wished there were a better way? Well, there is. If you understand what Lincoln had hoped to accomplish with the Emancipation Proclamation, for example, you will not need to memorize its provisions. You will know why it did not promise freedom to any of the slaves in states (like Maryland or Missouri) which remained loyal to the Union. You will know why the Proclamation did not go into effect until one hundred days after it was issued. You will not, in short, stumble over a question like: "Whom did the Emancipation Proclamation emancipate?"

Facts are by no means unimportant. It is essential to have something to think about. But it is generally more fun to pay attention to ideas. Lincoln, to pursue this example, was interested above all else in restoring the Union. He was perfectly willing, he said, to keep slavery if that would accomplish his purpose; he was equally willing to abolish slavery if that would do the trick. So there is no mystery that in the Emancipation Proclamation he gave the states of the Confederacy one hundred days to return to the Union on pain of losing their slaves if they did not. The same reason explains why the Proclamation did not apply to slave states still in the Union.

If you take care of the ideas, the facts will assemble themselves. There are two reasons for this happy state of affairs. One has to do with the way in which textbooks are written and courses taught. The other has to do with the way people learn.

No historian, including the authors of the text and your instructor, pretends that history is the story of everything that ever happened. Obviously, many things happened for which there are no surviving records. More importantly, scholars use the records that have survived in a highly selective way. Even though they are always interested in finding new information, and in finding new ways of using information already known, each individual work of history—be it an article, a doctoral dissertation, a monograph, a textbook, a course of lectures—represents hundreds and thousands of choices about what to include and what to omit. Much more is known, for example, about the signers of the Declaration of Independence than you will read in any textbook. What you actually encounter in this course, as a result, is here because the text authors or your teacher decided for some reason to include it. Usually the reason is that this particular bit of information helps explain or illustrate some pattern of behavior or thought. The moral for you should be clear. Focus on these patterns. They are what you should be thinking about.

If you do, learning theorists have some good news for you. They have found that while it is

difficult for the average person to recall disconnected bits of data (for example, which Pinckney was an emissary to France during the XYZ affair), it is comparatively easy to remember details of coherent stories. This is not a very startling finding. Details make sense once you see how they fit together. Let us return to the example of the Emancipation Proclamation. Lincoln's actions followed from: 1) his political priorities in which the integrity of the Union outranked achieving peace or ending slavery, 2) his analysis of the course of the war, and, 3) his perception of the choices open to him. Had Lincoln valued peace or ending slavery more highly than the Union, had easy victory or actual defeat seemed near at hand, had other inducements to the states of Confederacy to return to the Union seemed more promising, he would have acted differently. Once Lincoln's perception of the situation becomes clear to you, you will have little, if any, difficulty remembering what he did.

Neither compulsive underlining nor prodigious memorization will help you to understand these patterns. What will? We can rephrase the question: What does it mean to read and listen intelligently? For most of us, reading and listening are passive forms of behavior. We sit and wait to be told. Someone else, we expect, will provide the answers. Worse, we expect someone else will provide the questions. And, of course, they do. For our part, we limit ourselves to hi-liting and jotting notes. At best, this situation leaves us with a more or less adequate record of what someone else thinks we should know.

Most of what passes for studying involves not a conscientious effort to wrestle with the subject, but a determined effort to be prepared to answer likely questions. That is why we pay more heed to Silas Deane than to George Washington. It is why studying for exams is such a poor way to learn history. And, its chief drawback perhaps from your point of view, it is usually a recipe for earning a mediocre grade.

Letting your teacher or the authors of the text do your thinking for you also leads to tedium. The simple truth is that passivity is boring. Yet we rarely blame ourselves for being bored. It can not be our own fault. We are only "taking" the course. Someone else is "giving" it, and so we look to the instructor to liven things up a bit. Maybe some audio-visuals or a bit of humor, we think, would make the course less dreary. These hopes are misplaced for, while humor is a blessed thing and audio-visuals have their place, it is the nitty-gritty of the course that should interest us.

Boredom is almost always a self-inflicted wound. Students are bored because they expect the instructor to be interesting when it is they who must themselves take an interest. Teacher and students are equally responsible for the success of a course. Most of the students in American history courses will live out the rest of their lives in the United States. Their lives will be affected for both good and ill by what has happened in the American past. It follows that the simple desire to make sense of their own lives should lead them to take an interest in this course.

Taking an interest involves learning to read and listen actively. Intellectual activity begins with questions—Your own questions directed, in the first instance, to yourself and then to your teacher. Why is it, you might wonder, that the United States is the only industrialized country without a comprehensive national system of health care? Why did slavery last so long in the American South? Why did the Founding Fathers establish a republic? And why did a party system develop even though the founders were bitterly opposed to political parties? Why, for that matter, were they so set against parties in the first place?

You will not always find satisfactory answers. But you will have started to think about the meaning of the American past. And when you do, something quite desirable happens to all of those facts. They will take on life and become evidence, clues to the answers you are seeking. The questions, that is, will give you a rational basis for deciding which facts are important. And George Washington will finally receive his well-deserved priority over the Pinckneys.

All of this leads directly to the question of how you should study for this course. It is a truism that students do poorly when they are ill-prepared. But we too easily assume that the sole reason why we are sometimes ill-prepared is because we did not spend enough time getting ready. This is a half-truth, and a dangerous one. It ignores the critical fact that we often use the time we spend reviewing very inefficiently. And, since there is often no practical way of increasing the time we have to review (there being, after all, only so many working hours in the day), it makes far more sense to use the time we do have effectively instead of moaning about how we should have studied more.

How do you get ready for an exam? Do you get out your textbook and notes and pour over them again and again until the time runs out or the sheer boredom of it all crushes your good intentions? If so, then you have lots of company—a consolation of sorts. There is, on the other hand, a better way.

Find a quiet and comfortable spot (something not always easy to do in a dormitory). Bring along a blank pad and something to write with. Then jot down, just as they occur to you, whatever items you can remember about the course. Do not rush yourself. And do not try, at this stage, to put things in order. Just sit there and scribble down whatever pops into your mind. After a while you will have quite a large and varied mix of names, ideas, dates and events. Then see how much of this you can put together. There is no need to write out whole sentences or paragraphs. An arrow or a word or two will frequently be enough. You are not, after all, going to hand these scribbles in. You are just collecting your thoughts. Do not be concerned if this process seems to be taking up some of the limited time you have to study. It will prove to be time well spent.

Now look over what you have written. Where are the gaps? You will find that you know a fair bit about the material just from your previous reading of the text and from listening in class. But some topics will still be obscure. You may, for example, pretty well understand why Polk declared war on Mexico, but you may feel less sure about his negotiations with Great Britain over Oregon. All right. Now you know what you should be studying. There is no reason for you to go over the war with Mexico. Why study what you already know. And here is the nub of the matter, for an intelligent review is one that focuses on what you need to refresh your mind about.

You will doubtless have noticed that this strategy presupposes that you have read the textbook and taken good notes in class. Just what, you might wonder, are good notes? Many students think that the closer they come to transcribing the instructor's every word the better their notes are. They are mistaken. There are several reasons why. Unless your shorthand is topnotch, you will not succeed. Instead you will be frantically scrambling to catch up. In the process you will not only miss some of what is said, but you will pay attention to scarcely any of the lecture. At the end of class you will have: 1) a sore hand; 2) a great deal of barely legible notes; and 3) little if any idea of what the class was about.

Another reason not to attempt to transcribe lectures (taping them, by the way, is usually a poor idea) is that you will spend much of your time taking down information you either already know or can easily find in the textbook. How often do you need to see the fact that Jefferson Davis was the president of the Confederacy? A sensible person will decide once is enough.

The most important reason not to take down everything is that it prevents you from doing what you ought to be doing during class, listening intelligently. Your instructor is not simply transmitting information during a lecture but is also seeking to explain the hows and whys of the American past. It is these explanations you should be listening for, and your notes should focus on them. It is much easier to do this if you have read the relevant textbook chapters first. That way you will already know much of the factual information. And you will have, one hopes, some questions already in your mind. You will have, that is, something to listen for. And you can take notes sensibly. You can fill in explanations of points that had puzzled you, jot down unfamiliar facts, and devote most of your time to listening instead of writing. Your hand will not be sore; you will know what the class was about; and your notes will complement rather than duplicate what you already knew.

So far we have dealt mainly with the mechanics of studying—taking notes, reviewing for exams, and the like. Valuable as knowing the mechanics can be, and in terms of your grade they can be very valuable indeed, the real secret to studying history is learning how to think historically. History is both a body of knowledge about the past and a way of thinking about the human condition. You are probably familiar with the first of these two aspects of the subject. History is knowing about the Revolution, the Civil War, and so on. It is knowing, that is, that they happened, when they happened, and how they happened. It is also having some explanation of why they happened as they did, and of the differences their happening made. All of that is undoubtedly perfectly obvious to you. It may, in fact, seem to include the sum and substance of history. It does not.

History is also a way of thinking. It rests on the assumption that you understand what something is by finding out how it came to be that way. This is an assumption which, consciously or not, you share. When you ask friends how they are doing, for example, you are really asking what has happened to them since you last met. You are asking about the past—the recent past to be sure—but the past nonetheless. You accept, that is, the axiom that the past has consequences for the present and the future. If your roommate has just failed an organic chemistry final, to use a sad but not uncommon occurrence, you both know what that will mean for her chances of getting into medical school.

You also know, if you think about it for a minute, that the political beliefs of the Founding Fathers still matter. They matter not only because their beliefs continue to influence our own but also because we continue to use them as the standard against which we measure present-day political figures. You can even appreciate that the child-rearing practices of the Puritans are worth knowing about—not of course because they have been passed down unchanged from the seventeenth century nor because they provide a model for you in raising your own family, but because we can not understand changing cultural realities or social practices unless we first have a clear idea of what they were once like. Change, in short, is incomprehensible if we do not have a point of reference from which to measure it. And history alone can provide us with such a fixed point.

Learning to think historically is a simple necessity if we hope to make sense of the world around us. Fortunately, it involves nothing more than learning to employ in a disciplined way the same patterns of thought we already use on a daily basis. That your roommate failed organic chemistry is a historical fact just as Lincoln's victory in the presidential election of 1860 is. How your roommate failed, and how Lincoln won, can also be determined factually, to some degree. You can, that is, discover which questions your roommate got wrong, just as you can find out which states Lincoln carried. You can even begin to assemble facts which will help explain why your roommate missed those particular questions and why Lincoln won those particular states. With regard to your roommate, you might recall that she cut a number of classes. You could hypothesize that some of the material covered in those classes was on the exam. You might recall that your roommate had a political science paper to finish the week before the exam. Perhaps that kept her from studying chemistry thoroughly.

Similarly you could determine with some accuracy which voting blocs went for Lincoln. You could then analyze the campaign issues and speculate about how those constituencies lined up on those issues. In both cases you would be trying to marshall the facts so that they would support some interpretation. Clearly, if you could know all of the facts, and if there were only one possible explanation for them, your interpretation would be true in the same way that the facts themselves are true. You could say: it happened this way and no other.

Unfortunately, life is not so amenable to explanation. You will never have all the facts, and no explanation will ever be the only one possible. Consider your roommate's "F" in organic. You know which questions were missed. But the questions on the exam could have been different. Then your roommate's grade would, possibly, have also been different. So knowing which questions your roommate lost points on is not enough. You would also have to know why these particular questions, and not others, were on the test in the first place. Consider too that the test scores were probably "curved." A more forgiving curve might have allowed your roommate to pass. But to know why the curve was the way it was you would have to know why the other raw scores were the way they were. Your roommate's raw score, the actual points lost on particular questions, in other words, is only half the story. That score could, presumably, have become an "A" if other students in the course had done even worse than your roommate. There is no need to pursue the point any farther. It is clear that you could never be sure you knew all of the relevant facts. And if this be true for your roommate's "F", how much more obviously true it must be for Lincoln's election. There were millions of voters. Who could know why they all voted as they did?

Despite all of this you may feel—and quite sensibly—that your roommate's "F" is hardly an impenetrable enigma. You may not know everything about it, but you know enough. You can offer an explanation that fits the facts you do know and is congruent with what you know of your roommate's study habits, general intelligence, and so forth. What you have is an interpretation. So too with Lincoln's election. People may have had reasons for voting as they did that you will never know, but you can supply enough reasons to explain why he won. You can explain, that is, what is known, and your view is compatible with what is known about American elections during that period.

You can perhaps already see how to define a convincing interpretation. It is one that provides that simplest sensible account of why something happened. The goal of historical inquiry is interpretation. And while, as we have seen, interpretation is not synonymous with truth, it is something more than mere opinion.

Anyone can have an opinion. People claim that have a right to have opinions about anything and everything (some even seem to feel it is their duty to have an opinion about everything). But you have to earn the right to offer an interpretation because an interpretation is a thoughtful explanation based on a careful assessment of evidence. It follows that when you find scholars disagreeing over how to interpret the American Revolution, say, as Professors McDonald and Genovese do in one of their debates, you ought not to conclude that their dispute is "just a matter of opinion" or that the truth probably lies somewhere in the middle (an old saw that should be

permanently retired) or that one opinion (yours included) is just as good as another. Rather you need to ask: how well do these interpretations accord with what I know about the Revolution? How much sense can I make of what happened before and after it by using one or another of these explanations? The debates, in short, are an invitation to you to think about the meaning of American history. They should prompt you to struggle with the issues in your own mind and to come up with your own interpretation.

You may feel somewhat hesitant about putting your own interpretation forward, particularly if it differs markedly from those offered by your instructor or the authors of the text. And, within limits, you should be hesitant. A certain intellectual modesty is becoming in a beginning student. But you have read the material; you have listened intelligently in class; and you have thought about the issues. So you have the right to a view of your own. Teaching is not indoctrination. The object of the course is not to tell you what to think. The goal is to help you learn to think for yourself. You are therefore entitled to disagree.

When presenting your own interpretation, whether or not it agrees with one you have already encountered, you should always explain clearly how you reached that particular conclusion. This means explaining what evidence you found most important; it means explaining why that evidence struck you as important; and it means explaining the logic of your position. If you can do these three things, then you need not fear presenting your own ideas.

This appendix has an additional feature designed to help you think about how historical interpretations are developed and tested. This is a section on how to read the McDonald-Genovese debates. You will quickly realize, as you read the debates, that McDonald and Genovese rarely disagree over the facts of American history. They disagree over which facts are important and over how they should be interpreted. This section contains suggested exercises you can do on your own, or which your instructor can assign, that will enable you to read the debates more critically.

It is now time to see how these general considerations about studying history apply to specific tasks you will have to undertake in this course. We will start with how to take midterm and final examinations.

HOW TO TAKE EXAMS

In the best of all possible worlds examinations would hold no terrors. You would be so well prepared that no question, no matter how tricky or obscure, could shake your serene confidence. Unfortunately, the real world normally finds the average student in a different situation. Somehow it seems one's preparation is always less than complete. And so one approaches exams with some anxiety. "Of course," one says to oneself, "I should have studied more. But I did not. Now what?" This section can not tell you how to get A's without studying, but it can suggest some practical steps which can help you earn the highest grade compatible with what you do know.

The first step is to look over the entire exam before you start answering any of it. It is impossible to budget your time sensibly until you know what the whole exam looks like. And if you fail to allow enough time for each question, two things—both bad—are likely to happen. The first is that you may have to leave some questions out, including perhaps some you might have answered very effectively. How often have you muttered: "I really knew that one!"? The other unhappy consequence is that you may have to rush through the last part of the exam. Again, there may be questions you could have answered very well if you had had more time.

How do you budget your time effectively? The idea, after all, is to make sure that you have enough time to answer fully all the questions you do know. So the best plan is also the simplest. Answer those questions first. It may feel a bit odd at first answering question #7 before #4, but you will soon enough get used to it. And you will find that, if you still run out of time, you at least have the satisfaction of knowing you are rushing through or leaving out questions you could not have answered very well anyway. You will, in other words, have guaranteed that you will receive the maximum credit for what you do know.

There is another advantage to answering questions in the order of your knowledge instead of in the order asked. Most students are at least a little tense before an exam. If you answer the first several questions well, that tension will likely go away. As you relax, you will find it easier to remember names, dates, and other bits of information. Contrariwise, if you get off to a shaky start, that simple case of pre-exam jitters can become full-scale panic. Should that happen, you may have trouble remembering your own phone number, and your chances of recalling those facts which are just on the tip of your tongue will shrink to the vanishing point. Obviously, it is very important to get off to a good start. So do not trust to luck. Do not just hope the first couple of questions are easy. You can make sure you get off on the right foot by answering first whatever questions you are sure of.

Let us suppose you have gotten through everything you think you know on the exam and you still have some time left. What should you do? You can now try to pick up a few extra points with some judicious guessing. There is not much point to trying to guess with essay questions. In all probability you will write something so vague that you will not get any credit for it anyway. Rather you should try to score on the short-answer section. Some types of questions were made for shrewd guesswork. Matching columns are ideal. A process of elimination will often tell you what the answer has to be. Multiple choice questions are almost as good. Here too you can eliminate some of the possibilities. Most teachers feel obligated to give you a choice of four or five possible answers, but find it hard to come up with more than three that are plausible. So you can normally count on being able to recognize the one or two that are just there as padding.

Once you have narrowed the choices down to two or three, you are ready to make your educated guess. There are three rules. 1) Always play your hunches, however vague. Your hunch is based on something you heard or read even if you can not remember what it is. So go with it. 2) Do not take your time. If you can not think of the answer, just pick one and have done with it. 3) Try to avoid changing answers. There are a number of studies showing that you are more likely to change a right answer than to correct a wrong one.

Identifications are the type of short-answer question most resistant to guesswork. Unless you have a fairly strong hunch about the answer, you should leave this sort of question blank. The reason is that while it is true that an incorrect answer will cost you no more points than leaving the question out altogether, it is also true that an incorrect answer says something about the depths of your ignorance which a blank space does not. You want the exam as a whole to convey what you do know. Supplying a mass of misinformation usually creates a presumption that you do not know what you are talking about even on those sections of the exam when you really do. So be careful about wild guesses. They are almost sure to do more harm than good.

These suggestions are not substitutes for studying. They may, however, help you get the most out of what you know. They may, that is, spell the difference between a mediocre grade and a good one.

HOW TO WRITE BOOK REVIEWS

One goal of book reviews is to set forth clearly and succinctly who (if anyone) would benefit from reading the work in question. It follows that a good review indicates the scope of the book, identifies its point of view, summarizes its main conclusions, evaluates its use of evidence, and—where possible—compares the book with others on the subject.

It is highly likely that you have written book reviews in high school or in other college courses so it is important that you do not approach this kind of assignment with a false sense of security. It sounds easy, after all, to write a five-hundred-or-so word essay. And you have written lots of other reviews. But did those other reviews focus clearly on the questions a good review must address? If they did not, your previous experience is not going to prove especially helpful. It may even prove something of a handicap. You may have developed some bad habits.

Easily the worst habit is that of summarizing not the book's argument but its contents. Let us suppose you are reviewing a biography of George Washington. The temptation is to write about Washington rather than about the book. This is a sure path to disaster. Washington had, to put it mildly, an eventful career. You are certainly not going to do it justice in a few paragraphs. And you are not, in all probability, going to find that much that is fresh or interesting to say about him. Meanwhile you have ignored your primary responsibility which is to tell the reader whether this biography has anything fresh or interesting to say.

So you need to remind yourself as forcefully as possible that your job is to review the book and not the subject of the book. Does the book focus narrowly on Washington or does it also go into the general history of America during those years? Is the author sympathetic to Washington, tending to see things Washington's way? Does the writer attempt to psychoanalyze Washington or stick to political and military questions? Is there a firm command of the available evidence (this requires you, alas, to read the footnotes)? And, last but not least, does the author have something new to say about Washington and his times? If so, how well documented is this new interpretation?

It is less important to evaluate how well the author writes. While it is hard to imagine a poorly written novel that is still worth reading, it is common enough (unhappily) for important historical works to be written in a plodding fashion. So you should comment on the quality of the author's prose, but you should generally not make that an important part of your overall evaluation unless it is so good or so awful that it makes reading the work sheer bliss or unrelieved torture.

You should generally not comment on whether or not you enjoyed the book. That is undoubtedly an important consideration for you, but it is of little interest to anyone else. There are some occasions when you need to suffer in silence. This is one of them.

HOW TO SELECT A TERM PAPER TOPIC

Doing research, as you may already have had occasion to learn, is hard work. Worse yet, it is often boring. Typically it involves long periods of going through material that is not what you were looking for and is not particularly interesting. It also involves taking detailed and careful notes, many of which you will never use. These are the dues you must pay if you are ever to earn the excitement which comes when you finally find that missing piece of evidence and make sense of things.

Not everything about doing research is boring. Aside from the indescribable sensation of actually finding out what you wanted to know, there are also occasional happy accidents where you stumble across something which, while not relevant to your research, nonetheless pricks your imagination. Many a historian studying an old political campaign has read up on the pennant races or fashions or radio listings for that year. These are, as one scholar put it, oases in the desert of historical evidence. But, as he quickly added, no one crosses the desert just to get to the oasis. The truth of the matter is that you have to have a good reason for getting to the other side. This means a topic you are genuinely interested in.

The point cannot be overemphasized. If you have a question you really want to answer, you will find it much easier to endure the tedium of turning all those pages. You will have a motive for taking good notes and for keeping your facts straight. If you are not truly interested in your topic, on the other hand, you may be in trouble. You are going to be constantly tempted to take short-cuts. And even if you resist temptation, you are going to find it hard to think seriously about what you do find.

So the topic has to interest you. That, you may be thinking, is easy to say. But what if your interest in American history is less than compelling? What if, perish the thought, you do not give two figs about the whole American past? Are you then going to be stuck with some topic you could care little about? The answer is "No". "No," that is, unless it turns out that you have no curiosity about anything at all; and, if that is the case, you are probably dead already or nearly so. Anything that can be examined chronologically is fair game for the historian. There are histories of sports and of sciences, of sexual practices and jokes about them, of work and of recreation. It is odd, to say the least, that students so often choose to write of war, politics, and diplomacy even when their real interests lie elsewhere. If you use your imagination, you should be able to find a topic which you are genuinely interested in and which your teacher agrees merits serious study. This being true, you have no one to blame but yourself if you wind up writing on some question you are not passionately concerned with answering.

Once you have such a topic you need to find ways of defining it so that you can write an intelligent essay. "The Automobile in American Life" could well serve as the subject for a very long book. It is not going to work as a subject for a term paper, and for two compelling reasons. First, you could not possibly research so vast a topic in the time you have to work with. Second, your paper, however long, is not going to be of book length—in fact it is not likely to exceed 5,000 words. So you would be stuck with trying to compress an immense amount of information into a brief essay. The final product will be a disaster.

You need to focus on some aspect of the general topic which can be intelligently treated in the space and time you have to work with. Students usually look at this problem backwards. They complain about how long their papers have to be. They should complain about how short they have to be. Space is a luxury you normally can not afford. If you have done a fair amount of research on an interesting topic, your problem is going to be one of finding a way of getting all you have to say into your paper. Writing consists of choices about what you want to say. And if you have done your work properly, the hard choices involve deciding what to leave out.

"Fair enough," you may be thinking, "but I do not want to get stuck researching some minute bit of trivia, the 'gear shift level from 1940 to 1953,' for example. I want to study the automobile in American life." Here we come to the heart of the matter. Your topic must be narrowly defined so that you can do it justice, but it must also throw some light on the broad question that interested you in the first place. This is easier said than done, but it can be done. The trick is to decide just what it is about your topic—cars in this instance—that really interests you. Cars are means of transportation, of course, but they are also examples of technology, status symbols, and much else besides. Because of the automobile, cities and suburbs are designed in ways very different from how they were when people traveled by trolley or train. Because of the automobile, even teenage dating patterns are what they are. Having a driver's license, and regular access to a car, has become a crucial part of growing up.

The point is that you have to think about your topic and then decide what aspect of it to examine. If you wind up doing a treatise on changing methods of changing tires, you have only yourself to blame. You could have been studying sex and sexism in automobile advertising.

HOW TO LOCATE MATERIAL

Once you have worked up an interesting and practical topic for your term paper, you are ready to begin your research. For many students this means ambling over to the library and poking around in the card catalog. This may not be the best way to begin because the librarians who catalog the library's holdings, while skilled professionals, cannot possibly anticipate the needs of every individual researcher. So they catalog books by their main subject headings and then include obvious cross-references. Much of what you need, on the other hand, may not be obvious. So, for example, if you are interested in the causes of the Civil War, you will have no trouble finding a title like Kenneth Stampp's *And The War Came* listed under "U.S. History, Civil War." But will you find Roy Nichol's *Disruption of the American Democracy?* You may not.

The point is that there may be a number of important works in your library you will not be able to find if you start by checking the card catalog. What should you do instead? The first thing is to locate the *Harvard Guide To American History*. This is an invaluable tool. It will tell you the best (in the editors' opinion) books and articles on your subject. For each title prepare a separate card listing full bibliographic specifics (i.e., the author's full name, the complete title including subtitle, the place of publication, the edition, and if a journal article the volume and issue numbers). You will need all of this information.

Now you have the beginnings of a decent bibliography. Your next step should be to introduce yourself to the research librarian. This person's specialty is helping people look for information. Yet many students never consult with a librarian.

Do not pass up an opportunity to make your work easier! Ask your research librarian to help. Often he can point you to more specialized bibliographical guides, can show you where to learn of the most recent books and articles, and can help you refine your topic by indicating what aspects are easiest to get information on.

You now have a reasonably extensive set of cards. And you can now safely consult the card catalog to see which of these titles your library has. Prepare yourself for some disappointments. Even good undergraduate libraries will not have everything you need. They will have some (unless your library is very weak or your topic very esoteric). Virtually all college libraries participate in the inter-library loan system. This system, which the library staff will gladly explain to you, will permit you to get virtually any title you could wish for. The only catch is that you must give the library enough lead time. For books and articles which are not especially rare this normally means one to three weeks.

HOW TO TAKE NOTES

As you sift through the material you have found you will need to take careful notes. As you do, you should write down each piece of information which you believe might prove relevant on a notecard. You also will need to specify the full source for each piece of information.

If you follow these two bits of advice, you will save yourself much time and trouble. Finding information the first time, in your sources, is trouble enough. You do not want to have to find it all over again when you sit down to write your paper. But this is often just what students have to do because they discover that they did not bother to write down some bit of data (which, perhaps, seemed only marginally important at the time) or because they took all of their notes on loose leaf paper and now must search through every page to find this one fact. It is far easier, over the long run, to have a separate card for each piece, or closely related pieces, of information. Tell yourself that you are the last of the big time spenders and can afford to use up index cards as though they were blank pieces of paper. After all, that is what they are.

The general rule is that you should take extra pains when compiling your research notes so that the actual writing will be as trouble-free as possible. It follows from this that you should take lots of notes. Do not try to determine in advance whether or not you are going to use a particular bit of data. Always give yourself the benefit of the doubt. Similarly, do not try to decide in advance whether you will quote the source exactly or simply paraphrase it. If you take down the exact words, you can always decide to make the idea your own by qualifying it in various ways and putting it in your own words. When taking notes, in brief, your motto should be: the more the merrier.

WRITING TERM PAPERS AND OTHER ESSAYS

You have no doubt already learned that next to mastery of the subject matter nothing is more important for earning good grades than effective writing. You surely know people whose study habits are not all that they should be but whose grades are high. Nine times out of ten the secret of their success is their ability to write well. What they have to say may not always be all that impressive, but the way they say it is.

Students who are not among that relatively small group who write well sometimes think it unfair that writing skills should count so heavily. The course, some complain, is American History, not Creative Writing, and so their grade should not be influenced by their prose. Only what they know about history should count. But most teachers continue to believe that the ability to express what you know clearly and forcefully is an indispensable measure of how well you have learned the subject matter. So, like it or not, your writing is going to count. Writing well is an invaluable skill, and not only in college. Most good jobs (and most not-so-good ones) involve writing. There is correspondence, there are reports, there are memoranda. The writing will never stop.

No matter how poorly you write, you can learn to write effectively. This is not to say that anyone who desires it can become a brilliant prose stylist. Great talent is rare in every field. But anyone who can speak English effectively can learn to write it effectively. It is simply a matter of expressing your ideas clearly. This you can learn to do. It does not require genius, merely patience and practice.

Charity, St. Paul said, was the chief of all the virtues. In expository prose, however, the chief virtue is clarity. And like charity, it covers a multitude of sins. Be they ever so humble, or homely, your sentences will receive a sympathetic reading if they are clear. Why? There are a number of reasons. The first is that your papers, reviews, and essays—while they may seem very long to you when writing them—are in reality quite brief. A twenty-page paper, for example, only contains 5,000 words. This means that you do not have very much space to get your ideas across. The less space you have, the more carefully you have to choose your words. If it takes you four or five pages to get to the point, you have wasted a substantial portion of your essay. (If, on the other hand, you were writing a 500 page book, those four or five pages would not matter so much.)

It has perhaps crossed your mind that there are occasions when you are not very eager to get to the point. Sometimes you may not be sure just what the point is. Sometimes you do know, but are not convinced that your point is a very good one. At such times, a little obfuscation may seem a better idea than clarity. It is not. I can assure you, based on my experience as a college teacher (which has involved reading thousands of student papers), there is nothing more troubling than reading a paper where the author tried to hedge bets or fudge ideas. The very worst thing you can do is leave it up to your reader (also known as your instructor) to decide what you are trying to say. Teachers, as a group, have not heeded St. Paul. They conspicuously lack charity when reading student papers. They will not give you the benefit of the doubt. They will, more often than not, decide that you did not get to the point because you do not know the material. We teachers can be a heartless breed. So, no matter how weak your ideas seem to you, set them forth clearly. Something is always better than nothing.

Clarity is a virtue in part because so many papers from other students will not exemplify it. As a result, your teacher will be inclined to read yours more sympathetically. What you said may not have been brilliant, but it did make sense. And, contrary to popular reports, most teachers really are interested in helping students. It is much easier to help you if your instructor can figure out what you were trying to say.

My mistakes will stand out, you are thinking. That sounds very dangerous. We have all been conditioned to avoid detection. The last thing we want is for the teacher to find out that we do not know something. But teachers delight in watching students improve. The reason is obvious: they see it as proof that they are doing a good job. They take special pleasure in the progress of students who start off poorly but steadily get better over the course of the semester. You can do a lot worse than be one of those students.

Let us assume that you are willing to give clarify a try. How do you go about writing clearly? The first rule of thumb is to avoid complexity. You should strive to write simply and directly.

This does not mean that you are limited to a basic 1500-word vocabulary. There are hundreds of thousands of words in the language and you are entitled to use any of them, provided only that you use them correctly. You should not, on the other hand, go out of your way to find esoteric words or expressions. Use words that accurately express your meaning. Wherever possible use words that are part of your ordinary vocabulary. Above all, do not try to impress your instructor by using synonyms you located in a dictionary or, worse yet, a thesaurus. You run a high risk of using these words incorrectly because they may have connotations you are unaware of.

You should also avoid complicated grammatical structures. Do you know when to use the subjunctive mood? Do you know the rules about using semi-colons? Do you know which types of subordinate clauses require commas? If you have answered any or all of these questions negatively, then you should bone up on your grammar. And, in the meantime, you should avoid writing sentences where these kinds of questions arise. There is no reason to increase the probability of making an error. Grammatical errors can often be avoided simply by keeping your sentences fairly short. Qualifications of your main idea can go into separate sentences. You do not have to fit everything into a single sentence. Furthermore, your sentences will have more pace and rhythm if you keep them relatively short.

Grammatical difficulties—be they outright errors or merely negligent constructions—are a writer's nightmare. Each time you make an error or use an awkward phrase you distract the reader. He or she stops paying attention to what you are saying and instead focuses on how you are saying it. If you distract the reader often enough (four or five times a page will do it in most cases), you will have reduced your chances of getting your ideas across virtually to zero.

So it is vitally important to eliminate grammatical problems. This is, of course, easier said than done. But there are ways to do it. Many schools have writing centers where you can get help with your papers. If your school has such a center, use it. The improvement in both your prose and your G.P.A. can be dramatic. If your school lacks a writing workshop, ask your teacher to read over an early draft of your paper. This is the reader you have to please after all. So why not go straight to the source?

You may have observed that both of these suggestions presume that you will have completed an early draft. And so you should. But let us suppose that, like most college students, you write your papers by the dawn's early light just before they are due. You do not have an early draft. If you find yourself in this all-too-common situation, you may still be able to find someone who will, as a favor, read over your paper before you type the final version. There are college students who have a good working knowledge of grammar. You need to find one and get him or her to edit your work, that is, help you get rid of the most blatant errors. This person can also tell you if your paper is easy to follow. You should write so that someone unfamiliar with the subject but reasonably well informed in other respects can understand what you are saying. Such a person makes an excellent reader and can help you pinpoint the ideas you need to explain more fully.

Once you have worked out a scheme for eliminating grammatical shortcomings, you can turn to the equally crucial chore of articulating your ideas. This means deciding the most cogent sequence in which to present them, on the one hand, and explicating the connections between them on the other. The first order of business is making sure that your opening paragraphs clearly set out what your paper is about and how you are going to approach this topic. Your opening sentences should explain: what your topic involves; why it is worth investigating; and how you are going to look into it. If your topic were, for example, "Sex and Sexism in Automobile Advertising," you might write something like the following:

> The automobile is more than a means of transportation. It is also a powerful engine of change. Highways and suburbs have altered the human and physical geography of the nation. Shopping malls and drive-ins have transformed the retail economy. Social practices—from dating customs to recreational patterns—bear the imprint of the car. Cars have also come to symbolize status and prestige. Expensive models are perceived, and marketed, as visible signs of success. As a result, changing automotive advertising campaigns provide a wealth of data about how Americans have conceptualized the "good life" in this century.
>
> Success means different things to different people, but—if the car ads are to be believed—Americans tend to think of success in terms of power and sex.

You will note that this example sets the topic in a larger context, explains what the paper will examine (power and sex as components of the American idea of success), and how it will examine them (by analyzing changing patterns of au-

tomotive advertising). Further it explains why these ads are an important source of material for this topic.

"Well begun," the adage runs, "is half done." This is especially true in writing papers and essays. A good opening tells the reader what to expect. It piques curiosity and makes one eager to read on. A poor opening (one, that is, which leaves the reader still wondering what the paper is about or why a certain topic is important) does the opposite. So work on your openings! You may not have the time to write several drafts of your paper (although you should make the time), but you must take the time to rewrite your introduction as many times as necessary for it to sparkle.

You, as the author, have the responsibility of directing your reader's attention. You do this by explaining the logical connection(s) between the points you raise. You can not assume that your reader will figure out the logic of your paper. Your reader, you should recall, is a professional skeptic who starts from the assumption that you do not know what you are talking about. So it is the height of folly to assume that your instructor will supply logical connections for you. You have to supply them, and you do this—principally—by means of topic and transitional sentences.

Topic sentences introduce ideas. They belong at the beginning of paragraphs. All too often students bury their central ideas in the middle of paragraphs. Only the most attentive reader is likely to ferret them out. And while every teacher strives to be most attentive, the unvarnished truth of the matter is that there is usually a stack of papers to go through—a prospect that inspires a certain dread and tends to make one somewhat eager to get the whole business over with. So, despite our best intentions, we teachers are often less attentive than we should be. The lesson for you is clear. Do not risk having your best notions go unnoticed.

Transitional sentences explain connections. You can put them at the end of paragraphs if you wish. Wherever you put them, be sure you write them as carefully as you do your introduction and your topic sentences. A good topic sentence may also be a transitional device and improve the flow of your writing.

These few hints will not suffice to turn you into a good writer, but they can help you avoid fatal errors. If your writing is a problem, then you owe it to yourself to seek sustained professional help either in writing courses or at your school's writing center. Remember, a serviceable prose style will not only measurably improve your grade in this course (and many others), it will also improve your chances for success in whatever career you enter.

WHEN AND HOW TO USE FOOTNOTES

Many students apparently believe that the only thing worse than having to read footnotes is having to write them. It is easy to understand why they feel that way, but they are making much ado about very little. Footnotes are used to inform the reader (including your reader) where the information being used in the body of the paper can be found. That is the sum and substance of the matter.

So, when should you use a footnote? These are two occasions when you must. The first is when you are referring to someone's exact words whether by direct quotation or by paraphrase. The second is when you are referring to some bit of information that is not already well known or is someone's interpretation of the facts. How, you might wonder, can you tell whether or not something is already well-known? There is, fortunately, a simple rule. Any thing you can find in a standard textbook (like *Firsthand America*) does not need to be footnoted. Hence, for example, you do not need to footnote that George Washington was the first president of the United States. You do need to footnote an exact quotation from his "Farewell Address." You do not need to footnote that Henry Ford introduced the assembly line to the manufacture of automobiles. You do need to footnote your source for his political opinions.

As you can see from these examples, there is no mystery about using footnotes. If you are in doubt about a particular case, you still have two steps open to you. One is to ask your instructor, the reader you are seeking to inform in the first place. The other, if you find it impracticable to contact your teacher, is to use the footnote. Having an unnecessary footnote is a minor flaw. Not having a necessary one is a serious omission. So you can simply err on the safe side.

Now that you know when to use footnotes, you can consider the matter of how to use them. There are several commonly used formats. Simply ask your instructor which one is preferred. If your teacher has no preference, amble over to your campus bookstore and invest in the University of Chicago's *Manual of Style*. It is brief, clearly written, reliable, and cheap. It is very unlikely you will encounter a question the *Manual of Style* will not answer.

WHAT TO INCLUDE IN YOUR BIBLIOGRAPHY

Early in your research you compiled a list of possible sources. The temptation is to type out a bibliography from those cards. This is fine provided that you actually used all of those sources. Your bibliography should include all the sources you consulted and only the sources you consulted. So even though you have all sorts of cards, and even though your bibliography would look far more impressive if you included sources you looked up but did not use, do not. The game is not worth the candle. Your instructor will have a quite accurate sense of what sources you used just from reading your paper. So it is most unlikely that padding your bibliography will impress. In fact, your teacher is more than likely to challenge your reliability if any part of your paper seems padded. In scholarship, honesty really is the best policy.

A WORD ABOUT PLAGIARISM AND ABOUT ORIGINALITY

Plagiarism is the act of claiming another's work as your own. It is about as serious an offense as you can commit. Many colleges require teachers to report all instances of plagiarism and, while the punishment can vary, it is always stiff. Moreover, of all the various ways of cheating teachers find plagiarism the easiest to detect.

Some students even manage to plagiarize without realizing that this is what they are doing. They either quote or paraphrase a book or article without indicating that. (They omit the quotation marks or they omit the footnote.) They have, without necessarily intending to, passed off someone else's work as their own. Sometimes this results in nothing worse than a private lecture from the instructor on the necessity of correctly attributing all information. Even so it is embarrassing, and it creates the impression that you do not know what you are doing. So, be sure you indicate the sources not only of your information but also of the interpretations or ideas you include in your papers.

Teachers will often tell their students that their papers should be original. Since scholars use this word in a somewhat different sense than you might expect, a word of explanation may prove helpful. In ordinary speech something is original if it is the first of its kind or if it is the only one of its kind. Historians and other scholars mean something less dramatic than that. We refer to research as "original" if the researcher did the work himself. We do not mean that his conclusions have never been reached before or that no one else has ever used his source materials. The way you put familiar information and ideas together may be original.

Do not hesitate to make use of ideas from other historians. No one with any sense expects beginning students to make startling discoveries or to develop radically new perspectives on the past. Of course it would be wonderful if you did, but no one anticipates that you will. It is, accordingly, perfectly legitimate for you to use other people's insights. The only hitch is that you must always acknowledge where they came from.

A NOTE TO TEACHER AND STUDENT ON USING THE MCDONALD-GENOVESE DEBATES

How your teacher will decide to use the debates will depend upon her sense of what will work best. So rather than describing some idealized learning situation, the suggestions here are offered in ascending order or ambitiousness. They range from a project designed to improve your reading skills to a proposal for working out your own interpretations of the issues raised in the debates.

I. Identifying what the Debates are about.

You may have brought with you from high school courses the notion that history is merely a collection of facts. Moreover, your sense of what a "fact" is may also leave much to be desired. You may be used, for example, to treating the provisions of the Missouri Compromise and a summary listing of the causes of the Civil War as being equally matters of fact. But, whereas the provisions of the Compromises really are facts, that is, exactly known pieces of information, any list of the "causes" of the Civil War represents someone's judgment about why and how the war came. You, on the other hand, may not be used to routinely distinguishing between fact and interpretation. Anything likely to serve as an answer on a quiz or exam may be, so far as you are concerned, a fact. So the Debates between Forrest McDonald and Eugene Genovese and Elizabeth Fox-Genovese may well be your first systematic exposure to the ways historians put facts together to form interpretations.

Appreciating the interpretive process can enormously enrich your understanding of history by enabling you to share the intellectual excitement the study of history can generate. A crucial first step is to grasp the relationship between facts and interpretation. The following exercise may help.

EXERCISE 1

Identify in a few sentences the basic arguments advanced by Professors McDonald and Genovese. Then identify four to six facts each puts forward in support of his interpretation.

Once you have completed this diagram of each essay, make a brief list indicating central points of agreement and disagreement. You should then indicate which interpretation you prefer and explain the reasons for your choice, drawing on materials from the text.

This exercise is highly structured, and you may appreciate its step-by-step specificity. As the term proceeds and you become more experienced in reading the Debates, you will find that the need to diagram the relationships between fact and interpretation will disappear.

II. Testing Generalizations.

Once you have reached the point where you can analyze the arguments advanced in the Debates, you are ready to begin to make critical and informed judgments about the issues they raise. Reading and thinking critically are skills you may have had little opportunity to develop. Criticism is likely to mean little more than listing what you happen to dislike about something. This exercise is designed to introduce you to what scholars mean by criticism.

EXERCISE 2

The Debates focus on highly divergent readings of the meaning of the American past. Since each essay is relatively brief and yet must cover an extended period, the participants necessarily generalize a good deal. In writing about the Revolution, for example, Professor McDonald describes it as "a conservative crusade against the forces of modernism." Professor Genovese, to the contrary, claims it was "the furthest point of social transformation that the European world had so far achieved." Both agree that the Revolution brought widespread change, but while Professor McDonald sees this as ironic, and stresses the ways in which the former colonies came to adopt policies that resembled those Americans had "detested" when Parliament had sought to impose them, his opponent emphasizes the lasting radicalism of the revolutionary ideology of equality.

Note, for each essay, three or four such generalizations. Select one that you think is most central to its overall thesis, and then choose several events from the text or class lectures that, in your judgment, best enable you to test it. You should briefly state why you think these particular episodes are good measures of the generalizations. Then you should say how well each generalization meets the test. Your essay should be brief and to the point.

III. Thinking about the Interpretive Process.

Once you get to the point at which you can both identify and evaluate various interpretations, you can take up the basic question of why historians disagree about the past. Since the test of an interpretation is how cogently it explains the known facts, you might assume that all historiographical disputes are at bottom differences over what the facts are. In reality they are more usually over what the facts mean, and over what facts actually matter.

A first step is to see that facts do not interpret themselves. This is less simple than it sounds. You have probably not done any serious research and so can have almost no sense of how historians use evidence, nor can you have any notion of how vast, variegated, and yet incomplete the historical record actually is. So you might not immediately see the simple impossibility of assembling all the "facts" about some portion of the past. You may be equally unable to appreciate at first that the facts do not simply proclaim their own importance. What a source tells a historian depends, in part, on its own scope and quality, and you may see that side of things very clearly. But it also depends on the ingenuity of the historian in exploiting the source and on the questions about the past the historian is interested in, considerations you might not take into account at first.

EXERCISE 3

Anything that exists and can be dated even approximately (from a memory to a pyramid) is part of the historical record. Most can be classified as either documents (those which are or can be put in written form) or artifacts (objects).

For the first part of this exercise you are to locate a document from your own life (a letter, report card, newspaper story, recipe). Try to be imaginative in your choice; try, that is, to avoid birth certificates and the like. You are then to write a brief essay describing what the document is, and when, where, how, and by whom it was produced. Then indicate what a future historian might be able to learn about life in America from examining this document.

The second part of the exercise calls for you to

do the same things: only this time you are to locate an artifact from your own life. You are to provide the same information about it: what it is, and when, where, how, and by whom it was produced. What might an imaginative future historian learn about American life from examining it?

This exercise may help you begin to see for yourself something of the enormous variety of sources historians routinely draw upon as well as something of the ingenuity historical research demands. In particular, it should help you see that "facts" do not speak for themselves. It is the historian who does the speaking for them. So it is crucially important to determine the various perspectives from which historians approach the past.

EXERCISE 4

One clue to a historian's point of view is the type of questions about the past he or she regards as important. These questions, taken together, give us a good first approximation of the historian's interpretive framework.

Read over at least three Debates and list the questions about the past each participant seems most interested in. For each, decide whether there are certain kinds of developments (political, religious, economic, or cultural) and certain sorts of events (elections, inventions, religious revivals) he emphasizes more than others. How would you describe the priorities each displays?

At this point it should start to become apparent to you that you are encountering several distinct interpretations in this course. The Debates are the most obtrusive of these, but Professor Burner's narrative is a third while class lectures provide a fourth (and unquestionably the most important). The goal is to find your way to your own understanding of the past, the first step toward which is for you to learn to distinguish among the diverse versions of the past you are dealing with.

EXERCISE 5

Imagine that, for the second edition of *Firsthand America* the authors decided to include student rejoinders to the Debates. They have decided to ask you to write one of these.

Choose one of the Debates and write an interpretive essay giving your views on the topic. Do not feel obligated to comment on every point Professors McDonald, Fox-Genovese, and Genovese make: your primary goal should be to present your own analysis. But you should indicate major agreements and disagreements between your analysis and theirs.

On a separate sheet briefly describe your own

approach to history. What sorts of developments and events do you find especially significant? Why?

This exercise will provide you with a fair measure of how successfully you are learning to think for yourself about history. This may seem meager compensation for what might seem a good deal of effort on your part, but it is not. One reason is that learning to think about history is the surest and most satisfying way to do well in your course. Beyond that, historical analysis is a basic mode of human discourse and something you will use for the rest of your life. Why not learn to use it effectively and even pleasurably?

Glossary

abolitionism: The campaign, strengthened by religious passion, for the immediate end of slavery. Among the most famous abolitionists were William Lloyd Garrison and Theodore Dwight Weld. Themselves always in the minority, abolitionists combined with more compromising opponents of slavery to form a wide antislavery movement in the North by the eve of the Civil War.

antinomianism: The belief among Christians that salvation depends on the indwelling presence of the Holy Spirit, not obedience to earthly laws and codes.

apocalypse: A revelation or discovery. Christianity teaches that the final victory will be realized through the redemptive powers of Christ's Second Coming. Revelations, the Bible's final chapter, provides as Christians see it an apocalyptic vision of that fateful, final day.

armistice: A truce agreement between military opponents. The armistice that ended World War I, for example, was signed on November 11, 1918.

Articles of Confederation: The form of national government in the early days of the United States. The Articles, adopted in 1777, gave each state so much independence that the central government had difficulties in collecting revenue and establishing a national policy.

artisan: A skilled craftsman such as a blacksmith or carpenter.

assembly line production: A method of assembling standardized, interchangeable parts into an automobile or other item of mass consumption. Workers are assigned small, specialized tasks along the route of assembly, which increases efficiency, reduces production costs, and consequently lowers prices for the consumer. Of the nation's industrialists, Henry Ford was most closely identified with this form of production, using a conveyor belt system and making automobiles affordable to the middle class buyer.

balance of payments: The margin between the value of a nation's exports and the value of its imports.

balance of power: A system of international relations in which opposing alliances of countries seek to balance each other's military and diplomatic power. The confrontation between NATO (the North Atlantic Treaty Organization) and the Soviet-dominated Warsaw Pact is an example. See also **collective security**.

bank notes: Paper money issued by private banks and backed by the assets of those banks but not by any governmental agency.

Bank of the United States: A centralized financial institution designed to regulate the nation's economy through selective distribution of capital (loans and related transactions). As envisioned **by** Alexander Hamilton, the first Bank of the United States was to stimulate general economic growth through commercial investment, which in turn would make individual states more dependent on a strengthened national government. Andrew Jackson, in his assault upon the Second Bank of the United States, argued that such centralized control threatened the authority of the states and favored wealthy interests to the detriment of others.

bear market: A period of declining prices in the stock market or in any market. Speculators who agree to sell at some point in the future at lower than current prices are called bears since they can make a profit only if prices fall. See also **bull market**.

beat culture: A movement of the 1950s that rejected the nation's dominant values and mass culture. Beats, or beatniks, found little of worth in the decade's aggressive and confident capitalism and the generally rapid pace of American life. Instead they espoused individualism and nonconformity, which included Eastern religion, improvisational jazz, marijuana, and life on the road.

black nationalism: The belief that African Americans should seek an independent national or cultural existence. Marcus Garvey was the major proponent of this viewpoint in the 1920s. Black Muslims continue to promote this view. See also **Pan-Africanism.**

Bleeding Kansas: A phrase to describe the violent struggle between proslavery and antislavery forces in the Kansas territory after passage of the Kansas-Nebraska Act. Outside activists from both camps urged migration to Kansas to gain majority control of the territorial government and its decisions concerning slavery. Two separate governments were established, vigilante violence spread, and Congress, which had attempted to avoid the slavery issue, was forced to deal with the much intensified struggle. See also **popular sovereignty.**

blockade: The use of naval force to shut off passage to and from a hostile port or country. Used by England in its wars against Europe and the United States, by the North against the South during the Civil War, and by the United States in the twentieth century against such nations as Cuba and Iraq, blockades are designed to cripple a nation's economy and war machine by cutting off needed supplies.

bloody shirt (waving the): Taken from the waving in political campaigning of a shirt, actually or apparently bloody, said to belong to a supporter of the federal government killed by white southerners. The term "waving the bloody shirt" came to refer to the practice on the part of some Republican politicians late in the nineteenth century of arousing feelings among northern voters against the South, widely associated with the Democratic Party.

blue laws: Local laws, typically promoted by Protestant reformers, designed to keep Sundays reserved exclusively for worship and religious contemplation. Various immigrant and Catholic communities viewed the laws as discriminatory because they closed places used by these groups for social gatherings and cultural activities.

border states: Those states located between the North and the deep South, such as Delaware, Maryland, Kentucky, and Missouri, where slavery was legal but the plantation system was not widespread. A major task of Lincoln during the Civil War was to keep the border states in the Union.

brains trust: A popular nickname for the advisors Franklin D. Roosevelt gathered during his New Deal administration in the 1930s. Trust was another term for monopoly.

bull market: A stock market in which values are rising, to the benefit of investors who have bet on an increase in prices.

bullion: Gold used as backing for currency. See also **specie.**

capitalism: An economic system in which the means of production and exchange are privately owned (although one or more governmental agencies may regulate both) and market exchanges establish prices. Also referred to as the "free enterprise system." See also **socialism.**

cash crops: Agricultural produce grown for sale rather than for the farmer's own use. In the nineteenth century, cotton was the nation's most valuable cash crop.

checks and balances: The principle embedded in the Constitution that each branch of government be able to prevent any other from unilaterally deciding policy or imposing its will. The President, for example, can veto legislation and Congress can, with a two-thirds majority, override that veto.

civil liberties: Those rights of the individual citizen, as enumerated in the Bill of Rights in the Constitution, that limit the powers of the government. The First Amendment to the Constitution, for example, prohibits Congress from making any law that would restrict the free exercise of religious liberty.

civil rights: Rights to legal and social equality that everyone is supposed to possess regardless of race, creed, color, country of origin, age, gender, sexual orientation, or disability.

closed shop: The practice, made illegal by the Taft-Hartley Law, of requiring employers to hire only trade union members. See also **open shop** and **union shop.**

collective security: A system of diplomatic arrangements in which countries agree to act in unison to defend any one party to the agreement that is under armed attack or the threat of it. The United Nations seeks to embody this system on a global scale. See also **balance of power.**

conscription: Also known as the draft; a system in which young men (but, so far, not young women) are chosen and required to serve in the military for a specified period of time.

covenant: An agreement, like the Mayflower Compact, uniting a group of people for an expressed purpose. These agreements formed the basis for town settlement and government organization in regions where Puritans or Separatist groups took root. When establishing a new town, settlers signed a document (covenant) stating the spiritual purpose of their community and agreed to abide by Christian beliefs in their daily lives.

currency: Money, whether specie (that is, gold or silver) or paper. The total amount of money in circulation at any one time is the total of all currency not held in bank reserves, plus all outstanding credit orders.

dark horse (candidate): An office seeker regarded as a long shot in a race.

deflation: A period of declining prices and, therefore, of increasing purchasing power. During the last quarter of the nineteenth century, the longest sustained deflationary period in the nation's history, prices fell by a quarter, or a third. See also **inflation**.

depression: A severe economic slump in which the total amount of goods and services produced declines sharply. The decline in production decreases employment, the result is that the public has less money with which to purchase goods, and that further discourages production. A less severe decline is called a **recession**.

disarmament: A policy of reducing the size of a nation's military. Countries may undertake such a policy as part of an agreement with one or more other states. In that case the policy is called multilateral disarmament. Or it may disarm alone. That is called unilateral disarmament. Disarmament may involve particular weapons or types of weapons, such as intermediate range nuclear missiles, or may entail a general reduction in a country's military.

Dixiecrats: The name given to southern Democrats who bolted the 1948 nominating convention in protest over a civil rights plank in the party's platform. Forming the States Rights Party and nominating James Strom Thurmond as a third party presidential candidate, the Dixiecrats put forward a conservative program that pledged to preserve "social custom."

Dollar Diplomacy: A policy adopted by the United States during the administration of William Howard Taft (1909–1913) that relied upon economic incentives to persuade Latin American countries to cooperate with the policy initiatives of the United States.

Electoral College: Under the Constitution voters cannot directly elect the President or Vice President. Instead the Constitution provides that states are to elect the members of the Electoral College, who in turn elect the President and Vice President. Electors are not obligated to vote for the candidate with the highest popular vote in their state although, with rare exceptions, they have done so.

Enlightenment: Also known as the Age of Reason, this term refers to the scientific and philosophical achievements from the late seventeenth century to the outbreak of the French Revolution at the end of the eighteenth. "Enlightened" thinkers emphasized the power of human reason to discover scientific "laws" of human behavior.

fascism: A political doctrine, adopted in Italy in the 1920s and then in Germany under the Nazis in the 1930s, that exalted the state and military power.

freedmen: Generic term used in reference to all black men, women, and children freed from slavery during the Civil War. The Freedmen's Bureau, passed by Congress over Andrew Johnson's veto, was established to minister to the needs of these former slaves.

free soil: The political doctrine, embodied in the Wilmot Proviso of 1846 and the Free Soil Party in the presidential election of 1848, that western territories should be closed to slavery.

free trade: The policy of permitting other countries to sell their goods in a nation's domestic markets without paying fees or taxes, called tariffs. In the nineteenth century Great Britain adopted this policy with the expectation that the resulting free competition would reward its advanced manufacturing capabilities. See also **protectionism**.

frontier: Technically, the line marking the extent of settlement in the western territories; more broadly the term refers to the early period of settlement before such instruments of civilization as schools and churches had been established.

frontier thesis: Historian Frederick Jackson Turner's argument that the American frontier shaped the American character, more especially implanting habits of democracy, individualism, and enterprise.

fundamentalism: The belief in the literal truth of the Bible. For centuries it had been habitual for Christians to take the Bible as being literally accurate, but among some conservative Christians in the United States that way of reading Scripture became particularly insistent early in the twentieth century in reaction to scientific theory and to historical interpretation of the Bible. It is to this recent reaction that the term "fundamentalism" is applied.

gold standard: A monetary policy in which the amount of currency in circulation is based upon the amount of a country's gold reserves. The gold standard is often associated with the term "hard money."

Gospel of Wealth: The view, most strongly associated with Andrew Carnegie, that the wealthy were "stewards" of their riches and were to use them to benefit society. Carnegie's own philanthropy emphasized education and world peace.

Great Plains: The arid, treeless area of the United States between the Dakotas in the north to parts of Texas in the south.

Great Society: The label given to Lyndon B. Johnson's domestic program. Johnson, having grown up politically during Franklin D. Roosevelt's years in office, sought during his own presidency a program to fulfill the promise of the New Deal and complete the work left undone by John F. Kennedy's New Frontier.

greenbacks: Paper money first issued by the Lincoln administration and not redeemable in gold.

hard money: Currency backed by specie or redeemable in it. See also **soft money**.

holding company: A corporation that holds stock in other corporations and is therefore able to establish a monopoly.

impeachment: The first part of a process whereby a President, Vice President, or federal judge can be removed from office. The word refers to a finding by the House of Representatives, by a two-thirds majority, that there is reasonable evidence that the officeholder in question committed "high crimes or misdemeanors." After impeachment by the House, the official goes on trial before the Senate. If a majority of two thirds of that body finds the charges to be true, the defendant is removed from office.

imperialism: The policy of one nation's conquering other portions of the world and exercising political dominion over them. The term can also be applied to economic or cultural domination of one society by another.

indentured servant: An individual bound by a contract, called an indenture, to work for a specified period of time. During the length of the contract the servant is not free to leave his or her master's employ. Indentured service was common during the colonial era. Many entered into such contracts to finance their migration to North America. See also **redemptioners**.

industrialization: The process of substituting machine for human power in the manufacture of goods. In the United States this first happened on a large scale in the cotton textile industry, water power providing the primary source of energy.

inflation: A period of rising prices and therefore of decreasing purchasing power. Debtors favor inflation since it permits them to repay loans in dollars that are worth less than the ones they borrowed. Creditors have a corresponding preference for **deflation**.

integration: The policy of ending the legal or customary segregation (separation) of the races. It may also entail the adoption of active measures such as school busing to achieve racial balance.

internal improvements: The policy, first associated with the Federalists under Hamilton and later with the Whigs under Henry Clay, of getting the federal government to finance the construction of roads, railroad lines, canals, bridges, and other public works.

isolationism: The conviction that the United States could, and should, stay clear of "foreign entanglements." It was especially popular following the First World War. In its extreme form it called for the United States to abandon all unnecessary contact with the rest of the world; a more moderate version called upon the United States to act alone in protecting its interests.

Jim Crow: A colloquial name for the system of legal segregation of African Americans formally adopted in the South in the late 1890s and 1900s. See also **integration**.

laissez-faire: The economic doctrine, especially popular during the nineteenth century, that holds that the government should not interfere with the free working of economic markets.

lame duck: An officeholder who has not been reelected but has the remainder of a term to serve, or a President serving a second and therefore by law a final term.

land grant college: A college instituted and funded by resources made available under the Morill Land-Grant College Act of 1862. Each state was allotted federally owned land in proportion to the size of its congressional delegation, to be sold by the state for the establishment of an agricultural college.

loyalists: Those colonists who retained their allegiance to Great Britain during the American Revolution. They were also called Tories.

manifest destiny: The belief, especially popular in the 1840s, that the United States was destined to rule all or most of the Western Hemisphere. Supporters of the War with Mexico used it to justify the invasion of that country and the seizure of a third of its territory.

Medicare: A program of health care for the elderly championed by Lyndon B. Johnson and passed into law in 1965. During the next two years legislation was passed extending benefits to the poor and needy under the Medicaid program.

mercantilism: An economic policy under which a nation seeks to maximize exports and minimize imports on the theory that there is a finite amount of wealth and that one nation's gain is therefore another's loss. As applied by Great Britain during the eighteenth century, the policy held that colonial trade should be regulated in the interests of the empire as a whole as London perceived that whole.

millenialism: The religious doctrine that the Second Coming of Jesus Christ will begin a thousand-year-long reign of the just, or alternatively, that the Coming will follow the reign of the just. Milleniarians have often tried to predict the exact date of the Second Coming.

monopoly: Effective control over the supply of a product or service such that the holder can dictate its price. Some economists distinguish between "natural" monopolies, such as over a city's water supply, which should be permitted and regulated, and "artificial" ones, such as John D. Rockefeller's Standard Oil Company.

Monroe Doctrine: The policy adopted by the United States in 1823, proclaiming that in the future no European nation may establish a colony in the Western Hemisphere. See also **Roosevelt Corollary**.

muckraking: A derogatory term coined by Theodore Roosevelt for the investigative journalism of the Progressive Era.

nativism: Hostility to immigrants that has typically fed upon anti-Catholic or anti-Semitic notions or upon the belief that foreigners are the source of political radicalism. It is sometimes linked to **racism** when the immigrant group in question is non-white.

navigation acts: A series of measures enacted by the British Parliament to regulate colonial commerce. See **Mercantilism**.

Nazism: The German variant of Fascism. Nazis under Hitler sought German supremacy in Europe, the extermination of 'lesser' races such as Jews and Gypsies, and a totalitarian social order.

neutrality: A position of non-alignment adopted by a nation with respect to a real or potential international conflict. At the start of World War I, for example, President Woodrow Wilson pledged the United States to be neutral.

nullification: The constitutional theory, most notably associated with John C. Calhoun, that individual states could nullify and declare void within their own borders those acts of Congress the state believed to violate the Constitution. Used early by James Madison and Thomas Jefferson in their arguments against the Alien and Sedition Acts, and culminating in the nullification of the United States Constitution itself during southern seces-

sion, this theory was put asunder as legitimate constitutional interpretation with the defeat of the Confederacy and its radical assertion of states rights. See also **secession**.

Open Door (policy): The policy, adopted by Theodore Roosevelt's administration, that called for all states to have equal access to markets in China. By the end of the nineteenth century, several European powers had established spheres of influence in China that included monopolies of portions of that country's international trade.

open shop: The practicing of hiring non-union as well as union employees. See also **closed shop** and **union shop**.

pan-Africanism: The vision of the uniting of all "colored races" in a single, free African state. Promoted in one form by Marcus Garvey, the idea gained additional popular support among urban African Americans after World War I. It quickly lost momentum when Garvey fell prey to legal and financial troubles, culminating in his deportion to Jamaica in the late 1920s.

panic: A sharp economic downturn, believed to be caused by a sudden loss of confidence in one or more markets. Panics normally follow bursts of speculative investing in which values rise very rapidly and many speculators overextend their holdings by buying on credit.

political machine: A single-party political organization that dominates government and controls policy and practice. Most closely associated with the Democratic party in large northern cities during the late nineteenth and early twentieth centuries, the machine used patronage and corruption to consolidate a political power base that in turn provided opportunity for profit. George Washington Plunkitt, a boss in New York City's Tammany Hall machine, justified these practices, claiming they were merely the product of "honest graft."

popular sovereignty: A concept of self-rule built into the Kansas-Nebraska Act and other pre-Civil War legislation. People in the newer organized territories were empowered to decide whether to establish or prohibit slavery. Stephen Douglas and other architects of the policy hoped in vain to avoid contentious congressional and national debate over the extension of slavery, but in practice tensions between North and South intensified as evidenced by episodes such as "Bleeding Kansas."

populism: A radical political movement centered in the agricultural regions of the South and West of the late 1880s and the 1890s. Populists called for the federal regulation of railroads, the direct popular election of senators, federally guaranteed credit for farmers, the free coinage of silver, and numerous other reforms.

pragmatism: An American philosophy most closely associated with William James, Charles Pierce, and John Dewey that argues that the truth value of an idea is its utility in enabling the thinker to accomplish some purpose. This use of utility to assess truth is referred to as the "pragmatic test."

privateer: A ship of war owned and equipped by a private individual, yet sanctioned by a government to seize and plunder enemy vessels during war. Englishmen John Hawkins and Sir Francis Drake, for example, profited greatly in ventures against the Spanish during the sixteenth century, as did many Americans against the English during the War for Independence.

progressivism: A moderate political reform movement of the early twentieth century. Progressives sought to eliminate governmental corruption at all levels, to make cities safer and more liveable, and to use the federal government to correct abuses in business.

prohibition: The policy of enforcing temperance by outlawing the sale and non-medicinal use of alcohol. The Eighteenth Amendment to the Constitution, adopted in 1919, established prohibition throughout the nation. The Amendment was repealed in 1933.

protectionism: The economic policy of placing special fees or taxes (**tariffs**) on foreign or imported goods. The idea, in addition to raising revenue, is to aid domestic manufacturers whose goods would enjoy a protected position in their home markets.

racism: The belief that humanity is divided into distinct racial stocks and that one race is superior to others.

recession: See **depression**.

redemptioners: Laborers who contracted their services to pay for passage to the New World. Unlike indentured servants, who contracted through agents while still in Europe, redemptioners agreed to terms only after the Atlantic crossing. Most of them upon arrival were given two weeks to secure alternative means of payment through friends or family. If this failed, the newcomer's services would then be auctioned off. While indentured servants came singly, redemptioners generally came as whole families or even as small communities.

reparations: Payments exacted from Germany, principally by Great Britain and France, after World War I in payment for damage that, so the victors claimed, Germany had done during the war. The Treaty of Versailles of 1919 authorized the payments under a "war guilt" clause that assigned blame to Germany for causing the war.

revenue sharing: The policy of sharing federal tax dollars with state and local governments.

revivalism: A season of spiritual renewal among evangelical Christians. Revivalists, beginning with Jonathan Edwards in the eighteenth century, have called upon sinners to acknowledge their own sinful natures and throw themselves upon Jesus' infinite love and forgiveness. The revived believer is said to be converted and seeks to reorganize her or his life.

Roosevelt Corollary (to the Monroe Doctrine): In 1904 Theodore Roosevelt added this to the Monroe Doctrine. Under it the United States pledged to police the hemisphere to make sure, for example, that Latin American countries did not default upon debts to European nations.

secession: As a specific term in American history, the act of the eleven states of the Confederacy in removing themselves from the Union; also the doctrine justifying that decision. The theory of secession held that the Union was made up of sovereign states each of which retained the right to go its separate way.

sectionalism: A term used to describe the growing division between the North and the South in the decades prior to the Civil War. Each section increasingly identified more with its own regional interests than with national concerns.

sedition: The act of stirring up resistance to the government, inciting rebellion, or generally working for the destruction of the authority of the government.

segregation: The policy of maintaining a racially separate society. In 1896 the Supreme Court, rendering its decision in *Plessy v. Ferguson*, ruled that segregated "separate but equal" public facilities did not violate the Fourteenth Amendment. In 1954 the Court reversed itself through its decision in *Brown v. Board of Education*, holding that separate facilities were "inherently unequal."

separatists: Dissenting Christians who believed that separation from the **Anglican Church** and the establishment of independent congregations were necessary for the practice of a purified spiritual life. Puritans, although not separatists, nevertheless formed a congregational system that provided considerable independence for individual churches even.

slave codes: Laws regulating slaves in the Old South. Codes typically required slaves to possess a pass from their master in order to travel, prohibited slaves from learning to read, and banned slaves from testifying in court against whites. During Reconstruction these codes were revised, becoming known as black codes, as a means of controlling the freed slave population and subsequently enforced by newly formed vigilante groups, including the Ku Klux Klan.

Social Darwinism: The nineteenth-century social philosophy teaching that human progress mimics animal evolution, in which the strong and most "fit" win out, and that therefore government programs or private charities that seek to help the less "fit" such as the poor or the physically handicapped actually retard progress.

socialism: An economic system in which the workers collectively own the means of production. In the Soviet Union, collective ownership has translated into ownership by the state. Socialist thought in the West has envisioned control by smaller collective units with participation on the part of the individual worker.

soft money: Paper money not backed by **specie** (coin or hard money).

sharecropping: An agricultural system of tenancy in which landlord and tenant share the crop. The landlord provides the land and often credit for supplies; the tenant provides the labor. After the Civil War, this became a dominant system in the South.

specie: Gold or silver used as currency.

spoils system: The institutionalized practice of using the patronage system to full advantage. After an election and while in office, the victorious candidate or political party provides jobs and services ("spoils") to political supporters, party insiders, and others in order to consolidate a political power base and use the opportunities of office for partisan purposes.

subculture: A group of people united by ethnicity, social class, behavioral tendencies, or other defining characteristics that are identifiably distinct from the dominant culture. In the United States since the middle of the twentieth century, the term has often been used in reference to countercultural groups such as the beat generation of the 1950s or the cultural radicals of the 1960s.

suburbanization: The movement of urban dwellers to surrounding areas or "bedroom communities." Advances in transportation, especially the automobile, made it possible for individuals to live at considerable distances from the workplace. After World War II, suburban developments such

as Levittown, Long Island, provided thousands of identical, inexpensive homes for first-time buyers. Here, the "baby boom" flourished, and the power also of television, along with that of mass market consumerism, made American life appear increasingly standardized.

suffrage: The right to vote. During Reconstruction the Fifteenth Amendment was ratified, granting the vote to African American males. Women remained without a federal guarantee of the vote until 1920 when, after a century of organized political pressure, the Nineteenth Amendment was ratified.

tariff: A tax imposed upon goods or services imported into a country. When such taxes are used simply to help finance governmental operations, they are called revenue tariffs. When they are used to give domestic manufacturers a favored position by raising the prices of their foreign competitors, they are called **protective tariffs**.

temperance: The campaign against the non-medical use of alcohol. It was one of the largest reform movements of the nineteenth and early twentieth centuries.

Third World: A term used to designate non-Western countries that have yet to industrialize. The United States and its industrialized trading partners, and the Soviet Union and its satellites, make up the first two worlds.

trust: A combination of companies or other economic units that have joined to act in restraint of trade by setting prices or eliminating competition.

union shop: The practice of requiring new employees to join a trade union, usually within thirty to ninety days. Unlike the closed shop system, the union shop allows the employment of workers who are not members of a union at the time of their hiring; unlike the open shop, the union shop system forces them thereupon to join a union. See also **closed shop** and **open shop**.

vigilantes: Individuals who band together extralegally to enforce particular codes of behavior. In the South after the Civil War, white gangs lynched African Americans and whites who challenged the system of white supremacy; on the western frontier, vigilantes hanged cattle rustlers.

welfare state: The set of governmental programs that provides minimal care for the poor, the elderly, the disabled, and the unemployed. All industrialized societies have adopted welfare measures. In the United States the origins of the welfare state lie in Franklin Roosevelt's New Deal.

The Declaration of Independence

When in the Course of human events, it becomes necessary for one people to dissolve the political bands which have connected them with another, and to assume among the Powers of the earth, the separate and equal station to which the Laws of Nature and of Nature's God entitle them, a decent respect to the opinions of mankind requires that they should declare the causes which impel them to the separation.

We hold these truths to be self-evident, that all men are created equal, that they are endowed by their Creator with certain unalienable Rights, that among these are Life, Liberty and the pursuit of Happiness. That to secure these rights, Governments are instituted among Men, deriving their just powers from the consent of the governed, That whenever any Form of Government becomes destructive of these ends, it is the Right of the People to alter or to abolish it, and to institute new Government, laying its foundation on such principles and organizing its powers in such form, as to them shall seem most likely to effect their Safety and Happiness. Prudence, indeed, will dictate that Governments long established should not be changed for light and transient causes; and accordingly all experience hath shown, that mankind are more disposed to suffer, while evils are sufferable, than to right themselves by abolishing the forms to which they are accustomed. When a long train of abuses and usurpations, pursuing invariably the same Object evinces a design to reduce them under absolute Despotism, it is their right, it is their duty, to throw off such Government, and to provide new Guards for their future security.—Such has been the patient sufferance of these Colonies; and such is now the necessity which constrains them to alter their former Systems of Government. The history of the present King of Great Britain is a history of repeated injuries and usurpations, all having in direct object the establishment of an absolute Tyranny over these States. To prove this, let Facts be submitted to a candid world.

He has refused his Assent to Laws, the most wholesome and necessary for the public good.

He has forbidden his Governors to pass Laws of immediate and pressing importance, unless suspended in their operation till his Assent should be obtained; and when so suspended, he has utterly neglected to attend to them.

He has refused to pass other Laws for the accommodation of large districts of people, unless those people would relinquish the right of Representation in the Legislature, a right inestimable to them and formidable to tyrants only.

He has dissolved Representative Houses repeatedly, for opposing with manly firmness his invasions on the rights of the people.

He has refused for a long time, after such dissolutions, to cause others to be elected; whereby the Legislative Powers, incapable of Annihilation, have returned to the People at large for their exercise; the State remaining in the mean time exposed to all the dangers of invasion from without, and convulsions within.

He has endeavoured to prevent the population of these States; for that purpose obstructing the Laws of Naturalization of Foreigners; refusing to pass others to encourage their migration hither, and raising the conditions of new Appropriations of Lands.

He has obstructed the Administration of Justice, by refusing his Assent to Laws for establishing Judiciary Powers.

He has made Judges dependent on his Will alone, for the tenure of their offices, and the amount and payment of their salaries.

He has erected a multitude of New Offices, and sent hither swarms of Officers to harass our People, and eat out their substance.

He has kept among us, in times of peace, Standing Armies without the Consent of our legislature.

He has affected to render the Military independent of and superior to the Civil Power.

He has combined with others to subject us to a jurisdiction foreign to our constitution, and unacknowledged by our laws; giving his Assent to their acts of pretended legislation:

For quartering large bodies of armed troops among us:

For protecting them, by a mock Trial, from Punishment for any Murders which they should commit on the Inhabitants of these States:

For cutting off our Trade with all parts of the world:

For imposing taxes on us without our Consent:

For depriving us in many cases, of the benefits of Trial by Jury:

For transporting us beyond Seas to be tried for pretended offences:

For abolishing the free System of English Laws in a neighbouring Province, establishing therein an Arbitrary government, and enlarging its Boundaries so as to render it at once an example and fit instrument for introducing the same absolute rule into these Colonies:

For taking away our Charters, abolishing our most valuable Laws, and altering fundamentally the Forms of our Governments:

For suspending our own Legislature, and declaring themselves invested with Power to legislate for us in all cases whatsoever.

He has abdicated Government here, by declaring us out of his Protection and waging War against us.

He has plundered our seas, ravaged our Coasts, burnt our towns, and destroyed the lives of our people.

He is at this time transporting large armies of foreign mercenaries to compleat the works of death, desolation and tyranny, already begun with circumstances of Cruelty & perfidy scarcely paralleled in the most barbarous ages, and totally unworthy the Head of a civilized nation.

He has constrained our fellow Citizens taken Captive on the high Seas to bear Arms against their Country, to become the executioners of their friends and Brethren, or to fall themselves by their Hands.

He has excited domestic insurrections amongst us, and has endeavoured to bring on the inhabitants of our frontiers, the merciless Indian Savages, whose known rule of warfare, is an undistinguished destruction of all ages, sexes and conditions.

In every stage of these Oppressions We have Petitioned for Redress in the most humble terms: Our repeated Petitions have been answered only by repeated injury. A Prince, whose character is thus marked by every act which may define a Tyrant, is unfit to be the ruler of a free People.

Nor have We been wanting in attention to our British brethren. We have warned them from time to time of attempts by their legislature to extend an unwarrantable jurisdiction over us. We have reminded them of the circumstances of our emigration and settlement here. We have appealed to their native justice and magnanimity, and we have conjured them by the ties of our common kindred to disavow these usurpations, which, would inevitably interrupt our connections and correspondence. They too have been deaf to the voice of justice and of consanguinity. We must, therefore, acquiesce in the necessity, which denounces our Separation, and hold them, as we hold the rest of mankind, Enemies in War, in Peace Friends.

We, therefore, the Representatives of the United States of America, in General Congress, Assembled, appealing to the Supreme Judge of the world for the rectitude of our intentions, do, in the Name, and by Authority of the good People of these Colonies, solemnly publish and declare, That these United Colonies are, and of Right ought to be Free and Independent States; that they are Absolved from all Allegiance to the British Crown, and that all political connection between them and the State of Great Britain, is and ought to be totally dissolved; and that as Free and Independent States, they have full Power to levy War, conclude Peace, contract Alliances, establish Commerce, and to do all other Acts and Things which Independent States may of right do. And for the support of this Declaration, with a firm reliance on the Protection of Divine Providence, we mutually pledge to each other our Lives, our Fortunes and our sacred Honor.

The Constitution of the United States

We the people of the United States, in Order to form a more perfect Union, establish Justice, insure domestic Tranquility, provide for the common defense, promote the general Welfare, and secure the Blessings of Liberty to ourselves and our Posterity, do ordain and establish this CONSTITUTION for the United States of America.

ARTICLE 1

Section 1. All legislative Powers herein granted shall be vested in a Congress of the United States which shall consist of a Senate and House of Representatives.

Section 2. The House of Representatives shall be composed of Members chosen every second Year by the People of the several States, and the Electors in each State shall have the Qualifications requisite for Electors of the most numerous Branch of the State Legislature.

No Person shall be a Representative who shall not have attained to the Age of twenty-five Years, and been seven Years a Citizen of the United States, and who shall not, when elected, be an inhabitant of that State in which he shall be chosen.

Representatives and direct Taxes shall be apportioned among the several States which may be included within this Union, according to their respective Numbers, which shall be determined by adding to the whole Number of free Persons, including those bound to Service for a Term of Years and excluding Indians not taxed, three fifths of all other Persons. The actual Enumeration shall be made within three Years after the first Meeting of the Congress of the United States, and within every subsequent Term of ten Years, in such Manner as they shall by Law direct. The Number of Representatives shall not exceed one for every thirty Thousand, but each State shall have at Least one Representative; and until such enumeration shall be made, the State of New Hampshire shall be entitled to chuse three, Massachusetts eight, Rhode-Island and Providence Plantations one, Connecticut five, New-York six, New Jersey four, Pennsylvania eight, Delaware one, Maryland six, Virginia ten, North Carolina five, South Carolina five, and Georgia three.

When vacancies happen in the Representation from any State, the Executive Authority thereof shall issue Writs of Election to fill such Vacancies.

The House of Representatives shall chuse their Speaker and other Officers; and shall have the sole Power of Impeachment.

Section 3.   The Senate of the United States shall be composed of two Senators from each State, chosen by the Legislature thereof, for six Years; and each Senator shall have one Vote.

Immediately after they shall be assembled in Consequence of the first Election, they shall be divided as equally as may be into three Classes. The Seats of the Senators of the first Class shall be vacated at the Expiration of the second Year, of the second Class at the Expiration of the fourth Year, and of the third Class at the Expiration of the sixth Year, so that one-third may be chosen every second Year; and if Vacancies happen by Resignation, or otherwise, during the Recess of the Legislature of any State, the Executive thereof may make temporary Appointments until the next Meeting of the Legislature, which shall then fill such Vacancies.

No Person shall be a Senator who shall not have attained to the Age of thirty Years, and been nine Years a Citizen of the United States, and who shall not, when elected, be an Inhabitant of that State in which he shall be chosen.

The Vice President of the United States shall be President of the Senate, but shall have no vote, unless they be equally divided.

The Senate shall chuse their other Officers, and also a President pro tempore, in the absence of the Vice President, or when he shall exercise the Office of the President of the United States.

The Senate shall have the sole Power to try all Impeachments. When sitting for that purpose, they shall be on Oath or Affirmation. When the President of the United States is tried, the Chief Justice shall preside: And no person shall be convicted without the Concurrence of two thirds of the Members present.

Judgment in Cases of Impeachment shall not extend further than to removal from Office, and disqualification to hold and enjoy an Office of honor, Trust, or Profit under the United States: but the Party convicted shall nevertheless be liable and subject to Indictment, Trial, Judgment, and Punishment, according to Law.

Section 4.   The Times, Places and Manner of holding Elections for Senators and Representatives, shall be prescribed in each state by the Legislature thereof; but the Congress may at any time by Law make or alter such Regulations, except as to the Places of Chusing Senators.

The Congress shall assemble at least once in every Year, and such Meeting shall be on the first Monday in December, unless they shall by Law appoint a different Day.

Section 5.   Each House shall be the Judge of the Elections, Returns and Qualifications of its own Members, and a Majority of each shall constitute a Quorum to do Business from day to day, and may be authorized to compel the Attendance of absent Members, in such Manner, and under such Penalties, as each House may provide.

Each House may determine the Rules of its Proceedings, punish its Members for disorderly Behavior, and, with the Concurrence of two thirds, expel a Member.

Each House shall keep a Journal of its Proceedings, and from time to time publish the same, excepting such Parts as may in their Judgment require Secrecy; and the Yeas and Nays of the Members of either House on any question shall, at the Desire of one fifth of those Present, be entered on the Journal.

Neither House, during the Session of Congress, shall, without the Consent of the other, adjourn for more than three days, nor to any other Place than that in which the two Houses shall be sitting.

Section 6.   The Senators and Representatives shall receive a Compensation for their Services, to be ascertained by Law, and paid out of the Treasury of the United States. They shall in all Cases, except Treason, Felony, and Breach of the Peace, be privileged from Arrest during their Attendance at the Session of their respective Houses, and in going to and returning from the same; and for any Speech or Debate in either House, they shall not be questioned in any other Place.

No Senator or Representative shall, during the Time for which he was elected, be appointed to any civil Office under the Authority of the United States, which shall have been created, or the Emoluments whereof shall have been increased, during such time; and no Person holding any Office under the United States shall be a Member of either House during his continuance in Office.

Section 7. All Bills for raising Revenue shall originate in the House of Representatives; but the Senate may propose or concur with Amendments as on other bills.

Every Bill which shall have passed the House of Representatives and the Senate, shall, before it become a Law, be presented to the President of the United States. If he approve he shall sign it, but if not he shall return it, with his Objections, to that House in which it shall have originated, who shall enter the Objections at large on their Journal, and proceed to reconsider it. If after such Reconsideration two thirds of that House shall agree to pass the bill, it shall be sent, together with the objections, to the other House, by which it shall likewise be reconsidered, and if approved by two thirds of that House, it shall become a Law. But in all such Cases the Votes of both Houses shall be determined by Yeas and Nays, and the Names of the Persons voting for and against the Bill shall be entered on the Journal of each House respectively. If any Bill shall not be returned by the President within ten Days (Sundays excepted) after it shall have been presented to him, the Same shall be a Law, in like Manner as if he had signed it, unless the Congress by their Adjournment prevent its Return, in which Case it shall not be a Law.

Every Order, Resolution, or Vote to which the Concurrence of the Senate and House of Representatives may be necessary (except on a question of Adjournment) shall be presented to the President of the United States; and before the Same shall take Effect, shall be approved by him, or being disapproved by him, shall be repassed by two thirds of the Senate and House of Representatives, according to the Rules and Limitations prescribed in the Case of a Bill.

Section 8.   The Congress shall have Power To lay and collect Taxes, Duties, Imposts and Excises, to pay the Debts and provide for the common Defence and general Welfare of the United States; but all Duties, Imposts and Excises shall be uniform throughout the United States;

To borrow money on the credit of the United States;

To regulate Commerce with foreign Nations, and among the several States, and with the Indian Tribes;

To establish an uniform Rule of Naturalization, and uniform Laws on the subject of Bankruptcies throughout the United States;

To coin Money, regulate the Value thereof, and of foreign Coin, and fix the Standard of Weights and Measures;

To provide for the Punishment of counterfeiting the Securities and current Coin of the United States;

To establish Post Offices and post Roads;

To promote the Progress of Science and useful Arts, by securing for limited Times to Authors and Inventors the exclusive Right to their respective Writings and Discoveries;

To constitute Tribunals inferior to the Supreme Court;

To define and punish Piracies and Felonies committed on the high Seas, and Offences against the Law of Nations;

To declare War, grant Letters of Marque and Reprisal, and make Rules concerning Captures on Land and Water;

To raise and support Armies, but no Appropriation of Money to that Use shall be for a longer Term than two Years;

To provide and maintain a Navy;

To make Rules for the Government and Regulation of the land and naval forces;

To provide for calling forth the Militia to execute the Laws of the Union, suppress Insurrections and repel Invasions;

To provide for organizing, arming, and disciplining the Militia, and for governing such Part of them as may be employed in the Service of the United States, reserving to the States respectively, the Appointment of the Officers, and the Authority of training the Militia according to the discipline prescribed by Congress;

To exercise exclusive Legislation in all Cases whatsoever, over such District (not exceeding ten Miles square) as may, by Cession of particular States, and the acceptance of Congress, become the Seat of Government of the United States, and to exercise like Authority over all Places purchased by the Consent of the Legislature of the States in which the Same shall be, for the Erection of Forts, Magazines, Arsenals, dock-Yards, and other needful Buildings—And

To make all Laws which shall be necessary and proper for carrying into Execution the foregoing Powers, and all other Powers vested by this Constitution in the Government of the United States, or in any Department or Officer thereof.

Section 9. The Migration or Importation of such Persons as any of the States now existing shall think proper to admit, shall not be prohibited by the Congress prior to the Year one thousand eight hundred and eight, but a tax or duty may be imposed on such Importation, not exceeding ten dollars for each Person.

The privilege of the Writ of Habeas Corpus shall not be suspended, unless when in Cases of Rebellion or Invasion the public Safety may require it.

No Bill of Attainder or ex post facto Law shall be passed.

No capitation, or other direct, Tax shall be laid unless in Proportion to the Census or Enumeration herein before directed to be taken.

No Tax or Duty shall be laid on Articles exported from any State.

No Preference shall be given by any Regulation of Revenue to the Ports of one State over those of another: nor shall Vessels bound to, or from, one State, be obliged to enter, clear, or pay Duties in another.

No Money shall be drawn from the Treasury, but in Consequence of Appropriations made by Law; and a regular Statement and Account of the Receipts and Expenditures of all public Money shall be published from time to time.

No Title of Nobility shall be granted by the United States: And no Person holding any Office of Profit or Trust under them, shall, without the Consent of the Congress, accept of any present, Emolument, Office, or Title, of any kind whatever, from any King, Prince, or foreign State.

Section 10. No State shall enter any Treaty, alliance, or Confederation; grant Letters of Marque and Reprisal; coin Money; emit Bills of Credit; make any Thing but gold and silver Coin a Tender in Payment of Debts; pass any Bill of Attainder, ex post facto Law, or Law impairing the Obligation of Contracts, or grant any Title of Nobility.

No State shall, without the Consent of the Congress, lay any Imposts or Duties on Imports or Exports, except what may be absolutely necessary for executing its inspection Laws: and the net Produce of all Duties and Imposts, laid by any State on Imports or Exports, shall be for the Use of the Treasury of the United States; and all such Laws shall be subject to the Revision and Control of the Congress.

No State shall, without the Consent of Congress, lay any duty of Tonnage, keep Troops, or Ships of War in time of Peace, enter into any Agreement or Compact with another State, or with a foreign Power, or engage in War, unless actually invaded, or in such imminent Danger as will not admit of delay.

ARTICLE II

Section 1. The executive Power shall be vested in a President of the United States of America. He shall hold his Office during the Term of four years, and, together with the Vice-President, chosen for the same Term, be elected, as follows:

Each State shall appoint, in such Manner as the Legislature thereof may direct, a Number of Electors, equal to the whole Number of Senators and Representatives to which the State may be entitled in the Congress; but no Senator or Representative, or Person holding an Office of Trust or Profit under the United States, shall be appointed an Elector.

The Electors shall meet in their respective States, and vote by Ballot for two persons, of whom one at least shall not be an Inhabitant of the same State with themselves. And they shall make a List of all the Persons voted for, and of the Number of Votes for each; which List they shall sign and certify, and transmit sealed to the Seat of the Government of the United States, directed to the President of the Senate. The President of the Senate shall, in the Presence of the Senate and House of Representatives, open all the Certificates, and the Votes shall then be counted. The Person having the greatest Number of Votes shall be the President, if such Number be a Majority of the whole Number of Electors appointed; and if there be more than one who have such Majority, and have an equal Number of Votes, then the House of Representatives shall immediately chuse by Ballot one of them for President; and if no Person have a Majority, then from the five highest on the List the said House shall in like Manner chuse the President. But in chusing the President, the Votes shall be taken by States, the Representation from each State having one Vote; a quorum for this Purpose shall consist of a Member or Members from two-thirds of the States, and a Majority of all the States shall be necessary to a Choice. In every Case, after the Choice of the President, the Person having the greatest Number of Votes of the Electors shall be the Vice President. But if there should remain two or more who have equal votes, the Senate shall chuse from them by Ballot the Vice-President.

The Congress may determine the Time of chusing the Electors, and the Day on which they shall give their Votes; which Day shall be the same throughout the United States.

No person except a natural-born Citizen, or a Citizen of the United States, at the time of the Adoption of this Constitution, shall be eligible to the Office of President; neither shall any Person be eligible to that Office who shall not have attained to the Age of thirty-five years, and been fourteen Years a Resident within the United States.

In Case of the Removal of the President from Office, or of his Death, Resignation, or Inability to discharge the Powers and Duties of the said Office, the same shall devolve on the Vice-President, and the Congress may by Law provide for the Case of Removal, Death, Resignation, or Inability, both of the President and Vice-President, declaring what Officer shall then act as President, and such Officer shall act accordingly, until the disability be removed, or a President shall be elected.

The President shall, at stated Times, receive for his Services a Compensation, which shall neither be increased nor diminished during the Period for which he shall have been elected, and he shall not receive within that Period any other Emolument from the United States, or any of them.

Before he enter on the execution of his Office, he shall take the following Oath or Affirmation:— "I do solemnly swear (or affirm) that I will faithfully execute the Office of President of the United States, and will, to the best of my Ability, preserve, protect, and defend the Constitution of the United States."

Section 2.   The President shall be Commander in Chief of the Army and Navy of the United States, and of the Militia of the several States, when called into the actual Service of the United States; he may require the Opinion, in writing, of the principal Officer in each of the executive Departments, upon any subject relating to the Duties of their respective Offices, and he shall have Power to Grant Reprieves and Pardons for Offences against the United States, except in Cases of Impeachment.

He shall have Power, by and with the Advice and Consent of the Senate, to make Treaties, provided two thirds of the Senators present concur; and he shall nominate, and by and with the Advice and Consent of the Senate, shall appoint Ambassadors, other public Ministers and Counsuls, Judges of the Supreme Court, and all other Officers of the United States, whose Appointments are herein otherwise provided for, and which shall be established by Law: but the Congress may by Law vest the Appointments of such inferior Officers, as they think proper, in the President alone, in the Courts of Law, or in the Heads of Departments.

The President shall have Power to fill up all Vacancies that may happen during the Recess of the Senate, by granting Commissions which shall expire at the End of their next Session.

Section 3.   He shall from time to time give to the Congress Information of the State of the Union,

and recommend to their Consideration such Measures as he shall judge necessary and expedient; he may, on extraordinary occasions, convene both Houses, or either of them, and in Case of Disagreement between them, with respect to the Time of Adjournment, he may adjourn them to such Time as he shall think proper; he shall receive Ambassadors and other public Ministers; he shall take Care that the Laws be faithfully executed, and shall Commission all the Officers of the United States

Section 4.   The President, Vice President and all civil Officers of the United States, shall be removed from Office on Impeachment for, and Conviction of, Treason, Bribery, or other high Crimes and Misdemeanors.

ARTICLE III

Section 1.   The judicial Power of the United States, shall be vested in one supreme Court, and in such inferior Courts as the Congress may from time to time ordain and establish. The Judges, both of the supreme and inferior Courts, shall hold their Offices during good Behaviour, and shall, at stated Times, receive for their Services, a compensation, which shall not be diminished during their Continuance in Office.

Section 2.   The judicial Power shall extend to all Cases, in Law and Equity, arising under this constitution, the Laws of the United States, and treaties made, or which shall be made, under their Authority;—to all Cases affecting ambassadors, other public ministers and consuls;—to all cases of admiralty and maritime Jurisdiction;—to Controversies to which the United States shall be a Party;—to Controversies between two or more States;—between a State and Citizens of another State;—between Citizens of different States,—between Citizens of the same State claiming Lands under Grants of different States, and between a State, or the Citizens thereof, and foreign States, Citizens or Subjects.

In all Cases affecting Ambassadors, other public Ministers and Consuls, and those in which a State shall be Party, the supreme Court shall have original Jurisdiction. In all the other Cases before mentioned, the supreme Court shall have appellate Jurisdiction, both as to Law and Fact, with such Exception, and under such Regulations as the Congress shall make.

The trial of all Crimes, except in Cases of Impeachment, shall be by Jury; and such Trial shall be held in the State where the said Crimes shall have been committed; but when not committed within any State, the Trial shall be at such Place or Places as the Congress may by Law have directed.

Section 3.   Treason against the United States, shall consist only in levying War against them, or in adhering to their Enemies, giving them Aid and Comfort. No Person shall be convicted of Treason unless on the Testimony of two Witnesses to the same overt Act, or on Confession in open Court.

The Congress shall have power to declare the Punishment of Treason, but no Attainder of Treason shall work Corruption of Blood, or Forfeiture except during the Life of the Person attainted.

ARTICLE IV

Section 1.   Full Faith and Credit shall be given in each State to the public Acts, Records, and judicial Proceedings of every other State. And the Congress may by general laws prescribe the Manner in which such Acts, Records and Proceedings shall be proved, and the Effect thereof.

Section 2.   The Citizens of each State shall be entitled to all Privileges and Immunities of Citizens in the several States.

A Person charged in any State with Treason, Felony, or other Crime, who shall flee from Justice, and be found in another State, shall on demand of the executive Authority of the State from which he fled, be delivered up, to be removed to the State having Jurisdiction of the crime.

No Person held to Service or Labour in one State, under the Laws thereof, escaping into another, shall, in Consequence of any Law or Regulation therein, be discharged from such Service or Labour, but shall be delivered up on Claim of the Party to whom such Service or Labour may be due.

Section 3.   New States may be admitted by the Congress into this Union; but no new State shall be formed or erected within the Jurisdiction of any other State; nor any State be formed by the Junction of two or more States, or parts of States, without the Consent of the Legislatures of the States concerned as well as of the Congress.

The Congress shall have Power to dispose of and make all needful Rules and Regulations respecting the Territory or other Property belonging to the United States; and nothing in this constitution shall be so construed as to Prejudice any Claims of the United States, or of any particular State.

Section 4.   The United States shall guarantee to every State in this Union a Republican Form of Government, and shall protect each of them against Invasion; and on Application of the Legislature, or the Executive (when the Legislature cannot be convened) against domestic Violence.

ARTICLE V

The Congress, whenever two-thirds of both Houses shall deem it necessary, shall propose Amendments to this Constitution, or, on the Application of the Legislatures of two-thirds of the several States, shall call a Convention for proposing Amendments, which, in either Case, shall be valid to all Intents and Purposes, as part of this Constitution, when ratified by the Legislatures of three-fourths of the several States, or by Conventions in three-fourths thereof, as the one or the other Mode of Ratification may be proposed by the Congress; Provided that no Amendment which may be made prior to the Year One thousand eight hundred and eight shall in any Manner affect the first and fourth Clauses in the Ninth Section of the first Article; and that no State, without its Consent, shall be deprived of its equal Suffrage in the Senate.

ARTICLE VI

All Debts contracted and Engagements entered into, before the Adoption of this Constitution, shall be as valid against the United States under this Constitution, as under the Confederation.

This Constitution, and the Laws of the United States which shall be made in Pursuance thereof; and the Treaties made, or which shall be made, under the Authority of the United States, shall be the supreme Law of the Land; and the Judges in every State shall be bound thereby, any Thing in the Constitution of Laws of any State to the Contrary notwithstanding.

The Senators and Representatives before mentioned, and the Members of the several State Legislatures, and all executive and judicial Officers, both of the United States and of the several States, shall be bound by Oath or Affirmation to support this Constitution; but no religious Test shall ever be required as a qualification to any Office or public Trust under the United States.

ARTICLE VII

The Ratification of the Conventions of nine States shall be sufficient for the Establishment of this Constitution between the States so ratifying the same.

Done in Convention by the Unanimous Consent of the States present the Seventeenth Day of September in the Year of our Lord one thousand seven hundred and Eighty seven, and of the Independence of the United States of America the Twelfth. In Witness whereof We have hereunto subscribed our names.

Articles in Addition to, and Amendment of, the Constitution of the United States of America. Proposed by Congress, and Ratified by the Legislatures of the Several States, Pursuant to the Fifth Article of the Original Constitution.

AMENDMENT I [1791]

Congress shall make no law respecting an establishment of religion, or prohibiting the free exercise thereof; or abridging the freedom of speech, or of the press; or the right of the people peaceably to assemble, and to petition the Government for a redress of grievances.

AMENDMENT II [1791]

A well regulated Militia, being necessary to the security of a free State, the right of the people to keep and bear Arms shall not be infringed.

AMENDMENT III [1791]

No Soldier shall, in time of peace, be quartered in any house, without the consent of the Owner, nor in time of war, but in a manner to be prescribed by law.

AMENDMENT IV [1791]

The right of the people to be secure in their persons, houses, papers, and effects, against unreasonable searches and seizures, shall not be violated, and no Warrants shall issue, but upon probable cause, supported by Oath or affirmation, and particularly describing the place to be searched, and the persons or things to be seized.

AMENDMENT V [1791]

No person shall be held to answer for a capital or otherwise infamous crime, unless on a presentment or indictment of a Grand Jury, except in cases arising in the land or naval forces, or in the Militia, when in actual service in time of war or public danger; nor shall any person be subject for the same offence to be twice put in jeopardy of life or limb; nor shall be compelled in any criminal case to be a witness against himself, nor be deprived of life, liberty, or property, without due process of law; nor shall private property be taken for public use, without just compensation.

AMENDMENT VI [1791]

In all criminal prosecutions, the accused shall enjoy the right to a speedy and public trial, by an impartial jury of the State and district wherein the crime shall have been committed, which district shall have been previously ascertained by law, and to be informed of the nature and cause of the accusation; to be confronted with the witnesses against him; to have compulsory process for obtaining witnesses in his favor, and to have the Assistance of Counsel for his defence.

AMENDMENT VII [1791]

In suits at common law, where the value in controversy shall exceed twenty dollars, the right of trial by jury shall be preserved, and no fact tried by a jury, shall be otherwise reexamined in any Court of the United States, than according to the rules of the common law.

AMENDMENT VIII [1791]

Excessive bail shall not be required, nor excessive fines imposed, nor cruel and unusual punishments inflicted.

AMENDMENT IX [1791]

The enumeration in the Constitution, of certain rights, shall not be construed to deny or disparage others retained by the people.

AMENDMENT X [1791]

The powers not delegated to the United States by the Constitution, nor prohibited by it to the States, are reserved to the States respectively, or to the people.

AMENDMENT XI [1798]

The Judicial power of the United States shall not be construed to extend to any suit in law or equity, commenced or prosecuted against one of the United States by Citizens of another State, or by Citizens or Subjects of any Foreign State.

AMENDMENT XII [1804]

The Electors shall meet in their respective States and vote by ballot for President and Vice-President, one of whom, at least, shall not be an inhabitant of the same State with themselves; they shall name in their ballots the person voted for as President, and in distinct ballots the person voted for as Vice-President, and they shall make distinct lists of all persons voted for as President, and of all persons voted for as Vice-President, and of the number of votes for each, which lists they shall sign and certify, and transmit sealed to the seat of the government of the United States, directed to the President of the Senate;—The President of the Senate shall, in the presence of the Senate and House of Representatives, open all the certificates and the votes shall then be counted;—The person having the greatest number of votes for President, shall be the President, if such number by a majority of the whole number of Electors appointed; and if no person have such majority, then from the persons having the highest numbers not exceeding three on the list of those voted for as President, the House of Representatives shall choose immediately, by ballot, the President. But in choosing the President, the votes shall be taken by states, the representation from each state having one vote; a quorum for this purpose shall consist of a member or members from two-thirds of the states, and a majority of all the states shall be necessary to a choice. And if the House of Representatives shall not choose a President whenever the right of choice shall devolve upon them, before the fourth day of March next following, then the Vice-President shall act as President, as in the case of the death or other constitutional disability of the President.—The person having the greatest number of votes as Vice-President, shall be the Vice-President, if such number be a majority of the whole number of Electors appointed, and if no person have a majority, then from the two highest numbers on the list, the Senate shall choose the Vice-President; a quorum for the purpose shall consist of two-thirds of the whole number of Senators, and a majority of the whole number shall be necessary to a choice. But no person constitutionally ineligible to the office of President shall be eligible to that of Vice-President of the United States.

AMENDMENT XIII [1865]

Section 1.   Neither slavery nor involuntary servitude, except as a punishment for crime whereof the party shall have been duly convicted, shall exist within the United States, or any place subject to their jurisdiction.

Section 2.   Congress shall have power to enforce this article by appropriate legislation.

AMENDMENT XIV [1868]

Section 1.   All persons born or naturalized in the United States, and subject to the jurisdiction thereof, are citizens of the United States and of the State wherein they reside. No State shall make or enforce any law which shall abridge the privileges or immunities of citizens of the United States; nor shall any State deprive any person of life, liberty, or property, without due process of law; nor deny to any person within its jurisdiction the equal protection of the laws.

Section 2.   Representatives shall be apportioned among the several States according to their respective numbers, counting the whole number of persons in each State, excluding Indians not taxed. But when the right to vote at any election for the choice of electors for President and Vice-President of the United States, Representatives in Congress, the Executive and Judicial officers of a State, or the members of the Legislature thereof, is denied to any of the male inhabitants of such State, being twenty-one years of age, and citizens of the United States, or in any way abridged, except for participation in rebellion, or other crime, the basis of representation therein shall be reduced in the proportion which the number of such male citizens shall bear to the whole number of male citizens twenty-one years of age in such State.

Section 3.   No person shall be a Senator or Representative in Congress, or elector of President and

Vice-President, or hold any office, civil or military, under the United States, or under any State, who, having previously taken an oath, as a member of Congress, or as an officer of the United States, or as a member of any State legislature, or as an executive or judicial officer of any State, to support the Constitution of the United States, shall have engaged in insurrection or rebellion against the same, or given aid or comfort to the enemies thereof. But Congress may by a vote of two-thirds of each House, remove such disability.

Section 4. The validity of the public debt of the United States, authorized by law, including debts incurred for payment of pensions and bounties for services in suppressing insurrection or rebellion, shall not be questioned. But neither the United States nor any State shall assume or pay any debt or obligation incurred in aid of insurrection or rebellion against the United States or any claim for the loss or emancipation of any slave; but all such debts, obligations, and claims shall be held illegal and void.

Section 5. The Congress shall have the power to enforce, by appropriate legislation, the provisions of this article.

AMENDMENT XV [1870]

Section 1. The right of citizens of the United States to vote shall not be denied or abridged by the United States or by any State on account of race, color, or previous condition of servitude—

Section 2. The Congress shall have power to enforce this article by appropriate legislation.

AMENDMENT XVI [1913]

The Congress shall have power to lay and collect taxes on incomes, from whatever source derived, without apportionment among the several States, and without regard to any census or enumeration.

AMENDMENT XVII [1913]

The Senate of the United States shall be composed of two Senators from each State, elected by the people thereof, for six years; and each Senator shall have one vote. The electors in each State shall have the qualifications requisite for electors

of the most numerous branch of the State legislatures.

When vacancies happen in the representation of any State in the Senate, the executive authority of such State shall issue writs of election to fill such vacancies: *Provided,* That the legislature of any State may empower the executive thereof to make temporary appointments until the people fill the vacancies by election as the legislature may direct.

This amendment shall not be so construed as to affect the election or term of any Senator chosen before it becomes valid as part of the Constitution.

AMENDMENT XVIII [1919]

Section 1. After one year from the ratification of this article the manufacture, sale, or transportation of intoxicating liquors within, the importation thereof into, or the exportation thereof from the United States and all territory subject to the jurisdiction thereof for beverage purposes is hereby prohibited.

Section 2. The Congress and the several States shall have concurrent power to enforce this article by appropriate legislation.

Section 3. This article shall be inoperative unless it shall have been ratified as an amendment to the Constitution by the legislatures of the several States, as provided in the Constitution, within seven years from the date of the submission hereof to the States by the Congress.

AMENDMENT XIX [1920]

The right of citizens of the United States to vote shall not be denied or abridged by the United States or by any State on account of sex.

Congress shall have power to enforce this article by appropriate legislation.

AMENDMENT XX [1933]

Section 1. The terms of the President and Vice-President shall end at noon on the 20th day of January, and the terms of Senators and Representatives at noon on the 3d day of January, of the years in which such terms would have ended if this article had not been ratified; and the terms of their successors shall then begin.

Section 2. The Congress shall assemble at least once in every year, and such meeting shall begin at noon on the 3d day of January, unless they shall by law appoint a different day.

Section 3. If, at the time fixed for the beginning of the term of the President, the President elect shall have died, the Vice-President elect shall become President. If a President shall not have been chosen before the time fixed for the beginning of his term, or if the President elect shall have failed to qualify, then the Vice-President until a President shall have qualified; and the Congress may by law provide for the case wherein neither a President elect nor a Vice-President elect shall have qualified, declaring who shall then act as President, or the manner in which one who is to act shall be selected, and such person shall act accordingly until a President or Vice-President shall have qualified.

Section 4. The Congress may by law provide for the case of the death of any of the persons from whom the House of Representatives may choose a President whenever the right of choice shall have devolved upon them, and for the case of the death of any of the persons from whom the Senate may choose a Vice-President whenever the right of choice shall have devolved upon them.

Section 5. Sections 1 and 2 shall take effect on the 15th day of October following the ratification of this article.

Section 6. This article shall be inoperative unless it shall have been ratified as an amendment to the Constitution by the legislatures of three-fourths of the several States within seven years from the date of its submission.

AMENDMENT XXI [1933]

Section 1. The eighteenth article of amendment to the Constitution of the United States is hereby repealed.

Section 2. The transportation or importation into any State, Territory, or possession of the United States for delivery or use therein of intoxicating liquors, in violation of the laws thereof, is hereby prohibited.

Section 3. This article shall be inoperative unless it shall have been ratified as an amendment to the Constitution by conventions in the several States, as provided in the Constitution, within seven years from the date of the submission hereof to the States by the Congress.

AMENDMENT XXII [1951]

No person shall be elected to the office of the President more than twice, and no person who has held the office of President, or acted as President, for more than two years of a term to which some other person was elected President shall be elected to the office of the President more than once.

But this Article shall not apply to any person holding the office of President when this Article was proposed by the Congress, and shall not prevent any person who may be holding the office of President, or acting as President, during the term within which this Article becomes operative from holding the office of President or acting as President during the remainder of such term.

AMENDMENT XXIII [1961]

Section 1. The District constituting the seat of Government of the United States shall appoint in such manner as the Congress may direct:

A number of electors of President and Vice President equal to the whole number of Senators and Representatives in Congress to which the District would be entitled if it were a State, but in no event more than the least populous State; they shall be in addition to those appointed by the States, but they shall be considered, for the purposes of the election of President and Vice President, to be electors appointed by a State; and they shall meet in the District and perform such duties as provided by the twelfth article of amendment.

Section 2. The Congress shall have power to enforce this article by appropriate legislation.

AMENDMENT XXIV [1964]

Section 1. The right of citizens of the United States to vote in any primary or other election for President or Vice President, for electors for President or Vice President, or for Senator or Representative in Congress, shall not be denied or abridged by the United States or any State by reason of failure to pay any poll tax or other tax.

Section 2. The Congress shall have the power to enforce this article by appropriate legislation.

AMENDMENT XXV [1967]

Section 1. In case of the removal of the President from office or his death or resignation, the Vice President shall become President.

Section 2. Whenever there is a vacancy in the office of the Vice President, the President shall nominate a Vice President who shall take the office upon confirmation by a majority vote of both houses of Congress.

Section 3. Whenever the President transmits to the President pro tempore of the Senate and the Speaker of the House of Representatives his written declaration that he is unable to discharge the powers and duties of his office, and until he transmits to them a written declaration to the contrary, such powers and duties shall be discharged by the Vice President as Acting President.

Section 4. Whenever the Vice President and a majority of either the principal officers of the executive departments, or of such other body as Congress may by law provide, transmit to the President pro tempore of the Senate and the Speaker of the House of Representatives their written declaration that the President is unable to discharge the powers and duties of his office, the Vice President shall immediately assume the powers and duties of the office as Acting President.

Thereafter, when the President transmits to the President pro tempore of the Senate and the Speaker of the House of Representatives his written declaration that no inability exists, he shall resume the powers and duties of his office unless the Vice President and a majority of either the principal officers of the executive departments, or of such other body as Congress may by law provide, transmit within four days to the President pro tempore of the Senate and the Speaker of the House of Representatives their written declaration that the President is unable to discharge the powers and duties of his office. Thereupon Congress shall decide the issue, assembling within 48 hours for that purpose if not in session. If the Congress, within 21 days after receipt of the latter written declaration, or, if Congress is not in session, within 21 days after Congress is required to assemble, determines by two-thirds vote of both houses that the President is unable to discharge the powers and duties of his office, the Vice President shall continue to discharge the same as Acting President; otherwise, the President shall resume the powers and duties of his office.

Admission of States to the Union

1	Delaware	Dec. 7, 1787	26	Michigan	Jan. 26, 1837
2	Pennsylvania	Dec. 12, 1787	27	Florida	Mar. 3, 1845
3	New Jersey	Dec. 18, 1787	28	Texas	Dec. 29, 1845
4	Georgia	Jan. 2, 1788	29	Iowa	Dec. 28, 1846
5	Connecticut	Jan. 9, 1788	30	Wisconsin	May 29, 1848
6	Massachusetts	Feb. 6, 1788	31	California	Sept. 9, 1850
7	Maryland	Apr. 28, 1788	32	Minnesota	May 11, 1858
8	South Carolina	May 23, 1788	33	Oregon	Feb. 14, 1859
9	New Hampshire	June 21, 1788	34	Kansas	Jan. 29, 1861
10	Virginia	June 25, 1788	35	West Virginia	June 19, 1863
11	New York	July 26, 1788	36	Nevada	Oct. 31, 1864
12	North Carolina	Nov. 21, 1789	37	Nebraska	Mar. 1, 1867
13	Rhode Island	May 29, 1790	38	Colorado	Aug. 1, 1876
14	Vermont	Mar. 4, 1791	39	North Dakota	Nov. 2, 1889
15	Kentucky	June 1, 1792	40	South Dakota	Nov. 2, 1889
16	Tennessee	June 1, 1796	41	Montana	Nov. 8, 1889
17	Ohio	Mar. 1, 1803	42	Washington	Nov. 11, 1889
18	Louisiana	Apr. 30, 1812	43	Idaho	July 3, 1890
19	Indiana	Dec. 11, 1816	44	Wyoming	July 10, 1890
20	Mississippi	Dec. 10, 1817	45	Utah	Jan. 4, 1896
21	Illinois	Dec. 3, 1818	46	Oklahoma	Nov. 16, 1907
22	Alabama	Dec. 14, 1819	47	New Mexico	Jan. 6, 1912
23	Maine	Mar. 15, 1820	48	Arizona	Feb. 14, 1912
24	Missouri	Aug. 10, 1821	49	Alaska	Jan. 3, 1959
25	Arkansas	June 15, 1836	50	Hawaii	Aug. 21, 1959

Population of the United States, 1790–1990

YEAR	NUMBER OF STATES	POPULATION	PERCENT INCREASE
1790	13	3,929,214	
1800	16	5,308,483	35.1
1810	17	7,239,881	36.4
1820	23	9,638,453	33.1
1830	24	12,866,020	33.5
1840	26	17,069,453	32.7
1850	31	23,191,876	35.9
1860	33	31,443,321	35.6
1870	37	39,818,449	26.6
1880	38	50,155,783	26.0
1890	44	62,947,714	25.5
1900	45	75,994,575	20.7
1910	46	91,972,266	21.0
1920	48	105,710,620	14.9
1930	48	122,775,046	16.1
1940	48	131,669,275	7.2
1950	48	150,697,361	14.5
1960	50	179,323,175	19.0
1970	50	203,235,298	13.3
1980	50	226,504,825	11.4
1990	50	249,632,692	10.2

The Vice Presidents and the Cabinet

SECRETARY OF STATE
(1789–   )

Thomas Jefferson	1789	Daniel Webster	1850	Elihu Root	1905
Edmund Randolph	1794	Edward Everett	1852	Robert Bacon	1909
Timothy Pickering	1795	William L. Marcy	1853	Philander C. Knox	1909
John Marshall	1800	Lewis Cass	1857	William J. Bryan	1913
James Madison	1801	Jeremiah S. Black	1860	Robert Lansing	1915
Robert Smith	1809	William H. Seward	1861	Bainbridge Colby	1920
James Monroe	1811	E. B. Washburne	1869	Charles E. Hughes	1921
John Q. Adams	1817	Hamilton Fish	1869	Frank B. Kellogg	1925
Henry Clay	1825	William M. Evarts	1877	Henry L. Stimson	1929
Martin Van Buren	1829	James G. Blaine	1881	Cordell Hull	1933
Edward Livingston	1831	F. T. Frelinghuysen	1881	E. R. Stettinius, Jr.	1944
Louis McLane	1833	Thomas F. Bayard	1885	James F. Byrnes	1945
John Forsyth	1834	James G. Blaine	1889	George C. Marshall	1947
Daniel Webster	1841	John W. Foster	1892	Dean Acheson	1949
Hugh S. Legaré	1843	Walter Q. Gresham	1893	John Foster Dulles	1953
Abel P. Upshur	1843	Richard Olney	1895	Christian A. Herter	1959
John C. Calhoun	1844	John Sherman	1897	Dean Rusk	1961
James Buchanan	1845	William R. Day	1897	William P. Rogers	1969
John M. Clayton	1849	John Hay	1898	Henry A. Kissinger	1973

Cyrus Vance	1977
Edmund Muskie	1979
Alexander M. Haig, Jr.	1981
George Shultz	1982
James A. Baker III	1989

SECRETARY OF THE TREASURY (1789–   )

Alexander Hamilton	1789
Oliver Wolcott	1795
Samuel Dexter	1801
Albert Gallatin	1801
G. W. Campbell	1814
A. J. Dallas	1814
William H. Crawford	1816
Richard Rush	1825
Samuel D. Ingham	1829
Louis McLane	1831
William J. Duane	1833
Roger B. Taney	1833
Levi Woodbury	1834
Thomas Ewing	1841
Walter Forward	1841
John C. Spencer	1843
George M. Bibb	1844
Robert J. Walker	1845
William M. Meredith	1849
Thomas Corwin	1850
James Guthrie	1853
Howell Cobb	1857
Philip F. Thomas	1860
John A. Dix	1861
Salmon P. Chase	1861
Wm. P. Fessenden	1864
Hugh McCulloch	1865
George S. Boutwell	1869
William A. Richardson	1873
Benjamin H. Bristow	1874
Lot M. Morrill	1876
John Sherman	1877
William Windom	1881
Charles J. Folger	1881
Walter Q. Gresham	1884
Hugh McCulloch	1884
Daniel Manning	1885
Charles S. Fairchild	1887
William Windom	1889
Charles Foster	1891
John G. Carlisle	1893
Lyman J. Gage	1897
Leslie M. Shaw	1902
George B. Cortelyou	1907
Franklin MacVeagh	1909

William G. McAdoo	1913
Carter Glass	1919
David F. Houston	1919
Andrew W. Mellon	1921
Ogden L. Mills	1932
William H. Woodin	1933
Henry Morgenthau, Jr.	1934
Fred M. Vinson	1945
John W. Snyder	1946
George M. Humphrey	1953
Robert B. Anderson	1957
C. Douglas Dillon	1961
Henry H. Fowler	1965
David M. Kennedy	1969
John B. Connally	1970
George P. Shultz	1972
William E. Simon	1974
Michael W. Blumenthal	1977
G. William Miller	1979
Donald T. Regan	1981
James A. Baker III	1985
Nicholas Brady	1988

SECRETARY OF WAR (1789–1947)

Henry Knox	1789
Timothy Pickering	1795
James McHenry	1796
John Marshall	1800
Samuel Dexter	1800
Roger Griswold	1801
Henry Dearborn	1801
William Eustis	1809
John Armstrong	1813
James Monroe	1814
William H. Crawford	1815
Isaac Shelby	1817
George Graham	1817
John C. Calhoun	1817
James Barbour	1825
Peter B. Porter	1828
John H. Eaton	1829
Lewis Cass	1831
Benjamin F. Butler	1837
Joel R. Poinsett	1837
John Bell	1841
John McLean	1841
John C. Spencer	1841
James M. Porter	1843
William Wilkins	1844
William L. Marcy	1845
George W. Crawford	1849
Charles M. Conrad	1850

Jefferson Davis	1853
John B. Floyd	1857
Joseph Holt	1861
Simon Cameron	1861
Edwin M. Stanton	1862
Ulysses S. Grant	1867
Lorenzo Thomas	1868
John M. Schofield	1868
John A. Rawlins	1869
William T. Sherman	1869
William W. Belknap	1869
Alphonso Taft	1876
James D. Cameron	1876
George W. McCrary	1877
Alexander Ramsey	1879
Robert T. Lincoln	1881
William C. Endicott	1885
Redfield Proctor	1889
Stephen B. Elkins	1891
Daniel S. Lamont	1893
Russell A. Alger	1897
Elihu Root	1899
William H. Taft	1904
Luke E. Wright	1908
J. M. Dickinson	1909
Henry L. Stimson	1911
L. M. Garrison	1913
Newton D. Baker	1916
John W. Weeks	1921
Dwight F. Davis	1925
James W. Good	1929
Patrick J. Hurley	1929
George H. Dern	1933
H. A. Woodring	1936
Henry L. Stimson	1940
Robert P. Patterson	1945
Kenneth C. Royall	1947

SECRETARY OF THE NAVY (1798–1947)

Benjamin Stoddert	1798
Robert Smith	1801
Paul Hamilton	1809
William Jones	1813
B. W. Crowninshield	1814
Smith Thompson	1818
S. L. Southard	1823
John Branch	1829
Levi Woodbury	1831
Mahlon Dickerson	1834
James K. Paulding	1838
George E. Badger	1841
Abel P. Upshur	1841

David Henshaw	1843
Thomas W. Gilmer	1844
John Y. Mason	1844
George Bancroft	1845
John Y. Mason	1846
William B. Preston	1849
William A. Graham	1850
John P. Kennedy	1852
James C. Dobbin	1853
Isaac Toucey	1857
Gideon Welles	1861
Adolph E. Borie	1869
George M. Robeson	1869
R. W. Thompson	1877
Nathan Goff, Jr.	1881
William H. Hunt	1881
William E. Chandler	1881
William C. Whitney	1885
Benjamin F. Tracy	1889
Hilary A. Herbert	1893
John D. Long	1897
William H. Moody	1902
Paul Morton	1904
Charles J. Bonaparte	1905
Victor H. Metcalf	1907
T. H. Newberry	1908
George von L. Meyer	1909
Josephus Daniels	1913
Edwin Denby	1921
Curtis D. Wilbur	1924
Charles F. Adams	1929
Claude A. Swanson	1933
Charles Edison	1940
Frank Knox	1940
James V. Forrestal	1945

SECRETARY OF DEFENSE
(1947–   )

James V. Forrestal	1947
Louis A. Johnson	1949
George C. Marshall	1950
Robert A. Lovett	1951
Charles E. Wilson	1953
Neil H. McElroy	1957
Thomas S. Gates, Jr.	1959
Robert S. McNamara	1961
Clark M. Clifford	1968
Melvin R. Laird	1969
Elliot L. Richardson	1973
James R. Schlesinger	1973
Donald Rumsfield	1974
Harold Brown	1977
Caspar Weinberger	1981
Frank Carlucci	1988
Richard Cheney	1989

POSTMASTER GENERAL
(1789–1970)

Samuel Osgood	1789
Timothy Pickering	1791
Joseph Habersham	1795
Gideon Granger	1801
Return J. Meigs, Jr.	1814
John McLean	1823
William T. Barry	1829
Amos Kendall	1835
John M. Niles	1840
Francis Granger	1841
Charles A. Wickliffe	1841
Cave Johnson	1845
Jacob Collamer	1849
Nathan K. Hall	1850
Samuel D. Hubbard	1852
James Campbell	1853
Aaron V. Brown	1857
Joseph Holt	1859
Horatio King	1861
Montgomery Blair	1861
William Dennison	1864
Alexander W. Randall	1866
John A. J. Creswell	1869
James W. Marshall	1874
Marshall Jewell	1874
James N. Tyner	1876
David M. Key	1877
Horace Maynard	1880
Thomas L. James	1881
Timothy O. Howe	1881
Walter Q. Gresham	1883
Frank Hatton	1884
William F. Vilas	1885
Don M. Dickinson	1888
John Wanamaker	1889
Wilson S. Bissel	1893
William L. Wilson	1895
James A. Gary	1897
Charles E. Smith	1898
Henry C. Payne	1902
Robert J. Wynne	1904
George B. Cortelyou	1905
George von L. Meyer	1907
F. H. Hitchcock	1909
Albert S. Burleson	1913
Will H. Hays	1921
Hubert Work	1922
Harry S. New	1923
Walter F. Brown	1929
James A. Farley	1933
Frank C. Walker	1940
Robert E. Hannegan	1945
J. M. Donaldson	1947
A. E. Summerfield	1953

J. Edward Day	1961
John A. Gronouski	1963
Lawrence F. O'Brien	1965
W. Marvin Watson	1968
Winton M. Blount	1969

ATTORNEY GENERAL
(1789–   )

Edmund Randolph	1789
William Bradford	1794
Charles Lee	1795
Theophilus Parsons	1801
Levi Lincoln	1801
Robert Smith	1805
John Breckinridge	1805
Caesar A. Rodney	1807
William Pinkney	1811
Richard Rush	1814
William Wirt	1817
John M. Berrien	1829
Roger B. Taney	1831
Benjamin F. Butler	1833
Felix Grundy	1838
Henry D. Gilpin	1840
John J. Crittenden	1841
Hugh S. Legare	1841
John Nelson	1843
John Y. Mason	1845
Nathan Clifford	1846
Isaac Toucey	1848
Reverdy Johnson	1849
John J. Crittenden	1850
Caleb Cushing	1853
Jeremiah S. Black	1857
Edwin M. Stanton	1860
Edward Bates	1861
Titian J. Coffey	1863
James Speed	1864
Henry Stanbery	1866
William M. Evarts	1868
Ebenezer R. Hoar	1869
Amos T. Ackerman	1870
George H. Williams	1871
Edward Pierrepont	1875
Alphonso Taft	1876
Charles Devens	1877
Wayne MacVeagh	1881
Benjamin H. Brewster	1881
A. H. Garland	1885
William H. H. Miller	1889
Richard Olney	1893
Judson Harmon	1895
Joseph McKenna	1897
John W. Griggs	1897

Philander C. Knox	1901
William H. Moody	1904
Charles J. Bonaparte	1907
G. W. Wickersham	1909
J. C. McReynolds	1913
Thomas W. Gregory	1914
A. Mitchell Palmer	1919
H. M. Daugherty	1921
Harlan F. Stone	1924
John G. Sargent	1925
William D. Mitchell	1929
H. S. Cummings	1933
Frank Murphy	1939
Robert H. Jackson	1940
Francis Biddle	1941
Tom C. Clark	1945
J. H. McGrath	1949
J. P. McGranery	1952
H. Brownell, Jr.	1953
William P. Rogers	1957
Robert F. Kennedy	1961
Nicholas Katzenback	1964
Ramsey Clark	1967
John N. Mitchell	1969
Richard G. Kleindienst	1972
Elliot L. Richardson	1973
William Saxbe	1974
Edward H. Levi	1974
Griffin B. Bell	1977
Benjamin R. Civiletti	1979
William French Smith	1981
Edwin A. Meese III	1985
Richard Thornburgh	1988

**SECRETARY OF THE
INTERIOR (1849–   )**

Thomas Ewing	1849
T. M. T. McKennan	1850
Alexander H. H. Stuart	1850
Robert McClelland	1853
Jacob Thompson	1857
Caleb B. Smith	1861
John P. Usher	1863
James Harlan	1865
O. H. Browning	1866
Jacob D. Cox	1869
Columbus Delano	1870
Zachariah Chandler	1875
Carl Schurz	1877
Samuel J. Kirkwood	1881
Henry M. Teller	1881
L. Q. C. Lamar	1885
William F. Vilas	1888
John W. Noble	1889

Hoke Smith	1893
David R. Francis	1896
Cornelius N. Bliss	1897
E. A. Hitchcock	1899
James R. Garfield	1907
R. A. Ballinger	1909
Walter L. Fisher	1911
Franklin K. Lane	1913
John B. Payne	1920
Albert B. Fall	1921
Hubert Work	1923
Roy O. West	1928
Ray L. Wilbur	1929
Harold L. Ickes	1933
Julius A. Krug	1946
Oscar L. Chapman	1949
Douglas McKay	1953
Fred A. Seaton	1956
Steward L. Udall	1961
Walter J. Hickel	1969
Rogers C. B. Morton	1971
Thomas S. Kleppe	1975
Cecil D. Andrus	1977
James G. Watt	1981
William P. Clark, Jr.	1983
Donald P. Hodel	1985
Manuel Lujan	1989

**SECRETARY OF
AGRICULTURE
(1889–   )**

Norman J. Colman	1889
Jeremiah M. Rusk	1889
J. Sterling Morton	1893
James Wilson	1897
David F. Houston	1913
Edward T. Meredith	1920
Henry C. Wallace	1921
Howard M. Gore	1924
William M. Jardine	1925
Arthur M. Hyde	1929
Henry A. Wallace	1933
Claude R. Wickard	1940
Clinton P. Anderson	1945
Charles F. Brannan	1948
Ezra Taft Benson	1953
Orville L. Freeman	1961
Clifford M. Hardin	1969
Earl L. Butz	1971
John A. Knebel	1976
Bob Bergland	1977
John R. Block	1981
Richard E. Lyng	1986
Clayton Yeutter	1989

**SECRETARY OF COMMERCE
AND LABOR (1903–1913)**

George B. Cortelyou	1903
Victor H. Metcalf	1904
Oscar S. Straus	1906
Charles Nagel	1909

**SECRETARY OF COMMERCE
(1913–   )**

William C. Redfield	1913
Joshua W. Alexander	1919
Herbert Hoover	1921
William F. Whiting	1928
Robert P. Lamont	1929
Roy D. Chapin	1932
Daniel C. Roper	1933
Henry L. Hopkins	1939
Jesse Jones	1940
Henry A. Wallace	1945
W. A. Harriman	1946
Charles Sawyer	1948
Sinclair Weeks	1953
Lewis L. Strauss	1958
F. H. Mueller	1959
Luther Hodges	1961
John T. Connor	1965
A. B. Trowbridge	1967
C. R. Smith	1968
Maurice H. Stans	1969
Peter G. Peterson	1972
Frederick B. Dent	1973
Elliot L. Richardson	1974
Juanita M. Kreps	1977
Philip M. Klutznick	1979
Malcolm Baldridge	1981
C. William Verity, Jr.	1987
Robert Mosbacher	1989

**SECRETARY OF LABOR
(1913–   )**

William B. Wilson	1913
James J. Davis	1921
William N. Doak	1930
Frances Perkins	1933
L. B. Schwellenbach	1945
Maurice J. Tobin	1948
Martin P. Durkin	1953
James P. Mitchell	1953
Arthur J. Goldberg	1961
W. Willard Wirtz	1962
George P. Shultz	1969
James D. Hodgson	1970
Peter J. Brennan	1973

W. J. Usery, Jr.	1974
Ray Marshall	1977
Raymond J. Donovan	1981

SECRETARY OF HEALTH, EDUCATION, AND WELFARE
(1953–1979)

Oveta Culp Hobby	1953
Marion B. Folsom	1955
Arthur S. Flemming	1958
Abraham A. Ribicoff	1961
Anthony J. Celebrezze	1962
John W. Gardner	1965
Wilbur J. Cohen	1968
Robert H. Finch	1969
Elliot L. Richardson	1970
Caspar W. Weinberger	1973
David Matthews	1974
Joseph A. Califano, Jr.	1977

SECRETARY OF HEALTH AND HUMAN SERVICES
(1979–   )

Patricia R. Harris	1979
Richard S. Schweiker	1981
Margaret Heckler	1983
Otis R. Bowen	1985
Louis W. Sullivan	1989

SECRETARY OF HOUSING AND URBAN DEVELOPMENT
(1966–   )

Robert C. Weaver	1966
George W. Romney	1969
James T. Lynn	1973
Carla Anderson Hills	1974
Patricia Harris	1977

Moon Landrieu	1979
Samuel R. Pierce, Jr.	1981
Jack Kemp	1989

SECRETARY OF ENERGY
(1977–   )

James R. Schlesinger	1977
Charles W. Duncan, Jr.	1979
James B. Edwards	1981
Donald Hodel	1982
John S. Herrington	1985
James Watkins	1989

SECRETARY OF TRANSPORTATION
(1967–   )

Alan S. Boyd	1967
John A. Volpe	1969
Claude S. Brinegar	1973–74
William T. Coleman	1975–77
Brock Adams	1977–79
Neil E. Goldschmidt	1979–81
Andrew L. Lewis, Jr.	1981–83
Elizabeth Dole	1983–87
James L. Burnley IV	1987–89
Samuel Skinner	1989–

SECRETARY OF EDUCATION
(1979–   )

Shirley M. Hufstedler	1979
Terrel Bell	1981
William J. Bennett	1985
Laura F. Cavozos	1988

VICE PRESIDENT

John Adams	1789–97
Thomas Jefferson	1797–1801
Aaron Burr	1801–05
George Clinton	1805–13
Elbridge Gerry	1813–17
Daniel D. Tompkins	1817–25
John C. Calhoun	1825–33
Martin Van Buren	1833–37
Richard M. Johnson	1837–41
John Tyler	1841
George M. Dallas	1845–49
Millard Fillmore	1849–50
William R. King	1853–57
John C. Breckinridge	1857–61
Hannibal Hamlin	1861–65
Andrew Johnson	1865
Schuyler Colfax	1869–73
Henry Wilson	1873–77
William A. Wheeler	1877–81
Chester A. Arthur	1881
Thomas A. Hendricks	1885–89
Levi F. Morton	1889–93
Adlai E. Stevenson	1893–97
Garret A. Hobart	1897–1901
Theodore Roosevelt	1901
Charles W. Fairbanks	1905–09
James S. Sherman	1909–13
Thomas R. Marshall	1913–21
Calvin Coolidge	1921–23
Charles G. Dawes	1925–29
Charles Curtis	1929–33
John Nance Garner	1933–41
Henry A. Wallace	1941–45
Harry S Truman	1945
Alben W. Barkley	1949–53
Richard M. Nixon	1953–61
Lyndon B. Johnson	1961–63
Hubert H. Humphrey	1965–69
Spiro T. Agnew	1969–73
Gerald R. Ford	1973–74
Nelson W. Rockefeller	1974–77
Walter F. Mondale	1977–81
George Bush	1981–88
J. Danforth Quayle III	1989

Presidential Elections, 1789–1988

Year	Candidates	Party	Popular Vote	Electoral Vote
1789	**George Washington**			69
	John Adams			34
	Others			35
1792	**George Washington**			132
	John Adams			77
	George Clinton			50
	Others			5

Year	Candidates	Party	Popular Vote	Electoral Vote
1796	**John Adams**	Federalist		71
	Thomas Jefferson	Democratic-Republican		68
	Thomas Pinckney	Federalist		59
	Aaron Burr	Democratic-Republican		30
	Others			48
1800	**Thomas Jefferson**	Democratic-Republican		73
	Aaron Burr	Democratic-Republican		73
	John Adams	Federalist		65
	Charles C. Pinckney	Federalist		64
1804	**Thomas Jefferson**	Democratic-Republican		162
	Charles C. Pinckney	Federalist		14
1808	**James Madison**	Democratic-Republican		122
	Charles C. Pinckney	Federalist		47
	George Clinton	Independent-Republican		6
1812	**James Madison**	Democratic-Republican		128
	DeWitt Clinton	Federalist		89
1816	**James Monroe**	Democratic-Republican		183
	Rufus King	Federalist		34
1820	**James Monroe**	Democratic-Republican		231
	John Quincy Adams	Independent-Republican		1
1824	**John Quincy Adams**	Democratic-Republican	113,122 (30.9%)	84
	Andrew Jackson	Democratic-Republican	151,271 (41.3%)	99
	Henry Clay	Democratic-Republican	47,531 (12.9%)	37
	William H. Crawford	Democratic Republican	40,856 (11.1%)	41
1828	**Andrew Jackson**	Democratic	642,553 (55.9%)	178
	John Quincy Adams	National Republican	500,897 (43.6%)	83
1832	**Andrew Jackson**	Democratic	701,780 (54.2%)	219
	Henry Clay	National Republican	484,205 (37.4%)	49
	William Wirt	Anti-Masonic	100,715 (7.7%)	7
1836	**Martin Van Buren**	Democratic	763,176 (50.8%)	170
	William H. Harrison	Whig	550,816 (36.6%)	73
	Hugh L. White	Whig	146,107 (9.7%)	26
	Daniel Webster	Whig	41,201 (2.7%)	14
1840	**William H. Harrison** (**John Tyler**, 1841)	Whig	1,275,390 (52.8%)	234
	Martin Van Buren	Democratic	1,128,854 (46.8%)	60
1844	**James K. Polk**	Democratic	1,339,494 (49.5%)	170
	Henry Clay	Whig	1,300,004 (48.0%)	105
	James G. Birney	Liberty	62,103 (2.3%)	
1848	**Zachary Taylor** (**Millard Fillmore**, 1850)	Whig	1,361,393 (47.2%)	163
	Lewis Cass	Democratic	1,223,460 (42.4%)	127
	Martin Van Buren	Free Soil	291,501 (10.1%)	
1852	**Franklin Pierce**	Democratic	1,607,510 (50.8%)	254
	Winfield Scott	Whig	1,386,942 (43.8%)	42

Year	Candidates	Party	Popular Vote	Electoral Vote
1856	**James Buchanan**	Democratic	1,836,072 (45.2%)	174
	John C. Frémont	Republican	1,342,345 (33.1%)	114
	Millard Fillmore	American	873,053 (21.5%)	8
1860	**Abraham Lincoln**	Republican	1,865,908 (39.8%)	180
	Stephen A. Douglas	Democratic	1,382,202 (29.4%)	12
	John C. Breckinridge	Democratic	848,019 (18.0%)	72
	John Bell	Constitutional Union	591,901 (12.6%)	39
1864	**Abraham Lincoln** (Andrew Johnson, 1865)	Republican	2,218,388 (55.0%)	212
	George B. McClellan	Democratic	1,812,807 (44.9%)	21
1868	**Ulysses S. Grant**	Republican	3,013,650 (52.6%)	214
	Horatio Seymour	Democratic	2,708,744 (47.3%)	80
1872	**Ulysses S. Grant**	Republican	3,598,235 (55.6%)	286
	Horace Greeley	Democratic	2,834,761 (43.8%)	66
1876	**Rutherford B. Hayes**	Republican	4,034,311 (47.9%)	185
	Samuel J. Tilden	Democratic	4,288,546 (50.0%)	184
1880	**James A. Garfield** (Chester A. Arthur, 1881)	Republican	4,446,158 (48.2%)	214
	Winfield S. Hancock	Democratic	4,444,260 (48.2%)	155
	James B. Weaver	Greenback-Labor	305,997 (3.3%)	
1884	**Grover Cleveland**	Democratic	4,874,621 (48.5%)	219
	James G. Blaine	Republican	4,848,936 (48.2%)	182
	Benjamin F. Butler	Greenback-Labor	175,096 (1.7%)	
1888	**Benjamin Harrison**	Republican	5,443,892 (47.8%)	233
	Grover Cleveland	Democratic	5,534,488 (48.6%)	168
1892	**Grover Cleveland**	Democratic	5,551,883 (46.0%)	277
	Benjamin Harrison	Republican	5,179,244 (42.9%)	145
	James B. Weaver	People's	1,024,280 (8.5%)	22
1896	**William McKinley**	Republican	7,108,480 (51.0%)	271
	William J. Bryan	Democratic; Populist	6,511,495 (46.7%)	176
1900	**William McKinley** (Theodore Roosevelt, 1901)	Republican	7,218,039 (51.6%)	292
	William J. Bryan	Democratic; Populist	6,358,345 (45.5%)	155
1904	**Theodore Roosevelt**	Republican	7,626,593 (56.4%)	336
	Alton B. Parker	Democratic	5,082,898 (37.6%)	140
	Eugene V. Debs	Socialist	402,489 (2.9%)	
1908	**William H. Taft**	Republican	7,676,258 (51.5%)	321
	William J. Bryan	Democratic	6,406,801 (43.0%)	162
	Eugene V. Debs	Socialist	420,380 (2.8%)	
1912	**Woodrow Wilson**	Democratic	6,293,152 (41.8%)	435
	Theodore Roosevelt	Progressive	4,119,207 (27.3%)	88
	William H. Taft	Republican	3,486,383 (23.1%)	8
	Eugene V. Debs	Socialist	900,369 (5.9%)	
1916	**Woodrow Wilson**	Democratic	9,126,300 (49.2%)	277
	Charles E. Hughes	Republican	8,546,789 (46.1%)	254

Year	Candidates	Party	Popular Vote	Electoral Vote
1920	**Warren G. Harding** (**Calvin Coolidge,** 1923)	Republican	16,133,314 (60.3%)	404
	James M. Cox	Democratic	9,140,884 (34.1%)	127
	Eugene V. Debs	Socialist	913,664 (3.4%)	
1924	**Calvin Coolidge**	Republican	15,717,553 (54.0%)	382
	John W. Davis	Democratic	8,386,169 (28.8%)	136
	Robert M. La Follette	Progressive	4,814,050 (16.5%)	13
1928	**Herbert C. Hoover**	Republican	21,411,991 (58.2%)	444
	Alfred E. Smith	Democratic	15,000,185 (40.7%)	87
1932	**Franklin D. Roosevelt**	Democratic	22,825,016 (57.4%)	472
	Herbert C. Hoover	Republican	15,758,397 (39.6%)	59
	Norman Thomas	Socialist	883,990 (2.2%)	
1936	**Franklin D. Roosevelt**	Democratic	27,747,636 (60.7%)	523
	Alfred M. Landon	Republican	16,679,543 (36.5%)	8
	William Lemke	Union	892,492 (1.9%)	
1940	**Franklin D. Roosevelt**	Democratic	27,263,448 (54.7%)	449
	Wendell L. Wilkie	Republican	22,336,260 (44.8%)	82
1944	**Franklin D. Roosevelt** (**Harry S Truman,** 1945)	Democratic	25,611,936 (53.3%)	432
	Thomas E. Dewey	Republican	22,013,372 (45.8%)	99
1948	**Harry S Truman**	Democratic	24,105,587 (49.5%)	303
	Thomas E. Dewey	Republican	21,970,017 (45.1%)	189
	J. Strom Thurmond	States' Rights	1,169,134 (2.4%)	39
	Henry A. Wallace	Progressive	1,157,057 (2.3%)	
1952	**Dwight D. Eisenhower**	Republican	33,936,137 (55.1%)	442
	Adlai E. Stevenson	Democratic	27,314,649 (44.3%)	89
1956	**Dwight D. Eisenhower**	Republican	35,585,245 (57.3%)	457
	Adlai E. Stevenson	Democratic	26,030,172 (41.9%)	73
1960	**John F. Kennedy** (**Lyndon B. Johnson,** 1963)	Democratic	34,221,344 (49.7%)	303
	Richard M. Nixon	Republican	34,106,671 (49.5%)	219
1964	**Lyndon B. Johnson**	Democratic	43,126,584 (61.0%)	486
	Barry M. Goldwater	Republican	27,177,838 (38.4%)	52
1968	**Richard M. Nixon**	Republican	31,783,148 (43.4%)	301
	Hubert H. Humphrey	Democratic	31,274,503 (42.7%)	191
	George C. Wallace	Amer. Independent	9,901,151 (13.5%)	46
1972	**Richard M. Nixon**	Republican	47,170,179 (60.6%)	520
	George S. McGovern	Democratic	29,171,791 (37.5%)	17
1974	**Gerald R. Ford**	Republican	Appointed on August 9, 1974, as President after the resignation of Richard M. Nixon.	
1976	**Jimmy Carter**	Democratic	40,828,587 (50.1%)	297
	Gerald R. Ford	Republican	39,147,613 (48.0%)	240

Year	Candidates	Party	Popular Vote	Electoral Vote
1980	**Ronald Reagan**	Republican	43,899,248 (50.7%)	489
	Jimmy Carter	Democratic	35,481,435 (41.0%)	49
	John Anderson	Independent	5,719,437 (6.6%)	
	Ed Clark	Libertarian	920,859 (1.0%)	
1984	**Ronald Reagan**	Republican	54,451,521 (58.8%)	525
	Walter F. Mondale	Democratic	37,565,334 (40.5%)	13
1988	**George H. Bush**	Republican	47,946,422 (54.0%)	426
	Michael S. Dukakis	Democratic	41,016,429 (46.0%)	112

Index